D1482856

Dynamics of Populations

Dynamics of Populations

Proceedings of the
Advanced Study Institute on
'Dynamics of Numbers
in Populations',
Oosterbeek, the Netherlands,
7-18 September 1970

edited by P. J. den Boer and G. R. Gradwell

Centre for Agricultural Publishing and Documentation, Wageningen 1971

ISBN 90 220 0355 8

Organizing Committee

A. D. Voûte, president
K. Bakker, 1st secretary
C. W. Stortenbeker, 2nd secretary
D. Bakker
P. J. den Boer
P. Gruys
H. N. Kluyver
P. Korringa
D. J. Kuenen
L. Vlijm
H. Wolda

Assistants of the Committee
Miss M. van Wijngaarden
M. H. den Boer
S. Broekhuizen

Contents

Interactions between populations in general

Parasite-host and predator-prey relationships

Human intervention: the exploitation of marine populations

Human intervention: introduction into Australia

ﬠ

Preface

In the spring of 1968 a number of Dutch ecologists from various Universities and Research Institutes came together to discuss the possibility of organizing an international scientific meeting on population dynamics.

They all felt that such a meeting was long overdue. The last large conference on this subject was held in 1957 (The Cold Spring Harbor Symposium No 22 on Population Studies: Animal Ecology and Demography), and during the last decade many new ideas and methods have been developed and a considerable amount of research has been done. Therefore, discussions between workers studying various groups of organisms, plants as well as animals, and using different lines of approach might be expected to be very fruitful and be of benefit not only to those participating but also to the whole science of ecology.

The organization of an Advanced Study Institue offered an opportunity to achieve this goal. An Organizing Committee was formed which started its work by rawing up a list of topics to be discussed in the various sessions and, after consulting a number of prominent ecologists in Australia, France, Germany, Scandinavia, the United Kingdom and the USA, lecturers on these topics were invited.

Since it was the main objective of the meeting to promote an exchange of ideas among the participants, the number of lectures was restricted to only four per day. In this way ample time for discussions would be available. Further, it appeared necessary to re-examine a few important scientific controversies which had continued in the ecological literature for some 15 years, i.e. the controversy between those workers who emphasize the importance of density-dependent regulation and those who stress the importance of the heterogeneity of the environment both in space and time for the stabilization of numbers. By inviting prominent adherents of the opposing theories there would be an opportunity to discuss their views in a much more fundamental way than would have been possible in a short meeting crammed with a large number of short communications.

It was also felt necessary to attempt to bridge the gap between animal and plant ecology, which have developed independently for such a long time, and it is in the rapidly expanding field of plant population ecology that such bridges can be built.

It was the unanimous opinion of the participants that the Institute was very successful. Ecological workers on such diverse animal groups as flatworms, insects, fish, birds and mammals were brought together with plant population ecologists. These latter – together with the single plant epidemiologist – particularly expressed their gratitude for the opportunity to attend the Institute.

The participants were 'recruited' from such different groups as typical field ecologists, laboratory ecologists, model-builders, mathematical ecologists, genetic ecologists and conservationists. With such a diversity of interests it would not have been surprising had there been uncontrolled proliferation in the discussions and a great amount of semantic difficulties. That there were no such difficulties suggests that ecologists are now making conscious efforts to understand and appreciate one anothers points of view. A very fortunate aspect of the presence of so many experts on diverse fields of interest was that errors made during the discussions were generally immediately corrected.

The importance of the intensive contact made possible between workers in pure and applied scientific research in ecology was explicitly made clear by Dr Gulland of the FAO Department of Fisheries.

Finally, it was felt that the topics discussed at the Institute, though mainly of a pure scientific nature, were very relevant to the problems faced by mankind in his relationships with nature and natural resources, especially as regards the problem of the depletion of natural resources and the deterioration of the environment.

The results of most research projects discussed at this Institute were the fruits of long-term studies. The participants stressed the necessity for a change in the usual policy of organizations subsidizing scientific research in population ecology in such a way that well-planned research projects will receive subsidies for a far longer period than is now customary (3–4 years); however, it was realized that decisions about the continuation of these subsidies should be subject to regular scrutiny.

Another difficulty regarding research projects on population ecology that has been discussed is the lack of manpower. Most workers in this field unfortunately have to work individually, whereas most projects would benefit from having a team of specialists.

In the opinion of the Organizing Committee the topics discussed at this Institute give a representative picture of population dynamics as it is today, and therefore it was decided to publish this book.

The Editors have not attempted to give a historical report of the Institute, but have tried to compose the book in such a way that the transfer of information is as efficient as possible. The papers have been re-arranged, and the authors have been able to include in their text those points raised in the discussions which they thought suitable. This means that the printed text is not always identical to the text read at the Institute.

The rest of the discussions, together with remarks handed in later on, have been edited in such a way that the various problems discussed after each lecture are arranged according to their order of importance for population dynamics in general. As far as possible, the remarks of the different speakers are recorded in their own words, though often shortened.

The Editors are to be congratulated with the result of their efforts, and the Organizing Committee hopes that this book will fulfil its objective as a report on the state of affairs in population dynamics in 1970. Many thanks are due to Miss G. G. Gerding for typing the discussions and indices, and to the publishers, who have done all they could do to publish this volume within one year of the meeting.

The Organizing Committee wishes to express its gratitude to the Scientific Affairs Division of NATO, and to the Dutch Ministries of Education and Sciences, and of Agriculture and Fisheries, whose unconditional financial support made this very important and fertile meeting possible.

K. Bakker
1st secretary of the
Organizing Committee

List of participants in the Advanced Study Institute, Oosterbeek, the Netherlands, 7–18 September 1970

P. K. M. van der Aart, Zoölogisch Laboratorium der Rijksuniversiteit, Afdeling Oecologie, Kaiserstraat 63, Leiden, the Netherlands

W. Altenkirch, Niedersächsische Forstliche Versuchsanstalt, Abt. B, Forstschädlingsbekämpfung, Grätzelstrasse 2, 34 Göttingen, West Germany

F. S. Andersen, Statens Skadedyrlaboratorium, Skovbrynet 14, 2800 Lyngby, Denmark

H. G. Andrewartha, Department of Zoology, R. A. Fisher Laboratories, The University of Adelaide, Adelaide, South Australia 5001, Australia

D. Bakker, Laboratorium voor Plantenoecologie der Rijksuniversiteit, Kerklaan 30, Haren (Gr.), the Netherlands

K. Bakker, Zoölogisch Laboratorium der Rijksuniversiteit, Afdeling Oecologie, Kaiserstraat 63, Leiden, the Netherlands

J. H. van Balen, Instituut voor Oecologisch Onderzoek, Kemperbergerweg 11, Arnhem, the Netherlands

W. Baltensweiler, Entomologisches Institut der Eidgenossische Technische Hochschule, Universitätsstrasse 2, CH-8006 Zürich, Switzerland

K. R. Barbehenn, CBNS, Washington University, St. Louis, Missouri 63130, USA

J. J. Beukema, Nederlands Instituut voor Onderzoek der Zee, Postbus 59, Texel, the Netherlands

J. B. van Biezen, Rijksinstituut voor Natuurbeheer, Kemperbergerweg 11, Arnhem, the Netherlands

L. C. Birch, Zoology Building, The University of Sydney, Sydney 2006, Australia

M. H. den Boer, Rijksinstituut voor Natuurbeheer, Kemperbergerweg 11, Arnhem, the Netherlands

P. J. den Boer, Biologisch Station, Kampsweg 27, Wijster (Dr.), the Netherlands

A. M. J. Bouwerhuis, Zoölogisch Laboratorium, Driehuizerweg 200, Nijmegen, the Netherlands

E. Broadhead, The University of Leeds, Department of Zoology, Leeds LS2 9JT, England

S. Broekhuizen, Rijksinstituut voor Natuurbeheer, Kemperbergerweg 11, Arnhem, the Netherlands

P. F. Brussard, Cornell University, Division of Biological Sciences, Section of Ecology and Systematics, Building 6, Langmuir Laboratory, Ithaca, New York 14850–USA

J. B. Calhoun, National Institute of Mental Health, Mental Health Intramural Research Program, 9000 Rockville Pike, Bethesda, Maryland 20014, USA

J. P. Cancela da Fonceca, Station de Recherches de Lutte Biologique et de Biocénotique (INRA), F 78 La Minière par Versailles, France

P. B. Cavers, Department of Botany, The University of Western Ontario, London 72, Ontario, Canada

G. C. Clough, Department of Zoology, University of Rhode Island, Kingston, Rhode Island 02881, USA

J. H. Connell, Department of Biological Sciences, University of California, Santa Barbara, California 93106, USA

J. C. Coulson, Department of Zoology, University of Durham, South Road, Durham City, England

N. Croin Michielsen, Zoölogisch Laboratorium der Rijksuniversiteit, Kaiserstraat 63, Leiden, the Netherlands

J. P. Dempster, Monks Wood Experimental Station, Abbots Ripton, Huntingdonshire, England

A. Dhondt, Laboratorium voor Oecologie, Biogeografie en Algemene Biologie, Rijksuniversiteit te Gent, K. L. Ledeganckstraat 35, 9000 Gent, België

A. F. G. Dixon, Department of Zoology, The University, Glasgow W. 2, Scotland

P. J. Drent, Zoölogisch Laboratorium der Rijksuniversiteit, Kerklaan 30, Haren, the Netherlands

Walter D. Edgar, Department of Zoology, the University, Glasgow W.2, Scotland.

H. J. Egglishaw, Department of Agriculture and Fisheries for Scotland, Freshwater Fisheries Laboratory, Faskally, Pitlochry, Perthshire, Scotland

H. Eijsackers, Rijksinstituut voor Natuurbeheer, Kemperbergerweg 11, Arnhem, the Netherlands

F. Frank, Biologische Bundesanstalt für Land- und Forstwirtschaft, Messeweg 11/12, 33 Braunschweig, West Germany

H. G. Fransz, Zoölogisch Laboratorium der Landbouwhogeschool, Binnenhaven 7, Wageningen, the Netherlands

J. Friedman, Tel-Aviv University, Department of Botany, Tel-Aviv, Israel

J. M. F. Geelen, Zoölogisch Laboratorium, Driehuizerweg 200, Nijmegen, the Netherlands

J. J. van Gelder, Zoölogisch Laboratorium, Driehuizerweg 200, Nijmegen, the Netherlands

G. R. Gradwell, Department of Forestry, South Parks Road, Oxford, England

P. Gruys, Nedereindsestraat 35, Kesteren, the Netherlands

F. Gudmundsson, Museum of Natural History, P.O. Box 532, Reykjavik, Iceland

J. A. Gulland, Department of Fisheries, Food and Agriculture Organization of the United Nations, Viale delle terme di Caracalla, Rome 00100, Italy

D. A. Hancock, Fisheries Laboratory, Remembrance Avenue, Burnham-on-Crouch, Essex, England

M. P. Hassell, Imperial College Field Station, Silwood Park, Ascot, Berkshire, England

R. Hengeveld, Biologisch Station, Kampsweg 27, Wijster (Dr.), the Netherlands

W. M. Herrebout, Instituut voor Systematische Dierkunde der Rijksuniversiteit, Doezastraat 2, Leiden

C. B. Huffaker, Experiment Station, Division of Biological Control, University of California, Berkeley, California, USA

S. Iwao, Entomological Laboratory, College of Agriculture, Kyoto University, Kyoto, Japan

J. Jacobs, Zoologisches Institut der Universität München, Luisenstrasse 14, 8 München 2, West Germany

S. K. Jain, University of California, Davis Department of Agronomy and Range Science, Davis – California 95616 – USA

D. Jenkins, The Nature Conservancy, 12 Hope Terrace, Edinburgh EHG 2AS, Scotland

P. M. Jónasson, Ferskvandsbiologisk Laboratorium, Helsingørsgade 51, 3400 Hillerød, Denmark

A. Kessler, Zoölogisch Laboratorium der Vrije Universiteit, Amsterdam-Buitenveldert, the Netherlands

H. N. Kluyver, Van Goghstraat 11, Arnhem, the Netherlands

P. Korringa, Rijksinstituut voor Visserijonderzoek, Haringkade 1, IJmuiden, the Netherlands

C. J. Krebs, Department of Zoology, University of British Columbia, Vancouver 8, Canada

J. H. Kuchlein, Afdeling Dierkunde der Landbouwhogeschool, Binnenhaven 7, Wageningen, the Netherlands

M. Kruk-de Bruin, Zoölogisch Laboratorium der Rijksuniversiteit, Kaiserstraat 63, Leiden, the Netherlands

D. J. Kuenen, Rijksinstituut voor Natuurbeheer, Kemperbergerweg 11, Arnhem, the Netherlands

V. Labeyrie, Laboratoire d'Ecologie et de Biocoenotique Expérimentales, Parc Grandmont, Avenue Monge, 37 Tours, France

M. Lamotte, Université de Paris, Ecole Normale Supérieure, Laboratoire de Zoologie, 46 rue d'Ulm, Paris 5, France

R. Laughlin, The University of Adelaide, Waite Agricultural Research Institute, Department of Entomology, Glen Osmond, South Australia, Australia

J. H. Lawton, Animal Ecology Research Group, Department of Zoology, Oxford, England

J. C. van Lenteren, Zoölogisch Laboratorium der Rijksuniversiteit, Kaiserstraat 63, Leiden, the Netherlands

R. J. van der Linde, Rijksinstituut voor Natuurbeheer, Kemperbergerweg 11, Arnhem, the Netherlands

H. Löhrl, Vogelwarte Radolfzell Max-Planck-Just., Am Schlossberg, Möggingen, West Germany

A. R. Main, Zoology Department, University of Western Australia, Nedlands, Western Australia 6009, Australia

E. van der Meijden, Zoölogisch Laboratorium der Rijksuniversiteit, Kaiserstraat 63, Leiden, the Netherlands

J. A. J. Metz, Instituut voor Theoretische Biologie, Stationsweg 25, Leiden, the Netherlands

W. W. Murdoch, Department of Biological Science, University of California, Santa Barbara, California 93106, USA

R. K. Murton, The Nature Conservancy, Monks Wood Experimental Station, Abbots Ripton, Huntingdonshire, England

K. Myers, Division of Wildlife Research, CSIRO, P.O. Box 109 City, Canberra, A.C.T. 2601, Australia

15

B. Ohnesorge, Institut für Pflanzenschutz der Universität Hohenheim, 7000 Stuttgart Hohenheim, West Germany

H. C. J. Oomen, Zoölogisch Laboratorium, Driehuizerweg 200, Nijmegen, the Netherlands

L. M. Oosterhoff, Zoölogisch Laboratorium der Rijksuniversiteit, Kerklaan 30, Haren (Gr.), the Netherlands

I. Palmblad, Utah State University, Department of Botany, Logan, Utah 84321, USA

V. I. Pajunen, Department of Zoology, University of Helsinki, Helsinki, Finland

C. M. Perrins, Edward Grey Institute, Botanic Gardens, High Street, Oxford, England

D. Pimentel, Department of Entomology and Limnology, Cornell University, Ithaca, New York 14850, USA

T. Platt, Fisheries Research Board of Canada, Marine Ecology Laboratory, Bedford Institute, Dartmouth, Nova Scotia, Canada

J. E. Rabinovich, Universidad Central de Venezuela, Facultad de Ciencias, Institute de Zoologia Tropical, Apartado Los Chaguaramos 59058, Caracas, Venezuela

J. Reddingius, Zoölogisch Laboratorium der Rijksuniversiteit, Kerklaan 30, Haren (Gr.) the Netherlands

T. B. Reynoldson, Department of Zoology, University College of North Wales, Bangor Caernarvonshire, Wales

C. J. J. Richter, Université Libre du Congo, Boîte Postale 2012, Kinsangani, Republique Democratique du Congo

M. L. Rosenzweig, Department of Bioscience, State University of New York at Albany, Albany, New York 12203, USA

T. Royama, Forest Research Laboratory, P.O. Box 4000, Fredericton, New Brunswick, Canada

W. Scharloo, Genetisch Instituut der Rijksuniversiteit, Opaalweg 20, Utrecht, the Netherlands

M. E. Solomon, Research Station, Department of Agriculture and Horticulture, University of Bristol, Long Ashton, Bristol BS18 9AF, England

T. R. E. Southwood, Imperial College Field Station, Silwood Park, Sunninghill near Ascot, Berkshire, England

J. A. Springett, Forests Department, Perth, W. Australia 6000, Australia

C. W. Stortenbeker, Rijksinstituut voor Natuurbeheer, Kemperbergerweg 11, Arnhem, the Netherlands

S. J. ter Borg, Laboratorium voor Plantenoecologie der Rijksuniversiteit, Biologisch Centrum, Kerklaan 30, Haren (Gr.), the Netherlands

J. R. Tester, The Nature Conservancy, Blackhall, Banchory Kincardineshire, AB3 3PS, Scotland

W. J. Turnock, Science Secretariat Raivy Council Office, 207 Queenstreet, Ottawa, Ontario, Canada

G. C. Varley, Hope Department of Entomology, University Museum, Parks Road, Oxford, England

L. Vlijm, Zoölogisch Laboratorium der Vrije Universiteit, de Boelelaan 1087, Amsterdam-Buitenveldert, the Netherlands

A. D. Voûte, Bakenbergseweg 272a, Arnhem, the Netherlands

I. Walker, c/o Frau M. Walker, Laubholzstrasse 45, 8703 Erlenbach (ZH), Switzerland

N. Waloff, Department of Zoology, Imperial College of Science, Prince Consort Road, London S.W. 7, England

16

A. J. Wapshere, CNRS, Centre d'Etudes Phytosociologique et Ecologique, B.P. 1018, Route de Mende, 34-Montpellier, Hérault, France

A. Watson, The Nature Conservancy, Blackhall, Banchory, Kincardineshire, Scotland

K. E. F. Watt, Institute of Ecology, University of California, Davis, California 95616, USA

M. J. Way, Imperial College Field Station, Silwood Park, Sunninghill near Ascot, Berkshire, England

J. White, University College, Department of Botany, Belfield, Stillorgan Road, Dublin 4, Ireland

H. Wilbert, Institut für Pflanzenpathologie und Pflanzenschutz der Georg August Universität, Entomologische Abteilung, Grisebachstrasse 6, 34 Göttingen Weende, West Germany

M. H. Williamson, Department of Biology, University of York, Heslington, York Y0l 5DD, England

C. T. de Wit, Instituut voor Biologisch en Scheikundig Onderzoek van Landbouwgewassen, Bornsesteeg 65–67, Wageningen, the Netherlands

H. Wolda, Smithsonian Tropical Research Institute, P.O.Box 2072, Balboa, Canal Zone (Panama)

J. C. Zadoks, Laboratorium voor Fytopathologie der Landbouwhogeschool, Binnenhaven 9, Wageningen, the Netherlands

A. Zahavi, Tel-Aviv University, Institute for Nature Conservation Research, 155 Herzelstreet, Tel-Aviv, Israel

G. Zink, Vogelwarte Radolfzell, Schloss, Möggingen, West Germany

A. Zweep, Zoölogisch Laboratorium der Rijksuniversiteit, Kerklaan 30, Haren (Gr.), the Netherlands

H. Zwölfer, Commonwealth Institute of Biological Control, European Station, 1 Chemin des Grillons, Delemont, Switzerland

Proc. Adv. Study Inst. Dynamics Numbers Popul. (Oosterbeek, 1970) 19–28

Presidential Address for the Advanced
Study Institute on 'Dynamics of Numbers in Populations'

A. D. Voûte

This symposium has been organized in order to discuss the results that have been obtained up to now in the field of population dynamics. In the course of the next two weeks the many aspects of this subject will be brought to our attention by a number of speakers. It would, therefore, serve no useful purpose if I were to give you an overall picture of the research at this stage or of the courses that might be taken in future: any opinion that I now might defend could very well prove untenable in these next two weeks. It would seem to be more appropriate in the circumstances to have at the end of this symposium a short synopsis of the conclusions we reached together. However, before we start our discussions, it might be useful to determine why we are doing this research and what we are trying to achieve by it.

First of all, I think we should define the limits of population dynamics and give an indication of its relation to other biological sub-sciences, which deal with populations; naturally it would take me too long to discuss these various sciences here. Clearly, any subject concerned with individuals – that is to say the whole idiobiology – sooner or later has to bring the population into account, because in nature all individuals invariably are grouped in populations. There are, however, two other subsciences which specifically deal with populations, namely population genetics and population ecology, which should be clearly distinguished in order to understand the proper meaning of population dynamics as a subject.

Population dynamics

Population dynamics is a sub-science of biology, concerned with fluctuations in the numbers in which plants and animals occur, that is to say, concerned with the changes in population density resulting from interactions between the population and the environment, in so far as these are reflected as changes in reproduction, mortality and migration. This may raise the question as to a possible regulation of population densities. By this I mean the apparent tendency to maintain the population density at a certain level, or within certain specified limits.

Population dynamics aims to explain the fluctuations in population densities and thereby, should this prove possible, to predict them. Within a population the individual is the smallest unit which is worked with. The subject is causal-analytical in character.

Population genetics

Population genetics concerns itself with the genetic structure of populations and with the influence of external circumstances on this structure. If population dynamics works with numbers of individuals, population genetics works with ratios of genes. Like population dynamics, population genetics aims at explaining and predicting, and thus is also causal-analytical.

Population ecology

The definition of population ecology differs widely from scientist to scientist. It would be slightly exaggerating to say that in ecology there are as many different definitions as there are ecologists, but it is certainly true that there are many different points of view. Not so long ago I wrote an article for 'Acta Biotheoretica' (Vol. XVIII (1968) 143–164) in which I mentioned these various opinions, and you will, I hope, appreciate that I will stick to my opinion which I held then, and still do hold. But you will forgive me for not putting into words the whole of my argumentation anew, because that would take up too much time.

I should like to confine myself to saying that if one is to find a niche for ecology within the framework of biology, ecology would have to be defined as a final science. Seen in this context ecology is a science which deals with the relations between an organism – possibly a group of organisms or part of an organism – and its environment insofar as it is able to survive due to its ability to maintain itself in this environment, thereby making use of its adaptability. For the population ecologist, this adjustment is based largely on the genetic structure of the population. However, its survival is not a population genetical problem alone. The regulation of numbers (apart from genetics, and thus seen purely as a population dynamical datum) is equally important for a good understanding of population ecology. When observed phenomena have to be explained, population dynamics and population genetics serve as the most important auxiliary sciences for population ecology. Their role could be compared to that of causal physiology with regard to the final autecology. In this respect I should like to point out that final and causal could never be conflicting concepts; they are aligned and complement each other.

The aim of population dynamics

If we have in this way positioned population dynamics between the other related sciences, the question remains what is our purpose in trying to solve the problems which confront us in this particular field. Why are we doing this research and what do we hope to gain by it?

This is, in fact, a question which every researcher should – and must – ask himself. If it is not asked, it means that he has failed to take any responsibility for his research and for the use that will be made of his results. The scientist's attitude towards this question is not always the same and the answer to it will be greatly influenced by his attitude.

There is in the first place the researcher who works and thinks in terms of pure science. To him, solving problems could be an aim in itself. He want to know how nature is structured; which principles apply. His aim is to enlarge knowledge. It is this thirst for knowledge which drives him to go on with his research. There was a time when a scientist locked himself in an ivory tower, brushing aside as something inferior any pursuit that could not

20

be described as purely scientific. I am glad to say that these towers have all but dis-appeared, and with them any feelings of superiority. Pure science has remained, however, together with scientists dedicated to it.

Should the purely scientific researcher happen to be religiously inclined, then another argument for research could arise. For him, as for me, his 'Bible' is a Divine Revelation. This is also true for the Creation. Nature is also a Divine Revelation. To this scientist, therefore, scientific research is to read the book of nature and in doing so to gain an insight into the things the Supreme Being wishes to reveal to him. Seen in this light it is a religious experience. A religious scientist will read the book of nature with as much love and reverence as his 'Bible.' As 'Bible' and 'Book of Nature' do not overlap, but complement each other, the religious attitude cannot be of influence on the objectivity of the research or on the interpretation of the results gained by the experiments.

Nowadays, the number of researchers who work and think purely scientifically represent a small minority. Today, most scientists hope and expect that the results they obtain will – if not immediately, at least in the long run – be used for the benefit of mankind, and that they will help in the control, exploitation or management of nature. I should like to describe this particular group as 'applied scientists', whose research could be either fundamental or applied.

Both applied and pure scientists work the same way. Their methods of research and the way in which acquired data are interpreted, are exactly the same. The only difference lies in the ultimate aim of the work and, linked to this, the scientist's attitude. However, one should not see this difference too much in terms of black and white. I am sure no 'pure scientist' could fail to be pleased when his findings can be used for the benefit of mankind and, on the other hand, most 'applied scientists' will be most satisfied with results which, though they can never be applied, will all the same give us a clearer insight into the structure of nature.

What I have said about natural science in general, applies equally to population dynamics, in as much as most scientists have practical application as their ultimate aim. The question then arises: To what use can the results best be put? Which policies can benefit the most from them?

The use of population dynamics

When we consider our domestic animals and crops, we know that density is almost completely determined by man. Only in a few cases will population dynamical problems occur here, and even then only when the plants and animals in question compete with wild organisms, for example weeds in cultivated fields or meadows, or non-domestic herbivorous animals grazing on pastures meant for domestic animals (such as happens in Australia with rabbits and sheep).

The study of the population dynamics of plants has scarcely developed and therefore has, as yet, little practical significance. With animals, population dynamics could prove its use mainly in controlling the populations of wild, or semi-wild animals including those which have reverted to a wild state. Taking these groups together, we must make a distinction between

a. The species we want to protect in order to prevent them from dying out (the Pridzwalski horses, for example);

b. Those species we want to harvest by hunting or fishing; and

c. Those species we want to maintain at a lower population level than the natural one because they could otherwise be harmful to either man himself, to his domestic animals or to his crops, or to the preservation of nature.

In all these instances population dynamics will contribute to laying a foundation for effective management. Other sciences than population dynamics make their contribution – for example physiology and taxonomy – whilst influences like economics, traffic and recreation also make themselves felt. These latter are all subject to political decision-making. Thus, the basis for effective management will by no means be laid for reasons of population dynamics alone, however important its results may be and however dangerous it would be for effective management not to take the principles of population dynamics into consideration.

I should now like to discuss the forementioned three groups separately.

The protection of wildlife

We live in an age when it is increasingly difficult to preserve nature or what is left of it and to have these remains functioning properly. The intensive utilisation of the land (housing, industry, agriculture, fishery, recreation, etc.) and the widespread disposal of waste products, is making demands on the adaptability of many organisms which they cannot meet. Consequently, the areas of distribution of these organisms become smaller and smaller and the number of species of animals and plants that have become extinct or nearly so, is obviously ever-increasing. However, it must be said that man is increasingly willing to keep nature as rich and as varied as is possible. This means that as a counter-balance to the efficient but often rather destructive utilization of land, we must come to an equally efficient management of what remains of nature. This means that conditions must be created which will allow as great a number of species of organisms as possible to survive. This management should be focused on populations rather than on individuals. For example, the protection of rhinoceros in a territory in which only three old males are still alive is senseless, but creating the right conditions for a small rhino population to live and reproduce could very well save both this population and the species as a whole.

The same thing goes for those well-meant attempts to keep alive seabirds which have fallen victim to oil pollution. Whenever a species is threatened with extinction it can be saved only with far-reaching measures taken at a different level, like measures to check marine pollution.

Whenever a species is on the decline, one must determine whether with low densities the mortality rate still exceeds the rate of reproduction. Is regulation of the population possible under the prevailing conditions? If so, no immediate danger of extinction need exist, but if not, no time should be lost in taking effective measures, if necessary drastic ones.

For birds and mammals the zoos can sometimes bring respite. Here, the threatened species can be kept and bred until the conditions in the field have improved to such an extent that survival is possible and the species in one way or another can be controlled at a certain agreed density.

It is clear that management of animal populations requires expert knowledge of the regulations of numbers. Here we touch one of the controversies in the development of basic research in the field of population dynamics. Density-dependent factors can bring about regulation. Could this be done without those factors? If so, could something be said about the height of the level or about the range within which numbers fluctuate? In the

22

course of the next two weeks these matters will no doubt be amply discussed. I sincerely hope that this discussion will clear up many of the problems that confront us, because management of nature urgently needs the answers.

When protective measures are required our knowledge in the field of population dynamics is usually highly taxed, and more often than not science simply has not advanced enough to give sufficient support to the policy-making authorities. Since some course of action has to be taken, the necessary steps are usually based on common sense. Later research may sometimes make it necessary to change a policy. Understandably this can be painful. I can give you an example of this, with reference to the Netherlands.

Duck decoys. In earlier days those responsible for nature conservancy thought that ducks were in need of protection. No research on population dynamics had been done as yet. It seemed logical to reduce the mortality and to that end eliminate the wholesale killing of ducks as far as possible. This, it was thought, would automatically lead to an increase in the population density. The many duck decoys in use in the Netherlands – places where large quantities of duck were caught – had long been a thorn in the side of nature conservancy. Every year some 200,000 ducks were caught and killed in this way. Just think what an improvement it would be if these killings could be stopped! Our country had in the mean time signed the Convention of Paris and had agreed to abolish these methods of bird-catching. In short, the future policy had been well-established.

However, population dynamics research carried out by Eygenraam has since shown that these decoys have in fact a favourable effect on the inland mallard population; even to the extent that the population increases. By creating breeding places and providing protection for the brood, these decoys raise the number of full-fledged birds in such a way that this more than compensates for the catch. Moreover, the winter mortality is reduced because of the protection and care the birds receive in a period in which they are most vulnerable. It has also been established that to the population of migrating duck the decoys are certainly not detrimental. Although there is no actual proof of this, it seems reasonable to expect an increase rather than a decrease in the density of these migrating duck as there are strong indications that regulation takes place late in the winter. It is precisely at this time of the year – when the catching season is over – that the decoys bring about an improvement of the biotope.

It took a great deal of trouble to convince the authorities that the prohibition of these catching methods was not only senseless but, in so far as decoys were concerned, was even contrary to the interests of nature conservancy which, after all, was trying to increase the stock of duck. For ten years or more there was simply no convincing them.

However, they could not for ever turn a deaf ear to arguments based on the results of intensive research. In the last few years the authorities – also internationally I am glad to say – increasingly take into account the results of research and there is no longer such pressure for the abolition of duck decoys.

The cropping of wild animals

The harvesting of wildlife by means of hunting, trapping or catching – for reasons other than sports – should always be aimed at maintaining a large population intact, and at the same time furnishing a maximum yield. With over-hunting or over-catching the population density, as a rule, will fall off rapidly, this could eventually lead to extinction. In this connection we think for instance of the bison in northern America and the wisent, its European counterpart, which could only just be saved.

Even in our modern, technocratic world we should not fail to take into account that our wildlife could be an important source of food. In African countries, for example, it has been established already that the cropping of wild animals for the meat-market looks very promising. This harvest far exceeds that of cattle kept in the same area.

In the field of fisheries much work has been done already on population dynamics so that the authorities have at their disposal a reasonably well-established basis for management. Clearly, the same laws we have for land animals can be applied in principle to fish.

When in practice we often see such deplorable results – think for example of the whaling industry – then we find these are for the greater part caused by political or other influences which affect the control of international waters. This only shows how factors other than those based on population dynamics research effectively determine the basis for management.

Hunting just for sporting reasons should be mentioned separately. Its interests coincide largely with those I mentioned under the heading 'protection of wildlife'. The harvesting has no economic significance here – at most the hunter tries to cover part of his cost by selling the proceeds. By and large the same applies to fishing as a sport.

The same expert knowledge of the regulation of numbers that is required for the management of protected animals, is also required for the management of game. However, an additional question crops up. When does regulation occur? If it is competition for food which brings about regulation, then the period when there is shortage of food could, for herbivorous animals in temperate zones, be expected at the end of winter. If the hunting season is quite some time before that period, then a possible surplus will be cleared away and this could keep the population at a satisfactory level. The chances are that hunting pressure applied after the period of shortage will reduce the population.

In America as well as in Europe, more and more population dynamics research is being done on wildlife management. In particular, research on migratory birds should be mentioned. In many instances the results are still too incomplete to give a sound basis for future policy, but there is an encouraging degree of international co-operation so that in future we may come to a complete interchange of results.

Black grouse. Game living within certain restricted areas will often have to be properly managed if extinction is to be avoided. Here too, population dynamics can and must create a basis for efficient management. I will give you an example. In the 1940s the number of black grouse in the Netherlands was falling so rapidly that they were threatened with extinction. In many of the areas where grouse used to abound, the bird had completely disappeared. In other areas it became increasingly rare. The responsible authorities thought that the bird was slowly being driven out by civilization and they were convinced that its disappearance from our densely populated country was inevitable. They tried, however, to slow down the process as much as possible by means of severe restrictions on hunting. Later research, however, showed that this species was not retreating before civilization at all, but that it required regular rejuvenation of the heath. In the old days this used to be done by shepherds in order to provide their sheep with young shoots of heather. As soon as proper management was introduced in certain areas – rotational burning of small plots – the population in those areas yearly increased until a saturation level had been reached. From that moment on there could be no objection to hunting. What is more, well-thought-out hunting turned out to have a population-increasing effect.

Once more, this example shows us for how long a wrong course of action, based on faulty deductions, can make itself felt. Though it had been established beyond doubt that it was quite safe to harvest from a population at its maximum level, there was a general outcry when this actually happened in an entirely justifiable way in the northern part of the Veluwe. There were even questions in Parliament on the subject.

Pests

It has become clear that in many cases the aggressive manner in which we exploit our natural resources results not so much in the trouble it creates for the preservation of nature, but rather in massive occurrences of animals that are considered pests. Insect plagues and also those caused by other animals, are for the greater part man-made. Insect pests particularly are often in the news, and many of the insecticides used for their extermination scare people more than any other kind of environmental pollution. Applied entomology, therefore, has to concentrate increasingly on keeping these insect plagues under control whilst making a minimal use of insecticides, and thus turns to management of the populations in question. With this objective applied entomology has to call on the available knowledge of population dynamics or, when this knowledge is still incomplete, enlarge it. It is certainly no coincidence that population dynamics receives such a stimulus time and again from the research done by applied entomologists. Names like Nicholson, Thompson and many others are very well-known to all who study the dynamics of populations.

After the last war, population dynamics research in agriculture and horticulture became somewhat discredited by the great successes that were being scored with modern insecticides. It was thought that for the checking of plagues nature itself had become superfluous. In forestry, however, teams of scientists, sometimes composed of very distinguished experts, continued to work energetically on the subject. I should like to mention Switzerland and Canada in this respect where some excellent work was done. It is also significant that the International Union of Forest Research Organization (IUFRO) set up a discussion group on population dynamics which meets every other year and within which lively discussions take place on the problems of population dynamics as they affect forest entomology.

Lately, much of the earlier faith and enthusiasm in agriculture and horticulture with regard to the use of chemicals has vanished. It is felt that from now on the objective should be to produce an effective method of integrated or harmonious control of pests, and an interest in population dynamics has been revived.

Regulation

For the pest control branch of nature management the problem of regulation is of the greatest importance. Why are insects, as a rule, being kept at a certain low level? How does the mechanism work that seems to be responsible for this? In fact we can say that plagues occur when regulation fails. More than most of his colleagues in agriculture and horticulture, the forest entomologist realizes that of the hundreds of forest insects that represent a potential danger to our woods only a few occasionally occur on a large scale. Suddenly the regulation mechanism seems to fail. Why this happens is usually unknown, or only partly understood. Even in those cases when agriculture, horticulture or forestry prevented a plague by introducing natural enemies or diseases – the so-called biological control – they rarely succeeded in analysing the results in such a way that no doubts remain as to the way in which the enemy or disease regulated the population density.

In forestry, where no regular spraying schemes are used, one would prefer to know months beforehand when an outbreak is likely to occur. The same thing applies – be it in a lesser degree – to other branches of applied entomology; one has to anticipate a plague and not be taken by surprise. One must be able to predict an outbreak.

Certainly there is no field of population management in which the forecast of densities is more vital than in applied entomology. Therefore population dynamics is in the process of developing a mathematical methodology. This development requires an integration of mathematical and biological thinking, because otherwise the chances of a faulty interpretation of the acquired data would be great, maybe even unavoidable. This new development will undoubtedly be among the most important points of discussion during this symposium.

What I have said about insects which are harmful to agriculture and horticulture, equally applies to carriers of diseases like flies, mosquitoes, lice, fleas and ticks. Application of chemicals does not remove them permanently and it follows that also their populations have to be managed to keep them at such a level that they are no longer harmful.

Epidemiology of parasites

So far I have tried to establish which departments benefit from our knowledge in the field of population dynamics. This brings me automatically to the question whether there are other fields into which population dynamics has not yet penetrated, or only barely so. Indeed, these exist, and are to be found chiefly in the parasitological sector.

Research on the parasites of man and domestic animals has, as yet, almost never been aimed at regulating its population density at a low level. One has looked, of course, for methods of direct control, including the immunizing of the host. Apart from that, the main objects of study have so far been – and rightly so – the parasite's life-cycle, the manner in which it infects its host and consequently the finding of ways to break the contact between parasite and host. That the density of parasites, too, could be regulated in the same way as with free-living animals and that a diagnosis of their regulation mechanisms could benefit the control, has as yet hardly penetrated and for most parasitologists seems to be even a somewhat quaint idea.

Observations made on human ascarids have convinced me of the fact that here, for one, we have a field of research lying fallow which could be of great practical significance.

To what extent population dynamics will be of use in solving the epidemiological questions on plant parasites, I cannot say with any certainty. As far as I know, little or no work has been done on the subject. I am glad to see that at least one of you is occupying himself with this matter. One thing is certain, a fairly unexplored field lies open for research; and our experiences have taught us that such an exploration is never a disappointment. We already know from practice that plant parasites do not increase to an unlimited extent and that for them, too, a regulation mechanism may be assumed. It is to be hoped that population dynamics and parasitology will come together. It could well be that the epidemiology of parasites and diseases could open up completely new ground.

Population of man

In conclusion I should like to say something of the populations of man himself. The ever-growing population poses a problem with which mankind seems, as yet, unable to cope.

Let us try to view this problem solely from a population dynamics point of view – as a biological problem in fact. It immediately becomes clear that the regulation of human populations occurs in a way that is completely different from that in animal life. Predators, parasites and diseases which can bring about regulation in many species of animals, no longer have significance here; where the latter two may play a part of any importance, they do so less and less as a result of the immense advances in medical science. In our so-called prosperous countries, food certainly does not regulate population density. And yet – as we learn from the well-known curves by Pearl – there appears to be some kind of regulation even in the countries I have just mentioned. From a population dynamics point of view, there could be hardly an explanation for this phenomenon. The reason most probably is to be found in a conscious or unconscious family-planning that could be practised also by people living in more primitive circumstances. Family-planning is a sociological and not a biological process. Evidently, this form of regulation does not come within the range of population dynamics as a biological sub-science.

Several peoples exist, though, on which food has a direct or indirect regulating effect. In these cases it could be said that starvation is an integral part of the regulation, or, in other words: The more food there is, the more people there will be left to starve. In fact this is the same problem we observed in our own country when inefficient hunting failed to control our deer populations. Food regulated the density and throughout the populations symptoms of starvation were visible. From the moment efficient hunting succeeded in regulating the populations, these symptoms of starvation disappeared.

In the case of mankind, hunting cannot be used to gain this end. The world hunger is unsolvable from a population dynamics point of view. The responsible authorities, faced with population density problems, should aim at shifting the latter from the sphere of population dynamics into that of sociology.

This particular science will undoubtedly profit from the accumulated knowledge of population dynamics but will approach the problem from a different angle.

Conclusion

I gave you several examples of how population dynamics has been of use in matters of practical management. It should certainly not be assumed, however, that the fundamental knowledge is extensive enough to draw upon without difficulty in aid of nature management in all its various aspects. On the contrary. There are large gaps in our knowledge in almost every respect.

To my mind, it is an absolute necessity for applied ecology to increase the fundamental knowledge and to strive after a deeper understanding of the principles of population dynamics – and not only with future application in view.

Summing up I should like to say this: For the preservation of a rich and varied nature, for the harvesting of natural produce, for hunting and for the control of harmful organisms an efficient management of nature and all its living species is of the utmost importance. Due to rapid changes in the ways we utilize this earth, including the way in which we pollute our waters, our soil and atmosphere by a wholesale disposal of waste products, nature is being threatened more and more, and no more time should be lost in establishing a firm basis for nature management. Population dynamics will have to make an important contribution to the laying of this foundation. I sincerely hope that this may be a stimulus for us all to carry on with renewed strength and that this symposium will be an inducement to use this strength in the most efficient way.

I hereby declare the Advanced Study Institute open.

Proc. Adv. Study Inst. Dynamics Numbers Popul. (Oosterbeek, 1970) 29–40

Elements in the development of population dynamics

M. E. Solomon

Research Station, Long Ashton, Bristol, England

Abstract

There have been shortcomings both in field studies and in the formulation of theory, with too little contact between them. Theoretical differences have to some extent been resolved or clarified by discussion, by the results of long-term field studies, and by the use of new methods of analysis.

The general theories can be seen as variants of two alternative tenets: (1) that a population is not likely to persist for long unless it is subject to density-dependent regulation, or (2) that the diversity of the habitat and of the population adequately explains the persistence of many populations. Some recent studies aim to demonstrate the reduced amount of regulation that will suffice as diversity is increased.

Increasingly wide and varied use of population models, and of mathematics, can be anticipated. It is argued that: descriptive population work should lead on to analytical studies; hypotheses derived from the general theories should more often be tested in the field; critical discussion of theory should continue; more long-term analytical field studies should be supported; greater use should be made of field experiments; analytical methods should be improved; and greater resources should be devoted to population studies.

To understand the development of any science, we must know what have been the major problems formulated and pursued by those who have devoted themselves to the subject. In population dynamics, the chief questions that investigators and theorists have had in mind are probably somewhat as follows:

– What processes determine the numbers of a species in a habitat?

– What are the causes of variations in abundance through time and space, and by what processes are the range and extent of these numerical changes determined?

– Are the numbers of a species persisting in a habitat necessarily regulated (or should we say limited?), and if so, how?

Ecologists have sought the answers to such questions in several different ways. One way is by the study of populations in the field. Another is by means of experiments under artificial conditions in the laboratory. A third way is by resort to theoretical argument, the theories or models being founded on assumptions of uncertain general validity. It would probably be widely agreed that a great deal of field work on population ecology has been carried out with inadequate reference to any general theory, and that the formulation and discussion of general theories has continued with too little reference to field data (largely because of the shortage of adequate observations).

Although this is less true now than it was 10 years ago, it can scarcely be denied that, over the previous 40 years or so, theory and field observation each suffered from the short-comings of the other, and from the excessive separation of the two.

Many of the former controversies between opposing theorists are now being left behind, and replaced by more constructive efforts to understand the issues involved. I do not suggest that no important differences of opinion remain; but there is greater agreement on what these questions are and how they must be resolved.

The reason for this change is not only that discussion has clarified the questions at issue, but also that more long-term population studies have provided solid data and somewhat more decisive analyses than were formerly available. In the process, new methods of analysis (based on key factors, life tables, etc.) have been developed and applied to the study of population dynamics. There is no basis for complacency on any of these points – the subject is still in its youth; but the ways forward are probably clearer to more of its practitioners than was formerly the case (and not only because there are now more practitioners – another factor of some importance).

Descriptive studies

By descriptive work I mean such activities as the measurement of population density and its fluctuations, observations on the life cycle and on associated species, the recording of temperature, rainfall and other general features of the habitat that seem likely to be important. This is a necessary stage in the study of a population. It includes getting the relevant plants and animals identified, discovering which stages in the life cycle can be studied quantitatively, working out and testing sampling methods, and deciding what is practicable and what is beyond the resources available.

Some of these activities provide the technical basis for a more analytical study, in which causal relations are to be sought and evaluated. But many field studies have never made this transition to the analytical stage. They have been 'rounded off' when a research grant has come to an end; or the investigator has moved to another job or been diverted to other duties, or has decided to opt for something less difficult and more immediately rewarding. Left at a descriptive stage, such studies are very wasteful. If the efforts and resources that have gone into a few hundred of these enterprises could have been devoted to more searching studies of a few species, population ecology would be appreciably further advanced than it now is. Many short-term field studies are merely a training for beginners; but would not involvement in a more penetrating investigation be a better preparation for the sort of work that is most needed in population ecology?

Admittedly, I am looking at descriptive work from the viewpoint of what is needed for the rapid advance of our understanding of population dynamics. There are, no doubt, often compelling practical or economic reasons for the state of affairs I have criticised. Nevertheless, we should not fail to point out the scientific advantages of more penetrating studies.

Synoptic theories

The general theories of writers such as Nicholson, Thompson, and Andrewartha and Birch, can be called 'synoptic theories'. They are intended to be comprehensive; to include all the features that are important for an explanation of the numerical changes and of such degree of numerical constancy that populations are thought to exhibit.

The synoptic theories that different writers have presented differ among themselves in details or in matters of emphasis, yet they have all been variants of a few stereotypes. For convenience and brevity, we may regard the statements of general theory published in the last 30 years as falling into two groups. The first, stemming from Howard and Fiske (1911), Smith (1935) and Nicholson (1933), includes most of the post-war contributors to the subject; these theorists have attributed an essential role to the density-dependent regulation of numbers, and the nature of their argument has, I believe, been primarily deductive. The second, stemming from Thompson (1939, and his earlier writing reviewed there), is now chiefly represented by the statements of Andrewartha and Birch (1954 and elsewhere); they deny that density-dependent regulation is an essential feature of population ecology in general, and consider that the heterogeneity of the environment in space and time provides sufficient explanation of the observed population levels and changes of many species. Their argument is, I believe, primarily inductive.

Between Nicholson and Andrewartha & Birch there is, in fact, a fairly wide spectrum of views. It is not possible to survey them here, nor is it necessary, in view of the painstaking surveys by Huffaker and Messenger (1964) and by Clark et al. (1967), and the valuable analysis by Bakker (1964), all dealing with the whole range of theories.

Can diversity replace regulation?

It seems to me that density-dependent regulation theory rests primarily on the logical inference that a population is very unlikely to persist for a long period within an unchanging zone of abundance unless there is an element of density-dependent regulation.

Put in a different way, the idea could be formulated as an hypothesis. Certainly it has led ecologists to seek and evaluate density-dependent relationships. It does not exclude or discourage a search for density-independent influences; indeed, one would not normally try to find and study density-dependent relationships without also identifying and evaluating the density-independent influences which on the one hand cause fluctuations directly, and on the other hand modify the action of various density-dependent relationships, and so influence their relative importance.

When we adopt this approach we are led to undertake operations like the key-factor test and the analysis of life tables, as well as more direct tests of the density-relationships of processes we have reason to think may have a regulatory influence. Thus density-dependence theory (besides following in the wake of experience such as that of pest control) has led ecologists to seek relationships that have often in fact been found to exist and to play a major role in regulating abundance.

This, however, is scarcely a matter of dispute. The crucial question is whether some (or many) populations persist over many generations without density-dependent regulation. Years ago (Solomon, 1957) I expressed scepticism regarding this possibility, for reasons that may be stated as follows. Obviously, the longer the number of individuals in a population remains within an unchanged range of magnitude, the more closely does the overall net reproductive rate approach a value of one. Such a net reproductive rate could be maintained in only two different ways. The first is by density-dependent regulation opposing the tendency of the animals to increase, so that this tendency would be curbed with progressive intensity as density rose. (This is a highly simplified picture. More realistically, density-independent fluctuations would be superimposed, and the relationship between intensity of limitation and density would be somewhat variable, perhaps intermittent; also there might be a time-lag in the full development of suppressive influences, and in the relaxation when density fell.)

The second way in which the long-term net reproductive rate could approach and remain near zero would be for the physical and biological features of the habitat, on average over the period concerned, to be such that the overall mortality of this species more or less exactly cancels the reproductive rate (including migratory gains and losses), without density-dependent regulation. For any one species there must be very few habitats which happen to have such a set of conditions. Yet we find a particular species persisting in many different habitats; also, in one habitat many different species persist over long periods. How can such a striking long-term balance of gains and losses be maintained (except rarely by the chance matching of environmental conditions with a species' requirements), unless there are regulatory processes at work?

To make an adequate rebuttal of this argument by means of a model population curve, one would have to show that a multiplicity of density-independent influences would be sufficient to prevent the fluctuations from drifting predominantly upwards or downwards, that is, keep the net reproductive rate near zero. It does not meet the case to insert some form of limitation, for example a shortage of a resource such as food, and to exclude this from the category of density-dependent regulation. The argument requiring rebuttal is that, whether we call them regulation, or density-related limitation, or shortage of resources, or parasite-host interaction, some such relationships which penalise high density must be invoked to account for the common persistence of populations for long periods.

It is not convincing, either, to use a model that incorporates a net reproductive rate of zero as one of its initial assumptions. We should not begin by assuming the result that has to be demonstrated! Nor should the model population wander over too wide a range of abundance. In many real populations, the range of numerical variation is less than 10–fold, and even in some notably erratic insect populations the range of variation over considerable numbers of generations is less than 10^5–fold, over considerable numbers of generations (Solomon, 1954).

The above comments refer to attempts to demonstrate 'persistence without regulation'. Similar models are now being put to more instructive use by Reddingius and den Boer (1970; and see den Boer, these Proceedings), in a study of the extent to which diversity may reduce the amount or frequency of density-related limitation that is necessary to keep a population within bounds that might ensure its persistence. They demonstrate 'increase of stability' (reduction of the range of values covered by the variations in abundance) by introducing the following features into their models:
– increasing the number of factors influencing the population
– increasing the number of age-classes in the population
– dividing the population into 9 subpopulations with migratory exchange of individuals between them.
It seems to me that this sort of enquiry can make a most valuable contribution to the quantitative testing of the relative roles of regulation and diversity.

Hypotheses in population study

Scientific investigation proceeds to a great extent by the implicit or explicit testing of hypotheses. To be an effective tool, an hypothesis must make a clear statement that can be tested by resort to observation or experiment, or to existing but independent data. Hypotheses may be derived jointly from general experience or knowledge of 'the way things work' and from specific observations or the results of experiments on the situation to be analysed. Alternatively, they may be derived from mathematical or verbal models, or from one of the synoptic theories.

It has been stated that the two main lines of synoptic population theory are not distinguished from each other mainly by testable hypotheses. Certainly their proponents seldom explicitly put forward hypotheses by the testing of which the theories would stand or fall. This is partly a feature of their generalized form and all-embracing scope. Yet it is clearly important that a theory should be worked over and developed so as to yield adequate hypotheses.

As far as density-dependent regulation theory is concerned, it does provide hypotheses which some ecologists have put to the test. For example, Nicholson (1957) and others have pointed out that if a population is in a state of regulation, it should exhibit some degree of stable equilibrium (using this term in the physicists' sense) and show some power of recovery after its numbers have been artificially increased or reduced. Eisenberg (1966) carried out a test to determine whether a population of the snail *Lymnaea elodes* in a small pond in Southern Michigan exhibited this property. He subdivided part of the habitat with a number of snail-proof pens. In some pens he altered the numbers of adult snails to about one-fifth and five times the initial spring density of about 1,000 per pen, while others were left unaltered. Sampling during the summer showed there was an inverse relationship between the numbers of adults and the numbers of young. By the end of the egg-laying period there was no significant difference between the numbers of young in the different groups of pens (about 5,000 per pen), nor in the numbers of eggs. Further experiments supported the explanation that the fecundity of the snails was being limited by the supply of suitable food in the pond.

Of course, a test of one species and habitat is only a beginning. What we need to determine is how common this sort of stability is among animal populations, how rapid or slow the recovery is in varous circumstances, and so on (cf. Murdoch, 1970). We also require to know whether there are any populations which lack this property.

There is in fact a good deal of population work in which hypotheses derived from density-dependence theory have been tested, although the process has not often been explicitly sign-posted as such. Density-dependent processes have been identified and evaluated, and evidence about their role in population regulation has been produced. Methods such as life table analysis and key-factor analysis have been used in this sort of enquiry. Models of some density-dependent processes have been set up and tested.

To the extent that the two major theories are in contradiction, a single test may provide evidence against one and in support of the other. If some populations are found to remain at their new levels after an artificially imposed change of density in an unchanged environment, this is evidence against the presence of regulation. It is not so with all tests. A failure to find density relationships adequate to account for regulation is not convincing to anyone who appreciates the practical difficulties, unless a very thorough study of the dynamics of the population has been made.

The role of models

Models now play such a prominent part in population studies that it seems necessary to make a few general points here about their nature and function, although they are dealt with in more concrete and expert fashion by other contributors. A model is a representation in simplified or metaphorical form of aspects of a functioning system. It may take the form of a mechanical device, a mathematical equation, a diagram or even a verbal statement. Whatever their form, models have the same general function as mathematics: they are devices to assist thinking.

In general, models are not hypotheses nor theories. But a model, by revealing implications that were not obvious when it was constructed, may be a source of hypotheses, and some models do in fact serve as hypotheses, made clearer by being set down in model form. Models are generally more specific in their application and more readily disposable than are theories.

A model may be mainly descriptive, a convenient summary formula into which empirical data can be fed for the study of some straightforward relationship, e.g. Russell's equation

$$S_2 = S_1 + (A + G) - (C + M)$$

which states that the catchable stock of fish at the end of a year is equal to that at the beginning of the year, plus recruitment and growth, minus the year's catch and mortality. However, even such a simple model has an analytical aspect, laying down the categories involved and their mutual relationship.

At the opposite end of the scale to such descriptive or empirical models, we have purely deductive ones, developed from a set of assumptions, like that of Nicholson and Bailey (1935) for parasite-host interaction, or like the one presented by Royama (in these Proceedings). On another scale of reference, we may distinguish between deterministic and stochastic models.

A model may serve one or more of various purposes. It usually makes a clear statement of a set of relationships, perhaps representing the essence of some aspect of theory. It may serve to explore some of the consequences of its assumptions. It may have a didactic function, persuading us of the possibility of certain relationships. It may provide an analysis of a functioning system. A mathematical model provides a programme for calculation; it may be translated into a programme for a computer which then does the calculating. When fed sets of appropriate data, a model can derive predictions for testing or practical guidance. By providing predictions and hypotheses it can give impetus and direction to research.

In a more orderly world, models would always be constructed from assumptions whose validity has been tested and confirmed. In practice, this is often not done, and indeed a model when put to work may be used as a source of evidence regarding the validity of assumptions that are difficult to check directly. It is also desirable to check, when possible, whether the relationships embodied in the model exist in reality. Usually we seek to test the output of the model, to find to what extent its indications are qualitatively correct and quantitatively accurate.

Wilbert (in these Proceedings) has shown how cybernetic modelling may perhaps be used in the analysis of population dynamics; alternatively, it may suggest analagous methods derived directly from ecological bases.

Some requirements for progress

In this concluding section, I shall mention some more or less obvious points arising from the topics I have discussed above.

In relation to population theory, I should like to emphasize the valuable part played by

34

critical discussion. It seems to me to make at least as great a contribution to theory as do the original formulations. It is now generally better conducted than was once the case, and there is correspondingly less prejudice against 'theoretical controversy'.

Formulators of theory, and others, might usefully pay more attention to deriving testable hypotheses, and investigators could often enhance the general value of their work by making more use of hypotheses derived from theory, especially those bearing on the crucial differences.

The shortcomings of investigations which remain on the descriptive level emphasize the need for more penetrating studies. This might be met partly by a greater concentration on fewer projects. Certainly it calls for more team work continued over long periods. The team should often include, besides several ecologists, one or more specialists such as biometricians, physiologists, geneticists or biochemists, according to the demands of the problem. To achieve this on an adequate scale involves attracting greater resources for ecological work. In a world beset by many urgent population problems, there is a dangerous underinvestment in the subject.

Some of the specially valuable contributions to population study are the long-term comprehensive field studies of one or a few species. It would be a healthy development if other biologists could more often arrange to make specialised investigations on the same species as those being studied in these long-term projects.

Although most ecologists agree on their potential value, experimental methods have been relatively neglected in field studies. Efforts to overcome the obvious practical difficulties would probably be fully justified by the advances achieved.

The development of methods of detecting and analysing density-dependent and analogous relationships in the field have already made a substantial contribution to progress. There is, however, a great need for criticism and improvement of present methods, and for the development of better methods.

The use of models is making increasingly valuable contributions to the advance of the subject. In time, it may perhaps be possible to build a comprehensive compound model from fully tested elements; such a hyper-model having something like the status of a general population theory.

Mathematical methods are coming naturally, if belatedly, to play their natural predominant role in population study. A continuing problem is the frequent difficulty of communication between those who are expert at mathematics and ecologists who are not. Ecologists who have become biometricians often have better insight into the fieldworker's difficulties than has the professional statistician. (There are exceptions in both directions.) The main fault no doubt lies in the education of ecologists. Those who are now training will need all the mathematical knowledge and confidence they can acquire.

References

Andrewartha, H. G. & L. C. Birch, 1954. The distribution and abundance of animals. Chicago.
Bakker, K., 1964. Backgrounds of controversies about population theories and their terminologies. *Z. angew. Ent.* 53: 187–208.
Clark, L. R., P. W. Geier, R. D. Hughes & R. F. Morris, 1967. The ecology of insect populations in theory and practice. London.
Eisenberg, R. M., 1966. The regulation of density in a natural population of the pond snail, *Lymnaea elodes. Ecology* 47: 889–906.

Howard, L. O. & W. F. Fiske, 1911. The importation into the United States of the parasites of the gypsy moth and the brown-tail moth. *Bull. Bur. Ent. U.S. Dep. Agric.* 91.

Huffaker, C. B. & P. S. Messenger, 1964. In: Paul De Bach (Ed.), Biological control of insect pests and weeds, Chap. 3 and 4.

Murdoch, W. W., 1970. Population regulation and population inertia. *Ecology* 51: 497–502.

Nicholson, A. J., 1933. The balance of animal populations. *J. Anim. Ecol.* 2 (Suppl.); 132–178.

Nicholson, A. J. 1957. Discussion of Reynoldson, T. B. Population fluctuations in *Urceolaria mitra* (Peritricha) and *Enchytraeus albidus* (Oligochaeta) and their bearing on regulation. *Cold Spring Harb. Symp. quant. Biol.* 22: 313–327.

Nicholson, A. J. & V. A. Bailey, 1935. The balance of animal populations, Part. I. *Proc. zool. Soc. Lond.* 3: 551–598.

Reddingius, J. & P. J. den Boer, 1970. Simulation experiments illustrating stabilization of animal numbers by spreading of risk. *Oecologia (Berl.)* 5: 240–284.

Smith, H. S., 1935. The role of biotic factors in the determination of population densities. *J. econ. Ent.* 28: 873–898.

Solomon, M. E., 1957. Dynamics of insect populations. *A. Rev. Ent.* 2: 121–142.

Solomon, M. E., 1964. Analysis of processes involved in the natural control of insects. *Adv. Ecol. Res.* 2: 1–58.

Thompson, W. R., 1939. Biological control and the theories of the interactions of populations. *Parasitology* 31: 299–388.

Discussion

Participants: Solomon (Author), Andrewartha, Bakker (K.), den Boer (P. J.), Frank, Pimentel, Reddingius, Reynoldson, Scharloo, Varley, Vlijm and Wolda

Density-dependent factors and regulation

Evidently the argument about the need for density-dependent factors to explain the persistence of populations is still important for a number of reasons. Suppose an animal has separate generations and we express all population parameters in logarithms, with the increase F and mortality K; then

$$N_{t+1} - N_t = F - K \tag{1}$$

The actual values of F and K will vary from generation to generation for any species, but in any one area can be given mean values $\overline{F}$ and $\overline{K}$. $\overline{F}$ is a physiological property of the species only slowly altered by genetic change, $\overline{K}$ is a property of the interaction between an animal and its varying environment. If a species persists for a long time, then

$$\overline{F} - \overline{K} = 0 \tag{2}$$

which seems infinitely improbable if, over an animal's geographical range, there is no adjustment mechanism. Suppose the generation mortality includes a randomly variable component k_1 and a density-dependent component $k_2 = f(N)$. Then if $\overline{F} < \overline{k}_1$ the population becomes locally extinct, as at the edge of its range. If $\overline{F} > k_1$ the population rises until

$$\overline{F} = \overline{k}_1 + \overline{k}_2 = \overline{K} \tag{3}$$

The observed changes in N and K will now be random about mean values. Without life table data which separate k_1 and k_2, the cases 2 and 3 are indistinguishable. Do we have to (a) prove that density-dependent effects occur, or (b) disprove their presence? Technically we can only do (a) because the null hypothesis is refutable. The difference between the

36

views is neither trivial nor unimportant. Apparently Reddingius and den Boer have investigated the effects of diversity on stability using a model which lacks density-dependent effects. If in real situations density-dependent effects are hidden or undetectable in the observed variations of F or K, then stability can be explained over the whole geographical range of a species, and random walk to extinction becomes highly improbable until $\bar{F} = \bar{k}_1$ at the limits of the range (VARLEY).

To comment on Varley's statement:

– The model proposed by Reddingius and den Boer was not intended to be a realistic model of nature. We intended to indicate the importance of the number of factors, the heterogeneity in space and the heterogeneity of the population;

– If one is able to measure the influence of various mortality factors and assess their degree of density-dependence, a much more realistic and precise model can be built;

– For heterogeneously distributed populations which are perhaps themselves heterogeneous, the key-factor model will not work because it is a simple multiplicative model. In heterogeneous situations we need more complex models which then will have different mathematical properties. (REDDINGIUS).

It is not the presence of the density-dependent factor that matters; it is the magnitude of the density-dependent factor relative to the whole environment (ANDREWARTHA). It is indeed true that many density-dependent relationships are too feeble to be of much significance in regulation. On the other hand, there are also numerous examples of strong density-dependent relationships that play an important part in regulating abundance. This is taken to include regulation by a limited supply of food or other resources; the intensity of competition for the limiting resource is density-dependent. Also, it must be remembered that a relatively small density-dependent influence can exert regulation if there is a high and fairly constant density-independent mortality in each generation (AUTHOR).

It seems advisable to clear up something. If we discuss the relative importance of factors or processes we ultimately mean 'importance for the chance of survival (persistence) of the population' and we must try to test them in this way. Density-independent and density-dependent factors may both influence the chance of survival and, especially when many factors are acting together, it will be difficult not only to single out certain density-dependent effects but also to state that any of these effects is more important to the persistence of the population than others. Of course, a density may be reached – more or less frequently – at which limitation comes in, but this in itself is not the only important point; the critical point is what happens afterwards and to what extent the more or less density-dependent (or even hardly density-dependent) limitation or decrease of density has contributed to the survival of the population. We cannot solve these problems by discussing some simple averages; we shall have to study the pattern of density fluctuations through time itself, and also the frequency of local extinctions and of refoundings, the effects of dispersal and the influences of heterogeneity within the population and in its environment. Most controverses might be removed by shifting our attention from the degree of density-dependence of factors or processes, to the more general topic of the degree to which factors or (stochastic) processes may favourably influence the (chance of) survival of a population or species (DEN BOER). In population studies, we are often concerned with the importance of factors or processes as causes of fluctuation, or as agents of regulation, or as an influence on the level of abundance. Surely not many ecologists are so pre-occupied with population extinction that they would accept den Boer's dictum (AUTHOR).

The term 'self-regulation' seems appropriate only in cases like that of the aphids discussed by Way (in these Proceedings) when, for example, density limiting effects are self-imposed by an aggregation behaviour which is apparently not dictated by the pattern of the habitat. It might be used also when social animals (notably some insects, birds, and mammals) exhibit a behaviour pattern that limits the numbers in the social group; but perhaps 'social regulation' would then be more appropriate (AUTHOR's answer to REYNOLDSON).

Although investigations during 30 years by many entomologists did not provide any evidence for the operation of a regulating mechanism in tsetse flies, Buxton's conclusion is that a density-dependent factor *must* be regulating the density of *Glossina morsitans*. Is that conclusion realistic (ANDREWARTHA)? Buxton's expectation is very likely to be found correct. It seems very improbable that populations which persist as those of tsetse flies do, are not regulated in some way. It is highly desirable that some investigators should search (or continue to search) for regulatory aspects of the population dynamics of tsetse. If there is a natural regulatory process at work, it is surely important for the economic control of tsetse to know what this process is, and how it operates. One would like to know more, for example, about the reactions of their hosts to attacks by tsetse (AUTHOR).

Andrewartha remarked that the crucial point in tsetse ecology was not the actual amount of food, but its availability, and that therefore the density of the food supply did not depend on the density of tsetse. Now Glasgow in his book pointed out that tsetse had a definite preference for certain animals (warthogs) and appeared to be taking quite considerable amounts of blood from them. Warthogs may not be able to stand tsetse feeding indefinitely when tsetse density is high. Moreover, the animals are known to move away from high tsetse densities, because of the nuisance caused by them (BAKKER).

Solomon suggested as a possible density-dependent factor in the population dynamics of tsetse, the development of resistance in the host. Resistance is often genetically important. Does this not point to the possibility that genetic differences are important in population dynamics (SCHARLOO)? I do not know whether there is any evidence of genetic change in the resistance of mammalian hosts to tsetse. To be relevant to the argument, the genetic change in resistance would have to be recent, or still in progress, otherwise it would simply be classed along with the rest of the hosts' established characteristics. What I had in mind was the possibility of individually developed physiological resistance – immunity or allergic reactions (AUTHOR).

Importance of genetic components in the dynamics of populations

One of the differences between the two major schools of thought is, as Andrewartha and Birch explained, that one school is looking for regulatory mechanisms, whereas the other seeks to know what determines the fluctuation in numbers including regulatory processes. The latter seems to be more general. But whatever approach one has, the the importance of genetic factors is dismissed all too quickly as mere modifications or mere density-legislative factors. There are hypotheses which suggest that there may be regulation by genetic processes, and these have definitely not yet been refuted. Even if they should affect only the level about which populations fluctuate, they still cannot be ignored if we are to understand what determines the density of individuals in a population. The fact that only in a few cases it has been shown that genetic processes are important, may mean only that in all the other species that have been studied the investigators never examined the

38

genetics of that species; hence, the conclusion that genetic processes are important only in a few cases is at present unwarranted. If one starts to study genetic processes only when other processes do not produce an adequate explanation of a natural phenomenon it is analogous to saying that one is prepared to include predation in one's research only after it has been proven to be relevant. But how does one decide that predation (or genetic processes) are important if one does not study it (WOLDA)?

I agree with Wolda. We cannot dismiss genetics as Solomon has done. For example, how could one understand the dynamics of the numbers of parasites attacking the sawfly in Canada without investigating the genetics of their interaction? The sawfly became highly resistant to the parasite and reduced the parasite population to very low numbers (PIMENTEL).

I disagree completely with Wolda's opening remark. The widespread use of key-factor and life table analyses is one indication that adherents of the density-dependence approach are concerned with density-independent causes of fluctuations as well as with regulatory processes. There may be examples in which genetic changes play an important part in regulation, as modifying or legislative factors; the internal equivalent of external changes such as a rise in the mean temperature of the environment. I accept that the possibility of genetic feedback playing a more direct part in regulation cannot be dismissed a priori; but there are two reasons why most investigators of population dynamics (especially in the field) do not study the genetic changes in the population. The first is that the importance of one or more of the traditionally studied factors – e.g. weather, natural enemies, or food limitation – to the dynamics of the population is often obvious from an early stage. These major phenomena must be dealt with first. The study of these may supply an adequate explanation of fluctuation and regulation. Whether it does or not, many of the data from such a study would be essential as background for an investigation of the role played by genetic changes. The second reason is a simple practical one. Work on populations is very demanding of time and man-power. It is no mean achievement to complete an adequate study of the numerical aspects of the population dynamics of a single species. It is a matter of 'first things first'. It seems to me that if one is setting out to make such a study, it is unpractical, and against common sense, to assume that genetic changes are going to be important and to devote, say, half one's resources to this aspect. If, in the course of the study, evidence is found that genetic change is indeed a major factor, then certainly one should deploy the available resources accordingly. In brief, genetic changes, like other qualitative changes in organisms, may be important for the dynamics of some populations, but numerical studies should come first (AUTHOR).

Would it not be advisable to compare the numbers of a population (combined with the genetic variance) of ancient species (e.g. *Limulus*) with populations of species which are rather new in the fossil record (VLIJM?)

Evolution

Solomon should include Darwin in his scheme of population theories. Darwin's theory linked population regulation to natural selection. He started from four basic assumptions: (1) all organisms are able to increase strongly in numbers under favourable circumstances; (2) populations appear to be limited in size; (3) individuals have different properties; (4) part of this variability is genetically determined. If there were no limit to population size, no evolution would be possible. There has been a long-lasting difference of opinion between population geneticists who emphasise selection (Fisher and Ford) and those who stress the importance of random processes (Sewall Wright). This difference of opinion has disappeared, and we may hope that the same will happen as a result of this meeting as regards the difference between population ecologists emphasizing regulation and those emphasizing random processes (BAKKER). My presentation of the population theories had to be cursory. Besides omitting Darwin and other precursors I lumped together anonymously that large and varied band of postwar ecologists who base their views on the idea of regulation by density-dependent factors or processes. I was concerned to present as simply as possible the two mainstreams of modern thought on the subject. Although one of these can fairly be described as orthodox, in the sense of including the great majority of population ecologists, and the other as dissident, many of those who prefer the former standpoint will have also learned from the opposing one. The conflict between them will no doubt be left behind as the subject advances, a process which will be hastened by quantative studies of different sorts of relationship which influence the abundance of various animals in the field (AUTHOR).

I would like to support Bakker's remark. Undoubtedly we have to keep in mind that quantative changes or regulation are mostly linked with qualitative selection, and are thus a part of the major process of evolution. Therefore, the mechanisms of regulation must be in agreement with the principles and mechanisms of evolution and their genetical backgrounds. When we accept this, then we have to check our hypotheses on population dynamics against the principles of evolution, and reject those hypotheses which do not agree with the principles of evolution (FRANK). I agree that population fluctuations and regulation are likely to be often accompanied by selection – chiefly against the very young, the aged or the unlucky, but also sometimes against the genetically inferior with respect to the adverse conditions currently predominant. It is generally agreed that selection of genotypes is the basis of evolution. But it may well be that selection is generally of only minor importance for population dynamics, which is concerned with relatively short-term processes. Evolution is important for population dynamics chiefly as the provider of the organisms that act it out (AUTHOR).

Proc. Adv. Study Inst. Dynamics Numbers Popul. (Oosterbeek, 1970) 41–63

The dynamics of plant populations

J. L. Harper and J. White

School of Plant Biology, University College of North Wales, Bangor, Wales
Department of Botany, University College, Dublin, Ireland

Abstract

A schematic model is described for the successive stages that determine the regulation of number and mass in plant populations. This is envisaged as involving:
– the seed bank: the accumulated reserve of viable propagules present in and on the soil; the size of this is determined by the recruitment from the seed-rain and by the rates of loss by germination, predation etc.
– the environmental sieve: the factors in the heterogeneous soil environment, which, operating at the level of scale of individual seeds, determines whether or not a seed is recruited into a population of seedlings
– the correlated changes in plant number and size as a seedling population becomes thinned and individuals increase in size
– the phase of seed production which contributes to a new seed-rain.
  Analyses of examples from annual and biennial species and from forest trees illustrate the stages at which the regulation may occur. Studies of the population dynamics of herbaceous perennial species are difficult and laborious. Much of the most significant work in this field, e.g. of Rabotnov and his colleagues, is not widely known. An expansion of the simple schema originally proposed for the population dynamics of annual species and trees allows for the description of perennial systems. Feed-back systems are incorporated to represent the influence of young and mature perennial plants on Phases I–IV.

The major stimuli to the development of a study of the dynamics of plant populations are two, essentially paralleling those in animal population dynamics. The first stimulus, derived from Malthus, was Darwin's emphasis and re-emphasis of the struggle for existence that follows remorselessly from the capacity of organisms to increase their numbers exponentially. Here (in 'The origin of species') attention was focussed on reproduction and death, alike in animal and plant communities, in the struggle for existence. The second stimulus, paralleling the role of fisheries research and pest control problems in accelerating the pace of development of animal population dynamics, was the concern of agronomists with optimal plant densities for crops and with the interactions between the crops and associated plant species, weeds. These two stimuli, the one applied and concerned with optimizing plant yields, the other pure in its concern to understand evolutionary mechanisms and the diversity of natural vegetation have developed largely independently and still cross-fertilize very infrequently.

Although plants provide ideal material for formal studies of population behaviour, it is with animals that the greater part of empirical field and laboratory study has been made. Botanical studies started without the formal structure given by Verhulst and by Lotka and

Volterra, although it is interesting that apparently the first serious attempt to make a mathematical formulation of the population dynamics of closely related species living together was made by a botanist (Nägeli, who presented a theoretical mathematical model in 1874). His was apparently a dead-end in the botanical development of a theoretical population dynamics. In experimentation, it was not until 1917 that Tansley published his famous experiments involving the growth of two species of *Galium* in mixtures, on various soil types, and demonstrated that the resultant struggle for existence was resolved in favour of different species on different soils. Rather similar experiments were made in 1927 and 1928 in Russia by Sukatschew on *Taraxacum* and *Matricaria* and in the USA by Clements et al. (1929). It is interesting that these early studies were concerned to approach directly the problem of the relationships *between* species and to bypass any concern with the effects of density within single species stands. The logic of this order of priorities now seems misplaced to those reared on a Lotka-Volterra structured science in which the significance of interspecific activity is measured against intra-specific activity. Indeed, in 1945 at a meeting of the British Ecological Society the view was widely accepted that the problems of the ecology of closely related species and Gause's hypothesis were largely irrelevant to plants. It was not until de Wit's masterly contribution to the study of plant competiton in 1960 that an experimental structure was available for a deliberate and direct comparison of inter- and intraspecific interference in plant populations.

The agronomists' concern with optimal density of cropping led directly to the development of mathematically formulated relationships between components of crop yield and plant density worked out for single species stands, and focused attention on the plastic reaction to density stress, which is relatively unimportant in many animals. The plasticity of individual development and the vast range of size and reproductive output achieved under varying stress conditions derives from plants being of indeterminate growth. A consequence of the plasticity of individual plant growth is that counts of plant numbers as a measure of population size may be useful to a geneticist but have little meaning to an agronomist or a production ecologist, and consequently there are few data from the agronomic literature of relevance to the ecologist concerned with the dynamics of plant numbers. However, plasticity of development does offer to the plant ecologist, in the form of the extent of development of an individual, measures of the environmental stress; for the animal ecologist environmental stress may be reflected more often in changes in numbers rather than in individual size (there are of course major exceptions to this phenomenon, and many fish and some insects parallel closely a plant in showing variations in size and reproductive output that reflects the degree of crowding they have suffered).

Part of the Darwinian tradition in the study of plant population dynamics is the observation of the behaviour of plants in permanent plots over periods of time. Charting the fate of individual plants (to grow, to flower, to remain vegetative, to die) has been undertaken by few people. Observations on the longevity of populations, rates of turnover in their vegetative and reproductive composition, etc. are extremely laborious. The work of Tamm (1956), Sagar (1959) and the Moscow School of Rabotnov and co-workers since the 1940's hint at regularities in natural population dynamics that are quite surprising. There is an impressive tradition of field observation in Russia (Rabotnov and others) which has received too little attention hitherto. The long term data of foresters also provide valuable sources of information for the development of plant population dynamics (White and Harper, 1970) but they deal mainly with planted, managed systems.

The gap between the pure and applied plant sciences has been wide, and many ecologists and evolutionists have been unwilling to accept that experiments involving single species of plant (and cultivars at that) have relevance to problems of natural evolutionary ecology. It remains, of course, an act of faith, in ecology as in other experimental sciences, that an understanding of natural complexity can be approached by studying the behaviour of simple experimental populations. However, there is perhaps some real danger that the population ecology of plants may come to be concerned wholly with experimental models of simple systems and that their ultimate relevance to understanding natural complexity may be forgotten. It seems important that two types of experimental study which have been called 'synthetic' and 'analytic' (Harper, 1970) be pursued concurrently. In the synthetic approach, the study of the reaction of plants to each other in mixed and pure stands may be pursued in controlled environments and controlled densities, and detailed and sophisticated relationships established with a high degree of precision. The analytic approach involves direct manipulation of naturally occurring plant populations by artificial changes in their density, or the selective removal of individual species (Putwain and Harper, 1970). Modern herbicides used as ecological tools may facilitate this approach.

It is also important that some coherent body of theory should begin to evolve in plant populations studies and this cannot be achieved simply by absorbing the theories of animal ecologists. There are quite fundamental ways in which a generalised plant population theory must differ from that appropriate for animals (Harper, 1968). In particular the energy and nutrient supplies of a plant population do not represent a potentially exponentially growing food supply, whereas most animals live on food that is part of or produced by populations, and governed by population laws. Higher plants lack any choice in energy supply, and their population behaviour is fundamentally affected by the intensity and rhythm of the radiant energy they absorb. Furthermore, the plant's resources are not discrete except at the atomic or quantal level: there are no unit bodies of food or prey to be searched for or captured.

The remainder of the paper is an attempt to sketch a basic model that describes the behaviour of plant populations. It is presented in two parts, the first of which is principally derived from experimental studies involving one and two species populations (i.e. synthetic studies). The second part attempts to extend the model to systems of perennial plants accounting for various features of their behaviour which have been observed over longer periods than in the case of the experimental systems. The model may serve as a beginning of attempts at more complex model building in more sophisticated systems.

The model

Seed rain and sieve

It is convenient to consider a bare area onto which a rain of seeds of a single species is falling (Fig. 1, Phase I). In the case of a very low intensity of seed fall, a regular immigrant population is maintained, dependent simply on the frequency of the seed rain. Under these circumstances the regulatory forces operate from outside in determining the seed rain, and within the chosen area one may envisage a population maintained at low density in which individuals are far enough apart not to interfere with each other. (In nature the seed rain can be very high however; Roberts (1970) mentions influxes of up to $62 \times 10^3/m^2$ of viable seeds at the soil surface. Undoubtedly many may be eaten by animals but few quantitative assessments are available; e.g. Pinowski and Wojcik, 1968.) The seeds

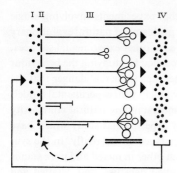

I II   III   IV

Fig. 1 Schema of the development of a plant population. Phase I represents the incoming seed rain. Phase II is the environmental mesh or sieve, determining the number of seeds which become established. Phase III incorporates various features of the development of the plants: they grow and reproduce within the limits of environmental constraints, shown as heavy double lines. During development some individuals may die, others reproduce in varying amounts, contributing a further seed rain (Phase IV) to a future generation.

landing may be dormant or non-dormant depending on the species (e.g. *Senecio vulgaris* and *Poa annua*, common annual weeds, produce many seeds which may germinate immediately on landing). Not all the seeds landing on the hypothetical bare area will land in sites suitable for germination. The soil surface may therefore be considered to operate as a sieve, determining what fraction of the incoming seed rain germinates to produce young plants (Fig. 1, Phase II). We therefore add to the intensity of the seed rain a factor describing the chance that a seed will produce a plant (even at densities so low that interference between established seedlings does not occur).

The concept of the soil surface acting as a sieve has been worked out in some detail by Harper, Sagar and others in a series of experiments in which it has been shown that quite slight variation in soil surface determine a minute scale heterogeneity of safe and unsafe sites, which selects from the seeds falling on the area those that will germinate and those that will not. Moreover, there is clearly a very strongly developed species subtlety in the requirement of safe sites, and the variations in seed sizes and shapes and their relevance to germination on heterogeneous media has recently been reviewed (Harper et al., 1970). For example, Bakker (1960) examined the germination biology of *Cirsium arvense* and *Tussilago farfara*, very common weeds of newly reclaimed polders, and found that they germinate to a maximum at high (30 °C) and strongly alternating (10–28 °C) temperatures – precisely the sort of temperature regime which occurs in the uppermost centimetres of the bare or thinly vegetated polder soils in the spring. The sowing depth for optimal germination is 0.5 cm for *Cirsium* and at the surface for *Tussilago*. White (1968) has shown that minute differences in seed size and surface texture can profoundly influence the percentage germination of seeds of *Brassica* and *Raphanus* cultivars (both with spherical seeds and each showing 96% germination on filter pads in petri dishes at about 15 °C: Fig. 2.). The safety of a microsite for a particular seed may be determined by its ability to extract sufficient water from the substrate and yet be protected against loss of water (Harper and Benton, 1966). With species showing seed polymorphism (genetic or somatic), two or more safe sites may be exploited by the seed population. Williams has described somatic polymorphisms in *Chenopodium* (Williams and Harper, 1965) of which four visually recognisable categories of seeds exist – brown-smooth, brown-reticulate, black-smooth and black-reticulate. The brown seeds germinate rapidly when supplied with water, even at temperatures down to 0 °C; the black-reticulate seed exhibit dormancy which is not broken by chilling, and the black-smooth seeds are partly released from dormancy by chilling. The ecological potentiality of each category is accordingly different. Such polymorphisms may vary in relation to the location of the seed on the parent plant (see Harper et al., 1970).

44

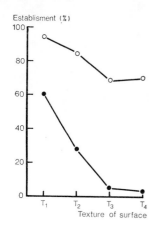

Establisment (%)

Texture of surface

Fig. 2. Establishment of seeds of different sizes on surfaces of varied textures. Seeds of *Brassica napus* ($\bigcirc$) and *Raphanus sativus* ($\bullet$), spherical seeds of 1.5 and 2.5 mm diam., respectively, were sown on vermiculite which had been passed through sieves to give four particle sizes, on the surfaces of which seeds were sown: $T_1 > 5.5, < 9.0$ mm; T_2 3.2–5.5 mm; T_3 2.1–3.1 mm; $T_4 < 2.1$ mm. The numbers established after four weeks are shown. Within two weeks 93% of the *Brassica* seeds had become established on T_1 and there was no further increase in this percentage. (Both species have over 90% germination within five days on germination pads).

To date, our understanding of the regulation of germination has not progressed beyond the recognition and study of some of the components of the microenvironment which are important for the seed to pass through the selective sieve. Temperature, water economy, depth in soil, intensity, spectral composition and periodicity of light are the environmental variables most commonly used by the seed for identifying its environment, and these have all been examined in experimental systems; their range and rhythms under natural conditions have scarcely been monitored. As a general principle one can agree with Koller (1969) that evolution has led to an almost universal imposition of regulating mechanisms on seed germination which will prevent the entire reproductive capacity of the species being used up in any given habitat at a given time, except where and when the probability of survival is maximal. Koller cites several examples of quantitative variability in dormancy of seeds from a single parent plant – their behaviour may be a directly adaptive counter to the 'uncertainty factor' in survival.

Phase II, the sieve, consequently selects out those seeds which can germinate at a given time and place. The remaining portion of the seed rain may be thrown (often by burial) into a state of induced or enforced dormancy from which it may emerge to contribute to a later generation of seedlings, or in which state it may die.

Dormancy of seeds

The study of the dynamics of this stored part of the population is interesting in itself. Roberts and Dawkins (1967) have shown that for weed seeds of horticultural soil, the buried seed population has apparently a constant death risk, so that it may be assigned a constant half-life. This half-life is species-specific and depends also on the frequency of cultivation. Even without cultivation the death risk remains constant. The exponential decline in the number of viable seeds is shown in Fig. 3. It should be noted that recruitment of new seeds to the population was prevented during the period of observation. There is little quantitative information to date on the relationship between buried viable seed populations and seedlings produced following soil disturbance by cultivation, but the seedlings appear to represent only a small proportion of the viable seeds present; Chancellor (1965), for instance, showed that a dense seedling stand of *Matricaria recutita* (1280/m²) represented only 4% of the number of viable seeds present in the soil. Roberts and Dawkins

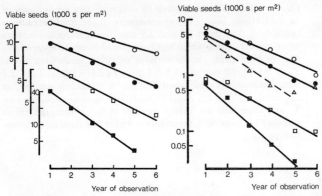

Viable seeds (1000 s per m²)

Viable seeds (1000 s per m²)

Year of observation

Year of observation

Fig. 3. Decrease in the numbers of viable arable weed seeds (in the absence of further seeding) on soils under various cultivation treatments.
Left: All species together: undisturbed soil, top 23 cm (○); cultivated twice a year, top 23 cm (●); cultivated four times a year, top 23 cm (□); cultivations involved in rotation of vegetable crops, top 15 cm (■). The exponential decay rate shown is about 23 % each year. (The scales on the ordinate are the same in each case, but the decay lines are displaced for clarity). (Redrawn from Roberts 1970).
Right: Species-specific rates of decrease on plots dug four times a year. *Chenopodium album* ○; *Capsella bursa-pastoris* ●; *Poa annua* △; *Solanum nigrum* □; *Stellaria media* ■. The decay rate is about 25 % per year, except for *Stellaria* (56 %). (Redawn from Roberts and Dawkins, 1967).

(1967) give some indication of the effect of a certain regime of soil disturbance on the proportion of viable stored seeds emerging in the top 23 cm of soil (Table 1). These were plots on which no new seed rain was allowed to fall. Although there was a rapid (exponential) decline in the total number of viable seeds in the soil, the percentage of the store which gave rise to seedlings varied comparatively little from year to year except on the undisturbed soil subsequent to 1961/62. This implies, of course, that the number of seedlings appearing declines exponentially from year to year; this is what happens (Roberts and Dawkins, 1967).

Table 1. Numbers of seedlings emerging per year as percentages of the numbers of viable seeds in the top 23 cm of soil present at the beginning of the year. (Data of Roberts and Dawkins, 1967.)

	1961	1962	1963	1964	1965	1966
Dug four times a year	10.7	6.1	9.4	8.3	8.7	9.6
Dug twice a year	7.8	4.7	6.7	6.1	9.0	7.2
Undisturbed	4.5	1.7	0.6	0.3	0.2	0.3

Table 2. Productivity of high density stands of *Helianthus annuus* (Data of Kuroiwa, 1960).

Plant classification	Number of plants/m²	Biomass (g/m²)	Net production (g/m²/day)
Dominant	16	105	4.8
Large intermediate	32	80	3.2
Intermediate	58	60	2.0
Small intermediate	64	35	0.4
Suppressed	30	8	–0.1

A recent pioneer study by Naylor (1970) has involved an attempt to use mark/recapture methods for seeds landing on a soil surface. He marked a part of the population of seed of *Alopecurus myosuroides* falling naturally on an area of arable land. The marking procedure involved spraying the spikelets with droplets of fluorescent paint; the seedlings emerging from the soil could then be recognized as belonging to the marked population. These experiments indicate that for this species in a ploughed environment, some 80% of the seedlings developing in a particular year were derived from seed that had fallen naturally in the previous year, only 20% of the population being from older seed. Attempts have been made to describe models of the dynamics of a plant population simply using the seed population in the soil as the index (Harper, 1960; Hayashi and Numata, 1967; Roberts, 1970), but although there are available measures of seed immigration, emigration, death rate, germination rate, for specific cases, no attempt has yet been made to measure all of these parameters of any single species in any single habitat.

Plant density and yield

The model has now taken a rain of seeds through an environmental sieve which has determined the density of seedling establishment; the subsequent relationship between individual plant weight and the density at which they develop has been the major type of agronomic contribution to plant population dynamics. It is apparent that over a very wide range of densities, many plant species reach a constant final yield of dry matter per unit area, independent of the densities that have been sown. This can be illustrated (Fig. 4) in the form of the relationship between the logarithm of plant weight and the logarithm of plant density (Kira et al., 1953). Over the range of densities at which plants interfere with each other, this relationship is linear and with progress of time achieves a slope of 1 (constant final yield): $w = Kp^{-a}$, where w is individual plant weight and p is plant density; K and a are constants, depending on the duration of growth after seeding, a being a measure of competitive stress. With progress of time the value of a rises from 0 at $t = 0$ to 1 at $t = \infty$. For a = 1, the equation degenerates into the form $y = c$; that is, the ultimate yield of an area of ground is independent of planting density. The reciprocal of individual plant dry weight plotted against density gives another convenient and effective way of describing the time sequence of the growth of plant populations. Shinozaki and Kira (1956), Holliday (1960) and de Wit (1960) independently derived the relationship, $1/w = Ap + B$, where w and p have the same meaning as in the previous equation. Such equations appear to be of

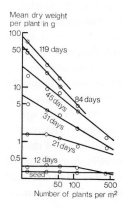

Fig. 4. The influence of density and time of harvest on the mean weight of individual soybean plants. (Redrawn from Kira et al., 1953)

wide generality, and seem to represent one of the fundamental quantitative principles underlying the time/space trend of intraspecific competition among higher plants. However, the yield of particular plant parts may sometimes decline at very high densities, and 'laws' of constant final yield may then need modification (Bleasdale, 1966; Farazdaghi and Harris, 1968). De Wit (1968) has pointed out how the growth habit of the plants may determine whether such relationships hold or not at high densities. Constancy of final yield sometimes also holds for seed yield, sometimes not. This depends on the fruiting pattern. Plants with terminate growing points and no alternative sinks (small grains, pineapple) may be 'miniaturised' by dense planting, without sacrificing seed yield per unit area. However, plants with auxilliary sinks besides ears or fruits (maize, oil palm, Brussels sprouts), divert more and more carbohydrate to these sinks at denser plantings and yield less and less seeds.

Self-thinning

In the majority of these studies, mortality has been negligible during the growth of the population or has been ignored. The agronomic models may often have been misleading in under-emphasising the role of mortality. The fact that in agricultural practice many of the species sown have large seeds, that attempts are made to space these evenly, to sow at optimal depth, all at the same time, giving more or less uniform emergence, probably minimises the amount of mortality occurring in a population during its natural life history. However, self-thinning is a well-known phenomenon in overcrowded forest nurseries and in horticultural practice, and it is not surprising that when natural and artificially created plant populations are examined carefully and the numbers of individuals are followed during the growth of the population, a process of natural thinning is often observed.

Yoda et al. (1963) have described the concomitant changes in plant numbers and individual weights in populations of *Erigeron canadensis* and other species, which suggest that self-thinning and the growth rate of survivors are interlinked. They showed that a graphical plot of changes in the logarithm of individual plant weight against the logarithm of changing plant density produces a linear relationship with a slope of $-3/2$. This has now been confirmed for a number of other species (White and Harper, 1970). We need, therefore, to build into the model description of plant populations such a process of reduction of numbers associated with increase in individual size of these plants which passed through the environmental sieve (Fig. 1, Phase III).

An example of the thinning 'law' is shown in Fig. 5. A feature of the relationship is clearly indicated; irrespective of the starting density of seedlings, crowded stands self-thin along a common line, the higher density stands thinning earlier. The relationship does not continue indefinitely, however. Subject to the physiological size which the plant is genetically capable of achieving, or the opportunity to develop governed by the growing season, an upper limit is set to individual plant size. Although the numbers decline, it should be noted that the environment under these conditions is more effectively utilized; the total biomass increases, since if the relation $w = C p^{-3/2}$ holds, its corollary $Y = wp = C p^{-1/2}$ also holds, where Y is the total yield per unit area. That is, Y increases with decreasing density, while thinning is proceeding. Eventually the relationship shown in Fig. 4 may be achieved – that is, a constant final yield per unit area. But the two relationships should be clearly distinguished. That shown in Fig. 4 is concerned with the relationships in stands of different density which started growth simultaneously and have continued to grow under

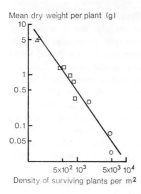

Mean dry weight per plant (g)

Density of surviving plants per m²

Fig. 5. Changes in numbers and individual plant weight of wheat undergoing self-thinning with time. Initial starting densities were approximately 5400 (○), 1078 (□) and 184 (△) plants/m². Thinning begins earlier in the stands of higher density. The regression equation is log w = 3.83 − 1.39* log p, where w is the mean weight per plant and p the corresponding, surviving plant density. (Redrawn from White and Harper, 1970).

* Within 2 degrees of − 1.5.

similar habitat conditions, whereas that in Fig. 5, the $^3/_2$ power relation, gives the interrelation between stands of different ages or starting densities on the same or different habitats. Further treatment of this distinction is given in Yoda et al. (1963).

In a single species population it is apparent that the frequency distribution of individual plant weights changes with time from a normal distribution through to a log-normal distribution as a proportion of the individuals present gain ascendency, and presumably control, over the availability of environmental resources. It is the weaklings in the population which are thinned. Kuroiwa (1960) classified individuals in a dense stand of *Helianthus annuus* into five groups, ranging from dominant to suppressed (Table 2). His results indicate the decline of net production in suppressed plants even beyond the compensation point, when the plants are respiring reserves presumably accumulated at an earlier stage in the population history, before the development of excessive skewness. However, it is worth noting that small suppressed individuals of perennial herbs and grasses may survive for many years (Tamm, 1948; Chippindale, 1948). Internode measurements and leaf scars on tree seedlings in forest shade suggest that these may remain close to compensation point for long periods. In dense populations, the skewed frequency distribution of plant weight indicates that a large proportion of the population falls into the suppressed class, so that a high rate of mortality is to be expected. Highly skewed weight distributions may be associated with approximately normal height distribution (Ogden, 1970) so that low-weight individuals in dense populations often struggle to reach a canopy provided by a few larger plants; they may as a result be lank and etiolated, with a relatively increased proportion of non-photosynthetic to photosynthetic tissue (stem to leaves).

Ross (1968) in a series of experiments introduced slight variations in sowing times of individual plants, and showed that relative timing was of great importance in determining the 'pecking order' in the log-normal distribution which develops. In one experiment he noted the time of emergence of each successive group of ten cocksfoot (*Dactylis glomerata*) seedlings, sown in pure stands at a density of approximately three seeds per cm². The broken line in Fig. 6 gives the regression which might be expected if the size of the plants were directly related to the time from emergence. (This line joins the starting capital at zero time to the mean weight of the earliest emerging group of seedlings.) 'However the mean weight of later emerging groups falls well below this line and the last group to emerge consisted of plants which had barely exceeded their starting capital 35 days after emergence. As it is unlikely that even the plants in the earliest emerging group had escaped interference, the real potential growth line is probably considerably

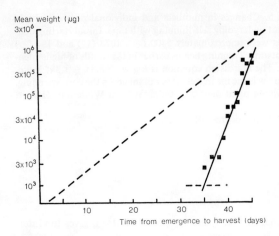

Fig. 6. Effect of time from emergence to harvest on the mean weight of plants of *Dactylis glomerata*. The broken line joins starting capital of seeds at zero time to the mean weight per plant of the earliest emerging group of the population. (Redrawn after Ross, 1968, omitting points for two replicates for clarity: the unbroken line is a fitted line for *three* replicated populations and accounts for 95.5% of the total variance of *all* sample points).

←— upper 95% confidence limit on seed capital.

steeper than shown and the proportionate suppression of later emerging groups even greater than the graph indicates. The advantage to a seedling of early emergence is manifest.' (Ross, 1968).

Other features of the model

The development of plant populations of single species to conform to the constant final yield irrespective of density implies an environmental restriction or resource limitation. The model (Fig. 1) therefore envisages a population emerging from the environmental sieve and developing by increasing plant weight and decreasing plant numbers within an environmental constraint that places limits on the total mass that the population may a-chieve. This in turn places limits on the rate at which new seed is produced from the plant population which will initiate the next cycle of generations. However, as pointed out previously, the actions of the 'environmental constraint' on the mass of plant tissue produced and on the number of reproductive units formed are not necessarily correlated, optimum seed production may occur before the upper limit of plant numbers or biomass per unit area has been achieved. Oxley (unpublished), for example, has shown this pattern of behaviour for *Digitalis purpurea*; at high plant densities the proportion of reproductive individuals declines (Fig. 7).

If two species are brought into this model, interest is focussed on the relative intensity of the seed rains and the extent to which the environmental sieves operate differentially upon them to determine the densities at which they start to interact among themselves and with each other, and subsequently (Phase III) the effect that each has on the other in the process of thinning and in the process of individual development. The elegant models of de Wit (1960), involving the use of the replacement series, have led to sophisticated ana-lyses of the competitive interrelationships of pairs of species and have enabled the accurate description of replacement rates of one species over another to be made in a way that is suitable for introduction to the model.

There are indications (Harper and McNaughton, 1962) that in mixed populations some species may react rather specifically to their own densities in determining their growth rate and mortality rate. The model, accordingly, has to allow for the existence of not only density-dependent but also frequency-dependent relationships dependent on the relative

50

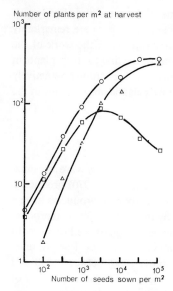

Number of plants per m² at harvest

Number of seeds sown per m²

Fig. 7. The relationship between seed density and the total number of plants/m² (○); the number of flowering plants/m² (□); the number of vegetative plants/m² (△) of *Digitalis purpurea*. (Unpublished data of R. Oxley.)

frequency of interacting species within Phase III.

A further major element to be brought into the model is the change that is brought about by the growth of one year's population on the nature and selectivity of the sieve, which may affect the performance of the next generation's seed rain. There is abundant evidence (see Knapp, 1967 for review) that the presence of growing vegetation affects the chance of seeds germinating on an area. The temperature and humidity of the soil surface are changed, as is the quality of the light. The germination of many seeds is influenced by the near-red/far-red light balance which they receive and Black (1969) has drawn attention to its importance in regulating germination under foliage: its influence on seed dormancy has so far received little attention from an ecological viewpoint. The character of the bare soil surface with which the model began will be drastically altered, to an extent that no seeds may pass through the environmental sieve at all. For example, McNaughton (1968) records an autotoxic regulation in populations of *Typha latifolia* by which exudations from the leaves inhibit the germination and growth of *Typha* seedlings. He suggests indeed that *Typha* marshes are unlikely sites for the establishment of *Typha* seedlings as a result ('auto-toxic feedback').

The model in relation to perennial plants

What are the population dynamics of perennial plants in relation to the model? Given the persistence of such plants, what is their reproductive life-span, their rates of replacement, their contribution to the seed rain each year? The answers to such queries are so far little known, since most of the statements and principles established to date about plant population dynamics concern annual species, predominantly crop plants. As Watt has emphasised elsewhere in these Proceedings, a preoccupation with economically important species living together at high densities, often unnaturally, may conceal certain very important features of the 'way the world works'. Theoretical models and the type of hypothesis they help to generate, may rely too heavily on the behavioural patterns of only a few species. Can the study of perennial plants add further to some of the principles already out-lined? Unfortunately, as in other branches of ecology, long runs of data are remarkably rare in plant population ecology. There is one important exception in the work of the Russian School of population ecologists. Shennikov was one of the first to study plants in permanent quadrats (1924), a Darwinian approach to population observation now actively pursued in the USSR, and dating principally from Rabotnov's classic observations in the 1940s (Rabotnov, 1950).

Reproductive strategies of perennial plants

Among perennial organisms the two strikingly different life-history strategies are recogniz-able, the repeating producers and the 'big-bang' (Gadgil and Bossert, 1970) producers. Most animals and perennial plants are of the first type. The big-bang reproducers have a reproductive effort of zero for many age classes followed by the single suicidal reproduc-tive effort; this category includes organisms such as the Pacific salmon or the Foxglove. In plants either kind may occur depending on environmental circumstances. For example, *Trifolium pratense* (red clover) has been observed (Rabotnov, 1960) between 1940 and 1959 on sub-alpine meadows at 1950 m O.D. and on floodplain meadows in the valley of the Oka River. The number of clover plants in the floodplain meadows fluctuates so great-ly as to constitute an agronomic problem. Here the plants usually flower once, within two years of seedling establishment, and then die; in years of favourable meteorological con-ditions vegetative individuals are transformed en masse into luxuriant reproductive ones, followed as a rule by mass death. For example, in 1948, of 308 individuals in a plot of 5 m², 288 (93.5%) developed reproductive shoots and by 1949 75% of them had died, 22% re-mained vegetative and only 3% flowered again. All the individuals which survived until 1949 were dead by 1950. A new population is formed by seedling establishment; there is a rapid turnover of the population as a result of a 'big-bang' method of reproduction. On the other hand, the red clover in the sub-alpine meadows grows under less favourable con-ditions and becomes polycarpic. Plants do not flower until they are 5 to 10 years old, their reproductive period may be 10 years (some plants flowering every year, some every two or three years), and the life-span of some individuals reaches 20 years. Such longevity is com-bined with low seed yield and slow replacement. The rates of population turnover in the two areas are, accordingly, strikingly different; the different frequency in each case with which seedling populations are constrained to go through selective environmental sieves must have profound evolutionary consequences.

A graphical representation of the behaviour of a system involving perennial plants is given in Fig. 8, an extension of the model shown in Fig. 1. The varying patterns of fre-quency of seed production by individuals are depicted, together with some indications of mortality and recruitment. The influence of growing plants on the sieve (Phase II) is shown; many seeds may germinate but not become established through failure to negotiate the complex network of selective barriers that constitute the sieve. The seed population in this model (Phase I) may exist largely in a dormant condition and be released from the seed bank after relaxation of factors enforcing dormancy. A proportion of this seed reservoir will suffer death and decay before an opportunity arises for individuals to germinate: as shown previously, the mortality patterns displayed may be quite regular in some cases (Roberts, 1970). A few seeds may have the capacity to germinate directly on being shed from the parents.

52

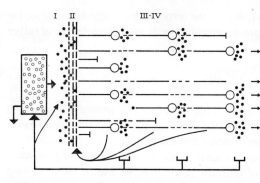

Fig. 8. Schema incorporating some of the features of the development of populations of perennial plants. Phase I represents the viable seed component of the population; much of this may be in a dormant condition in a seed reservoir, from which a certain amount may be released occasionally. Some seeds may die before the dormancy mechanisms are relaxed. Phase II is the environmental sieve, more complex than in Fig. 1 because of the presence of growing vegetation; some seeds may penetrate some of the barriers but not all. Those seedlings which become established grow and reproduce to varying degrees in Phase III; continous or intermittent fruiting may occur. The seeds produced (Phase IV) replenish the seedbank in Phase I, or may germinate directly.

Viable seed population

A comprehensive schema of population dynamics of plants under natural conditions must take account of all the phases outlined in the diagram. With regard to Phase I, Major and Pyott (1966) have emphasised the importance of the buried, viable seed population in nature as an essential part of the total plant population. A tendency to keep what is 'out of sight, out of mind' should be avoided. It may be very difficult to determine this component of population structure, but a few observations have testified to its significance. Rabotnov (1956) lists a number of perennial plants, prominent in the vegetation of meadows, whose seeds were not found in the soil at all; of 33 species growing in the meadows, 19 were not found as buried seeds and of the buried seeds many were not found in the meadows as mature plants. Golubeva (1962) corroborates this data and adds other species of steppe grasses: only 2% of the buried viable seeds were of the dominant perennial grass species in a meadow investigated by her, a phenomenon she ascribes to the great variation of fruiting in different years and to the lack of adaptations in most species to long preservation of viability. Major and Pyott (1966) also found that buried seed populations do not correlate well with the growing vegetation on the same site; of the perennials none had buried seeds. They inferred that seed production by perennials was less vital to population maintenance than seed production by annuals. Champness and Morris (1948) reported that perennials had a disproportionately low representation in the buried seed population compared with annuals. Hence, it would appear that for some perennial plant populations the component of the population spectrum represented by seeds is quite meagre.

Most of the reports of buried, viable seed populations have been of agricultural, mostly annual, weeds, such as the extensive data of Brenchley and Warrington (1930), dealing with arable soils, where populations of up to 75,000 viable seeds per m^2 have been recorded. Meadow communities studied by Rabotnov (1956) and by Golubeva (1962) have up to 20,000 seeds per m^2. The size and even the presence of a seed reservoir as shown in Phase I varies with the species, with a major distinction between them based primarily on the life-cycle strategy (annual/perennial) of the plant. It is important also to note that some plant populations in nature may exist only as buried seeds in certain areas. This frequently occurs when earlier stages in a plant succession are replaced by later ones. For example, Karpov (quoted by Major and Pyott, 1966) described a 100-year-old *Picea* forest in detail,

53

and of the buried, viable seeds only one species of the spruce forest was represented (to the extent of $\frac{1}{2}\%$ of all seeds); all the other plants present as seeds were characteristic of earlier stages in the succession.

Age distribution in perennials

Data which might contribute towards the formulation of general principles concerning Phases III and IV of the model (Fig. 8), that is, the variation in numbers from year to year of plants of perennial species, their rates of decay and the frequency and productivity of seed yield, are very rare. Tamm (1956) has documented the behaviour of individual plants in permanent quadrats over a period of fourteen years. Figs. 9a and b, redrawn from Tamm's data for *Sanicula europea* and *Anemone hepatica*, show the very stable populations of mature plants of both species which are maintained in the plots he observed in a spruce forest. In both cases there have been large seedling recruitments to the populations, but only small fractions have persisted: reproduction by seedlings is not very important for population maintenance. The fluctuations in the total population more closely reflect the changes in the numbers of juveniles (seedlings and older plants which have never flowered) than variations in the numbers of mature plants (those which have flowered at least once). The proportion of the total number of mature plants flowering each year is quite different for the two species. From Tamm's data, intermittent flowering of individuals is quite a striking feature of *Sanicula*, whereas most individual individuals of *Anemone* flower every year. Harper (1967) has shown for a few of the other species mentioned by Tamm that the rates of decay of populations (though only of plants present from the beginning of the ob-

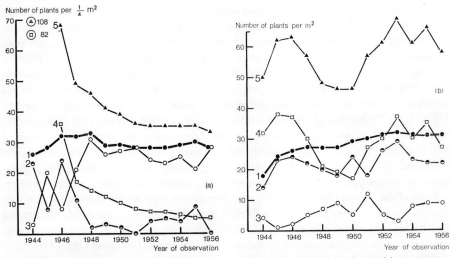

Fig. 9. Changes in population composition of two herbaceous perennials observed in permanent plots in Spruce forest. (a) *Sanicula europaea*; (b) *Anemone hepatica*; 1. total population of plants which have reached reproductive maturity; 2. plants currently flowering; 3. plants not currently flowering but which have flowered at least once before; 4. juvenile plants which have never reproduced; 5. total population. Data on the number of juveniles of *Sanicula* in 1945 are lacking. The numbers for 1944 are indicated in the top left-hand corner of the graph. (Redrawn from data in Fig. 10 and 5, respectively, of Tamm, 1956.)

servation period and excluding all new recruits) are exponential, with species-specific half-lives. However, some perennial plant populations probably have a half-life so long as not to be measurable even over a decade.

In the foregoing data there are no indications of the ages of the individual plants, related to their reproductive behaviour. Although the importance of age on fecundity has been a dominant theme in animal population dynamics, scant attention has been given to this relationship in plants. Attempts to formulate age structures of any kind are generally absent from the literature of plant population dynamics, although they should have a part in the plant ecologist's modelling. In general, it has been suggested that plant populations do not show stable age distributions; Richards (1952), for example, asserts that tropical rain forest trees, because of their sporadic reproduction do not. Rabotnov (1950, 1960, 1964a) has been able to determine the age of perennial plants by anatomical study of perennating organs. This technique can only be used for a few species and the results of age determination are not always precise. Kershaw (1960, 1962) has also assessed the age of perennial plants by ring counts and rhizome morphology, and by using vegetative characters, unfortunately not reproductive ones, has been able to demonstrate clear relationships between age and performance. Rabotnov considers that the age of individuals is insufficient to characterize a population, because individuals of the same age in the same community can differ considerably in vigour. He therefore defines the distribution of individuals in terms of their 'age state' (Rabotnov, 1969a). Juvenile plants are weakly developed individuals with few leaves, a condition that may persist for many years. According to the biological properties of the species and the effects of environment, they gradually or quickly develop into mature plants, although an intermediate 'immature phase' is distinguished on morphological criteria. The ability of plants to persist for long periods as juvenile or immature plants on very low nutrient and light resources, is considered by Rabotnov to be of great importance in the structure of perennial herbaceous plant populations. The diversity of 'age state' composition in plant populations (and the spectrum includes the buried, viable seed populations) enable species, in spite of considerable changes in environment, to persist as components of communities, sometimes with quite small changes in the numbers of individuals.

The age distribution of reproductive plants of a perennial species in four different types of sub-alpine meadow community are shown in Fig. 10 (Rabotnov, 1950). All the plants in a given area were collected and their age determined by anatomical investigation. The onset of the reproductive phase, its duration and its peak are quite distinct in each community. Two attempts to determine the age structures of plant populations from tabulated da-

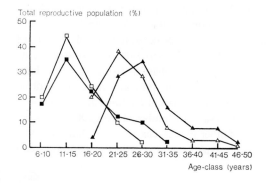

Fig. 10. Age of reproductive individuals of *Libanotis transcaucasia* on different types of subalpine meadow, expressed as proportions of the total reproductive population in each age class. Each symbol represents a different meadow community. (Redrawn from Rabotnov 1950).

55

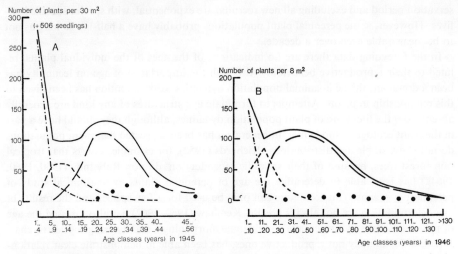

Fig. 11. Age composition of (a) *Anemone fasciculata* and (b) *Polygonum carneum* in areas of sub-alpine meadow in autumn 1945, and Summer 1946, respectively. (———) total population; (— —) mature vegetative plants; (– – – –) semi-mature plants; (– · – · – · –) juvenile plants; (●) reproductive plants. (Drawn from data in Tables 32 and 37, respectively, of Rabotnov, 1950).

ta (Rabotnov, 1950) are shown in graphical form in Fig. 11a and b. An important feature of the diagrams is the length of time over which, apparently, individuals may persist and continue to reproduce. Plants of *Anemone* appear to reach a reproductive peak from 30 to 40 years of age, whereas *Polygonum* has a constant, very low proportion of individuals of all ages byond twenty years reproducing. The bulk of the mature plants in both cases are non-reproductive, although to what extent this may be typical of such populations at other times is uncertain. However, these diagrams do represent almost unique attempts to determine age spectra of plant populations. Table 3 gives the age spectra for these and the other populations examined by Rabotnov. In most cases the proportion of plants in the reproductive phase is quite small.

More recently, Zhukova and Ermakova (1967) have analysed in great detail the population structure of *Deschampsia caespitosa* in meadow communities, by partitioning populations into as many as eight morphological types from seedlings to senile plants. Shorina (1968) and Smirnova (1968) have also made significant contributions to this tradition of population investigation.

One final example of the value of detailed observations on permanent plots is shown in Fig. 12 (Rabotnov, 1964b). Starting with seedling populations in 1958, the fate of mono-carpic species was followed over five years. Reproductive peaks were reached in the third year and thereafter declined. The decline in numbers of *Barbarea* shows a constant decay rate, or half-life, of 11 months, but *Tragopogon* has a two-phase decay curve, with a half-life of 34 months until the peak of flowering is reached in 1961 and thereafter a rapid decline with a half-life of 7 months. 13 % of all the individuals of *Barbarea* and almost 50 % of *Tragopogon* flowered during the period of observation. Golubeva (1964, 1965, 1966) has carried out similar observations for a variety of other species, charting the relative proportions of juvenile, vegetative, reproductive, and senile components in populations over a number of years.

56

Table 3. Age spectra for perennial herbaceous plant populations in meadow communities. Data are expressed as proportions of the total population, excluding seedlings (*Libanotis* excepted). (From Rabotnov, 1950).

	Total number of plants	Area (m²)	Juvenile	Immature	Mature	
					vegetative	reproduc-tive
Anemone hepatica	1087	30	29	18	44	9
Pedicularis condensata	51	15	8	18	49	25
Peucedanum pschavicum	283	not given	17	8	69	6
Polygonum carneum	874	8	18	15	64	3
Libanotis transcaucasia						
data from three	3388	25	31[1]	11	55	3
different meadow	5560	25	29[1]	8	50	13
communities	3737	18	26[1]	20	52	2

[1] Including seedlings

Reproduction in perennials

Phase IV of the model (Fig. 8) is concerned with seed production. Plant species differ in the fraction of their net annual income of assimilates which is devoted to reproductive effort. Ogden (in Harper et. al., 1970) has given a crude estimate of 10% for polycarpic herbaceous perennials, compared with about 30% for most grain crops. In general, it appears that colonizing species have a high reproductive effort and a high rate of natural increase, whereas perennials, mostly plants of stable habitats, devote a greater proportion of available energy to persistent vegetative organs, conferring advantages in a crowded,

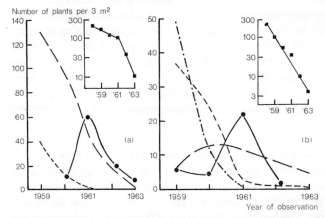

Fig. 12. Changes in numbers and morphology of populations of monocarpic perennials, (a) *Tragopogon orientalis* and (b) *Barbarea vulgaris*, on permanent plots, starting with seedling densities of 205 and 222, respectively, in 1958. The changes in the 'age states' are shown as (– . – . – .) juvenile; (– – – – –) immature; (— —) mature vegetative; (— ● —) reproductive plants, defined on morphological criteria. An insert on each graph shows, on a logarithmic scale, the decline of the population (to which there was no further recruitment) from the initial seedling stage. Numbers of plants are shown on the ordinate and dates on the abscissa. (Drawn from data in Tables 1 and 2 of Rabotnov, 1964).

resource-limited environment. These might be regarded as 'r' species and 'K' species respectively in the sense of MacArthur and Wilson (1967).

In terms of the actual numbers of seeds produced by perennial plants there are very meagre data available. Rabotnov (1969b) has collated much of the available information, which shows that there is considerable variation between species, and within species in different years or under varied environmental conditions. Of 102 species studied by him in a subalpine meadow, 8% produced less than 100 seeds/100 m², 38% produced 100–1000 seeds/100 m² and 16% produced over 10,000 seeds/100 m². For a given species, the seed production varies with its age groups (Golubeva, 1968; Rabotnov, 1950) and the seed production of individual species in a community varies more than does the average seed production of the community as a whole. The total number of seeds produced in stable habitats apparently can be high; 7,500–8,000 seeds/m² in subalpine meadows in the Caucasus (Rabotnov, 1950); up to 67,000 seeds/m² in *Nardus stricta* communities of the Carpathians (Malinovski, 1959). Perennial plants commonly reproduce vegetatively, of course, but there is little information available on the relative importance of vegetatively-derived and seed-derived plants in the maintenance of populations. Wilson (1959) found that multiplication by seed was of much greater importance than the production of vegetative offshoots in the bulbous perennial *Endymion nonscriptus*; 78–89% of the plants examined in three woodlands were estimated to have been derived from seeds. Harberd, in a series of papers (1961, 1962, 1963, 1967, and with Owen, 1969), has demonstrated the significance of vegetative propagation for the persistence of populations. Of 1481 isolates of *Festuca rubra* from a 100m² (approximately) quadrat, all except 150 were referrable to one or other of only 17 genotypes, and 51% were of a single clone. He estimated that the age of some clones, considering their current growth rates and their present-day extent, to be of the order of 400 years. Indeed, the community, he reckons, may be composed of the genotypes of the original colonizers. Harberd (1961) questions whether, in a closed community of perennials, sexual reproduction plays any part at all since the seeds of many species stand little chance of survival. Plants produced asexually have perhaps the advantages of belonging to genotypes already tested for suitability in the environment and of obtaining from the parent a good material start in life. Harberd (1967) in a population of 58 isolates of *Holcus mollis* found four plant types only, with major discontinuities between them and little heterogeneity within them; he argues that each plant type, though in one case occurring in places up to a half mile apart, corresponds to a single colonizing seedling.

The role of animals

The role of predation and disease in plant population dynamics is still very little explored, except in relation to biological control. Harper (1969) has made an attempt to discuss the role of herbivores in vegetational diversity. It may however be useful in future studies of plant-animal relationships to consider the action of herbivores in relation to the models proposed in the present paper. The herbivore, clearly, can influence plant population size and composition by influencing the seed rain (birds and insects feeding on seed before dispersal) and on the sieve which determines which seeds are exposed to further predation after landing. The co-occurring processes of individual plant growth and mortality are affected by the timing of activity of grazing animals and their grazing selectivity.

The models presented in Fig. 1 and 8 in simple diagrammatic form account for and integrate, in a convenient manner, the results of a large number of experimental studies and

painstaking long-term observations. They are clearly capable of a much greater sophistication and susceptible to systems modelling. It is hoped, however, that their main value will
be in focussing with a little more precision the sorts of experimentation and observation
that might be made in the logical development of a science of plant population dynamics.

References

Bakker, D., 1960. A comparative life-history study of *Cirsium arvense* (L.) Scop. and *Tussilago farfara* L., the most troublesome weeds in the newly reclaimed polders of the former Zuiderzee. In: J. L. Harper (Ed.), The biology of weeds, p. 205–222. Oxford.

Black, M., 1969. Light-controlled germination of seeds. In: H. W. Woolhouse (Ed.), Dormancy and survival. *Symp. Soc. Exp. Biol.* 23: 193–219.

Bleasdale, J. K. A., 1966. Plant growth and crop yield. *Ann. appl. Biol.* 57: 173–182.

Brenchley, W. E. & K. Warrington, 1930. The weed seed population of arable soil. 1. Numerical estimation of viable seeds and observations on their natural dormancy. *J. Ecol.* 18: 235–272.

Champness, S. S. & K. Morris, 1948. Populations of buried viable seeds in relation to contrasting pasture and soil types. *J. Ecol.* 36: 149–173.

Chancellor, R. J., 1965. Weed seeds in the soil. *Rep. A.R.C. Weed Res. Org.* (1960–64) 15–19.

Chippindale, H. G., 1948. Resistance to inanition in grass seedlings. *Nature, London.* 161: 65.

Clements, F. E., J. E. Weaver & H. C. Hanson, 1929. Plant competition. *Carnegie Inst. Wash. Publ.* 398, pp. 340.

Farazdaghi, H. & P. M. Harris, 1968. Plant competition and crop yield. *Nature, Lond.* 217: 289–290.

Gadgil, M. & W. H. Bossert, 1970. Life historical consequences of natural selection. *Am. Nat.* 104: 1–24.

Golubeva, I. V., 1962. Some data on the reserves of living seeds in the soil under meadow- steppe vegetation. *Byull. mosk. Obshch. Ispyt. Prir.* 67: 76–89 (Russian).

Golubeva, I. V., 1964. Age composition and dynamics of numbers in populations of *Stipa pennata* L. in meadow steppe. Sci. mem. Moscow Region Pedagog. Inst. 153 (Russian).

Golubeva, I. V., 1965. Age composition and dynamics of numbers in populations or *Trifolium montanum* L. and *Onobrychis arenaria* (Kit.) Ser. in different conditions of meadow steppe. *Trans. Central. Chernozem. Reserve* 8: 37–67. (Russian).

Golubeva, I. V., 1966. Age composition and dynamics of numbers in populations of some plant species in different conditions of meadow steppe. Moscow Region Pedagog. Inst., pp. 18. (Russian).

Golubeva, I. V., 1968. The dynamics of the seed productivity of *Trifolium montanum* L. and *Stipa pennata* L. populations under different phytocoenotic conditions of a meadow steppe. *Bot. Zh. USSR* 53: 1604–1611. (Russian).

Harberd, D. J., 1961. Observations on population structure and longevity of *Festuca rubra* L. *New Phytol.* 60: 184–206.

Harberd, D. J., 1962. Some observations on natural clones in *Festuca ovina. New Phytol.* 61: 85–100.

Harberd, D. J., 1963. Observations on natural clones of *Trifolium repens* L. *New Phytol.* 62: 198–204.

Harberd, D. J., 1967. Observations on natural clones in *Holcus mollis. New Phytol.* 66: 401–408.

Harberd, D. J. & M. Owen, 1969. Some experimental observations on the clone structure of a natural population of *Festuca rubra* L. *New Phytol.* 68: 93–104.

Harper, J. L., 1960. Factors controlling plant numbers. In: J. L. Harper (Ed.), The biology of weeds, p. 119–132. Oxford.

Harper, J. L., 1967. A Darwinian approach to plant ecology. *J. Ecol.* 55: 247–270.

Harper, J. L., 1968. The regulation of numbers and mass in plant populations. In: R. C. Lewontin (Ed.), Population biology and evolution, p. 139–158. Syracuse.

Harper, J. L., 1970. The role of predation in vegetation diversity. Diversity and stability in ecological systems. Brookhaven National Laboratory, New York, p. 48–62.

Harper, J. L., 1970. The population biology of plants. In: A. Allison (Ed.), Population control, p. 32–44. Harmondsworth.

Harper, J. L. & R. A. Benton, 1966. The behaviour of seeds in soil. II. The germination of seeds on the surface of a water supplying substrate. *J. Ecol.* 54: 151–166.

Harper, J. L., P. H. Lovell & K. G. Moore, 1970. The shapes and sizes of seeds. *Adv. Ecol. Syst.* 1 (in press)

Harper, J. L. & I. H. McNaughton, 1962. The comparative biology of closely related species living in the same area. VII. Interference between individuals in pure and mixed populations of *Papaver* species. *New Phytol.* 61: 175–188.

Hayashi, I. & M. Numata, 1967. Ecology of pioneer species of early stages in secondary succession. I. *Bot. Mag. Tokyo* 80: 11–22.

Holliday, R., 1960. Plant population and crop yield. *Nature, Lond.* 186: 22–24.

Kershaw, K. A., 1960. Cyclic and pattern phenomena as exhibited by *Alchemilla alpina*. *J. Ecol.* 48: 443–453.

Kershaw, K. A., 1962. Quantitative ecological studies from Landmannahellir, Iceland. III. The variation of performance of *Carex bigelowii*. *J. Ecol.* 50: 393–399.

Kira, T., H. Ogawa & N. Sakazaki, 1953. Intraspecific competition among higher plants. I. Competition-yield-density interrelationship in regularly dispersed populations. *J. Inst. Polytech. Osaka City Univ.* D4: 1–16.

Knapp, R., 1967. Experimentelle Soziologie und gegenseitige Beeinflussung der Pflanzen. Stuttgart.

Koller, D., 1969. The physiology of dormancy and survival of plants in desert environments. In: H.W.Woolhouse (Ed.), Dormancy and survival. *Symp. Soc. Exp. Biol.* 23: 449–469. Cambridge.

Kuroiwa, S., 1960. Intraspecific competition in artificial sunflower communities. *Bot. Mag. Tokyo* 73: 300–309.

MacArthur, R. H. & E. O. Wilson, 1967. The theory of island biogeography. Princeton.

Major, J. & W. T. Pyott, 1966. Buried, viable seeds in two California bunchgrass sites and their bearing on the definition of a flora. *Vegetatio* 13: 253–282.

Malinovski, K. A., 1959. *Nardus stricta* pastures of the subalpine belt of the Ukrainian Carpathians. *Izd. Akad. Nauk USSR.* (Russian). Quoted by Rabotnov (1969b).

McNaughton, S. J., 1968. Autotoxic feedback in the regulation of *Typha* populations. *Ecology* 49: 367–369.

Nägeli, C., 1874. Verdrängung der Pflanzenformen durch ihre Mitbewerber. *Sitzb. Akad. Wiss. München* 11: 109–164.

Naylor, R. D., 1970. Weed Research. (in press)

Ogden, J., 1970. Plant population structure and productivity. *Proc. N.Z. Ecol. Soc.* 17: 1–9.

Pinowski, J. & Z. Wojcik, 1968. Production of weeds in fields and the degree to which their seeds are consumed by the tree sparrow (*Passer montanus* L.). *Ekol. pol.* B14: 297–301.

Putwain, P. D. & J. L. Harper, 1970. Studies in the dynamics of plant populations. III. The influence of associated species on populations of *Rumex acetosa* L. and *R. acetosella* L. in grassland. *J. Ecol.* 58: 251–264.

Rabotnov, T. A., 1950. Life cycles of perennial herbage plants in meadow communities. *Proc. Komarov Bot. Inst. Akad. Sci. USSR*, Ser. 3 (6) 7–240 (Russian).

Rabotnov, T. A., 1956. Some data on the content of living seeds in soils of meadow communities. In Akademiku V.N. Sukachevu k 75-letiyu so dnya rozhdeniya. *Izd. Akad. Nauk USSR*: 481–499. (Russian).

Rabotnov, T. A., 1960. Some problems in increasing the proportion of leguminous species in permanent meadows. *Proc. 8th Int. Grassld. Congr.* 260–264.

Rabotnov, T. A., 1964a. Determination of the age composition of species populations in communities. *Field Geobot.* 3: 132–145 (Russian).

Rabotnov, T. A., 1964b. On the biology of monocarpic perennial plants. *Bull. Moscow Soc. Nat.* 71: 47–55 (Russian).

Rabotnov, T. A., 1969a. On coenopopulations of perennial herbaceous plants in natural coenoses. *Vegetatio* 19: 87–95.

Rabotnov, T. A., 1969b. Plant regeneration from seed in meadows of the USSR. *Herbage Abstr.* 39: 269–277.

Richards, P. W., 1952. The tropical rain forest. Cambridge.

Roberts, H. A. 1970. Viable weed seeds in cultivated soils. *Rep. Natn. Veg. Res. Stn* (1969): 25–38.

Roberts, H. A. & P. A. Dawkins, 1967. Effect of cultivation on the numbers of viable weed seeds in soil. *Weed Res.* 7: 290–301.

Ross, M., 1968. The establishment of seedlings in grassland. Ph. D. Thesis, University of Wales.

Sagar, G. R., 1959. The biology of some sympatric species of grassland. Phil. D. Thesis, University of Oxford.

Shennikov, A. P. & E. P. Baratynskaya, 1924. Studies on structure and variability of meadow coenoses. *Zh. russk. bot. Obshch.* 9: 75–82 (Russian). Quoted by Rabotnov (1969b).

Shinozaki, K. & T. Kira, 1956. Interspecific competition among higher plants. VII. Logistic theory of the C-D effect. *J. Inst. Polytech. Osaka City Univ.* D7: 35–72.

Shorina, N. I., 1968. Age spectrum and numbers in populations of meadow saffron (*Colchicum speciosum* Stev.) in forests in the subalpine zone of Western Transcaucasia. In: A. A. Uranov et al. (Ed.), Problems of morphogenesis of flowering plants and the structure of their populations, p. 125–154. Moscow (Russian).

Smirnova, O. V., 1968. Number and age composition of populations of some components of the herbaceous cover of oak woods. In A. A. Uranov et al. (Ed.), Problems of morphogenesis of flowering plants and the structure of their populations, p. 155–182. Moscow (Russian).

Sukatschew, W., 1927. Einige experimentelle Untersuchungen über den Kampf ums Dasein zwischen Biotypen derselben Art. *Z. Indukt. Abstamm.- u. Vererblehre* 47: 54–74.

Sukatschew, W., 1928. Plant communities. Moscow (Russian).

Tamm, C. O., 1948. Observations on reproduction and survival of some perennial herbs. *Bot. Notiser* 3: 305–321.

Tamm, C. O., 1956. Further observations on the survival and flowering of some perennial herbs *Oikos* 7: 273–292.

Tansley, A., 1917. On competition between *Galium saxatile* L. (*G. hercynium* Weig.) and *Galium silvestre* Poll. (*G. asperum* Schreib.) on different types of soil. *J. Ecol.* 5: 173–179.

White, J., 1968. Studies on the behaviour of plant populations in model systems. M. Sc. thesis University of Wales.

White, J. & J. L. Harper, 1970. Correlated changes in plant size and number in plant populations. *J. Ecol.* 58: 467–485.

Williams, J. T. & J. L. Harper, 1965. Seed polymorphism and germination. 1. The influence of nitrates and low temperatures on the germination of *Chenopodium album*. *Weed Res.* 5: 141–150.

Wilson, J. Y., 1959. Vegetative reproduction in the bluebell, *Endymion nonscriptus* (L.) Garcke. *New Phytol.* 58: 155–163.

Wit, C. T. de, 1960. On competition. *Versl. landbouwk. Onderz.* 66.8.

Wit, C. T. de, 1968. Plant production. *Misc. Pap. LandbHogesch. Wageningen* 1968 (3) 25–50.

Yoda, K., T. Kira, H. Ogawa & K. Hozumi, 1963. Intraspecific competition among higher plants XI. Self-thinning in overcrowded pure stands under cultivated and natural conditions. *J. Biol. Osaka City Univ.* 14: 107–129.

Zhukova, L. A. & I. M. Ermakova, 1967. Change in age composition of populations of *Deschampsia caespitosa* P.B. on flood and upland meadows in Moscow region. In: A. A. Uranov (Ed.), Ontogenesis and age composition of populations of flowering plants, p. 114–131. Moscow (Russian).

Discussion

Participants: Harper and White (Authors), Bakker (K.), Hancock, Jain, Laughlin, Varley, Watt, Way and de Wit

It is delightful to know that there are some generalizations coming from plant ecology. There is a large body of material in animal studies that is exactly like the self-thinning relationship of Yoda et al.; the work done in various countries on pond fish culture. In this, an effort is made to find out the number and mixture of fish that maximize production from a pond. The studies of Swingle and Smith in Alabama show that, regardless of the number introduced into the pond at the beginning of the year, a constant biomass of fish was produced. This suggests that a universal law is being observed, of the form $w = Cp^{3/2}$, where C is the carrying capacity of the environment (WATT). The thinning relationship certainly holds for a large number of plants, ranging from short-lived annuals to forest trees. In a recent paper (White and Harper, 1970) several examples have been documented, and possible ways of deriving the relationship are indicated (AUTHORS).

There is a striking similarity between the results of self-thinning experiments (intra-specific competition) and competition between species of plants, and the experiments which I did in 1969 on competition within and between *Drosophila* strains. One example is the 'constant total yield' over a large range of initial densities (in *Drosophila*, 'constant total biomass') (BAKKER).

In the early stages of crop growth, a field is not closed, and exponential growth occurs because the newly formed leaves contribute to the interception of light. However, as soon as a closed crop surface is reached, new leaves increase the mutual shading and do not con-tribute to the interception of more light. As a consequence, crop growth proceeds in a linear fashion, the linear growth rate being the same for various densities. The yield dif-ference existing at the time when the most sparsely planted crop closes the field then stays absolutely the same, but decreases relatively. By the time that the experimental technique is no longer sophisticated enough to establish the difference, a 'density-independent yield' is said to occur. However, we should not obscure our lack of sophistication by calling this phenomenon a law and by introducing a 'law of constant yield' (DE WIT).

My experience with a population of overcrowded cockles (*Cardium edule*) was that from thinning experiments it was never possible to achieve a better biomass than that in nature, although this might have been possible if they were thinned out less drastically or if the growth season had continued longer. Any gain in yield was from the additional biomass obtained from the thinnings together with the larger size to which individuals could grow (HANCOCK).

Too much attention may be paid to intermediate stages in competition experiments. Would it not be simpler, from the point of view of population dynamics, firstly to plot Reproduction Curves (as Ricker did for fish), and plot viable seeds of generation N + 1 against seeds of generation N?. The next stage would be to construct life-tables for the plants (VARLEY).

Is there any evidence that interspecific competition between plants creates greater diver-sity within the competing species than does intraspecific competition (WAY)?

On the question of intraspecies diversity in situations with one or few species versus many species: There is a beautiful example from studies on the California grassland spe-cies. In *Avena*, for instance, using the degree of genetic polymorphism as measured in terms of genotypic frequencies of marker loci, it was found that mixed stands of two spe-cies showed less intraspecies variation than pure stands. The same sort of evidence is avail-able from the estimates of coefficients of variation for several morphological characters taking two *Avena* and three *Bromus* species in their natural stands where they vary in their relative abundances. Thus, it appears that species competition results in a greater occupan-cy of favoured niches by each species, and reduces genotypic and phenotypic diversity (JAIN).

The exponent in the equation $w = C\, p^{-3/2}$ looks like a relationship linking surface area and volume. Might not this equation be simply doing that (LAUGHLIN)? Plants may indeed be treated as geometrical objects, although not necessarily as regular cones, cylinders, etc.; some coniferous trees do, in fact, appear very like regular cones. These three-dimensional structures may be treated as occupying surface area on the ground. Presumably, relationships might be developed on these two frames of reference, for a formal theory of the growth and development of plant populations. But I am unaware of any such published treatment. Ross (1968, vide supra) has attempted something along these lines. Plant form itself has been subjected to geometrical analyses by Shinozaki et al. (1964a, 1964b) and by Newnham (1966), for example (AUTHORS).

Additional references

Bakker, K., 1969. Selection for rate of growth and its influence on competitive ability of larvae of *Drosophila melanogaster*. *Neth. J. Zool.* 19: 541–595.

Newnham, R. N., 1966. Stand structure and diameter growth of individual trees in a young Red Pine stand. Unpublished report, Canada Dept. of Forestry, pp. 19.

Shinozaki, K., K. Yoda, K. Hozumi & T. Kira, 1964a. A quantitative analysis of plant form – the pipe model theory. I. Basic analyses. *Jap. J. Ecol.* 14: 97–105.

Shinozaki, K., K. Yoda, K. Hozumi & T. Kira, 1964b. A quantitative analysis of plant form – the pipe model theory. II. Further evidence of the theory and its applications in forest ecology. *Jap. J. Ecol.* 14: 133–139.

Proc. Adv. Study Inst. Dynamics Numbers Popul. (Oosterbeek, 1970) 64–76

Models as research tools

J. Reddingius

Zoological Laboratory of the State University at Groningen, Haren (Gr.), the Netherlands

Abstract

This paper discusses the uses of mathematical and computational models in theory and practice. In theoretical research, models may be used for testing lines of reasoning and checking arguments; a model may either demonstrate the plausibility of a certain theoretical explanation or serve as a counterexample showing that something is wrong. In practical research, models may be used to represent the hypotheses one wishes to test. Both in the 'strong inference method' discussed by Platt (1964) and in applications of mathematical statistics the use of such models is obvious. Some problems connected with the use of models are discussed. Because of the rigor and exactness required for good models, simplifications and the introduction of special assumptions cannot always be avoided. Models used for testing purposes should be distinguishable from others, yet be robust in other respects. For certain purposes, models need not be very realistic. Modern mathematics provides us with many techniques to cope with qualitative problems, and this lessens the need for quantitative specifications that are unwarranted.

The concepts of 'distinguishability' and 'robustness', however, are not yet too well understood and should be further investigated.

Although I cannot claim to be a population ecologist, I gladly accepted the invitation to speak to this meeting where most people know a great deal more about animal populations than I do. Carelessly I suggested that I should talk about the use of models in research, because that is a subject I have rather strong feelings about. Of course, when I settled down to prepare this paper it turned out that lots of philosophers, cyberneticians, systems analysts, biologists and even ecologists had written articles or books on the subject, or had made important remarks on it in articles or books on other subjects. With only a few months to work on this paper and only 45 minutes to present it, it is both impossible to say something very original and to give a complete survey of all that has already been said. So I will only offer some reflections arising out of my own experience as a theoretician, and only quote a couple of papers that impressed me some way or other when I, rather by chance, happened to thumb through them.

The term 'model' may mean different things to different people. (See e.g. Models and analogues in biology). You might think of, for example, a model of the human eye made out of plastic and used for classroom demonstrations. Or you might think of some machine, an electrical one or a mechanical one, which simulates a certain natural process or at least is supposed to do so, such as the apparatus designed by Pearson (1960) to simulate population dynamics. Or you might think of a set of definitions, assumptions and propositions stated in some language and supposed to give a mental picture of a certain natura phenomenon. (See e.g. Kacser, 1960). Or finally, you might think of a carefully controlled laboratory experiment with real organisms used to simulate processes that are supposed to take place in more natural situations (cf. Neyman, Park and Scott, 1955; and Hassell, these Proceedings). In this talk, I will have in mind mainly mathematical and computational models and also machine-like models in so far as these may be seen as analogue computers simulating computational models. These are models of the mental-picture type, and they are characterized by their being, in part, stated in mathematical language or in a programming language, or in both. This means that I will not be interested in the problems concerning the realization of someone's ideas in hardware machinery, and that I will leave laboratory models out of the discussion entirely because real organisms are not equivalent to statements in any language. So, for the time being, 'models' are conceived as expressions of thoughts and ideas in language, with all of the charms and the dangers that ideas may have. As it was so candidly put by Pearson (1960): 'It should be pointed out that I have designed the machine to function in a manner that I believe populations function in the wild. Consequently, it is nothing more than a mechanical expression of my own notions about populations and as such is perfectly capable of reproducing over and over all of the misconceptions of its designer'. There are two more characteristics of our models that have to be pointed out. Firstly, when speaking of a model we think of a device that is rather rigorously and exactly defined; it will have to be built out of a well-defined set of either hardware parts or mathematical symbols or admissible statements in some programming language. This has something to do with the distinction between theories and models. In a sense, any theory might be called a model inasmuch as it is a mental picture of natural phenomena. But theories may contain vague concepts, unproven conjectures and provisory lines of reasoning that should be lacking in a model. Secondly, models not only give nothing more than an expression of our ideas, but often give less – in the sense that in order to construct a machine, a program or a mathematical structure that really can be put to work we often have to simplify our original notions quite a bit, and also have to introduce arbitrary assumptions that we did not originally make. This point is related to the first one about rigor and exactness. Just because the models have to be rigorously defined and have to be specified down to all the details relevant to a proper functioning, we have to omit complications that might mess up the whole thing, and we have to introduce specifications without which the thing wouldn't work. Levins (1966) points out that it is impossible to construct models of population systems that are general as well as realistic and precise. General, realistic and precise models cannot be had because such models would have to be so unwieldy and complicated that they could not be handled or even understood, and because the number of parameters to be measured in order to match the model to reality would be far too large.

Now, what uses can be made of models in scientific research? I will mention some examples with which I have had a little bit of personal experience. Roughly speaking, one may use models for theoretical purposes or for practical purposes; but there is no sharp borderline between the two, as will become apparent in a moment. Let me first comment on using models for theoretical purposes. The thing modeled in such cases is not a 'real' system, but rather a theory about such a system. It is obvious that theorizing is an important scientific activity; scientific research does not merely consist of collecting and describing data. We even need some theorizing before we can state what will be considered to be 'data'. Now, in our theorizing we often start with rather vague and general notions and intellectual guesswork. Our aim is, of course, to build a 'good' theory in the long run, a theory that explains all there is to explain in an unambiguous and precise fashion. So one of the first things we may try to do is to investigate what happens if we construct models of our provisory theory. If we attempt this, it often turns out to be an enlightening exercise because we have to think really hard on what it is exactly that we wish to demonstrate; we become aware of all the vagueness and arbitrariness that is in our ideas and of all the gaps in our factual knowledge. Maybe a first requirement that should be met by a scientific theory is that it should be possible to construct a model for that theory. Such a model may then be used to investigate possible consequences of certain ideas, or to see whether some idea works or might work the way we conjecture that it will. There are several examples of this kind of work, for example the models presented by Royama in these Proceedings. An example of the use of such theoretical models is also provided by den Boer and myself (Reddingius and den Boer, 1970); in that paper we discuss models that illustrate certain ideas about risk distribution (the spreading of risk) and stabilization of animal numbers proposed by den Boer (1968 and these Proceedings). The results obtained by simulating these models do not show, of course, that den Boer's theory is right, for that theory cannot yet be formalized into a manageable model; but these results do show that den Boer's ideas might work. We thought that such a provisory check on a theory was worth while to perform, the more so since the theory touches upon a subject that has been controversial since 1928 or thereabouts, namely, the balance-of-nature idea.

We may also work the other way round. If we suspect that a certain theory, or a certain line of reasoning, is not generally valid, we may try to construct a model that provides us with a counter-example showing what is wrong. This is a very powerful theoretical method, and if we make a combined use of examples and counter-examples we may improve our theory to such an extent that we are better able to set up a research program based on that theory. The mathematical reasoning that goes with constructing mathematical models for theories can do valuable work towards finding better definitions of concepts that play a crucial role in the theory, and better formulations of all the basic assumptions underlying the theory. Let us discuss one example. It deals with the well-known saying that animal populations fluctuate about equilibrium levels. Let us agree for the moment that deterministic population models are basically unrealistic except for large populations governed by only a few environmental variables. So, the simplest sort of population models we may wish to consider would assume that population density N behaves with time as a realization of a Markov chain. Thus we have to talk about the conditional probability that $N(t + 1) = m$, given that $N(t) = k$, p_{mk}, say, for all possible pairs m, k. We may let these conditional probabilities depend on k in any way we like, so we will be able to provide for any kind of 'density-dependence'. Now to me it seems reasonable to assume that $p_{10} \neq O, p_{21} \neq O, p_{32} \neq O$ and so on; that is, I want to assume that it is always possible that we shall have one animal per unit area less than we had before, even if there was only one animal left. It follows that, however small these probabilities may be, the probability that the population density becomes zero after a finite number of steps is still positive. But then the law of large numbers tells us that extinction of the population will surely occur some time – if only we wait long enough, especially if we allow for the fact that there is an upper boundary to all densities. For example, you cannot have a million elephants per cm². So I arrive at a theorem which states that

$$\lim_{t \to \infty} P \{N(t) = 0\} = 1$$

I think that this is a robust theorem; that is, I think that it will hold also for a set of models larger than the set of Markov chains, provided there is an absorbing state, the zero state, from which no return is possible. However we govern, regulate or control a population, we can never totally exclude the possibility that a series of 'bad years', or some catastrophe, will destroy it. Let us now have a look at the equilibrium concept. In a deterministic model it is easy and straightforward to define the concept of 'equilibrium density'. We might call a density n an equilibrium density if $N(t) = n$ implies $N(t + u) = n$ either for all $u > 0$ or maybe for $u = 0,1,2,...$ ad inf. Once a density (at a certain time of the year) is at equilibrium, this will remain so ever after (at the same time of the year). However, this definition is useless for a stochastic model because there we want to allow for a non-zero probability that $N(t + u)$ will differ from n even if $N(t) = n$. Then in any realization there will occur random fluctuations that will move density away from equilibrium. Might we find a statistical definition of the equilibrium concept? Yes, maybe, but the difficulty is that for any reasonable definition it will turn out that there exists one, and only one, stable equilibrium, namely, the zero density! So the problem is not at all trivial and calls for more mathematical reasoning. It is discussed in some detail in my thesis (Reddingius, 1968).

It may well turn out to be true that any concept can only be meaningfully defined within a certain set of models, and often we will only discover this after having considered alternative models. For example, in the discussion to Way's paper (these Proceedings) it turned out that 'stability' could be defined in many possible ways depending on the model we have in mind.

This discussion maybe demonstrates that models used for theoretical purposes need not always be very general or realistic, as long as they are suitable for making a point. Maybe a Markov chain is a much too simple and unrealistic model for an animal population, but the theoretical difficulty I pointed out a while ago makes sense from a biological point of view. We might even say that an unrealistic model under certain circumstances may help to show how far away we still are from realism. In this connection it may be noted that often deterministic models are very useful in spite of their lack of realism because they are more easily understood and more easily handled than stochastic models. On the other hand, one of our aims of course, is to build a general and realistic theory that is so well-defined and rigorous that it may be called a model, or at least can be modeled in a straightforward fashion. But a general and realistic population theory will be qualitative in nature because, of course, no theory can ever predict exact numbers for all populations in the world simultaneously; rather, it will deal with general propositions concerning the influence of, e.g., weather factors, predators, competitors, pathogens, age distribution, sex ratio, genetic constitution and so on. Levins (1966) says that for general and realistic models we have to sacrifice precision. In my opinion, we are then talking about a precision that is worth sacrificing because it would be a spurious precision arising out of unwarranted specifications of our models. Of course, if a general model is to be applied to a special case, it should be possible to specify it in such a way that it attains more numerical precision. I think that during this conference we have seen cases where the building of a quantitative model is essential for a further development of the subject. Conversely, we may hope that by constructing a set of realistic and numerically precise models, we may combine them into one more general and still realistic model (cf. Holling, 1968) but still such a general model will be more qualitative and less quantitative than the special-case models upon which it is based. In this connection, it is worth while to remark that modern mathematics contains much that is qualitative and general rather than quantitative and specified; we have general set theory, topology, measure theory and functional analysis to teach us how to think about qualitative problems in a precise fashion. It is therefore not always necessary, and hence not always desirable, to boil down our models to computational formulae. For example, we might perhaps prove interesting theorems by assuming that the amount of food taken by a consumer per unit of time will be a nondecreasing function of food density (that is, no consumer will eat less when more food becomes available). (cf. Reddingius, 1963.) Then it is unneccessary and undesirable to state that it is exactly proportional to food density. Be this as it may, it still remains true that most of the models we use in order to illustrate a theory will contain certain assumptions that are unrealistic or otherwise unwarranted. In these cases we hope that our models be robust. This means that we hope that certain conclusions we have arrived at by investigating the properties or the behavior of models will be valid also in the more general case; that is, for a larger set of models including the models we played with. This question of robustness is highly interesting and I feel that more theoretical research has to be done in order to define the concept of 'robustness' more exactly and to develop methods for finding out how robust a given model is (cf. van der Vaart, 1963). One method suggested by Levins (1966) is to use different models for the same problem. All of these models have some amount of unrealism or unwarranted specification, but the unrealistic and unwarranted specifications differ for different models. Then if by means of different models we arrive at the same conclusion, we may think these models to be robust as far as this conclusion is concerned, or you might call the conclusion itself a robust one. In Levins' words: 'Our truth will be the intersection of independent lies'. This suggests a sort of set-theoretic approach to the problem: Suppose a model is a set of interconnected propositions, part of which will be unwarranted; let us, for convenience, call the unwarranted ones 'lies' and, by a similar abuse of language, 'truths' will designate premises which we think are justified and propositions derived from these. Suppose we have models M_1, M_2, ..., M_k. Each model, in a sense, is a set. So we may go and find the intersection of M_1, M_2, ..., and M_k. Now, if the 'lie-contents' of these models are disjoint, or, weaker, if no lie is contained in all of the sets, then the propositions contained in the intersection will hold in all models and will not be lies, and so we may hope that their truth does not depend on any of the lies; that is, we may hope that they are deducible from a (partially unknown) set of acceptable premises. However, there remains a problem; clearly, we cannot tell by mere logic which of the propositions are not lies and do not depend on lies, and equally we can never be wholly sure that the intersection will contain only propositions which are independent of any lie. Furthermore, robustness seems to be a relative concept. If we add new models M_{k+1}, ... M_n, the intersection could become smaller and might even become empty, so in fact we may only talk about robustness within a well-defined set of models. One then would like to characterize this set by other means than a simple enumeration of all the models contained in it. Another idea would be to try and find a topology on a set of models, and call two models the more robust with respect to each other the closer they are according to this topology. I do not see yet how this could be done, except perhaps in certain simple cases.

All of this perhaps sounds so theoretical that some of you are losing your patience. Such an irritation would be very understandable. It is our job to do research on populations, not to sit in an armchair and dream up theories. Yet I definitely have the feeling that a little bit of abstract theorizing will do no harm to population ecology. To illustrate this, I recall that in the 'fifties' and 'sixties' population ecologists were divided into at least two antagonistic groups, each group favoring its own general population theory. To a certain extent the division still exists. Now controversies may be all right if they give rise to suggestions as to how to disprove an opposing theory. But this was not the case. People kept calling one theory or the other unscientific and illogical and what not, and nothing came out of it. The controversy, in fact, has existed since about 1930 (Bodenheimer, 1928; Nicholson, 1933; Smith, 1935; Thompson, 1939; Andrewartha and Birch, 1954; Nicholson, 1954; Thompson, 1956, Milne, 1957; Schwerdtfeger, 1958; Andrewartha, 1961; Klomp, 1962; Milne, 1962; Smith, 1961; Andrewartha, 1963; Smith, 1963; to give a small anthology). I did some theoretical work in order to find out what was wrong (and of course, I was not the only one, but allow me to talk about my own attempts, these being the ones I am best acquainted with). I will not bother you with the terminological and logical cleaning-up that has to be performed, but will just concentrate on the main issue: Is it possible that populations persist without being regulated by density-governing factors, or negative feedback, or how you wish to call it? No, says Nicholson, they cannot, as a matter of logic. Well, the others said, your logic has no sound scientific basis and you cannot prove empirical propositions by mere logic. As I pointed out above, populations, whether governed or not, cannot persist indefinitely. On the other hand, computer simulations of stochastic models show that even non-governed populations may persist for a long time (here we have the counterexample method again). So in the case of some real population studied over a finite time, density-governing factors might or might not be at work. But if we state it in this way, we have an interesting problem for practical research: Given a natural population, do density-governing (or, more generally, density-dependent) factors have an important influence on fluctuations and persistence, and if not, how is it that the population doesn't quickly become extinct? We may design experiments or sampling schemes in order to investigate these problems, and we have reached the realm of what Platt (1964) has called 'strong inference'. Strong inference is the method of devising a set of mutually exclusive hypotheses and planning crucial experiments or observations in order to falsify or disprove at least some of these hypotheses. As Platt (1964) remarks: 'A failure to agree for 30 years is public advertisement of a failure to disprove'. In population ecology there has been a failure to agree for at least 35 years and this is really too bad.

In order that a scientific theory be fruitful, it should not merely summarize and explain all current knowledge, but it should also expound all open questions and unsolved issues as clearly as is possible in order to provide a basis for the strong inference method. This will enable us to leave our armchairs and go into the field or the laboratory to do some real work. Formally, we might conceive of a scientific theory as a set of hypotheses all of which are compatible with our factual knowledge, and it should be possible to partition this set into mutually exclusive subsets. Each of the subsets we obtain may be called a hypothesis, if we allow that the union of a set of hypotheses is again a hypothesis. Now abstractly speaking a set containing two or more elements can always be partitioned in many ways, and in concrete cases this may play a role also. If in your mind you play around with ideas of density-governing factors, density dependent factors of various sorts, density-independent factors, equilibria, persistence, amount of fluctuation and so on, you will imagine that there are lots of ways of partitioning the set of admissible hypotheses about some population's dynamics into disjoint hypotheses. So our job is to find the partition that offers the best opportunity to perform crucial experiments or to use powerful statistical tests in order to narrow down the set of admissible hypotheses by excluding one or more of the subsets of the partition. There may exist inadequate partitionings; if we have an inadequate one it may turn out that there are hypotheses between which no choice can be made on the basis of observations, or only with great difficulty. An example might be the partition of the set of admissible hypotheses about, say, the human population of Asia such that the first hypothesis, H_1, states that this population will persist for one million years counting from now, and the second hypothesis, H_2, states that the population will have died out before one million years have elapsed. It is a nice partition all right, but nobody is going to be able to see which of the two hypotheses is correct except in the trivial and extremely unlikely case that the population will happen to die out within the next 60 years or so. Hypotheses between which no choice can be made on the basis of feasible observations will be called unidentifiable. If we have two or more hypotheses and a set of propositions about feasible observations such that the truth or falsehood of these propositions enables us to exclude all but one of the hypotheses, the hypotheses will be called identifiable. Identifiability is, in part, a matter of using operational concepts in formulating the theory and operational definitions of the hypotheses of the partition, but we have also to deal with the restrictions imposed on us by experimental and statistical technicalities, the limited amounts of time and money available and so on.

So, if we have found a clever partition, we may proceed to perform experiments and gather data and eliminate all but one of the hypotheses. The remaining hypothesis then will be partitioned in its turn, and the cycle starts again. Now in this whole business models may play an important role. One of the things we might do is the following: For each hypothesis of our partition we construct a model that represents the hypothesis in that all of the typical characteristics that define the hypothesis are found in the model. The choice between hypotheses is then boiled down to a choice between models, and this choice is often easier to make. A requirement that such models then have to fulfil is that they be identifiable with respect to each other, but robust within the set of hypotheses they represent. If we have models M and N representing hypotheses H and G, then M and N should be identifiable, i.e. there must exist an operational test to choose between them; but M must be a robust model of H and N must be a robust model of G. This may lead to a problem; if H is accepted and G rejected then H will be partitioned in its turn, but it may be difficult to use M again. The partitioning of M will perhaps not be very successful because of the robustness of M.

I hope I have now about made the point that inasmuch as theories have to lead to experiments and observations and the latter again have to be accounted for in theory, model building is an important activity both from a theoretical and a practical point of view. Useful references on the subject are e.g. van der Vaart (1961, 1962), Levins (1966), Holling (1963, 1964, 1966, 1968), Watt (1961, 1962), George (1960) and other papers in 'Models and analogues in biology', Beck (1957), various papers in Watt (1966) and Mesarović (1963), Andrewartha (1957) and many others.

However, let us now become entirely practical. We are not going to build any fancy models of population systems, we are just going to gather some relevant data about population density, reproduction, mortality, and migration. I presume, however, that we will have to do some statistics. For one thing, population ecology is in a sense a statistical science (Reddingius, 1968). To illustrate this, consider mortality. If you have 10,000 animals and 5,000 of them die during a certain time interval, it makes sense to state that a 50% mortality occurred. However, none of the 10,000 animals that we had originally was submitted to a 50% mortality; each one either died or survived. But we are not interested in the fates of separate individuals, we are interested in a frequency or, if you like, a probability. This is very clearly stated in Andrewartha and Birch (1954). However, in order to talk about probabilities and such, you need a whole mathematical apparatus, you have to postulate certain things, accept certain rules of inference and so on; in other words, you have to use a mathematical model. Let us go one step further; in many cases we cannot even count the exact number of animals present, but this number has to be estimated. The animals that die during a given time usually are not found lying around waiting to be counted either. The sampling techniques and computing schemes that are used all presuppose certain mathematical models. If we have the sound working knowledge of statistics that we are supposed to have (Andrewartha and Birch, 1954) we will moreover want to obtain a measure of the reliability of our estimates, and often we shall want to test hypotheses, such as: Is average mortality higher in cold winters than in moderate winters? What I wish to emphasize right now is that a sound working knowledge of statistics is not just a matter of knowing some bunch of recipes which tells us how to cook up our data. What we need is a good insight into the model that is presupposed by a given statistical method. We have to know what statistics is all about. Let us now throw a quick glance at the theory of statistics. We there encounter the following sort of problem: Suppose we perform an experiment (which may consist of just observing something). Suppose also that the outcome of the experiment may be considered a chance event. That is, suppose we can specify the set of possible outcomes of the experiment; we call this the sample space. Now, we may have a probability measure defined on the set of all chance events that can in some way be defined in terms of events in the sample space (we have to bypass certain technicalities here). There may exist a great many of such probability measures. We believe there is some 'true' probability measure, generated maybe by some law of nature. If we knew such a law, we would have a stochastic model of our experiment. Statistics comes in when we consider a set of hypotheses about what the true probability measure might be. Maybe such hypotheses state exact forms for these measures, maybe only certain characteristic features of the probability distributions are specified, such as the median, or the mean, or the probability that something is less than something else. The job of a statistician is to construct a decision rule prescribing how to choose a hypothesis from the given set, given that the outcome of the experiment is known, or, if you like, how to reject a hypothesis in the given set. The decision rule must be such that for each outcome of the experiment there is just one decision. Three special cases are well-known:

1. Hypothesis testing. The set of hypotheses consists of just two hypotheses, one of which has to be rejected;

2. Point estimation. The set of hypotheses contains an infinite number of hypotheses that are distinguished by the value of some parameter; estimating the parameter means choosing that hypothesis (or that subset of the original set) for which the parameter has a certain value computed from the outcome of the experiment;

3. Interval estimation. The set of hypotheses is similar to that in the previous case, but now we are going to state an interval or, more generally, a set, the borderlines of which depend on the outcome of the experiment, and we will accept the hypothesis that the true value of the parameter is within this set, which is called the confidence set.

As you know, for each possible decision there is associated a probability that the decision is wrong and, in fact, in the construction of the decision rule these probabilities play an essential role. Also we have to remark that sometimes we also allow for the decision not to choose any of the hypotheses, because the data are not sufficient for the probability of a wrong decision to be small. Be this as it may, it is clear that we are back at the same formal scheme I proposed when discussing scientific theory in general; we have a set of admissible hypotheses, we are going to partition it and reject certain hypotheses of the partition and accept others. The problem I mentioned about partitionings (having to do with design of experiments), about robustness and indentifiability, are well known among theoretical statisticians and the statistical literature would be the obvious source to look at for suggestions as to how to solve the problems that may arise. It furthermore turns out that there is a lot to say about the criteria by which hypotheses are to be rejected or accepted. There apparently does not exist an optimum criterion that may serve to construct decision rules for all problems. (See e.g. Lehmann, 1959). It is also well-known that, in order to obtain a powerful decision rule, it is often desirable to specify in some detail the set of probability models we are going to partition, in fact in more detail than is provided by the scientific problem that motivated the mathematical one. For example, it often helps a lot if we can specify that certain probability distributions are of the normal, or Gaussian, type. But just as for some problems we may use qualitative mathematics rather than computational equations, we may sometimes use distribution free statistics to get an answer to certain questions; in the latter case we have again to 'sacrifice' a certain amount of numerical precision. In short, there is no essential difference whatsoever between my previous scheme symbolizing theory of strong inference and a scheme symbolizing theoretical statistics; in both cases the theory has direct consequences for our methods of doing empirical research. So, if someone were to criticize the use of mathematical models for the reason that these models are nearly always unrealistic simplifications of nature – animals being too complex to be represented by mathematical symbols – and yet at the same time were to see no harm in using statistical correlation and regression techniques for interpreting field data, he would be very inconsistent. Correlation and regression analyses presuppose a family of linear models with independent errors distributed according to the normal probability law, which family then is partitioned in the way we discussed a while ago.

The title of this paper, 'Models as research tools', was designed to emphasize that I did not want to look at the subject of Hypotheses and Facts in the manner of: This is Dr Jones, and this is His Model, but rather to stress that for better or worse we must, and do, work with models of various kinds much in the same way that we must, and do, work with all kinds of measuring instruments, field glasses, notebooks, computers and cameras. All tools have their limitations and problems. Field glasses limit your field of vision, cameras give only two-dimensional pictures, notebooks may contain just notes and not a full description of reality. But we cannot do without these tools, limited though they may be. The important thing is to have a clear insight into what you can and what you cannot do with them, and into how you may interpret data obtained with the aid of certain tools. For a pair of field glasses this is far easier to tell than for a mathematical method and that is why I thought it worth while to spend some time on this outline of my ideas on the subject.

References

Andrewartha, H. G., 1957. The use of conceptual models in population ecology. *Cold Spring Harb. Symp. quant. Biol.* 22: 219–236.
Andrewartha, H. G., 1961. Introduction to the study of animal populations. Univ. of Chicago Press, Chicago.
Andrewartha, H. G., 1963. Density-dependence in the Australian thrips. *Ecology* 44: 218–220.
Andrewartha, H. G. & L. C. Birch, 1954. The distribution and abundance of animals. Univ. of Chicago Press, Chicago.

Beck, W. S., 1957. Modern science and the nature of life. Harcourt, Brace & Cy, New York.

Bodenheimer, F. S., 1928. Welche Faktoren regulieren die Individuenzahl einer Insektenart in der Natur? *Biol. Zbl.* 48: 714–739.

Boer, P. J. den, 1968. Spreading of risk and stabilization of animal numbers. *Acta biotheor.* 18: 165–194.

D'Ancona, U., 1954. The struggle for existence. *Bibliotheca Biotheoretica* Vol. 6, Brill, Leiden.

George, F. H., 1960. Models in cybernetics. In: Models and analogues in biology, Cambridge Univ. Press, Cambridge. p. 169–171.

Holling, C. S., 1963. An experimental component analysis of population processes. *Mem. ent. Soc. Can.* 32: 22–32.

Holling, C. S., 1964. The analysis of complex population processes. *Can. Ent.* 96: 335–347.

Holling, C. S., 1966. The functional response of invertebrate predators to prey density. *Mem. ent. Soc. Can.* 48: 9–86.

Holling, C. S., 1968. The tactics of a predator. In: T.R.E.Southwood (Ed.), Insect abundance. *Symp. R. ent. Soc. Lond.* 4: 47–58. Blackwell, Oxford and Edingburgh.

Kacser, H., 1960. Kinetic models of development and heredity. In: Models and analogues in biology, p. 13–27. Cambridge Univ. Press, Cambridge.

Klomp, H., 1962. The influence of climate and weather on the mean density level, the fluctuations and the regulation of animal populations. *Arch. néerl. Zool.* 15: 68–109.

Lehmann, E., 1959. Testing statistical hypotheses. Wiley, New York.

Levins, R., 1966. The strategy of model building in population biology. *Am. Scient.* 54: 421–431.

Mesarović, M. D. (Ed.), 1963. Systems theory and biology. *Proc. 3rd Systems Symp. Case Inst. Technol.* Springer, Berlin.

Models and analogues in biology, 1960. *Symp. Soc. exp. Biol.* 14. Cambridge Univ. Press, Cambridge.

Morris, R. F., 1963. The development of a population model for the spruce budworm through the analysis of survival rates. In: R. F. Morris (Ed.), The dynamics of epidemic spruce budworm populations. *Mem. ent. Soc. Can.* 31: 30–32.

Neyman, J., T. Park & E. L. Scott, 1955. Struggle for existence – The Tribolium model: biological and statistical aspects. *Proc. 3rd Berkeley Symp. Math. Stat. Prob.*, (reprinted in General Systems Yearbook 3 (1958) 152–179).

Nicholson, A. J., 1933. The balance of animal populations. *J. anim. Ecol.* 2: 132–178.

Nicholson, A. J., 1954. An outline of the dynamics of animal populations. *Aust. J. Zool.* 2: 9–64.

Pearson, O. P., 1960. A mechanical model for the study of population dynamics. *Ecology* 41: 494–508.

Platt, J. R., 1964. Strong inference. *Science* 146 (3642): 347–353.

Reddingius, J., 1963. A mathematical note on a model of a consumer-food relation in which the food is continually replaced. *Acta Biotheor.* 16: 183–198.

Reddingius, J., 1968. Gambling for existence. A discussion of some theoretical problems in animal population ecology. Thesis, Groningen (to be published in the series *Bibliotheca Biotheoretica* by Brill, Leiden).

Reddingius, J. & P. J. den Boer, 1970. Simulation experiments illustrating stabilization of animal numbers by spreading of risk. *Oecologia* 5: 240–284.

Schwerdtfeger, F., 1958. Is the density of animal populations regulated by mechanisms or by chance? *Proc. 10th Int. Congr. Ent.* 4: 115–122.

Smith, H. S., 1935. The role of biotic factors in the determination of population density. *J. econ. Ent.* 28: 873–898.

Smith, F. E., 1961. Density-dependence in the Australian thrips. *Ecology* 42: 403–407.

Smith, F. E., 1963. Density-dependence. *Ecology* 44: 220.

Symposium on cycles in animal populations. *J. Wildl. Mgmt.* 18, 1–112.

Thompson, W. R., 1939. Biological control and the theories of the interactions of populations. *Parasitology* 31: 299–388.

Thompson, W. R., 1956. The fundamental theory of natural and biological control. *A. Rev. Ent.* 1: 379–402.

Vaart, H. R. van der, 1961. The role of mathematical models in biological research. *Bull. Inst. Int. Statistique*, 33e Session (Paris): 1–30.

Vaart, H. R. van der, 1963. A survey of problems and methods in mathematical biology. In:

H. L. Lucas Jr. (Ed.), The Cullowhee conference on training in biomathematics 1961. p. 52–57. Typing Service, NCSU, Raleigh, N.C.

Vaart, H. R. van der, 1963. On the robustness of mathematical models in biology. Handout for the Univ. of Texas Postgraduate School of Medicine Symposium on Biomathematics and Computer Science in the Life Sciences, 1963. Biomathematics Program. Institute of Statistics NCSU, Raleigh, N.C.

Volterra, V., 1931. Leçons sur la théorie mathématique de la lutte pour la vie. Gauthier-Villars, Paris.

Watt, K. E. F., 1961. Mathematical models for use in insect pest control. *Can. Ent.*, Suppl. 19 acc. Vol. 93. (reprinted in General Systems Yearbook 7 (1962): 195–230).

Watt, K. E. F., 1962. Use of mathematics in population ecology. *A. Rev. Ent.* 7: 243–260.

Watt, K. E. F. (Ed.), 1966. Systems analysis in ecology. Academic Press, New York-London.

Discussion

Participants: Reddingius (Author), Andersen, van Biezen, Gradwell, Laughlin, Metz, Rosenzweig, Royama, Watt and de Wit

As research tools models could be used as base line showing how much of the variation could be explained on certain assumptions (ANDERSEN). This seems, indeed, what one tries to do. However, with respect to the simple models Andersen is emphasizing we have to realize that the procedure may be quite misleading. The logistic model for population growth may be fitted to growth data for sheep populations, *Drosophila* populations, or the human population of the USA, but we know very well that as an explanatory model it is inadequate just because of its simplicity. (AUTHOR).

In modeling a complex system it is advisable to use a systems approach; the model is constructed with several building blocks, each of which should be separately testable. After having tested all blocks separately, we derive predictions from the whole model which are then again tested against reality. From the discrepancies that arise, one obtains hunches about what is wrong in the setup, one works on them, tests the new submodels and feeds the result back into the large model and so forth. One should keep the hypothesis and the testing separate (DE WIT). Simple models have a tendency to be robust, they don't have a high credibility. With respect to de Wit's statements this means that such simple models are nice descriptions of the blocks whose effect you are not really interested in (METZ). In such cases what one is doing is equivalent to curve fitting (AUTHOR).

It seems advisable to discuss the difference between theory and hypothesis. In particular it seems that a hypothesis is an educated guess. It may be arrived at by induction or by theorization. Theorization includes at least one deductive step. The process of deduction must proceed according to the rules of logic thus presenting an added chance for error (a chance often worth taking however, since the hypotheses resulting from theorization are frequently not obvious from the data alone). A model is the explicit representation of data classes and their underlying hypothetical relationships in such a form that they are ready for either simulation or direct deduction. Thus we see the role of simulation in attempting to substitute for logical analysis and produce quasi-deduction. The deductions or quasi-deductions become the working hypotheses for future tests. A theory is therefore a complex containing some assumptions (some of which are a posteriori) organized into a model which has by deductive logic been forced to produce testable hypotheses (ROSENZWEIG). It will be difficult to draw sharp borderlines between 'theory', 'hypothesis' and 'model', and it may be doubted whether it is very useful to try and do so. Models may be more precise than theories, and in a theory we are more free to let our minds go. Several philosophers of science have argued that any scientific theory is to be considered as a hypothesis, or set of hypotheses, because scientific propositions, with the exception of mathematical theorems and other tautological statements, can never be proven by logic (AUTHOR).

In the paper it was accepted that it may be impossible to prove a theory. Equally well it is impossible to disprove one. Yet, at the beginning of the paper, ecologists were criticized for not performing experiments to disprove one or other of the opposing theories which are still being contested. Will the information we have to date allow us to say that one or other of these theories is wrong? And, if not, what sort of evidence is needed to constitute disproof (GRADWELL)? In the first place, in the present context 'proof' and 'disproof' are taken in the sense in which they are, rather loosely, used by scientists, and not in the strict logical sense. We should really talk about accepting or rejecting hypotheses rather than of proving or disproving them. In the second place, however, hypotheses and theories can be disproved. For example, if one has a deterministic model, this may be considered disproved as soon as we have found just one case where the model doesn't fit the facts. We can never prove such a model to be correct because from the fact that it did fit in a great number of cases it cannot be inferred that a bad fit will never turn up. With the statistical testing of (stochastic) hypotheses one accepts a certain risk of being wrong, so in that case a strict 'disproof' cannot be given either. With respect to population theories, the hypotheses generated by such theories should be tested for each special case by crucial experiments or statistical testing. Governing of density in flour beetles does not tell us too much about antarctic penguins (AUTHOR).

Accepting a hypothesis is an inappropriate expression which should be read as: not rejecting it. Since the probability of not rejecting a hypothesis when it is in fact wrong is to be made as small as possible, it is of great importance to set up a good experimental design before actually performing experiments (VAN BIEZEN). Although this is right, of course, in cases where the number of observations is large and the test applied is powerful, one should not hesitate to accept the hypothesis that is not rejected, although this really means to accept a set of hypotheses in a 'small neighbourhood' of the not-rejected one (AUTHOR).

What is the meaning of the words 'realistic' and 'unrealistic'? To give an example: Aristotle considered that a cart pulled by a horse moves with constant speed but comes to rest as soon as the horse is removed. From this Aristotle concluded that a thing moves as long as a force is applied but stops when the force is removed. Galileo, however, objected to this view and said: 'A ship floating on a perfectly smooth water will move if it is pushed and will keep going without the application of further force'. Now Aristotle's view is more realistic than Galileo's in the sense that the former can be observed around us while the latter situation is highly idealized and would not normally be observed. Can we consider a deterministic model to be this kind of idealization, which though unrealistic, may be useful for the formulation of a hypothesis (ROYAMA)? Any model is only an approximation to reality. Therefore, in certain instances, deterministic models, even while lacking realism, may be more useful than stochastic ones because they may give more 'insight' (whatever that may be) or are better manageable. Of course, the success of the theories of Galileo and his followers over the Aristotelean theory was accomplished by the former providing a simpler and better fitting model of reality than the latter. The lack of 'realism' that is apparent in Royama's example is justified by a gain in 'realism' in other respects. We may now account for the fact that the horse may trot faster the smoother the road, and the fact that the ship will not move a great distance if it floats on sugar syrup. However, 'reality' is a rather difficult concept about which we cannot say too much in the present discussion, and finally it must be emphasized that as soon as statistical methods are used, stochastic models are to be postulated (AUTHOR).

If one has the time and money to make just 100 observations all 100 can be made by one method, or 10 methods can be thought up to make 10 observations by each method. Which system is the best (LAUGHLIN)? There is no definite answer to this because it depends on the problem and what one thinks important. Statisticians will usually prefer the first method but there are many situations in which the second is preferable, if only because there does not always exist a nice and clearcut statistical solution to the problem (AUTHOR).

Whether or not 100 samples should be taken, all the same way, or 10 samples, by each of 10 techniques, depends on whether the principal pitfall in any situation is accuracy or precision. If there is some important source of bias in the technique or the situation, then 10 samples or 10 techniques are required to cross-check the validity of the assumptions. If precision is a bigger problem than accuracy, 10 samples by the same technique will give a measure of precision which, in that instance, would be more important than accuracy (WATT).

Proc. Adv. Study Inst. Dynamics Numbers Popul. (Oosterbeek, 1970) 77–97

Stabilization of animal numbers and the heterogeneity of the environment: The problem of the persistence of sparse populations[1]

P. J. den Boer

Biological Station, Wijster, the Netherlands

Abstract

To understand the persistence of sparse insect populations it must be supposed that the fluctuations in density are small and that the average in net reproduction is close to zero. By simulation experiments and by field observations it has been demonstrated that a relative restriction of density fluctuations may result both from heterogeneity of the environment (and from heterogeneity within the population) and from the number of 'factors' influencing net reproduction. It is argued that when an increase in the complexity of a biocoenosis is accompanied by an increase in the number of species, this will not only result in a decrease in the density fluctuations of many populations but also – because of a growing asymmetry in the distribution of the 'factors' according to their influence on net reproduction – in a lowering of the density level and in the keeping down of a potential upward trend in density.

Because my first experiences with natural populations were the experiences of an insect collector, I have always been impressed by the amazing number of insect species that may be found in a restricted natural locality. I was still more puzzled by the fact that, in most cases, the greater part of these insect species appeared to be relatively rare (cf. Williams, 1964). Although, in the course of years, I learned that some of these supposed rare species are mainly rare in insect collections, the apparent commonness of sparse insect populations remained a fascinating natural phenomenon in the background of my thoughts. Hence, it was almost inevitable that I should test the different population theories I came across on the degree to which they gave an explanation of the apparent persistence of sparse insect populations. However, most population theories – as far as they are based on concepts that can be tested by studying natural populations – appeared to be concerned with overcrowding or, at least, with phenomena connected with relatively high densities. Up till now remarkably little attention has been paid to phenomena connected with low densities, and it seems to me that it is not enough to state that low densites will be followed by higher densities or sometimes by extinction.

Restriction of density fluctuations

If we try to look at high and low densities with the same kind of interest, one thing will be evident: the less frequently the density approaches extremely high or low values the greater will be the population's chance to survive (see also Williams, 1966, p. 107). In other words,

---

[1] Communication 158 of the Biological Station, Wijster.

when we are equally interested in the persistence of dense and of sparse populations our problem is not only 'How are high densities limited?', but more generally 'How are the fluctuations of density restricted?' or 'How is density kept fluctuating between certain (safe) limits?' (See also Reddingius, 1970). When our problem is formulated in this way we also see a possible theoretical explanation for the persistence of sparse populations. If in a sparse population the density fluctuates between narrow limits, its chance to reach density zero need not be greater than in the case of a correspondingly dense population in which density tends to fluctuate much more violently.

Fluctuation characteristics

In order to be able to compare the patterns of density fluctuations of different populations, it will be necessary to calculate some adequate fluctuation characteristics (Reddingius and den Boer, 1970):

1. The difference between the logarithms of the greatest density and of the smallest density that was reached during a certain number of generations: 'logarithmic range' (LR). This measures the limits between which the density has been fluctuating. Of course, for different cases only the LR values of the same number of generations can be compared.

2. The variance of net reproduction (R: density in generation n divided by density in generation n–1) during a certain number of generations: var R. This measures the violence of density fluctuations and thus the chance of reaching values which differ greatly from the mean.

3. The average logarithm of net reproduction during a certain number of generations ($=$ logarithm of the geometric mean of R): average ln R. For m generations the average ln R is simply $1/m\,(\ln[n(m)] - \ln[n(o)])$. This measures the overall trend which density fluctuations have shown. It must be noted that, in any case, the longer a population is observed to persist the closer the average ln R will be to zero; this is a statistical truism which in itself has nothing to do with 'regulation'.

Our problem can now be formulated: Which circumstances in natural environments and/or in natural populations may generally favour such a restriction of density fluctuations that the persistence of sparse insect populations may be at least imagined? In other words, which circumstances will generally decrease the 'logarithmic range' and 'var R' of natural populations and will keep 'average ln R' close to zero?

Heterogeneity and the spreading of risk

Such general circumstances were found to be the heterogeneity in time and space of the natural population itself and of its effective environment (den Boer, 1968a). Because the habitats of natural populations generally are very heterogeneous, there will be local differences in microweather, food, natural enemies, etc. Therefore, the chances of surviving and of reproducing will be different for individuals living in different sites within a natural habitat, even when they are phenotypically identical. Hence, for each generation in turn, the change in numbers may be expected to be different in different parts of the habitat of a natural population; this means that, for the population as a whole, the effect of relatively extreme conditions in one place will be damped to some degree by the effect of less extreme conditions in others. In other words, from generation to generation the risk of wide fluctuation in animal numbers is spread unequally over a number of local

78

groups within the population; this will result in a levelling of the fluctuations in the size of the population as a whole. Moreover, the animals may move from one place to another within the habitat and such movements, even if they occur wholly at random, will contribute to this stabilizing tendency of spatial heterogeneity, since in this way very high or low numbers in some places will be levelled out more thoroughly. Although it is outside the scope of this paper, it must be noted here that heterogeneity within the population will also contribute to the relative stabilization of animal numbers; changes in numbers in one phenotypic or age group will be more or less counterbalanced by changes in other such groups. In this way, the effect of fluctuating environmental factors on the population as a whole is continuously damped to some degree by the phenotypic variation and/or by the variation in age composition (by this variation the range of tolerance of the population is increased as compared with that of the individual animals). (See den Boer, 1968a).

Subpopulations model

To check the correctness of these thoughts Reddingius did some simulation experiments (Reddingius and den Boer, 1970). A population is assumed to consist of 9 subpopulations, each of which occupies an area of unit size (total population with area of 9 units). Each subpopulation consists of animals in either one or three age classes. The time unit is 'a generation' (year). In each generation we have a reproduction period, and a migration period with separate emigration and immigration. It is assumed that during the reproductive period the animals stay in the subpopulations where they are, and that individuals do not reproduce during migration. Survival and reproduction are random variables, emigration and immigration are either both density-independent or both desity-dependent. To get density-dependence of migration it was assumed in our model that the greater the density in a given subpopulation the greater the probability of an animal emigrating from, and the smaller the probability of an animal immigrating into, that subpopulation. Several cases were then compared:
1. NMSP (no migration, similar populations). All subpopulations consist of one age class only and have the same parameters; there is no migration. Simulation of this model serves as a kind of 'control experiment'; there is no spreading of risk.
2. DIMSP (density-independent migration, similar populations). Subpopulations as in 1, but now density-independent migration occurs.
3. DIMDP (density-independent migration, different populations). As in 1 and 2, but there are now 3 groups of subpopulations with different parameters.
4. DDMDP (density-dependent migration, different populations). As in 3, but now migration is density-dependent.
5. NMHP (no migration, heterogeneous populations). Each subpopulation consists of 3 age classes with different parameters; apart from this heterogeneity within subpopulations, the subpopulations are similar and there is no migration.
6. DIMHP (density-independent migration, heterogeneous populations). As in 3 (with 3 groups of subpopulations with different parameters) but now the subpopulations each consist of 3 age classes.
7. DDMHP (density-dependent migration, heterogeneous populations). As in 6, but now migration is density-dependent.
For a detailed discussion see: Reddingius and den Boer (1970).
   It was evident from these simulations that NMSP (1) is much less stable than all other

79

Table 1. Fluctuation characteristics of simulation experiments (explanation see text). (From Reddingius and den Boer, 1970.)

	LR	var R	Average ln R
1. NMSP	5.318	0.417	—0.067
2. DIMSP	2.366	0.062	—0.014
3. DIMDP	3.608	0.068	—0.024
4. DDMDP	1.761	0.078	—0.005
5. NMHP	2.112	0.113	+0.004
6. DIMHP	1.521	0.054	—0.006
7. DDMHP	1.767	0.040	+0.019

cases. When we consider LR and var R (Table 1) most cases with 3 age classes appear to do better than the corresponding ones with only one age class; this is most apparent when comparing NMSP (1) and NMHP (5). All cases with migration are more stable than those without, whereas density-dependent exchange is not distinctly more favourable than density-independent exchange. From this simulation experiment it appears that the spreading of risk brought about by exchange between subpopulations and by heterogeneity according to age within subpopulations, may importantly contribute to a restriction of density fluctuations in the population as a whole and, therefore, to a stabilization of animal numbers. Moreover, the occurrence of exchange appears to be more important than whether or not such an exchange is density-dependent.

Stabilization of numbers in carabid populations

Now that we have shown that a stabilization of numbers by spreading of risk may occur in some imaginary populations, one may ask whether it may also occur in natural populations. Although there are suggestive indications that in some carabid populations phenotypic variation and variation in age composition may contribute to a stabilization of numbers (some preliminary notes in den Boer, 1968b), I will restrict myself here to the possible effect of spatial heterogeneity.

In the northern part of the Netherlands (Drenthe, Fig. 1) on the Heath of Kralo (Fig. 2), during a number of years carabid beetles were sampled in a number of different sites with standard sets of pitfalls. From capture-recapture experiments (Table 2) it was concluded that, in general, the pitfall-catches of a carabid species summed over the period of activity is itself a useful measure of relative density. From such measurements it is possible to estimate the net rate of reproduction (r) from year to year for a number of subpopulations occurring in those sites in which the catches were continued during a succession of years. For a number of species such data are available; the two most reliable cases will be discussed here (Tables 3 and 4). In these cases we may be sure that direct exchange of individuals between sample sites will be quantitatively unimportant (with the possible exception of sites AT, BH and BJ); dispersal occurs by running, and within one year only very few individuals are able to cover distances of 100 m or more as was shown by capture-recapture experiments with different species. However, because the Heath of Kralo will be more or less uninterruptedly populated by these two species, indirect exchange in the course of a number of generations over far greater distances may be important. Hence a comparison

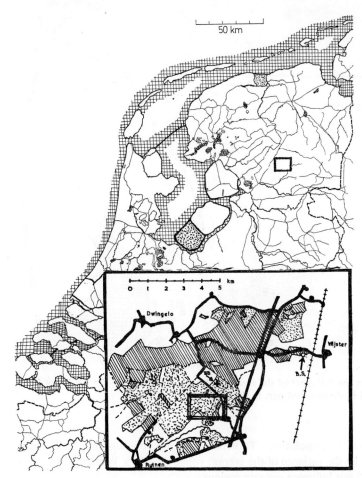

Fig. 1. Situation of the area of investigation in the northern part of the Netherlands (rectangle), enlarged in the lower right; the outlined area is enlarged again in Fig. 2.

of the density changes in different sites – in which the possible results of indirect exchange between sites are included – may give some impression of the relative contribution of these sites to the overall density changes in that area. 'Var R' seems to be the most adequate measure for such a comparison (see Fig. 7 and Reddingius and den Boer, 1970). For each row (site) 's_j^2' gives an estimate of the violence of density fluctuations. The weighted average of these row variances (S_p^2) gives some impression of how violent density fluctuations were in an average site on the Heath of Kralo. Not in all sites, however, did density fluctuate in parallel and to the same degree; for each column (pair of years) 'v_i^2' gives an estimate of the degree of dissimilarity of density changes in the sites concerned. The weighted average of these column-variances (S_t^2) gives some impression of how different the density changes were in different sites during an average pair of years. In the case of *Pterostichus coerulescens* (Table 3) S_p^2 and S_t^2 are of the same magnitude, which may indicate that the differences between sites might be great enough to counterbalance the density changes in

81

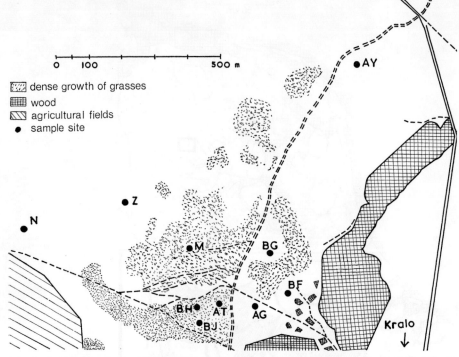

Fig. 2. Sample sites in the S.E.-part of the Heath of Kralo. Note: sample-site BB is not in the picture; it is indicated in the outlined part in the lower right of Fig. 1.

time within a group of subpopulations. To what degree this compensation really occurs is roughly estimated by the variance of the average column-r's (S_r^2). We may also use var R_i (S_R^2) but this will not influence our conclusions.

In *P. coerulescens* (Table 3) S_r^2 is much smaller than S_p^2, which may indicate that, in this group of subpopulations on the Heath of Kralo, there is a considerable levelling down of density fluctuations as a result of effective differences between the sites. This, indeed, corroborates my statement that in many natural populations the risk of wide fluctuation is spread from generation to generation over a number of local groups within the population, and that this will result in a relative stabilization of numbers in the population as a whole (see also Fig. 3).

In *Calathus melanocephalus* (Table 4), however, S_t^2 is much smaller than S_p^2, which indicates that the differences between sites have not been great enough to counterbalance the density changes in time within this group of subpopulations. This seems to be confirmed by the fact that the difference between S_r^2 and S_p^2 is relatively much smaller in this species than in the case of *P. coerulescens* (see also Fig. 4). Hence, on the Heath of Kralo the population of *P. coerulescens* seems to be more favoured by spatial spreading of the risk of extinction than is that of *C. melanocephalus*. We do not yet know what are the causes of this difference between the two species.

Table 2. *Pitfall-catches as a relative measure of mean density* (carabid beetles).
For most weeks during the reproductive period of some populations, reliable estimates of density could be derived from capture-recapture experiments (Jolly's stochastic method: 1965). The mean density (per week) during the same (main) part of the reproductive period in two successive years (or in two sites in the same year) was compared with the total number of unmarked individuals caught during that period. (All available data are presented.)

The same site in two successive years	Total number of unmarked individuals (not caught before)			Mean density (from capture-recapture exp.) per week			Difference between the quotient of pitfall-catches and that of densities
	year n-1	year n	year n / year n-1	year n-1	year n	year n / year n-1	
Agonum assimile PAYK. 1966-'67: 8 weeks	459	670	1.46	474.2	785.8	1.66	$\chi^2 = 2.287$ P ≈ 0.15
Agonum assimile PAYK. 1968-'69: 17 weeks	1048	1011	0.96	560.1	462.8	0.83	$\chi^2 = 3.963$ P ≈ 0.05
Calathus erratus SAHLB. 1968-'69: 15 weeks	1649	1207	0.73	1956.0	1552.1	0.79	$\chi^2 = 2.484$ P ≈ 0.13
Nebria brevicollis F. 1968-'69: 10 weeks	231	264	1.14	158.0	205.8	1.30	$\chi^2 = 0.943$ P ≈ 0.35
Pterostichus oblongopunctatus F 1968-'69: 14 weeks	644	1151	1.79	371.8	690.6	1.86	$\chi^2 = 0.235$ P ≈ 0.60
Two sites during the same year	site I	site II	site I / site II	site I	site II	site I / site II	
Calathus erratus SAHLB. 1969: 6 weeks	458	383	1.20	999.5	788.0	1.27	$\chi^2 = 0.07$ P ≈ 0.80

Note that: *Agonum assimile* and *Pterostichus oblongopunctatus* (both studied in a small deciduous wood) reproduce in spring, whereas *Nebria brevicollis* (studied in a small deciduous wood) and *Calathus erratus* (studied in an area of blown sand) reproduce in late summer and autumn.

Table 3. *Pterostichus coerulescens* L. (Col., *Carabidae*) in different sites on the Heath of Kralo (the Netherlands, Drenthe: Fig. 2).

$n_{j,i}$: number of individuals caught during year i in site j; $r_{ji}: \dfrac{n_{j,i}}{n_{j,i-1}}$

Sub-population (j)	n_{ji} / r_{ji}	1959	1960 '60/'59	1961 '61/'60	1962 '62/'61	1963 '63/'62	1964 '64/'63	1965 '65/'64	1966 '66/'65	1967 '67/'66	1968 '68/'67	1969 '69/'68	s_j^2	k_j
N	n_{1i}	202	246	206	230	223	206	154	86			162	0.048	7
	r_{1i}		1.22	0.84	1.11	0.93	0.92	0.75	0.56					
Z	n_{2i}		150	317	493	550	525	163	83			148	0.460	6
	r_{2i}			2.15	1.55	1.11	0.95	0.31	0.51					
AG	n_{3i}			209	282	393	265	412	283	354		336	0.142	6
	r_{3i}				1.35	1.39	0.67	1.55	0.69	1.25		0.66		
AT	n_{4i}					132	139	196	133	353	506		0.541	6
	r_{4i}						1.05	1.41	0.68	2.65	1.43			
AY	n_{5i}						367	264	163			21	0.005	2
	r_{5i}							0.72	0.62			0.66		
BB	n_{6i}							595	625	755	543	485	0.044	4
	r_{6i}								1.05	1.21	0.72	0.89		
M	n_{7i}	45	55	72	37	30	13	4	3				0.148	7
	r_{7i}		1.22	1.33	0.56	0.81	0.43	0.31	0.75					
BF	n_{8i}							256	260	315			0.018	2
	r_{8i}								1.02	1.21				
BG	n_{9i}							463	548	405			0.097	2
	r_{9i}								1.18	0.74				
BH	n_{10i}							119	287	410	444	292	0.557	4
	r_{10i}								2.41	1.43	1.08	0.66		
BJ	n_{11i}							114	157	202	320	209	0.162	4
	r_{11i}								1.38	1.29	1.58	0.65		
	v_i^2		0.000	0.438	0.183	0.064	0.063	0.283	0.300	0.351	0.148	0.014		
	$\bar{r}_{.i}$		1.22	1.44	1.14	1.06	0.80	0.84	0.99	1.40	1.20	0.72		
	R_i		1.22	1.32	1.30	1.15	0.86	0.79	0.96	1.22	1.05	0.73		
	$(R_i - \bar{r}_{.i})^2$		0.000	0.014	0.026	0.008	0.004	0.003	0.001	0.032	0.023	0.0001		
	m_i		2	3	4	4	5	6	11	7	4	4		

$i = 1, 2, \ldots t$
$j = 1, 2, \ldots p$

$$s_j^2 = \frac{\Sigma(r_{j.} - \bar{r}_{j.})^2}{k_j - 1}$$

$$v_i^2 = \frac{\Sigma(r_{.i} - \bar{r}_{.i})^2}{m_i - 1}$$

$S_p^2 = \dfrac{\Sigma(k_j-1)s_j^2}{\Sigma(k_j-1)} = 0.2384$; $S_t^2 = \dfrac{\Sigma(m_i-1)v_i^2}{\Sigma(m_i-1)} = 0.2218$; $S_p^2/S_t^2 = 1.07$; $S_r^2 = var\, \bar{r}_{.i} = 0.0604$; $S_R^2 = var\, R_i = 0.0462$; $S_{(R-\bar{r})}^2 = 0.0122$

Note that $R_i = \dfrac{\Sigma n_{j,i}}{\Sigma n_{j,i-1}}$ for those subpopulations that were sampled during both successive years. Compare: Fig. 3

84

$n_{j,i}$: number of individuals caught during year i in site j; $r_{j,i}$: $\dfrac{n_{j,i}}{n_{i,i-1}}$.

Subpopulation (j)	n_{J1} / r_{J1}	1959	1960 '60/'59	1961 '61/'60	1962 '62/'61	1963 '63/'62	1964 '64/'63	1965 '65/'64	1966 '66/'65	1967 '67/'66	1968 '68/'67	1969 '69/'68	s_j^2	k_j
N	n_{11}	129	517	360	1131	661	177	61	63			7	2.256	7
	r_{11}		4.01	0.70	3.14	0.58	0.27	0.34	1.03					
Z	n_{21}		196	384	606	569	257	43	45			10	0.450	6
	r_{21}			1.96	1.58	0.94	0.45	0.17	1.04					
AG	n_{31}			652	2591	2445	758	317	352	457		(69)	1.809	6
	r_{31}				3.97	0.94	0.31	0.42	1.11	1.30				
AT	n_{41}					2408	926	238	138	685	97	50	3.527	6
	r_{41}						0.38	0.26	0.58	4.96	0.14	0.52		
AY	n_{51}						813	518	509			47	0.058	2
	r_{51}							0.64	0.98					
BB	n_{61}							155	481	2125	691	221	4.194	4
	r_{61}								3.11	4.42	0.33	0.35		
M	n_{71}	156	145	76	155	322	143	9	9				0.634	7
	r_{71}		0.96	0.52	2.10	2.08	0.44	0.06	1.00					
BF	n_{81}							143	259	309			0.192	2
	r_{81}								1.81	1.19				
BG	n_{91}							269	485	485			0.309	2
	r_{91}								1.80	1.00				
BH	n_{10t}							222	660	772	187	33	1.693	4
	r_{10t}								2.97	1.17	0.24	0.18		
BJ	n_{11t}							310	560	824	162	12	0.778	4
	r_{11t}								1.81	1.47	0.20	0.07		
v_i^2			4.650	0.616	1.140	0.426	0.006	0.041	0.694	2.901	0.006	0.039		
$\bar r_{.i}$			2.49	1.06	2.70	1.14	0.37	0.32	1.48	2.22	0.23	0.28		
R_i			2.32	0.96	3.28	0.89	0.35	0.39	1.56	1.93	0.26	0.28		
$(R_i-\bar r_{.i})^2$			0.029	0.010	0.336	0.063	0.0004	0.005	0.006	0.084	0.001	0.000		
m_i			2	3	4	4	5	6	11	7	4	4		

$i = 1, 2, \dots t$
$j = 1, 2, \dots p$

$$s_j^2 = \frac{\Sigma(r_{j.}-\bar r_{j.})^2}{k_j-1}$$

$$v_i^2 = \frac{\Sigma(r_{j.}-\bar r_{.i})^2}{m_i-1}$$

$$\frac{\Sigma(R_i-\bar r_{.i})^2}{9} = 0.0594$$

$S_p^2 = \dfrac{\Sigma(k_j-1)s_j^2}{\Sigma(k_j-1)} = 1.7136$; $\quad S_t^2 = \dfrac{\Sigma(m_i-1)v_i^2}{\Sigma(m_i-1)} = 0.8822$; $\quad S_p^2/S_t^2 = 1.94$; $\quad S_r^2 = \mathrm{var}\, r_{j,i} = 0.9220$; $\quad S_R^2 = \mathrm{var}\, R_i = 1.0547$; $\quad S_{(R-\bar r)}^2 = \dfrac{\Sigma(R_i-\bar r_{.i})^2}{9} = 0.0594$

Note that $R_i = \dfrac{\Sigma n_{j,i}}{\Sigma n_{j,i-1}}$ for those subpopulations that were sampled during successive years. Compare: Fig. 4.

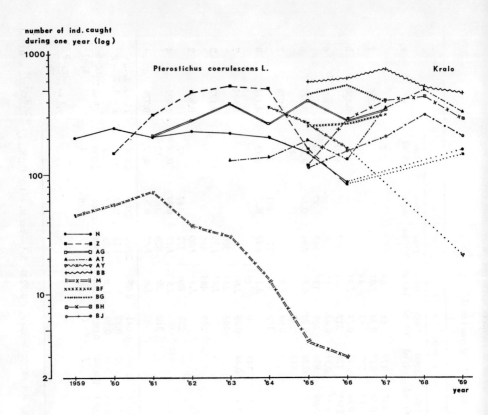

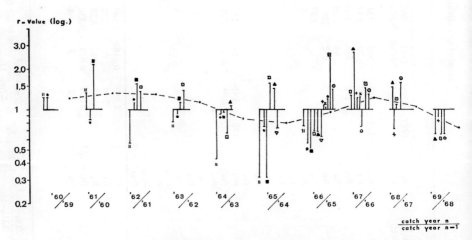

Fig. 3. Catches of *Pterostichus coerulescens* L. in sample-sites on the Heath of Kralo (Fig. 2). In the lower part of the figure are values of r_{ji} (vertical lines) and values of R_i (broken line) (See Table 3).

Fig. 4. Catches of *Calathus melanocephalus* L. in sample-sites on the Heath of Kralo (Fig. 2). In the lower part of the figure are values of r_{ji} (vertical lines) and values of R_i (broken line) (See Table 4).

◄

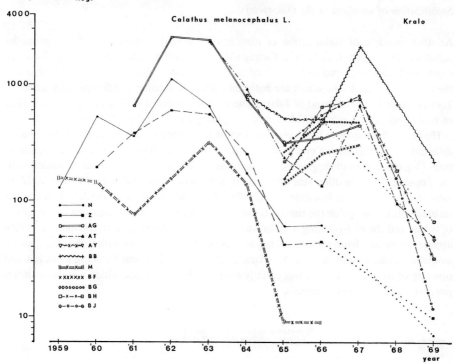

number of ind. caught
during one year (log)

Calathus melanocephalus L.   Kralo

Legend:
● N
■ Z
▫ AG
▲ AT
▽ A Y
+ BB
‖ M
× B F
○ B G
▫ B H
⊙ B J

year

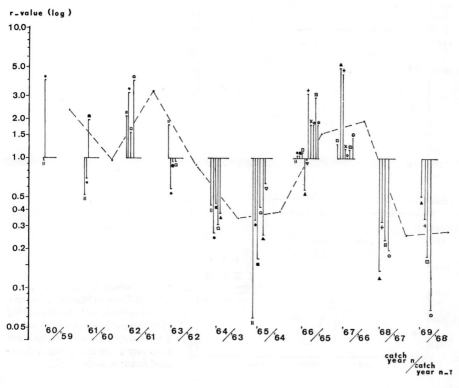

r_value (log)

'60/59 '61/60 '62/61 '63/62 '64/63 '65/64 '66/65 '67/66 '68/67 '69/68

catch
year n / catch
year n_1

Another example of stabilization of numbers by spatial spreading of risk is given by Schütte (1957) for the Oak tortrix, *Tortrix viridana* L. in the vicinity of Münster. The chief mortality factor appeared to be: lack of coincidence between the hatching of larvae and the opening of oak buds, which are both influenced by weather conditions. The larvae of *Tortrix* hatch within a period of 7 days, whereas there is considerable variation in the time of bud-opening between individual oaks; 19 days in 1952 and 26 days in 1953.

However, the sequence in which a number of trees open their buds remains the same in different years, this allows one to distinguish between 'early-opening' and 'late-opening' trees (4 groups were distinguished). In some years the hatching of larvae coincided with early opening oaks, in other years with late opening oaks. The dynamics of *Tortrix viridana* were studied by Schütte in 4 plots of oaks (Fig. 5). He discovered that the density was most stable in plot A in which the mortality due to a lack of coincidence between the hatching of larvae and the bud-opening of oaks was nearly constant (60%). This constant mortality apparently results from the oaks being distributed almost equally within the four groups. In other words, in plot A the risk of lack of coincidence between hatching of larvae and opening of oaks is spread almost equally over the different trees, which results in an important stabilization of numbers.

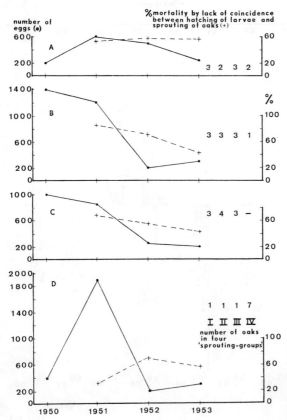

Fig. 5. Density of eggs, and % mortality of *Tortrix viridana* L. due to a lack of coincidence between hatching of larvae and bud-opening of oaks in 4 plots with different distribution of oaks over 4 'opening groups'. (Modified from: Schütte, 1957).

Number-of-factors model

The stabilization of animal numbers does not only result from spatial heterogeneity in the effective environment (and from heterogeneity within the population), but also from the number of 'factors' that influence density. Animal numbers will be influenced by a smaller or greater number of meteorological 'factors', of species of natural enemies, of kinds of food, of kinds of hiding places, etc, and sometimes some of these 'factors' may tend to counterbalance the effects of some others. In fact this is only another way of looking at the influence of the complexity of natural situations, a view, however, that has been put forward already by different authors in various forms, e.g. by Thompson (1929, 1939, 1956), Andrewartha and Birch (1954), Glen (1954), Milne (1957, 1962), Schwerdtfeger (1958), Richards (1961).

We attempted to demonstrate the supposed stabilizing influence of an increasing number of factors affecting net reproduction by a model (Reddingius and den Boer, 1970). In this model net reproduction was allowed to vary between a very low value $r_{min} = 0.02$ and a very high value $r_{max} = 50$ under the influence of 1, 2, etc. up to 10 meteorological 'factors' such as average temperature, total rainfall, etc. over a given month. These 'factors' were taken, irrespective of whether they would be serially correlated in time or not and/or whether their frequency distributions would be about normal or not; in fact one or more of these features appeared to occur in some of the factors (Reddingius and den Boer, 1970). The values of the meteorological 'factors', the only kind of environmental 'factors' of which real values over long series of consecutive years are available, were taken from published tables of the Meteorological Institute, De Bilt, the Netherlands. Each factor f_i was allowed to influence net reproduction between certain limits u_i and b_i corresponding with r_{min} and r_{max}; u_i and b_i were fixed arbitrary somewhere outside the values of the tables, which resulted in quantitatively different influences in different factors. The meteorological data were used in the same annual sequence in which they appear in the original tables and in the same sequence values of r were given by

$$y(t) = \ln[r(t)] = y_{min} + \frac{y_{max} - y_{min}}{\sum\limits_{j=1}^{k} |b_i - u_i|} \cdot \sum\limits_{j=1}^{k} |f_i(t) - u_i|.$$

In this way a number of populations were simulated which were influenced by a different number of factors; all possible combinations of up to 10 factors were simulated and the calculated values of the fluctuation characteristics for the total number of combinations were averaged. It must be noted that by increasing the number of factors one certainly does not decrease 'LR' and 'var R' in all individual cases (individual results are highly variable). Therefore, averages were calculated to show the general trend with which we are concerned in these theoretical considerations. Two versions of this additive linear model were used:

A. Very different 'factors' (air temperature, rainfall, evaporation, sunshine, soil temperature) during 30 years.

B. Only values on temperature and rainfall during a period of 210 years (the longest series available).

To be sure that our modeled populations would 'persist' for some time it was assumed that, in the case with 10 factors after a given sequence of years (30 in version A and 100 in

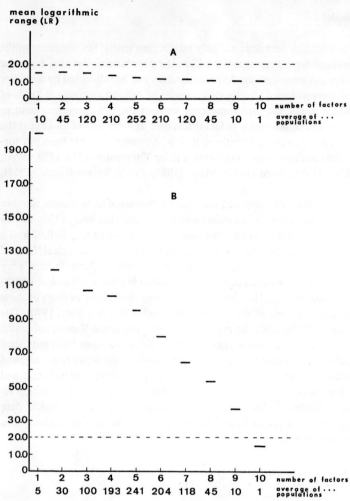

Fig. 6. Mean logarithmic range (LR) of density fluctuations in simulation experiments on the stabilizing influence of the number of (meteorological) factors determining the net rate of reproduction. The experiment was repeated for each possible combination of 2, 3, etc. factors out of 10, except cases in which population density became too high (higher than 10^{130}: Experiment B). LR was averaged over all calculated combinations (populations) with the same number of factors.
A. Models for 30 generations (years) with very different meteorological factors.
B. Models for 210 generations (years) with only mean air temperature and/or total rainfall over a given month (the only data available).

version B), density attains about the initial value once more (see Reddingius and den Boer, 1970). Hence, the case with 10 factors did not show a strong trend in density.

In both versions, LR steadily decreases with an increase in the number of factors (Fig. 6); in the case with 210 years, LR starts, of course, with much higher values and the decrease is much steeper than in the case with 30 years. The decrease of var R with increase of the number of factors is very convincing in both versions (Fig. 7). From this figure (compare A and B) one even gets the impression that the number of factors may have a

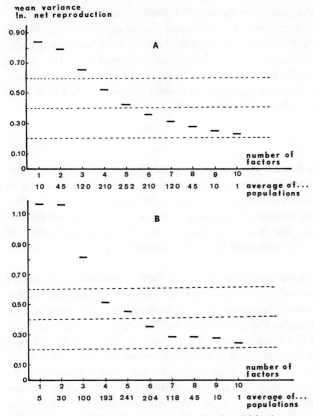

Fig. 7. Mean variance of ln net reproduction (var R) in the same simulation experiments as those in Fig. 6.

more important influence on var R than the 'kind of factor' and/or than the number of years over which var R was calculated (this latter feature of var R is used in the interpretation of Tables 3 and 4). The correctness of this interpretation was made probably by Reddingius (Reddingius and den Boer, 1970); he was able to prove that within the premises of our model, even when this was weakened regarding the limits b_i and u_i, var R approaches zero when the number of factors becomes infinite. The factors need not be uncorrelated among themselves and in all probability they may even depend on density.

Trends in density

Hence, under the conditions of our model we may get density fluctuations as small as we want by assuming the influence of an appropriately large number of 'factors' on density, and this may serve as a conceptual model for the persistence of sparse insect populations; but in that case it must also be assumed that 'average ln R' is close to zero. In an overall highly unfavourable environment most 'factors' during most of the time will have an unfavourable influence, and density will show an overall downward trend albeit with small fluctuations. In an overall highly favourable environment density will show an upward

91

trend and, in the long run, the sparse population will become a dense one unless the environment shows some limiting tendency. Although some kind of density-dependent limitation may, of course, keep 'lnR' close to zero, such limitation is not a 'conditio sine qua non'. Even some very incidental random crashes in random years (once in 30–100 years in the population with 10 factors in our model with 210 years) may keep in persistence a population which otherwise would have shown an overall upward trend. For a more detailed discussion see: Reddingius and den Boer (1970).

Environmental resistance

But another line of thought is possible to introduce some limiting tendency of the environment; in many cases, such a limiting tendency appears to be theoretically necessary to keep down a strong upward trend and thus to supplement the restriction of density fluctuations resulting from a great number of 'factors'. Let us imagine some animal population influenced only by a small number of 'factors', e.g.: a homogeneous population of some not very polyphageous phytophageous insect in a homogeneous environment poor in animal species.

If we now visualise that for some reason the number of 'factors' gradually increases, we may wonder what 'kind of factors' most probably will be added. The population will become more heterogeneous; more phenotypes, a more heterogeneous age composition, more variation in development, etc. The environment will become more heterogeneously structured, which will result in a breaking up of the population into a number of local groups, each with an effective environment (e.g. microweather; see den Boer and Sanders, 1970) somewhat different from that of the other groups. Perhaps there will also be more variation in the distribution, the composition and the quality of the food, etc. This increase in the number of 'factors' will result, of course, in a decrease of density fluctuations; but there is no reason to suppose that – averaged over a great number of such cases – the overall favourability of the circumstances always will be altered in one and the same direction i.e. that 'average ln R' always will shift significantly in the same direction. However, we have left out another 'kind of factors' that must also take action in our 'concept adding procedure'. The number of other species will also increase, and among them the number of species of parasites, predators, competitors and other enemies generally will greatly outnumber the number of beneficial species (indifferent species need not be considered). Hence, adding this kind of factors will result in a relative increase in the limiting tendency of the environment, increase of 'environmental resistance' (Chapman, 1928); contrary to Chapman this term does not imply here any 'mechanism(s)', whether density-dependent or not, but only points to the existence of some general limitation or resistance.

In my opinion there are good reasons to suppose that an increase in the number of species of a biocoenosis will not only contribute – via an increase in the number of 'factors' – to a relative reduction of density fluctuations in many populations, but will also result in an increase of some general kind of 'environmental resistance'. The latter – mainly resulting from an asymmetrical increase of different kinds of factors (beneficial, indifferent, limiting) – will lower the density level of many populations and may keep down possible upward trends in density which might have become manifest under less complex circumstances.

In a very simple – but appropriate – situation, an experiment by Utida (1957) nicely demonstrates that in a population of the azuki bean weevil (*Callosobruchus chinensis* L.)

an increase in the number of parasite species from one to two (other things being equal) not only results in a decrease of density fluctuations (Fig. 8 compare ln-range and var R in A and B), but also in a lowering of the density level of the host population. Moreover 'average ln R' is indeed closer to zero in the case with two parasite species (0.0176) than in the case with one (0.0281). The experiment also illustrates that hypotheses on stabilization of numbers by spreading of risk may be tested experimentally.

Density-related limitation

It may be expected that the total action of all kinds of predators, parasites and competitors ('environmental resistance') will often be related to density in a very broad sense. In general, dense populations will be affected more than sparse ones, especially when polyphageous predators (and parasites?) are able to develop 'specific searching images' (Tinbergen, 1960) for numerous prey species; sparse prey species will then experience some 'protection' from severe predation. But a relative 'protection' of sparse prey species may also result from other circumstances, e.g. a more 'clustered' distribution of individuals in some numerous species than in sparse ones, the occurrence of Batesian mimicry, adequate differences in hiding abilities, patterns of activity, palatability, etc. between some numerous species and sparse ones. However, this kind of limiting tendency of the environment also

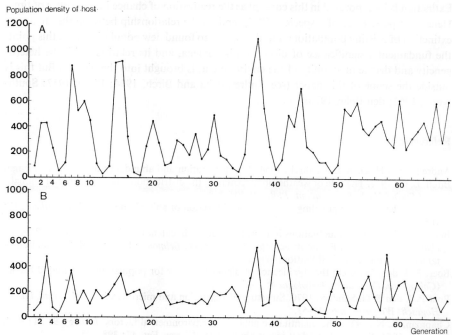

Fig. 8. Density fluctuations in experimental populations of the azuki bean weevil *(Callosobruchus chinensis* L.) during 68 generations.
A. Culture with one parasite species; ln range 4.00733; variance R 4.6437; average ln R 0.0281.
B. Culture with two parasite species; ln range 2.87437; variance R 2.1855; average ln R 0.0176.
(Modified from: Utida, 1957).

93

must be seen as part of a very complex pattern of environmental (and 'populational') influences on net reproduction (number of factors) from which separate density-dependent 'factors' generally cannot easily be singled out. Moreover, it may be expected that, in general, the greater the complexity the smaller will be the specific effect of individual 'factors' – e.g. the density-dependent effect of some of these 'factors' – and the smaller will be the significance of these special influences for the overall stabilization of numbers. This does not imply that I would deny that density- dependent limitation of density can make an important contribution to the stabilization of animal numbers in some or in many cases. However, it may generally be expected that, in these cases, the limitation or decrease of density will be more important than the degree to which it is density-dependent (see also den Boer, 1968a).

Sparse insect populations

Returning to our problem 'the apparent persistence of sparse insect populations', I should like to pose the following hypothesis:

> In a complex biocoenosis many species will show restricted density fluctuations as a result of the great number of 'factors' affecting net reproduction; such a situation – by a relative preponderance of mainly non-specific density-limiting factors – results in a kind of 'environmental resistance' keeping down both the density level of many populations and any possible tendencies for an upward trend in density.

Extinction is incorporated in this concept as the realization of chance in the course of time. Hence, the persistence of a species will depend on the relationship between the chance of extinction of existing populations and the chance to found new populations. On this point, the fundamental significance of dispersal phenomena, and its relations with the heterogeneity and degree of stability of the environment, is brought into the picture. But this is outside the scope of this paper (see Andrewartha and Birch, 1954; Birch, 1957; Southwood, 1962; den Boer, 1970).

References

Andrewartha, H. G. & L. C. Birch, 1954. The distribution and abundance of animals. Chicago.

Birch, L. C., 1957. The role of weather in determining the distribution and abundance of animals. *Cold Spring Harb. Symp. quant. Biol.* 22: 203–218.

Boer, P. J. den, 1968a. Spreading of risk and stabilization of animal numbers. *Acta biotheor.* 18: 165–194.

Boer, P. J. den, 1968b. Fluctuations in morph frequency in catches of the ground beetle *Pterostichus oblongopunctatus* F. and its ecological significance, *Belmontia* 13. II: Ecology. Can be obtained from the Biological Station, Wijster.

Boer, P. J. den, 1970. On the significance of dispersal power for populations of Carabid beetles (*Coleoptera, Carabidae*). *Oecologia* 4: 1–28.

Boer P. J. den & G. Sanders, 1970. Structure of vegetation and microweather. *Misc. Pap. Landb. Hogesch. Wageningen* 6: 33–53.

Chapman, R. N., 1928. The quantitative analysis of environmental factors. *Ecology* 9: 111–122.

Glen, R., 1954. Factors that affect insect abundance. *J. econ. Ent.* 47: 398–405.

Jolly, G. N., 1965. Explicit estimates from capture-recapture data with both death and immigration – stochastic model. *Biometrika* 52: 225–247.

Milne, A., 1957. Theories on natural control of insect populations. *Cold Spring Harb. Symp. quant. Biol.* 22: 253–271.

Milne, A., 1962. A theory of natural control of insect populations. *J. theor. Biol.* 3: 19–50.

Reddingius, J., 1970. Gambling for existence. Thesis, Groningen, 1968. To be published in *Bibliotheca biotheor*.

Reddingius, J. & P. J. den Boer, 1970. Simulation experiments illustrating stabilization of animal numbers by spreading of risk. *Oecologia* 5: 240–284.

Richards, O. W., 1961. The theoretical and practical study of natural insect populations. *A. Rev. Ent.* 6: 147–162.

Schütte, F., 1957. Untersuchungen über die Populationsdynamik des Eichenwicklers (*Tortrix viridana* L.) *Z. angew. Ent.* 40: 1–36; 285–331.

Schwerdtfeger, F., 1958. Is the density of animal populations regulated by mechanisms or by chance? *Proc. 10th. Int. Congr. Ent.* (1956) 4: 115–122.

Southwood, T. R. E., 1962. Migration of terrestrial arthropods in relation to habitat. *Biol. Rev.* 37: 171–214.

Thompson, W. R., 1929. On natural control. *Parasitology* 21: 269–281.

Thompson, W. R., 1939. Biological control and the theories of the interactions of populations. *Parasitology* 31: 299–388.

Thompson, W. R., 1956. The fundamental theory of natural and biological control. *A. Rev. Ent.* 1: 397–402.

Tinbergen, L., 1960. The natural control of insects in pine woods. I. Factors influencing the intensivity of predation by song birds. *Arch neerl. Zool.* 13: 265–336.

Utida, S., 1957. Population fluctuation, an experimental and theoretical approach. *Cold Spring Harb. Symp. quant. Biol.* 22: 139–151.

Williams, C. B., 1964. Patterns in the balance of nature. London.

Williams, G. C., 1966. Adaption and natural selection. University of Princeton Press.

Discussion

Participants: den Boer (Author), Beukema, Frank, Gradwell, Jacobs, Jain, Lawton, Murdoch, Ohnesorge, Platt, Royama, Solomon, Southwood and Walker

The initial discussion concerned the features of the number-of-factors model. Many of these points can be clarified by referring to Reddingius and den Boer (1970), but some need to be mentioned here too –

Simple models of population fluctuation often have a built-in balance inasmuch as the chances of increase and decrease are made quantitatively equal. It seems unlikely that many populations would be matched to their habitats in this way, for habitats vary, and such a balance could exist for only one or a few among the many in which the species is found. It seems that in nature populations would mostly have an overall net reproductive rate above the value needed just to replace regular losses, and that the consequent tendency to net increase would be offset by density-dependent processes (SOLOMON). Hence, models for which density dependent factors are not essential to prevent eventual overpopulation or extinction are concerned with fluctuations rather than with trends and will have a built-in balance (SOUTHWOOD). A distinction between long-term trends in the numbers and fluctuations around that trend is fine in a model. In nature, however, we have time to observe rather few fluctuations in annual species, and, thus, purely by observing changes in numbers it is very difficult to distinguish between fluctuations around a trendline (or 'equilibrium' level) and changes in the trend itself (MURDOCH).

I admit that the distinction between amplitude of fluctuations and long-term trend is essential in the models. Fluctuations could be made as small as one wanted by increasing the number of 'factors' but to be sure that the model 'populations' would 'persist' for some time (no pronounced trend) a very crude 'safety-valve' had to be built in, as is mentioned in the paper. The models are only intended to give a possible understanding of the often observed restriction of density fluctuations in supposedly persisting populations, which is illustrated by some examples. It is hardly possible at this moment to give sensible thoughts about the problem of the supposed persistence (absence of trend) of populations itself. To make an attempt:

1. One can deny the problem by stating that there is a more or less continuous 'turnover' of populations (extinction and refounding) ending ultimately in extinction of the species (in different species the time-scale of this 'turnover' may be very different).

2. As is discussed in this paper, one can accept eventual extinction (the end of a downward trend) of populations as a realization of chance, and state that the eventual keeping down of upward trends may be a function of the complexity of the effective biotic environment as a whole ('environmental resistance').

3. One can state that 'self-regulatory mechanisms' are necessary to prevent overpopulation and/or extinction in the long run (no pronounced trend). Although at this moment I guess that the possibilities (1) and (2) will turn out to present the more general cases, I am sure that at least in a number of cases possibility (3) will be involved to some degree (if 'regulation' is not defined too strictly in a Nicholsonian sense) (AUTHOR).

Some kind of environmental predictability was not incorporated into the models, because the environment is hardly supposed to show it (except for the existence of seasons); real meteorological data are used (AUTHOR to LAWTON).

In many cases adding a factor actually decreases stability, because the factors are not selected to have special features and are taken together in all possible combinations; the stabilizing trend becomes especially apparent when considering the averages (AUTHOR to JACOBS).

It is difficult to see how the number of factors is important to stability unless their effects are very similar, and there is no single dominating factor (FRANK, GRADWELL, OHNESOR-GE). The very different (arbitrary) values of the limits b_i and u_i prevent the factors from having very similar quantitative effects, although it is not expected that one factor will dominate the quantitative effects of all the others. Because population numbers are undoubtedly influenced by many factors, to obtain a generalization it seemed more relevant at the moment to test the influence of the number of factors rather than to study what kinds of effects of some single factor may still be measured against the background of the effects of many others. Of course, very different relationships between factors can be imagined, which can hardly ever all be covered by simulation models. On the other hand, we expect that the conclusions drawn are valid for a more general class of models as well. But it will always be possible to construct exceptional situations or even to trace them in nature (AUTHOR).

'LR' and 'var R' cannot be mathematically independent because a small 'LR' can hardly coincide with a great 'var R', but they measure different features of a set of fluctuations, 'LR' being more susceptible to trend than 'var R' (AUTHOR to BEUKEMA).

No special features of 'model animals' are taken into account besides perhaps the values of r_{min} and r_{max} and the – arbitrary taken – parameters in the subpopulations model (AUTHOR to ROYAMA).

What kind of differences in the environment are important for carabid beetles? (FRANK), how are they quantified? (WALKER), and which quantitative operational measure of the spatial heterogeneity of a natural environment may be used or suggested? (PLATT) In order to effectively measure heterogeneity, it would be necessary to know the variation in space and time of all factors significantly influencing density. As a start, we tried to develop techniques for measuring spatial and temporal variation in the temperature and humidity of the surface layer, and we hope to develop techniques for measuring the spatial structure of vegetation, because these factors are found to correlate highly – in an estimated ordinal scale – with habitat-selection. But apart from this we may simply observe that changes of density are different in different places within the habitat of a population, and try to estimate how this affects a group of such subpopulations in order to learn whether stability is favoured by such a situation or not (AUTHOR).

Several ideas (Mayr, Wright) invoke 'regular' or occasional bottlenecks of numbers to allow 'genetic revolution' – a new breakthrough in the genetic system. The role of drift or founder effect is directly relevant to fluctuations in numbers, either locally or to the species as a whole. If sparser species would indeed show relatively greater stability, one may wonder whether their being sparse may imply a lack of such 'genetic revolution events' (JAIN).

Proc. Adv. Study Inst. Dynamics Numbers Popul. (Oosterbeek, 1970) 98–108

Ecological variation and its implications for the dynamics of populations of the landsnail Cepaea nemoralis

H. Wolda

Zoological Laboratory of the State University at Groningen, Haren (Gr.), the Netherlands

Abstract

Attention is drawn to the fact that in natural populations there may be a large variation in ecologically important characters such as fecundity, dispersal tendency, survival under specific conditions and growth rate. It is argued that in order to understand the dynamics of a population such variation should not be ignored.

This is illustrated with some data on variation in the growth-rate in the landsnail *Cepaea nemoralis* (L.) Within populations there is a large variation in the growth-rate. Between populations there also are differences in the growth-rate per season. These differences are caused by some unidentified factors early in the season since later in the season there are no differences in the growth-rate per unit of time. Such differences have large consequences for the number of adult individuals in a population.

The aim of population dynamics is to understand the 'chances to survive' of species of organisms in nature. In practice this means the 'chances to survive' of single-species populations of animals, plants or micro-organisms.

The number of a individuals in a population is a convenient parameter to use in a study of that population, but it is not the only one. Most hypotheses and research projects take it as the only parameter and ignore others such as changes in the phenotypic or genotypic composition of a population. This is understandable as a first approach, as the present hypotheses are complicated enough already and ignoring variation between individuals and between populations is one way of simplifying matters. However, I think we have reached the stage where such variation should no longer be ignored. This is no new idea; several ecologists, such as Birch (1960), Chitty (1960, 1967), Krebs (1970), Pimentel (1961, 1964), Schwerdtfeger (1969) and Wellington (1957, 1960), have made attempts to incorporate ecological variation in their ideas and research. In several papers presented in these Proceedings the importance of variation between individuals has also been emphasized. Such ideas, unfortunately, do not seem to have received the attention they deserve and I hope that the present discussion will help us to understand the consequences of variation for the 'chances to survive' of natural populations. With variation I do not refer to polymorphism or variation in bristle numbers, but rather to variation in ecologically important characters, such as growth rate, fecundity, dispersal tendency and 'chances to survive'.

In the past few decades, population geneticists have shown that in natural populations there is a tremendous genetic variation. They have shown that natural selection operates in

Present adress: Smithsonian Tropical Research Institute, P.O.Box 2072, Balboa, Canal Zone.

nature so that changes may occur in the genetic make-up of a population, sometimes in a surprisingly short time. They have also shown that the degree of variation as well as the kind of variation may have considerable effects on the number of individuals in a population. The causes of the changes in numbers will thus partly be found in the direct action of some environmental factors, but may also be the result of indirect actions of the environment through changes in the composition of the populations; i.e. changes in mean and/or variance of ecologically important characters.

One approach to the study of the population dynamics of some organism in nature is to compare the number of individuals in a population in a number of successive generations and to find out which environmental factors have caused the changes observed. However, there is the possibility, or even the probability, that natural selection has occurred so that the quality of the individuals in later generations may be different from that at the beginning of the observations. This would mean that the various generations are not quite comparable in terms of numbers only, and that the picture obtained for the variation in numbers contains only part of the relevant information – or may even be misleading.

Conclusions are often inferred by comparing the number of individuals in different populations. This is even more hazardous, as it has become quite obvious that large differences in quality of the individuals may exist between different populations of the same species.

I don't intend to overemphasize the importance of genetic variation among the various processes that determine the number of individuals in a population. One still has to make life tables and study the role of predation, parasites etc. In some populations, during the period of observation, there may be no effects caused by changes in the genetic constitution; in others the effects of predation or parasites can be ignored. However, ignoring a priori (as is often explicitly done) the possible role of variation 'until the evidence shows that it has to be taken into account' is just as foolish and even more dangerous than a priori forgetting about predation. It is more dangerous because one may come across predators eating individuals of the species under consideration or find carcasses as evidence of predation, while the chances of coming across even important genetic changes are rather remote unless one specifically looks for such changes with the appropriate techniques. Studying changes in genetic constitution only if it has been shown that all other known processes fail to explain the observed phenomena in a population, where changes in genetic compositions happens to be relatively important, means that one has wasted a lot of time by studying the other processes exhaustively. To me, the most efficient approach to understand the dynamics of a population is to start by surveying all the processes that could be relevant, and only in a later stage select those that are likely to be rather important. Any a priori selection may lead on the wrong track and thus to a waste of time and effort.

What one would like to do is at each census determine not only the number of individuals present but also their quality; that is mean and variance of characters such as fecundity, growth rate, dispersal tendency and survival under specific conditions. This is no easy task, but it is not impossible either. In order to be able to do this, one has to start by studying such characters in detail. One has to find out how such characters can be measured and what such measures mean.

I chose to work with the landsnail *Cepaea nemoralis* (L.). Our program is to evaluate the various causes of changes in numbers. This includes a determination of the amount of genetic and phenotypic variation that exists both within and between populations, and of changes in the composition of the population that may be associated with changes in numbers. The available data suggest that there is a large ecological variation. Snails from different populations have been found to differ in dispersal tendency, oviposition frequency and mating frequency. The fact that different morphs have been found to differ in dispersal tendency, clutch size, oviposition frequency, juvenile mortality and survival under thrush predations and at extreme temperatures, demonstrates that there may be a large genetic variation in ecologically important characters within a population (Boettger, 1954; Cain and Sheppard, 1954; Sheppard, 1951; Wolda, 1963, 1965, 1967). In the present paper I will concentrate on some data on variation in the growth rate.

Procedures

Cepaea nemoralis is a pulmonate landsnail of the family *Helicidae*. It is a hermaphroditic with obligatory crossfertilization. The species is well-known for its polymorphism which has been extensively studied, especially by Cain and Sheppard and their students in Britain and by Lamotte in France (Cain and Sheppard, 1954; Cain and Currey, 1963, 1968; Lamotte, 1951, 1959; Wolda, 1969a, b). During the winter the snails hibernate in the soil or among dead vegetation on the ground. By the end of March they 'wake up' and soon afterwards the first mating pairs can be observed. Eggs are produced between the end of May and the beginning of August. The eggs are laid in clutches in holes dug into the soil. After some two years the snails complete the growth of their shell and are then called adults, although generally it takes another year for them to participate in the reproductive activities of the population. Eggs are eaten by the predatory snail *Oxychilus cellarius*, crushed by worms or killed by drought. Small juveniles are eaten by small birds and some carabid beetles. Larger juveniles may be killed in large quantities by blackbirds (*Turdus merula*) and other predators – frogs, toads, small rodents and shrews. Still larger juveniles and adults are killed by thrushes (*Turdus ericetorum*) and rats. Although the snails very often have some parasitic trematodes this does not seem to affect their ability to survive and multiply.

Data are collected in a number of natural populations, but mainly in a series of experimental outdoor-populations and in the laboratory. The experimental populations are in the botanic gardens near our laboratory. There are 8 plots, 12×23 m each, surrounded by fences with an electric barrier (Wolda, 1970) to prevent the exchange of individuals between plots and between the 'snail-garden' as a whole and the surrounding botanic gardens. The populations were started in 1966 with large juveniles collected from a large number of natural populations. Great care was taken to have each natural population equally represented in all 8 plots in order to make the genetic background of all 8 populations as identical as possible. There were, however, some differences as some populations were given initial morph frequencies different from those in others; statistically speaking, populations 2 and 8 are identical in composition as are 6 and 7 and 1, 3, 4 and 5. Populations 3, 6 and 8 started with 3000 and the others with 1000 individuals.

The populations are all sampled twice a year and all the adult individuals are marked by drilling a pattern of holes into the shell (Wolda, 1963).

Growth can be determined by measuring the increase in size of the shell. Except in the very small individuals, the size during the last winter can easily be determined as this is indicated by a varix on the shell (Fig. 1). Growth until time t (G_t) is the diameter of the shell at that time (D_t) minus the diameter during last winter (D_w). If D_w cannot be directly determined because too much of the shell has been overgrown, it can be determined indirectly by measuring the distance d_w, which is closely correlated with D_w (Oosterhoff,

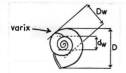

Fig. 1. The measurement of growth. D = diameter of the shell at the moment of sampling. D_w = diameter at the beginning of the season. d_w = 'top'-diameter at beginning of season which can be used to determine D_w if this diameter cannot be directly measured.

pers. comm.). Measuring growth as an increment in diameter works rather well in *Cepaea*. It so happens that the increase in diameter is independent of initial size, so that snails of all sizes can be lumped to obtain an average and variance of growth. Apparently the shell, which formally can be described by a logarithmic spiral, is sufficiently close to a spiral of Archimedes (Thompson, 1961). If it were not so, the data would have had to be transformed to make the growth data independent of initial size. One could have measured growth by taking log. weight or log. volume, but these measurements will be closely correlated with my measure of increment in diameter.

Results

From the size distribution of the juveniles and from changes in this distribution in time (Wolda, 1963; Fig. 18), it was concluded that it usually takes two years for a newly hatched individual to become adult, and from the time at which they became adults it was assumed that they usually do not take part in the reproductive activities of the population during that same season. I, therefore, started off with the hypotheses:
1. It takes always two years to become adult.
2. It always take another year before the snails produce any progeny.

The data from my experimental populations showed that both hypotheses have to be rejected (Wolda, 1970). Sometimes it takes only one year to become adult, sometimes at least three years. Sometimes the snails do reproduce in the same season in which they completed the growth of their shell. There is a fairly large variation in growth-rate both within and between populations.

The significance of this for the dynamics of a *Cepaea* population can best be illustrated by a descriptive model of such a population (Fig. 2). This model becomes much more complicated if the existing variation is taken into account. In my opinion this means that one cannot hope to understand fully what is going on in the population if variation in this character, and in others, is ignored.

A

0	0	p_{1s}	p_{2s}	p_{3s}	·	·		n_s
p_{sL}	0	0	0	0	·	·		n_L
0	p_{L1}	0	0	0	·	·		n_1
0	0	p_{12}	0	0	·	·		n_2
0	0	0	p_{23}	0	·	·		n_3
·	·	·	·	·	·	·		·

B

p_{ss}	p_{Ls}	p_{1s}	p_{2s}	p_{3s}	·	·		n_s
p_{sL}	p_{LL}	p_{1L}	p_{2L}	p_{3L}	·	·		n_L
p_{s1}	p_{L1}	0	0	0	·	·		n_1
0	0	p_{12}	0	0	·	·		n_2
0	0	0	p_{23}	0	·	·		n_3
·	·	·	·	·	·	·		·

Fig. 2. A descriptive model of a *Cepaea* population. In the population vector n = number of individuals while the suffixes s, L, 1, 2, 3 refer respectively to small juveniles, large juveniles and 1st, 2nd and 3rd year adults. In the net reproduction matrix, p_{ij} is the contribution per individual of age class i to age class j next year. 'A' gives the model if variation in growth-rate is ignored, 'B' when it is taken into account.

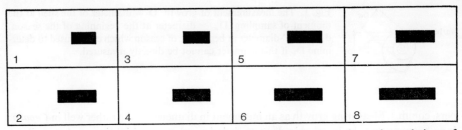

Fig. 3. Mean growth from the beginning of 1970 till 20 May in 8 experimental populations of *Cepaea nemoralis*. Populations 6 and 8 had grown much more than 1 and 3, while the other populations were intermediate.

The next question is: What circumstances make some snails to become adult within one year and what makes them reproduce in the same season they became adult?

We do know that part of the variation in growth rate is genetic (Wolda, 1970), but the effects of the environment are considerable. The relevant environmental factors have to be identified and then quantified. The fact that not all experimental populations grew equally fast might provide a clue as to what environmental factors are important. The mean growth per population up to 20 May 1970 is given in Fig. 3. It will be seen that the snails in populations 6 and 8 had grown most, while the ones in population 1 and 3 were relatively slow growing. These differences already existed in 1967 (Wolda, 1970); that is, right at the beginning of the experimental populations. Because of the way they were set up it can safely be concluded that the differences then were not genetic so, probably, the differences between the populations in 1970 were not genetic either. A study of the stomach contents and faeces in a relatively fast (6) and a slow growing population (3) did not suggest that the differences in growth rate were caused by differences in food. *Cepaea* seems to take a more or less random sample of the vegetation present. The vegetation in population 3 is different from that in population 6 and thus there are differences in diet. We do not know enough about the nutritional requirements of *Cepaea* to be able to see the significance of such differences in diet, but my guess at present is that they are not important. There did not seem to be any differences in microweather either. Therefore, I decided to study the growth curves in the populations in order to see whether any clues might be provided there.

At first, however, I had to find out how such growth curves can be obtained. Fig. 4 gives an example of the difficulties involved. Early in the season the increase in diameter of the shell is independent of the winter diameter, and the same seems to be true later in the season although the wide scattering of points make it less easy to establish this fact. However, it will be assumed that it is independent of size at the beginning of the season. Some snails become adult and that means they have stopped growing. The ones that were rather large during last winter become adults first and smaller ones become adults later, on the average. Such adults should be left out when calculating the growth rate. But then the juveniles that failed to become adults although they were rather large initially also have to be ignored; these are the relatively slow growing individuals and thus are a biased sample of the population. Therefore, it was decided to calculate the mean growth rate only for those snails that were too small initially to have become adults at the time of census. Fig. 4, by the way, illustrates again that some first-year juveniles – i.e. belonging to the left

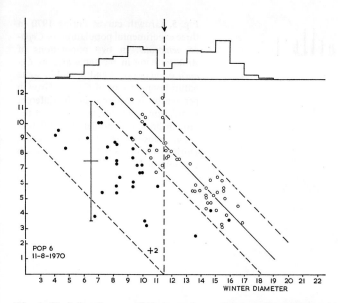

Fig. 4. Variation in growth in experimental population 6 from the beginning of 1970 till 11 August. Full circles refer to juveniles and open circles to new adults. At the beginning of the season the transition between small juveniles (born in 1969) and large juveniles (born in 1968) was at 11.5 mm. Mean growth plus and minus twice the standard error is given together with mean adult diameter plus and minus twice the standard error. The ordinate gives the increase in diameter in mm.

peak of the winter size-distribution – may become adult within one year.

I then determined mean and variance of growth for a series of samples taken in three selected populations in my snail-garden; a relatively fast (6) and intermediate (4) and a slow growing population (3). I also used some data from natural populations, also collected during 1970, and from the populations of *Arianta arbustorum* in populations 3 and 4. *Arianta* is also a pulmonate land snail, of about the same size and shape as *Cepaea*. It is very abundant in six out of the eight experimental populations. The results were rather surprising (Fig. 5). The differences in growth over the whole season are definitely there, but the growth lines seem to be nicely parallel. In other words, growth rate during the season is the same in all populations studied; also *Arianta* does not differ in growth rate from *Cepaea*. It is now clear why no clues were found about the causes of differences in growth rate by studying food or weather, because such differences during the season do not exist! The differences in growth over the whole season are already present in early May and must have been caused very early in the season. Either some populations start earlier than others or there are differences in growth rate in April or early May which disappear later. The data suggest that the latter hypothesis is true. It is difficult to believe that the natural population of Brekenpolder (top line in Fig. 5) was also parallel with the experimental populations early in the season, as this would imply that they started very early in April. This is extremely unlikely as spring started very late in 1970. However, we have the impression that *Arianta* starts somewhat earlier than *Cepaea*. Anyway, we now know that we have to look for clues in April. What caused the difference between the populations I still don't know. It could be food.

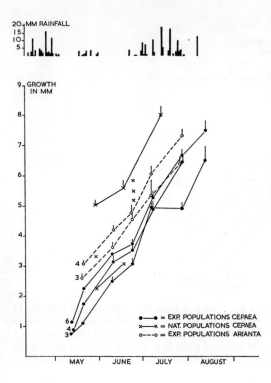

Fig. 5. Growth curves during 1970 in three experimental populations of *Cepaea nemoralis*, in two populations of *Arianta* living in the same area as *Cepaea* populations 3 and 4, and in some natural populations of *Cepaea*. Growth per season is different in the different populations, but during the season the growth lines are parallel. The differences are caused very early in the season. During the dry spell in June growth was retarded.

Fig. 5 shows something else as well. During June, growth was definitely less than during the rest of the season. This was a very dry month as can be seen from the distribution of rainfall. So apparently growth is inhibited during drought. In the period immediately after drought, however, growth was faster than ever, suggesting that the snails make up for periods of adverse conditions. Some experiments that are being carried out now suggest that this effect is real (Oosterhoff, pers. comm.).

Other environmental influences on growth rate are effects of temperature, availability of chalk and density (Oosterhoff, pers. comm.). The density effects found by Miss Oosterhoff are interesting as these occur at the very low levels such as are commonly found in nature. It seems to be produced by the trails of mucus the snails make.

The effects of growth rate and its variation on the number of adults produced per season or at some date early enough to enable the new adults to produce some eggs during that season, can best be summarized in a model. Size during winter is given by the stochastic variable $\underline{d}_w$, at any time t by $\underline{d}_t$. Growth until time t is given by G_t with mean $\overline{G}_t$ and variance S_t^2. Then:

$$\underline{d}_t = \underline{d}_w + \overline{G}_t + \underline{Z}_G \qquad (1)$$

Where $\underline{Z}_G$ is a stochastic variable, normally distributed, with mean O and variance S_G^2.

The diameter of the adults is normally distributed with a mean $\overline{D}$ and variance S_D^2. The probability that any juvenile will form a lip and become adult is given by this distribution. Then, theoretically, juveniles of any size have a positive chance of becoming adult at that size, but in practice one could say that any snail where the d_t calculated according to Eq. 1 is smaller than $\overline{D} - 2S_D$ is still a juvenile (the theoretical chance of being adult at $d_t = \overline{D} - 2S_D$ which is 0.02). All snails with the calculated d_t larger than $D + 2S_D$ are assumed to be adult with an actual adult diameter somewhere between $\overline{D} - 2S_D$ and $\overline{D} + 2S_D$. Any snail with a calculated d_t between these limits has a probability of being adult given by the normal distribution of D, and the actual size is given by the same distribution (Fig. 6).

The parameters that matter here are $\overline{G}$, $\overline{D}$, S_G^2 and S_D^2. The influences on these parameters have to be identified and quantified in order to make a predictive model for the effects of growth rate. The admittedly few data we have now show that the variances are dependent on the means, but no conspicuous differences in variance between populations, apart from differences caused by differences in means, have yet been found. We do know that part of the variance is caused by genetic factors (Cook, 1967; Wolda, 1970) and differences in individual environment probably play a large role as well.

The mean growth ($\overline{G}_t$) is affected by temperature (T), availability of chalk (Ca), drought (H), density (N) and genetic factors (C_G). The mean diameter of adults ($\overline{D}$) is determined by mean growth rate ($\overline{G}_t$) and genetic factors (C_D). Other influences probably exist as well. The equations $\overline{G}_t = F(T, Ca, H, N, C_G,...)$ and $\overline{D} = F'(\overline{G}_t, C_D,...)$ must now be made more specific.

If the idea that short adverse conditions are compensated for later when conditions are more favorable is true, it could be that growth is largely independent of drought and temperature. This would simplify matters a great deal. However, there may be complications.

Some of our data suggest that there may be an accumulation of slow growing juveniles at the larger sizes. In other words, that the lower limit to G in Fig. 6 is not quite horizontal but tapers off towards the right. This would mean that $\overline{G}_t$ is not independent of initial size.

In our experiments in the laboratory, slow growing individuals suffered a larger mortality. If this is true in nature as well, the model has to be corrected for this. Some data also suggest that faster growing snails are more active and have a larger dispersal tendency. This would mean that the loss of individuals through emigration is dependent on growth rate, and this also calls for a modification of the model. In closed populations such as the

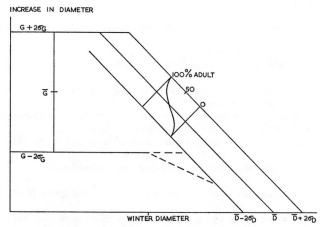

Fig. 6. A model of growth-rate in *Cepaea*. See text.

ones in my snail garden this is, of course, of no consequence. In the laboratory slow growing individuals seem to be less fecund when adult (Oosterhoff, pers. comm.).

The maintenance of genetic variation in the growth rate is still a mystery as slow growing individuals seem to have only disadvantages. It could be that some mechanism such as heterozygote advantage is present, but as long as there are no relevant data there is little point in making any such assumption as this might sound a bit like a quasi-explanation.

Discussion

It has been shown in the present paper and in Wolda (1970) that in *Cepaea* there is a considerable amount of variation in an ecologically important character, i.e. growth rate, and that part of this variation is genetic. Other characters in *Cepaea* have yet to be studied in detail, but the available evidence suggests that there the variation is also far from negligible. This is not surprising as in many other animals or plants where such variation has been looked for it has been shown to exist. I suggest that such variation is the rule rather than the exception.

It has also been shown (Wolda, 1970) that the mean growth per season may have large consequences for the number of individuals in a population. Slight differences in mean growth rate between populations caused striking differences in the rate at which the numbers in these populations built up. This is not surprising either as, in fact, this is what one would expect. For other characters and for other species one would expect similar, rather large effects.

Variance in the growth rate is large. Part of this variance is genetic and another part is environmental. The larger the additive genetic component of this variance, the larger the possibility for natural selection to act and change the genetic constitution of the population. A large environmental component of the variance means that the individuals concerned are fairly susceptible to environmental influences. This means that either all sorts of misfits are produced under adverse conditions or that the individuals are flexible enough to adjust to such adverse conditions. The first effect calls for selection towards a more stable phenotype. The fact that in *Cepaea* environmental influences on growth rate are so large, suggests that such selection has not occurred and that possibly the observed flexibility is somehow advantageous.

References

Birch, L. C., 1960. The genetic factor in population ecology. *Am. Nat.* 94: 5–24.
Boettger, C. R., 1954. Zur Frage der Verteilung bestimmter Varianten bei den Schnirkelschnecken-gattung *Cepaea* Held. *Biol. Zbl.* 73: 318–333.
Cain, A. J. & P. M. Sheppard, 1954. Natural selection in *Cepaea*. *Genetics* 39: 89–116.
Cain, A. J. & J. D. Currey, 1963. Area effects in *Cepaea*. *Phil. Trans. R. Soc. Ser. B.* 246: 1–81.
Cain, A. J. & J. D. Currey, 1968. Studies on *Cepaea*. III. Ecogenetics of a population of *Cepaea nemoralis* (L.) subject to strong area effects. *Phil. Trans. R. Soc. Ser. B.* 253: 447–482.
Krebs, Ch. J., 1970. *Microtus* populationbiology, Behavioural changes associated with the population cycle in *M. ochrogaster* and *M. pensylvanicus*. *Ecology* 51: 34–52.
Lamotte, M., 1951. Recherches sur la structure génétique des populations naturelles de *Cepaea nemoralis*. *Bull. biol. Fr.* 35: 1–239.
Lamotte, M., 1959. Polymorphism of natural populations of *Cepaea nemoralis*. *Cold Spring Harb. Symp. quant. Biol.* 24: 65–86.
Pimentel, D., 1961. Animal population regulation by the genetic feedback mechanism. *Am. Nat.* 95: 65–80.

Pimentel, D., 1964. Population ecology and the genetic feedback mechanism. *Proc. XI Congr. Genetics* 2: 483–487.

Schwerdtfeger, F., 1969. Disposition und Determination im Massenwechsel der Insekten. In: Voordrachten ter gelegenheid van het afscheid van Dr. A. D. Voûte als directeur van het ITBON, p. 10–17.

Sheppard, P. M., 1951. Fluctuations in the selective value of certain phenotypes in the polymorphic landsnail *Cepaea nemoralis. Heredity* 5: 125–134.

Thompson, D. A. W., 1961. On growth and form. Cambridge University Press.

Wellington, W. G., 1957. Individual differences as a factor in population dynamics. *Can. J. Zool.* 35: 293–323.

Wellington, W. G., 1960. Qualitative changes in natural populations during changes in abundance. *Can. J. Zool.* 38: 289–314.

Wolda, H., 1963. Natural populations of the polymorphic landsnail *Cepaea nemoralis* (L.) *Archs néerl. Zool.* 15: 381–471.

Wolda, H., 1965. Some preliminary observations on the distribution of the various morphs within natural populations of the polymorphic landsnail *Cepaea nemoralis* (L.) *Archs néerl. Zool.* 16: 280–292.

Wolda, H., 1967. The effect of temperature on reproduction in some morphs of the landsnail *Cepaea nemoralis* (L.). *Evolution* 21: 117–129.

Wolda, H., 1969a. Fine distribution of morph frequencies in the snail *Cepaea nemoralis* near Groningen. *J. Anim. Ecol.* 38: 305–327.

Wolda, H., 1969b. Stability of a steep cline in morph frequencies of the snail *Cepaea nemoralis* (L.). *J. Anim. Ecol.* 38: 623–635.

Wolda, H., 1970. Variation in growth rate in the landsnail *Cepaea nemoralis. Res. Pop. Ecol.* 12: 185–204.

Discussion

Participants: Wolda (Author), Perrins, Turnock and Zwölfer

Are growth rates related to morph type? How good are the genes involved in polymorphism as markers for ecologically more important characters (Turnock)? No differences in growth rate were found between different morphs. The genes involved in the shell polymorphism are usually in one single linkage group with only two major genes, the one for 'midbanded' (pattern 00300) and 'threebanded' (pattern 00345) being exceptions. As *Cepaea* has a haploid number of 22 chromosomes it is not surprising that they do not act as markers for many ecologically important characters. For a gene to act as a suitable marker it must be rather closely linked with the genes one is interested in, and there must be a fairly strong linkage disequilibrium. Therefore, I do not expect that the approach to the study of genetic variation in ecologically important characters by using some arbitrarily chosen 'marker genes' will be very profitable. One can only expect very limited results unless the 'marker genes' in question have a pleitrophic effect on the characters under consideration (compare with the discussion of Krebs's paper). Generally, one may expect much more clearcut results if one studies the ecologically important characters directly. To give an example. Suppose that in *Cepaea* the gene for banding pattern 00000 (= unbanded) had a strong effect on, say, reproduction and, therefore, was important from an ecological point of view. This gene is closely linked with the gene for colour, and their is a strong linkage disequilibrium in most populations. If one wants to study this by using colour as a marker gene, one would get nowhere because the percentage of 'yellow' in a population gives little or no indication of the frequency of the character 'unbanded'. (Author)

The environmental factors involved in the trend for growth rates among the different enclosures are not known (AUTHOR to PERRINS).

Later eggs are not smaller than the first eggs in *Cepaea* and do not produce slower growing snails, as was found by Wellington in the western Tent Caterpillar. Larger eggs do produce larger hatchlings and faster growing snails: see Wolda (1970) (AUTHOR to ZWÖLFER).

Proc. Adv. Study Inst. Dynamics Numbers Popul. (Oosterbeek, 1970) 109–128

The role of environmental heterogeneity and genetical heterogeneity in determining distribution and abundance

L. C. Birch

School of Biological Sciences, University of Sydney, Sydney, Australia

Abstract

Environmental and genetical heterogeneity increase the chance of a species to survive and reproduce. In this paper examples are given of the role of both components in determining distribution and abundance; this includes reduction of the chance of extinction.

Rabbit and mouse populations in semi-arid Australia survive by virtue of the existence of relatively small areas that act as refuges in adverse seasons. In favourable seasons other areas are much more favourable, but the species cannot continuously exist here; because of this the refuges serve as centres from which recolonization can occur.

The very small overwintering populations of the fruit fly *Dacus tryoni* act as a similar sort of foci from which the orchards are repopulated each spring.

In a number of moths and butterflies, changes in the number of individuals in different localities are relatively independent. For *Cactoblastis cactorum* some cactus plants are more favourable than others and, therefore, some plants survive while others are destroyed; because of this, and because in another season the previously unfavourable plants may become favourable, both the insect and the plant survive.

Adaptive differences have evolved between local populations of the fruit flies *Dacus tryoni* and *D. neohumeralis*. There is a continuous production of much variability, which is non-directionally selected in permanently occupied places and directionally selected in new environments.

These findings are consistent with the models of Andrewartha and Birch (1954), Sewall Wright (1931, 1937) and Dobzhansky (1970).

The model

The model of animal populations discussed in this paper is essentially stochastic. Its principal components are environmental heterogeneity and genetical heterogeneity in space and time. I shall illustrate its applicability to a number of natural populations without implying that it has a general applicability, though how generally it may apply remains to be seen.

The population is not homogeneous in its genetical composition nor is the environment it occupies homogeneous in space or in time. Nothing remains the same. The population of the species consists of a number of more or less isolated local populations which may be close together or far apart. Each local population has its own distinctive environment. The changes in numbers in different local populations may be quite different from one another; some local populations may be on the way to extinction, others may be increasing and others may be stable. The differences between numbers in local populations reflect (a) differences in the chance of being colonized, and (b) differences in local environment.

In unfavourable environments, most local populations may become extinct or nearly so, leaving relatively few local populations surviving to act as foci for recolonization when favourable conditions return later on. The surviving foci occupy the most favourable sites during unfavourable conditions; but these sites may not be amongst the most favourable sites when favourable conditions return. There are other sites which may be far more favourable for survival and reproduction. The concrete shelter that protects us in a hurricane may be the best place to be then, but not in the interim between hurricanes. The species survives, despite the highly unfavourable conditions it often experiences, because the heterogeniety of the environment provides local situations where survival and reproduction are possible when they are not possible in other places. The extinction of the species would consist of the extinction of its last surviving local population. The chance of this happening may depend upon the number and distribution of those sites which provide some degree of favourability in unfavourable times. In this model, the causes of changes in distribution and abundance of the species can only be understood through studying the causes of changes in many local populations.

There is nothing new about this model. It was included as a part of the general theory on population numbers of Andrewartha and Birch (1954), but for some ecologists it seemed then to lack credibility. A comparable view on 'spreading of risk' is given by den Boer (1968). The 'balance of nature' theorists have not been sympathetic to stochastic models that allow a species a chance of becoming extinct, remote though that may be in short periods of time; furthermore, the chaos aspect of this model seemed to threaten the more idealistic picture of nature in balance – which of course it does. The 'balance of nature' may be a myth, useful for political purposes, but hardly for a scientific understanding of what is going on. There are two approaches in the development of ideas on the heterogeneity model of animal numbers. One is computer simulation which, of all the theoretical approaches, sacrifices least data for the sake of generalization. Work on these lines is being done by Ehrlich (unpublished), Reddingius (1968) and Reddingius and den Boer (1970). Another approach is the analysis of natural populations with the perspective of this model in mind. I shall follow this latter path and illustrate the model with four case histories which, I believe, indicate the reality of this type of model.

Superimposed on the model of heterogeneity of environment and changing numbers in local populations is genetic heterogeneity. Genetical heterogeneity and its concommitant, genetical plasticity, decrease the chance of extinction of the last local populations and hence the chance of extinction of the species. It enhances the chance of all local populations to survive and multiply. Furthermore, genetical plasticity provides the possibility of new colonies of the species being established in previously unoccupied environments by means of adaptive evolution. The biologist does not hesitate to claim that a potentiality for genetical change has been essential for the survival and evolution of species in the distant past; therefore he should not be reluctant to accept it as an important factor in ecological studies today. It is realistic to superimpose this genetical model upon the ecological model and to look for both ecological and genetical components operating together in natural populations. I shall leave out the interesting possibility of genetic feedback between a population and some of its living components of environment, since this is dealt with by Pimentel (in these Proceedings). There is nothing new in this genetical model. It is essentially the one proposed by Sewall Wright (1931, 1937) for the most rapid evolution of a population; namely, a series of more or less isolated populations of different size and number subject to different selective pressure, some subject to genetic 'drift', with periods of isolation followed by a certain amount of gene exchange. It would, of course, be nice to be able to illustrate the operation of all aspects of this genetical model in the ecological case histories to be discussed. This is not possible. However, some pointers are provided by these studies, particularly the final one on fruit flies of the genus *Dacus*. The particular 'genetic strategy' that turns out to be the 'best' for a population at a particular time may be one of a great number of possibilities. The relationship of 'genetic strategy' to the ecological problem of survival of local populations has been integrated into a single subject of study by Lewontin (1965a, 1965b), and the extent to which genetic polymorphism in *Drosophila* may be attributed to environmental heterogeneity had been reviewed by Beardmore (1970).

Survival of the moth Cactoblastis cactorum and its host cacti as a result of heterogeneity in quality of the host cacti and selective behaviour of the moth

In the first decades of this century, the prickly pears *Opuntia inermis* and *Opuntia stricta* existed in dense stands over a huge area in eastern Australia in the states of Queensland and New South Wales. Since the 1930s prickly pears have become sparse due to the predations of caterpillars of the moth *Cactoblastis cactorum*. Today, both cactus and moth coexist over a huge area of Australia which is similar in extent to the original distribution of the cactus at the height of its abundance. But, within this area both cactus and moth now exist at densities which, relative to their former state of abundance, are quite low. From the point of view of biological control of the cactus, it is indeed fortunate that *Cactoblastis* does not eat *Opuntia* and itself out of existence over the areas formerly occupied by dense forests of 'pear'.

But why does this not happen? Andrewartha and Birch (1954) suggested, on the basis of statements made by Nicholson (1947), that a game of 'hide and seek' between cactus and *Cactoblastis* kept both populations in being. Although *Cactoblastis* had large powers of increase and large powers of dispersal, it was prevented from finding and destroying all the cactus at once by the patchy dispersion of the cactus and the ready dispersal of its fruits. Monro (1967) has re-examined the dispersion and abundance of both cactus and *Cactoblastis*. He has produced evidence to indicate that the theory of 'hide and seek' may be applicable to some marginal areas where both cactus and *Cactoblastis* are quite rare, and where the cactus plants are separated from each other by large distances. However, this is evidently not the case in the vast areas which are favourable to both cactus and *Cactoblastis*. There, Monro believes that the answer is to be found in the behaviour of female moths, which do not disperse their eggs at random but concentrate on some plants and leave others free, at least for a time. In such favourable areas, cactus plants are spaced some 5 to 20 metres apart; most of them are no more than a couple of feet high, though occasionally a larger plant or group of plants can be found. In these areas the quantity of cactus remains remarkably constant from year to year, as measured by the number of cactus segments per hectare (Monro, unpublished work). In the southern half of its range, there are two complete generations of *Cactoblastis* each year during which time some plants are completely destroyed, others are partly destroyed and still others remain uninfested with *Cactoblastis*. On balance, about the same amount of cactus grows each year as is destroyed over any area.

The clue to this interesting situation appears to be in the dispersion of the eggs of *Cactoblastis*. Female moths do not lay their eggs either at random or evenly with respect to whole plants. They cluster their eggs on some plants more than on others. Table 1 shows the observed distribution of eggs compared with that expected if eggs were laid at random in a typically favourable area of 3.3 ha in Queensland. More plants were free of eggs than would be expected from a random distribution; other plants had on them far more eggs than would be expected from a random distribution. Why some plants should be favoured more than others is not known, though Monro (unpublished work) has evidence that the clustering is due not to the attractiveness of eggs already laid on plants but to some intrinsic difference between plants in their attractiveness to moths. However, these differences are of a subtle nature, for a plant that is unattractive one season may be heavily loaded in another season. This could be interpreted as a heterogeneity in quality of plants for egg laying. The plants are sufficiently close to one another that the wide ranging moths are not likely to have difficulty in finding every plant over an area as such in the example of Table 1, and this situation is quite typical of favourable areas.

Table 1. Distribution of egg sticks of *Cactoblastis* per plant of *Opuntia* at a central site in the distribution of 3.3 hectares. The mean egg sticks per plant was 2.42. Each egg stick contains about 30 to 100 eggs. (After Monro, 1967).

Number of egg sticks per plant	Observed number of plants	Expected number of plants (Poisson)
0	25	9.01
1	27	21.8
2	16	26.41
3	7	23.60
4	6	12.90
5	6	
6	1	
7	3	
8	4	19
9	3	6.28
10	1	
11	0	
12	1	

The effect of clustered dispersion of eggs is that some plants escape *Cactoblastis* and others are overloaded in the sense that they have more *Cactoblastis* on them than is necessary to destroy them. About 0.25 egg sticks per segment of cactus is a minimum overload density. On overloaded plants there is a wastage of eggs; many of them will not give rise to moths because there is not enough food for all the caterpillars that hatch out. Monro (1967) called this a 'distributional wastage of eggs'. The extent of this wastage is illustrated in Fig. 1, which shows the proportion of eggs which are laid on overloaded plants. The distributional wastage is greatest for the highest egg densities. At high egg densities (four of the eight localities of Fig. 1) this distributional wastage is greater than would have been the case had eggs been distributed either randomly or evenly with respect to plants. If *Cactoblastis* had spread its eggs evenly on segments of the cactus (Fig. 1), no eggs would have been on overloaded plants at the low densities, but at the two highest densities all eggs would have been on overloaded plants. In this model such an even dispersion would increase survival of *Cactoblastis* at low densities, but this would lead to a rapid increase in

112

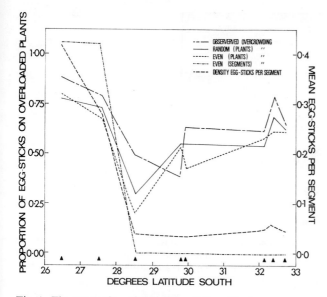

Fig. 1. The proportion of egg-sticks of *Cactoblastis cactorum* on 'overloaded' cactus plants (ob served overcrowding) at different densities of egg-sticks per plant compared with proportion of egg-sticks on overloaded plants expected if eggs were distributed: randomly per plant, evenly per plant and evenly per segment. (After Monro, 1967.) The sites, at 8 different latitudes are indicated by the solid triangles.

density. There would be a sudden and complete destruction of the resource when the density of eggs reached the critical density (100 % of eggs on overloaded plants; (Fig. 1) 'even (segments) overcrowding'). That situation is 'avoided' by the clustering of eggs on some plants. The effect of this is to increase the chance of both cactus and *Cactoblastis* surviving. It reduces the rate at which *Cactoblastis* could destroy its limiting resource, the retardation being greatest the higher the density of *Cactoblastis* eggs on the plants. Monro (1967) argues cogently that the effect of this will be for the resource and the predator to be maintained at more or less constant levels over quite small areas, which, indeed, is what he observes.

Survival of the European rabbit Oryctolagus cuniculus in semi-arid areas of Australia in relation to heterogeneity of habitats in space and time

Studies by Myers and his colleagues (in these Proceedings) over many years have shown that the continued existence of rabbits in semi-arid parts of its distribution in Australia is dependent upon the existence, in these regions, of niches which are sufficiently favourable in drought years for survival of rabbits. In favourable years populations are widespread. In years of severe drought most local populations become extinct, except the few that happen to be in the few remaining favourable niches. When favourable weather returns to the region, these niches act as foci from which the region is recolonized.

Fig. 2 shows the five major physiographic and vegetational zones in an area of 250 mile² of Tero Creek in semi-arid north-west New South Wales. The distribution of rabbit warrens in this whole area was mapped by Myers and Parker (1965) in the favourable years

113

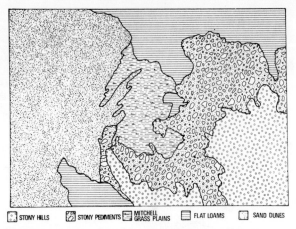

STONY HILLS · STONY PEDIMENTS · MITCHELL GRASS PLAINS · FLAT LOAMS · SAND DUNES

Fig. 2. The distribution of five main physiographic-vegetational regions in an area of 250 miles² at Tero Creek in New South Wales. This is within the semi-arid part of the distribution of the rabbit in Australia. The dispersion of rabbit warrens in the stony hills and pediments is shown in Fig. 3 (From aerial photo in Myers and Parker, 1965.)

1963–1964. They mapped a total of 4,910 warrens having a total of 32,225 burrow entrances. That the different zones were very different in favourability for rabbits is shown by the density of warrens in each zone (Table 2). Sand dunes were the most favourable habitats in good seasons. They provided plenty of food in the form of annual grasses and the soils were suitable for making burrows. In favourable years, the production of rabbits is greatest in this zone. The Mitchell grass plains, in contrast, are not occupied by rabbits at all. The stony habitats are not as favourable in good seasons as the sand dunes; water runs off readily and plant growth stops earlier in the season. In good seasons, they produce fewer rabbits than the sand dunes (Myers and Parker, 1965; Wood, unpublished data.). Even in favourable years the dispersion of rabbits is very patchy as can be seen, for example, in Fig. 3 which shows dispersion of warrens in part of the stony hills and pediments of Tero Creek in 1963–1964. The stony hills are on the right of the figure; warrens occur there in discrete clumps. In the less favourable stony pediments on the left, warrens are strung out along drainage channels and occur in small clumps where shales outcrop. Still, over much of the area there are no warrens at all.

In drought years the whole picture changes dramatically. In the sand dunes, which were

Table 2. The number of rabbit warrens per square mile in five main physiographic and vegetation zones of Tero Creek (1963–1964). (After Myers and Parker, 1965)

Zone	Area (mile²)	Warrens/mile²
Sand dunes	90	38
Stony hills	43	19
Flat loams	42	8
Stony pediments	58	6
Mitchell grass plains	25	0

114

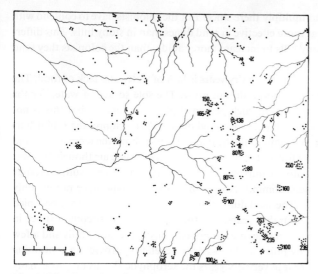

Fig. 3. The dispersion of rabbit warrens in the stony hills and pediments of Tero Creek (see Fig. 2). Each dot represents a rabbit warren. The number beside a clump of warrens is the total number of entrances in that particular clump of warrens. These numbers are given only when the number of entrances exceeds 80. The stony hills are on the right and there warrens tend to be clumped where outcrops of soft shale occur. The stony pediments are on the left and there warrens tend to be strung out along drainage canals. (After aerial photo in Myers and Parker, 1965.)

previously the most favourable habitats, rabbits become completely extinct, while the stony hills are amongst the few places where any local populations survive (Table 3). The data in Table 3 were supported by extensive transect counts of rabbits made at the same time. In 1966, a very dry year, only two warrens were left in 55 mile² of sand dunes, and there were no active entrances and no surviving rabbits. By contrast, on the stony hills there were 1,251 warrens with 0.05 active entrances per warren. Apart from a few isolated foci adjacent to former swamps and along creek beds, the stony hills were the only habitats where rabbits survived. Table 3 also shows that, despite their extinction in sand dunes in 1966, recolonization began in 1967 from the few foci that remained elsewhere and local

Table 3. The number of warrens and the mean number of active entrances to burrows per warren in two zones: sand dunes and stony hills at Tero Creek from 1963–69. (Myers, pers. comm.)

Year	Sand dunes (55 mile²)		Stony hills (42 mile²)	
	total warrens	mean active entrances	total warrens	mean active entrances
1963	1649	4.98	717+	6.37
1965	648	0.12	1025+	0.20
1966	2	0.00	1251	0.05
1967	13	0.23	1436	1.16
1968	23	2.22	971	3.45
1969	322	3.36	1420	3.97

populations have continued to multiply there since. But the colonists have to contend with a predator, the fox, which is far more effective in sand dunes than in stony hills. This difference enables rabbits in the stony hills to increase more rapidly than the colonists they send to the dunes (Myers, pers. comm.).

The critical features of the sand dunes in dry years is lack of water and lack of food. The annual grasses, which are the main food, do not grow. The sole source of water for the rabbit is from leaves, bark and roots of such perennial plants as survive, but this is not enough to offset body water loss in the hot dry sand dunes. Furthermore, the rabbit burrows get hot and rabbits soon succumb to the heat and dryness; both the temperature and relative humidity inside burrows follow the fluctuations of the outside air though at lower levels. In addition, sand blows into the burrows and blocks them up; as a result, no refuge is left for the rabbits (Myers, pers. comm.). No new burrows are made since rabbits only make burrows prior to breeding. The sand dunes thus seem to be areas which are occupied by local populations during favourable years, but these populations become extinct in drought years. The permanent foci reside in local populations in the stony hills and a few other isolated places. In the stony hills the shrub-steppe vegetation provides a continuing source of food, despite the fact that in very dry years the xerophytic shrubs may lose many of their leaves. Food is the sole source of water for the rabbit. Warrens built in the stony shales have a lower daily temperature fluctuation and a higher relative humidity than the outside summer air, and rabbits inhabiting such warrens lose less body water than those in sand dunes. The rabbits still have a tough time in these places but some of them always manage to survive.

The favourability of a habitat for a local population is primarily determined by the availability of food and water and the existence of suitable soil for burrows. Food shortage is caused primarily not by rabbits but by lack of rain. Myers has not observed over-utilization of food in the semi-arid areas, though others have considered that this does sometimes happen. If sheep are present on sand dunes they destroy such perennial plants as may otherwise survive, but even in the absence of sheep the sand dunes do not provide enough moisture for the rabbit to survive in drought years. The abundance of the two necessary components, food and moisture is largely independent of the density of rabbits. The ceiling reached by a local population is a function of the duration of favourable weather. Favourable weather in sand dunes results in high reproductive rates and high survival though in early stages of colonization survival is low due to predation by foxes. In stony hills the reproductive rate is lower. However, in drought years survival is cut to zero in sand dunes but not in stony hills (Myers and Parker, 1965; Myers, pers. comm.). It is clear from this account that rabbits could not exist as a permanent population in an area that consists of sand dunes alone, despite the fact that in favourable years this is quite the most favourable habitat for survival and multiplication of rabbits. The distribution and abundance of rabbits in sand dunes, or in any other area, could not possibly be understood except in relation to the heterogeneity of the total area in both space and time. The clue to understanding distribution and abundance in this example has been the study of local populations in a diversity of habitats.

A somewhat analagous situation applies to the mouse *Mus musculus* in wheat fields in Australia. During the 1960s there have been seven plagues of mice in the Australian wheat belt (Newsome, 1969a). Mice multiply in the wheat fields in a succession of favourable years, reaching plague numbers if unfavourable weather does not interrupt the steady increase. For example, in 1961–1962 mice were abundant in an area of about 4000 mile^2 in the wheat belt of South Australia. It would seem, therefore, that wheat fields are highly favourable for the increase of mice. However, Newsome (1969a) found that mice in wheat fields live a largely opportunistic existence. In most winters, the wheat fields were completely inhospitable for mice, especially when the soil becomes waterlogged and mice can no longer live in cracks and burrows in the soil. In summertime, the soil is too hard for burrowing and the mice rarely breed. If mice only had wheat fields to live in, they would not be able to maintain their populations. What usually happens is that wheat fields become colonized each year from more permanent local colonies in habitats, such as reed beds, that provide more suitable permanent homes for the mice (Newsome, 1969b). The numbers of mice in wheat fields were controlled by the supply of colonists, the suitability of soil for burrowing and the food supply, in that order; but it is not often that the soil is suitable for the establishment of colonies. The wheat fields for the mice are similar to the sand dunes for the rabbits. The mice survive and multiply best there in favourable weather, but in unfavourable weather they are unable to multiply and mortality is very high. The reed beds correspond with the stony hills for the rabbits, they were less favourable than wheat fields in good years and are patchily distributed. In unfavourable years, however, they were the only sort of place where mice could survive and multiply. Little is known about genetical heterogeneity in either rabbits or mice in these field populations, though this might well be a fertile field for study (Birch, 1965). Such an investigation has, however, been made on *Microtus* populations by Tamarin and Krebs (1969). They demonstrated a correlation between density and frequency of an allele responsible for a specific serum protein. In *M. pennsylvanicus*, for example, decreasing population density favoured the gene, but in increasing population density it was selected against.

Independence of changes in numbers and genetic structure of isolated but neighbouring local populations of butterflies and moths

Despite their apparent mobility, many species of butterflies and moths exist in a series of isolated or nearly isolated local populations which change in numbers independently. Examples of this are documented in the studies of Dowdeswell et al. (1940, 1949), Ford (1964), Ehrlich (1965), Sheppard (1951), Turner (1963, 1968), Keller et al. (1966), and Dempster (in these Proceedings). Similar findings on the snail *Cepaea nemoralis* are reviewed by Wolda (1969 and in these Proceedings).

For several years, Ehrlich (1965) studied populations of the checkerspot butterfly *Euphydras editha* on Jasper Ridge in the San Fransicco Bay region. His populations were on an island of grassland on the top of the ridge. The grassland was a mile long and was surrounded by woodland. The closest neighbouring colony of checkerspot butterfly was $3\frac{1}{2}$ miles away. These butterflies only colonize serpentine outcroppings on the area where their food plant *Plantago erecta* is especially abundant. These outcroppings have a patchy distribution which results in a patchy dispersion of the butterfly, this is further accentuated by the non-colonization of some of the serpentine outcrops which appear to be suitable habitats.

Within the mile long grassland on Jasper Ridge, Ehrlich (1965) identified three quite discrete and isolated local populations. In 1960–64, he found no exchange of butterflies between these local populations, although the distance between them was only a matter of hundreds of yards. Furthermore, he found that movement within the local populations was surprisingly restricted. Over these years, the numbers of the butterflies in the three populations changed considerably but the three populations changed independently of each other; one steadily increased in size from about 150 to 3200 adult butterflies, another fluctuated between about 70 and 400, while the third dropped from 50 to extinction. Ehrlich (pers. comm.) has found that this population has since become re-established. The three local populations were separated by areas containing no butterflies, despite the fact that these appeared to be habitats with an abundance of the required food plants.

One could easily imagine that someone might have counted the butterflies on Jasper Ridge without identifying the three local populations; but such a study would have completely missed what was actually going on, namely, that one population increased steadily in size, another fluctuated and the third decreased to extinction. In commenting on this Ehrlich and Birch (1967) wrote: 'A series of isolated populations with an array of different densities (including extinctions and re-establishment by migrants) may give the same superficial impression as a continuous population under rather tight 'control'. That is, to the casual observer, the species will be present each year. However, from the point of view of the way numbers change in nature, the two situations are entirely different.'

Much larger populations of a moth which appear to fluctuate independently in different localities are those of the Grey Larch Tortrix *Zeiraphera griseana* in the European Alps. Baltensweiler (1968) has studied the various populations in different parts of the Alps at altitudes between 1700 and 2000 m; they were considered by him to be 'independent populations'. Over a number of years in which their fluctuations were studied, their numbers rose and fell in an unsynchronized way. Furthermore, when numbers were reduced to low levels by adverse weather, environmental heterogeneity acted as a 'buffer' (Baltensweiler, 1966).

In contrast to *Euphydras editha* and those butterflies and moths studied by the authors cited above, the satyrnine butterfly *Erebia epipsodea* is quite different (Brussard and Ehrlich, 1970). It is unlike any other butterfly which has been studied in detail. Instead of being divided into numerous small populations which only rarely exchange individuals, *E. epipsodea* occurs in vast more or less panmictic populations which may cover hundreds of square miles. Unsuitable habitats do not impose barriers to the movements of the butterflies which wander widely over a large terrain.

Within isolated, yet neighbouring, populations of both *Maniola jurtina* and *Panaxia dominula*, Ford (1964) identified changes in gene frequency which were independent in the separate colonies. This suggests that local populations may evolve gene frequencies fitted to the particular environment of the local population. Ford remarked; 'When populations are cut off in restricted areas they can be adapted by selection to the special features of their environment in a way that is not possible when they occupy a large and usually, therefore, a more diversified territory.' The particular interest of Ford's findings was that local gene frequency differences occurred between populations that were geographically very close together.

Ehrlich and Mason (1966) measured the changes in frequency of 12 characters in the three local populations of *Euphydras editha* on Jasper Ridge from 1959 to 1964. Two of the 12 characters were in different frequencies in the three populations, and neither of these varied in frequency from year to year. There were significant trends in the year to year changes in the frequency of four characters; the trends being strikingly similar in differing local populations despite the fact that there was little or no gene flow between local populations. These trends in the four characters were interpreted by Ehrlich and Mason as being probably the result of changing selection pressure.

In the wide ranging and relatively panmictic *Erebia epipsodea* Brussard and Ehrlich (1970) were unable to find, by phenetic and isozyme analyses, any local variations in gene frequencies. They suggest that, in the 'wide rangers' the strategy may be to favour genetic combinations that have high average fitness in a wide variety of local environments. Wellington (1960) and Baltensweiler (1968 and in these Proceedings) have accounted for the qualitative changes they have observed in the course of developing outbreaks by postulating that genetic and/or phenotypic changes occur in populations of moths in relation to the changes in density.

Populations of the butterfly *Colias eurytheme* in central Texas are exceedingly variable in relation to the alleles of the autosomal locus controlling the production of an esterase (Burns and Johnson, 1967). Few wild individuals are genetically identical at this locus. Burns and Johnson (1967) speculate that this striking esterase polymorphism together with other polymorphisms in this species, may facilitate the rapid expansion of the butterfly into unoccupied areas in favourable seasons when food plants become available in these areas. In unfavourable seasons, the butterfly has a very discontinuous distribution which changes to a more continuous one in favourable seasons. This hypothesis is supported by the finding of clinal variations in the frequencies of several of the many alleles present at this esterase locus (Richmond, 1970). The role of natural selection in maintaining latitudinal clinal variation at an esterase locus has been demonstrated by Koehn (1969) in the freshwater fish *Catostomes clarkii*. Further, Koehn hass hown that the enzyme activity of the allele which is more frequent in the colder latitude increases as temperature decreases; the activity of the allele which is more frequent in the warmer latitudes increases as temperature increases. Thus, he has demonstrated a correlation between the physiological effects of the gene and the temperature of the environment where it is common.

The role of genetical plasticity in the survival and distribution of the fruit flies Dacus tryoni and Dacus neohumeralis in eastern Australia.

Dacus tryoni and *Dacus neohumeralis* are essentially tropical species of Tephritid fruit flies presumed to be native to northern tropical Australia (Queensland). As one proceeds south of the tropics or west of the moist coastal zone, the environment becomes less favourable for survival and reproduction of both species. The southern limit of both species is apparently imposed by temperature (Bateman, 1967). *D. neohumeralis* does not occur south of latitude 30°S, and *D. tryoni* does not occur south of latitude 38°S (Birch, 1965). The western limit of *D. tryoni* (and possibly also of *D. neohumeralis*) is almost certainly imposed by dryness during the summer months. Bateman (1968), for example, has shown that, in a local population studied near Sydney, a high proportion of the variability in numbers of *D. tryoni* between years is accounted for by fluctuations in the summer rainfall. It acts mainly through its effects on the survival of pupae and newly emerged adults, the fecundity of mature females and the rate of immigration. When there is little summer rain, the population dwindles almost to extinction. Superimposed on this distribution are genetical differences. Tropical populations are adapted to a relatively low range of extreme temperatures, whereas the southern populations are adapted to survive at both high and low extreme temperatures characteristic of the temperate climatic regions (Bateman, 1967). There is evidence that the differences between tropical populations and temperate populations have evolved within the past 90 years (Birch, 1965). A mechanism for this evolutionary change has been suggested by Lewontin and Birch (1966).

119

I would like to be able to present a picture of the dispersion of these two species of fruit flies in eastern Australia in the way that Myers (see earlier in this paper) has been able to do for rabbits. I would like, then, to be able to show how genetical changes of an adaptive nature are continuously occurring in populations, and that these are adaptively different in different climatic regions and, possibly too, that new adaptive complexes are arising on the dry and the cold peripheries of the distribution which might later result in a yet further extension of the distribution of the species. That whole story cannot yet be told because (i) we do not yet know the extent to which local populations are isolated from one another; and (ii) we have not made studies in the field of short term genetical changes in adaptive characters, though we hope to do this later. However, we do know something about dispersion and dispersal and also something about genetical plasticity of phenetic characters and long term evolutionary changes.

Bateman and Fletcher (unpublished) have shown that a population they studied for five years in a field station near Sydney, received immigrants from a distance of 20 or more miles away, and it sent off migrants to unknown destinations. This population, in a forty acre orchard, was very much a population in flux whose residents did not necessarily stay long; how long they stayed depended on many things, especially the age of the fly and the availability of fruit. They also showed that, in the Sydney latitude, populations are reduced to very low numbers in winter; the only overwintering individuals being adults which are patchily distributed. They survive in particular habitats where the foliage cover is dense; these may be individual trees or shrubs widely separated from one another. These refuge populations provide the colonists that, in Spring, repopulate places depopulated at the onset of winter.

On the genetical side of this study we have had to satisfy ourselves, at this stage, with a study of phenetic variation in five characters in a number of localities in widely different latitudes (Birch and Vogt, 1970). The picture that emerges is:

a. The median values for the five phenetic characters are quite different for the two species, but are fairly constant as from one place to another and from time to time; if there are trends, the wide range for each character makes it difficult to pick them up;

b. Within any locality there is a constant and rapid production of variants about the mean of each character, but there is strong selection against these variants;

c. Within a few generations, the means of each of the characters can be moved either by natural selection in different environments in the laboratory, or by artificial selection; but such directional selection has not yet been demonstrated in the field.

The importance of these findings, from the point of view of the subject of this paper, is that they demonstrate both continuous production of variation and intense stabilizing selection acting within local populations. We need only extend the story to adaptive characters and we have a picture of a continuously evolving population poised for new ecological opportunities, and actively adapting to the natural, fluctuating environment. That this may be true for *Dacus tryoni* is reinforced by our knowledge that within the past 90 years, it has evolved to adapt from tropical to temperate climatic regions.

The five phenetic characters studied by Birch and Vogt (1970) were: the extent of yellow and brown areas on the humeral callus: the area of dark pigmentation on the ventral surface of the mesothoracic femur (femoral darkness): the area of darkness of two longitudinal lines on either side of the midline of the dorsal surface of the thorax (thoracic darkness); and the area and darkness of two areas on the genae (the upper and lower genal spots). Each character covers a range which is a continuum that extends from one

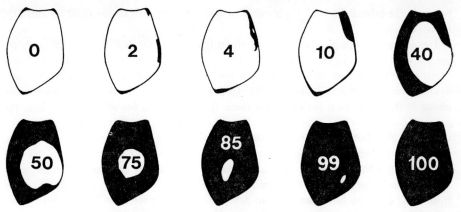

Fig. 4. The range of 'percentage of brown area' on the humeral callus of *Dacus tryoni* (0%–80%) and *D. neohumeralis* (45%–100%). (After Birch and Vogt, 1970).

species to another with a certain amount of overlap in the middle. In classifying the humeral callus, 10 arbitrary grades were recognized according to the proportion of callus that was brown; the rest being yellow (Fig. 4). In the field, *Dacus tryoni* typically has a mostly yellow humeral callus (0% brown) but the range extends from 0 to 80% brown. *D. neohumeralis*, in the field, typically has a mostly brown humeral callus, but the range extends from 100 to 45% brown. Fig. 5 shows the frequency of different callus types in populations of fruit flies collected from tropical, northern Australia (Cairns) to the more southern, temperate Sydney. The frequency of brown callus (*D. neohumeralis*) falls off from north to south; conversely the frequency of yellow callus (*D. tryoni*) increases from north to south. As can be seen in Fig. 5, the Sydney population consists of *D. tryoni* alone,

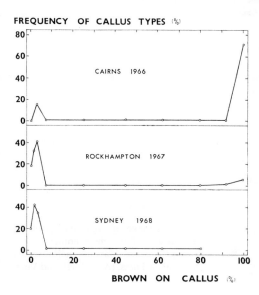

Fig. 5. The distribution of callus types (percentage of brown on callus) in populations of adult flies of *Dacus tryoni* and *D. neohumeralis* bred from fruit collected in three localities on a north-south transect of eastern Australia (Cairns 16° 55′S.; Rockhampton 23° 24′S.; Sydney 33° 51′S.). All points shown on the graph are above 0% though in the horizontal section of each graph the frequency of callus types is of the order of only 1% or less. (After Birch and Vogt, 1970).

121

but its range extends beyond 0 % brown to a very small number of flies (0.02 %) with 80 % brown callus.

There is nothing particularly unusual about the data so far described except, perhaps, for the wide overlap in the callus character for the two species. However, the situation is more complicated than this. When *D. tryoni*, from any locality between Cairns and Sydney, with 3 % brown humeral callus (which are common in field populations) are mated in the laboratory, their progeny range from 0 to 92 % brown callus, i.e. into the range of *D. neohumeralis*. When we consider the offspring from other humeral types mated with their like kind, it is evident that the types which are rare in the field are, nevertheless, frequent in laboratory matings. Moreover, such matings must be common in the field since mating within the species appears to be non-selective. By comparing the frequency of genotypes in the eggs of *D. tryoni* laid in the field with the frequency of adults that come from these eggs, we have been able to demonstrate strong selection in the field against callus types 7 to 92 % brown.

The first evidence that 'humeral callus' is readily subject to selection was provided by Wolda (1967), who showed that the amount of brown and yellow on the callus was readily changed by artificial selection. From parents whose callus was almost entirely yellow (*D. tryoni*) he selected for brown callus, and by the third generation he had produced flies with a nearly all brown callus. Similarly, by selecting from flies that had an all brown callus (*D. neohumeralis*) he produced, in three generations, flies that had a mostly yellow callus. Since then, we have also found that the modal value for callus type moves quite rapidly under natural selection in laboratory cultures with different environments.

The second phenetic character studied was 'femoral darkness'. The ventral surface of the mesothoracic femur in *D. neohumeralis* and *D. tryoni* varies from having almost no melanic pigment to having a large area of pigment (Fig. 6). Eight arbitrary grades were

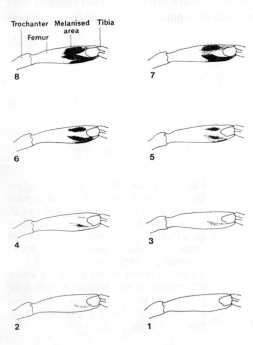

Fig. 6. The range of pigmentation of the inner surface of the mesothoracic femur showing the lower limits for each category of femoral darkness. (After Birch and Vogt, 1970)

122

recognized. Fig. 7 shows a typical frequency distribution of femoral types in the two species *D. tryoni* and *D. neohumeralis*. As with humeral callus, there is an overlap of the character in the two species. Most *D. tryoni* are in grades 1–2 and most *D. neohumeralis* are in grades 5–8. Hybrids of the two species mated in the laboratory have a mean for the character which is in between that of the two species (Fig. 7). Femoral darkness is also subject to selection. In laboratory populations, the median value of the character moves to new values in different environments. Further, this character is readily selected in artificial selection (Fig. 8). *D. tryoni* flies (with light femurs) when selected for dark femurs produced, within four generations, flies with femurs nearly as dark as the mean for *D. neohumeralis* (Fig. 8A). Similarly, *D. neohumeralis* (with dark femurs) when selected for light femurs produced, within three generations, flies that had femurs as light as the mean for *D. tryoni* (Fig. 8B).

A similar story applies to the remaining three phenetic characters. All characters have a high hereditability, but there is only a low correlation between the characters indicating that variation in the five characters is mainly under the control of different genes.

The genetical question posed by these data is: Why are the populations not 'purified' by

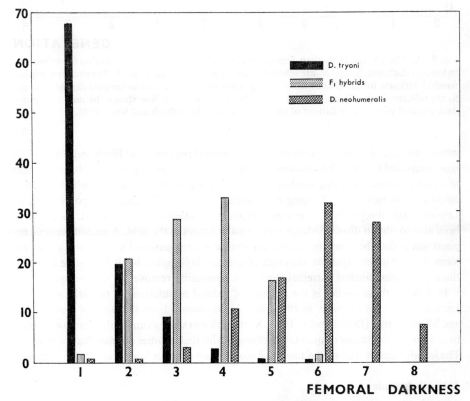

Fig. 7. The frequencies of the different grades of femoral darkness for a population of flies bred from fruit collected at Rockhampton (1968) and for a population of hybrids. (After Birch and Vogt, 1970).

FEMORAL DARKNESS

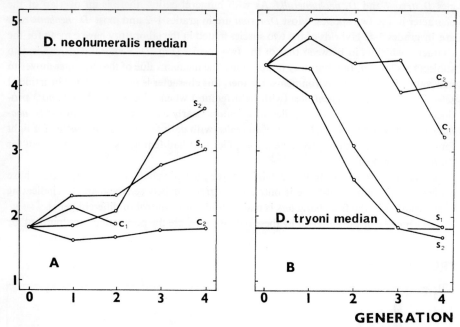

Fig. 8. A. The change in median femoral darkness for *D. tryoni* during selection for an increase in femoral darkness. S_1 and S_2 are selected lines, C_1 and C_2 are controls. B. The change in median femoral darkness for *D. neohumeralis* during selection for a decrease in femoral darkness. S_1 and S_2 are selected lines, C_1 and C_2 are controls. The horizontal line shows the median femoral darkness in the initial populations of the other species. (After Birch and Vogt, 1970.)

continuous selection against extreme types in natural populations? Birch and Vogt (1970) have suggested two possible answers. Some crossing between the two species may occur in natural populations; this would provide a rich source of variation on which selection could operate rapidly in changing environments as shown in laboratory populations by Lewontin and Birch (1966). The species cross in the laboratory, but, as yet, we have not been able to obtain direct evidence that crossing occurs in the field. A second possible explanation is that the characters may each involve several gene loci with several alleles per locus. In such genetic systems, the effect of selection is complex, but it is possible that continuous selection against extremes would not necessarily remove the variability.

In none of these studies is the genetics of natural populations in the field at all well known, as it is, for example, in *Drosophila pseudoobscura* from the work of Dobzhansky and his colleagues (Dobzhansky, 1970). Such work can serve as an inspiration to ecologists to combine such studies of qualitative changes with their studies on quantitative changes. The hopeful sign is that such a fusion of ecology and genetics is gradually taking place.

Acknowledgments

Different parts of the manuscript were read and criticized by Mr K. F. Myers, CSIRO, Division of Wildlife Research, Canberra; Dr J. Monro, Biology Department, New South

Wales Institute of Technology, Sydney; and Dr M. A. Bateman and Dr B. S. Fletcher, Joint University-CSIRO Unit of Animal Ecology, The University of Sydney. Each of them also provided me with unpublished data of their own. I gratefully acknowledge their help and criticism.

References

Andrewartha, H. G. & L. C. Birch, 1954. The distribution and abundance of animals. University of Chicago Press.

Baltensweiler, W., 1966. The influence of climate and weather on population age distribution and its consequences. *Proc. F.A.O. Symp. integr. Pest Control* 2: 15–24.

Baltensweiler, W., 1968. The cyclic population dynamics of the grey larch tortrix *Zeiraphera griseana* Hübner (Lepidoptera: Tortricidae). *Symp. R. ent. Soc. Lond.* 4 (Insect abundance) 88–97.

Bateman, M. A., 1967. Adaptations to temperature in geographic races of the Queensland fruit fly *Dacus (Stumeta) tryoni. Aust. J. Zool.* 15: 1141–1161.

Bateman, M. A., 1968. Determinants of abundance in a population of the Queensland fruit fly. *Symp. R. ent. Soc. Lond.* 4 (Insect Abundance) 119–131.

Beardmore, J., 1970. Ecological factors and the variability of gene pools in *Drosophila.* In: M. K. Hecht & W. C. Steere (Ed.), Essays in evolution and genetics in honour of Theodosius Dobzhansky. (Supplement to Evolutionary biology.) Appleton-Century-Crofts, New York, p. 299–314.

Birch, L. C., 1965. Evolutionary opportunity for insects and mammals in Australia. In: H. G. Baker & G. L. Stebbins (Ed.), Genetics of colonizing species. Academic Press, New York, p. 197–213.

Birch, L. C. & W. G. Vogt, 1970. Plasticity of taxonomic characters of the Queensland fruit fly *Dacus tryoni* and *Dacus neohumeralis* (Tephritidae). *Evolution* 24: 321–343.

Boer, P. J. den, 1968. Spreading of risk and stabilisation of animal numbers. *Acta biotheor.* 18: 165–194.

Brussard, P. F. & P. R. Ehrlich, 1970. The population structure of *Erebia epipsodea* (Lepidoptera: Satyrinae). *Ecology* 51: 119–129.

Burns, J. M. & F. M. Johnson, 1967. Esterase polymorphism in natural populations of a Sulpur butterfly *Colias eurytheme. Science* 156: 93–96.

Dobzhansky, Th., 1970. Genetics of the evolutionary process. Columbia University Press, New York.

Dowdeswell, W. H. R., R. A. Fisher & E. B. Ford, 1940. The quantitative study of populations in the Lepidoptera. 1. *Polyommatus icarus* Roth. *Ann. Eugenics* 10: 123–136.

Dowdeswell, W. H. R., R. A. Fisher & E. B. Ford, 1949. The quantitative study of populations in the Lepidoptera. 2. *Maniola jurtina* L. *Heredity* 3: 67–84.

Ehrlich, P. R., 1965. The population biology of the butterfly *Euphydras editha* II. The structure of the Jasper Ridge colony. *Evolution* 19: 327–336.

Ehrlich, P. R. & L. C. Birch, 1967. The 'Balance of Nature' and 'Population Control'. *Am. Nat.* 101: 97–107.

Ehrlich, P. R. & L. G. Mason, 1966. The population biology of the butterfly *Euphydras editha.* III. Selection and the phenetics of the Jasper Ridge Colony. *Evolution* 20: 165–173.

Ford, E. B., 1964. Ecological genetics. Methuen, London.

Keller, E. L., R. H. T. Mattoni & M. S. B. Seiger, 1966. Preferential return of artificially displaced butterflies. *Anim. Behav.* 14: 197–200.

Koehn, R. K., 1969. Esterase heterogeneity: Dynamics of polymorphism. *Science* 163: 943–944.

Lewontin, R. C., 1965a. Selection in and of populations. In: J. A. Moore (Ed.), Ideas in modern biology. Natural History Press, New York, p. 299–310.

Lewontin, R. C., 1965b. Selection for colonizing ability. In: H. G. Baker & G. L. Stebbins (Ed.) The genetics of colonizing species. Academic Press, New York.

Lewontin, R. C. & L. C. Birch, 1966. Hybridization as a source of variation for adaptation to new environments. *Evolution* 20: 315–336.

Monro, J., 1967. The exploitation and conservation of resources by populations of insects. *J. Anim. Ecol.* 36: 531–547.

Myers, K. & B. S. Parker, 1965. A study of the biology of the wild rabbit in climatically different regions in eastern Australia. *CSIRO Wildl. Res.* 10: 1–32.

Newsome, A. E., 1969a. A population study of house mice temporarily inhabiting a South Australian wheatfield. *J. Anim. Ecol.* 39: 341–359.

Newsome, A. E., 1969b. A population study of house-mice permanently inhabiting a reed bed in South Australia. *J. Anim. Ecol.* 38: 361–377.

Nicholson, A. J., 1947. Fluctuations of animal populations. *Rep. 26th Meet. Aust. N.Z. Ass. Advt Sci.*

Reddingius, J., 1968. Gambling for existence. Unpublished Thesis, Groningen.

Reddingius J. & P. J. den Boer, 1970. Simulation experiments illustrating stabilization of animal numbers by spreading of risk. *Oecologia* 5: 240–284.

Richmond, R., 1970. Non-Darwinian evolution: a critique. *Nature, Lond.* 225: 1025–1028.

Sheppard, P. M., 1951. A quantitative study of two populations of moth *Panaxia dominula* L. *Heredity* 5: 349–378.

Tamarin, R. H. & C. J. Krebs, 1969. *Microtus* population biology. II. Genetic changes at the transferrin locus in fluctuating populations of two vole species. *Evolution* 23: 183–211.

Turner, J. R. G., 1963. A quantitative study of a Welsh colony of the large heath butterfly *Coenonympha tullia* Muller (Lepidoptera).

Turner, J. R. G., 1968. The ecological genetics of *Acleris comariana* (Zeller) (Lepidoptera: Tortricidae), a pest of strawberry. *J. Anim. Ecol.* 37: 489–520.

Wellington, W. G., 1960. Qualitative changes in natural populations during changes in abundance. *Canad. J. Zool.* 38: 289–314.

Wolda, H., 1967. Reproductive isolation between two closely related species of Queensland fruit fly, *Dacus tryoni* (Frogg.) and *D. neohumeralis* Hardy (Diptera: Tephritidae) II. Genetic variation in humeral callus pattern in each species as compared with laboratory bred hybrids. *Aust. J. Zool.* 15: 515–539.

Wolda, H., 1969. Fine distribution of morph frequencies in the snail *Cepaea nemoralis* near Groningen. *J. Anim. Ecol.* 38: 305–327.

Wright, Sewall, 1931. Evolution of Mendelian populations. *Genetics* 16: 97–159.

Wright, Sewall, 1937. The distribution of gene frequencies in populations. *Proc. Nat. Acad. Sci. Wash.* 23: 307–320.

Discussion

Participants: Birch (Author), den Boer (P. J.), Jain, Pimentel, Reynoldson, Rosenzweig, Varley, Voûte and Zwölfer.

Not all stochastic models are more useful than the corresponding deterministic model. Random variables used in generating a stochastic process do not always give the most general or most well known distribution (normal, Poisson, etc.) We should try to determine the actual distribution (JAIN). Stochastic – and especially simulation – models are difficult, if not impossible, to treat analytically. To obtain generalizations one must begin with good, analyzable, deterministic models. Though these simplify reality, they do not necessarily oversimplify it. Empirical tests should eliminate those that do. Certainly not enough deterministic models include aspects of heterogeneity, but they can and should. (ROSENZWEIG). One may wonder whether it is always necessary to treat a model analytically to obtain generalization. Deterministic models simplify reality in a causal way, whereas stochastic models simplify reality in a descriptive way, i.e. a multi-causal complex of relations (e.g. weather) is replaced by some relevant frequency distribution(s). If one is not interested in the (very complex) causation of some kind of heterogeneity (e.g. weather) but only in its consequences for, say, animal numbers, a very straightforward way to study the probability of some supposed consequences is to construct stochastic models in which this kind of heterogeneity is represented by some relevant frequency distribution(s) and the output is animal numbers. As long as we have no deterministic models to obtain this kind of generalization, stochastic models will have to do the job and there may even be cases (especially in ecology) in which they will always have to do it (BIRCH and DEN BOER). (See also Reddingius' paper in these Proceedings).

One, of course, would like to see the hypothesis of expanding and contracting ranges in good and bad years tested further. In particular, one would like to see results of tests outside Australia. Australia's high success in accepting introductions suggests that there are many open evolutionary opportunities. The question arises: How important is an irregular occupation of a habitat to a fauna which has reached evolutionary saturation (ROSENZWEIG)? One would also like to know when, if ever, a fauna 'has reached evolutionary saturation', and when, if ever, an area has many or only few 'evolutionary opportunities', and how this is supposed to interfere with the spatial differences and temporal fluctuations in the favourability of habitats for, say, the rabbit and for *Cactoblastis* in Australia. If change is a perpetual characteristic of environments, then one might well question whether the concept of 'evolutionary saturation' has any meaning at all. Is it not more likely to be the case that evolutionary change is characteristic rather than exceptional, and that Australian environments are no more exceptional in this respect than say North American environments? (AUTHOR).

Heterogeneity is an important influence, but does the frequent and intensive intraspecific competition in *Cactoblastis* and in the rabbit also play a significant part in determining their population numbers and quality (REYNOLDSON)? Monro's measure – 'percentage eggsticks of *Cactoblastis* on overloaded plants' – is an index of the extent of crowding of larvae in cactus plants. This crowding or 'competition' is quite intense and results in the destruction of cactus plants on a large scale. However, the relevant aspect of this case history is not the 'amount of competition' but the fact that some plants escape predation by *Cactoblastis*, at least for that generation. There is obviously a great deal of 'competition' between caterpillars for food in most cactus plants. If this were true of all cactus plants then neither *Cactoblastis* nor cactus would survive. As far as the rabbits, there is no evidence to suggest that as the drought advances rabbits crowd into the few remaining local places where food still exists. They appear more to wander around in an exhausted state. Those that happen to be near a swamp or are in a stony habitat have a relatively greater chance of surviving. There is no evidence that these survivors 'compete' for the resources in these habitats; but perhaps they do, and if so this would simply mean that the number of survivors would decrease still more. 'Competition' does not provide the key clue to an understanding of the main factors responsible for determining numbers in either rabbits or *Cactoblastis*; the key clues are in the behaviour of the animals in relation to the heterogeneity of plants and to spatial heterogeneity (AUTHOR).

Commenting on the statement that the considered non-random distribution of egg-sticks of *Cactoblastis* on *Opuntia* plants would favour the survival of both cactus and moth: In order to generate some testable hypotheses on the strategy of the supposed evolution, variation in genetics, behaviour, dispersal, environment, etc. must be given. How is this system thought to have been selected for (JAIN, PIMENTEL)? The evolutionary problem in this case is, that a possible genetic variant of *Cactoblastis* that was able to lay its eggs on all plants would tend to spread and hence to increase the chance of annihilation of all plants. Plants may develop characteristics that give them some resistance to insect attacks. Perhaps such co-evolution of insect and plant is involved with *Cactoblastis* and *Opuntia*. It is difficult to imagine a way in which an insect could evolve with an 'altruistic' behaviour of deliberately refraining from laying eggs on a certain proportion of its hosts (AUTHOR).

A similar distribution pattern of eggs and a similar waste of eggs was observed in *Altica carduorum* Guer. feeding on *Cirsium arvense* L. in western France. In this case the distribution pattern of eggs results from a semi-gregarious behaviour of the adult insects (ZWÖLFER).

Sometimes no eggs of a certain forest insect are laid on a tree even when population-density is high. In some years only a few trees seem to be attractive, and in other years eggs are laid on the greater part of the trees; examples: *Diprion sertifer, Diprion pini, Evetria buoliana* (VOÛTE).

The non-randomness of the distribution of egg-sticks need not contradict the potential ability of *Cactoblastis* to lay eggs on all plants. All kinds of subtleties in the distribution of the plants, in the environment, in the behaviour of the animals, etc, may prevent all plants from being equally attainable; also, all plants may not be equally attractive to alight on and/or to deposit eggs upon. The same curious escape of some plants amidst an overall heavy infestation of some insect is often observed and I guess that in many of these cases – although generally not tested – the distribution will appear to be non-random (DEN BOER).

Why are the eggs of *Cactoblastis* laid in sticks? There must be some advantage in clumping eggs (VARLEY). Clumping of eggs is common in insects. In the case of *Cactoblastis* I can suggest two possible functions of this: (1). A group of larvae may more readily enter the surface of a cactus segment than single larvae; (2) Egg-sticks look very like cactus spines and so perhaps they are cryptically concealed from predators. It would be interesting to study this in the original habitat. *Opuntia inermis* and *O. stricta* came from Central America, whereas *Cactoblastis* came from Argentina and Brazil; however, in Brazil *Cactoblastis* feeds on *Opuntia* species which have a similar growth form to the two species it feeds on in Australia (AUTHOR).

Proc. Adv. Study Inst. Dynamics Number Popul. (Oosterbeek, 1970) 129–147

Dynamics of numbers of a phytophagous lady-beetle, Epilachna vigintioctomaculata, living in patchily distributed habitats

Syun'iti Iwao

Entomological Laboratory, College of Agriculture, Kyoto University, Kyoto, Japan

Abstract

The dynamics of numbers in a small population of a phytophagous lady beetle, *Epilachna vigin-tioctomaculata*, was studied in 1960–63. Particular attention was paid to adult movements between patchily-distributed habitats. The species has one generation a year, even in a southern fringe of its distribution range where the study area is located. Larvae develop on potato plants in spring but newly-emerged adults disperse to egg plants and some other crops and feed on them until they enter hibernation in late autumn. The study area is topographically isolated from other areas, and the food plants are distributed in small patches in varying combinations.

Results of marking-recapture experiments indicated that adult mobility was restricted to a small range, and that the population under study was nearly self-contained. Because of the patchy distri-bution of habitats, the population was split up into several subpopulations that were interconnec-ted by the movements of adults between them. The numbers in the respective subpopulations tended to be stabilized through population interchange among them, density-dependent adult mortality (possibly losses involved in dispersal process), and larval competition for food. During 4 consecutive generations, the whole population in the study area was fairly stable in numbers. The stabilization of numbers in the whole population is considered to be brought about by density-dependent mortality processes operating locally in the area.

Since the habitat for any species of animal is neither homogeneous nor continuous, the population in a given area tends to be split up into many minor units or subpopulations that are interconnected with each other to varying degrees. Elton (1949) rightly pointed out that it is important to know how the splitting up of a population into partly isolated units affects the mechanism of natural control of an animal population in a wider area. Many population theorists, notably Thompson (1939, 1956), Andrewartha and Birch (1954), Ehrlich and Birch (1967) and den Boer (1968), also have emphasized the impor-tance of such spatial structure of animal populations to the dynamics of their numbers. In field population studies, therefore, we should recognize natural population units in larger and smaller spatial scales, and relate the changes in numbers within different spatial units to each other. The assessment of animal movements is of vital importance for this purpose. To my knowledge, however, little detailed studies have been done from such a point of view, though there are several attempts to delimit natural insect populations spatially through a marking-recapture census (e.g., Ford, 1964; Ehrlich, 1965; see also Birch in these Proceedings.)

We have studied a small population of a phytophagous lady-beetle, *Epilachna vigintioc-tomaculata*. We have paid particular attention to the changes in numbers in patchily dis-tributed habitats, and have investigated the role of population interchange among them in the dynamics of numbers in these patches as well as in the whole study area. The species has one generation a year. Eggs are laid on potato plants in spring. Adults emerge in July, disperse to several kinds of vegetables such as egg plant, kidney bean, cucumber, tomato, etc, and feed on them until they enter hibernation in October–November. Thus, the adult has a 9-month life span but its mobility is restricted to a relatively short period of time. The study area is topographically well-defined and within it non-commercial farms of very small sizes are distributed spottedly. The situation is therefore suited for a detailed study by a small research team.

The study area and field methods

The study was conducted in 1960–63 at Kurama, the northern suburb of Kyoto City. The study area is in a valley and forms a strip less than one km in length along the stream Kurama-gawa (Area A in Fig. 1). To both the north-east and south-west of the strip there were no cultivated fields within 1.5 km. In 1960, the nearest farm area (Area C) was also subjected to a marking-recapture survey of adults, but no population interchange could be detected between this and the study area. In later years, therefore, Area C was surveyed only occasionally. In the study area, the village people cultivated several kinds of vegetables only for their own use and, hence, small patches of cultivated fields were distributed spottedly and no insecticidal control was being practised.

The number of fields chosen for population survey varied from year to year and with the stage of development of the insect, but from the summer of 1961 to the spring of 1963

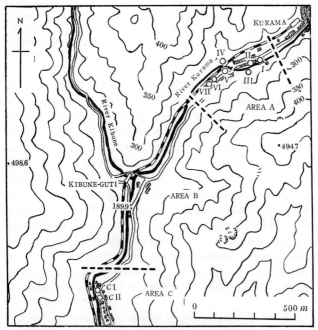

Fig. 1. Map of the study area and its vicinity. Open circles indicate local patches of food plants. The study was focused on the population in the area A.

all of the fields containing the food plants of this insect were examined. In 1962, the total number of plants were as follows: potato 1846; egg plant 156; kidney bean 756; cucumber 464; red pepper 50; and tomato 5. These were distributed in seven patches, so that each patchy habitat was composed of several hundreds of potato plants and several tens of each of other food plants.

For an adult census, every plant in each census field was examined, usually at intervals of 1–2 weeks, throughout the season. During limited periods of time in summer (period of adult emergence), autumn (before hibernation) and spring (reproductive season) all the adults discovered were marked with lacquer paint. Marking was done in such a way that individual adults could be identified for capture history in terms of place and time; the adults captured or recaptured were released on the same plant on which they were caught. The number of eggs, larvae and pupae were counted at intervals of one week throughout the growing season of potato. Egg masses were labelled to avoid double counting on the next sampling day. Except early in the season, eggs and larvae were counted, without removing them, on about 10 percent of the plants in each census field. Population surveys were done most intensively for the 1962–63 generation; those in earlier years were less complete.

Quantitative description of life history in the study area

Seasonal fluctuations in numbers in the whole study area for 1962–63 are shown in Fig. 2. In early May, overwintered adults appeared in potato fields and laid eggs in masses (average number of eggs per mass 28). The period of oviposition covered the whole growing

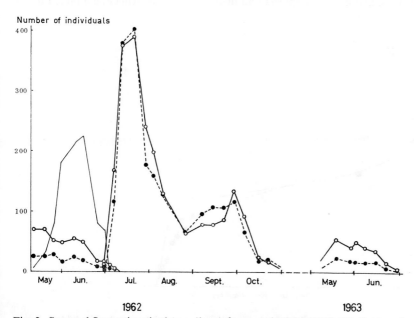

Fig. 2. Seasonal fluctuations in the numbers of eggs and adults (1962–63). Open and solid circles show the observed numbers of female and male adults on sampling days. The thin line (left) indicates the oviposition curve based on egg-mass counts.

season of potato plants, resulting in a wide overlapping of various developmental stages. The adults emerged in early to mid July and they moved to other food plants because potato plants were withered up by early July. In mid summer, the number of adults on plants decreased due to their aestivation in soil crevice, etc. They reappeared in September and fed exclusively on egg plants (other food plants were withered by this time) and they entered hibernation in late October-early November.

Fig. 3 shows a survivorship curve constructed for the 1962–63 generation. The total number of adults emerging in summer, and the survivors in autumn and spring were estimated by applying Jolly's stochastic model (Jolly, 1965) to the marking-recapture data. Although the details of the problems of population estimation will be reported in a separate paper (Iwao et al., in preparation), an example is given in Table 1 for the period of adult emergence, where the total number of adults emerged is estimated as $\hat{N}_1 + \Sigma(\hat{B}_i / \hat{\phi}_i^{\frac{1}{2}})$. The potential fertility is calculated as the estimated number of adult females in spring of 1962 (160) multiplied by 700, the average fecundity of laboratory-reared females. The number of eggs laid and egg mortality could be estimated with a relatively high accuracy, because each egg mass discovered was labelled. However, the numbers of young larvae and pupae proved to be underestimated, so that the number of 4th (final) instar larvae only was estimated by the graphical method given by Southwood and Jepson (1962).

Causes of mortalities could not be assessed quantitatively. It is peculiar, however, that there was no parasite in any stage of *Epilachna's* life cycle in the area. Egg mortality was mainly due to predation by Coccinellids, *Harmonia axiridis* and *Coccinella septempunctata*, and other insect predators. Also, adult beetles sometimes ate their eggs, though the percentage killed by this factor was unknown. Larvae and pupae were preyed upon by spiders and coccinellids, and adults by spiders and mantids. Since the females continued to lay

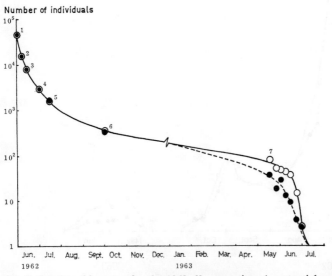

Fig. 3. Survivorship curve for the 1962–63 generation. 1. potential eggs; 2. eggs laid; 3. larvae hatched; 4. 4th-instar larvae; 5. adults emerged; 6. adults surviving in autumn; 7. adults surviving to reproductive season. Open and solid circles indicate female and male respectively.

Table 1. Estimation of population parameters for newly-emerged adults in 1962.

Sex	Sampling date (i)	Total catch	Number recaptured	Population size $\hat{N}_i \pm \sqrt{V(\hat{N}_i)}$	Survival rate $\hat{\theta}_i \pm \sqrt{V(\hat{\theta}_i)}$	Number recruited $\hat{B}_i \pm \sqrt{V(\hat{B}_i)}$
Male	6 July (1)	114	–	285.0	0.500±0.098	672.1
	13 July (2)	376	26	824.6±183.4	0.427±0.054	468.9±105.3
	20 July (3)	397	84	820.7±107.4	0.427±0.054	198.7±56.7
	28 July (4)	177	67	549.5± 75.3	0.600±0.089	69.7±39.9
	3 Aug.(5)	157	75	399.6± 57.5		
	10 Aug.(6)	124	73			
Female	6 July (1)	167	–	383.0	0.309±0.059	568.1
	13 July (2)	372	28	686.6±133.3	0.439±0.044	479.9± 85.1
	20 July (3)	389	86	781.1± 83.2	0.593±0.057	188.9± 57.2
	28 July (4)	241	104	651.8± 68.1	0.616±0.077	33.1± 32.5
	3 Aug.(5)	194	115	434.4± 52.0		
	10 Aug.(6)	126	85			

Total number emerged $\hat{N}_1 + \sum\limits_{i=1}^{4} (\hat{B}_i/\hat{\Phi}_i^{1/2})$: 2349.6 ♂♂ and 2416.2 ♀♀

Average sampling ratio $\bar{f}_i$: 0.400 (♂) and 0.436 (♀).

eggs over the growing season of potato plants, about 30% of larvae that hatched out later than mid June were inevitably killed by deprivation of food. The process was intensified when the potato plants were severely damaged by larval feeding. Some late-instar larvae that suffered from starvation migrated to nearby plants such as egg-plant, cucumber and kidney beans. When larvae fed on these plants, the ensuing adults were small in size and tended to be eliminated by the next spring.

About 4% of the potential egg supply, or 15% of eggs laid, reached the adult stage. Of adults, 85% were killed by autumn, this seemed to be due to high temperature during summer as well as losses during dispersal; also 80% of females and 90% of males in the autumn population were killed during the winter. As a result, the proportion of females in the population changed from 50% to nearly 70% in the next spring. Generation mortality in females amounted to 99.86% on the basis of potential egg supply, or 99.5% on the basis of eggs laid in this particular generation.

Behaviour of reproductive females and survival of immature stage insects

In both 1962 and 1963, more than 80% of the total population of spring (overwintered) adults were finally marked in potato fields, but none of them moved from field to field. Thus, spring adults are extremely sluggish and rarely move across the foodless space after they arrive in a potato field from the hibernation quarter (Iwao et al., 1963). Even within a single field, the average distance of their movement was as small as 1.6 m in females and 3.0 m in males per week. Larval mobility, also, is limited to a range of few potato plants. In the period of reproduction and larval development, therefore, the subpopulations in different potato fields are considered to be independent of each other.

In 1962, mean densities per m² of successive stages, from potential egg supply to adult emergence, were calculated for each potato field (Fig. 4, left). Varley and Gradwell's (1960)

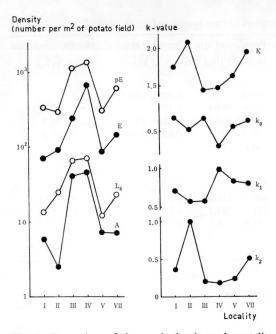

Fig. 4. Comparison of changes in density and mortality among different subpopulations for the period from potential egg supply to adult emergence (1962).

Left: density changes. pE = potential eggs; E = eggs laid; L_4 = 4th-instar larvae; A = emerged adults.

Right: changes in mortality expressed by k values. K = total mortality; K_0 = reduced fertility; k_1 = mortality from egg laying to 4th-instar stage; k_2 = mortality from 4th instar to adult stage.

key factor analysis was then used to detect the differences in mortality patterns among subpopulations (Fig. 4, right). Since the number of adults in each field was too small to apply Jolly's formulae directly, the population size in a field was estimated as the cumulative total number of adults that were marked in that patch multiplied by the ratio of marked to estimated total population in the whole area. The sum of such estimates was consistent with the estimate of total population calculated by Jolly's method.

It is suggested from Fig. 4 that the mortality during the period from 4th instar to adult emergence is the key factor causing the variation of total mortality among different subpopulations. The potato plant was dying off or harvested in late June to early July, at this time only small differences in the timing of food deprivation could exert a large influence on the percentage of successful emergences. The mortality during egg to 4th instar stages, on the other hand, appeared to be partially compensatory, though it was not sufficient to counter the local variations in the initial population densities.

To make clear the possible density dependence in larval mortality, the relation between egg density and the survival to 4th instar was examined by adding supplementary data from other years. Since the eggs laid in the latter half of June inevitably died due to deprivation of food, only the eggs laid by mid June were considered. As shown in Fig. 5, there seems to be some indication of density dependence, though the points at low egg densities are widely scattered. Late-instar larvae are vigorous feeders and they are distributed contagiously within a field, so that many plants are severely damaged when the lar-

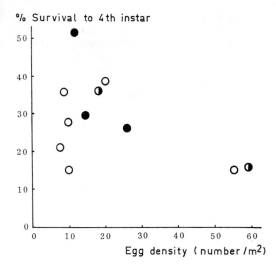

Fig. 5. Relationship between egg density and the survival rate to 4th instar stage. Different symbols indicate years (solid = 1960; semisolid = 1961; open = 1962).

val density is high. For example, on 23 June, 1960 the highest number of 4th instar in Locality III was 63, and one half of the plants were completely skeletonized. Under such circumstances, smaller larvae would have a high probability of death due to starvation. This kind of competition for food is probably the main cause of the reduced survival rates at high densities.

Dispersal of newly-emerged adults

The adults that emerge in July disperse to egg-plant and some other crops because potato plant is no longer available. At this time adults are polyphagous and they tend to feed on food plants which are located in close proximity to the place where they emerged. Fig. 6 illustrates the process of such dispersal. In this particular instance, a row of kidney beans was adjacent to the potato field and then, further away, there was a row of cucumbers. Many adults which emerged in the potato field moved to kidney beans, fewer to cucumbers, and only a small fraction to the other field which was 30 m away. Numbers on kidney beans were kept at high levels during the first week and then decreased gradually, whereas numbers on cucumbers increased with a time lag of a few days. On kidney beans, the population was mostly the immigrants from potatoes during the early period, but the individuals once arrived tended to stay there for two or more sampling intervals. On cucumbers, immigrants came from kidney beans as well as directly from potatoes, and a considerable percentage of the adults moved to 'the other field' after a short stay. Thus, the process of dispersal proceeded rather slowly. In another instance where the spatial arrangement of crops was reversed relative to potato field, the opposite tendency of dispersal was observed. When egg plants were available in the neighbourhood, the percentage moving to other fields was usually smaller than in the above-mentioned example.

The effect of population density on dispersal rate was examined by using the percentages of marked individuals recaptured on the same plant species in the same patch. (Fig. 7). On all of the three species of food plants, the percentage of recaptures after one week tended to be lower at high initial densities. On egg plants, the percentage of recaptures consist-

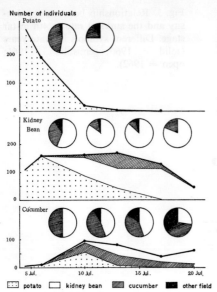

Fig. 6. An example showing the process of dispersal of newly emerged adults. Changes are shown in adult numbers on each food plant species (heavy line) and in the proportion of immigrants from other plants. Circular diagrams indicate the proportions of residents and emigrants of various classes during the interval of two successive sampling days.

ently decreased with increasing density, whereas it tended to be highest at intermediate densities on kidney beans and cucumbers. The reason for this difference is not clear. Food-choice experiments in the laboratory indicated that kidney bean and cucumber, particularly the former, were not preferred hosts for adult beetles. Judged from the percentage of resident recaptures, however, kidney bean seems to be as good as egg plant. The distribution of adults per plant was more aggregative on kidney beans and cucumbers than on egg plants. One possibility, then, is that aggregation of several adults tends to facilitate the feeding activity on these rather unsuitable food plants.

Fig. 7 also shows the percentage of recaptures on different species of plants in the same patch and that of total recaptures over the study area. The percentage of emigrated recaptures was lowest among the adults released on egg plants, intermediate among those released on kidney beans and highest among those on cucumber. It is interesting that on egg plants and kidney beans the percentage of total recaptures was even lower at high initial densities, but on cucumbers it was roughly constant regardless of initial density. The former indicates the occurrence of higher mortality (losses during dispersal or due to other causes) at high densities since, in this period, dispersal is restricted to a small range (see next chapter).

Seasonal change in adult numbers and interconnection by movements among subpopulations

The change in adult numbers in the different patches, and the degree of interchange of individuals among them, are schematically shown in Fig. 8 for the period from summer of 1961 to spring of 1963. Although the subpopulations in different patches are connected with each other through the movements of adults, in autumn the majority of individuals remained in the original place where they emerged as long as the suitable food (egg plant) was available there. If egg plants were not there, all the adults moved to other places

136

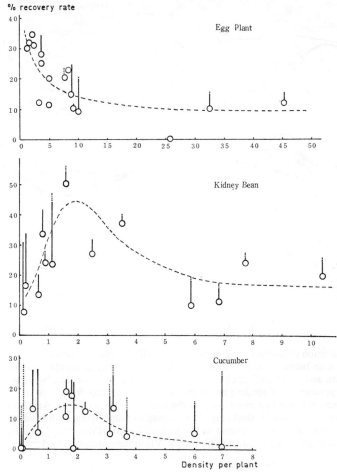

% recovery rate

Egg Plant

Kidney Bean

Cucumber

Density per plant

Fig. 7. The relation between adult density and the percentage recovery of marked individuals after 1 week, with reference to plant species. The % recovery on the same plant species is shown by a circle. The % of recovery from a different plant species in the same patch and that from different patches are indicated by the respective lengths of solid and dotted lines attached to each circle.

because other kinds of food plants, such as kidney bean and cucumber, were withered up by autumn (e.g. patch II in 1962-63 generation). During the successive seasons of adult life, from summer to the next spring, the variation in population sizes among patches appeared to be diminished. This tendency will be analyzed in the next chapter.

Several marked adults that were first liberated in summer were recaptured in the next spring, but their numbers were too small to assess the rate of migration between patches. Table 2 shows the relation between the place of release in summer or autumn and that of recapture in the next spring. In 1960, some patches in Area C, 1.5 km south of the study area, were included for marking-recapture study, but none of the adults marked in one area were recaptured in the other area. The overall percentage of recaptures of summer adults in the next spring varied from 0.4 to 0.7%, and 12.5-50.0% of recaptures were found in the same patches where they were liberated.

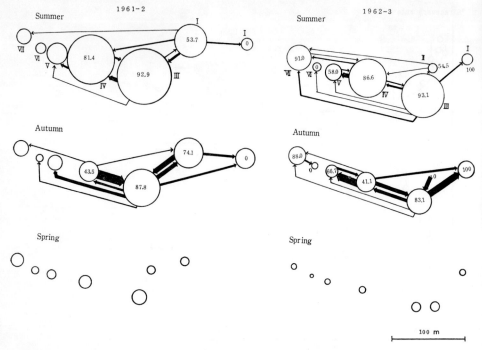

Fig. 8. Schematic representation of changes in adult numbers in different subpopulations and the interconnection by movements between them. The centre of each circle indicates the approximate location of a patchy habitat, and the area of the circle is proportional to population size. Numerals in the circle indicate the percentage of resident recaptures to total recaptures from a group of marked individuals that were released in a given patch at the time of adult emergence. An arrow indicates the direction of movement and the thickness of line is roughly proportional to the number of emigrants. Amounts of migration from summer to the next spring could not be determined. (see text). Also, no marked insects were liberated in patches V–VII in the summer of 1961.

The low percentage of recaptures is not only due to mortality but also due to detachment of marks during the 10-month period. In 1962, the rates of detachment of marks were estimated by double-marking method given by Beverton and Holt (1957). The method is based on the assumptions that the detachment of marks is due to a local event operating on each mark independently, and that the instantaneous rate of detachment of marks is constant over the period under consideration. The rate of detachment of marks can be assessed by another way: From the distribution of recaptures in autumn (see Fig. 8) it is inferred, with assurance, that there was no emigration from, and immigration into, the study area by this time, so that the difference between the proportion of marked adults in the summer and autumn populations must be entirely due to detachment of marks. Then, the following relationship can be deduced by assuming a constant rate of detachment of marks:

$$p_t / p_o = e^{-at}$$

where p_o and p_t are the proportion of marked insects in the summer and autumn popula-

138

Table 2. Distribution of recaptures in spring from groups of individuals that were marked and released in summer or autumn of the previous year.

Recaptured in the next spring from:	Released in summer of:															Released in autumn of 1961 at patch:				
	1960 at patch:					1961 at patch:				1962 at patch:										
	I	III	IV	VII	C I	I	II	IV	V	I	II	III	IV	V	VII	I	III	IV	V	VII
I	1*	3				2*	1									1*		1		
II						2											1			
III	2	4*				2	1*	2					4			2	2*			1
IV		2				1					1		1*	1		1			3	1
V									1										1*	
VI																				
VII				2*		1	1	2					1			1				12
C I					1*															
C II					1															
total number released	2275					2425				1997						514				
% recoveries	0.7					0.7				0.4						5.3				

*Figures indicate the number of marked adults that were recaptured from the same patches.

tions, respectively, and a indicates the rate at which marked individuals lose their marks per month. This method can be applied to the data for 1961 and 1962.

The expected proportion of marked insects in the spring population, calculated by these methods, agrees reasonably well with the observed proportion (Table 3). Since virtually no detachment of marks occurred during the first month after marking, the assumption of constant instantaneous rate of detachment is valid only as a crude approximation. Nevertheless, the above-mentioned results indicate that there was no population interchange between the study area and the surrounding area. This conclusion is consistent with the results from surveys that were carried out occasionally in the neighbouring area. Thus, the population in the whole study area is considered to be nearly self-contained at least during the period of this study.

Table 3. Estimation of rate of detachment of marks.

Time of release	Number released	% marked in population			Expected % marked		
		summer	autumn	spring	in autumn	in spring	
					method I	method I	method II
summer 1962	1997	59.5	37.2	5.4	34.3	3.8	5.4
autumn 1962	506	–	72.1	14.0	–	13.6	13.4
summer 1961	2435	35.0	22.4	7.0	–	–	3.8
autumn 1961	514	–	35.4	11.7	–	–	7.4

Method I: double-marking method (Beverton & Holt, 1957). Loss rate per mark per month 0.300. This value was then corrected by the average number of marks per individual.
Method II: see text. Loss rate per individual per month 0.240.

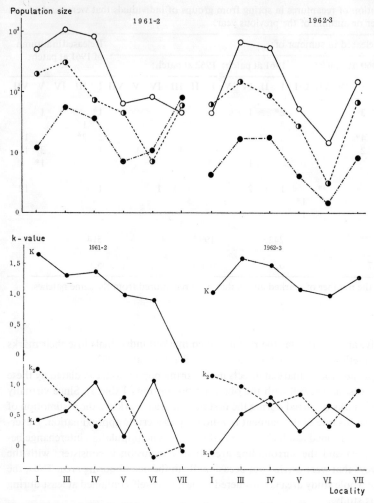

Fig. 9. Comparison of within-generation changes in adult numbers among subpopulations. The upper figure shows the changes in numbers from summer (open circles), through autumn (semi-solid circles), to the next spring (solid circles). The lower figure indicates by k-values the variation in 'mortality' (k_1: from summer to autumn; k_2: autumn to spring).

Fig. 10. Relationship between density and the rate of population change during successive periods of adult life. Solid circle: 1961; open circle: 1962.

140

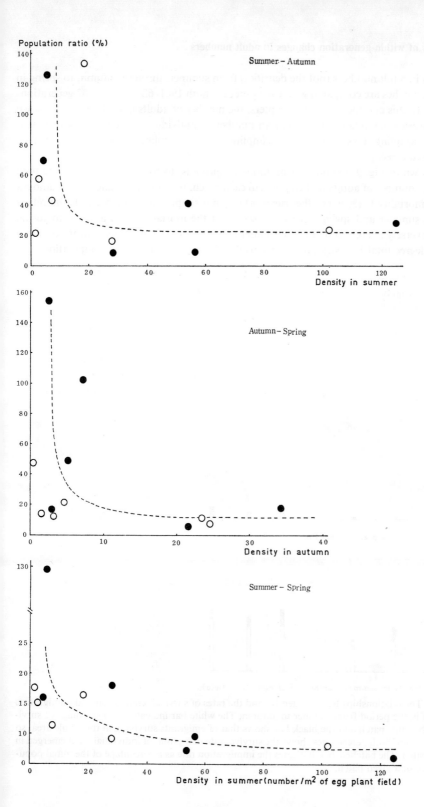

141

Analysis of within-generation changes in adult numbers

Changes in adult numbers (not the densities) from summer, through autumn, to spring in different patches are compared with each other for both 1961–62 and 1962–63 generations (Fig. 9). In this and the following chapters, the number of adults in each season is shown by the average abundance, i.e. the mean number of individuals caught over 4 or 5 consecutive sampling days corrected by sampling ratio. (Sampling ratio was estimated by marking-and-recapture data).

As shown in Fig. 9, the number of adults in spring is, to some extent, correlated with the initial number of adults that emerged in each patch, but also it is related to the amount of total mortality K (K is not the true mortality but simply the difference in log numbers between summer and spring). It can be seen that the mortality from autumn to spring (k_2) is inversely related to that from summer to autumn (k_1) in both generations but, to a certain degree total K is still positively correlated with the initial size of population.

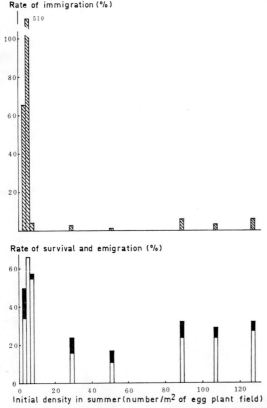

Fig. 11. The relationships between density and the rates of survival, emigration and immigration of adults in the period from summer to autumn. The white bar indicates the percentage of survivors in the same patch and the black bar shows that of emigrants surviving in the whole area, so that the sum of both percentages shows the survival rate of a group of individuals that emerged in a given patch. The hatched bar indicates the immigration rate as a percentage of the initial population size in a given patch.

142

Since adults feed on several different food plants, it is somewhat difficult to determine what is the reasonable criterion on which to detect density relationships. Here, we have adopted the mean number of individuals per m² of egg-plant field in each patch. This is because other plants are withered up by September and the presence of egg plant is essential for the maintenance of subpopulations in a patch. Then, the rate of population change is expressed by the ratio of population sizes (absolute numbers) during the two successive seasons and this is plotted against density.

As shown in Fig. 10, there is a clear negative relationship between the initial density and the population ratio in any of the periods of summer-autumn, autumn-spring, or summer-spring, thus indicating the presence of some density-stabilizing processes in the adult stage. Since population interchange occurred between patches, in some places the numbers even increased at a later season. From the recapture data of marked adults in autumn, we can estimate the proportion of immigrants in a given subpopulation and that of emigrants among the total survivors that were originally living in the same patch. Then we can get approximate estimates of the rates of immigration and emigration as well as the survival rate in terms of the initial population in summer, even when some marks were detached by autumn. As shown in Fig. 11, the rate of emigration has no clear relationship with initial density, whereas the rate of immigration tends to be high at low initial densities. Also, the total survival rate (ratio of residents plus emigrants to initial population) becomes low at high densities, indicating the operation of some density-dependent mortality process. Thus, the negative relationship between summer density and the rate of population change between summer and autumn seems to result from both higher rates of immigration and survival at low initial densities. The result can be interpreted in either of the following two ways: (1) Dispersal occurred density dependently, but high mortality during dispersal as well as influences of other factors (e.g., qualitative composition of food plants in a patch and distance between patches) and sampling errors masked density dependence in the rate of successful emigration; or (2) The dispersal process was essentially independent of density, and some density-dependent mortality took place in resident populations. In either case, high rates of immigration at low initial densities may result from a density-unrelated redistribution of migrants among patches (see Discussion). Since our observation has suggested no important mortality factor that possibly acts on a resident population density dependently, the case (1) seems to be more plausible.

No further analysis can be made for the autumn-spring period because of the small number of recaptures in spring.

Changes in numbers over several generations

Although we have no long-term population data, the changes in numbers of spring adults during 4 consecutive generations from 1960 to 1963 have been recorded for patches I, III, V and VII. These are considered to be representative of the population trend in the study area during this period of time. As shown in Fig. 12, the total population of spring adults in these patches was relatively stable; during these 4 years, the difference between the highest and lowest numbers was only two times. This resulted from different population trends in different patches; the numbers were fairly constant in patches III and V but fluctuated remarkably in VII.

The number of potato plants cultivated in each year differed to some extent; the total numbers were 1134, 970, 1161 and 766 for 1960–1963, respectively. The number of spring

143

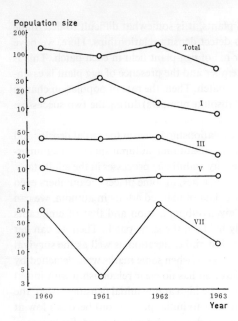

Fig. 12. Annual fluctuation in numbers of adults in the reproductive season.

adults appearing in a particular year was independent of the number of potato plants in that year, but somewhat related to the number of potato plants in the previous year. Therefore, the ratio of adult numbers (not the densities) between two successive generations is plotted against the population density in the first of the two generations, in order to detect a density relationship (Fig. 13). As can be seen from the figure, there is a clear tendency for there to be a density-related reduction in the rate of population change in both the total populations and the subpopulations in the different patches. The available

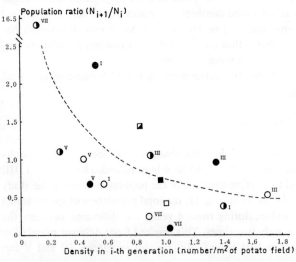

Fig. 13. Relationship between density and the rate of population change during two successive generations. A rectangle indicates the total population and a circle indicates a composite subpopulation. Solid symbol = 1960–61; semi-solid = 1961–62; open = 1962–63.

evidence, given in the foregoing chapters, indicates that the stabilization of density in local patches is more or less related to the relative amounts of emigration and immigration as well as to some density-dependence in larval and adult mortalities, the latter of which may be responsible for the stablization of numbers in the whole study area.

Discussion

As outlined above, the spatio-temporal dynamics of numbers in a natural population of this phytophagous insect involves complex processes. The species requires potato plant for reproduction in spring, egg plant and some other plants for adult feeding during summer and autumn, and hibernation places (leaf litter, various kinds of crevices) in winter. Since it has a limited mobility, the combination of these habitat components within a short distance is very important for survival of individuals. Although the hibernation sites seem to be available anywhere in the study area, the food plants are distributed patchily with varying combinations and quantities. Accordingly, the population is split up into subpopulations. Under such circumstances, for an understanding of the dynamics of the whole population under study we should analyze the changes in numbers in the respective subpopulations and their interrelationships. The results presented here indicate that larval competition for food, population interchanges by adult movements and density-dependent adult mortality from unknown cause are the important factors involved in the stabilization of numbers in subpopulations. Although no evidence has been obtained of density dependence in the rate of successful emigration, population interchange may tend to stabilize the density of each subpopulation and reduce the variation in density among subpopulations even if both exodus and redistribution of individuals among different patches occur density independently (Iwao and Kuno, 1970). However, it can not influence the population stability in the whole area unless it is associated with some mortality. Density-dependent adult mortality, possibly involved in the dispersal process, seems to be most important for stabilization of numbers in subpopulations as well as the whole population in the area.

Different patches in the area are different in their favourability and stability as habitats for the species; in a favourable patch, such as III, a fairly stable population was maintained at a high level and it formed a main stock of the population in the area. In a place like VII, the numbers changed violently from generation to generation, and the population there appeared to be frequently restocked by immigration from other patches. Some patches were available only temporarily for the insects. It seems likely, therefore, that the stability of the whole population in the area is basically guaranteed by the density-dependent processes going on in the subpopulations living in favourable patches, and it is reinforced by the occasional operation of such processes in subpopulations that are under less favourable or unstable habitat conditions.

Den Boer (1968) suggested that the splitting up of a population into subpopulations that are interconnected by migration may have a considerable effect on the stabilization of numbers in the whole population by the spreading of risk, even if the occurrence of mortality and migration are independent of local density. This possibility has been illustrated by Reddingius and den Boer (1970) through simulation experiments. Our observation suggests that the *Epilachna* population in the study area has been maintained over 18 years without violent fluctuation in numbers, though we have no quantitative data before 1960. The spreading of risk by splitting up of the population may be advantageous for the continued existence of the species in the area, but is seems not to be sufficient to keep such a small population, that comprises several hundred adults in the reproductive season, within a restricted range of fluctuation in numbers if no density dependent mechanism is included.

It may be worth mentioning that the study area is located in a southern fringe of the distribution range of this species; the actual boundary of distribution lies only 2 km south of the area. Since it is generally believed that in fringe areas the population is under strong influences of density-disturbing factors (e.g., Huffaker and Messenger, 1964; Richards and Southwood, 1968), the persistence of a fairly stable population in the study area is rather surprising. This may be due, partly, to topographical features of the area which make the local climate cooler and more humid than would be expected from its geographical location. And, the presence of sets of food plants as small patches may favour the survival of individuals of this species as mentioned earlier.

The rather complex environment of the insect discussed here is not an exception to the general case; the habitats for any species of animal are distributed discontinuously over a wide area, and their quality and quantity are constantly changing in space and in time. In the present instance, such a pattern simply occurs within a small area. In any study of animal population dynamics, therefore, changes in population size with time should be analyzed in relation to the spatial structure of the population under study.

Acknowledgments

I should like to thank Messrs Kuniyasu Mizuta, Hiroshi Nakamura, Jojiro Nishigaki, Tsutomu Oda, Tetsuo Okauchi and Yasuo Sato for their cooperation in the field work. Thanks are also due to Dr Eizi Kuno for his invaluable suggestions.

References

Andrewartha, H. G. & L. C. Birch, 1954. The distribution and abundance of animals. Chicago.

Beverton, R. J. H. & S. J. Holt, 1957. On the dynamics of exploited fish populations. London.

Boer, P. J. den, 1968. Spreading of risk and stabilization of animal numbers. *Acta biotheor.* 18: 165–194.

Ehrlich, P. R., 1965. The population biology of the butterfly, *Euphydryas editha*. II. The structure of the Jasper Ridge colony. *Evolution* 19: 327–336.

Ehrlich, P. R. & L. C. Birch, 1967. The 'balance of nature' and 'population control'. *Am. Nat.* 101: 97–107.

Elton, C., 1949. Population interspersion: An essay on animal community patterns. *J. Ecol.* 37: 1–23.

Ford, E. B., 1964. Ecological genetics. London.

Huffaker, C. B. & P. S. Messenger, 1964. The concept and significance of natural control. In: P. de Bach (Ed.), Biological control of insect pests and weeds. p. 74–117. London.

Iwao, S. & E. Kuno, 1971. An approach to the analysis of aggregation pattern in biological populations. In: G. P. Patil, E. C. Pielou & W. E. Waters (Ed.), Statistical ecology, Vol. I, p. 461–513, Pennsylvania State University Press.

Iwao, S., K. Mizuta, H. Nakamura, T. Oda & Y. Sato, 1963. Studies on a natural population of the large 28-spotted lady beetle, *Epilachna vigintioctomaculata* MOTSCHULSKY. I. Preliminary analysis of the overwintered adult population by means of marking-and-recapture method. *Jap. J. Ecol.* 13: 109–117.

Jolly, G. M., 1965. Explicit estimates from capture-recapture data with both death and immigration- Stochastic model. *Biometrika* 52: 225–247.

Reddingius, J. & P. J. den Boer, 1970. Simulation experiments illustrating stabilization of animal numbers by spreading of risk. *Oecologia* 5: 240–284.

Richards, O. W. & T. R. E. Southwood, 1968. The abundance of insects: Introduction. In: T. R. E. Southwood (Ed.), Insect abundance. *Symp. R. ent. Soc., Lond.* 4: 1–7.

Southwood, T. R. E. & W. F. Jepson, 1962. Studies on the population of *Oscinella frit* L. (Dipt.: Chloropidae) in the oat crop. *J. Anim. Ecol.* 31: 481–495.

Thompson, W. R., 1939. Biological control and the theories of the interactions of populations. *Parasitology* 31: 299–388.

Thompson, W. R., 1956. The fundamental theory of natural and biological control. *A. Rev. Ent.* 1: 379–402.

Varley, G. C. & G. R. Gradwell, 1960. Key factors in population studies. *J. Anim. Ecol.* 29: 399–401.

Discussion

Participants: Iwao (Author), Andrewartha, Baltensweiler, Reddingius, Solomon, Southwood, Varley, Watt and Way

The discussion opened on the possible causes of the stability of the population studied –

Perhaps the population is stable because the amount of resource is kept relatively stable by the farmer, who will plant about the same quantity each year, independent of the density of *Epilachna* in the previous year. Hence, there would be a limited and rather constant amount of resource (ANDREWARTHA). Were the insects at all short of food, so that they may have been limited by the food supply (SOLOMON)? Stability in the annual supply of food plants certainly is a basic requirement for the maintenance of a stable population in the area as a whole. The beetles cause heavy destruction of plants in some patches, but never affect more than about a quarter of the crop in the area. The process of stabilization of numbers is, therefore, more complex than a simple story of absolute food shortage (AUTHOR).

While movements between subplots is levelling out numbers in different local populations, there must also be movement out of the area of investigation. Could this be acting in a density dependent manner and help to explain the observed adult 'mortality' (WAY)? Marked individuals released in the study area were always recaptured within it. Cumulative recaptures of beetles within the area tended to change with changes in density in a way that suggests that there is higher mortality at higher densities (AUTHOR).

The study area lies within a few kilometers of the southern limit of the species range. Is this boundery due to climate or due to lack of the egg plant (BALTENSWEILER)? Is there a sudden geographical discontinuity just south of the study area (SOUTHWOOD)? The distribution of the species has nothing to do with the distribution of the egg plant, but coincides approximately with the isocline of average annual temperature of 14 °C. The valley where the beetles live is cool and shady, whereas a few kilometers to the south the country opens up and the temperature is higher. This may form a climate barrier (AUTHOR).

The discussion then turned to a consideration of the best way to detect density-dependence.

If N_{t+1}/N_t is plotted against N_t, this will produce a hyperbola, even with random numbers (WATT). Random numbers have a lower and upper limit (Eberhardt: *Ecology* 51 (1970) 306) and this in a broad sense is equivalent to the assumption of some density-dependent mechanism (AUTHOR). The appropriate test is plotting N_{t+1} against N_t (WATT). I agree with Watt, see Varley and Gradwell (1968) (VARLEY). I do not agree, because it makes no difference whether you plot N_{t+1}/N_t or N_{t+1} against N_t; in both cases you may obtain a suggestion of density-dependence even when it is absent. This problem is discussed in : Reddingius, Gambling for existence. *Bibl. Bioth.*, 8.2 (in press) (REDDINGIUS).

Proc. Adv. Study Inst. Dynamics Numbers Popul. (Oosterbeek, 1970) 148–158

Adaptation of Arctocorisa carinata (Sahlb.) and Callocorixa producta (Reut.) populations to a rock pool environment

V. Ilmari Pajunen

Department of Zoology, University of Helsinki, Helsinki, Finland

Abstract

The rock pools of the outer archipelago of the Baltic are inhabited by two boreoalpine species of Corixidae, *Arctocorisa carinata* and *Callicorixa producta*. The adaptation of the species to their heterogeneous and fragmentary environment rests on their high capacity for dispersal by flight and their high reproductive capacity, making rapid repopulation possible after rapid areal changes caused by periods of drought. The adults are able to choose shallow temporary pools for the reproductive period, and they choose large deep pools in the autumn since they overwinter in places where free water remains below the ice. Factors limiting reproduction include an arrest of ovarian maturation in females during the late reproductive period and an eating of eggs, but the continuous existence of populations seems mainly to rest on the effect of the heterogeneous environment, making reproduction successful in at least some subunits of the habitat.

In evaluating the significance of the heterogeneity of the environment for population dynamics, an obvious line of approach is a comparison between related species, some living in a more homogeneous, others in a more heterogeneous habitat. As regards aquatic habitats small bodies of water have an inherent heterogeneity. They are more or less temporary, their distribution is often fragmentary, and even relatively mild external changes tend to have a more profound influence than is the case in larger bodies of water.

In Northern Europe, the Corixidae form a fairly homogeneous ecological group, whose members, however, are specialized for a variety of habitats, and a group of species favouring small bodies of water can be distinguished. In the Scandinavian fauna, two species, *Arctocorisa carinata* and *Callicorixa producta*, are extreme types which occupy only temporary rock pools of the outer archipelago in the area of the Baltic.

These rock pool populations are presumably cut off from the other parts of the ranges of the species, which in Scandinavia cover only Lapland and the Norwegian mountain area. Both species have a more or less typical boreoalpine distribution.

Since, in the Baltic area, the two species seem to depend solely on the bizarre habitat of rock pools which no other corixid species seems able to colonize permanently, they must be specially adapted to the peculiarities of this very heterogeneous and fragmentary habitat. This paper is an attempt to discuss these adaptations in the light of the results of work still in progress on the south coast of Finland, and to present a comparison with species living in more permanent habitats.

The life history of rock pool species is typical of most North-European Corixidae. The adults that have succeeded in surviving the winter leave the deep pools in May, oviposition starts in the shallow pools in late May and the first adults of the new summer generation appear at the end of June. These rapidly mature and continue oviposition up to the end of August. However, the females terminating larval development after the middle of July remain callow and do not oviposit until the following spring. Larvae of all five stages occur simultaneously for most of the reproductive period.

Rock pool corixids are predators, principally attacking chironomid larvae and other bottom-living animals. At least in the laboratory, they also attack planktonic Crustacea, culicid larvae, and presumably most living small animals.

Environment

The islands of the outer archipelago of the Baltic are characterized by open flat shores of Precambrian rock. Brackish sea-water and rain-water collect in the depressions of the rock, forming pools of varying size and permanence. Most of the pools are shallow, 10–40 cm deep, and their surface areas vary from $\frac{1}{2}$ to $10m^2$. Large deep pools are rare, distances of several kilometres between them being by no means exceptional.

Rock pools occur in great numbers on the islands of the outer archipelago of southern Finland and in the south-eastern archipelago of Sweden wherever the structure of the rock is favourable. The pools vary considerably, and a series of main types is readily distinguishable. New pools are continuously being formed as a result of land upheaval and those already existing slowly come to be farther from the water-line. The pools nearest the water-line contain brackish seawater and are frequently exposed to the waves. During periods of drought their salinity often rises to many fold. Farther from the sea, rain-water has a stronger diluting effect and ultimately the pools contain fresh water. The lowermost pools are occasionally exposed to wave action, which precludes the accumulation of bottom material; in less exposed sites the mineral and vegetable matter forms a sediment. Ultimately the pools are filled with moss and vascular plants, and end up as discrete small bogs. The pools may also acquire dissolved humus matter, or become contaminated with bird excrement. The classification of pool types has been discussed by Levander (1900) and Lindberg (1944); hydrographic data on different types were presented in Järnefelt (1940).

The animals living in pools generally use them as their sole or principal habitat. Most species have rather strict requirements, being specialized only to certain types of pools (Levander, 1900; Lindberg, 1944). Although the number of rock pool species is considerable, the community of a single pool is normally extremely simple, with simple food-webs, and accordingly is rather unstable. The most important predators are the two species of Corixidae, and one dytiscid beetle, *Deronectes griseostriatus*, which all seem to tolerate a variety of pool types.

Both species of Corixidae prefer fresh-water pools with little or no bottom material, but are normally lacking only from the pools nearest to the shore-line and from those with dense emergent vegetation. They tolerate even the brackish water of the Baltic, but do not live in the sea.

In addition to the spatial heterogeneity of the discontinuous pool habitat, with its diversity of pool types, the drying of the pools in summer and their freezing in winter cause profound temporal changes. The existence of the fresh-water pools is wholly dependent on rain; even a short spell of drought considerably decreases the available habitat, as the pools lose several centimetres of water by evaporation in a week. On the other hand, a single shower is often sufficient to refill most of them.

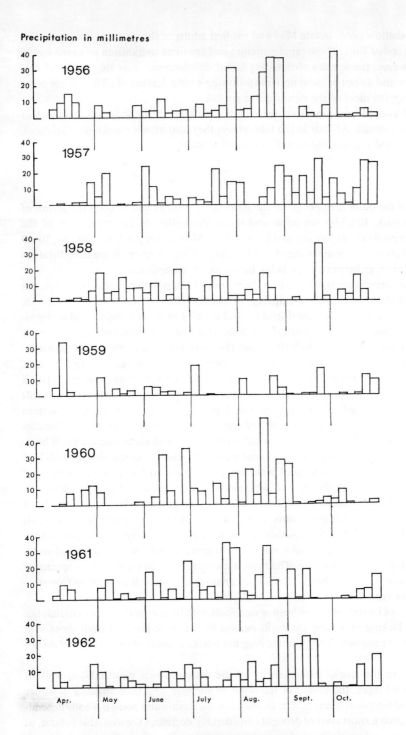

Precipitation in millimetres

Fig. 1. Rainfall expressed as total precipitation during five- or six-day periods for April – October of 1956 – 1969 on Russarö, southern archipelago of Finland.

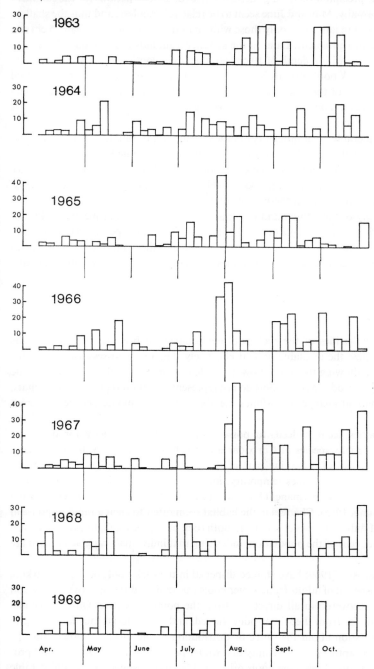

Fig. 1 shows the precipitation during successive five- or six-day periods for the summers of 1956–1969. Normally, May and June seem to be relatively rainless, and thus the shallow pools tend to dry out in late June; only those with an initial depth of more than 25 cm can be regarded as at all permanent. Later in the summer, rain falls more frequently, and in most years even pools with a depth of 10 cm can then exist continuously. Thus, the early breeding season of rock pool corixids is characterized by a decrease of pool area and pool number to about 10% of the area available in May, with a sudden and more permanent expansion of the area in late summer. Even during exceptionally rainy and dry years this pattern is usually observable.

There are considerable areal differences in the distribution of rain along the coast, and even during a serious drought there may be plenty of pools in some limited areas.

Most pools freeze totally in winter and only those with a depth of more than one metre have any free water left below the ice. Pools of this type are rare and only a few of the islands contain them. It is only in these pools that corixids can survive.

The heterogeneity of the habitat and the drastic seasonal changes in the availability of the pools are obviously not the sole factors limiting the number of species able to colonize them. For example, the high temperatures encountered and the profound daily temperature fluctuation considerably exceed the values normally occurring in northern aquatic habitats.

Dispersal

Regarding the peculiarities of the rock pool environment, it becomes clear that if the corixids are to utilize the available habitat effectively they must possess a considerable ability to disperse, allowing them to follow its sudden expansions in the spring and at the termination of dry periods. Winter pools do not represent optimum reproductive habitats, and a seasonal habitat change necessitates the ability to discriminate between different types of pools.

Rock pool species seem, indeed, to possess an exceptional capacity for dispersal. Although adults of many species of Corixidae are structurally capable of flight, in many cases the flight muscles of a varying part of the population may fail to develop fully, causing permanent, or sometimes temporary, inability to fly. Flightlessness seems to be more common in species of permanent habitats, the population differences observed being considerable (Young, 1965). Changes in the habitat seem often to elicit a rapid response in the frequencies of different types of adults. In both rock pool species, flightless adults form only about one per cent of the population, indicating that individuals capable of flight are highly favoured.

Pajunen and Jansson (1969) have studied dispersal in the rock pool species by marking and recapture. Dispersal of adults from winter pools was rapid, taking only two weeks, and individuals were recovered in all directions from the point of release. Only occasional records were made far from the winter pool studied, and the material thus failed to give any precise information about the range or distribution of the distances flown. But the low frequency of recaptures in the vicinity of a winter pool showed that only a small proportion of the adults in the shallow pools originated from this, suggesting a considerable mixing of individuals from different areas. Further evidence of the strength of the spring dispersal and the considerable length of the flights involved was obtained in years when the adults in the local winter pools were exterminated during strong winters. In these years a rapid repopulation from unknown sources was recorded. The spring dispersal thus resulted in an even distribution of adults in all suitable pools in May. Even solitary outer islands with no safe winter pools contain adults prior to the start of the reproductive period. The flight speed of corixids are of the order of one metre per second (Popham, 1952), and evidently winds considerably influence long-distance flights.

At the maturation of the females in June the dispersive activity diminishes, but marking studies indicated that even then an average of 5–10% of adults in *Arctocorisa carinata* and 10–20% in *Callicorixa producta* left their pools daily. Although the limited study area makes it difficult to assess the distribution of the lengths of the flights, long distances were evidently covered continuously. However, a considerable number of marked adults were repeatedly recovered from an area of 300 m in radius, giving an impression of a diffusion-like mobility through the pools available. As a result, larvae were subsequently found in every pool in the area, although the density of the overwintered generation was low and, at a given moment, not all the pools contained adults.

The flight activity of the adults can be described as spontaneous in the sense that it does not occur in response to adverse factors. The significance of this behaviour seems to lie mainly in the efficient utilization of all suitable pools as oviposition sites, so that successful reproduction is secured in at least some places.

During the periods of drought the adults move to the remaining pools, and at the start of rainy periods they readily repopulate the refilled shallow pools by ovipositing into them, and thus periods sufficiently long for completion of larval development are effectively utilized.

The greater mobility of *Callicorixa producta* allows it to use the shallow pools more effectively, and it is normally the dominant species in them in the late summer. In refilled temporary pools, several species of Chironomidae specialized to this habitat very rapidly form dense populations, and thus provide more ample food than is available in the permanently exploited deeper pools. As a result, *Callicorixa* is normally able to reproduce more effectively in late summer.

It is not known whether the adults are able to discriminate between pools with different densities of corixid larvae, but a random dispersal would be sufficient to cause the distribution observed.

In August, the flight activity tends to increase to some degree; the flight distances, especially, tended to become longer. This suggests that at this time, when an increasing proportion of the females are callow, the flights are more dispersive. In September, flight activity tended to remain at its former level in spite of the rapidly decreasing temperature; flight activity was terminated in November when temperatures fell below 10 °C.

In other European Corixidae, adults capable of flight seem to exhibit a corresponding seasonal variation in flight activity. There is a period of intense dispersal in the spring and autumn, while in the summer flights are less frequent, and some species do not fly at all (Brown, 1951; Crisp, 1962b; Fernando, 1959; Popham, 1964; Young, 1966). Species favouring small aquatic habitats seem to be more apt to fly (Brown, 1951). Popham (1964) has attempted to correlate the incidence of flights with favourable climatic factors, but innate dispersive tendency also clearly displays seasonal variation.

At the time of more intense dispersive activity in the autumn, the rock pool corixids also change their preference from small to large pools as destinations. The result is a marked increase in the numbers of adults in these pools in September – November. The topography of the surrounding terrain also has its effects, and in suitable places an increase of over tenfold in adult numbers has been detected (Pajunen and Jansson, 1969). A corresponding increase also occurs in medium-sized pools in September, but later they, too, lose their adults. Dispersal from shallower pools of larger area corresponds approximately to that from small pools; thus the increase in numbers is largely the result of a net increase in the numbers of adults arriving, rather than due to a smaller dispersal from large pools. Only in very deep pools does the low water temperature affect dispersal, here the animals that alight become trapped and are unable to take wing again. As pools with a large surface area are, in general, deeper, the adult behaviour is significant in securing a suitable winter habitat for a substantial part of the populations. However, many adults remain in pools that are too shallow, and the total winter losses always seem to exceed 90 % of the population.

Several other species occurred in the area studied by Pajunen and Jansson (1969), the most significant being *Sigara striata* (L.) in the shallow sheltered littoral areas of the Baltic, and *S. distincta* (Fieb.), *S. semistriata* (Fieb.) and *Corixa dentipes* (Thoms.) in a large pond on one island. Individuals of these species were regularly observed in rock pools in the autumn at the time of intense dispersal of the rock pool species, but only a few sporadic records exist for the reproductive period. These observations strongly suggest that rock pool species are peculiar in having a high summer flight activity. *Sigara nigrolineata* (Fieb.) was the only species frequently observed, a mass invasion to the area occurred (Pajunen, 1970a), but even this species was not able to colonize the pools permanently.

Reproduction

As the immature stages of corixids are confined to their pools, the drying up of pools and other sudden environmental changes cause a high mortality not encountered in more permanent environments. To compensate for these losses, the reproductive capacity of the species must be sufficiently high.

The rate of oviposition of rock pool corixids has been studied by confining solitary females in small plastic vessels immersed in pools for twentyfour hours. In order to gain an impression of the actual rate in natural conditions, only freshly caught females were used. Oviposition seemed to continue to the end of August, the mean daily rate in June – July being fairly constant, 8–10 eggs per female in both species. In August, oviposition was greatly influenced by food shortage in the study period, but in suitable conditions rates comparable with those of earlier months seem to exist.

Crisp (1962a) reported a daily oviposition rate of 2 eggs per female in natural conditions in *Arctocorisa germari* (Fieb.), a species taxonomically very close to *Arctocorisa carinata*, but preferring deep permanent habitats. Young (1965) has reported rates of 1.7–2.6 eggs per female in *S. scotti* (Fieb.) and 2.6–4.2 eggs per female in *S. dorsalis* (Leach) in the laboratory. From these few data it may be seen that the two rock pool species have a considerably higher reproductive capacity, as the total oviposition period seems in all cases to be the same.

In a single pool, the instability of a simple community strongly affects the success of reproduction. On occasions of food shortage, the corixid larvae, which constantly exploit nearly all the food available, have no alternative type of prey or other, less preferred, stratum of the habitat to move to. Accordingly, the pressure for the evolution of some specific mechanism limiting the density to the suitable level can be assumed to be considerable in pool populations.

154

However, the pronounced heterogeneity of the environment in general compensates for the instability of the individual pool. Even between the pools of a single island there are considerable differences in the density of corixids, caused either by different preferences for different pool types or by topographic factors influencing arrival at pools or flight, or even by random variation. Similar variation also exists in the populations of prey animals, species differing greatly in their habitat preferences and phenology. An example of this in pool chironomids is given by Lindeberg (1958). Even the vulnerability of the prey can be assumed to vary with the amount and composition of the bottom material. Thus, although the density of corixids in many pools may rise to a level causing acute starvation and high larval mortality, there always seem to be pools where this is not the case, and the great heterogeneity of the environment has a clear buffering effect on the population.

Two mechanisms limiting egg production exist in Corixidae. The first is an arrest of ovarian maturation in females completing their development in late summer. In rock pool species, only females moulting before the middle of July mature directly, the rest remaining callow until the following spring (Pajunen, 1970b). This diapause thus effectively limits the number of reproductive females of the summer generation in the later part of the breeding season. In normal years, their numbers seem to correspond closely to that of an average spring generation. Although the diapause has no regulating capacity, except possibly when an exceptionally dense spring population might have caused food shortage early in the season and subsequent retardation of development, it is of considerable significance. If the total reproductive capacity of the summer adults were fully expressed, the larval density would clearly exceed the levels allowed by habitat. Not much is known about the mechanism of the diapause. Some experimental evidence suggests that the larvae respond to the direction of the change in day-length, reproductive females only appearing when the day-length is increasing. This type of diapause is probably common in northern Corixidae, which are either univoltine or have a partial second generation; the difference evidently depending more on the rate of development in a given habitat than on species-specific factors (Young, 1965).

A second limiting factor is the tendency of the females to suck their eggs during oviposition. In rock pool populations the proportion of destroyed eggs in oviposition experiments showed a clear seasonal trend from nil in June to 20% in *Callicorixa* and to 25–50% in *Arctocorisa* in late July. The seriousness of the losses could be readily correlated with the level of food shortage and high density in the pools, the highest values being recorded at times when starvation had proceeded to the stage at which attacks were made on insects that had dropped on the water and there was cannibalism on moulting larvae.

The provision of adequate food during oviposition did not reduce the losses. The applicability of the results to the situations existing in the pools is not known with certainty, but the same general trend evidently exists.

When eggs were introduced into pools, losses of 30 to 90% were recorded during their development. The extent of losses could not be correlated with adult or larval densities, and was evidently mainly due to other predators.

The sucking of eggs forms an effective way to secure a rapid limitation of reproduction in the event of sudden food shortage. Prolonged starvation probably affects egg production directly.

The eating of eggs is not limited to rock pool species. Crisp (1961) has recorded losses of about 6% in a population of *Arctocorisa germari*. *Sigara scotti* has been found to destroy 2% and *S. dorsalis* up to 40% of their eggs in laboratory cultures (Young, 1965).

However, even in normal years the density of adult and larval corixids in preferred pools tends to rise to the level causing starvation. No quantitative data on the effects of predation on a pool community is at present available but, at least in pools with little bottom sediment, the increase in the numbers and size of corixid predators rapidly affects the numbers of chironomid larvae, and in many cases leads to total elimination of prey.

At the present, no quantitative data on the mortality of corixid larvae are available, but even qualitative observations seem to indicate that high densities mainly increase the mortality of young larvae, and thus the simultaneous presence of all five larval stages certainly acts as a stabilizing agent. This mortality may in part be due to cannibalism, but there are also indications that at high density young larvae are less viable, even when subsequently kept in optimal conditions in the laboratory. The high density seems also to lead to a decrease in the size of the larvae at later stages. Thus starvation results in compensatory mortality in the youngest larval stages, but the older larvae are possibly able to complete their development even in adverse conditions. With the resultant decrease in density, prey animals are able to recolonize the pools from other, less intensively exploited sources.

Thus no regulating mechanisms specific to rock pool species seem to exist. The populations are mainly maintained by the high fecundity of the animals and by the heterogeneity of the environment. Reproduction is always successful in some subunits, and adverse periods of drought and food shortage are always of short duration when compared with the rather long reproductive season of three and half months.

The adaptation of rock pool corixids to their environment is thus mainly based on a special behavioural repertoire; a strong tendency to fly, and an ability to choose pools suitable for the seasonally varying needs, according to a few characteristics. The two species are extremely similar in their behaviour, a fact indicating the narrowness of the niche available. Much of the continuous existence of populations is due to the fact that the environment is sufficiently complex to ensure that the conditions required always exist in at least some limited areas.

The size of the populations is ultimately determined by the availability of the habitat; a greater permanent pool area means a more successful reproduction, and an increased number of deep pools allows an increased winter survival. Even without quantitative data, it is apparent that the density of adults in the autumn is considerably higher in years with much rain.

References

Brown, E. S., 1951. The relation between migration-rate and type of habitat in aquatic insects, with special reference to certain species of Corixidae. *Proc. zool. Soc. Lond.* 121: 539–545.

Crisp, D. T., 1961. A study of egg mortality in *Corixa germari* Fieb. (Hem., Corixidae). *Entomologist's mon. Mag.* 96; 131–132.

Crisp, D. T., 1962a. Estimates of the annual production of *Corixa germari* (Fieb.) in an upland reservoir. *Archs Hydrobiol.* 58: 210–223.

Crisp, D. T., 1962b. Observations on the biology of *Corixa germari* (Fieb.) (Hemiptera, Heteroptera) in an upland reservoir. *Archs Hydrobiol.* 58: 261–280.

Fernando, C. H., 1959. The colonization of small fresh-water habitats by aquatic insects. 2. Hemiptera (The water-bugs). *Ceylon J. biol. Sci.* 2: 5–32.

Järnefelt, H., 1940. Beobachtungen über die Hydrologie einiger Schärentümpel. *Verh. int. Verein. theor. angew. Limnolog.* 9: 79–101.

Levander, K. M., 1900. Zur Kenntnis des Lebens in den stehenden Kleingewässern auf den Skäreninseln. *Acta Soc. Fauna Flora fenn.* 18 (6) 1–107.

Lindberg, H., 1944. Ökologisch-geographische Untersuchungen zur Insektenfauna der Felsentümpel an den Küsten Finnlands. *Acta zool. fenn.* 41: 1–178.

Lindeberg, B., 1958. A new trap for collecting emerging insects from small rock-pools, with some examples of the results obtained. *Suom. hyönt. Aikak.* 24: 186–191.

Pajunen, V. I., 1970a. A case of mass flight of *Sigara nigrolineata* (Fieb.) (Heteroptera, Corixidae). *Annls zool. fenn.* 7: 191–192.

Pajunen, V. I., 1970b. Phenology of the arrest of ovarian maturation in rock pool corixids (Heteroptera, Corixidae). *Annls zool. fenn.* 7: 270–272.

Pojunen, V. I. & A. Jansson, 1969. Dispersal of the rock pool corixids *Arctocorisa carinata* (Sahlb.) and *Callicorixa producta* (Reut.) (Heteroptera, Corixidae). *Annls zool. fenn.* 6: 391–427.

Popham, E. J., 1952. Observation on the behaviour of aquatic insects during the drying up of a moorland pond. *Entomologist's mon. Mag.* 88: 180–181.

Popham, E. J., 1964. The migration of aquatic bugs with special reference to the Corixidae (Hemiptera, Heteroptera). *Archs Hydrobiol.* 60: 450–496.

Young, E. C., 1965. Flight muscle polymorphism in British Corixidae: ecological observations. *J. Anim. Ecol.* 34: 353–389.

Young, E. J., 1966. Observations on migration in Corixidae (Hemiptera: Heteroptera) in southern England. *Entomologist's mon. Mag.* 101: 217–229.

Discussion

Participants: Pajunen (Author), van der Aart, Andersen, den Boer (P. J.), Frank, Jacobs, Kuenen, Varley, Whittaker and Wolda

To be sure that some characters of the corixids (behaviour of winged individuals, percentage of flightless individuals, fecundity) are adaptations to the unstable environment of the rock pools, some populations of these species living in more stable environments should be studied – if possible – as a comparison (WOLDA).

Is there a positive correlation between the oviposition rate and the total number of eggs laid per female (JACOBS)?

The oviposition rate is higher in rock pools, but the oviposition period is about the same there as elsewhere; thus, the total number of eggs laid in rock pools is higher. The observed higher reproduction rate in less stable habitats was explained in the paper as enabling the species to cope with the effects of less stable habitats. Another explanation might be: Rock pools (less stable habitats) are more shallow, and water temperatures are higher; these higher temperatures might result in a higher reproduction rate (VAN DER AART). My explanation was meant in an evolutionary sense. In more unstable habitats there must be some compensation for the greater chance of extinction, otherwise the species would not have been able to survive. The causal mechanism of this compensation might well be the favourable influence of higher temperatures (AUTHOR).

The situation in Lappland and other Fjäll-regions of Scandinavia is very similar to that in the Tvärminne archipelago. The same corixids live there in small rock pools which become completely frozen in winter, so that the animals have to disperse in the way described by Pajunen. The advantages of this way of life may be that the larvae of mosquitoes are concentrated in the small pools and are easy to catch in the shallow water (FRANK).

Do the animals fly during the reproductive period even when there is no obvious need to do so (shortage of food or high densities), and thus put their eggs in many different pools? Does this behaviour result in a spreading of the risk of larval death over a number of pools (DEN BOER)? The corixids fly spontaneously all the time. The smaller pools are relatively warm and stimulate flight. In the autumn the adults concentrate in the bigger rock pools because they begin to favour the pools with a larger surface area, and because these are often deep and cold and thus prevent further flight. This is the whole point; since the larger pools freeze less in winter they are also more favourable as a place to hibernate (AUTHOR).

Have known numbers been added to a pool to observe whether dispersal increases (VARLEY)? Enormous densities are necessary to cause significantly increased dispersal. If corixids are kept in small containers at very high densities they are likely to take wing (AUTHOR).

C. H. Fernando in Oxford found he could trap corixids using sloping sheets of glass and a detergent-filled gutter. Probably such experiments can help to study dispersal (VARLEY).

Are flights directed by wind direction or by the position of the sun (KUENEN)? I do not have many observations. Corixids are slow fliers and disperse in all directions. When they are flying, they move in directions given by the prevailing conditions; wind affects the direction of flight very much (AUTHOR). Corixids mainly fly by day (AUTHOR's answer to ANDERSEN).

Do the corixids alight on the surface of small inlets of the sea which are almost surrounded by rock and must appear very similar to rock pools (WHITTAKER)? I never found them in the sea, but in a sea-water aquarium the rate of dispersal is not greater than in the natural habitat. The pools near the sea have a special vegetation, the presence of which may exclude corixids. Perhaps the large body of reflecting water of the sea disturb their ability to find the pools close by (AUTHOR).

Proc. Adv. Study Inst. Dynamics Numbers Popul. (Oosterbeek, 1970) 159–173

Measures of wellbeing in populations of herbivorous macropod marsupials

A. R. Main

Zoology Department, University of Western Australia, Nedlands, W. A., Australia

Abstract

Populations of four species of macropod marsupials (wallabies and kangaroos) have been studied, viz quokka (*Setonix brachyurus*), tammar (*Macropus eugenii*), euro (*Macropus robustus*) and red kangaroo (*Megaleia rufa*). All show a decline in weght as the quality (nitrogen) of forage declines during seasonal drought. Analyses suggest that weight losses are also affected by salt loading and dehydration (the quokka), energy deficiency (the tammar) and dehydration and salt deficiency (the euro and red kangaroo).

In Western Australia, which spans a wide latitudinal range, the climate varies from tropical in the north to temperate Mediterranean in the south, and rainfall is always seasonal with summertime peaks in the north and wintertime peaks in the south. The resulting seasonal drought is of irregular duration and varying intensity and it is often possible, even for the casual observer, to see the deterioration of condition in animal populations. When field populations subject to drought conditions are intensively studied, e.g. by a repeated field census, it is possible to document the decline in condition and loss of weight of marked individuals and in many cases observe their death.

From the decline in numbers following such conditions, it is quite apparent that the populations change their size as the incidence of mortality on the adults and recruits varies. Populations living under such conditions offer the opportunity to interpret the data on changing body condition as it indicates morbidity and relates to population dynamics. In a sense these populations are not to be regarded as typical or representative; however, insofar as such populations allow the study of the way the individuals of the population respond to environmental conditions, they afford a simplified situation for interpretation.

Problems of interpretation of population data can be considered under the following headings:
1. Changes in total size of the population
2. Changes in composition, e.g. sex and age structure
3. Changes in recruitment
4. Changes in measures of wellbeing or general condition
5. Proximal causes of death
6. Changes in the carrying capacity of the environment consequent upon seasonal or other changes, especially as it regulates 1, 2 and 3 above.

Interpretations under 1, 2 and 3 are primarily limited by census and statistical considerations, while interpretations under items 4, 5 and 6 are limited by our knowledge of:

a. The needs of the animal
b. The way the animal satisfies its needs in the field situation
c. The way the animal withstands deleterious environmental conditions, e.g. heat, water deprivation, inadequate diet.

The distinction between b and c is to some extent arbitrary. However, despite this, the distinction offers a convenient and useful framework for analysis.

This paper discusses the above by reviewing published and unpublished studies on the seasonal condition and possible causes of mortality in a range of macropod marsupial populations subject to irregular or seasonal drought under contrasting environmental conditions (see Fig. 1).

The study areas for the species have been selected because they are readily accessible and have populations of a size and density suitable for study. Two of these populations are insular – the quokka on Rottnest Island and the tammar on East Wallabi Island, Houtman's Abrolhos. The euro and red kangaroo have been studied where they occur together on Mundabullenganah Station about 50 miles south of Port Hedland in southern tropical Western Australia (see Fig. 1).

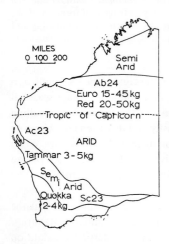

Fig. 1. Map showing localities where the 4 species of macropods were studied: quokka (*Setonix brachyurus* Quoy & Gaimard), tammar (*Macropus eugenii* Desmarest); euro (*Macropus robustus* Gould) and red kangaroo (*Megaleia rufa* Desmarest). The boundaries of the arid and semi-arid climatic zones are shown.
Symbols: A = arid; S = semi-arid; a = no marked season of precipitation; b = summer precipitation; c = winter precipitation.
1st digit indicates mean temperature of coldest month, 2nd digit indicates mean temperature of warmest month:
1 = 0° to 10°C; 2 = 10 to 20°C; 3 = 20 to 30°C; 4 = more than 30°C.
Arid lands classified after W. G. McGinnies, B. J. Goldman & P. Paylore, Deserts of the world. University of Arizona Press, Tucson, 1968 (1–XXVIII), pp. 788.

General biology of macropods

The four macropod species under review are herbivores and ruminant-like in their digestion (Moir et al, 1956). A characteristic of this type of digestion is that, in the large sacculated fore-gut, there is a fauna of protozoa and a flora of bacteria; these ferment and break down the fibrous ingesta during the relatively long period that it is held in the functional 'rumen'. As a result of this fermentation, the host derives its energy requirements as volatile fatty acids derived from the breakdown of cellulose, while its protein requirements are satisfied by the digestion of the abundant bacterial flora and protozoa as the ingesta passes from the foregut into the duodenum.

In order that such a system can function, it is necessary for the bacteria to have access to a readily fermentable source of energy. When energy is present, bacteria can utilize nitrogen sources other than protein or amino acids as a nitrogen source from which to synthesise their own protein. Thus it is possible for macropods to utilize urea as a protein source in lieu of casein in nitrogen balance feeding trials, and similarly to utilize injected

160

urea (by passing it across to stomach wall). It is possible that under appropriate field conditions, e.g. where the diet is low as a nitrogen (protein) source but energy adequate, the macropod could recycle its own urea to the 'rumen' where it could be synthesised to bacterial protein and then digested as a protein source so supplementing the dietary nitrogen. This system is thus potentially able to turn a waste product, whose excretion would require water, into a supplementary food source. Since the food plants in all the localities studied show a marked decline in protein during drought, recycling of urea potentially has considerable biological value.

The uniform development of ruminant-like digestion in all macropod marsupials, together with the attribute of such a system of utilizing low quality forage and recycling urea, suggested that the principal adaptation of macropods is to poor quality forage. As a consequence, a great deal of attention has been paid to establishing, by laboratory feeding trials, the precise nitrogen and energy requirements of the commoner macropods (Brown, 1964; Brown and Main, 1967; Brown, 1968). At the same time attention has been paid to the diet in the field. Analysis of the nitrogen content of common forage plants invariably shows low values during the peak of the summer drought. Nevertheless, it is possible that by selective grazing an animal could materially raise the nitrogen content of its diet. In order to establish whether this is so, Storr (1961) developed a method of identifying plant epidermis in faeces. By measuring the area of epidermis of each plant species in the faecal sample, Storr (1961) was able to convert his readings to volume of plant species eaten and, incidentally, determine either water or nitrogen ingested with food. Information gained in this way for the quokka is given in Storr (1964) and for the euro and red kangeroo in Storr (1968). Storr was also able to measure the daily dry matter intake of macropods (Storr, 1963). By means of the techniques developed, Storr was able to show that, as measured by the percentage nitrogen of the ingesta, neither the quokka, euro or red kangaroo could overcome the fall in generally available nitrogen during the season of drought (see Table 1).

Table 1. Nitrogen content (% dry weight) of ingesta – water content (% of wet weight) in brackets (data from Storr, 1964, 1968).

Species	Summer	Autumn	Winter	Late spring
Quokka	0.8–1.3	1.0–1.5	2.3–2.5	1.3–1.8
	(71–86)	(77–88)	(81–89)	(78–86)
Euro	1.3	1.1	1.0	0.8
	(62)	(55)	(48)	(31)
Red	1.6	1.2	1.1	0.8
	(77)	(57)	(53)	(30)

Concurrent studies on field populations of the four species showed that, depending on the duration and intensity of the drought season (which may vary from year to year), there is a more or less marked decline in the weight of field caught animals coincident with the middle and end of the drought (see Fig. 2 where data are presented for the four species). These data do not represent the results of particularly intense drought seasons – for example, Mundabullenganah had an excess of 17 inches (43 cm) of rain in the summer (January/March) of 1961. From laboratory trials on the quokka, euro and red (Brown,

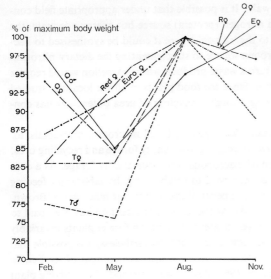

Fig. 2. Changes in weight during a year expressed as a percentage of the heaviest weight; quokka (Q), tammar (T), euro (E), and red kangaroo (R), Calculations from data in Main (1968) and Kinnear (unpublished).

1968; Brown and Main, 1967), and from field studies on the same species (Storr, 1964, 1968; Main, 1968), it seems fairly clear that during drought the nitrogen intake falls below the daily requirement and it is conceivable that starvation is reflected in the seasonal decline in weight.

Shield (1958, 1959) studied the quokka population on Rottnest Island over a number of years and showed that, coincident with the seasonal decline in the quality of forage (particularly in nitrogen) there is not only a weight decline but also a pronounced anaemia. The anaemia is not accompanied by either an increase in the white cell count or a rise in the sedimentation rate, and Shield (1958, 1959) interpreted the anaemia as a protein deficiency anaemia. At the same time, Shield showed, by means of the tooth eruption pattern of the skulls of recently dead animals, that the peak of mortality occurred during the period between the peak and end of seasonal drought. In a subsequent study, Holdsworth (1964) showed that individual animals could lose 30–40% of their body weight during drought, and that when this occurred they were subsequently caught only infrequently, suggesting that most had died.

The relationships between low protein level of the diet, low haemoglobin levels of the blood and low body weights of the Euro was shown by Ealey (1962) and Ealey and Main (1967). These workers showed that white cell counts did not vary and that sedimentation rates only rose when filarial worms were present in the blood.

Taken together the foregoing suggest a very simple picture, namely a herbivore specially adapted to taking advantage of low-quality forage with low nitrogen intake, yet suffering to such an extent from low plant-protein levels during each seasonal drought that there is a marked decline in weight associated with a fall in haemoglobin values and a marked anaemia. In the quokka, at least, these changes are implicated as being the primary factors leading to the considerable seasonal deaths recorded during severe drought on Rottnest.

The question arises as to whether the foregoing is the complete interpretation. Admittedly, in all species the weight changes are always associated with decline in quality of the forage, but drought is always associated with this event and drought is always associated

162

with change in energy status of the plants and reduced availability of water, which could possibly lead to water shortage and problems with electrolytes. It is clear that these questions have to be investigated and the results are given in the sections which follow.

Quokka and tammar

By holding field-caught quokkas in metabolism cages, Ramsay (1966) was able to establish the mean daily urine volumes of quokkas in the months of February (at the height of the summer drought, but the collections were made after 0.003 inches of rain), May (cool autumn) and October (warm late spring), 1965. At the same time, she was able to compare coastal and inland animals. Her results are set out in Table 2.

Table 2. Mean values and standard errors of urine volumes (ml/day) from Rottnest Island quokkas in 1965.

Month	Origin of Animal	
	coastal	inland
February (post-rain)	57.6 ± 22.9 (7)	51.6 ± 17.6 (18)
May	190.8 ± 34.5 (10)	158.4 ± 53.6 (8)
October	216.1 ± 40.2 (14)	171.9 ± 63.9 (13)

Although the table shows that inland animals always produced less urine than coastal animals, the differences only reach statistical significance in October ($P < 0.05$). Table 3 lists the concentrations of electrolytes and urea in the urine during the same months of 1965. The concentrations show considerable variation and Ramsay used the measured urine volumes to calculate the mean daily excretion of urea and electrolytes which are shown in Table 4. These data suggest that coastal animals excrete a good deal more salt than inland animals. Ramsay interpreted this as being due in part to the incidence of salt spray on plants in coastal situations. Looking at the data on electrolyte concentration of plasma and urine in Table 3, it seems that the high plasma sodium values of February 1965 (pre-rain) could be due to dehydration while the lower values for May reflect a relief from midsummer dehydration during the cool autumn. On the other hand, the high values for June reflect a salt load derived from the first spray brought ashore with the first winter storm. The low October and November values reflect the persistence of rain and plant growth into the spring without strong winds and storms.

The tammar on East Wallabi appears not to be salt-loaded by wind-borne salt spray. However, the island is considerably drier than Rottnest and yet it is apparent that the tammar regulates plasma electrolytes within closer limits than the quokka (see Table 5). Over the four sampling periods from February 1966 to April 1967 plasma electrolytes did not change. However, over this same period the plasma urea levels fell consistently so that by April 1967 the circulating levels were only half those of February 1966. The circulating levels of February 1967 and April 1967 are not significantly different, but they are both significantly lower than December or February 1966.

The urine urea levels show a different pattern. The early summer levels (December 1966) are significantly higher than at other periods. The two mid-summer levels (February 1966,

Table 3. Rottnest Island, 1965; quokka, both sexes, electrolytes and urea in plasma and urine

Month	Plasma			Urine		
	Na meq/l	K meq/l	urea mg/100 ml	Na meq/l	K meq/l	urea mg/100 ml
February 1965						
Coastal	152.5 ± 2.5 (6)	9.0 ± 2.2 (6)	22.3 ± 5.0 (6)	366.4 ± 120.4	84.7 ± 54.7	524.8 ± 347.3
Inland						
Pre-rain				318.5 ± 102.9	132.2 ± 41.8	964.5 ± 537.6
Post-rain				273.8 ± 87.8	117.6 ± 45.8	556.4 ± 298.3
May 1965						
Inland	138.9 ± 3.6 (18)	6.6 ± 0.9 (18)	–	134.5 ± 33.2	37.3 ± 15.4	364.8 ± 97.9
Coastal				177.9 ± 40.3	23.2 ± 5.3	264.0 ± 71.9
June 1965	151.7 ± 5.4 (6)	7.2 ± 1.4 (6)	22.8 ± 3.3 (6)			
October 1965	141.4 ± 4.5 (25)	5.4 ± 1.0 (25)	17.6 ± 3.6 (16)			
Inland				120.6 ± 34.6	43.4 ± 15.2	325.0 ± 119.1
Coastal				120.6 ± 24.6	34.7 ± 13.0	284.7 ± 91.4
November 1965	144.0 ± 2.1 (5)	5.8 ± 1.3 (5)	17.5 ± 3.2 (5)			

Tabel 4. Mean daily electrolyte and urea excretion for Rottnest Island quokkas

Month	A. Sodium excretion (meq/day)		B. Potassium excretion (meq/day)		C. Daily urea nitrogen excretion (mg/day)	
	coastal	inland	coastal	inland	coastal	inland
February (post-rain)	20.0 ± 7.6 (7)	13.4 ± 4.3 (18)	3.9 ± 1.8 (7)	5.8 ± 2.4 (18)	–	–
May	30.3 ± 6.4 (10)	17.2 ± 7.8 (8)	4.3 ± 1.0 (10)	4.1 ± 1.0 (8)	641 (10)	716 (8)
October	26.8 ± 5.6 (14)	20.2 ± 6.0 (13)	8.3 ± 3.0 (14)	7.5 ± 3.0 (13)	891 (13)	807 (13)

A. All coastal animals excrete significantly more sodium than inland animals.
B. There is no significant difference in potassium excretion between coastal and inland animals.

Table 5. East Wallabi Island tammar, both sexes – electrolytes and urea in plasma and urine

Month	Plasma			Urine		
	Na meq/1	K meq/1	urea mg/100 ml	Na meq/1	K meq/1	urea mg/100 ml
February 1966	142.3 ± 2.1	5.3 ± 0.8	24.8 ± 4.2	370.4 ± 74.4	150.5 ± 45.9	168.6 ± 77.8
December 1966	147.2 ± 2.4	5.8 ± 0.5	21.1 ± 4.5	366.0 ± 75.2	130.2 ± 35.0	324.2 ± 117.8
February 1967	145.3 ± 4.6	5.2 ± 0.5	15.2 ± 6.8	323.6 ± 59.9	118.2 ± 68.4	165.8 ± 119.6
April 1967	145.6 ± 3.9	4.9 ± 1.1	12.0 ± 7.5	427.3 ± 66.9	95.6 ± 16.6	95.9 ± 64.7

February 1967) are not significantly different from one another, but are significantly lower than the December 1966 levels and significantly higher than the late summer values for April 1967. These values can be interpreted as indicating urea recycling during mid and late summer.

During the period, urine electrolytes remained constant until April 1967 when sodium levels rose and potassium levels fell significantly. Such a pattern, of rising sodium levels in late summer, could indicate dehydration and that the animals were either contracting their fluid space and regulating plasma sodium levels, or supplementing the water present in their diet by drinking sea water. The significant fall in potassium in April 1967 suggests that tissue catabolism is not high, despite the lower body weights at this time (see Table 4B). Such an interpretation suggests that body weight reduction is largely caused by reduction of body water. On the other hand, if the urine is close to the maximum concentrating ability of the kidney, potassium derived from tissue catabolism may be retained. The plasma levels do not suggest that this is happening.

During the period February 1966 to April 1967, Kinnear (unpublished) attempted to see whether there was any limiting process in the nutrition of field animals. Having noted that the tammar is ruminant-like in its digestion, and that the nitrogen values of the forage fall during the summer, Kinnear hypothesised that nitrogen balance could be achieved only by recycling urea, but that this could be limiting if:
– insufficient urea was present, or if
– urea transport e.g. to the gut was limiting, or if
– the diet in late summer contained insufficient of a readily digestible energy source for bacterial metabolism. Such a state of affairs would have as its consequence an inability of bacteria to synthesise bacterial protein from recycled urea.

In order to check the above hypothesis Kinnear did the following in an appropriate statistical design:
1. He caught field animals and while they were held in the field cages he administered urea, collected urine and compared the amount of urea injected with the amount excreted. These experimental animals were then compared with untreated controls;
2. Field-caught animals were held in cages in the field and treated as follows: controls (no treatment), given urea, given starch (energy) or given urea and starch.

From 1 above Kinnear found that if urea is injected, animals will partially utilize the urea in December and April, suggesting that the microbial flora will fix more recycled nitrogen if the rate of flux is increased. No urea retention was found in February. When starch (2 above) was administered Kinnear found that it promoted the utilization of urea but that when starch and urea were administered together even more urea was utilized. These findings suggest that the flux – determined by plasma levels – and the energy level of the diet are both limiting during summer on East Wallabi Island, Abrolhos.

It is not clear to what degree these limiting factors have contributed to the decline in weight observed during the summer. However, it is clear that single factors alone, e.g. dietary inadequacies or problems of urea flux or problems of dehydration, are not uniquely responsible, and that the observed weight changes reflect the total influence of these factors. It is conceivable that the individual contribution of each of these factors to the total weight loss could be different in different summer seasons, but that the total loss (about 20 %) might be similar in every summer. It follows that while a measured weight loss may suggest that death is imminent, it is not by itself sufficient to suggest the proximal cause of death.

The euro was first studied in the Pilbara by Ealey (1962, 1967a, b, c), Ealey et al. (1965) and Ealey and Main (1967). From 1961 onwards, the euro and red kangaroo have been studied together at Mundabullenganah, a coastal situation in contrast with the inland localities at which Ealey worked. Ealey et al. (1965) showed that the total concentration of the urine did not vary throughout the year; however, the relative concentration of the constituents of the urine did vary. In particular, when water was scarce the amount of sodium in the urine relative to potassium increased, but decreased after drinking. In general the data from Mundabullenganah for 1961 (Table 6) agrees with that reported by Ealey et al; however, 1961 was a year of very good rainfall and the collection of February was immediately following 17.66 inches of rain (45 cm). During this sampling, water was abundant, forage plants were well hydrated and animals were not seen to drink. The data for both sexes of each species are given in Table 6. It is noteworthy that the average sodium values for euros and red kangaroos are much lower than those recorded for the quokka or tammar. On the other hand, urine urea concentrations are much higher. Furthermore, the standard errors of the values for weight and sodium excretion of the euro and red kangaroo are relatively greater than those for the two wallabies.

In order to study the reason for this greater variability among the kangaroos, I attempted to relate pes length (a measure of size), body weight and urine constituents. Previous attempts to regress body weight on pes length have shown a great scatter and low correlation (Sadleir, 1961). Storr (1968) followed Sadleir and explained the scatter by assuming that kangaroos grow throughout their life, and that young animals with long pes had yet to reach their adult weight. Storr's (1968) published weights of euros and red kangaroos for 1961 have been adjusted on the foregoing assumption. However, I used the same data as Storr and by ranking animals in order of increasing pes length and then within each pes length in order of decreasing weight, it was soon apparent that low body weight corresponds with low urine sodium excretions as indicated by low sodium/potassium ratios. In the samples collected, about 30 % of the animals had low body weights and low to very low urine sodium levels.

Since during February and May 1961 water and plant growth were both abundant, it is apparent that animals conserving sodium (low sodium/potassium ratio in urine) are depleted of sodium. If this is so, the low body weight suggests inability to take in water because of sodium depletion. It was thought that sodium depletion of such magnitude should be apparent from plasma sodium values. In April 1963 plasma sodium values ranged from 113 to 144 meq/l and, apart from some exceptions, showed a relationship of low plasma sodium and low urine sodium values. The coincidence of low plasma sodium values and low urine sodium values suggest sodium conservation.

From Table 6 it is apparent that the red kangaroo is excreting urine with high average urine urea concentrations throughout the year. However, in the euro urea values decline during May and August (Females: February vs. May $P < 0.01$, February vs. August not significant. Males: February vs. May $P < 0.02$, February vs. August < 0.01). This is at a time when the euros, but not the red kangaroos, are eating seed heads of native grasses. Collections of euros made during February 1962, November 1963, September 1964, January 1965, September 1965 and August 1966, show variations in the foregoing depending on the season. In particular, the dehydration associated with the drought of January 1965 is reflected in the very high sodium values in the urine.

Table 6. Urinary electrolytes and urea measured in samples of euro and red kangaroo shot at Mundabullenganah in the months of February, May, August and November 1961.

Sex and species	February			May			August			November		
	Na	K	urea	Na	K	urea	Na	K	urea	Na	K	urea
♀ Euro	138 ± 102 (14)	344.6 ± 114.9 (14)	2144 ± 1017 (13)	145 ± 111.2 (17)	506.2 ± 113.6 (17)	767 ± 820 (12)	191.5 ± 107.7 (15)	476.3 ± 151 (15)	1294 ± 978.4 (10)	254 ± 116.6 (11)	407.3 ± 119.4 (11)	—
♀ Red	112 ± 74.9 (13)	422 ± 85.8 (13)	2085 ± 888.8 (12)	164 ± 122 (17)	499.7 ± 172 (17)	2607 ± 1055.6 (16)	324 ± 152.2 (11)	495.5 ± 162 (11)	1795.9 ± 1063.4 (11)	196.6 ± 169.7 (14)	539.6 ± 196.9 (14)	1274.8 ± 625.6 (10)
♂ Euro	138 ± 89.5 (7)	419.3 ± 94 (7)	2020.3 ± 1001.4 (7)	184 ± 92.9 (8)	398.8 ± 131.8 (8)	720.9 ± 631.7 (7)	283 ± 121 (10)	374 ± 119.7 (10)	588.7 ± 491.8 (8)	171 ± 86.8 (10)	429.0 ± 111.7 (10)	—
♂ Red	203 ± 84.6 (3)	375 ± 114.6 (3)	1832 ± 339.4 (2)	96 ± 28.7 (4)	612.5 ± 160.1 (4)	2314.5 ± 344.3 (4)	266 ± 139.6 (4)	425 ± 122.5 (4)	1445.5 ± 824.2 (4)	252 ± 95.2 (5)	545 ± 67.1 (5)	2582.8 ± 1752 (5)

It was thought that urine volumes would indicate whether animals were dehydrated or not. Since the daily excretion of creatinine was shown by Frazer and Kinnear (1969) to be constant for the euro, the total daily urine production was calculated from the amount of creatinine in a known urine volume. The values so calculated give no indication of gross differences in daily urine production between those with normal or with low sodium. These findings tended to confirm the opinion of Ealey et al. (1965) that the euro never consumes an excess of water. However, these calculations do confirm that the low sodium concentration of the urine is not due to dilution resulting from high urine flows (an unlikely event because the urine potassium values were usually high).

Finally it seemed that the difference in the urine solutes could only be due to one or a combination of the following:
– genetic differences with respect to sodium balance;
– dietary differences imposed because of choice of food plants by the animal, and the locality in which the animal chose to live and hence a restriction in the plants available as forage;
– differences with respect to shelter, particularly heat refuges. It was thought that poor or few heat refuges would lead to dehydration and a consequent greater need to drink.

The labour involved in making a complete dietary analysis, such as that done in 1961 by Storr (1968), was regarded as being too great so during the collections of November 1963, September 1964, September 1965 and August 1966, the food plants actually in the mouth at the time the animal was shot were taken as an indication of the diet. There was no difference between sexes in urine production (ml/kg/day) and electrolyte concentration, so the results were pooled. They are summarised in Table 7. The mean sodium concentrations are significantly different (p < 0.001) but mean urine production and potassium concentrations are not different. From the above it is clear that a grouping of animals depending on the mouth contents leads to a very clear dichotomy with respect to the urine sodium levels but not the calculated urine flow expressed as ml/kg/day. An analysis of the spinifex and other native grasses found in the diet and which grow in the deep sands showed no sodium. On the other hand, grasses such as *Cenchrus* and *Eriachne* which grow on loams and clays between the dunes show values of 0.0191 meq/g (Buffel), 0.3690 meq/g (Birdwood) and 0.4515 meq/g (*Eriachne aristidea*).

Table 7. Mean urine volume (ml/kg/day) and concentration of sodium and potassium in the urine of euros of both sexes feeding on *Triodia* and *Cenchrus*.

	Diet	
	Triodia	*Cenchrus*
Urine (ml/kg)	6.3 ± 5.9 (23)	6.4 ± 3.9 (14)
Sodium meq/l	43.7 ± 73.9 (23)	237.1 ± 108.1 (14)
Potassium meq/l	369.3 ± 127.1 (23)	390.1 ± 95.3 (14)

These findings show clearly that the differences in urinary sodium levels are due to differences in the diet. However there is also a relationship between low urinary sodium and low body weight (see earlier) which suggests an inability to rehydrate because of insufficient sodium. Such a situation could come about if an animal was situated in a home range with poor shelter and heat refuges so that it was repeatedly subjected to dehydration, contraction of fluid space and regulation of plasma sodium with attendant salt loss. Should it have a home range with few or no loamy or clay flats with salt-containing forage, it would be unable to rehydrate fully because it could not replace the salt lost. Analysis of the drinking waters in the vicinity of the study area showed sodium levels ranging from 4 to 40 meq/1. Under such circumstances euros could not replace the sodium lost unless they changed their home range.

Discussion

The biology of the four macropod species as outlined in the introduction gave a story which may be summarised in point form as follows:
1. The macropods are ruminant-like in their nutrition;
2. Ruminant-like nutrition allows the animal to supplement its dietary nitrogen by recycling urea;
3. Nitrogen values of forage plants show a seasonal cycle in abundance. The lowest values occur during seasonal drought;
4. Coincident with the decline in dietary nitrogen, field animals suffer a decline in weight;
5. In the quokka weight losses are associated with a pronounced protein deficiency anaemia;
6. Severe weight loss appears not to be accompanied by symptoms of disease but often leads to the death of the animal;
7. The foregoing may be generalised by stating that weight losses during times of drought are likely to be due to decline in nutritional (principally nitrogen)levels of the diet, and that weight loss is a manifestation of the incidence of malnutrition or starvation.

Such an explanation, while plausible, does not take into account the other changes, e.g. the availability of water, taking place concurrently with the decline in dietary nitrogen, and it has been the purpose of this review to compare the four species with respect to other measures of their physiological state.

In summary the findings show:
1. Urine sodium levels rise during drought as would be expected if the animals were conserving water with ADH;
2. The mainland species (euro and red kangaroo), but not the insular species (quokka and tammar), show exceedingly low urine sodium levels during and just following the break of drought;
3. In the euro and red kangaroo, low urinary sodium levels frequently correspond with low body weights;
4. Urinary urea levels show great variability;
5. In the euro, the low urinary urea levels correspond with times when grass seeds are abundant and being eaten;
6. Low urinary urea values suggest that urea is being recycled;
7. With the tammar, field experiments at East Wallabi Island suggest that early in the summer nitrogen is limiting and more urea could be recycled; later in the summer it seems that both nitrogen and energy are in short supply;
8. It is likely that the environment of the quokka is similar to that of the tammar with respect to shortage of nitrogen and energy in late summer;
9. Neither the quokka nor the tammar is short of salt. The qoukka is salt loaded during early winter and the tammar may have to supplement plant water by drinking sea water late in the summer drought;

170

10. Low urinary sodium values and low body weights suggest that such animals have undergone repeated cycles of dehydration during which sodium was excreted. The subsequent replacement of lost water was dependent on replacement of lost sodium, and this was in short supply;

11. The sodium level of forage plants is dependent on the soil type on which the plant occurs. Plants on loams and clays have adequate salt; those on sand have a negligible sodium content. Drinking waters have low sodium content;

12. Whether animals are subject to dehydration and salt deprivation will depend on two factors:

a. The site of the home range, the included soil types and the kind of plants found growing there;

b. The nature of the heat refuges within the home range. Good heat refuges will allow the animal to be economical with respect to water, while poor refuges will cause the animal to expend much water in heat regulation with a consequent increased risk of dehydration and salt loss. Those animals with a home range on clay or loam soils and poor heat refuges but with access to drinking water, will be better off than those with home range on sandy soils and access to drinking water.

The significance of the foregoing for the size of the population of any of the species in an area lies in the carrying capacity of the land. In general we may say that populations will be high when the carrying capacity is high. Usually we do not specify what makes for high carrying, but we commonly regard adequate food and shelter as being the prime regulating factors. The data on the field populations of the four macropods indicate that the components of food are complex, and that the interactions between these components and the quality of shelter are quite intricate.

In the presence of energy, a shortage of nitrogen is not likely to lead to great and rapid loss of weight. Without energy, however, recycling cannot proceed and in such a case, and irrespective of the adequacy of N in the diet, N deficiency may be apparent as anaemia or weight loss.

Shortage of water will be accentuated when shelter is inadequate and will lead to dehydration. Dehydration becomes more serious when plasma sodium levels are regulated and there is no ready source in the environment from which sodium can be replaced. In such cases, animals remain in voluntary dehydration and may show considerable weight reduction even in the presence of adequate nitrogen and energy in the diet.

In an earlier paper (Main, 1968), I proposed that the carrying capacity of land with respect to kangaroos and wallabies could be defined by the amount of nitrogen fixed in the system. From the foregoing, it is clear that nitrogen will only limit the carrying capacity in cases where salt is not limiting.

It should also be noted that, from Table 6 and individual records, when urea excretion is high, sodium excretion is low; similarly, when urea excretion is low (presumed recycling) sodium excretion is high. Should these apparent relationships be a physiological necessity, then it is apparent that sodium-depleted animals will be at a disadvantage if they should also be ingesting a nitrogen deficient diet.

Drought-induced weight loss may be a prelude to death; but, without a good deal of natural history knowledge, one cannot ascribe the population mortality during drought to any particular one of the following possible causes: prolonged nitrogen deficiency, energy deficiency, salt deficiency, water deficiency, inadequate shelter.

It is likely that, prior to European settlement, kangaroos were more restricted in their distribution due to an absence of drinking water. In these times, they were limited by the abundance of good heat refuges. With the advent of pastoral settlement, the supply of abundant drinking water has allowed the species to expand, and the limiting factor is now the ability to restore the salt balance after dehydration.

Acknowledgments

The work reported has been supported by grants from: the CSIRO for work on marsupials, the University of Western Australia Research Grants Committee and the Australian Research Grants Committee.

Professor H. Waring and Dr S. D. Bradshaw read and criticised the manuscript. J. E. Kinnear kindly permitted me to use some of his unpublished data on the Abrolhos Islands. B. T. Clay and P. S. Kennington assisted in gathering the field data and performed the subsequent chemical analyses.

References

Brown, G. D., 1964. The nitrogen requirements of macropod marsupials. Ph. D. thesis, University of Western Australia, pp. 224.

Brown, G. D., 1968. The nitrogen and energy requirements of the Euro *Macropus robustus* and other species of macropod marsupials. *Proc. Ecol. Soc. Aust.* 3: 106–112.

Brown, G. D. & A. R. Main, 1967. Studies on marsupial nutrition. V. The nitrogen requirements of the Euro *Macropus robustus*. *Aust. J. Zool*, 15: 7–27.

Ealey, E. H. M., 1962. The biology of the euro. Ph. D. thesis, University of Western Australia, pp. 313.

Ealey, E. H. M., 1967a. Ecology of the euro *Macropus robustus* (Gould) in North-western Australia. 1. The environment and changes in euro and sheep populations. *CSIRO Wildl. Res.* 12: 9–25.

Ealey, E. H. M., 1967b. Ecology of the euro *Macropus robustus* (Gould) in North-western Australia. 2. Behaviour movement and drinking pattern. *CSIRO Wildl. Res.* 12: 27–51.

Ealey, E. H. M., 1967c. Ecology of the euro *Macropus robustus* (Gould) in North-western Australia. 4. Age and growth. *CSIRO Wildl. Res.* 12: 67–80.

Ealey, E. H. M., P. J. Bentley & A. R. Main, 1965. Studies on water metabolism of the hill kangaroo *Macropus robustus* (Gould) in Western Australia. *Ecology* 46: 473–479.

Ealey, E. H. M. & A. R. Main, 1967. Ecology of the euro *Macropus robustus* (Gould) in North-western Australia. iii. Seasonal changes in nutrition. *CSRIO Wildl. Res.* 12: 53–65.

Fraser, E. Hope & J. E. Kinnear, 1969. Urinary creatinine excretion by macropod marsupials. *Comp. Biochem. Physiol.* 28: 685–692.

Holdsworth, W. N., 1964. Marsupial behaviour with special reference to population homeostasis in the quokka on the West End of Rottnest Island. Ph. D. thesis, University Western Australia, pp. 196.

Main, A. R., 1968. Physiology in the management of kangaroos and wallabies. *Proc. Ecol. Soc. Aust.* 3: 96–105.

Moir, R. J., M. Somers & H. Waring, 1956. Studies on marsupial nutrition. I. Ruminant-like digestion in a herbivorous marsupial (*Setonix brachyurus* Quoy & Gaimard). *Aust. J. biol. Sci.* 9: 293–304.

Ramsay, B. A., 1966. Field nutrition in the quokka. M.Sc. thesis, University of Western Australia, pp. 152.

Sadlier, R. M., 1961. Fertility studies of macropods. Ph.D. thesis, University of Western Australia, pp. 162.

Shield, J. W., 1958. Aspects of field ecology of the quokka [*Setonix brachyurus* (Quoy & Gaimard)]. Ph.D. thesis, University of Western Australia, pp. 153.

Shield, J. W., 1959. Rottnest field station studies concerned with the quokka. *J. R. Soc. W. Aust.* 42: 76–78.

Storr, G. M., 1961. Microscopic analysis of faeces, a technique for ascertaining the diet of herbivorous mammals. *Aust. J. biol. Sci.* 14: 157–164.

Storr, G. M., 1963. Estimation of dry matter intake in wild herbivores. *Nature, Lond.* 197: 307–308.

Storr, G. M., 1964. Studies in marsupial nutrition. iv. Diet of quokka [*Setonix brachyurus* (Quoy & Gaimard)] on Rottnest Island. *Aust. J. biol. Sci.* 17: 469–481.

Storr, G. M., 1968. Studies on marsupial nutrition. Diet of kangaroos (*Megaleia rufa* & *Macropus robustus*) and merino sheep near Port Hedland, Western Australia. *J. R. Soc. W. Aust.* 51: 25–32.

Discussion

Participants: Main (Author), Jacobs, Jenkins and Watt

How much of the nitrogen requirements can be supplied by recycling? (JACOBS) In the laboratory, using a high energy diet, urea is as satisfactory as casein as a nitrogen source. In the field, the effectiveness of recycling will vary with energy intake. Up to 20% of the nitrogen requirement is possibly supplied in this way (AUTHOR).

How have these results been used in conservation planning? (JENKINS) Reservations for these animals must supply all the animal's requirements, such as sodium and nitrogen. The latter is only fixed by the blue-green algae and bacteria, and these provide nitrogen for the whole natural system. Reserves must therefore have a diversity of habitats. Even so, on the poor land available the carrying capacity is 1 euro per 30 acres and 1–3 red kangaroos per square mile. It is not feasible politically to take back the better land which is now being used by the pastoral industry (AUTHOR).

The work in Rhodesia has suggested that the efficiency of native game on native pasture in building up protein is greater than that of imported cattle. Would it not pay to crop these marsupials on the better land? (WATT) Macropods have a high protein/fat ratio; but since their metabolic rate is 2/3rd that of eutherians they take longer to produce the same weight of protein. This introduces a longer production routine. Also, in nature the animals occur at low densities, so that a high yield sustained harvest is not possible (Main, 1969) (AUTHOR).

Additional reference

Main, A. K., 1969. Native annual resources. In: R. O. Slayter & R. A. Perrey (Ed.), Arid lands of Australia, Chap 6. Australian University Press, Canberra.

Proc. Adv. Study Inst. Dynamics Numbers Popul. (Oosterbeek, 1970) 174–188

Feedback control by competition

H. Wilbert

Institut für Pflanzenpathologie und Pflanzenschutz der Georg August Universität, Entomologische Abteilung, Göttingen – Weende, West Germany

Abstract

The population can be described as an integral element of a system. Upon logarithmic transformation, the net rate of increase is the input variable and population density is the output variable of this element.

The net rate of increase is partly dependent on the 'degree of saturation' of the population with certain requisites. This degree is composed of the density of requisites as well as of the searching ability and the requirements of the animals.

If the animals compete for the requisites, competition acts upon population like a proportional controller. Consequently, it stops the variations of population density that are caused by independent variables (disturbance variables), but it cannot nullify them. Therefore, a definite final state of population density is coordinated to every combination of disturbance variables (and command variables). This state, however, is probably seldom attained because the disturbances change too frequently.

The degree of saturation with requisites is the controlled condition of a second control loop. It is controlled by the behaviour of the animals, which also acts like a proportional controller by changing the searching ability. In this loop, the feedback effect is attenuated by way of competition. Both control loops influence each other in a manifold manner.

If population is delineated in such a way that both control loops are enclosed, a proportional element results, because a definite final value of population density (output variable) is coordinated to every combination of values of the input variables. Consequently, in the long term, population density remains between finite limits if the variation pattern of the input variables makes those final states of the density which are too extreme either sufficiently improbable or so transient that they cannot be reached by the density. Additional controllers (enemy or prey populations), however, are able to confine or shift the range of variation of population density.

Who so ever wants to integrate his special field of research into the frame of sciences has at his disposal two main criteria. He may start from the concrete object or from the problem of his research. If he starts from the object, investigating population dynamics of pest insects for instance, he will consider himself an entomologist; consequently, he will strive to contact other entomologists. If he emphasizes the problem, he will meet colleagues who investigate similar problems with other animals. He shares with these colleagues a common field of inquiry; they all are working on population dynamics. If he proceeds one further step in this direction removing himself further from the object, he will debate with the disciples of that branch of science which claims to deal with any dynamic system, be it alive or artificial. That branch is called cybernetics.

Sharing common problems promotes the exchange of knowledge which results in new ideas, new problems, and new methods of solution. The general validity of such solutions, however, is naturally restricted. That which is taken over has to be carefully examined in every case. Such precautions also apply if one attacks problems of population dynamics by cybernetical way of reasoning in order to see what can thereby be gained.

Because I am not a cyberneticist I only hope to demonstrate here that concepts from the theory of feedback control can indeed be utilized at least to describe certain simple processes in population dynamics, and that by this means insight into more complex situations may be improved.

Mathematical formulations may be omitted in these general considerations; they are, however, indispensable for more detailed studies. Some of the processes that will be discussed here have not yet been investigated sufficiently by experiments. In such cases, theory is not supposed to substitute for experimental findings, but rather to indicate which kind of information is needed most. Of course the theory has to be revised or extended if experimental results so demand.

The population as an element of a system

Cybernetics deduces the dynamic properties of a system from the properties of its single elements and from the nature of their connexions. The population is such an element within a larger system (Watt, 1966; Mott, 1967) called 'Gradocön' (Schwerdtfeger, 1941) or 'Life system' (Geier, 1965). In a schematic diagram it is represented by a block (Fig. 1). The density of the population is of particular interest because it influences other elements of the system. Population density therefore, is the 'output variable' of the element population, represented by an arrow called 'line of influence'.

Fig. 1. The population as a single element with input variable (net rate of increase) and output variable (density).

If we express fecundity by the factor of increase per unit of time and mortality by the factor of decrease, then the total increase and decrease of population density depend on the ratio of fecundity to mortality (if necessary, immigration and emigration are to be included). I want to call this ratio here 'net rate of increase'. Some simplification is achieved if the logarithms are taken of these and all other quantities. Then the ratio is substituted by the difference between the logarithms. This difference is the 'input variable' of the population, represented again by an arrow. These lines of thought are further simplified by considering only populations with continuous reproduction, i.e., those having no distinct generations.

Very different types of elements exist in the theory of feedback control. All of them connect their outputs in various ways with the inputs. Some of them attach a definite value of the output variable to every value of the input variable. A heated room is an example of such an element, for a definite room temperature (output) corresponds to each definite heat supply. When the heat supply is changed, a new room temperature will arise after some transition time. In the most simple case, elements of this kind shift their output variables proportionally to the changes of the input variables; therefore, they are called 'proportional elements'. Usually they are so designated even if the relation between both variables is represented by a 'characteristic curve' that is more or less bent, because for practical purposes linear approximate functions are often used in such cases.

175

Other elements connect a distinct speed of change in their output with every value of the input variable. A water vessel with influx and outflow is an example. The water level (output variable) remains constant as long as influx exactly equals outflow and, accordingly, the difference between both (input variable) equals zero. If influx starts to deviate from this particular value, the water level begins to change. The more the influx differs from the outflow, the faster the water level will change. It does not stop changing until the influx has returned to its former value. Then the water level is constant again but on another value. Hence in this case, the value of the ouput variable (water level) is not directly connected to the input variable; it is rather proportional to the time integral of the latter. Such an element is therefore called 'integral element'.

Water vessel and heated room act differently because the vessel stores the water, whereas the room cannot retain the heat. The more its temperature increases, the more heat will pour through the walls into the surroundings per unit of time. Therefore, in the room an equilibrium is soon established automatically, but this is not so in the water vessel.

In which of these two groups of elements must the population be classified? Is it analogous to the water vessel or to the heated room? Support for both alternatives can be presented (see later). If, however, the whole net rate of increase of the population is defined as input variable (Fig. 1), then the answer is obvious. Density change is possible only by way of this input variable. The density remains constant as long as the net rate equals zero; it changes as long as the net rate deviates from zero. The speed of this change increases with increasing deviation. In this light, the population is an integral element. It houses the animals; hence it is analogous to the water vessel.

The influence of certain requisites on numbers in the population

The degree of saturation of the population

The net rate of increase is influenced by a great number of factors which need not be specified here. Only one of them will be considered in detail. All animals need some specific requisites which are often available only in a limited amount. Some of them – like food – are destroyed when they are used by the animals. In this paper it is assumed that such requisites are produced continuously. Other requisites, like many hiding places, are indestructible.

The need for these requisites can be met to a greater or lesser degree. Therefore, the net rate of increase is partially dependent on a variable that can be called 'degree of saturation' of the population with the requisites.

This situation can be shown schematically by a 'block-diagram' (Fig. 2). The net rate is composed of two components; one of them (b_r) corresponds to the share that the satura-

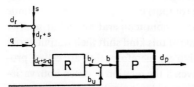

Fig. 2. Block-diagram: The net rate of increase (b) depends partly on the degree of saturation ($d_r + s - q$). P = population, R = transformation of the degree of saturation into fecundity and/or mortality, s = searching ability, d_r = requisite density, q = requirements per animal, b_r = component of the net rate of increase dependent on the degree of saturation, b_u = component of the net rate dependent on the totality of all other factors, d_p = population density. All values are in logarithms.

tion contributes to the total net rate, the other (b_u) represents the remainder. Both are connected (in the logarithmic model) by simple addition (but may as well be connected by a more complicated method). In the steady state condition of the population, b_r equals $-b_u$, because the total net rate (b) then equals zero.

b_r is the output of a further element R, which represents the transformation of the degree of saturation into the fecundity and/or mortality of the population. Consequently, the degree of saturation (logarithm) is its input variable. This degree, on the other hand, results from a division of the medium number of utilized requisites per animal by its requirements. These can be defined as the number of requisites per animal that enables b_r either to reach its maximum or to attain a certain mean value. In the logarithmic model, therefore, the degree of saturation is represented by the difference between the number of utilized requisites and the requirements (q) per animal.

In most cases, the animals have to search for requisites before they can utilize them. The mean number of utilized requisites per animal and per unit of time, therefore, increases with the density of requisites as well as with the searching ability of the animals. Searching ability at a fixed requisite density is here understood to be a combination of all properties that influence the number of utilized requisites (e.g., searching activity, capacity of sense-organs, ability to acquire encountered requisites). Hence searching ability depends on the species, but is dependent as well on the surrounding conditions such as weather (for dependence on saturation see later). If the units of measure are chosen appropriately, the mean number of utilized requisites per animal is equal to the product of density and searching ability; in the model it equals the sum of the logarithms of these two quantities (d_r, s). Consequently, saturation is equal to $d_r + s - q$.

The element R relates a definite value of b_r to every value of its input variable; this relation, however, is probably not linear, especially not in the logarithmic model discussed here. R therefore belongs to the group of proportional elements in a broad sense. The connexion between the two variables depends partly on how the requisites are distributed among the animals. If hiding places are the requisites, the need of each single animal is either completely satisfied or completely unsatisfied (neglecting differences in requisite quality); in the case of food, however, the individual need may also be partially satisfied. If, for instance, the mean degree of saturation is $\frac{1}{4}$ in both cases, then the hiding places protect 25% of the animals, whereas food, because of its more even distribution among the population, may hardly be sufficient to save a few individuals from starvation. This difference corresponds to the distinction between 'contest-type' and 'scramble-type' of competition made by Nicholson (1954).

Under fixed environmental conditions (that is, with a fixed value of b_u) b_r equals $- b_u$ only if a very special degree of saturation is reached; then population density is constant. If the degree of saturation deviates from this value, density increases or decreases. Here the principle of 'relative shortage of food' is effective; this principle was originally put forward by Andrewartha and Birch (1954) and was discussed in greater detail by Andrewartha and Browning (1961). Its effect has been excellently demonstrated by Potts and Jackson (1953) with some species of *Glossina* and by Dethier (1959) with larvae of *Melitaea harrisii*. I think that this principle is important more generally than has hitherto been accepted.

Under natural conditions, b_u is not constant; on the contrary, its value is continuously changing. Only if the degree of saturation can be incessantly adapted to all these changes, can population density be held constant. It stands to reason that such an ('openloop') control of density is impossible.

The definite connection of the output variable b_r with the input variable by the element R is limited by one restriction. When the input variable changes, the shift is transferred to the output variable only with delay. If the degree of saturation could be suddenly reduced, b_r would not at all occupy its corresponding new value at the same time. It takes a certain time for fecundity or mortality to react to that change. An interval of this kind is called 'dead time' in feedback control theory. The output variable does not begin to change before this time has passed. But even then the change will probably not be abrupt; b_r will rather approach its new value continuously. The function that describes the response of the output variable during the time after a sudden change of the input variable is called 'step response'. Its diagram possibly looks like that of a 'second-order element' (Fig. 3).

It is a matter of great concern for the general theory of feedback control to investigate the time behaviour of the single elements, because it is significant for the dynamic qualities of the whole system. In ecological systems the variables from the outside (e.g., d_r, s, q, b_u) are varying permanently. In this way the input variables of all elements are nearly incessantly changing. Therefore the time behaviour of the single elements is of particular interest here. Unfortunately, our knowledge is still very scanty in this respect. Perhaps it would improve considerably our understanding of ecological systems. Hutchinson (1948, 1954), Wangerski and Cunningham (1956, 1957), and Leslie (1959) have put forth appropriate lines of thought.

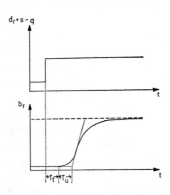

Fig. 3. Step response of a second-order element. Change of the output variable (below) as a function of time (t) after a sudden change of the input variable (above). T_t = dead time, T_u = delay.

Competition for requisites

Competition as controller of population density (control loop I)

When the members of a population are searching for requisites, they compete with each other in most cases, because each one can utilize only that which has not yet been utilized by others. The density of requisites usable for any single animal is therefore reduced by the activity of the others. This effect operates, although to a lesser degree, even if the number of requisites within the habitat were to be principally sufficient to satisfy the requirements of all members of the population (that is, if there were only a relative shortage of requisites).

Competition reduces the density of usable requisites by a certain factor. Consequently the logarithm (c) of that factor has to be subtracted from d_r (Fig. 4). c is the output varia-

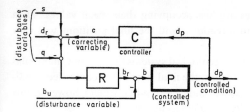

Fig. 4. Closed-loop control of population density by competition. C = competition, c = intensity of competition;
other designations as in Fig. 2.

ble of an additional element C that symbolizes competition. The density of the population is its input variable, represented by a branch of the line of influence. Since the element C connects a definite value of c with every value of population density, it has to be regarded as a proportional element in a broader sense. The degree of saturation is now equal to $d_r - c + s - q$.

In this way the output variable d_p of the population is fed back negatively to the input variable; we have a closed loop of influence. Hence b_r is now adapted automatically to changes in b_u; the former open-loop control which was only speculative has been replaced by a 'closed-loop control' or 'automatic control' of population density. The population P (together with R) can be regarded as the controlled system', d_p as the 'controlled condition' or 'controlled variable', b_u as a 'disturbance variable', C as the 'regulator' or 'controller', and c as the 'correcting variable' (automatic control terminology according to Broadbent 1967).

b_u is not the only disturbance variable for population density. d_r, s, and q are also independent variables which influence the net rate b (by way of b_r) in an unpredictable manner. Therefore they must also be viewed as disturbances.

The final states of the feedback control system

There is one major limitation of automatic control by intraspecific competition. If mortality, for instance, is reduced by weather influences, the amount of b_u is smaller. Consequently, population density increases. Without competition it would deviate more and more from its starting point. With increasing competition, however, $d_r - c$ decreases. Hence, the degree of saturation also decreases until, finally, b_r equals $-b_u$ again. At this moment population density comes to a standstill; the system has attained a new 'final state'. This state is not changed as long as the disturbance variable b_u keeps its new value. In this way, increase and decrease of density are certainly stopped but not reversed by competition. More cannot be accomplished by it because a definite value of its output variable is connected with every value of the input variable; i.e., because competition functions like a 'proportional controller' ('p-controller').

All proportional controllers work in this way even in technology. If man installs a feedback control system, he usually prescribes a 'set point' of the controlled condition (e.g., a definite temperature or a course). That set point has to be observed by the controller. But only an 'integral controller' ('i-controller') can reverse all deviations from that value. With a p-controller the 'transient deviation' turns into a 'steady state deviation' as soon as the controlled condition attaines its new final state. Consequently, a distinct final value is co-ordinated to every combination of values of the disturbances; a range of variation of final values corresponds to the range of variation of the disturbances. The controller is best installed in such a way as to attain the desired value of the controlled condition ap-

179

proximately when all disturbance variables are just occupying their mean values. Then steady state deviations will appear in both directions, and the final positions will vary about the fixed set point.

No set point is prescribed from the outside on ecological systems that are not manipulated by man. In case an integral controller is at work, the final state of the controlled condition can be empirically ascertained and called set point. With p-controllers, however, this procedure is impossible. If population density is regulated by competition, there are various final states depending on the values of the disturbance variables, and no one of them is distinguished in any way from the others. At best, the mean value of all these states can be empirically ascertained during a period which seems to be sufficiently representative. But this procedure, too, is rarely practicable, because the disturbances change too frequently. In most cases the new final state is probably shifted again before it can be attained by population density. Then density has a continuously changing goal, so to speak.

Delays within the feedback control system

When population density begins to change under the influence of a disturbance variable, the negative feedback action does not begin immediately but rather after a time interval composed of all dead times of the control loop. Even then it does not set in at once with full power, but slowly increases according to the step responses of the single elements. Because of this delay, the controlled condition overshoots its new final state in the first instance and then swings back. It may oscillate up and down several times before it finally rests. Consequently, dead times within a control loop produce oscillations.

Such oscillations, therefore, are by no means limited to the well-known simple enemy-prey systems. Those systems consist of two populations – i.e., of two integral elements. Hence they must produce oscillations if no other processes intervene (Wilbert, 1970a). Population and competition, however, constitute a system of one integral and one (or more) proportional element(s). Such systems can oscillate as Nicholson (1954, 1957) has demonstrated impressively by his experiments with *Lucilia cuprina*. These oscillations need not even be damped. The risk of instability by increasing oscillations increases with the 'proportional control factor' of the p-element and with the sum of dead times (and delays) within the control loop. It remains to be investigated whether population and competition in certain cases are able to produce increasing amplitudes. Overexploitation of the habitat would be the consequence. The permanent density oscillations in the experiments of Nicholson suggest that they were primarily undamped, prevented from increasing only by additional processes.

Disturbance variables and command variables at control loops with p-controllers

Thus far the effect of searching ability has not been taken completely into account. Competition too is influenced by it. The more requisites are used by the single animal, the greater the competition felt by others, as Franz (1965) has already stated. Higher searching ability, therefore, has the same effect on competition as increased population density. Consequently, s has to be also added to population density. Then $d_P + s$ is the input variable of C, as is illustrated in Fig. 5 by a branching-off line of influence.

Every change of s now affects the density of requisites in a twofold manner; directly as well as in a roundabout way via C with opposite sign. The second effect partly cancels the

180

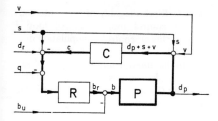

Fig. 5. Block-diagram of feedback control with compensation of searching ability (s) at the input of competition. v = deviation of the animals from a random spatial distribution. All other designations as in figures 2 and 4. The control loop is distinguished by thicker lines.

first one. By this 'compensation' of the disturbance variable s, the feedback control system is less susceptible to changes of that quantity.

The spatial distribution of competitors is another variable that interferes with the control loop between controlled system and controller. If ecological conditions cause the animals to concentrate more or less at certain places within their habitat, the searching routes will, on the average, cross each other more often. Hence, competition is more intense than in the case of random distribution. Consequently, in the block diagram a certain variable v must be added to $d_p + s$ before entering the element C (Fig. 5). v is a measure of the deviation of animals from random distribution.

If a variable interferes with the control loop between controlled system and controller, the 'information' which the latter receives from the controlled system is changed. It acts, however, as if the changed value were still the real value of the controlled condition. Therefore, it now tries to observe a correspondingly different value. Variables interfering between controlled system and controller consequently shift the set point of the controlled condition; they operate like 'command variables'.

Such command variables are of special importance for integral controllers with their well-defined set points, like enemy populations for instance. As p-controllers, of course, they also shift the final state of the respective controlled condition, but in this respect they do not differ in principle from disturbance variables. This is especially true of biological systems with their numberless equivalent final states. The different point of interference with the control loop merely implies that, contrary to the disturbance variables, these quantities are converted together with the controlled condition in the controller, where they are also subject to the same delay.

Degree of saturation and behaviour of animals

Behaviour as controller of the degree of saturation (control loop II)

Thus far the factor s has been considered to be an independent variable. If this assumption were correct, the behaviour of animals towards their requisites would not be influenced by their success in searching and thereby by the degree of saturation. This may by correct with some species, but certainly not with most of them. An occasional success may enhance the searching activity, repeated success may reduce it or may raise the liminal thresholds of certain reactions.

There are many possibilities for the degree of saturation to influence the behaviour of animals, as has been demonstrated by several lecturers during this conference. Only one of these possibilities will be discussed here; the decrease in searching activity or in readiness to use discovered requisites with an increasing degree of saturation. In the block diagram

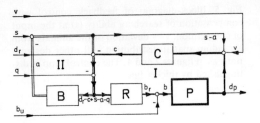

Fig. 6. Block-diagram of two interconnected control loops. Control loop I (thicker lines); control of population density (d_p) by competition (C). Control loop II (double lines); control of degree of saturation ($d_r - c + s - a - q$) by the behaviour (B). a = amount of change in behaviour. All other designations as in Fig. 5.

this influence can be demonstrated by the aid of a further element B (behaviour) (Fig. 6) which has the same input variable as the element R. Its output variable a (amount of change in behaviour) has to be added to s with a negative sign. Apart from eventual delays, this output is again coordinated clearly to the input; consequently, B also is a p-element in a broader sense.

A new loop has been closed by the element B. Its output is fed back negatively to its input, that is the degree of saturation, $d_r - c + s - a - q$. Therefore, the latter is controlled, and B acts like a p-controller. A controlled system cannot be defined in this case. The new control loop is distinguished in Fig. 6 by double lines of influence and by insertion of a II. The feedback effect in this loop is accomplished by way of the searching ability. Consequently, changes of the correcting variable a are added together with s to the input of C; in this way they are attenuated. Hence the feedback effect in this loop is more or less weakened.

Interaction between the control loops

The system composed of the two loops discussed here is still a relatively simple one. Nevertheless, it is difficult to survey all possible interactions. Therefore only a few relationships can be singled out here.

s, d_r, c, and q are disturbance variables at the control loop II. Controller B counteracts their effects on the degree of saturation. Being a p-controller, it cannot neutralize these effects. Every change of one of the disturbances still alters the degree of saturation; the alterations, however, are less pronounced due to the influence of B.

Three of the disturbance variables mentioned above are also disturbances at the control loop I: s, d_r, and q. As well as attenuating their effect on the degree of saturation, the control loop II also reduces their influence on R and thereby on the population. Hence population density increases or decreases more slowly when one of these variables changes; it takes a longer time for c to neutralize the changes and, consequently, for population density to reach its new final state. The state itself is not changed by the control loop II. Variations of v have similar consequences. This variable primarily alters the intensity of competition, and the effects of these changes are attenuated also by the control loop II.

Only b_u is not influenced by the control loop II. The effects of this variable on the population can be neutralized only by corresponding shifts of b_r, accomplished by the controller C. The correcting variable c, however, loses part of its influence on R by the action of the control loop II; hence the intensity of competition has to change more violently than before to cause the necessary alterations of b_r. Consequently, population density increases or decreases by a greater amount before the balance is adjusted again by means of the controller C. Due to control loop II, the influence of b_u on the final state of population density is enhanced.

182

The connection between output (correcting variable) and input of the controllers C and B is not linear. Whatever the formulae of their characteristic curves may be, they certainly do not result in straight lines. Both correcting variables approach the threshold zero asymptotically with decreasing values of the input variables because, by definition, a negative intensity of competition is just as impossible as a negative value of a change in behaviour. With increasing values of the input variables, however, c and a approach the values of these variables (proportional control factors → 1). The characteristic curves of both controllers therefore are bent, thereby making the mathematical treatment of the whole system difficult. It has still to be investigated to what extent linear approximate functions will suffice.

Because of these curvatures, both controllers do not always work with the same intensity. The smaller the input variable of the single controller in the steady state, the weaker the feedback effect in the respective control loop after a perturbation of this state. Control loop I has its greatest efficacy at high population density, whereas control loop II works most effectively at high density of requisites. Various densities of both classes of objects therefore give different importance to the control loops. Time behaviour of all elements complicates the situation even more.

Conclusions

The model discussed here is not complete at all. There are numerous details and relationships that have not yet been taken into account. Therefore it has to be improved in many respects. Then we shall know whether or not cybernetics in its present state is able to deal with all these complications in ecological systems. The model can also be extended in several directions. Above all, most of the variables considered here as independent are in fact dependent in some way on population density. This applies, for instance, to d_r if the requisites are also living organisms; then the population of those organisms (prey) together with the population P constitutes a further control loop (Wilbert, 1970b). The deviation of animals from the spatial random distribution (v) may also be density dependent. It must be noted that b_u often contains density dependent components, e.g., the effects of enemies or of (additional) prey populations; on the other hand, it can be influenced in an inversely density dependent manner by the frequency of copulation (Klomp et al., 1964)

What has been discussed so far is only a small part of a considerably larger system of interconnected control loops, but this part is composed of elements which are correlated in a particular manner, competition for requisites and changes in behaviour with increasing saturation are processes which can hardly be separated from population. It is even reasonable to maintain the view that the concept of population should include these vital functions. Then all processes discussed here take place within the population, which is identical to the partial system.

In order to illustrate this situation in the scheme, the elements and the loops are surrounded in Fig. 7a by a wider rectangle. The population so delineated is affected from the outside by the former disturbance and command variables. The changes of these variables are transferred to the density as a result of the internal structure of the population. If for some reason this structure is not interesting, it need not be represented. In this case there remains only a black box, one single element with several input variables and one output variable (Fig. 7b). How is this element to be clasified?

In the control loop I a definite final state of d_p is coordinated to every combination of

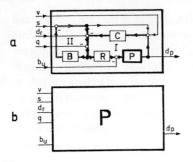

a

b

Fig. 7. Delineation of a new element 'population' that includes the control loops I and II (cf. Fig. 6). In Fig. 7b this element is presented as black box. Consequently, population density is controlled by an open loop.

values of the independent variables (see earlier). This situation is not altered by control loop II; this loop influences the value of the final state and the time behaviour of the first loop, but the clear coordination of a final state of d_p to every combination of values is not affected. Consequently, the newly delineated population has the quality of a proportional element (in a broader sense); it coordinates (apart from transition phenomena) a definite value of its output variable to every combination of values of its input variables. Certainly this value is hardly ever reached because the input variables change too frequently; but in this respect other proportional elements do not really differ.

In this way, the control loops are no longer objects of investigation because there is now an 'open-loop control' of population density by the independent variables. The newly delineated population is analogous not to the water vessel, but to the heated room. In the room, the compensation is attained by a different demission of heat dependent on room temperature; here it is accomplished by the control loop of competition.

As far as these considerations are valid, I believe a problem, which in past years has given abundant occasion for debates and which has been discussed more recently by Bakker (1964), Clark et al. (1967), Ehrlich and Birch (1967), and Schwerdtfeger (1968) no longer exists, the problem of natural control or regulation of population densities. According to Wilbert (1962) a population is regulated when its density in the long run remains between finite limits, no matter where these limits may lie in the individual case. With p-elements, the range of variation of the ouptut variable is always limited only if the input variables are correspondingly limited. As everybody knows, the temperature within a heated room cannot increase or decrease unlimitedly even without any control mechanism. Consequently, in the case of a population, regulation is ensued if the variation pattern of the input variables makes those final states of d_p which are too extreme either sufficiently improbable or so transient that they cannot be reached by the density. Only when the variation range of the output variable is to be more confined or to be shifted is a controlling mechanism necessary as well as, for instance, in a climatic chamber. The intended or unintended introduction of new enemy or prey populations has demonshifted by strated clearly that the variation range of population densities can also be confined or additional controllers.

A great part of the past controversies about natural control of animal populations seems to originate from different opinions about the delineation of populations according to Fig. 7. Thompson (1929), for instance, does not investigate the control loops, but he presupposes the loop I when he takes into account that the animals, after an increase in density, necessarily disperse into less favourable parts of their habitat where the rate of multiplication diminishes. Nicholson (1933, 1958) considers primarily the loop I (besides

184

the enemy-prey relations). On the other hand, Andrewartha and Birch (1954) are also correct in stating that one has only to count the auger-holes in the fencing-posts in order to learn the population density of certain bees (genus *Megachile*). The holes are requisites for the bees and the density of requisites controls (by open loop) the density of bees in the sense of Fig. 7b. Milne (1957, 1962), who classifies intraspecific competition as the only perfectly density dependent factor, looks at the control loop I again; he considers that it is only able to prevent overcrowding but not able to stop decrease.

To unite separate elements mentally or to split them up further is a typical method of cybernetical reasoning. Of course, in this way reality is not altered, but the view of the whole or the insight into details are improved at will. The single element can only describe but not explain a certain relationship. Who so ever wants to know why the output variable depends on the input variable just in this peculiar way, should not be content with the black box; rather, he has to analyse the processes within the respective element. That applies to the elements P, R, C, and B (c.f., for instance: Holling, 1965; Griffith and Holling, 1969), but it particularly applies to the partial system regarded as a single element. The clear connection of a definite final value of population density to every combination of values of outside variables is accomplished by the control loop I, probably also by additional control loops. Feedback control systems, however, can be grasped mentally only with surprising difficulty. One has to agree with Ferner (1960, p. 174) when he states: 'Selten werden einem die Grenzen der Denkfähigkeit so bewußt wie bei dem Versuch, ohne geeignete Hilfsmittel in die Dynamik von geschlossenen Regelkreisen einzudringen.' (Seldom one becomes as conscious of the limitation of reasoning power as in the attempt to invade the dynamics of closed control loops without suitable auxiliary means.)

References

Andrewartha, H. G. & L. C. Birch, 1954. The distribution and abundance of animals. Chicago.
Andrewartha, H. G. & T O. Browning, 1961. An analysis of the idea of 'resources' in animal ecology. *J. theor. Biol.* 1: 83–97.
Bakker, K., 1964. Backgrounds of controversies about population theories and their terminologies. *Z. angew. Ent.* 53: 187–208.
Broadbent, D. T. (Ed.), 1967. Multilingual dictionary of automatic control terminology. Pittsburg.
Clark, L. R., P. W. Geier, R. D. Hughes & R. F. Morris, 1967. The ecology of insect populations in theory and practice. London.
Dethier, V. G., 1959. Food-plant distribution and density and larval dispersal as factors affecting insect populations. *Can. Ent.* 91: 581–596.
Ehrlich, P. R. & L. C. Birch, 1967. The 'balance of nature' and 'population control'. *Am. Nat.* 101: 97–107.
Ferner, V., 1960. Anschauliche Regelungstechnik. 2. Aufl. Berlin.
Franz, J. M., 1965. Qualität und intraspezifische Konkurrenz im Regulationsprozeß von Insektenpopulationen. *Z. angew. Ent.* 55: 319–325.
Geier, P. W., 1965. Spatial favourableness and patterns of numerical causation. *Proc. 12th Int. Congr. Ent.*, 368–369.
Griffith, K. J. & C. S. Holling, 1969. A competition submodel for parasites and predators. *Can. Ent.* 101: 785–818.
Holling, C. S., 1965. The functional response of predators to prey density and its role in mimicry and population regulation. *Mem. Ent. Soc. Can.* 45.
Hutchinson, G. E., 1948. Circular causal systems in Ecology. *Ann. N.Y. Acad. Sci.* 50: 221–246.
Hutchinson, G. E., 1954. Theoretical notes on oscillatory populations. *J. Wildl. Mgmt* 18: 107–109.

Klomp, H., M. A. J. van Montfort & P. M. L. Tammes, 1964. Sexual reproduction and under-population. *Archs néerl. Zool.* 16: 105–110.

Leslie, P. H., 1959. The properties of certain lag type of population growth and the influence of an external random factor on a number of such populations. *Physiol. Zool.* 32: 151–159.

Milne, A., 1957. The natural control of insect populations. *Can. Ent.* 89: 193–213.

Milne, A., 1962. On a theory of natural control of insect populations. *J. theor. Biol.* 3: 19–50.

Mott, G. D., 1967. Dynamic models for population systems. *Proc. Forest Insect Popul. Dynamics Workshop, West Haven*, 53–72.

Nicholson, A. J., 1933. The balance of animal populations. *J. anim. Ecol.* 2: 132–177.

Nicholson, A. J., 1954. An outline of the dynamics of animal populations. *Aust. J. Zool.* 2: 9–65.

Nicholson, A. J., 1957. The self-adjustment of populations to change. *Cold Spring Harb. Symp. quant. Biol.* 22: 153–173.

Nicholson, A. J., 1958. Dynamics of insect populations. *A. Rev. Ent.* 3: 107–136.

Potts, W. H. & C. H. N. Jackson, 1953. The Shinyanga game-destruction experiment. *Bull. ent. Res.* 43: 365–374.

Schwerdtfeger, F., 1941. Über die Ursachen des Massenwechsels der Insekten. *Z. angew. Ent.* 28: 254–303.

Schwerdtfeger, F., 1968. Eine integrierte Theorie zur Abundanzdynamik tierischer Populationen. *Oecologia (Berl.)* 1: 265–295.

Thompson. W. R., 1929. On natural control. *Parasitology* 21: 269–281.

Wangerski, P. J. & W. J. Cunningham, 1956. On time lags in equations of growth. *Proc. nat. Acad. Sci. USA* 42: 699–702.

Wangerski, P. J. & W. J. Cunningham, 1957. Time-lag in prey-predator population models. *Ecology* 38: 136–139.

Watt, K. E. F., 1966. The nature of systems analysis. In: K. E. F. Watt (Ed.), Systems analysis in ecology. New York/London. p. 1–14.

Wilbert, H., 1962. Über Festlegung und Einhaltung der mittleren Dichte von Insektenpopulationen. *Z. Morph. Ökol. Tiere* 50: 576–615.

Wilbert, H., 1970a. Cybernetic concepts in population dynamics. *Acta biotheor.* 19: 54–81.

Wilbert, H., 1970b. Feind-Beute-Systeme in kybernetischer Sicht. *Oecologia (Berl.)* 5: 347–373.

Discussion

Participants: Wilbert (Author), Bakker, (K), van Biezen, Jacobs, Rabinovich, Solomon, Varley, Vlijm, Walker, Williamson, de Wit and Wolda

There are various ways in which the usefulness of a model can be evaluated. The degree to which it can interact with actual research seems the most important criterion. Does the feedback model generate any new hypotheses? What kind of hypotheses are these, and does the model indicate which of the hypotheses it is more important to test (WOLDA)? Feedback control theory, in the first place, improves our ability to reflect on dynamic systems. Therefore, the main intention of the model is to clarify thinking and to interact with actual research. Moreover, it tells us which qualities of the single elements should be tested because they are important for the functioning of the whole system (AUTHOR).

Two main points can be concluded from the paper, namely (1) that the cybernetics approach essentially helps to clear our thinking on particular problems, and (2) that until we make the black boxes transparent we have not gained any insight into the processes. With the flow diagrams of digital computer programs we can, similarly, think clearly about the processes and, at the same time, we can solve the mathematical problems by numerical methods. Because cybernetic block diagrams usually end in a nonsolvable nonlinear system of equations, it seems better to give up this approach to population ecology (RABINOVICH). The cybernetic approach may give much insight into complex interactions without making the black boxes fully transparent, and this more easily than by computer programs. Because of the possible difficulties with nonlinear systems of equations, I do not think that all the problems of population dynamics can be solved by feedback control theory. However, the usefulness of linear approximate functions is yet to be investigated (AUTHOR).

At present too little is known about the mathematical functions within the boxes; but perhaps in future feedback control theory may help to predict population densities (AUTHOR to VAN BIEZEN).

Hence, the scheme represents a 'didactical' model and *not* one from which testable hypotheses can be drawn (BAKKER).

A number of speakers were confused by the use of technical analogies –

Feedback controls in technology and physiology are *real final* processes, where a specific mapping in a physical substrate is determining where the process is going. In populations, so far as we can tell, there is no such set goal. Another point is the arrangement of parts; in a technical system there are regulating parts, input-parts ... etc. linked by channels in which information flows in defined directions. In Wilbert's model we have only the population. Density is *within* the population, reproduction is *within* the population, competition is *within* the population. There is really no analogy between the material and functional pattern of our population systems and the patterns of physiological and technical systems as expressed by cybernetic methods (WALKER).

Technical terms are assigned to certain aspects of population regulation, such as population = 'controlled system', or competition = 'controller'. Could not the 'controller' (or any other) function be assigned to any one of the members of a circle of biological causes with an uneven number of negative signs (JACOBS)?

It would be better to restrict any notions about 'controllers' to homeostatic situations (VLIJM).

We should be careful about the use of the engineering terminology. Engineers make a factory after a model, and not the model after the factory. Moreover, the kinds of flow (of material and information) and the integrals are not specified in the diagrams (DE WIT).

Although finality may be essential in the two main fields of cybernetic application, technology and physiology, I do not think that the conclusion is justified that feedback control theory can only deal with final processes. Some terms like 'set point', controller' etc. may be a little confusing; but they are accepted terms in cybernetics which cannot be changed at will. We have to free ourselves from mental associations with finality, homeostasis, etc., which belong to other fields of application. The spatial arrangement of the system's elements is not essential; the block-diagram is not a geographical map, but a schematic presentation of assumed causal interactions. Whether or not analogies between ecological and technical or physiological systems on this level of abstraction can be of some help remains to be seen. In technology, man installs feedback control systems to regulate certain variables. His purpose determines which quantity is to be regarded as the controlled condition and, with that, the functions of all other quantities are fixed. In every case, however, the whole loop tends to certain final states and, therefore, all quantities within it are controlled. In ecology man seldom installs control loops; he only finds them, waiting for investigation. Therefore, it is a matter of interpretation which variable shall be considered the controlled condition. For example, in control loop I the degree of saturation may be interpreted as the controlled condition; in this case, P can be regarded as the i-controller of that condition which, every time, brings back the degree of saturation to the respective set point, even in the case of a lasting change of a disturbance variable. Insight into the system is improved by this variability of interpretation. The feedback control terminology is *not* a part of the engineering terminology, because engineering is only one field of application of feedback control theory. This theory deals with causal interactions and not with physical substrates. Engineers construct something, ecologists analyse something; why should not both of them use models of the same type? (AUTHOR).

It seems possible that the cybernetic model may provide what we have been hoping to see – a master model of population dynamics and a precise language with which to manipulate and modify it. Perhaps existing models of parts of the system (e.g. parasite-host interaction) can be translated into cybernetic terms and incorporated into such a master-model. Whether or not such a model provides hypotheses as such, it at least seems to suggest functional models of phenomena like the fluctuations in Nicholson's blowfly experiments: such functional models need not be accepted at face value but their ability to represent what happens in the experiments can presumably be tested (SOLOMON). I think, that that the 'dead time' between the incidence of competition and the numerical response of the population caused the fluctuations in Nicholson's blow-fly experiments (AUTHOR).

Oscillations within a single loop can be permanent only if very specific conditions are satisfied. However, it is very easy to get permanent oscillations by addition of further elements. Each element represents only one process. The two populations of enemy-prey systems react primarily like two integrating elements, causing oscillations if no other processes intervene. Additional processes may smooth the oscillations; competition of predators for prey, for example, may be such an additional process (AUTHOR to WILLIAMSON).

The reference to Nicholson's blow-fly population 'oscillations' illustrates a terminological confusion. Nicholson had previously used the term oscillation for parasite-host interactions with discrete generations. Each generation number was represented by a point – and points were joined by lines. Logically a histogram should have been used because the line represents nothing. In the blow-fly work, weekly counts within a generation gave curves which are the frequency distributions of successive or alternating large and small generations. In fact, the density dependent recruitment curve given by Nicholson contains most of the information to generate his population curves. This can be done simply with the aid of Ricker's reproduction curves (VARLEY).

Proc. Adv. Study Inst. Dynamics Numbers Popul. (Oosterbeek, 1970) 189–198

The concept of local population and the mechanisms of negative feedback in natural populations

H. G. Andrewartha

Department of Zoology, R. A. Fisher Laboratories, The University of Adelaide, Adelaide, S. A., Australia

Abstract

In seeking philosophical rigour for thinking about populations, ecologists should take pains to discriminate between like and unlike. For example, if the animals in local populations seem to have substantially different environments it might be better to use the statistical device of stratified sampling rather than simple randomization when estimating the numbers in the whole population. This point is illustrated by reference to a population of red kangaroos. Similarly in formulating theoretical principles the decision as to what is to be regarded as like or unlike should be taken rigorously. For example, it is shown that species which demonstrate territorial behaviour with respect to a resource are not necessarily all alike in the way that the density of the population interacts with the supply of resource for future generations.

Population is a technical word in statistics as well as in ecology. In statistics 'population' defines a set of measurements in which there is no recognizable sub-set. The operative word is recognizable. If some of the objects that are to be measured are physically recognizable as distinct from some others and it is wished to define a single population, then the sub-sets are made statistically unrecognizable by an appropriate randomising process.

If ecologists are to aim at a similar rigour in their treatment of the concept of population, they should strive to be well informed about the sorts of sub-sets that they might wish to make 'unrecognizable' for the purpose of analysis; and they should have good statistical techniques for analysing the population in which certain sub-sets have been made statistically unrecognizable. In this paper I shall address myself to these two aspects of the problem of interpreting population data, dealing with the second aspect first.

Stratified sampling: red kangaroo

Newsome (1965), in the course of a study of the ecology of the red kangaroo *Megaleia rufa*, estimated the number of kangaroos on 6730 km² of arid rangeland in central Australia. For sampling, Newsome used the method of random quadrats, counting every kangaroo in each quadrat. The counting was done while flying in a small aeroplane about 90 m above the surface. The quadrats were rectangles having a length equal to the distance flown by the aeroplane in 10 sec and width that was defined by a mark on each wing of the aeroplane. The quadrats were wider in open plain than in woodland. The area of a quadrat in open plain was 0.31 km² and in woodland 0.07 km².

Open plain and woodland were two of 14 different land systems which Newsome could recognize. The whole area had been photographed from the air, so the distribution of the land systems were mapped from the aerial photographs and, by combining certain land systems, the whole study area was divided into 10 blocks. A large number of parallel transects were laid down on the map and, in any one sampling, a certain number of transects were chosen at random. The whole area was thus sampled by the procedure of placing random quadrats over it, but the records for the 10 blocks were kept separate. The mean number of kangaroos per km^2 and the variance of the mean was estimated for each block separately and then the estimate for the 10 blocks were pooled to give an estimate of the number of kangaroos in the whole study-area. In this way, estimates with quite reasonably narrow fiducial limits were obtained. For example, on one occasion towards the end of a prolonged drought the number of kangaroos on the area ($6730 km^2$) was estimated at 3927 with fiducial limits ($P < 0.05$) of 3322 and 4532. On another occasion after good rains had fallen the population was estimated as 4914 with fiducial limits ($P < 0.05$) of 4093 and 5735.

Had this method of stratified sampling not been used (i.e. had the quadrats been distributed simply at random over the whole area without regard to its stratification into diverse land systems), the variance would have been so large and the fiducial limits so wide that the estimate of the population would have lacked any useful precision. The variance would have been large because the density of the local 'populations' on the different land systems varied extremely, but the variability between quadrats in any one land system was small. The analysis of the stratified sample depends on the statistical theorem that:

Variance of $(A + B + C...) = Var A + Var B + Var C...$

The stratified sampling, in this instance, produced an additional bonus because it allowed the nomadism of the red kangaroo to be documented. During drought, they concentrate on the open plain especially along the 'gilgais' which mark the course of the water that drains from the surrounding hills after rain. The gilgais support perennial grasses and forbs that supply a little green picking late into the drought when there is very little suitable food anywhere else. After a substantial rain, ephemeral grasses and forbs grow for a season quite widely but especially in the mulga woodland. At such times, the kangaroos are dispersed widely especially in the extensive areas of mulga woodland.

Clearly, it would make nonsense of the ecology of the red kangaroo to treat the local population in any one land system as an ecological population. These sub-sets must be recognizable ecologically but unrecognizable statistically.

Territorial behaviour

I want now to discuss certain aspects of territorial behaviour in animals, because territorial behaviour is one of the ways in which recognizable sub-sets may be generated in natural populations and so the interpretation of territorial behaviour may have a bearing on the interpretation of population data. To begin, I shall summarize three well known case histories of animals that show territorial behaviour, leaving the interpretation until I have described all three.

Nezara and Asolcus

The eggs of the bug *Nezara viridula* are laid in a 'raft'; this consists of up to 90 barrel-shaped eggs which stand upright and side-by-side. A single egg contains enough food to

190

allow a larva of *Asolcus basalis* to grow to maturity. The female *Asolcus* pierces the egg of the bug with her ovipositor and lays her own egg inside the egg of the bug. If more than one egg is laid into the same egg of *Nezara*, one of the larval *Asolcus* will eat the others so that usually one, but never more than one, *Asolcus* emerges from a *Nezara* egg that has had one or several *Asolcus* eggs laid into it. But, according to Wilson (1961), it is unusual for a *Nezara* egg to have more than one *Asolcus* egg laid into it.

Wilson described how a female *Asolcus* which is ovipositing on a raft of bug eggs, examines each thoroughly with her antennae before either inserting or not inserting her ovipositor into the egg. If she pierces the egg, she usually (on 93 % of occasions in one experiment) lays an egg into it. If she lays an egg, she invariably marks the bug egg with a pheromone; 'painting' the pheromone over the top of the bug egg by stroking the tip of her ovipositor over it. The presence of this mark is highly effective in inhibiting herself or any other female from laying another egg into a marked bug egg. Table 1 gives the distribution of 'stings' when 75 eggs of *Nezara* were exposed to either one or two females of *Asolcus*. A 'sting' was counted when a female was seen to pierce an egg with her ovipositor. On 5 occasions out of 85 a female pierced an egg without laying an egg into it. The values of χ^2 at the foot of the table show that there is no significant difference between the two empirical frequency distributions, but that both of the empirical distributions were significantly different ($P < 0.001$) from the theoretical Poisson distribution.

Table 1. Distribution of 'stings' in 75 eggs of *Nezara* exposed to 1 or 2 females of *Asolcus*. (After Wilson, 1961).

Number of stings	Number of eggs (f)			
(x)	observed		expected on a random distribution	
	1 female	2 females	1 female	2 females
0	1	2	23	21
1	66	57	27	27
2	5	11	16	17
3	1	4	6	7
4	2	1	2	3
χ^2	non-significant		86.5	55.4

When more than one female was present on an egg-raft, they took little notice of each other at first but towards the end, when most of the bug eggs had been marked, one female usually became highly aggressive, driving all the others away; she then continued searching on her own for unmarked eggs.

The important feature of this behaviour is not so much the marking of the egg with pheromone by the fortunate firstcomer, but rather the capacity of the latecomers to recognise the mark and so avoid wasting their eggs. The eggs laid after the first one will be eaten; so the firstcomer is assured of a representative in the next generation without making the mark. The latecomers, however, have no chance of contributing to the next generation by laying their eggs in a place that is already occupied, whereas they may have a chance of finding an unoccupied one if they continue the search elsewhere. Of course, the firstcomer, by marking the egg, enhances its own chance of having more than one representative in the next generation; but, afterfirst the egg has been laid, the mark merely puts the firstcomer on the same level as the latecomers.

Codling moth

The adult codling moth *Cydia pomonella* lays its eggs on the outside of an apple. On hatching, the caterpillar burrows into the core of the apple where it remains, feeding largely on seeds, until it is mature. Then it cuts a way out of the apple and seeks a place to pupate. Usually, *Cydia* is rare relative to its food because, in a well kept orchard, it runs a big risk of being poisoned by insecticide and, in a neglected orchard, it is likely to experience an extrinsic relative shortage of food. Consequently, an apple rarely contains more than one caterpillar, despite occasional signs of more than one entry into the same apple. But artificially, by withholding insecticide from an otherwise well run orchard, it is possible to provide *Cydia* with an abundance of readily accessible non-poisonous food. In these circumstances, *Cydia* may multiply beyond the limits of its food and many caterpillars may seek to feed in one apple at the same time. Then the territorial behaviour of the caterpillars becomes clearly manifest; the core is divided into 'territories' which contain just enough food for a larva to grow to maturity. The unsuccessful contestants die; most of them are probably eaten by the successful ones. Geier (1963) found that the core of a 'small' apple would support only one or occasionally two caterpillars but the core of a 'large' apple would support two or three (Table 2). Apparently the caterpillars showed little tendency to defend a territory larger than their needs and, even under intense crowding, they could rarely be forced to accept a territory that was too small for their needs. The crowded diapausing larvae developed into adults that were significantly smaller than the uncrowded ones.

Table 2. Reduction in size of territory in response to crowding in *Cydia pomonella* (After Geier, 1963)

Initial number of caterpillars per apple	Small apples		Large apples		
	mean number mature larvae per apple	mean weight of adult females (g)	mean number of mature larvae per apple	mean weight adult females (g)	
				diapausing	non-diapausing
1	0.93	26.9	0.93 ⎫		
2	1.11 ⎫		1.54 ⎭	32.7*	22.2
3 or more	1.13 ⎭	26.1	–	–	–
3–5			2.25 ⎫	29.8*	21.6
6–10			2.26 ⎭		

* Difference significant at P < 0.01

Rabbits in Australia

Territorial behaviour in the European rabbit in Australia has been studied by Mykytowycz (1958, 1959, 1960, 1961, 1968) and by Myers and Poole (1959, 1961, 1962, 1963a, 1963b).

192

The rabbits breed during the winter when they can feed on green growing herbage. At the beginning of the breeding season, females in breeding condition begin to renovate and extend burrows and to undertake other home-making activities. In this condition, females are both gregarious and aggressive towards each other. The presence of a female digging a burrow, especially one in an old well developed warren, attracts other females. They fight fiercely and some may be driven away, but some persist. The end result is that a group of 3–5 females is formed which claims joint possession of a cluster of burrows. One female dominates all the others and she takes first choice of the best sites in the territory; the others also arrange themselves in a hierarchy of dominance. It is an uneasy but persistent truce. Meanwhile, males fight fiercely among themselves for 'ownership' of a group of females. Most of the contestants leave the area and, as the fighting subsides, one emerges as the victor, but usually one or two others remain; these seem to be accepted by the victor because they accept subordinate rank and make scarcely any attempt at retaliation. If there is more than one subordinate, one will dominate the others. So the typical social group comprises 2–3 males and 3–5 females, the members of each sex being arranged in a social hierarchy clearly dominated by the individual with the highest social status.

The outcome of the contests for status depend largely on tradition, age and weight. When the contest takes place in an established territory, it is mostly the yearlings from the previous breeding season that are driven out; and usually last year's dominants retain their status. When the contest occurs in new territory, victory usually goes to the oldest or the heaviest. (Usually age and weight go together.) It has not been shown that breeding has much influence on an animal's chance of becoming a dominant. However, it has been observed that at least some of those that are slow to find a place in a social group are so because they aspire to the dominant position but have not been successful in the first few groups that they have tackled. On the other hand, some of those that fail to enter a group seem to belong to the other extreme.

Each group defends a territory centred on its cluster of burrows. The territory is marked with pheromones. A secretion from the inguinal gland is smeared on faeces which are dropped in conspicuous and strategic places, especially on the main pathways leading from the burrows. Sticks, stones and other landmarks, even heaps of old faeces, or any faeces dropped by a stranger, are marked with the secretion of the chin gland; urine is also used. The dominant male is most active in marking, so his odours pervade the territory.

The territory, once marked, is defended strongly especially during the breeding season. All members of the group will join in the defence of the territory, but individuals react more strongly against intruders of their own sex. The dominants of both sexes are most vigorous in defence. The burrows, and the immediate approaches to the burrows, are policed most vigorously. As might be expected, the strictness and the vigour of the defence declines with distance from the burrow. It is likely that the characteristic odour of the group and its territory gives confidence to the members of the group and, conversely, saps the confidence of the intruder. Certainly this impression is confirmed by watching the behaviour of an intruder; its demeanour changes to one of marked and obvious wariness and diffidence as soon as it can be seen to pick up the odours of a strange well-marked territory. Because the odours are stronger near the burrows, the defenders are fiercer and more persistent the closer they are to the burrows and the intruder correspondingly less so; but as the fight or the chase approaches the boundary of the marked territory the difference between the antagonists might disappear or might be reversed.

Not only are the individuals in a social group bound to their territory by the odours of

193

the dominant male, but they are also bound to each other in the same way. As a pregnant female approaches her term, the dominant male consorts with her and drives away all other males; during the post-partum oestrus he copulates with her. During courtship and after copulation he urinates over her and smears the secretion from his chin gland on her. At other times he 'chins' the females, the kittens and the juveniles in the group. It seems that by chinning the kittens and the juveniles he protects them from the aggression of the females; it has been shown that females will accept strange juveniles that have been chinned by the dominant male of their group, whereas they will drive out others that have not been so marked (Mykytowycz, pers. comm.).

When social groups are being formed or re-established at the beginning of the breeding season, those rabbits that are evicted from, or fail to gain access to, established territories may form new social groups, especially if the ancestral warren is not heavily populated, or if there are derelict warrens nearby that can be taken over and renovated. But when the population is dense, there are usually a number of expatriate outcasts living solitary in the no-man's-land between warrens.

Myers and Poole studied the rabbits' ability to maintain their social groups though densely crowded. They put varying numbers of rabbits, in breeding condition, into three 2-acre enclosures where there was a good pasture of clover and grass. The rabbits bred during two successive winters but many of the young died during the summer. Table 3 shows that, no matter how intense the crowding, the rabbits did not vary the size of the social group; they responded to crowding by reducing the size of the territory.

Table 3. The influence of the density of the population in an enclosure and the size and number of social groups. (After Myers and Poole, 1959.)

Year	Enclosure	Number of adult rabbits	Number of social groups	Mean number per group		Mean size of territory (acres)	Number of outcast males
				♂	♀		
1957	A	6	1	2.0	4.0	2.00	0
	B	10	2	2.0	3.0	0.88	0
	C	19	3	2.3	3.3	0.66	2
1958	A	38	6	2.5	3.8	0.35	2
	B	51	7	2.3	4.7	0.29	2
	C	49	8	2.3	3.3	0.33	0

Clearly, the behaviour that causes rabbits to live in social groups of about 8 is strongly ingrained in them. The selective advantage seems to come from being a member of the group per se; it is not confined to the dominants or the subordinates although both are necessary for the persistence of the group. Natural selection has ensured the persistence of both sorts in the population partly by gearing dominances to tradition, age and weight and partly by not allowing either dominant or subordinate an exclusive advantage. Within the social groups, Myers and Poole could find no evidence that dominant females contributed more or stronger progeny to posterity than the subordinates; but the dominant males seemed to have an advantage over the subordinates (see above). Even so, there seemed to be selection pressures to offset this advantage, notably the strong tendency of the females in a group to synchronise their reproductive cycles. This tended to spread paternity because it is difficult for the dominant male to attend more than one pregnant female at a time.

Because the rabbits' territories are readily compressible, the territorial behaviour of the rabbit does not seem to result in the 'hoarding' of food against emergencies for the benefit of the residents and at the expense of the expatriates. Indeed, before myxomatosis was introduced into Australia it was a common experience to come across dense populations of rabbits which were starving because they had been overtaken by a drought.

The most obvious advantages of belonging to a group are:

– A group, by virtue of its ability to defend a cluster of burrows, can retain the same burrows throughout the breeding season or for several seasons. This allows the group to develop its burrows; the more elaborate the burrows are the better is the protection that they afford against the weather and predators. A group can make a more elaborate system of burrows than can a solitary rabbit. The more elaborate the burrows become, the more attractive they are to strangers and the greater the need for a well-knit group to defend them.

– By living within their territory, the rabbits become familiar with it, and gain confidence through familiarity; hence they have greater security when seeking food and avoiding predators.

Perhaps these advantages to the member of a group are sufficient to explain the social behaviour of the rabbit; in which case, social behaviour in the rabbit is best seen as an adaptation that allows the rabbit to make better use of a resource (burrows) by improving its quality. In the ecological context, there is not much difference between such a behavioural adaptation and a physiological adaptation such as the development of a caecum wich allows the rabbit to make better use of fibrous food. The evolutionary principles that have been proved in the study of physiological adaptations are equally relevant to the evolution of behaviour (Ewer, 1968).

Negative feedback

It will be seen from Table 4 that the major subdivision A caters for those species that may generate a negative feed-back between the density of the population and the supply of resource for future generations; these are the species that may have the potential of becoming effective agents of biological control. Indeed, *Asolcus* is a most effective agent for the biological control of *Nezara* in Australia.

The minor subdivision b characterizes species that show territorial behaviour; any species that falls into the classification b in this table may be said to do so by virtue of its territorial behaviour. Because there are species belonging to category b in both the major subdivision A (which defines species that generate a negative feed-back) and in B (which defines species that do not generate a negative feed-back), it seems clear that the capacity to generate a negative feed-back is not a necessary consequence of territorial behaviour.

This, to me, seems to be an interesting discovery, because one frequently comes across statements in the literature in which the existence of territorial behaviour is taken as sufficient evidence for a self-regulatory mechanism – which implies a negative feed-back.

It seems to me that territorial behaviour is best regarded merely as an adaptation that gives the animal that posesses it a better chance to survive and reproduce. Sometimes it forms part of a regulatory mechanism but sometimes it does not.

Table 4. Classification of the relationships that occur between animals and their resources in conditions of absolute shortage. (After Andrewartha and Browning, 1961.)

A. The supply of resource for future generations depends on the number of animals in the present generation using the resource.		B. The supply of resource for future generations is independent of the number of animals in the present generation using the resource.	
a. The amount of resource used effectively* by the present generation depends upon the absolute shortage that they experience.	b. The amount of resource used effectively by the present generation is independent of the absolute shortage that they experience.	a. The amount of resource used effectively by the present generation depends upon the absolute shortage that they experience.	b. The amount of resource used effectively by the present generation is independent of the absolute shortage that they experience.
Deer on Kaibab, *Cactoblastis*, cats on Berlenga.	*Asolcus*	*Lucilia*, certain parasites, most 'detritus feeders'.	*Parus, Cydia, Oryctolagus* (burrows)

* 'Effective' is used in the sense defined by Andrewartha & Birch (1954, p. 498), i.e. it refers to that part of the resource that is actually used by those individuals that get enough to mature and so have a chance to contribute to the next generation.

References

Andrewartha, H. G. & T. O. Browning, 1961. An analysis of the idea of 'resources' in animal ecology', *J. theor. Biol.* 1: 83–97.

Ewer, R. F., 1968. The ethology of mammals. Logos, London.

Geier, P. W., 1963. The life history of the codling moth *Cydia pomonella* (L.) (Lepidoptera: Tortricidae), in the Australian Capital Territory. *Aust. J. Zool.* 11: 323–367.

Myers, K. & W. E. Poole, 1959. A study of the biology of the wild rabbit in confined populations: I. The effect of density on home range and the formation of breeding groups. *CSIRO Wildl. Res.* 4: 14–26.

Myers, K. & W. E. Poole, 1961. A study of the biology of the wild rabbit in confined populations. II. The effects of season and population growth on behaviour. *CSIRO Wildl. Res.* 6: 1–41.

Myers, K. & W. E. Poole, 1962. A study of the biology of the wild rabbit in confined populations. III. Reproduction. *Aust. J. Zool.* 10: 225–267.

Myers, K. & W. E. Poole, 1963a. A study of the biology of the wild rabbit in confined populations. IV. The effect of rabbit grazing on sown pastures. *J. Ecol.* 51: 435–451.

Myers, K. & W. E. Poole, 1963b. A study of the biology of the wild rabbit in confined populations. V. Population dynamics. *CSIRO Wildl. Res.* 8: 166–203.

Mykytowycz, R., 1958. Social behaviour of an experimental colony of wild rabbits, *Oryctolagus cuniculus* (L). I. Establishment of the colony. *CSIRO Wildl. Res.* 3: 7–25.

Mykytowycz, R., 1959. Social behaviour of an experimental colony of wild rabbits, *Oryctolagus cuniculus* (L). II. First breeding season. *CSIRO Wildl. Res.* 4: 1–13.

Mykytowycz, R., 1960. Social behaviour in an experimental colony of wild rabbits *Oryctolagus cuniculus* (L). III. Second breeding season. *CSIRO Wildl. Res.* 5: 1–20.

Mykytowycz, R., 1961. Social behaviour in an experimental colony of wild rabbits *Oryctolagus cuniculus* (L). IV. Conclusions, outbreak of myxomatosis, third breeding season and starvation. *CSIRO Wildl. Res.*, 6: 142–155.

Mykytowycz, R., 1968. Territorial marking by wild rabbits. *Scient. Am.* 218: 116–119.

Newsome, A. E., 1965. The abundance of red kangaroos. *Megaleia rufa* (Desmarest), in central Australia. *Aust. J. Zool.* 13: (2) 269–287.

Wilson, F., 1961. Adult reproductive behaviour in *Asolcus basalis* (Hymenoptera: Scelionidae). *Aust. J. Zool.* 9: 737–751.

Discussion

Participants: Andrewartha (Author), Bakker (K.), Gradwell, Jacobs, Laughlin, Lawton, Murdoch, Murton, Reynoldson, Solomon, Varley, Walker, Watson.

There was much discussion on the appropriate use of the term negative feedback. A number of speakers pointed to the possible confusion deriving from an already established but different use of the term in cybernetics, technics and physiology; in these, the regulated system is visualized as having a built-in 'set point', either fixed or variable and the feedback signal is the difference between the real value and the set-point. Populations seem to have nothing analogous to an independently determined set-point, unless it is the average density; this average, however, is set by the environment as a whole, and is calculated from the densities themselves. Moreover, with 'negative feedback' a special property of the population is suggested which cannot be derived from the individual. The general feeling was that in biology the term 'feedback' should be restricted to the responses of individuals or to physiological processes within individuals (LAUGHLIN, LAWTON, MURDOCH,MURTON, WALKER). I cannot see any good reason why ecologists should not make use of it; after all, the physiologists has borrowed the term 'negative feedback' from cybernetics, and I think it a useful one (AUTHOR). See also the discussion after the paper of Wilbert.

How do you distinguish between 'negative feedback' and density-dependent'', and is 'negative feedback' considered synonymous with either 'direct' or 'delayed density-dependent' (GRADWELL)? I use 'negative feed-back' to imply that the density of the population in the present generation (or cohort) influences, in a negative way, the activity of a component of the environment (here a resource) in the next generation (or cohort). 'Density-dependent' has generally been used in a much wider sense than this. 'Delayed density-dependent' is, indeed, often used in the present context (AUTHOR).

Can we agree that a term nowadays needs a verbal definition; that, if it involves numbers it needs a mathematical definition and that it also needs a statistical test to decide whether or not a given situation comes within the category? Can we also agree that subsequent users of a term should stick to the original definitions? In this connection: how does one measure and test for 'negative feedback' (VARLEY)? I agree.I would measure the activity of the environment in the appropriate units – numbers, grams, degrees, etc. – and would then compare the differences by standard statistical tests (AUTHOR).

We should not allow ourselves to become too gloomy about the terminology of population dynamics. Although some of the terms are not too well defined, and although beginners may have difficulties, it seems that nowadays most ecologists understand each other pretty well. A high degree of precision in definition is only occasionally necessary; for most of the time, the meaning of a term is made clear by the context in which it is used (SOLOMON).

I do not believe it is right to separate the two aspects of quality and numbers. If competition is important for the qualitative aspects, it must also be important in the dynamics of numbers. The concept of 'effective' and 'ineffective food' is, in fact, the same as Nicholson's concept of 'scramble' and 'contest competition' (BAKKER).

I admit that my concept makes the same distinction as does Nicholson's. But I prefer to avoid the word 'competition' because, in ecological writings, it has become so attenuated as to have no meaning. I prefer to talk about 'resources' because these are components of the environment, and I like to analyse the influence of components of the environment on an animal's chance to survive and reproduce. There is a close interaction between ecology and evolution, but, nevertheless, we should recognize that different theories are possible to explain changes in numbers of individuals and in frequencies of genotypes (AUTHOR).

In the paper the statement is made that territorialism and feed back control can be independent of each other – and the codling moth is cited as an example. This example is an artificial one, because the apple is a domesticated species, which is reproduced vegetatively. Presumably, the territorialism of the moth evolved on some wild apple which reproduced by seed: feedback will have been involved in this evolution (JACOBS). I see territorial behaviour as an adaption that enhances the individual's chance to survive and reproduce. Admittedly, most known cases of territorial behaviour seem to be related to resources that might be used ineffectively if the territory were compressible. But territorial behaviour can also evolve in relation with resources which are not liable to be used ineffectively, e.g. the rabbit will be territorial chiefly with respect to its burrows (AUTHOR).

Is there in the rabbit any difference between the resorbtion of embryos at high densities (small territories) and at low densities (larger territories) (REYNOLDSEN)? Myers has shown that when rabbits are densely crowded they become less fecund and that resorbtion is one of the causes of this reduced fecundity. However, at densities normally found in nature the effects are small (AUTHOR).

The experiments within enclosures do not refute the possibility that territory size is related to food resources in the wild, because at very high densities the type of social structure may be changed (WATSON).

Proc. Adv. Study Inst. Dynamics Numbers Popul. (Oosterbeek, 1970) 199–207

Mutual interference in Bupalus piniarius (Lepidoptera, Geometridae)

P. Gruys

Research Institute for Nature Management, Arnhem, the Netherlands

Abstract

Mutual interference between larvae of *Bupalus piniarius*, in which contact transmission of fluid gut contents seems to be involved, reduces growth and hence results in smaller and less fertile moths. This effect occurs in the field over a range of relatively low population densities. It is suggested that it is not a self-regulatory mechanism, but rather an adaptation for avoiding, by dispersal, the effects of density-related mortality.

To gain an insight into the population dynamics of animals, long series of population censuses are an indispensable basis. But as a complement to this general framework, single processes that seem to be important must be analysed in greater detail. The present paper summarizes a study of the latter type. A detailed description of the work has been published elsewhere (Gruys, 1970).

Bupalus piniarius L., the pine looper, lives in Scots pine forests and completes one generation per year. The pupae hibernate in the litter under the trees. The moths emerge in June, and lay their eggs in rows of up to 25 on the pine needles. The larvae have solitary habits; they descend to the soil to pupate in the autumn.

In a long-continued investigation of a natural population of *Bupalus*, Klomp (1958, 1966) has found that size of larvae and pupae, and fecundity of adults, are negatively correlated with larval population density. This density-dependent reproduction, which occurs over a range of population densities at which only a slight fraction of the foliage is consumed, might play some role in the numerical changes of the population, and it might even have something to do with the regulation of numbers, as a sort of self-regulatory mechanism. Therefore, a separate study of the relationship between density and growth seemed worthwhile.

The effect of density

The puzzling thing about the relationships mentioned above is that the population density is very low relative to an abundant supply of food, and also the pine looper larvae are sluggish and well dispersed. Competion for food can therefore be excluded as a cause, and also, at first sight, mutual interference seems improbable. The relationship between density and growth need not necessarily be causal: it could arise from the dependence of both density and growth on a third factor, for instance weather. Several experiments, however, have shown the causality of the relationship.

Table 1. Influence of larval density on weight (mg) of pupae in insectary rearings. Mean, standard deviation and number of observations are given.

Number of larvae per 0.37 liter jar	Males	Females
1	139 ± 11.7 (44)	209 ± 19.4 (50)
2	118 ± 11.6 (33)	168 ± 19.6 (47)
5	115 ± 17.5 (21)	158 ± 19.4 (19)

The first (Table 1) is the obvious trial in insectary rearings, with different numbers of larvae per jar and abundant food. Rearing two larvae together in a jar gives a pronounced effect on size. The effect is greatest in females, and the greatest part of the maximum effect is already attained with this first step of density increase. In the following discussion, I shall only refer to females, in order to simplify the presentation of the results. Females are the most sensitive to grouping and, as procuders and carriers of the eggs, the most interesting as well.

A second trial to experimentally produce variations in density was conducted in a forest with a very low natural population density. By introducing laboratory-reared eggs in the trees, I obtained groups of trees with different densities of larvae. The highest experimental density turned out to be six times the lowest, and pupal size of females showed a significant decreasing trend with increasing density of larvae (Table 2). Data from Klomp's (1966) study for years with similar densities show that there is a fair agreement between the effects of density in the natural and the experimental populations and in the laboratory rearings. Therefore, the detailed analysis of the density effect could be restricted to laboratory experiments.

Table 2. Effect of larval density on pupal size in a field experiment, compared with Klomp's (1966) results from a natural population. SE is standard error.

Experiment		Natural population	
number of larvae per shoot	diameter of female pupae (mm)	number of larvae per shoot	diameter of female pupae (mm)
0.030	4.97 (SE 0.04)	0.026	4.80
0.012	5.08	0.011	4.98
0.006	5.15	0.006	5.22
0.005	5.12	0.004	5.08

In a number of rearings in different years, the effect of grouping was highly significant, but considerable differences were found between experiments as regards the absolute and relative effects of grouping. In seven experiments the range of reduction of female pupal weight was 12–24%. The cause of this variation remains unknown. Each sex had the same influence on members of its own as upon those of the opposite sex.

I made a preliminary test of possible genetic differences in susceptibility for grouping effects. From the eggs of each of 24 pairs of adults (from a homogeneous batch reared singly in the previous year), 24 larvae were reared singly and 24 in groups of six. An analysis of variance, conducted on the logarithms of pupal weight, showed a significant interaction between the factors 'progenies' and 'densities'. This means that the percentage effect of grouping was small, or possibly absent, in some progenies and large in others. There was an indication that grouping reduced growth in families of large larvae more severely than in families of small individuals.

I found no effect of grouping on larval mortality, nor on pupal mortality and longevity of adults. Colouration of the larvae was not affected. Some physiological changes in the larvae due to grouping are summarized in Fig. 1. The graphs show the ratio of means of grouped larvae to means of single larvae for certain properties, and for each of the five larval stages separately. Grouping lengthened the duration of the larval stages and reduced weight increase per stage; hence, weight increase per day was greatly reduced by grouping (Fig. 1: a, b and c). Finally, weight increase per unit faeces was reduced by grouping (Fig. 1: d). Since faeces production was found to be a good measure of food intake, this means that the conversion of the ingested food into body substance was less efficient in the grouped larvae. The influence of grouping occurred in the second to the fourth instars, and there was no effect in either the first or the last instar.

Larval behaviour was examined in several series of continuous observation over one or several days. Its pattern was not changed by grouping. The first instar loopers were active during the day; particularly at sunrise and sunset. After the first instar, their activity was concentrated at dawn and dusk, and during the night, but nearly always the larvae rested during daytime. The level of activity was low; even at night, some 70% of the time was spent resting. Most of the activity was feeding. There were two or three bouts of feeding per night, coinciding more or less with dawn and dusk. The larvae moved around for some minutes before and after each period of feeding. When two larvae met, which occasionally

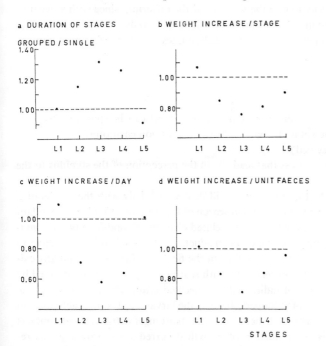

Fig. 1. Difference between single and grouped larvae in duration of stages and growth.

occurred when two individuals inhabited the same shoot, they usually showed sharp behavioural reactions; swinging with the anterior part of the body, or dropping off the
needle on silk. But this excitation did not cause any significant difference between density
categories in the level of activity.

Morphological measurements of the moths showed that grouping gives a proportional
reduction of size, that is, all linear dimensions measured were reduced to about the same
extent. We had a particular interest in wing area and wing loading because of a possible
relationship between density and dispersal. Wing area was not disproportionally large
after grouping of the larvae but wing loading, that is the weight that the animal has to
carry per unit wing area, was reduced. This is not surprising, because weight increases with
the cube of linear dimensions and wing area with their square.

After grouping, the females produced fewer eggs (on the average: solitary females, 228
eggs; grouped females, 189 eggs). The regression of number of eggs on pupal weight was
significantly steeper in crowded than in single females, which means that body weight is
more efficiently used for reproduction after grouping. Accordingly, eggs of grouped females were slightly lighter in weight.

I have tested viability in relation to larval aggregation of the parents in several laboratory experiments, with contradictory results. The first experiments (Klomp and Gruys,
1965) suggested a reduced viability of eggs and young larvae after grouping. But continuation of this line of experimentation has not confirmed these first results. In addition to
this, survival of offspring from a forest with a high, and another with a low density in the
previous year, was tested under natural conditions in the field; we found no difference
between high and low density offspring.

There is no satisfactory explanation for this inconsistency. It is clear that a high density
of parents does not necessarily reduce the viability of the offspring; since such a negative
effect was in fact only found in one out of five experiments, its reliability is very questionable. Therefore, I have not incorporated it into the hypothesis about the function of mutual interference.

Mechanism

The question of the mechanism underlying the density effect can be split up into:
1. what is the nature of the stimulus that the larvae exert upon each other?
2. how is the stimulus perceived?
3. what is the physiological process that leads from the perception of the stimulus to the
effect on growth?

I have studied only the first question, and will deal very briefly with the results of a
rather long series of experiments conducted in search of the stimulus. Food was abundant
enough to prevent competition for it. Density related changes of food quality, or conta-
mination of the food with possible excretory products, were found to be ineffective in
several experiments in the laboratory as well as in the field. Neither did we find any evidence for olfactory stimulation in experiments with rearing compartments partitioned by
double screens. These two sorts of indirect stimuli seemed intuitively most likely in the
sessile, and sparsely occurring, pine loopers. In fact, the larvae must touch each other in
order to get the effect on growth and, because of the pattern of activity, these contacts
occur at night. Accordingly, no reduction of growth occurred when grouping was restricted to the day, whereas it did when two larvae were kept together at night. As a result

of the (rather few) nocturnal encounters that provoke vehement behavioural reactions, grouped larvae interrupt each other's feeding bouts from time to time; but it was experimentally shown that the reduced opportunity to feed caused in this way cannot explain the effect of density. The excitation, as such, aroused by encounters, also does not reduce growth. This could easily be tested because pine loopers behave in an identical way after any kind of stimulation, whether artificial or by their own species.

The stimulus that did show effects was regurgitated gut fluid; although its experimental transmission onto solitary test larvae did not match the effect of grouping completely in all respects. Efforts to find the source of the active principle have not been successful. The substance is not present on the skin of the larvae, as is the case with a pheromone of male desert locusts (Loher, 1961). Also, experiments with extracts of the larvae's mandibular glands gave negative results.

Whatever the source of the substance, contacts between larvae are necessary for its transmission. How probable are encounters under field conditions? The probability is very high for newly hatched larvae at all densities, because the eggs are laid in rows. But, as we have seen, these contacts remain without effect. The young larvae start to disperse soon after hatching. Moreover, mortality in the first stage is high, and this increases the average distance between survivors. Therefore, I suggest that the initial aggregative distribution does not prevent overall population density from acting as a determinative factor for growth.

Another point is, whether or not the distance between caterpillars in the susceptible stages is too far for encounters to occur. The observations that I have on the areas of pine foliage visited during a certain time, indicate that contacts can be expected in the field at the medium to high values of naturally occurring population densities.

Function: a hypothesis

Summing up now, what we have is that aggregation reduces growth and fecundity. Certain abiotic factors can also do this, but density is much more determinative for average size than the abiotic factors. Mortality is not affected, and there is insufficient evidence that density influences the viability of the next generation. These changes are brought about by a rather specific mechanism. An important thing is that individual differences in susceptibility exist. If these are genetic, there is a basis for selection against the density effect. However, that this effect has been demonstrated shows that it has not been eliminated by selection. It is therefore reasonable to suppose that it must have survival value; that is, that the disadvantage of lowered fecundity is outweighed by some advantage. This – its possible function – is the most intriguing problem about the density effect. I can only present a hypothesis about it.

Since one of the environmental factors that may determine survival of parents and offspring is density of its own population, the ability of an animal to respond in some way or other to changes in population density can have survival value for itself or for its progeny, and thus give a selective advantage. This general principle can take various forms.

Firstly, high density may cause the depletion of certain resources, and mutual interference may induce a timely escape reaction, such as dispersal or diapause (e.g. Iwao, 1962; Tsuji, 1959).

Secondly, there may be a response in order to escape density-related mortality arising from natural enemies. Such responses can be expected to occur already at low population densities. They can either serve to escape mortality in the same generation (e.g. Sharov, 1953) or to avoid high mortality among the progeny. Adult migration, in the latter case, could be functional in avoiding eradication of the progeny by natural enemies. Some species of army worms can be considered as examples of this (Brown, 1962; Iwao, 1962; Whellan, 1954).

A third possibility is that high density is not deleterious by itself, but rather warns against approaching physical unfavourableness (Kennedy, 1956).

Density effects of the type encountered in *Bupalus*, i.e. chronic changes in certain characters resulting from mutual interference and occurring at natural population densities, have been found in several insects (Gruys, 1970). The way in which the properties of the animals are changed is very variable, but it appears in many cases that dispersal is in some way involved. Apart from Johnson's (1969) book which contains several instances, reference may be made to the recent papers of Shaw (1970) and Dixon (1969) on aphids and Nayar and Sauerman (1968), on mosquitos.

Klomp (1966) has shown that the chance of survival of *Bupalus* larvae decreases with increasing density. Therefore, females could increase their effective reproduction by moving away from their place of birth to more scarcely populated areas. The function of mutual interference in *Bupalus* could be to increase the tendency of the adult females to disperse, through the greater ease of flight that results from reduced weight. Decreased weight also entails a reduction of fecundity, but this seems a small price at which a greater gain is purchased, namely greater effective reproduction.

Although *Bupalus* is not migratory in a strict sense, light trap catches show that females do leave the forest. We obtained evidence that males are more active fliers than females, but that females have a greater tendency to fly out of the forest than males. Females caught outside the forest carried part (roughly one third) of their initial egg supply.

The crucial point with respect to this hypothesis is, of course, whether dispersal of females is related to larval population density. A release-recapture experiment with females from high and low density cultures has failed to produce evidence on this point because of poor recaptures. Similarly, our captures of wild moths outside the forest were too few to find a relationship between size of the moths and distance from the forest. However, some of Klomp's (1966) data favour the hypothesis. In his life tables, he gives a mortality index of female moths which is the ratio between the actual and the expected egg density. Strictly, this index indicates moth disappearance, and it may as well indicate dispersal as mortality.

This disappearance shows some correlation with the density of the larvae from which the moths have issued, and it is also correlated with pupal size (Figs. 2 and 3). Such correlations are more probable when disappearance is due to dispersal, than when it is due to mortality. It is not surprizing that the correlations are weak, because several factors contribute to the disappearance of moths.

Klomp's (1966, Fig. 36) data on generation survival in relation to egg density can be used to estimate the advantage that can be gained by density-related moth dispersal. At high density and without an effect of mutual interference, fecundity would average 200 eggs per female and the females would not disperse. The survival of the progeny generation would be 0.16 % and hence one female would produce 0.32 new adults. At high density and with the effect of mutual interference, fecundity would be 150 eggs per female on the average and the females would disperse. If they succeed in laying all their eggs in places with low density, survival of the progeny generation would be 2.8 %; thus, one female

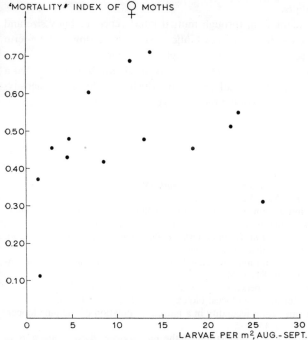

Fig. 2. Relation between larval population density and disappearance of female moths in the following spring (data from Klomp, 1966). Kendall's $\tau = 0.29$, $P = 0.16$.

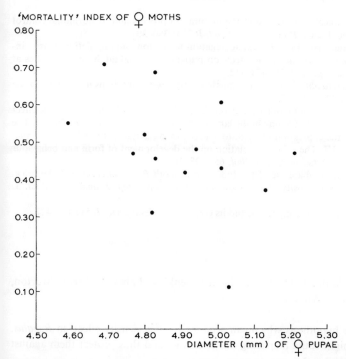

Fig. 3. Relation between pupal size and disappearance of female moths (data from Klomp, 1966). Kendall's $\tau = -0.36$, $P = 0.08$.

would give rise to 4.2 new adults.

Besides quick, short-term adaptation, through mutual interference, of body size and dispersal to rapidly changing conditions of the biotic environment, slower, long-term adaptation through shifts in genotypic size could conceivably occur.

In conclusion, I suggest that the density effect in *Bupalus* should not be considered as a self-regulatory mechanism, but rather as an adaptation by which mortality due to density-related processes can be escaped by exploiting the heterogeneity of density occurring over extensive areas.

References

Brown, E. S., 1962. The African army worm *Spodoptera exempta* (WALKER) (Lep. Noct.), a review of the literature. Commonw. Inst. Ent., Lond. pp. 57.

Dixon, A. F. G., 1969. Population dynamics of the sycamore aphid *Drepanosiphum platanoïdes* (SCHR.) (Hemiptera: *Aphididae*): migratory and trivial flight activity. *J. Anim. Ecol.* 38: 585–606.

Gruys, P., 1970. Growth in *Bupalus piniarius* (Lepidoptera: *Geometridae*) in relation to larval population density. *Agric. Res. Rep.* (Pudoc, Wageningen) 742, pp. 127.

Iwao, S., 1962. Studies on the phase variation and related phenomena in some lepidopterous insects. *Mem. Coll. Agric. Kyoto Univ.* 84: 1–80.

Johnson, C. G., 1969. Migration and dispersal of insects by flight. London. pp. 763.

Kennedy, J. S., 1956. Phase transformation in locust biology. *Biol. Rev.* 31: 349–370.

Klomp, H., 1958. Larval density and adult fecundity in a natural population of the pine looper. *Archs néerl. Zool.* 13, Suppl. 1: 319–334.

Klomp, H., 1966. The dynamics of a field population of the pine looper, *Bupalus piniarius* L. (Lep., Geom.). *Adv. ecol. Res.* 3: 207–305.

Klomp, H. & P. Gruys, 1965. The analysis of factors affecting reproduction and mortality in a natural population of the pine looper, *Bupalus piniarius* L. *Proc. XII Int. Congr. Ent. (Lond. 1964)*: 369–372.

Loher, W., 1961. The chemical acceleration of the maturation process and its hormonal control in the male of the desert locust. *Proc. R. Soc. Lond. B* 153: 380–397.

Nayar, J. K. & D. M. Sauerman, 1968. Larval aggregation formation and population density interrelations in *Aedes taeniorhynchus*, their effects on pupal ecdysis and adult characteristics at emergence. *Entomologia exp. appl.* 11: 423–442.

Sharov, A. G., 1953. *Exaereta ulmi* SCHIFF., a noxious insect of forest plantations in the steppe zone (In Russian). *Zool. Zh.* 32: 594–607.

Shaw, M. J. P., 1970. Effects of population density on alienicolae of *Aphis fabae* SCOP. I. The effect of crowding on the production of alatae in the laboratory. *Ann. appl. Biol.* 65: 191–196. II. The effects of crowding on the expression of migratory urge among alatae in the laboratory. *Ann. appl. Biol.* 65: 197–203. III. The effect of isolation on the development of form and behaviour of alatae in a laboratory clone. *Ann. appl. Biol.* 65: 205–212.

Tsuji, H., 1959. Studies on the diapause of the Indian meal moth *Plodia interpunctella* HÜBNER. II. The effect of population density on the induction of diapause. *Jap. J. appl. Ent. Zool.* 3: 34–40.

Whellan, J. A., 1954. The African army worm and its control. *Rhodesia agric. J.* 51: 415–427.

Discussion

Participants: Gruys (Author), Dempster, Jacobs, Jenkins, Labeyrie, Metz, Murton, Pimentel, Rabinovich and Wilbert.

There is an alternative hypothesis which can account for the 'density effect' in *Bupalus*. Mutual interference might cause a spacing out of larvae, and thus protect them against predators that hunt by sight. This hypothesis is supported by the fact that: larvae feed only at night, and have solitary behaviour and protective colouration, whereas the adult moth seems not well designed for dispersal (PIMENTEL). There are some similarities with the situation in Cinnabar moth where, also, the eggs are laid in clusters, the young larvae do not react to one another while the older larvae space themselves out (DEMPSTER). However, the observed effects of mutual interference in *Bupalus* do not favour this alternative explanation. No indication was found of an increased tendency for the larvae to disperse under grouped conditions; the reduction in weight and fecundity caused by mutual interference must also be accounted for by any alternative hypotheses (AUTHOR). In seed eating birds, the searching behaviour is related to clumped or scattered distributions and can change relatively suddenly; hence, these different distributions in themselves do not provide an a priori explanation of prey behaviour (MURTON).

Several comments refered to the relation between size of the moth, power of dispersal, and fecundity –

Rather than wingload, the size of the flight muscles relative to body weight (in which the weight of the flight muscles is included) is determinative for flying power; this may well turn out to the advantage of large moths (JACOBS). However, the force generated by a muscle is usually assumed to be proportional to the square of its linear dimension rather than to the cube of it, and this favours smaller animals (METZ). The effort of a long flight might well reduce fecundity and thus put dispersing moths at a disadvantage (RABINOVICH). These points, as well as the behaviour of moths originating from single and grouped conditions, need further study (AUTHOR).

Do *Bupalus* populations reach such high densities in nature that they affect their food supply?, and might the density effect delay starvation for some individuals (JENKINS)? In Holland, such high densities are unknown, and in countries in which they do occur (Germany, for instance), no research has been conducted to ascertain the density effect. It would be interesting to study the density effect in outbreak areas (AUTHOR).

No evidence was found of differences in sexual attractiveness between females from single and grouped conditions (AUTHOR to LABEYRIE).

There is no evidence that the secretion of gut content has a defensive role against parasites and predators (AUTHOR to WILBERT).

207

Proc. Adv. Study Inst. Dynamics Numbers Popul. (Oosterbeek, 1970) 208–219

The relevance of changes in the composition of larch bud moth populations for the dynamics of its numbers*

W. Baltensweiler

Entomologisches Institut, Eidg. Technische Hochschule, Zürich, Switzerland

Abstract

Population ecology is, for many reasons, in great need of long term quantitative population studies. The research project on *Zeiraphera diniana* covers 20 annual generations of a cyclic fluctuation type of population change, 18 years of irregular and 5 years of rather stable fluctuations, along an altitudinal gradient in the Swiss Alps. These fluctuation types are illustrated by means of a reproduction curve. The differences in abundance in time and space are caused by the climate through its selective action on two distinct ecotypes; directly in the suboptimum area and indirectly, by allowing population increase until the depletion – and ensuing temporary deterioration – of the food resource, in the optimum area.

Selection for the intermediate (in larval colour) ecotype, however, is not restricted to climatic and trophic stresses, the same selection phenomenon was observed as a consequence of a large scale DDT-spray programme.

Thus, genetic polymorphism is a basic strategy in the population dynamics of this species of *Zeiraphera* and analogous to the phenotypic response to crowding shown by many noctuid moths.

In the final paper of this Advanced Study Institute, Watt stresses the biased approach of present ecology which is aptly described by the research question 'Why do these populations fluctuate from time to time the way they do?' This critical remark itself has merit, but what are the reasons for this situation? Watt points to the great economic importance of the various species studied: cod, sardines, locusts, spruce budworm, fur bearers and others. In view of human requirements there was and still is a great need for sound knowledge in order to manage any one of these species.

In addition to this, however, I feel that the great numerical changes, which all these species have in common, considerably influenced their selection for basic research. Conspicuous changes in population numbers imply two advantages for ecological research:
1. Population numbers may be considered, in a relative sense, as one of the most readily measured population parameters over a long period of time;
2. Although the knowledge of changes in population numbers in time and space is essential, it is by no means sufficient for an understanding of the underlying causes of population dynamics. However, it is hoped that these causes of numerical changes may be more readily recognized the greater the variations are.

Naturalists who were confronted with the quantitative and qualitative complexity of

* Contribution No 41 of the working group, under the direction of Prof. Dr Bovey, on the population dynamics of *Zeiraphera diniana*. The research was aided by a grant of the Swiss National Funds for Scientific Research.

Nature had to start with the study of simple ecological situations. This, of course, led to the many biased theories, summarized by Solomon (1949), which are characteristic of the development of ecology. As yet this process is not finished, since there is a growing awareness among ecologists that intraspecific variation, either geno- or phenotypical, has been neglected to an unjustified extent until recently, as stated by Wilson, 1967, at the London Symposium on Insect Abundance.

This paper deals with the role of intraspecific variation in relation to the population dynamics of a tortricid species (*Zeiraphera diniana* GN.) on larch (*Larix decidua*) in Switzerland. The study of this forest pest in the Alps started in 1949, and it is only fair to say that I shall rely upon results from many colleagues who contributed to the research team during this 20 year's period. The study, initially triggered for economic reasons, has gained very much impetus from the qualification of the research object for basic research. After a very brief description of the biology of the bud moth, I shall discuss its various types of population fluctuation with regard to the concepts on the reproduction curve by Takahashi (1964). Next, the kind of intraspecific variation, as expressed by larval morphotypes, will be described and its ecological significance evaluated. Finally, general inferences are drawn in relation to relevant information from the literature.

Biology of the larch bud moth

The biology of the larch bud moth is as simple as it can be. The female moth flies in summer and deposits her eggs on the branches of the larch. The eggs, after development to the gastrula stage (Bassand, 1965), overwinter in an obligatory diapause until the following spring. The eggs hatch in coincidence with the sprouting of the larch. The feeding of the first three instars occurs within the short shoots of the larch, but the ultimate, fifth instar larva is an open feeder which hides in webbing along the branch axis. The mature larva drops to the ground from where, after a 3–4 weeks pupation period, the moth emerges again to start a new generation.

This phenology of the life cycle may vary by up to two months for any given place, under the influence of weather; but in addition to this, the species exhibits enough plasticity to spread over the full altitudinal range from 400 m to 2200 m. Within the range of climatic zones there is an increased phenological variation; for the egg hatch of up to three months and for the moth flight of up to four months. Due to the alpine topography, there are good chances for individuals to migrate up and down the altitudinal profile. But nevertheless, as large as the plasticity of the species appears to be, climate and weather impose definite trends on survival. In summary it may be said that eggs laid before August have a low survival rate due to temperature induced mortality and, on the other hand moths flying after August are not able to contribute the full egg potential to population growth because temperature limits the period of activity (Baltensweiler, 1966; Baltensweiler, Giese and Auer, 1970). Therefore, the physical environment defines a zone where population growth is fastest. This zone is readily demonstrated to lie at 1700–1900 m altitude by the delimitation of complete defoliation of the host-trees within extensive larch stands. The reality of this optimum zone is further characterized by the periodic occurrence of defoliation at intervals of 8.38 $\pm$ 0.4 years since 1855 (Baltensweiler, 1964). This qualitative schema, derived from experimental research and observation by the forest service, is fully verified by the results of the quantitative census of the fourth and fifth instar larvae (Auer, 1960). This census is based on 400 randomly distributed sampling units within 1300 ha of

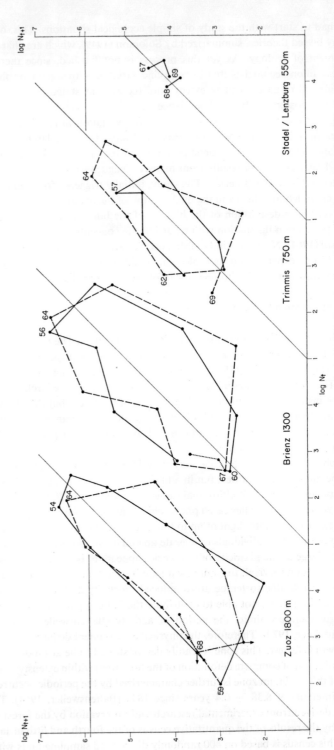

Zeiraphera diniana Gn

N_t = number of insects in any generation
N_{t+1} = number of insects in next generation at same point in life cycle

Density: number of larvae per 7500 kg larch branches

Fig. 1a. Fluctuation of larval numbers of Z. diniana at 4 sites during the period 1950–1969. Density log. 5.8 = density of general defoliation in the area.

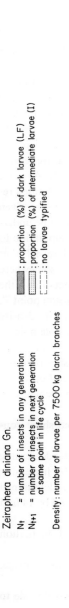

Zeiraphera diniana Gn.

N_t = number of insects in any generation

N_{t+1} = number of insects in next generation at same point in life cycle

Density: number of larvae per 7500 kg larch branches

: proportion (%) of dark larvae (LF)

: proportion (%) of intermediate larvae (I)

: no larvae typified

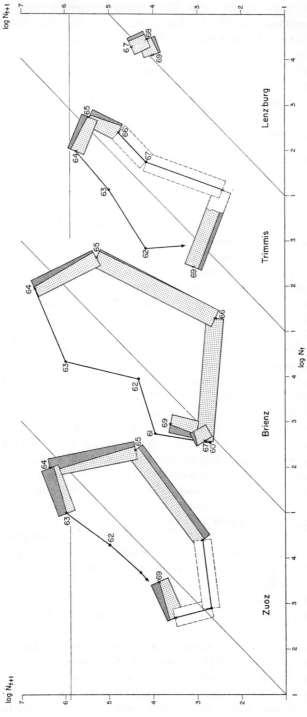

Fig. 1b. Fluctuation of larval numbers and of the proportions of dark and intermediate ecotypes of Z. diniana at 4 sites during the period 1960–1969.

211

forest in the Upper-Engadin Valley. The Engadin represents a largely autonomous biotic unit in the optimum zone. Outside this optimum zone, from the subalpine conifer region to the colline broad leaf tree forest on the northern slope of the Alps, larch distribution becomes more patchy and sampling is restricted to 6 stations with 20 sampling units each. The sampling unit consists of 7.5 kg (or fractions of this) of larch branches taken throughout the larch crown. I am greatful to my colleague Auer for permission to use unpublished density-figures from his census in the following discussion.

Population fluctuations

The quantitative population census of the bud moth yields only one density figure per generation; it seems, therefore, appropriate for the interpretation of the long term fluctuation to apply Takahashi's (1964) concept of the reproduction curve. The rate of reproduction (r) is defined as $r = N_{n+1}/N_n$, where N_n and N_{n+1} are the population densities of the same stage in the nth and $n + 1^{th}$ generation respectively. The most simple case of constant and unlimited population increase would be represented by a straight line above the 45° line which itself indicates equal densities in two subsequent generations (compare the Fig. 1 and 2). The intersects of the normal reproduction curve with the 45° line are termed the stable upper and lower equilibrium points, E and T, and the release point R. At point T any further population increase is limited by intraspecific competition for a limited resource; density T corresponds, therefore, to the maximum carrying capacity of a given ecological situation. The processes around the lower equilibrium point E cannot be understood in a straight forward deterministic manner, the change of a declining population to an increasing trend is a stochastic process. A completion of Takahashi's graph reveals that the reproduction curve leads either to extinction or has to intersect the 45° line somewhere below point R. It seems logical to extend Takahashi's reasoning to the problem of how the population increases from the lower equilibrium point E to the upper equilibrium point T, also to the reversal of the population at the lower density limit. Then the entire density range below R is included in a multitude of stochastic processes and the unstable point E should be recognized more aptly as the lower equilibrium range.

The reproduction curve of the bud moth is presented in Fig. 2 for three sites (two optimal sites – Sils, Zuoz – and a suboptimal site – (Celerina)) within the general optimum area of the Upper-Engadin (Baltensweiler, 1969). The following points are recognized:
1. The time period from 1949–1969 covers two full population cycles;
2. The two cycles at both sites agree quite well at the upper density limit but show considerable differences between sites as well between cycles at the lower limit;
3. The form of the reproduction curve differs from either the increasing or the decreasing phase of the cycle between cycles and sites. Considering the pattern of points for increasing populations only, the rate of increase may be calculated by regression for a determined period and site (Morris, 1959). Thus, populations increase by 6 fold at Zuoz and by 14 fold at Celerina.

From a comparison of the reproduction curves for representative types of fluctuation along the altitudinal gradient (Fig. 1a) we may summarize:
1. The upper density limit is stabilized at a fixed density for sites with defoliation damage, and decreases to a medium density in the suboptimum area;
2. The lower density limit is for all sites considered rather variable but, worthwhile to note, lowest in the optimum area for the period observed.

212

3. The correlation coefficient *r* for population growth decreases gradually from a maximum value 0.98 (Zuoz) to 0.30 (Lenzburg) when populations at high and low altitudes are compared.

It is evident, therefore, that populations outside the optimum area are much more affected by the variability of one or more weather-factors.

From forestry records we know that at intermediate altitudes (Brienz site), the defoliation pattern is not as regular as in the Engadin. Therefore it would be most interesting to follow up a population increase which is stopped before reaching the carrying capacity of the site. Unfortunately, from our point of view, larval populations of both the last two cycles caused defoliation.

Because of this, the processes in the optimum area will be summarized from more detailed information which was gathered during the last two cycles and has been presented in various papers by my colleagues or myself (Fig. 2). At defoliation densities, populations of the fourth and fifth instar larvae suffer from great losses due to lethal temperatures during their movements on the soil surface in search of food. Whenever defoliation ex-

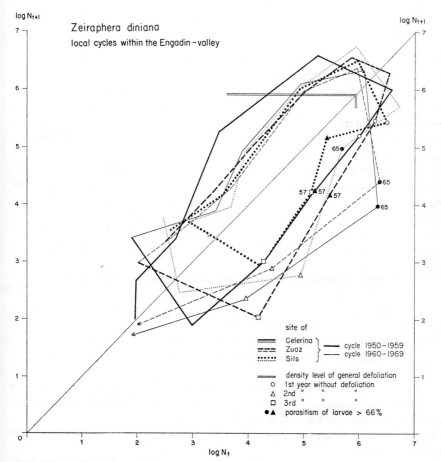

Fig. 2. Fluctuation of larval numbers of *Z. diniana* at 3 sites within the Engadin during the period 1950–1969.

ceeds 50% of the foliage, the larch grows needles for a second time in late summer; this affects the food quality in the following year (Benz, pers. comm.) which, in turn, influences the fresh weight and respiration rate of crowded larvae (Gerig, 1967), fecundity (Baltensweiler, 1968) and survival. An epizootic virus disease caused heavy mortality in 1954 (Martignoni, 1957) but was enzootic only in 1963 (Benz, pers. comm.). Larval parasitism increases from approximately 20% at peak density to 80% in the regression phase (Baltensweiler, 1968).

Colour-forms in the fifth instar larvae

However, populations continue to decrease even after all these regulating processes have ceased to exert their influence. This rather surprising phenomenon may be explained by a process whose investigation was begun in 1961. The evaluation of the larval population census with regard to parasitism, fecundity etc. revealed great variability in fifth instar colouration. Subsequently a classification scheme for colourtypes was set up and their genetical and ecological relationships were studied. The knowledge of dark and light colour-forms of the bud moth, confined either to larch (*Larix decidua* MILLER) or the cembran pine (*Pinus cembra* L.) (Bovey and Maksymov, 1959) was used for the classification; the colours of the head capsule, thoracic shield, anal plate and body were assigned to 7, 4, 4 and 7 classes respectively, ranging from black (1) to light orange (4) or yellow (7). Thus, the individuals of the extreme colour phases were characterized by the symbol 1111 and 7447 respectively. For ease of discussion, populations will be characterized in three classes; dark, intermediate and light colour phases. Crossing experiments between the two extreme forms yield the full range of intermediate colour phases in the F_1-generation, but there is a definite trend towards the darker colour classes; this fact is most evident in body colour and least evident in the anal plate criterion. It seems, however, that higher proportions of the dark anal-plate are linked with the dark criterion of the male parent. In general, the male sex is darker than the female sex. Field populations of the bud moth on larch generally include only a few individuals of the light form (at best a few percent), they consist of various proportions of dark and intermediate colour classes.

The evaluation of ecological differences between colour classes of the larch form was guided by a knowledge of differences between larch and cembran pine forms. Thus, Bovey and Maksymov (1959) found:
1. earlier hatching of the larch form larvae in spring in agreement with the phenology of the respective host trees, and
2. an extremely high mortality of the larch form when reared on cembran pine, but which does not apply to the cembran pine form reared on larch.

From experimental work in the laboratory the following facts were obtained:
1. There is no significant difference in fecundity between dark and intermediate colour-phases of the larch form.
2. High temperatures (34 °C) during the prediapause period of the egg stage cause twice as high a mortality to eggs of the dark colour-phase as to those of the intermediate colour-phase (Baltensweiler and Vaclena, in prep.).
3. Eggs of the dark colourphase show a faster postdiapause development than eggs of the intermediate phase.
4. Larvae of the dark colour-phase exhibit a higher susceptibility to food stress than intermediate ones (Baltensweiler and Day, in prep.).

214

These facts allow us to infer (a) that the colourphases represent ecotypes, and (b) that the diversity in fitness of these ecotypes should be reflected by variable proportions according to changes in the environment.

Selective influence of spatial heterogeneity

I would like to present this schematically by comparing the influence of climate and weather in the areas with cyclic and with latent population fluctuations with respect to the egg stage and the hatching process (Table 1). The climate of the subalpine region is heterogenous with regard to the abiotic weather factors, this is due to topography and the intense radiation. The spatial heterogeneity in temperature therefore induces great differences in the phenology of instars and other stages in different parts of the population. In the temperate zone of low altitude, temperature is very much the same throughout the larch stand.

With respect to weather, variability in time may occur in both regions. The two following extreme situations of spring and summer weather serve to show the possible consequences on the egg-stage of the bud moth population: (1) a hot summer or a cool, cloudy summer, and (2) an early warm spring or a delayed, cool spring season.

With respect to metabolism, the egg stage is partitioned into three stages; prediapause, diapause and postdiapause.

At low altitude the eggs are laid in June and July when temperatures quite frequently reach 30 °C or more. This causes heavy egg mortality and the intermediate ecotpye is selected. In the optimum area at 1800 m egg laying begins only at the end of July and temperatures rarely reach 30 °. Therefore, a hot summer is detrimental and a cool summer favorable for population growth at low altitude, but neither situation affects either numbers or selection in the optimum area.

The spring weather has identical effects on survival and selection in both areas; an early spring season reduces postdiapause mortality and increases the proportion of black morphotypes. At sites of low altitude, however, the enhanced development in early spring increases the risk of high egg-mortality in the prediapause stage of the following generation, due to coincidence with summer-maxima temperatures. In the optimum area the two extreme spring weather situations impose pronounced differences on the spatial growth

Table 1. Environmental diversity.

Region	Space (climate)	Time (weather)			
		spring		summer	
		early, warm	late, cool	hot	cool
subalpine (1800–2000 m)	heterogenous	more or less homogenous	heterogenous	heterogenous	heterogenous
	+	+	−	+	+
colline <1000 m	more or less homogenous	more or less homogenous	more or less homogenous	more or less homogenous	more or less homogenous
	−	+	−	−	+

+ = inducing population increase/favouring selection for dark morphotype.
− = inducing population decrease/favouring selection for intermediate morphotype.

pattern within the Engadin. The early warm spring homogenizes the timing of snow-melting, the sprouting of the larch tree and the egg hatch throughout the Engadin. If such a situation occurs two or three times out of four years of population increase, defoliation damage occurs simultaneously all over the valley in the first year of defoliation. Such a situation is termed 'an accelerated cycle' (Baltensweiler, 1964). However, in normal or cool springs snow melting is very patchy, but always in the same spatial sequence. In areas with a late snow cover, there is a lack of coincidence due to earlier egg-hatching and delayed sprouting, and this imposes a heterogenous growth pattern (Baltensweiler, 1969). Under these conditions, the black morphotype suffers relatively higher mortality due to their faster postdiapause development; however, the heterogeneity of the environment counterbalances this selection. A sequence of three or four years of normal or cool spring weather leads to a rather patchy defoliation on the warmest sites in the first year of defoliation, and the maximum extension of defoliation is reached only one or even two years later. Such a cycle is termed 'normal'. The year after first defoliation the dark morphotype suffers high mortality because of the poorer food condition.

These conclusions on morphotype frequencies are verified by the varying proportions of morphotypes as derived from the census material during the course of the last population cycle. We find in the optimum area a greater proportion of dark ecotypes at peak densities which later are replaced by the intermediate ecotype. Therefore, the cyclic fluctuation type may be understood as a process involving an alternate directional selection at intervals of three to four generations. The determination of the upper density limit is provided by the maximum carrying capacity of the biotope, and the ensuing density induced change in food quality selects for the more resistent intermediate ecotype. Interestingly enough, the sympatric light cembran pine form shows a similar trend towards intermediate colour phases at the end of the cycle. From this observation an increased panmixia between the larch and cembran pine forms might be expected to occur at lower densities. The latent fluctuation type, however, is determined by the climatically induced selection for the intermediate ecotype; the regulating processes for this are not yet understood. Relevant life-table studies were initiated in 1968.

Generalization of the determinative selection against the two ecotypes is corroborated by the fact that the slopes for population increase, but not those for population decrease, differ significantly from each other according to climatic zones. Directional selection in the bud moth is due to the fact that the density induced change in food quality lasts at least for two and possibly for three generations. Selection for the intermediate ecotpye, however, is not restricted to climatic and trophic stresses; an analogous selection was observed as a consequence of a large scale spray programme (Bovey, 1966) with DDT and Phosphamidon (Baltensweiler, in prep.).

Polymorphism

Polymorphism is not necessarily linked only with selection; there exists an extensive literature on phenotypic, density dependent polymorphism associated with regulation of numbers of gregarious insects, especially amongst noctuid moths (Iwao, 1968). It was found that phenotypic adaptation functions by a change in metabolic rate; i.e. the rate increases in crowded, dark populations and is low in uncrowded, pale populations. Titova (1968) presented evidence from experiments and from the literature that insecticidal treatments lead to the selection of individuals with lowered metabolism. With regards to these

216

results and the findings of the work on the larch bud moth, we are able to postulate the following generalization: The change in the composition of populations is an intrinsic mechanism which enables a species to cope with the variability of the environment. This mechanism functions in its most simply conceived form on the basis of two different physiological types and operates either by selection or by modification.

References

Auer, Chr., 1961. Ergebnisse zwölfjähriger quantitativer Untersuchungen der Populationsbewegung des Grauen Lärchenwicklers (*Zeiraphera griseana* HB.) im Oberengadin, 1949–1958. *Mitt. schweiz. Anst. forstl. VersWes.* 37: 175–263.

Baltensweiler, W., 1964. The case of *Zeiraphera griseana* HB. (= *diniana* GN.) (Lep., Tortricidae) in the European Alps. A contribution to the problem of cycles. *Can. Ent.* 96: 790–800.

Baltensweiler, W., 1966. Influence of climate and weather on population age distribution and its consequences, with special reference to the population dynamics of *Zeiraphera griseana* (HB.) (*Z. diniana* GN.) in the European Alps. *Proc. FAO Symp. Integrated Pest Control* 2: 15–24.

Baltensweiler, W., 1968. The cyclic population dynamics of the Grey Larch Tortrix, *Zeiraphera griseana* HÜBNER (= *Semasia diniana* GUENÉE) (Lepidoptera: Tortricidae). *Symp. R. ent. Soc. Lond.* 4: 88–97.

Baltensweiler, W., 1969. The influence of climate and weather on the population dynamics of the larch bud moth, *Zeiraphera diniana* GN. in the Engadin. *Biometeorology* 4 (2) 47.

Baltensweiler, W. & K. Day. Comparative mortality of larval ecotypes of *Zeiraphera diniana* GN. (in prep.).

Baltensweiler, W. & K. Vaclena. Comparative egg-mortality due to temperature of ecotypes of *Zeiraphera diniana* GN. (in prep.).

Bassand, D., 1965. Contribution à l'étude de la diapause embryonnaire et de l'embryogenèse de *Zeiraphera griseana* HÜBNER (*Z. diniana* GN.) (Lepid.: Tortricidae). *Revue suisse Zool.* 72: 429–542.

Bovey, P., 1966. Le problème de la Tordeuse grise du mélèze (*Zeiraphera diniana* GN.) dans les forêts alpines. *Bull. Murithienne* 83: 1–33.

Bovey, P. & J. K. Maksymov, 1959. Le problème des races biologiques chez la Tordeuse grise du mélèze, *Zeiraphera griseana* (HB.) (Note préliminaire). *Vjschr. naturf. Ges.* 104, Festschrift: 264–274.

Gerig, L., 1967. Physiologische Untersuchungen am Grauen Lärchenwickler *Zeiraphera diniana* GN. (= *Z. griseana* HB.) während einer Periode der Massenvermehrung. *Z. angew. Ent.* 59: 187–211.

Iwao, S., 1968. Some effects of grouping in lepidopterous insects. In: L'effet de groupe chez animaux. *Colloques int. Cent. natn. Rech. scient.* 173.

Martignoni, M. E. & Ch. Auer, 1957. Contributo alla conoscenza di una granulosi du *Eucosma griseana* (HÜBNER) (Tortricidae, Lepidoptera) quale fattore limitante il pullulamento dell'insetto nella Engadina alta. *Mem. Ist. svizzero Ric. for.* 32: 371–418.

Takahashi, F., 1964. Reproduction curve with two equilibrium points: a consideration of the fluctuation of insect populations. *Res. Popul. Ecol.* 4: 28–36.

Titova, E. V., 1968. Qualitative changes in insect pest populations under the influence of chemical treatment. *Ent. Rev.* 4: 437–445.

Solomon, M. E., 1949. The natural control of animal populations. *J. Anim. Ecol.* 18: 1–35.

Wilson, F., 1968. Insect abundance: Prospect. *Symp. R. ent. Soc. Lond.* 4: 143–158.

Discussion

Participants: Baltensweiler (Author), Iwao, Jacobs, Jain, Pimentel, Turnock, Varley, Watt and Zwölfer.

It must be possible to find here one or more factors with two-stage carry-over effects. One of these was given in the paper: the effect of defoliation on the quality of food in the following year, and hence on larval survival the year after that. A powerful general principle for ecology shows up here; the pattern regularity in population fluctuations depends on the relative importance of two-and-more-year lag effects. Such lags build inertia into population trends. Declines as well as increasing trends tend to continue. This means that log N_t does not by itself tell us enough to show the impact of density-dependent factors on log N_{t+1}. In addition we need two or more time-interval lags, such as log N_{t-1}, log N_{t-2} (WATT). See also the discussion after the paper of Watson.

Why are the very detailed census data not transformed into life tables? The comparison between even one year of decline and one year of population increase would reveal the main driving mechanism here. Can the genetic changes supply the cause – not the effect – of the unobserved mortality (VARLEY)? Life table studies are in progress for the third generation in the areas of cyclic and latent fluctuation. The most important difference between the increasing and decreasing phase of the cycle lies in the mortality of small larvae, which is negligible in the increasing phase, but considerable in the decreasing part of the cycle. The question whether ecotypes, i.e. genetic changes are the cause and not the effect of the cycle does not seem very pertinent to the cycle. The driving force is nothing other than the inherent pressure of the organism to multiply which at the carrying capacity leads to a density-induced change in environment. The organism is able to cope with this by being selected towards a different ecotype (AUTHOR).

With regard to the cause-and-effect relationship between genetic changes and population regulation: The driving force is basically found to be the energy flow, although external resource variations may also occur as argued by Watt. Genetic and ecological variables are simultaneously involved, and circularity need not interfere with either the overall energy flow or an instantaneous study of different subprocesses (JAIN). See also Jain's and Soutwood's comments in the discussion to Krebs' paper.

What form would the density cycles take, if there were only one ecotype? Intuitively, one guesses that the presence of polymorphism decreases the amplitude of density fluctuations, because the accumulation of dark forms during the upswing hastens the start of the downswing since the dark forms are selected against as overall density increases (JACOBS). There is no possibility at this moment to test this point. Assuming that only the dark ecotype exists, the population would increase in its optimal environment until the carrying capacity is reached. Then the dark-ecotype population would become extinct because the environment is very much unsuitable for it, and it can no longer adapt by shifting to other ecotypes (AUTHOR).

The colour phases in the larvae cannot be changed by artificially modifying the density at which they are reared (AUTHOR to TURNOCK and IWAO). Furthermore, rearing experiments on different food qualities resulted in differential mortalities, and hence, the ecotypes must be genotypes (AUTHOR to IWAO).

Do larval parasites and mortality by disease influence the balance of polymorphism in Z. griseana (ZWÖLFER)? In the summer of 1970, an experiment was made to test whether differences in susceptibility to virus disease exist between the ecotypes. The results are not yet worked out. Parallel to the change in ecotypes from progression to regression phase of the cycle a similar change between various parasite species was observed. However, within the same parasite species, no definite discrimination between dark and intermediate ecotypes was found (AUTHOR).

218

The nutritional quality of larch needles was investigated by Benz. From observation and needle-length measurements one gets the impression that three years after complete defoliation the quality is back to normal again. A change in food quality may be expected when defoliation has been more than 50%. Such a change causes a change in the feeding behaviour of the larvae, growth is slowed down and mortality of small instars is increased. The larches in the Engadin area are all autochtonous (AUTHOR to PIMENTEL).

Proc. Adv. Study Inst. Dynamics Numbers Popul. (Oosterbeek, 1970) 220–231

Population studies on Chironomus anthracinus

P. M. Jónasson

University of Copenhagen, Hillerød, Denmark

Abstract

The essential relationships between environment, food, larval growth and life cycles in *Chironomus anthracinus* are analysed.

Fluctuations in number were studied through 17 years. A life cycle of two-years was observed in populations at 20 m depth. High initial population densities and large number remaining after the first years emergence prevent a new generation from becoming established. When density is low after the first year's emergence, a new generation becomes established every year. As a result of such alternating recruitment the benthic fauna at any one time contains larvae from only a single generation of eggs, but during the period of annual recruitment the larvae are a mixture of two generations.

As a contrast at 11 and 14 m the periods both of growth and of exposure to predation are of long duration. This results in higher larval weight and lower number per m². At 11 m depth the larvae are consistently able to complete their life cycle in one year. The transitional zone between one and two-year life cycles is found at 14–17 m since at the latter depth the larvae are unable to make a successful recruitment of larvae every year. At 14 m depth the larvae succeed in having a yearly recruitment in some years. Thus at 17 m and 20 m depth a 2-year life cycle dominates. Population size also increases with depth. This seems primarily due to reduced predation.

Environment

A lake consists of a shallow littoral region and a deep profundal region. Bottom animals are among the commonest of freshwater invertebrates and they form an important link in the food web of lakes. Many are microphagous, feeding on either phytoplankton or organic mud constituents. In their turn, they are eaten by many aquatic predators. They show a great variety of adaptations to their semisessile mode of life. They adapt to the substratum, to the amplitude and rhythm of physical and chemical factors and to the exploitation of food resources.

In the profundal sub-ecosystem the environment is relatively homogenous and the species diversity is very much reduced. The bottom fauna fits into an ecological pattern set by primary production of algae, submerged macrophytes, and physical and chemical factors of a lake. The physico-chemical factors affect the size and seasonal trend of primary production whereas the latter determines the range of various physical and chemical factors at the bottom.

The investigations were carried out in Lake Esrom, Northern Sealand, 35 km north of Copenhagen. Lake Esrom, the second largest lake in Denmark, has proved admirably suited for this purpose since it is large, 17.3 km², and consists of a single regular basin without submerged banks or depressions of which 10 km² form a muddy, uniform habitat, mostly 0.5 m thick. Physiographical information of interest for Lake Esrom, with special reference to primary production of food and to bottom fauna, is given by Berg (1938), Jónasson and Mathiesen (1959), Jónasson and Kristiansen (1967, Fig. 1), and Jónasson (1969, Fig. 1).

In the profundal of Lake Esrom *Chironomus anthracinus*, both in numbers (up to 70,000 individuals/m²) and weight, is the most important species. The larvae inhabit the mud bottom from 10–22 m depth. *C. anthracinus* ZETT. (syn. *bathophilus* KIEFF and *liebeli* KIEFF) is a circumpolar, holarctic and widely distributed species which prefers the muddy profundal zone of medium eutrophic lakes of north and temperate latitudes (Brundin, 1949).

Growth

This section is a summary of previous papers (Jónasson, 1964, see Fig. 1 and 2; Jónasson and Kristiansen, 1967, see Fig. 15). The growth of *C. anthracinus* at a depth of 20 m depends on environmental factors, lake rhythm and food in the following way.
1. During winter, growth depends upon the production of food by the phytoplankton. Temperatures of 2.2–4.4 °C are not limiting, as might be expected, but ice-cover stops the primary production during the first few months of the year and larval growth during the whole ice-period. A considerable production of Chlorophyceae (green algae) in March-April under the ice does not facilitate the growth of larvae. (Jónasson and Kristiansen, 1967, Table 8 and 9).
2. In spring, larval growth follows the rhythm of the spring maximum of phytoplankton (90% Bacillariophyceae – diatoms). The average growth increase of first-year larvae is 72% in wet weight and 171% in dry weight.
3. In early summer, growth takes place when Chlorophyceae are quantitatively important in the plankton. In late summer during the peak of primary production, growth stops due to oxygen lack. Thus, the larvae in the bottom of deep water (hypolimnion) are not able to use the very high production of bluegreen algae as food.
4. The importance of oxygen as a growth regulating factor is shown by the fact that the average weight of first-year larvae increases 900% within 3–4 weeks after the autumn turnover, while primary production rapidly decreases. Growth stops in October as a result of lack of food and at a temperature above 11 °C; primary production at this time is approximately 0.2 g C/m² lake surface/day.
5. Growth, population size and oxygen uptake show that the food requirements of the larvae, in some cases, are higher than the phytoplankton production.

Population dynamics

The above-mentioned relationships between lake rhythm, primary production and accumulation of organic matter in the larvae, is a necessary basis for understanding the population dynamics of *C. anthracinus*.

Emergence and swarming

The larvae inhabit the mud bottom where they live in vertical tubes lined with salivary secretion, as described by Jónasson (1971). The metamorphosis from larva to pupa takes place gradually over a longer period within the same tube. At the beginning of May the tubes contain pupae ready for emergence. The pupae ascend to the surface like a Cartesian diver. On reaching the surface, the pupa behaves like a boat. The anterior dorsal part of the pupal skin then opens and the first pair of legs of the imago appear through the rupture. Within a few seconds metamorphosis is complete and the imago flies away. At the same time the dark red colour of the larva and pupa changes into the black of the imago. This complicated process lasts for only 35 seconds.

The ascent of pupae from the bottom to the surface is restricted to the night hours, from 19.00 to 1.00 h (Jónasson, 1961, Fig. 5). The moment is well chosen since the lake is usually more quiet then than at any other time and risk of hatching failure is therefore much reduced. In 1956, 500 individuals emerged per m² per night, which amounts to about 5 billions from the whole lake in one night. Since the emergence takes place during the night when temperatures are low, the imagines are not able to fly and the lake surface appears to be covered by a greyish brown carpet (the colour of the wings) consisting of millions of imagines. Just after sunrise they fly away.

The emergence takes place at temperatures between 6.2 and 7.2 °C. It is limited to 3 to 6 days and is completed a few days before the thermocline is established (Jónasson, 1971). There is no doubt that temperature is an important stimulus since emergence does not take place when a temperature gradient is established; the influence of temperature seems restricted to the very last phase of the life-cycle as shown by the following experiment. Larvae were placed at a temperature of 2.5 and 6.5 to 7.0 °C respectively. After 48 hours the relative composition of developmental stages was quite different in the two groups (Table 1):

Table 1. The moulting of larvae to imago at two different temperatures.

Temperature (°C)	Number of		
	larvae	pupae	imagines
2.5	27	71	0
6.5–7.0	25	24	23

The result is that at the lower temperature the larvae only pupate but at the higher temperature, similar to that at the lake, they develop through to the imago. Similarly, fullgrown larvae kept at low temperatures for months may pupate, but very seldom emerge. The most important factor which determines the time of emergence is the accumulation of fat in the body, since it is a fuel for flight (Jónasson, 1965, Table 1). The timing of larval growth is related to the timing of the spring maximum of phytoplankton (Jónasson, 1964, 1965; Jónasson and Kristiansen, 1967), consequently the time of emergence varies between years, e.g.: 1954, from 6th to 14th May; 1955, from 15th to 18th May; 1956, from 11th to 17th May.

The data for Lake Esrom during the period 1954 to 1966 show that the emergence period has varied between the 3rd and 22nd of May (cf. Thienemann, 1951).

The absolute size of the emergence varies greatly (in 1956 it was 10 times higher than in

1954 and 1955). This depends partly on the size of larval population and partly on the proportion of first year larvae which emerge. Weight is also very important. If the larvae in spring reach the weight of about 13 mg they emerge and those which are left weigh only 10 mg.

The average proportion emerging at the end of first year varies between years, but for the years 1955, 1957, 1959 and 1961 the average percentage was between 23% and 38%. Between sampling stations in the lake within the same year there is also a difference ranging from 9% to 47%.

Swarming occurs mainly in the shelter of the forest on the west coast. Swarming needs dead calm and other parts of the lake are too windy. The lake is usually most calm about sunset, and swarming is most active at that time. The swarms consist mainly of males. A rough estimate of catches in swarms showed a male-female ratio of 50:1. Females are common in the grass along the shore.

Egg laying occurs mainly about sunset and continues until darkness. The females fly with drooping hind legs and with a curved abdomen under which the brown egg mass is placed in the angle near the end. The female dips the end of the abdomen into the water and the egg mass is then free. The dry egg mass is about 2×2.5 mm in diameter, but its gel swells in water to about 100 times its volume. Since specific gravity is nearly the same as that of water the egg masses sink slowly. As mentioned, the beech forest on the west side of the lake is of vital importance as shelter for swarm formation since the prevailing wind direction is south, southwest and west, and *C. anthracinus* swarms only in dead calm. Therefore, the bulk of egg masses may be expected to be deposited on the western lake shore. The south and south-western winds move the egg masses to the north and north-eastern part of the lake. This fact becomes clear from counts in different places of the initial numbers of young larvae of the 1956 generation. The number of individuals per m² increases from south to north of the lake in the folloling way: Slotspark, 38,184; Endrup, 42,360; Kobæks Vig, 56,072 and Skovlund 70,920.

After westerly winds during swarming and egg laying, the distribution of young larvae is quite different. The eastern station, Kobæks Vig, then shows the largest initial number.

The pattern of emergence means that *C. anthracinus* is extremely vulnerable at this time. The effect of unfavourable weather, especially wind and rain, during the short period of emergence can be very deleterious. If the weather is rough, fewer imagines hatch and the resultant number of juvenile larvae is small. If it is favourable, the number of juvenile larvae is large.

Effect of seasonal events

The seasonal variation in numbers of *C. anthracinus* larvae over a period of 2 years at 20 m depth is shown in Fig. 1 A. As already mentioned, part of the population has a one-year cycle (emergence 1955) and the other a two-year cycle (emergence 1956). The arrows indicate the influence of external factors and the curve indicates the response of the larval population.

It shows clearly that larval mortality is comparatively low during July, August and until the 20th of September; the population was reduced by 1,500 individuals/m² over this period. The low mortality is due to the stratification of the lake water, which prevents fish from living in the hypolimnion during this period, so that no predation occurs. The larval population is thus protected against fish predation, and the low death rate which occurs is

223

due to other less tangible causes which can be referred to as 'natural mortality'. The autumn overturn results in higher temperature and oxygenated water. The larval activity increases and fish predation begins. The large drop in larval numbers by approximately 4,000 individuals/m^2 during this period, is mainly due to fish predation. During the winter the activity of poikilothermic animals is low (e.g. the eels burrow into the mud), fish predation ceases and larval numbers remain constant.

Experiments with silver eels (*Anguilla anguilla* L.) show that the respiration rate remains at a constant level from air saturated water down to 50% or even 20% saturation; below this the ventilation rate declines and finally stops (Boëtius unpublished data, cf. Lindroth, 1947). Young eels are the most important predators of the larvae and it is essential to know their critical oxygen limit, because at the time when they leave the profundal their consumption of the larvae stops. A comparison with oxygen data (Jónasson, 1971, Fig. 31) shows that in 1958 this critical low oxygen level was reached in the bottom layer during the first half of July and in 1959 as early as in June. The eels are able to return again after autumn overturn.

In the profundal zone of Lake Esrom it is thus possible to separately estimate mortality from fish predation and other forms of mortality in the population of *C. anthracinus* at different seasons of the year.

In the second year (1955 to 1956) the timing of the fluctuations is largely the same as in the first year, but they are smaller because the larvae are now full-grown.

It is rather surprising that no new generation appeared at 20 m in 1955 and that, in general, a new generation is produced only every second year. In fact, alternating generations should not be expected. The most likely explanation is that the eggs of the emerging population which reach the deeper profundal are eaten by the *C. anthracinus* larvae population which remain there. In the spring of 1955 this population amounted to 7000–7500 per m^2. and their feeding on the mud surface is sufficiently effective to clear it of eggs and small larvae.

During feeding, second and third instar *Chironomus* larvae sweep the surface (Jónasson, 1971). Measurements show that the larvae extend 3/4 of their body length out of their tubes. If we assume this to be the feeding area, then burrows of the newborn and young larvae cover the surface of the mud completely, without overlapping. After the first autumn overturn and the resulting larval growth, feeding areas overlap to such an extent that they amount to three times the area of the mud surface. Because of increased larval size, areas of feeding continue to overlap at this high level despite the reduction in numbers in autumn and partial emergence in spring. A reduction in feeding area occurs only when the population declines during the second autumn of a two year cycle. After the emergence in May 1956 there were no larvae left to feed (Fig. 1B).

On the basis of the above data, 2,000 fully grown larvae per m^2 would completely cover the sediment surface during their feeding activities. If the population exceeds this size, neither eggs nor young larvae could survive on the surface sediment. If the population is below this number, a new generation of larvae is able to settle and a mixed population of one-year old and newly hatched larvae occurs. This mechanism seems to determine whether or not a new population is established each year (Jónasson, 1971, Fig. 58 A). From Figs. 2 and 3 it can be seen that if the larval population is very small then young larvae are recruited to the population every year; e.g. at 11 and 14 m depth in Tumlingehus, and at Endrup every year from 1964 to 1967.

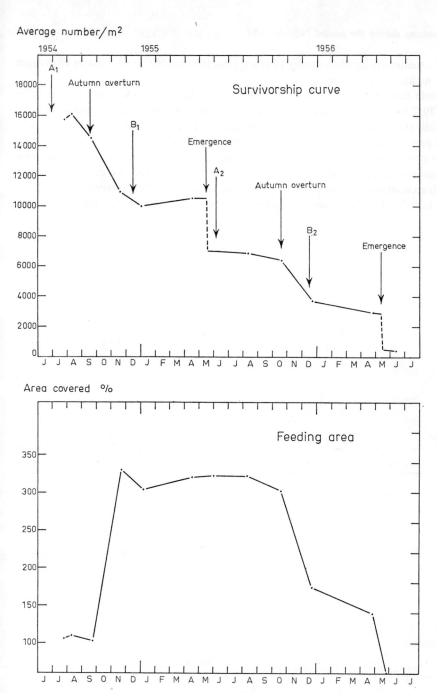

Fig. 1A. The seasonal fluctuations in numbers per m² during a two-year larval life cycle of the population of *C. anthracinus* (1954 to 1956) in relation to external factors. A_1 and A_2 indicate the beginning of summer stagnation period in first and second year of life cycle. B_1 and B_2 indicate that fish predation ceases, caused by decrease in temperature.

Fig. 1B. The seasonal variation in the area covered by the substrate feeding *C. anthracinus*.

The fluctuations in numbers during 14 years, from 1953 to 1967, in mid-lake at 20 m depth (Endrup) are shown in Fig. 2.

A main characteristic is the two-year life-cycle each beginning in an even numbered year from 1952 to 1962. A general feature of these life-cycles is the high population density, especially the big initial numbers. The large number remaining after the first year's emergence prevents a new generation from becoming established. If these conditions are no longer present, and the population density after first year's emergence is low, the new generation is able to occupy the vacant space and become established every year.

This accounts for the successful recruitment of larvae at two year intervals from 1952 to 1962; but after 1962 recruitment occurred every year until 1968. During this last period a

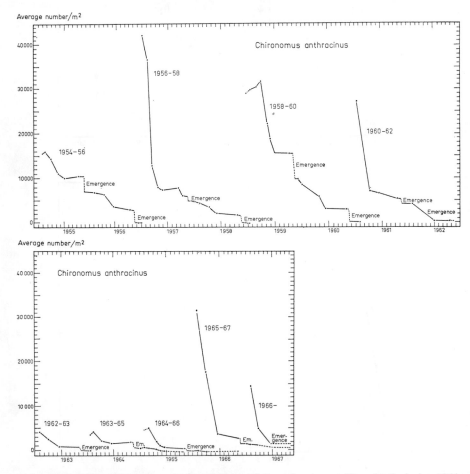

Fig. 2. The seasonal fluctuations in the numbers of *C. anthracinus* at 20 m depth during 1954–1967. Two-year life cycles dominate the period from 1954 to 1962 and they begin in the even numbered years i.e. 1954–1956–1958 and 1960. A one-year life cycle is found in 1962–63. The succeeding life cycles are two-year life cycles i.e. 1963 to 1965, 1964 to 1966, 1965 to 1967. Sewage introduced from 1962 onwards.

two-year life-cycle was replaced by a one-year life-cycle only once, in 1962 to 1963.

As a result of such alternating recruitment during 1952 to 1962 the benthic fauna at any one time contains larvae only from a single generation of eggs, but during the period of annual recruitment the larvae are a mixture of two generations.

It may be worth pointing out that there is a change in the numbers of final instar larvae before and after 1962. Prior to this time they were numerous, and afterwards they are fewer. The high recruitment in 1965 suggests that this is not primarily related to the numbers of imagos emerging but to a higher survival rate during the first larval stages. These facts seem to suggest some basic changes in the lake ecosystem which became detectable in 1962 and which were due to the introduction of sewage.

How may we explain such differences in the life cycle of the same species?

If the weather is favourable during emergence and during the adult swarming season, the larval population of the succeeding year is large, e.g. 1956. A small larval population may result, as in 1962, if unfavourable conditions for swarming occur after there has been a small larval population (230 individuals/m²) during the preceding season.

In his monograph of the bottom animals of Lake Esrom, Berg (1938) describes *C. anthracinus* as having a one-year life-cycle. However, scrutiny of his primary data shows that the species had, in fact, a two-year life-cycle which, at that time, began in odd numbered years (1931 and 1933). This must have been due to the occurrence of either a one-year life cycle or an alternating two-year life cycle. The evidence gained about external factors and food during the last 15 years allows us to predict the environmental conditions necessary for a one-year life cycle. The larvae must get a 'flying start' in early larval life and reach a fresh weight of about 6 mg before the summer stagnation period. After an early autumn overturn a long period of growth during the autumn is necessary to allow a weight of about 10 mg to be reached. The final spring increase to 13 mg is then easily attained. This happened in 1962, and is entirely different from former conditions when at the end of autumn the larvae had a weight of only 6 mg.

The effect of seasonal events was discussed in the previous section. However, during a long span of years, variations occur which are not observed during a single life cycle. An early autumn circulation exposes the larvae to a prolonged period of predation by fish, and causes the larval population to decrease rapidly e.g. during the period 5 September to 19 September 1956, the number of individuals/m² was reduced by 24,000 and, similarly, during the period 28 September to 10 October 1960, numbers were reduced by 18,000 individuals/m². If autumn overturn occurs late the period of predation is short and the decrease in larval numbers less, e.g. in 1958 there was a reduction by 10,000 individuals/m² during the period 24 October to 27 November.

These variations in the length of predation period result in different population levels at the end of autumn.

Big initial populations of the order of 16,000 – 42,000 individuals per m² may, after the first autumn season, result in various population levels (4,000–15,000 (or even 18,000) individuals per m²) during the winter. Since the winter level seems rather constant, the next variation in population density occurs at the time of emergence. The timing of this period in relation to primary production is discussed (in Jónasson, 1971). The question now is whether the absolute size of emergence is influenced by primary production. This is difficult to answer, because a more intensive sampling procedure is needed. After an ice-cover, a short peak of primary production occurs and this results in high emergence numbers (e.g. 1955). In ice-free years the emergence numbers may be either low (e.g. 1961) or extremely high (e.g. 1959). The reason may well be that in icefree years the primary production occurs over a long period during which the larvae grow rather slowly at a low temperature, and this results in lower emergence numbers.

Populations dynamics at different depths

An attempt has now been made to analyse and explain the influence of the external factors on the life-cycle and population dynamics of *C. anthracinus*. The analysis should now be followed by a synthesis. *C. anthracinus* lives at depths from 10-22m. At shallower depths, from 11 and 14 m, both the growth period and exposure to predation are long. This means that there is a higher larval weight and a lower number per m². Fig. 3 shows that at 11 m depth the larvae are consistently able to complete their life cycle in one year. The transitional zone between one- and two-year life cycles is found to be at 14–17 m because at the

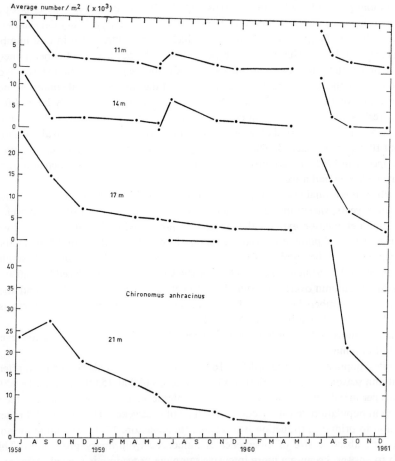

Fig. 3. The seasonal fluctuations in the numbers of *C. anthracinus* at different depths at the Tumlingehus section during 1958–1962. One-year life cycles are found in shallower water (11 and 14 m) and two-year cycles in deeper water (17 and 21 m).

latter depth a successful recruitment of larvae does not occur every year (cf. Fig. 3). At the 14 m depth successful annual recruitment is intermittent. At 17 and 21 m depth a 2-year life cycle dominates. The population curves also show clearly the fact that larval populations increase with depth. This seems mainly due to reduced predation, since the actual predation period decreases with increasing depth. This ability of the larval population to change its life history in response to a change in environmental conditions raises the question of how many larvae per unit area left over from the previous generation are necessary to prevent a new generation of eggs from settling. From the measurements shown in Fig. 3 it is possible to estimate that the necessary number of fullgrown larvae is approximately 2000 per m². A scrutiny of the number per m² at Tumlingehus confirms these measurements. At 11 m depth larval numbers in spring are always below 2000 individuals per m² and an annual recruitment takes place. At 14 m depth both annual and biennial recruitment takes place depending on the actual size of larval population in spring. Thus at 14m depth, numbers in spring were low during the period 1958 to 1960 and an annual recruitment took place while in the odd numbered years 1955 and 1957 the spring number still was high and a biennial recruitment took place.

Berg (1938) showed that in September the average weight of larvae was 7.4 mg at 11 m depth; 7.6 mg at 14 m, 3.9 mg at 17m and 1.6 mg at 20 m.

These weights describe clearly the fundamental difference in life conditions above and below the thermocline. This is in good agreement with the observation that emergence begins first at 14 m then at 11 m and 17 m and at last at 21 m as shown by Jónasson (1971, Table 29).

References

Berg, K., 1938. Studies on the bottom animals of Esrom Lake. *K. danske Vidensk. Selsk. Skr. Nat. Math. Afd.* 9 Rk. 8: 1–225.

Berg, K., P. M. Jónasson & K. W. Ockelmann, 1962. The respiration of some animals from the profundal zone of a lake. *Hydrobiologia* 19: 1–40.

Berg, K. & P. M. Jónasson, 1965. Oxygen consumption of profundal lake animals at low oxygen content of the water. *Hydrobiologia* 26: 131–144.

Brundin, L., 1949. Chironomiden und andere Bodentiere der südschwedischen Urgebirgsseen. *Rep. Freshw. Res. Drottningholm* 30: 1–914.

Jónasson, P. M., 1954. An improved funnel trap for capturing emerging aquatic insects, with some preliminary results. *Oikos* 5: 179–189.

Jónasson, P. M., 1955. The efficiency of sieving techniques for sampling freshwater bottom fauna. *Oikos* 6: 183–208.

Jónasson, P. M., 1961. Population dynamics in Chironomus anthracinus ZETT. in the profundal zone of Lake Esrom. *Verh. Int. Ver. Limnol.* 14: 196–203.

Jónasson, P. M., 1964. The relationship between primary production and production of profundal bottom invertebrates in a Danish eutrophic lake. *Verh. Int. Ver. Limnol.* 15: 471–479.

Jónasson, P. M., 1965. Factors determining population size of Chironomus anthracinus in Lake Esrom. *Mitt. Int. Verein. Limnol.* 13: 139–162.

Jónasson, P. M., 1969. Bottom fauna and eutrophication. Eutrophication: causes, consequences, correctives p. 274–305. National Academy of Sciences, Washington D.C. USA.

Jónasson, P. M., 1971. Ecology of profundal fauna in relation to phytoplankton in Lake Esrom. (in press).

Jónasson, P. M. & Hans Mathiesen, 1959. Measurements of primary production in two Danish eutrophic lakes. Esrom Sø and Furesø. *Oikos* 10: 137–167.

Jónasson, P. M. & Jørgen Kristiansen, 1967. Primary and secondary production in Lake Esrom. Growth of *Chironomus anthracinus* in relation to seasonal cycles of phytoplankton and dissolved oxygen. *Int. Revue. ges. Hydrobiol.* 52: 163–217.

Keyl, H. G. & I. Keyl, 1960. Die cytologische Diagnostik der Chironomiden. I. *Arch. Hydrobiol.*
56: 43–47.

Keyl, H. G., 1960. Die cytologische Diagnostik der Chironomiden. II. *Arch. Hydrobiol.* 57: 187–
195.

Keyl, H. G., 1961. Die cytologische Diagnostik der Chironomiden. III. *Arch. Hydrobiol.* 58:
1–6.

Lindroth, Arne, 1947. Vattenförorening och vattenfaunans andningsproblem. *Vattenhygien* 2:
32–43.

Plagens, U., E. J. Fittkau, P. M. Jónasson & G. Braunitzer, 1970. Vergleichende Untersuchungen
der Hämoglobine verschiedener Chironomiden. Auszug aus Dissertation U. Plagens. Naturwiss.
Fakult. der Univ. München. (in Vorbereitung).

Thienemann, A., 1951. Das Schwärmen von *Chironomus bathophilus* K. (= *anthracinus* ZETT.) im
Plöner Seengebiet 1918–1950. *Arch. Hydrobiol.* Suppl. Bd. 18: 692–704.

Discussion

Participants: Jónasson (Author), Jacobs, Labeyrie, Varley and Zahavi

What happens to the eggs laid by the first-year imagos? It seems highly improbable, if only on statistical grounds that none of these eggs at all should survive and start a new generation. Should there not be other reasons than cannibalism to account for the lack of a one-year cycle? (JACOBS). Experiments show that the larvae are extremely efficient substrate feeders (Jónasson, 1971, Fig. 41), and they cover the sediment surface up to three times or more (Fig. 1), depending on the population size in spring. The head diameter of these fullgrown larvae is 690 μm, and their mouth size approximately 250 μm. Thus, they are easily able to predate both eggs and first instar larvae which have a diameter of 119 and 113 μm respectively (AUTHOR).

The problem of cannibalism may be examined by diluting the population and then seeing if all larvae will emerge at the same time. (ZAHAVI). It is easy to design, but difficult to carry out such an experiment, because it is difficult to make observations on a soft bottom in deep water and complete darkness. In fact, such an experiment is carried out in the transect mentioned at depths from 11 to 21 m with different densities of larvae (AUTHOR).

There must be a difference between the two types of animals that emerge in different years because of differential hatching. (JACOBS). The two different life cycles are the result of ecological contrasts in the habitat at the time of egg deposition, particularly whether larvae are abundant or not (AUTHOR).

What is the evolutionary importance of the emergence after one year when all the eggs are destroyed by cannibalism? (LABEYRIE). The retention of both one- and two-year life cycles is the result of differences in the utilization of food and availability of oxygen at the depth the larvae are living. The emerging larvae in spring weigh 13.1 mg and these have big, fat bodies, but those left over weigh only 10.3 mg (AUTHOR).

There are no larvae with a three-year cycle (AUTHOR to ZAHAVI).

The insect must be able to detect light at the bottom of the lake, otherwise there would be no diurnal rhythm for the emergence of the pupae to the surface. (VARLEY). It seems reasonable to suggest that light is the immediate mechanism. Light measurements and calculation show that the approximate light penetration into Lake Esrom is 1 % of sub-surface light at 7 m, 0,1 % at 10,5 m, 0.01 % at 14 m and 0.001 % at 21 m. Light meters can measure down to 0.01 % and light penetration is due to seasonal variation. Further, hypolimnion water might be clearer than epilimnion water. The human eye is able to perceive light intensities of 0.01 % subsurface light. However, the larvae must be more sensitive than either instruments or the human eye (Author).

Proc. Adv. Study Inst. Dynamics Numbers Popul. (Oosterbeek, 1970) 232–242

Self regulation in aphid populations

M. J. Way and M. E. Cammell

Department of Zoology and Applied Entomology, Imperial College, London

Abstract

Animals with unstable populations (show large numerical changes) may have as well developed self-regulatory, or other stabilising mechanisms as species with more stable populations. The latter may owe this stability in part to their intrinsic sluggishness in ability to respond to environmental changes. Stabilising mechanisms may be even more necessary in species, like many aphids, that must adjust to an unstable environment than in species living in a more stable environment.

Possible self-regulating mechanisms in some aphids are briefly reviewed; they seem to result from complex interactions between the behavioural attributes of the species, the density of the population and the quality and quantity of the food supply.

The interactions between self regulatory processes and natural enemy action are also discussed. It is considered that aphid pest problems, especially of annual monocultures, arise when self-regulatory mechanisms fail to prevent increase in numbers. The delayed density dependent action of natural enemies may then induce violent oscillations in numbers. Therefore, the growing of crops may put the aphid population at risk during the troughs created by such cyclic changes. Self-regulation seems to be most clearly defined in aphids whose dispersion behaviour on plants makes them relatively unavailable to natural enemies.

The numbers of some aphid species change violently over short periods of time and thus their populations appear to be 'unstable'. Such aphids are succeeding in a way of life which each season requires the exploitation of a sequence of temporary host plants which vary enormously in space and time in terms of quality, quantity and pattern of dispersion. Thus in Western Europe, *Aphis fabae* SCOP. occurs from October to May on the shrub *Euonymus europaeus* which is absent or rare over large areas but sometimes locally common in hedgerows and scrubland. From May to July the aphid colonises certain annual weeds which, although qualitatively attractive at this time, may be scarce and scattered except in arable areas where there are also locally dense concentrations of certain very attractive crop hosts. Several annual weed species of very varying quality and pattern of dispersion are the main hosts in August and September after which the aphid returns to *E. europaeus*. Therefore, while there is the appearance of instability it is also a fact that the species is succeeding in violently changing circumstances; this implies the existence of self regulating mechanisms that are perhaps more sensitive than those possessed by species with so-called stable populations that live in relatively stable environments. The nature of self-regulating mechanisms in aphids will therefore be examined briefly, particularly in those aphids that colonise a succession of host plants.

Life histories

Aphid species vary from those that can maintain permanent populations on particular perennial host plants (e.g. *Drepanosiphum platanoides* on *Acer platanoides*, or *Therioaphis trifolii* (MONELL) on alfalfa), through those which can stay on a particular annual or biennual plant throughout all or most of its season (e.g. *Brevicoryne brassicae* L. on Cruciferae) to those, like *A. fabae* and *Myzus persicae* SULZ. which successively colonise several annual hosts during the season.

Aphids are plant parasites dependent on the soluble nutrients in phloem sap which is imbibed through the proboscis. This readily assimilated food for animals which are parthenogenetic, viviparous and have telescoped generations, permits very rapid multiplication of wingless forms (apterae) on a host plant. Winged forms (alatae) are produced which colonise new hosts; the original hosts may remain colonised or be deserted depending on the aphid and plant species involved.

Colonisation by alatae

The alate must first alight and 'taste' a plant before it can assess whether or not it is a host species which is at a nutritionally suitable stage of growth – aphids can assimilate the soluble sugars and amino-acids present in immature or senescent growth but normally do not colonise mature growth in which soluble nutrients are scarce relative to insoluble ones. In fact, the colonising alate is hypersensitive to the physiological state of the plant and thus the great majority of alate *A. fabae* and *M. persicae* failed to stay and colonise host plants which physiologically seemed highly attractive (Kennedy and Stroyan, 1959). That such plants can support aphid populations was shown by the normal development and reproduction of apterae cultured on them (Way and Banks, 1968). The sensitivity of the alate is such that the strength of flight elicited by a rejected plant is related to its degree of unsuitability (Kennedy, 1966). The aphid will therefore tend to disperse away from a seemingly very unsuitable host plant environment whilst remaining in the more favourable vicinity of better hosts. The colonising behaviour of such alate aphids is thus a sophisticated example of a situation – which is becoming increasingly well documented – where the food plant is abundant but in fact may be limiting. It is analogous to that where *Cactoblastis* fails to colonise seemingly suitable *Opuntia* (Birch, these Proceedings). In aphids, this restriction on colonisation happens not only when the plant is inherently unsuitable but also because it has seemingly become of selective value for aphids to be hypersensitive even to what is suitable. This appears to be a self-limiting mechanism which helps to ensure that the host plant population is not over-exploited while, at the same time enhancing the success of those aphid populations which became established since these are on maximally nutritious plants. As discussed later, this behaviour may create problems in agriculture where monocultures comprising large numbers of plants may be simultaneously available in an exceptionally attractive condition.

Population development on the plant

An alate may produce groups of up to about 20 progeny which reproduce to form either a dense aggregate on a leaf or stem – as do *B. brassicae* and *A. fabae*, or a more 'spaced out' but still gregarious population, e.g. *M. persicae*. At first, aggregation benefits the aphids;

as indicated by increased reproductive rates and large size of individuals in aggregates initiated by about 8–20 individuals compared with smaller or larger initial aggregates (Way and Banks, 1967; Murdie, 1970; Way and Cammell, 1970). This effect is, however, short lived because aggregation begins to slow the multiplication rate once the population has reached a critical size of perhaps only 40 individuals. Thus in one field study with *A. fabae* (Way, 1968; Way and Banks, 1967), where mortality from other sources such as natural enemies was prevented by a large field cage, the multiplication rate of the newly established field population was 30 after 14 days whereas the potential multiplication calculated from the observed multiplication rates of successive generations of aphids kept uncrowded on plants was 89. After 21 days the figures were 39 and 490 respectively. It can be said, therefore, that self-induced competition caused by the tendency to aggregate begins to limit population increase at an early stage of population growth, and well in advance of the time when there is an absolute shortage of food. What then is the possible selective value of such behaviour?

Experimental populations of *B. brassicae* were confined to one leaf of each of a set of small brassica plants and their development was compared with ones kept dispersed throughout all leaves of another set of plants. More and larger alatae were produced by the one-leaf colonised plants (Way and Cammell, 1970). Furthermore, when the experiment ended, the one-leaf colonised plants were still alive whereas the others had been killed by the aphids. The fact that an aphid population on a single leaf of a small plant can ultimately be more productive than when dispersed over the plant is perhaps partly because only one leaf is mechanically injured and contaminated by the aphids. However, the success of this method of exploiting the plant derives primarily from the ability of the aphid aggregate to divert food to its leaf from other leaves of the plant via the phloem (Way and Cammell, 1970). The aphids appear to be acting like a 'sink' which is equivalent, for example, to the meristematic region of a plant.

In *B. brassicae* and perhaps in other aphids the restriction in the rate of increase of numbers is not caused by a decrease in the proportion of reproducing adult apterae in the population but by a decrease in reproduction by apterae; these maintain a remarkably constant proportion (about 7%) of the population irrespective of aggregate size varying from about 200 to 4000 individuals (Way, 1968). During this time, however, the proportion of newly born aphids in the aggregate may decrease from about 80% to about 10% while that of aphids destined to be migrant alatae increases from less than 5% to over 50%. Apart from slowing down of multiplication rate and qualitative change represented by increased proportion of alatae, adult aphids both alate and apterous, become smaller, commonly to 1/4th or 1/5th with a limit of about 1/10th in *A. fabae* (Way and Banks, 1967). This seems to be an adaptation to deteriorating conditions which enables the maximum number of individuals to become adult. There is also evidence that the smaller apterae are better adapted to crowded conditions since their fecundity is less decreased by crowding than that of larger ones. Although the small aphids are inherently less fecund than the large ones and their progeny are smaller, this does not debilitate subsequent generations since their progeny grow relatively more during development and are almost as large when adult and as fecund as the progeny of large apterae. Thus in one generation there is complete recovery from density induced size decrease.

Production of alatae

As already indicated, the proportion of alatae increases as an aggregate of *B. brassicae* or *A. fabae* on a leaf or stem grows and ages. The production and migration of alatae not only limits local increase in the aggregate and on the plant as a whole but, in a species which only lives ephemerally as a local population, it has the vital function of perpetuating the regional population of the species on its succession of host plants. In a few species there is evidence that food quantity or quality can directly influence the switch from aptera to alate production and vice-versa (Mittler and Sutherland, 1969) but this is probably of minor significance compared with tactile stimuli from other aphids (Lees, 1922). Such stimuli are a natural consequence of aggregation behaviour and are accentuated by conditions – such as starvation – that make the aphids restless. Starvation therefore acts indirectly as well as sometimes directly. That alatae are produced early in the life of an aggregate of *B. brassicae* is probably due to jostling of growing aphids in the aggregate which at this stage is most dense (300 per cm^2) but well fed as indicated by the large size of the adult aphids. Later the density decreases and, in a deteriorating aggregate, falls below 10 per cm^2, but by then the aphids have become much more restless presumably due to deterioration in the food supply from the damaged leaf. Thus tactile stimuli increase despite the less crowded conditions. The controlling mechanism is delicate; for example, in some species aphids conditioned to become alatae may nevertheless revert to apterae if they are removed from the crowding stimulus soon after birth (Johnson, 1966). Furthermore, the sensitivity of aphids to the crowding stimulus is modified by past as well as by immediate conditions. Thus, adult *A. fabae* are more sensitive to a particular crowding stimulus (i.e. produce more alate progeny relative to apterous) if they have been crowded rather than uncrowded during their development (Shaw, 1970a). Furthermore, it is now known that alatae may vary qualitatively; some winged individuals do not have the urge to fly and behave as apterae, others probably fly only short distances before they begin to seek new host plants, while others have the characteristics of long distance 'migrants'. In *A. fabae* the proportion of 'migrants' among their alate progeny increases with increasing density of the parents, and is relatively greater if the parents are crowded rather than uncrowded during their development (Shaw, 1970b). Similar differences occur among *M. persicae* and *B. brassicae* alatae (Way and Cammell, unpubl.).

It is concluded from this evidence that some aphids possess an array of self-regulating responses elicited by density change interacting with changing food supply within a framework provided by the aggregation behaviour of the particular aphid species. Thus, the control of reproduction and of alate production acts through a sensitive feed back mechanism adjusting the local population to the changing conditions of the growing plant and also providing different kinds of alatae to ensure dispersion of the species to new hosts both locally and at a distance. Except when very young or old, a single aggregate of *B. brassicae*, for example, is simultaneously producing the full range of forms; the proportion of each varies with the size and age of the aggregate and the condition of the host. Large apterae, newly moulted alatae and a large proportion of newly born aphids are present in the densely crowded 'leading edge' of the growing aggregate whereas the part first colonised may be relatively sparsely occupied by small alatae and late instar alate larvae.

The aggregate is therefore considered to be the basic population unit. The population on the plant consists of one or more groups of competing aggregates which exploit the plant piecemeal and the local population consists of all aggregates on a group of nearby plants.

Population regulation however must depend on interactions occurring on a regional basis, the size of the region and the attributes of the regional population depending crucially on the quality and quantity of the alatae which in turn depend on interactions within the individual aggregates.

Discussion

The numbers of some aphids can vary enormously from month to month or even weekly. This is made possible by the ability to multiply rapidly, to vary reproduction rate within wide limits and to produce migrants with little delay in sensitive response to changing density and food supply. These qualities enable aphid numbers to adjust very quickly to the quickly changing food supply of a particular growing plant as well as to changes in quality, overall abundance and pattern of dispersion of available food plants. The large numerical change in these aphid populations – brought about by the ability to respond quickly and delicately to changes in food supply – is no doubt a successful adaptation to a particular way of life. Many animals with so-called stable populations do not have such attributes, their prolonged life cycle and smaller fecundity makes it impossible for them to respond at all sensitively to changes in their food supply. Thus most animals, normally regarded as having stable populations, have an intrinsic sluggishness of response to changing environmental conditions and this sluggishness in some ways puts less of a premium on the need for self-regulating mechanisms in such animals than in those, like aphids, which can and do react much more sensitively to changing food supply.

If these aphids can react sensitively to food supply, why then do they sometimes reach excessive and crippling numbers as crop pests? Such occurrences do not give the impression that self-regulation is in operation! While certain aphids have qualities which enable them to colonise annual crop habitats, this does not mean that as species they are well adapted to crop conditions. Such aphids evolved before crops occurred and even now, with aphids like *A. fabae* and *M. persicae*, the area of their overall habitat occupied by suitable crops is a very small proportion of the whole. There is therefore likely to be continued selection for adaptation to the 'natural' situation consisting of a diverse environment containing scattered, more or less, isolated host plants varying in age, maturity and vigour. At any one time, success in finding the possibly small proportion of physiologically suitable plants growing in these conditions no doubt depends on the production of very many alatae as an insurance against necessarily large mortalities during migration. Crops, however, unlike the wild host in natural conditions, are grown in such a way (rows of green plants against a bare soil background) that they are highly attractive visually to colonising aphids. They may also lack natural resistance mechanisms possessed by wild plants and are usually nutritionally much more attractive to aphids. Their most attractive stage often coincides in time with late spring/early summer aphid migration and then all plants in a crop are attractive simultaneously. A very large number of alatae of some aphids that would otherwise fail to find suitable host plants, may therefore reach and extensively colonise certain crops. In circumstances where most plants of a field of beans, for example, are colonised by early migrants of *Aphis fabae* the populations on different plants, once they are developed, are continually receiving recruits of crawling apterae and flying alatae from each other. Density induced loss by dispersal is partly nullified. This is particularly important because even on a crop plant like field beans (*Vicia faba* L.) a population of *A. fabae* is able to adjust to the food supply of the plant – provided density induced dispersal is not impeded (Way and Banks, 1967). In these circumstances, the natural processes of altered reproduction and loss of alatae and of some adult apterae ensures that by the time the plant begins to fail, almost all aphids produced on it have become adult – mostly alatae. This happens even in the absence of natural enemies which would, at least, cut short the life-time of the population on the plant and would certainly consume the 'tail' of immature forms that might otherwise be left when the plant failed. The situation is further complicated by natural enemies. The sudden arrival of many aphids on a large area of newly planted crop usually makes chance predation relatively insignificant as a mortality factor compared with 'natural' situations. However, the large food supply permits multiplication of natural enemies leading to a characteristic delayed-density dependent effect which in aphids like *A. fabae* seems to be responsible for a basic 2-year population cycle in parts of Western Europe (Way, 1967; Way and Banks 1967). This starts with a large regional build up of the aphids on different crops and arable weeds which then provide the abundant food for multiplication of predators in particular. The delayed build-up of natural enemies may have little effect on aphid numbers on the crop plants until after intraspecific effects have already halted the aphids' population increase. The natural enemies may thus act mainly by hastening the decline and disappearance of aphids from those particular plants. However, later in the summer the large population of regionally dispersing natural enemies reach newly established populations of aphids and their action, combined with that of nutritionally less suitable plants (many are now mature weeds rather than attractively immature crops), has a catastrophic effect on the aphid numbers during the late summer and autumn. These depressive effects last into the spring and early summer of the following year, so populations on crops become relatively small; by then, however, natural enemies have also become scarce. Aphid numbers begin to increase in the late summer and autumn and there are again over-abundant populations on crops in the next year. The evidence as a whole therefore implies that, with aphids like *A. fabae*, the growing of annual crops tends to interfere with density induced dispersal as a self-regulatory mechanism and also accentuates the delayed density dependent action of natural enemies. Thus, rather than benefiting from the large and rich source of food, the species may even be put at risk during the troughs of the cyclic changes in numbers that are promoted. These conclusions apply only to those ephemerally colonising aphids that form large populations on plants. In contrast, *Myzus persicae*, for example, occurs characteristically as sparse populations in temperate regions maintained as such by its spacing-out behaviour, its sensitivity to plant food quality and its sensitivity to alate producing stimuli. In these circumstances, where inherent qualities and dispersal behaviour limit numbers, the plant population remains most of the time at a low density. Such populations are incidentally preyed upon but their dispersion at low density seemingly discourages density dependent natural-enemy induced cyclical change. Nevertheless this might still happen as a side effect of changes in overall natural enemy abundance created by large cyclical changes in the numbers of other crop aphids.

Perhaps the situation in *M. persicae* is comparable to that of *Bupalus* (Gruys, these Proceedings) where density induced dispersal, while not necessarily regulatory, may nevertheless minimize mortality from potentially disturbing density related processes. In this context it is significant that, in laboratory studies, *M. persicae* has invariably proved to be as good as or better than any other aphids tested as food for several coccinellid, syrphid, anthocorid and chrysopid species (Blackman 1967a, b; Mondal, pers. comm.). Perhaps its self induced low density has decreased selection pressure for other protective mechanisms

237

against over-predation, whereas the dense-population, predator-associated species like *A. fabae* and *B. brassicae* are almost invariably less good as food even to the extent that some aphid-predator species cannot breed on them.

So far, only aphids associated with ephemeral annual plant food sources have been considered. In striking contrast are those species which retain permanent populations on perennial host plants e.g. *Drepanosiphum platanoides* on sycamore trees. Various characteristics of the leaves – nutritional, structural and spatial greatly limit the number of leaves on a tree that are suitable for colonisation at any one time. Food and space are therefore severely limiting despite apparent abundance. Spaced-out gregariousness also limits population size, and warning mechanisms and escape reactions provide considerable protection trom predators which therefore seem to be unimportant as causes of mortality. In these circumstances, where the density disturbing effects of natural enemies are minimal, the stabilisation of numbers on a tree is made possible through density induced dispersal of individuals in excess of those that can find space on the available leaves, and also by reproductive diapause involving complete inhibition of reproduction among the aphids occupying the available space. If, however, the available space is under-occupied, dispersal is decreased and diapause is not elicited so the insect continues to reproduce (Dixon, 1966, 1969, 1970; Dixon and McKay, 1970; Kennedy and Crawley, 1967). There is, therefore, good evidence that self-regulating mechanisms are not only controlling increase but also setting an upper limit to the numbers of the species.

For the annual crop aphids we have shown that the complex of self-regulatory mechanisms has several functions, including efficient exploitation of the growing plant by limiting the rate of increase, preservation of some of the local plant population for future generations of the pest and control of quality and quantity of migrants needed to maintain the species regionally. However, this does not mean that they are necessarily concerned in setting an upper limit to the numbers of the regional population. We are faced with a situation where migration may be so extensive that the size and complexity of the region within which the population is truly regulated must often be enormous. In these circumstances, and in the absence of mechanisms like density induced diapause, it is difficult to appreciate how self regulatory processes are able to set a limit on population increase except crudely by starvation on some overpopulated crops. Great environmental heterogeneity in space combined with other elements of heterogeneity may provide the limiting mechanisms (see den Boer, these Proceedings). Furthermore, the regulating effect of density dependent natural enemy action may be important regionally even if its local and short term effect is density disturbing.

References

Birch, L. C., 1971. The role of dispersion and genetic plasticity in determining distribution and abundance. *Proc. Adv. Study Inst. Dynamics Numbers Popul.* (*Oosterbeek, 1970*) 109–128 (these Proceedings).

Blackman, R. L., 1967a. The effects of different aphid foods on *Adalia bipunctata* L. and *Coccinella 7-punctata* L. *Ann. appl. Biol.* 59: 207–219.

Blackman, R. L., 1967b. Selection of aphid prey by *Adalia bipunctata* L. and *Coccinella 7-punctata* L. *Ann. appl. Biol.* 59: 331–338.

Boer, P. J. den, 1971. Stabilization of animal numbers and the heterogeneity of the environment. *Proc. Adv. Study Inst. Dynamics Numbers Popul.* (*Oosterbeek, 1970*) 77–97 (these Proceedings).

Dixon, A. F. G., 1966. The effect of population density and nutritive status of the host on the summer reproductive activity of the sycamore aphid, *Drepanosiphum platanoides* (SCHR.). *J. Anim. Ecol.* 35: 105–112.

Dixon, A. F. G., 1969. Population dynamics of the sycamore aphid *Drepanosiphum platanoides* (SCHR.) (Hemiptera: Aphididae): migratory and trivial flight activity. *J. Anim. Ecol.* 38: 585–606.

Dixon, A. F. G., 1970. Quality and availability of food for a sycamore aphid population. In: A. Watson (Ed.), Animal populations in relation to their food resources p. 271–287. Oxford.

Dixon, A. F.G. & S. McKay, 1970. Aggregation in the sycamore aphid *Drepanosiphum platanoides* (SCHR.) (Hemiptera: Aphididae) and its relevance to the regulation of population growth. *J. Anim. Ecol.* 39: 439–454.

Gruys, P., 1971. On the influence of mutual interference on growth in *Bupalus piniarius. Proc. Adv. Study Inst. Dynamics Numbers Popul. (Oosterbeek, 1970)* 199–207 (these Proceedings).

Johnson, B., 1966. Wing polymorphism in aphids. III. The influence of the host plant. *Entomologia exp. appl.* 9: 213–222.

Kennedy, J. S., 1966. The balance between antagonistic induction and depression of flight activity in *Aphis fabae. J. exp. Biol.* 45: 215–228.

Kennedy, J. S. & L. Crawley, 1967. Spaced-out gregariousness in sycamore aphids, *Drepanosiphum platanoides* (SCHRANK) (Hemiptera, Callaphididae). *J. Anim. Ecol.* 36: 147–170.

Kennedy, J. S. & H. L. G. Stroyan, 1959. Biology of aphids. *A. Rev. Ent.* 4: 139–160.

Lees, A. D., 1966. The control of polymorphism in aphids. *Adv. Insect Physiol.* 3: 207–277.

Mittler, T. E. & O. R. W. Sutherland, 1969. Dietary influences on aphid polymorphism. *Entomologia exp. appl.* 703–713.

Murdie, G., 1969. Some causes of size variation in the pea aphid *Acyrthosiphon pisum. Trans. R. ent. Soc.* 121: 423–442.

Shaw, M. J. P., 1970a. Effects of population density on alienicolae of *Aphis fabae* SCOP. I. The effect of crowding on the production of alatae in the laboratory. *Ann. appl. Biol.* 65: 191–196.

Shaw, M. J. P., 1970b. Effects of population density on alienicolae of *Aphis fabae* SCOP. II. The effects of crowding on the expression of migratory urge among alatae in the laboratory. *Ann. appl. Biol.* 65: 197–203.

Way, M. J., 1967. The nature and causes of annual fluctuations in numbers of *Aphis fabae* SCOP. on field beans (*Vicia faba*). *Ann. appl. Biol.* 59: 175–188.

Way, M. J., 1968. Intra-specific mechanisms with special reference to aphid populations. In: T.R.E. Southwood (Ed.), Insect Abundance. p. 18–36. London.

Way, M. J. & C. J. Banks. 1967. Intra-specific mechanisms in relation to the natural regulation of numbers of *Aphis fabae* SCOP. *Ann. appl. Biol.* 59: 189–205.

Way, M. J. & C. J. Banks, 1968. Population studies on the active stages of the black bean aphid, *Aphis fabae* SCOP. on its winter host *Euonymus europaeus* L. *Ann. appl. Biol.* 62: 177–197.

Way, M. J. & M. Cammell, 1970. Aggregation behaviour in relation to food utilization by aphids. In: A. Watson (Ed.), Animal Populations in relation to their food resources. *Proc. Brit. Ecol. Soc. Symp.* 10: 229–247. Oxford.

Discussion

Participants: Way and Cammel (Authors), Huffaker, Kuenen, Pimentel, Rosenzweig, Royama, Solomon, Southwood, Turnock, Watson, Watt, de Wit and Zwölfer

The group of aphid species showing unstable populations have characteristics which enable them to cope with ephemeral food supplies. In contrast, aphid species with relatively stable food plants have more stable populations and regulatory mechanisms which are related to this situation. If the food source of the second group is artifically increased e.g. by monoculture, does this group lack the necessary characteristics to stabilise its populations in the new situation (TURNOCK)? The second group would be associated with perennial or semi-perennial host plants where natural enemies may be the major regulating mechanism. In these species the selective pressure for the development of self-regulatory mechanisms may be weak; as shown by Messenger in alfalfa aphid populations. Alternatively, as Dixon has shown in *D. platanoides*, the aphid may be little affected by natural enemies but be delicately self-regulated to its food supply. There is no reason why a mechanism such as density induced diapause should not maintain stability in *D. platanoides* irrespective of whether the host is abundant or scarce (AUTHORS).

That instability may result from increasing a host's supply of limiting resources is a general principle. Huffaker showed it in the laboratory for a mite-mite interaction. Recently I have shown that six realistic models of host-parasite differential equations possess this property. The only way systems can resist this tendency is for the parasite to possess a large degree of self-regulation (e.g. by territoriality) (ROSENZWEIG). This general principle must be accepted with caution. There are several examples such as Ulyett's work with brassica pests where increasing the hosts' supply of food creates conditions favouring its control by natural enemies. The result is greater stability rather than instability. Conversely there must be many situations where decreasing the supply of a resource below a critical level also creates instability (AUTHORS).

What is instability? We would rank the instability of different species differently depending on whether we measure variation through time in raw counts, or logarithms of counts which correct for the mean value. The definition of 'instability' is made difficult because there are three different patterns of fluctuation in biological systems: (a) highly irregular (*Bupalus piniarius* in Europe) (b) highly regular (Lynx in Canada) (c) alternating endemic and eruptive periods (influenza and plague) (WATT).

It seems a pity to use the terms 'stable' and 'unstable' to describe the state of relatively constant or variable populations when all we know about them is that the numbers change little or much, as the case may be. We have the words constant and variable for these situations. In mechanics, 'stability' is the property of returning to an original position after displacement from it. A few populations, at least, have been demonstrated to have this property. I suggest that 'stability' should be kept to describe this state of affairs in population dynamics, and 'instability' its opposite (SOLOMON).

It was said that aphid enemies generally are not a stabilizing factor. What types of enemies are involved and what is their degree of host specificity (ZWÖLFER)? I was referring only to situations that arise with certain aphids which colonise successive annual plants each for periods of perhaps 8–12 weeks. The main natural enemies are insect predators. Insect parasites seem relatively unimportant sometimes because hyperparasites arrive simultaneously. The predators tend to be general aphid feeders and not specific to the species studied (AUTHOR).

Natural enemies may have a controlling effect on their aphid hosts, as is shown by the results from biological control introductions in California. Three species, the spotted alfalfa aphid, the pea aphid and the walnut aphid have been brought under very good biological control, mainly by introduced parasites, whereas they were formerly real problems (HUFFAKER). The annual crop situations that I was describing are similar to those which arise with aphids on a newly sown alfalfa crop. In these circumstances the species arrive out of phase and, with short term annual crops, time is too short to establish a low density equilibrium. This can, however, develop on the walnut tree and also on established semi-perennial crops like alfalfa. One might consequently expect the pea aphid to be much better controlled by natural enemies on alfalfa than, for example, on an annual pea crop (AUTHOR).

The advantage of a high production of flying aphids in high density conditions is elaborated, but could not the advantage of a low production in low density conditions be elaborated too (DE WIT)? I can only speculate that in low density conditions the decreased proportion of alatae produced relative to apterae, encourages multiplication on the host plant and thus increases the probability of a high density outcome. The relatively few alatae produced by small populations would also tend to be short-distance 'flyers' colonising nearby plants rather than be 'migrants' subject to the hazards involved in finding distant host plants. Under low density conditions, the populations would thus tend to be conserved locally and not dispersed regionally (AUTHOR).

It was shown that early experience as larvae affected adult numbers and adult quality. This would probably fit the idea of sensitivity in population adjustments to food quality. However, it was said that some of this pre-determination went back to the previous generation. The introduction of a lag due to a maternal effect of this sort would seem to be evidence against a very fine sensitivity of adjustment, unless there is also a similar lag in nutritive value of the food plant (WATSON). I was referring to situations where the switch from winglessness to winged was determined in the mother. Some lag is inevitable and the minimum, as shown by some aphid species, is from the second instar onwards when the wings are forming. Therefore it is correct to imply that maternal determination is evidence against fine sensitivity of adjustment though there may however be re-adjustment. Thus, in some species an individual that has been determined by its mother as an alata will revert to an aptera if, after it is born and before the end of the second instar, it is given aptera producing conditions (uncrowded, good nutrition) (AUTHOR).

What kind of evolutionary mechanism might cause aphids to develop an ability to avoid the over-exploitation of their food-resources (ROYAMA)? It seems feasible that any aphid population which over-exploited a particular host plant would produce fewer and weaker alatae; these would be less likely to find and colonise new host plants than others which were able to regulate their exploitation of the host plant. In these circumstances, there could be quite rapid selection of the latter, especially in conditions of host plant scarcity such as might arise from over-exploitation (AUTHOR). I can add to this that, due to parthenogenesis, all the aphids in a colony are genetically identical and group selection is therefore a possibility (SOUTHWOOD).

If natural selection has been important in the development of this self-regulatory system, has there not been sufficient time for the aphids to evolve adaptation to man's manner of cultivating crops – they have had more than 500 years to adapt? We know for insecticide resistance that this adaptation has taken place within a few years (PIMENTEL). Adaptation to crop conditions seems very likely in species like *B. brassicae* that nowadays occur almost exclusively on crops. In areas which are extensively treated with insecticides, this aphid may perhaps be changing in ways other than by developing resistance. Thus insecticides are decreasing the selection pressure for a maintainance of some self-regulatory mechanisms, because they are keeping populations well below the level where these need to be invoked. In contrast to *B. brassicae* a species like *A. fabae*, which I suggested may be put at risk by the growing of crops, has a wide range of wild hosts with relatively small localised areas occupied by crop hosts on which it forms significant populations for only about 8–12 weeks during the year. In these very diverse and mainly non-crop conditions, it might be argued that the species will not have become significantly adapted to crop conditions (AUTHOR).

Does this work help at all in the finding of a solution to the control of aphids on field crops (KUENEN)? It suggests fanciful possibilities such as the use of a chemical which will induce all aphids to become alate migrants. Otherwise the work seems to be helpful only indirectly or in a negative way. Thus, it reinforces the view that, in certain circumstances, natural enemies are likely to be unreliable or useless in practical control. The discovery of qualitative differences in alatae may prove valuable in pin-pointing sources of aphid infestations and of virus spread. It may be forseen that, in the future, methods based on a suppression of alternate or other hosts will provide an increasingly important contribution to integrated control (AUTHOR).

Proc. Adv. Study Inst. Dynamics Numbers Popul. (Oosterbeek, 1970) 243–256

Genetic and behavioral studies on fluctuating vole populations

C. J. Krebs

Department of Zoology, Indiana University, Bloomington, Ind., USA*

Abstract

A five-year study of two small rodent species, *Microtus ochrogaster* and *M. pennsylvanicus*, has concentrated on describing the demographic machinery producing population fluctuations, and on measuring changes in aggressive behaviour and changes in the genetic composition of these vole populations. These studies have been done in southern Indiana, in eastern USA.

A repeatable syndrome of changes in birth, death, and growth rates has accompanied population fluctuations in these two *Microtus* species. This syndrome is complex, which involves both reproduction and mortality and affects more than one age group.

Male aggressive behaviour changed throughout a population fluctuation in both species. In *Microtus pennsylvanicus*, male aggressive behaviour scores are correlated with the mean rate of population increase, but the relationship is not very strong. This may mean that female aggressiveness is more important, but we have not studied this.

Two polymorphic loci have been studied in relation to these population events. Both genetic systems have shown changes in gene frequency that can be associated with the demographic changes. This association may be causal because the properties of the genotypes change in relation to population phase and are repeatable in time and space. The intensity of natural selection may be very strong in these vole populations, and the possibility of a genetic mechanism underlying these fluctuations cannot be dismissed.

Small mammal populations often fluctuate greatly in abundance from year to year, sometimes in regular 'cycles'. Voles and lemmings show these fluctuations, and studies on these rodents have thus formed a small subset of population dynamics. Almost all vole populations that have been studied have fluctuated in numbers, and consequently emphasis has been placed on explaining these *fluctuations*. Students of small mammal populations find discussions of *stability* irrelevant to these rodent systems.

There is at present no agreement about what factors cause these population fluctuations in voles and lemmings. What variables must we measure to be able to predict future population trends? This question still receives a wide variety of responses, ranging from quality of food, or predators, to physiological stress, or aggressive behaviour. For the past five years my students and I have studied fluctuations in *Microtus pennsylvanicus* and *M. ochrogaster* populations in southern Indiana. We have attempted to measure changes in aggressive behaviour in these voles and to monitor genetic changes through serum protein marker systems. We have tried to answer two questions: (1) Does aggressive behaviour

* Present address: Institute of Animal Resource Ecology, University of British Columbia, Vancouver 8, Canada.

change during a population fluctuation?; and (2) Is the genetic composition of these populations labile on a short term basis? Our purpose in doing this is to test Chitty's (1967) hypothesis regarding these fluctuations.

Methods

Our techniques involve live trapping every two weeks, throughout the year with an excess of live traps in 0.8 hectare fields. We are thus able to capture virtually the whole adult population of *Microtus*. Voles were bled in the field either from the toes or from the suborbital sinus of the eye. Male voles have been removed to the laboratory for up to 2 days for behavioral testing.

The trapping techniques were described in Krebs, Keller, and Tamarin (1969). The bleeding techniques and electrophoresis work are discussed by Tamarin and Krebs (1969) and by Gaines (1970). The measurement of aggressive behavior has been described in Krebs (1970).

Results

Population changes

Both *Microtus* species have shown population fluctuations in southern Indiana but we do not know whether these fluctuations are 'cyclic'. The *Microtus pennsylvanicus* populations we have studied have tended to reach peak densities at two-year intervals, and the *M. ochrogaster* populations at three-or four-year intervals, but periodicities may be affected by agricultural practices. The disturbances, which occurred every year, from the plowing of old fields and the seeding of new grasslands in the agricultural areas surrounding our study plots may have resulted in an atypical timing of highs and lows.

Details of the population changes we have observed have been shown by Krebs et al. (1969), Gaines (1970) and Myers (1970). I will not repeat them here.

One of our more striking experimental observations is that voles enclosed in large, fenced areas (0.8 ha) increased in density at unusually high rates, reached densities 3–4 times those of unfenced populations, and overgrazed their habitat (Krebs et al. 1969). Fig. 1 documents a second case of this 'fence-effect', and shows that it is a repeatable event. Thirty-two *Microtus ochrogaster* were removed from a field immediately adjoining an unfenced grid (H) in August 1967. These were split at random into two groups, and 9 females and 7 males were introduced into each of fenced grids B and D. These subsamples from the increasing grid H population showed similar population trends, and reached very high numbers in the winter of 1968/69 (grid B, 277 voles; grid D, 370 voles). Unfenced populations on comparable areas normally peaked at approximately 80 voles. This 'fence-effect' is probably the result of their being no dispersal from these enclosed populations; it is not associated with reduced predation losses (Krebs et al., 1969). Myers (1970) has recently evaluated the role of dispersal in these *Microtus* populations, and these results will be reported elsewhere.

On areas that are unfenced and unmanipulated, population changes are due to the action of four variables: (1) reproductive rate, measured by the percentage of adult females that are lactating when live trapped; (2) juvenile survival, measured by the mean number of young voles recruited into the trappable population per lactating female; (3) male sur-

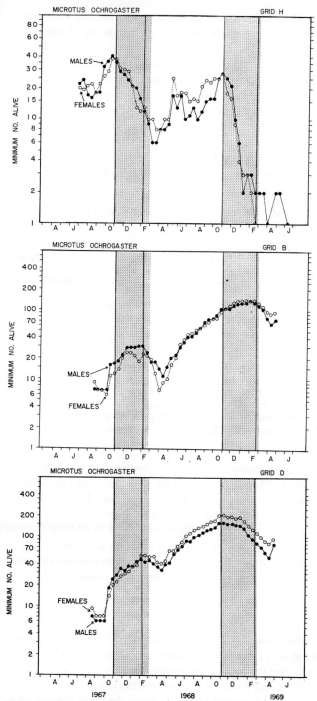

Fig. 1. Density changes in *Microtus ochrogaster* populations on unfenced grid H and fenced grids B and D. Voles removed from a field next to grid H were seeded into fenced areas B and D in August 1967.

245

vival; and (4) female survival. These survival rates for males and females are measured by direct enumeration of voles by live trapping and are given as the rate per 14 days. Since survival is equated with staying on the live-trapping area, poor survival may be due to a high emigration rate or high death rate, or to both. Mean values were obtained for these four variables for each trapping grid for two periods each year (summer, winter). Multiple regression analysis (Table 1) was used to measure the relative effect of each of these four components on variations in the mean rate of population growth (Snedecor, 1956: p. 416). For both *Microtus* species, the population growth rate can be predicted without any data on male survival. The other three variables – reproductive rate, early juvenile survival, and female survival – are all of approximately equal importance in determining variations in the rate of population growth. This is shown for *M. pennsylvanicus* in Fig. 2–4.

Table 1. Relative importance of reproductive and mortality components in determining the rate of population growth in *Microtus ochrogaster* and *M. pennsylvanicus*. Data pooled from all open populations, 1965–1970.

Demographic variable[1]	Ratios of standard partial regression coefficients	
	M. ochrogaster[2]	*M. pennsylvanicus*[3]
Percent adults lactating	0.71	1.00
Early juvenile survival	1.00	0.74
Male survival rate	0.33[1]	0.28[1]
Female survival rate	0.71	0.98

[1] These variables can be deleted from the multiple regression with no loss of power to predict rate of population growth.
[2] Multiple regression for *M. ochrogaster*: Mean rate of population growth = $-0.4017 + 0.00117$ (lactation) $+ 0.0441$ (juvenile survival) $+ 0.3771$ (female survival).
[3] Multiple regression for *M. pennsylvanicus*: Mean rate of population growth = $-0.2935 + 0.00180$ (lactation) $+ 0.0234$ (juvenile survival) $+ 0.2697$ (female survival).

The syndrome of changes which produce population fluctuations in these *Microtus* is thus complex and does not involve only one stage of the life-cycle. Increasing populations survive well and reproduce rapidly because they breed through the winter period and mature at lighter weights than usual (Keller and Krebs, 1970). In peak populations, reproductive rates and juvenile survival are lower; in the decline phase, in addition to these negative effects, adult females survive less well. This syndrome has never been found in fenced populations. Theories which proport to explain these fluctuations therefore cannot rely solely on mortality factors or solely on reproductive changes as causal forces.

Behavioural changes

Behavioural variations among individuals cannot readily be studied in field populations of voles, so we have been forced to adopt standard laboratory testing procedures in order to look for behavioural changes during the population fluctuations. A preliminary report of this work is given in Krebs (1970), and I will summarize here the remainder.

Aggressive behaviour was measured by recording for 10 minutes the number of approaches, attacks, retaliations, avoidances, and threats for two male voles in a neutral fighting arena (see Krebs (1970) for details). Only males have been studied; this was probably

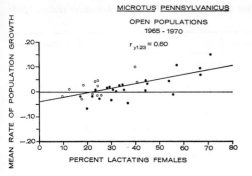

Fig. 2. Relationship between the percentage of adult females which were lactating and the rate of population increase. Each point represents one season (summer ●, winter ○) for one grid population.

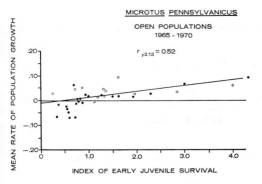

Fig. 3. Relationship between the index of early juvenile survival (number of young recruited per lactation) and the rate of population increase. ● = summer, ○ = winter.

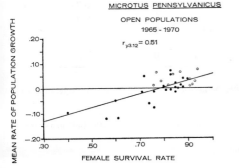

Fig. 4. Relationship between the female minimum survival rate per 14 days and the rate of population growth. ● = summer, ○ = winter.

a mistake and we should have studied females as well.

These data were subjected to factor analysis (Program BMD 03M) and the results are given in Tables 2 and 3. Previous analysis (Krebs, 1970) was done with multiple discriminant functions, but the results of these two types of analyses are not very different. Factor analysis is a more descriptive technique and avoids the assumption that voles must fit into discrete 'types'.

Mean factor scores for males from unfenced populations were correlated with the demographic variables described previously. Weighted multiple regressions were used and, on the whole, the results (Table 4) confirm those obtained in the earlier study, There is a significant correlation between mean rate of population growth and the aggressive behaviour factor scores for *Microtus pennsylvanicus*, but there is no such relationship for

Table 2. Factor analysis of aggressive behavior test scores for *Microtus ochrogaster* males, 1965–1969. Sample size is 1450.

Original variables	Factor loadings			Communalities[1]
	factor 1	factor 2	factor 3	
Approaches	0.834	−0.164	−0.019	0.72
Attacks	0.951	0.162	−0.082	0.94
Retaliations	−0.006	0.887	0.043	0.79
Avoidance	−0.122	0.070	0.982	0.98
Threats	0.134	0.834	0.044	0.72
Attacks per approach	0.671	0.379	−0.182	0.63
Eigenvalues	2.35	1.55	0.88	
Cumulative proportion of total variance	0.39	0.65	0.80	

[1] The communalities give the proportion of the variance of each of the original variables which is preserved in the factor solution.

Table 3. Factor analysis of aggressive behavior test scores for *Microtus pennsylvanicus* males, 1965–1969. Samples size is 1140.

Original variables	Factor loadings				Communalities
	factor 1	factor 2	factor 3	factor 4	
Approaches	0.128	0.005	−0.059	0.959	0.94
Attacks	0.842	0.171	−0.001	0.395	0.90
Retaliations	0.170	0.837	0.024	−0.184	0.76
Avoidances	0.001	0.014	0.998	−0.055	1.00
Threats	0.081	0.855	−0.004	0.212	0.78
Attacks per approach	0.953	0.119	0.001	−0.063	0.93
Eigenvalues	2.18	1.26	1.01	0.86	
Cumulative proportion of total variance	0.36	0.57	0.74	0.88	

Table 4. Multiple correlations between aggressive behavior factor scores and demographic variables. All open populations pooled, 1965–1970.

Demographic variable (y)	Multiple R	Significant partial correlations
Microtus pennsylvanicus[1]		
Mean rate of population growth	0.35*	factor 3
Percent adults lactating	0.48**	factor 1
Index of early juvenile survival	0.31	−
Male survival rate	0.25	−
Female survival rate	0.42*	factor 3
Microtus ochrogaster[2]		
Mean rate of population growth	0.19	−
Percent adults lactating	0.36	−
Index of early juvenile survival	0.31	−
Male survival rate	0.61**	factors 1, 2, 3
Female survival rate	0.42	−

[1] n = 36 for *M. pennsylvanicus*
[2] n = 29 for *M. ochrogaster*.
* = significant at 5%, ** = significant at 1%.

M. ochrogaster. Even for the first species, however, the correlation is low, and little of the variation observed in the rates of population growth can be ascribed to changes in the aggressive behaviour of males.

The net conclusion from this work on aggressive behaviour is that the aggressiveness of male voles changes, and that some of these changes can be significantly associated with population parameters in *Microtus pennsylvanicus*. The relationships between behaviour and demography are very weak, and there may be three explanations for this. First, aggressive behaviour of female voles may be the principal mechanism, and variations in male aggressiveness may be poorly correlated with this. Second, male aggressive behaviour may be the principal mechanism, but my measurements of this set of behaviours may be a poor index of the important behaviours used in social groups in nature. Third, aggressive behaviour may not be the principal causal mechanism involved in these population fluctuations. On the present information any of these three might be true.

Genetic changes

There are two approaches one can use to investigate the relationship between changes in population density and the genetic composition of the population. First, one can determine ecologically important variations in populations, e.g. in growth rate, ability to breed during winter, or aggressiveness, and then determine the extent of genetic influence on these traits. This type of work has been done extensively on *Drosophila* (Robertson, 1965) and could be done on other species. We have not followed this approach in our *Microtus* work. A second approach is to obtain genetic markers, 'randomly' chosen polymorphic loci, which can be used to estimate the extent to which selection is operating in these vole fluctuations and to obtain some estimate of how intensive selection might be. This is the approach we have used in our work. Note that these marker loci are marking a part (or all) of a chromosome, and that in studying these loci we are studying a whole linkage group.

We have studied two polymorphic systems. The transferrin polymorphism (Fig. 5) was worked out by R. H. Tamarin (Tamarin and Krebs, 1969) and has been studied from 1965 to 1970. The leucine aminopeptidase (LAP) polymorphism (Fig. 6) was analyzed by M. S. Gaines (Gaines, 1970) and has been studied from 1967 to 1970. Gaines (1970) has shown by laboratory crosses that each polymorphism is controlled by a simple autosomal locus and that these two loci are not linked in *Microtus ochrogaster*.

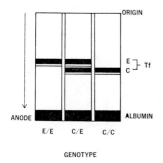

Fig. 5. Schematic diagram of starch gel showing transferrin (Tf) polymorphism in *Microtus pennsylvanicus*.

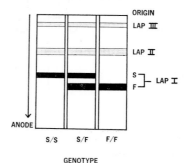

Fig. 6. Schematic diagram of starch gel showing leucine aminopeptidase (LAP) polymorphism in *Microtus* spp.

249

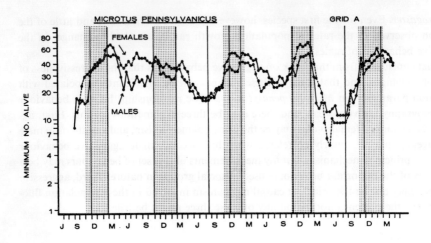

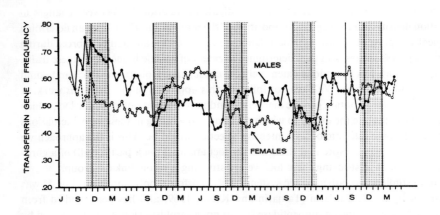

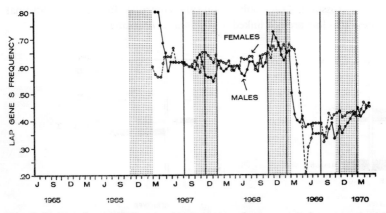

Fig. 7. Changes in population density (top), transferrin gene E frequency (middle) and leucine aminopeptidase gene S frequency (bottom) from 1965–1970 for the unfenced grid A population of *Microtus pennsylvanicus*.

Fig. 7 shows for one population the types of changes observed in population density, transferrin gene frequency, and LAP gene frequency. These types of changes have been analyzed in detail by Tamarin and Krebs (1969) and by Gaines (1970). Note that male and female gene frequencies may remain quite disparate for several months and that gene frequency changes may be quite different in the two sexes. Note also that very rapid changes in gene frequency may occur within a short period of time (e.g. spring 1969 population decline). The pattern of these changes has been consistent over a number of different populations (Gaines, 1970), and this repeatability seems to rule out random drift as a possible explanation. Gaines (1970) has also shown that there is no evidence of subdivision of these vole populations into very small demes, as has been suggested for commensal populations of house mice (Petras, 1967).

The details of one population decline in *Microtus ochrogaster* are shown in Fig. 8. This decline began at the end of the summer breeding season, when the lack of recruits together with a decrease in survival caused numbers to fall off very rapidly. This decline was associated with selection against transferrin gene E, which in males amounted to an average loss of gene E of 0.7 % per week, and in females to an average loss of 3.1 % per week. Since this decline occurred after most breeding had stopped, the main cause of the selection was differential survival. The probabilities of survival per 14 days for males during the decline were: Tf^E/Tf^E, 0.57; Tf^E/Tf^F, 0.75. For females this difference was even more pronounced: Tf^E/Tf^E, 0.60; Tf^E/Tf^F, 0.91.

The general picture that we have obtained of selection during these population fluctuations is as follows. During the increase phase, survival is typically good and the selective premium rests with those genotypes which have a high reproductive rate, a high growth rate, and early age at sexual maturity. Some genotypes seem to survive worse than others, or perhaps to disperse more readily. During the decline phase, survival is very poor, the reproductive rate is reduced, and juvenile losses are high. The selective premium now rests with genotypes having a relatively high survival rate, and less importance is attached to reproductive or growth abilities.

There are two possible kinds of genotypes in this situation. The first set of genotypes

Table 5. Minimum survival rates per 14 days for transferrin genotypes of female *Microtus pennsylvanicus* on unfenced grid I, 1967–70. Highest survival rates for each time period are in italics.

	Tf^C/Tf^C	Tf^C/Tf^E	Tf^E/Tf^E
Increase phase			
fall 1967	*0.92*	0.80	0.85
winter 1967–68	*0.91*	0.84	0.82
Peak phase			
summer 1968	0.83	*0.90*	0.81
winter 1968–69	0.73	*0.84*	0.70
Decline phase			
summer 1969	0.68	0.72	*0.79*
Increase phase			
fall 1969	*0.89*	0.72	0.81
winter 1969–70	*0.84*	0.76	0.67
Peak phase			
summer 1970	0.71	*0.75*	0.60

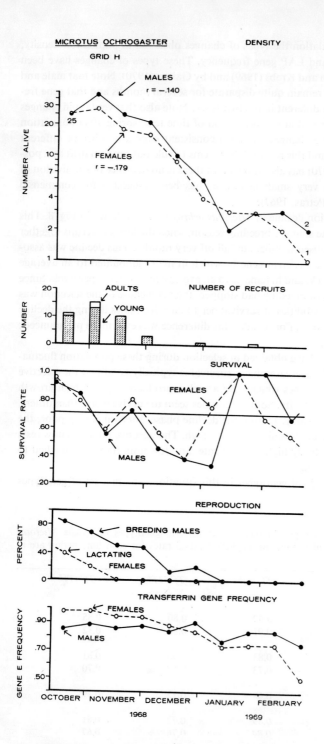

Fig. 8. Detailed profile of a population decline in *Microtus ochrogaster* during the winter of 1968–1969.

could have properties which were constant and independent of population phase or density. Thus, for example, genotype A might always have slightly better chances of survival than genotype B, while genotype B might always grow slightly faster than genotype A. This type of system would produce fluctuations in gene frequencies in association with the population fluctuations, but these genetic changes would be the *effect* of the population density changes. Thus, if these population fluctuations were produced by predator pressure (or some other extrinsic factor), these gene frequency changes would still occur. This set of genotypes is clearly *not* what Chitty's (1967) hypothesis relates to population events.

A second set of genotypes could have properties which were variable and dependent on population phase or density. For example, genotype X might survive less well than genotype Y in increasing populations, but survive better in declining populations. This type of genetic system would also produce fluctuations in gene frequencies in association with population fluctuations, and these genetic changes *might* be a principal cause of the density changes. They could, of course, be minor side effects as well.

The critical experiment to distinguish between these two opposing views for any genotypic array is to drive the genotypic frequencies in opposite directions in two adjacent field populations. The first view predicts little demographic difference between populations that are 90% A, 10% B, compared with populations that are 10% A, 90% B. If the genetic system involved is of major importance, the second view would predict large demographic effects from this type of experiment. For voles, this experiment would have to be done in open populations which permit dispersal. We have already done experiments similar to this in enclosed areas but the results cannot be extrapolated to natural populations because of the 'fence-effect'.

The two genetic systems we have studied seem to fit the second type described above. Table 5 shows one example of how the 'chances of surviving' of different genotypes changed during one fluctuation in numbers. The properties of these genotypes seem to change in relation to population phase in both *Microtus* species (Tamarin and Krebs, 1969; Gaines, 1970), but we do not know the role of these genetic changes in causing the population density fluctuations.

Acknowledgments

I thank my students Michael Gaines, Barry Keller, Judy Myers, Robert Tamarin, Paul Whitney and Pam Fraker for their energy in making this work possible. This research has been supported by grants from the National Science Foundation.

References

Chitty, D., 1967. The natural selection of self-regulatory behaviour in animal populations. *Proc. Ecol. Soc. Aust.* 2: 51–78.

Gaines, M. S., 1970. Genetic changes in fluctuating vole populations. Ph. D. thesis, Indiana University, Department of Zoology. pp. 95.

Keller, B. L. & C. J. Krebs, 1970. *Microtus* population biology. III. Reproductive changes in fluctuating populations of *M. ochrogaster* and *M. pennsylvanicus* in southern Indiana, 1965–67. *Ecol. Monog.* 40: 263–294.

Krebs, C. J., 1970. *Microtus* population biology: behavioral changes associated with the population cycle in *M. ochrogaster* and *M. pennsylvanicus. Ecology* 51: 34–52.

Krebs, C. J., B. L. Keller & R. H. Tamarin, 1969. *Microtus* population biology: demographic changes in fluctuating populations of *M. ochrogaster* and *M. pennsylvanicus* in southern Indiana. *Ecology* 50: 587–607.

Myers, J. H., 1970. Genetic, behavioral, and reproductive attributes of dispersing field voles, *Microtus pennsylvanicus* and *Microtus ochrogaster*. Ph.D. thesis, Indiana University, Department of Zoology. pp. 95.

Petras, M. L., 1967. Studies of natural populations of *Mus*. I. Biochemical polymorphisms and their bearing on breeding structure. *Evolution* 21: 259–274.

Robertson, F. W., 1965. The analysis and interpretation of population differences. In: H. G. Baker and G. L. Stebbins (Ed.), The genetics of colonizing species. p. 95–113. New York.

Snedecor, G. W., 1956. Statistical methods. Ames.

Discussion

Participants: Krebs (Author), Brussard, Frank, Gulland, Jacobs, Jain, Murdoch, Myers, Reddingius, Rosenzweig, Scharloo, Solomon, Southwood, Watt and Zahavi

Several speakers raised the point whether studying frequency changes of 'marker' genes is relevant to the mechanisms underlying population changes –

Changes in gene frequencies may merely be the result of population changes (GULLAND, JACOBS, REDDINGIUS, SOLOMON, SOUTHWOOD). Moreover, selection for reproductive advantages and selection for survival advantages are often produced by quite different causes (JACOBS). The description of such a mechanism of fluctuations is like a person who comes to Holland, observes all the bicycles, clearly describes the wheels and chains, but fails to notice the girl's legs that are pushing the pedals. We should look to the environment for the driving force. If we accept the interpretation of Krebs, the hypothesis can be diagrammed as:

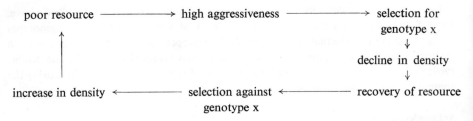

The perturbation experiments proposed by Krebs do not help us to decide what the 'poor resource' is for these animals (SOUTHWOOD). The perturbation experiments I proposed are based on the assumption that the driving force for these fluctuations is a behavioral-genetic polymorphism operating through the resource of 'space'. If you believe that food shortage is the important resource involved, you must view these genetic experiments as meaningless because you would design quite different experiments to study food shortages. Similarly, if you believe that predation is the driving force, you would view food shortage experiments as meaningless (AUTHOR).

Shortage of suitable food, quantitatively or qualitatively, may indeed result in both the density changes and the genetic changes (SOLOMON). There has certainly been a shortage of good experimental work on this question, but the few studies that have been done have not encouraged one to think this is a major cause of population fluctuations in small rodents. In southern Indiana I have been able to produce rapidly expanding populations in fenced enclosures year after year (in fact three times within one year), and I find it difficult to see any clear suggestion that these populations peak and decline occur because something is wrong with the food supply (AUTHOR).

254

It is amazing to see the resistance shown by so many participants to the idea that genetic factors can be involved in the problems of regulation and fluctuation of populations. Because selection does not work on single loci, but on highly organized gene complexes, it is not surprising that these changes are observed at a few loci that may or may not have an easily understood physiological relation to the events observed (BRUSSARD). Population geneticists have a good deal of evidence that the genetic composition of populations can affect their density and demography. Genetic variance in the relative fitness of population members is then assumed to account for a fraction of total death rates and for adaptive changes over time. While we may argue about the net regulatory effects, these associations do point to the necessity of looking at genetic systems. The apparent circularity of density $\rightleftharpoons$ genetic composition should not raise serious objections at this stage, because cause-and-effect 'circularity' is imperative due to the way genetic differences in ecological parameters are analyzed (JAIN). Much more work is needed on this question of the relationship between genetic heterogeneity and the classical problems of population dynamics. Perhaps genetic changes are indeed most easily viewed as the effects of changes in population density, and not as the driving mechanism. But we cannot conclude this without further experimental evidence (AUTHOR). See also the discussion after the paper of Solomon.

MacArthur's generalized theorems of natural selection show that genetic changes are most easily viewed as effects of oscillation, and may not be the driving mechanism (ROSENZWEIG).

Year-to-year variations in the precipitation regime might be the pacemaker for rodent fluctuations. Both Cox and Butler have commented on mammal cycles which are out of phase, and have suggested that precipitation is of prime importance. Butler identified the epicenters for mammal cycles in North America as regions of great year-to-year variability in precipitation. Green and Evans showed that the survival of young hares is correlated with snowfall. All this suggests the causal pathway: precipitation → plant productivity → rodent starvation → survival of offspring (WATT). It seems likely that the causal pathway is more complex and, for reasons suggested above, may not operate through food supply. Perhaps direct effects of weather on the probability of survival (or reproduction) of different genotypes is involved. Synchrony is not absolute in these vole fluctuations, and populations a few hundred meters apart can be out-of-phase (AUTHOR).

Upsets in the development of a young mammal – especially around the perinatal period – may have effects on its physiology and behaviour which last for the rest of its life. If the stimuli necessary for such changes occur in relation to density, it might provide a logical explanation for the kinds of fluctuations observed; although, of course, genetic effects may be involved in this (MYERS). Unfortunately, these types of effects have not been studied in voles (AUTHOR).

From my experience with breeding microtines, there are remarkable differences in the aggressiveness of individuals which apparently have a genetic basis. There is also much variation in the succes of individual females in rearing litters in nature, and this may have a genetic basis as well. Thus, it is very important to extend the behavioral observations to adult females – which can be very aggressive. The behaviour of male voles is less important and might be ignored altogether. If the behavioral-genetic changes cause the changes in numbers, one would expect that more than one genetic locus is involved (FRANK).

In this type of work the loci studied are marking part of a chromosome and consequently one is studying the effects of closely linked genes, as well as pleiotropic effects, that are not distinguishable operationally in this work. More marker loci could be studied and no one knows at present what fraction of loci might show changes in gene frequency correlated with population events (AUTHOR to SCHARLOO).

Any genetic system of the type proposed may drift to fixation of one genotype or another sooner or later. This would make it difficult to maintain the polymorphism (MURDOCH). Such fixation may in fact occur, and dispersal will help to keep local populations polymorphic. Mass outbreaks of rodents might represent a drift to fixation over large areas (AUTHOR).

Such a genetical control mechanism cannot continue by itself indefinitely. There seem to exist unutilized food resources in this system, and this would produce powerful selection for individuals to break away from a behavioral-genetic set of controls and thus to utilize food up to its carrying capacity. Hence, the mechanism must be continuously under positive selection pressure from some factor outside the control mechanism itself in order to be continuously effective (ZAHAVI). But there are always resources in excess supply for all populations (for example, oxygen for voles), and there is no effective selection for this because the population has exhausted another resource – in the voles this is postulated to be *space*, space free of other hostile individuals (AUTHOR).

Proc. Adv. Study Inst. Dynamics Numbers Popul. (Oosterbeek, 1971) 257–268

Competition for breeding sites causing segregation and reduced young production in colonial animals

J. C. Coulson

Department of Zoology, University of Durham, England

Abstract

In several colonial species, breeding is restricted to suitable sites within the colony or group. This results in severe competition for the better sites and also in segregation of individuals by age and quality.

In the Grey Seal, an increase in the social crowding may decrease the calf survival from about 80–57% in the first five weeks of life. So far, no selective advantage has been discovered to account for the more intense crowding.

Marked changes in a Shag population have presented the opportunity to examine the effects of age and nest-site quality on young production. The reduction in the population resulted in an appreciable improvement in the average physical qualities of the nest-sites and in the numbers of young reared per pair, particularly amongst the young birds. It is suggested that the social structure reduces the production of young, particularly of young birds, and hence the overall production of the population.

The Kittiwake shows marked segregation between the birds recruited into the centre and at the edge of the colony. The central males live longer, are recruited at a slightly higher weight and are more productive annually.

In these colonial species the good and less good individuals are not randomly distributed in the breeding colonies and the social aspect becomes an important variable in the population dynamics. There is an indication in the Shag and the Grey Seal that at high densities the breeding success is lower. Thus, there is a reservoir of potential reproductive capacity which can be utilised if the breeding population is reduced by either natural or human predation.

It is often convenient to consider each animal in a population as a single, equal unit. Every ecologist appreciates that this equality is not real and that individual animals differ in fecundity, longevity and many other factors, but this assumption is often made in order to apply life-tables and other concepts of population dynamics. Often, this assumption can be justified on the grounds that the good and the less good animals are distributed randomly with respect to each other and, for example, a sample of, say, a hundred animals will correspond closely to another sample of the same size. In other words, it is usual to ignore the differences between the individual animals since these average out over a large sample.

However, it is not always justifiable to make the assumption that the individuals of different quality are randomly distributed throughout the population. In the case of social or colonial animals, the intense competition between individuals in close proximity can result in the segregation of animals into spacially distinct groups. Unless this separation is taken into account, in cropping or culling operations, for example, it could produce appreciably different effects on the population than that expected from calculations from an overall life-table.

The segregation of animals of a single population into groups which differ markedly is more readily seen in colonial species. It is not part of my thesis that this applies only to social animals; these differences could well occur (but are more difficult to detect) in species with a greater distance between individuals.

The demonstration of differences in survival or reproductive powers of individuals in certain groups raises the question as to the source of such differences. Obviously some of these differences could have a genetic basis, but in some social species at least, the difference appears to have a strong environmental component and, in particular, poorer survival or reproductive success can be induced by the social conditions in the group. In such situations, the breeding success of the groups is influenced by the degree of competition for some commodity that is socially but not actually in short supply. For example, suitable breeding sites may be in excess but the social convention necessitates that the individual or the pair must normally restrict their breeding activities to the existing groups, and within these groups suitable sites are often in short supply. In this manner, breeding success can be influenced, resulting, for example, in non-breeding or poorer overall breeding success.

I propose to illustrate these situations with examples from three socially breeding vertebrates; the Grey Seal *Halchoerus grypus*, the Kittiwake *Rissa tridactyla* and the Shag *Phalacrocorax aristotelis*.

Grey Seal

Typically, the Grey Seal is a social breeding animal although in the Baltic it breeds in isolated pairs on the frozen sea. Investigations of the breeding biology on the Farne Islands, Northumberland indicate that there is considerable calf mortality induced by crowding, yet other neighbouring and suitable islands still remain unoccupied (Coulson and Hickling, 1964).

The calf mortality occurs in at least two stages; those which die on the breeding island and those with a poor growth rate during suckling but which do not die until some time after they leave the breeding area.

Only four of the Farne Islands are used for breeding although a further five are suitable. During the period of study only two of these islands were nearly fully saturated by breeding seals, while the other two were only partially occupied and considerable areas were left unused. Calf mortality was always higher on the crowded islands. Density, expressed in terms of seals per unit area, was not closely correlated with the calf mortality. A much better relationship was found between calf mortality rate and the number of calves born behind 100 m of accessible shore-line. Since the cows move frequently between the sea and their calves, the greatest interaction occurs near the tide-line and it is easy to appreciate that the greatest amount of aggression occurs where there are more seals moving through a particualr length of shore. Table 1 and 2 show that the mortality rate of calves is closely correlated with shoreline density, and the extrapolation of the regression indicates that about 9% mortality of calves would occur when the density is minimal; mortality above this level is density induced. The average mortality rates on the four breeding islands are shown in Table 2. On Staple Island over half of the mortality is density induced, with lower levels on the other breeding islands.

The mortality of calves after leaving the islands is closely correlated with their growth rate whilst suckling. A newly born calf weighs about 13.6 kg (30 lb) and puts on 1.8 kg

258

Table 1. The percentage mortality of Grey Seal calves born on individual islands in years with above and below average numbers and density (after Coulson and Hickling, 1964).

Island	Four years with largest numbers		Three years with lowest numbers	
	number of calves	mortality rate	number of calves	mortality rate
Staple	476	19.9	329	16.8
North Wamses	388	13.1	251	11.7
Brownsman	196	12.9	59	10.1
South Wamses	71	9.9	55	9.7

Table 2. Percentage mortality of Grey Seal calves on individual breeding islands, 1956–61 (after Coulson and Hickling, 1964).

Island	Mean mortality rate	Mean number of calves per 100 m of accessible shore
Staple	18.6	77
North Wamses	12.5	42
Brownsman	11.9	14
South Wamses	9.8	10
All islands	14.9	

(4 lb) per day. This rapid growth, which results in a well fed calf doubling its birth weight in about 8 days, is almost completely due to the deposition of lipid (blubber); at the end of the suckling period the calf may weigh over 45 kg (100 lb). The survival of calves can be shown to be closely correlated with their growth rates. The growth rates of calves were determined by weighing them at least twice during their suckling period; they were individually recognisable by numbered tail tags. All calves which died on the breeding islands were excluded from consideration. An arbitrary distinction for successful survival has been taken at 5 weeks after birth, that is about $2\frac{1}{2}$ weeks after suckling ceases. In Table 3 the known cases of death before this period and of survival beyond this time are shown in relation to the growth rate. The index of the proportion surviving varies from 0–100%

Table 3. The survival of Grey Seal calves in relation to growth rate (after Coulson and Hickling, 1964).

	Growth rate per day (kg)					
	−0.5 to 0.0	0.0 to 0.4	0.5 to 0.9	0.9 to 1.3	1.4 to 1.8	>1.8
A. Number found dead less than 5 weeks old	10	2	3	3	1	0
B. Number known to have lived more than 5 weeks	0	1	3	8	9	15
Percentage known to survive more than 5 weeks	0	33	50	73	90	100

259

and this extensive range suggests that these proportions probably closely represent the actual proportions which survived this period.

On both the crowded and less crowded islands, the growth rate of calves declines with the lateness in the season at which birth occurs (Table 4). This decrease corresponds to the progressive increase in the degree of crowding on the breeding islands; the final slight increase in the growth rate at the end of the breeding season is in response to the decrease in density which occurs at the late part of the breeding season. From the distribution of growth rates of calves which survive to leave the islands, it is possible to calculate the mortality at sea in the first five weeks of life and add this to the deaths which have already taken place on the islands. Using the growth rates given as means in Table 5 for individual islands, the mortality rate up to 5 weeks of life has been calculated (Table 6). Clearly, the overall mortality is appreciably higher on the crowded islands.

The higher mortality under crowded conditions would appear to be a considerable

Table 4. The growth rates (kg/day) of Grey Seal calves born at different times of the breeding season on a crowded (Staple) and less crowded (Brownsman) island.

Born in week commencing	Crowded (Staple)	Less crowded (Brownsman)
21 October	1.77	1.80
28 October	1.59	1.87
4 November	1.36	1.65
11 November	1.00	1.70
18 November	0.88	1.45
25 November	1.14	1.05
2 December	–	1.13

Table 5. Mean growth rate of calves on four islands in the Farnes group.

Island	Sample size	Mean growth-rate kg per day
Staple	76	1.40 ± 0.04
North Wamses	38	1.48 ± 0.06
Brownsman	25	1.58 ± 0.08
South Wamses	10	1.56 ± 0.11

Table 6. Estimated Grey Seal calf survival rates during the first 5 weeks of life in relation to the island of birth.

	Survival rate on island (%)	Survival rate in the sea (%)	Overall survival to five weeks old (%)
Staple	81.4	70	57
North Wamses	87.5	74	65
Brownsman	88.1	90	79
South Wamses	90.2	89	80

selective disadvantage unless there is an equal or greater advantage in highly social breeding. The evidence suggests that the grey seals would rear more young if the cows spread themselves out onto other neighbouring islands at a similar density to that on Brownsman and South Wamses.

It is worth while attempting to identify the disadvantage to less gregarious breeding. Predation does not account for social breeding, as the only predators of the Grey Seal would appear to be man and the Killer Whale *Orca grampus*. The latter cannot pursue the seals onto land and the former would not be intimidated by groups of seals together, and there are reasons to believe that man would be a more efficient predator when the seals are grouped. There is a possible advantage in limited grouping together to facilitate a greater mating success, but there is little indication of lower breeding rate when the Farnes breeding colony was several times smaller than it is now, while in the Baltic pairs of Grey Seals breed successfully in isolation from other seals.

If the Grey Seal became less gregarious during breeding, there is reason to suppose that the numbers of young reared could be as much as 20–30% larger than occurs on the Farne Islands at the present time. The very social system employed by the seals increases the calf mortality as the population of breeding cows and the density of seals increases. This progressive increase in overall mortality has been observed since 1956 during which time the population has increased 3 fold. Consequently, any cull of breeding animals will have the effect of lowering the overall density which, in turn, will introduce a compensatory reduction in calf mortality. There are reasons why the Grey Seal population on the Farne Islands should be limited and when such measures are taken, it is to be hoped that they will be such that they will give further insight into the social organisation of the seals and that the social factors will be included in estimates of proposed culls, otherwise much effort will be wasted in killing cows and calves which will themselves contribute little to the next generation.

Shag

The Shag is a colonial breeding sea-bird which can occasionally nest in isolation. However, these isolated breeders are predominantly older birds, and young individuals seem to need the influence of an established group before being able to breed themselves. Typically, young Shags attach themselves to the periphery of a group and are forced into nesting in poorer sites as the best situations are taken by older birds early in the breeding season before the arrival of the younger birds.

Shags usually lay three eggs but the overall annual breeding success is only one young. In all age classes, the breeding success of any pair is increased with an improvement in the quality of the nest site; a typical result is shown in Table 7.

The catastrophic decrease in the Shag population on the Farne Islands in 1968 occurred when the neurotoxin produced by a 'Red Tide' (Protozoan *Gonyaulax* outbreak) killed

Table 7. The influence of nest-site quality on the production of young by Shag. The effect of age taken into account. Site-quality improves from 0 to 4.

Site-quality	0	1	2	3	4
Number of extra young compared with nest-site quality 0	0	0.06	0.15	0.21	0.42

Table 8. Mean nest-site quality of Shags before and after the population crash in 1968.

	First breeders	Older
Before crash	1.61	1.92
After crash	2.24	2.31

Note: nest-site quality is on a scale from 0 to 4 and is based upon: (a) the position of the nest-site in relation to ready access to the sea, (b) ability of the site to withstand the effects of heavy rain, (c) the protection afforded by the site to the effects of rough seas and heavy swells, (d) the capacity of the site to hold fully grown birds.

Table 9. Mean number of young reared per pair of Shags before and after the population crash in 1968.

	First breeders	Older
Before crash (1963–67)	0.90	1.27
After crash (1969–70)	1.64	1.73

80% of the breeding population in 10 days (Coulson et al. 1968). This allowed the surviving young birds a much better choice of nest sites in 1969 and 1970. Table 8 shows that the average nest-site quality increased markedly, but was greater in the young birds. Correspondingly, the number of young reared per pair also increased (Table 9) and again the increase was more marked amongst the young birds. Although other factors, such as good weather, also helped to increase the overall number of young reared per pair in 1969 and 1970, the improved nest site quality was the major contributory factor and those birds in good nest-sites continued to produce more young than did those in poorer sites. Within breeding groups of Shags, good nest-sites are in short supply so that whilst order 4 are the best nest sites, the average is just over order 2 (Table 8). The quality of a nest-site depends entirely on the site's physical qualities, and it is evident that there are many good quality sites on the cliffs on the Farne Islands which are outside of the breeding groups of Shags and are not even used by birds with poorer sites within the groups. Thus the social convention of Shags typically needing to nest in groups results in a contrived shortage of good quality sites available to prospecting birds. As a colony increases in size, some of the previously unused good nest-sites are taken up as the nesting groups expand. Whilst there are obvious disadvantages in Shags nesting in good sites in isolation, particularly in defence against predators, the social system does force young birds into poor sites where they have a correspondingly poor breeding success. When this system is altered (as in 1968) and young birds can move into better sites, there is a corresponding increase in the breeding performance of the young birds almost to the level of the older birds. Young Shags are not poor breeders solely because they are inexperienced; they are also poor breeders because the social system enables the best sites to be taken by the old birds and, in general, the younger birds have to select from the remaining poorer sites within the sub-colony group.

Kittiwake

The Kittiwake is an intensely colonial sea-bird and there are no known instances of pairs nesting in isolation; the species has lost the ability for individual pairs to breed in isolation and each pair requires stimulation from neighbouring pairs before nesting can be successful.

Unlike the situation in the Shag, the physical properties of the nest-sites used in this study were identical inasmuch as they were on similar window ledges of a warehouse at North Shields, Northumberland, and differences in breeding success cannot be attributed to variation in the quality of the nest-site. Further, there is virtually no predation of the eggs, young or adults at this colony. The birds nesting in the colony have been divided into two groups of approximately equal size according to the distribution of nests in the colony when it was half its present size. The original area is mainly the central part of the present colony and is termed the 'centre' whilst the more recently colonized part is referred to as the 'edge'. Since young birds tend to colonize the edge of the colony, in the ensuing analyses consideration has been given to age of the birds. There is no indication of an age component affecting the mortality rate of the adult Kittiwake.

An analysis of the mortality rate of Kittiwakes nesting at the edge and in the centre of

Table 10. The mortality rates of male and female Kittiwakes nesting in the centre and at the edge of the colony.

Sex	Colony position	Bird-years at risk	Number dying	Percentage annual mortality	Expectation of further life (years)
Male	centre	555	75	13.6	7
	edge	432	87	20.1	4.5
Female	centre	570	66	11.6	8
	edge	454	59	13.1	7

Note: The difference between the mortality rates of males in the centre and at the edge of the colony is significant ($P < 0.01$). The difference between the two groups of females is not significant.

Table 11. Weight of male and female Kittiwakes at time of recruitment in relation to (A) area of colonisation and (B) subsequent survival (sample size in parenthesis).

A	Centre		Edge	
	number	weight (g)	number	weight (g)
Males	161	394.4	158	386.2
Females	140	350.6	126	350.9

The difference in weight of males is significant ($P < 0.01$).

B	Centre		Edge	
	died within 5 years	survived over 5 years	died within 5 years	survived over 5 years
Males	392	395	381	392
	(64)	(68)	(71)	(47)
Females	349	356	346	354
	(55)	(60)	(54)	(42)

the colony showed no significant difference in the females, but a highly significant difference in the males (Table 10) with an appreciably lower mortality rate in those nesting at the centre. (Coulson, 1968). The difference in survival is evident in the first year of colonization, and since males rarely move their nest-site the segregation into two groups persists for life.

Even at the time of recruitment to the colony, there are small but significant differences in the weight of males and it has been demonstrated for both sexes in both the edge and the centre of a colony that survival is related to the body weight at recruitment (Table 11).

The higher male mortality rate at the edge of the colony results in more pairs being formed for the first time in this area than in the centre. Even amongst the pairs in which both members survive to the next breeding season, the proportion of individuals which change their mate is appreciably higher in edge birds; this is further enhanced by the average age of edge birds being lower than central birds, since younger birds are also more liable to change mate.

The retention of the mate from the previous breeding season is, in general, an advantage in the Kittiwake and results in greater breeding success per pair. In Table 12 the number

Table 12. The mean clutch size of Kittiwakes according to breeding experience, pair status and position in the colony. Sample sizes in parenthesis.

| | Breeding experience | | | | | |
| | 1st season | | 2nd–4th season | | 5th–16th season | |
	edge	centre	edge	centre	edge	centre
Same mate as last year			2.06 (64)	2.20 (83)	2.23 (74)	2.31 (150)
	1.88 (93)	1.86 (99)				
Change of mate since last year			1.99 (74)	2.05 (60)	2.04 (65)	2.06 (68)

Mean difference of edge and centre = 0.06 eggs.
Mean difference of age = 0.07 eggs.
Mean effect of change of mate = 0.16 eggs.

Table 13. The mean number of young successfully fledged per pair of Kittiwakes according to breeding experience, pair status and position in the colony. Sample sizes as in Table 12.

| | Breeding experience | | | | | |
| | 1st season | | 2nd–4th season | | 5th–16th season | |
	edge	centre	edge	centre	edge	centre
Same mate as last year			1.37	1.43	1.51	1.62
	1.16	1.06				
Change of mate since last year			1.20	1.30	1.30	1.39

Mean difference of edge and centre = 0.09 young.
Mean difference of age = 0.13 young.
Mean effect of change of mate = 0.19 young.

of eggs laid per pair is shown in relation to nest position, breeding experience of the female, and pair status. Similar data are given in Table 13 for the number of young fledged per pair. In both instances, the birds in central positions in the colony lay more eggs and rear even more young when all other factors are equal. Since pair change is appreciably more frequent at the edge of the colony, and this also leads to fewer young being reared, birds in a central position, on average, rear about 13% more young each breeding season. Taking into account age and the difference in expectation of life, a typical central male will rear nearly 11 young in its lifetime, a value which is 74% greater than an average edge male's production.

There is considerable variation in the quality of both male and female Kittiwakes and detailed measurements of these differences are now in progress. It would appear that a good breeding male is, typically, successful all of his life. The most successful male in the colony has successfully reared 29 young from 30 eggs in 15 years while several males have failed to rear any young in five years, some even failing to obtain mates in certain years.

Clearly, it would be wrong to consider all birds in a Kittiwake colony as equal. At the present time it is not known whether the differences between an edge bird and a central one is genetical or induced by the situation created by the social system. Clearly competition can be more severe under colonial conditions since the frequency of contact with other individuals is much higher. In the Kittiwake, this competition segregates birds into groups which have different breeding success and the males have different expectations of life. Attempts to encourage potential 'edge' males into the centre of the colony have been attempted but too few results have been obtained and in any case the recruitment to colonies is such that it cannot, with certainty, be assumed that males which nest on additional sites created in the centre of the colony are 'edge' birds, since potential 'centre' birds may be attracted from neighbouring and much larger colonies.

Conclusions

In this review of the effects of social breeding, examples have been presented showing that in two species, the Grey Seal and the Shag, the breeding potential of the group is being kept below its potential by restraints induced by colonial breeding. In the Grey Seal, it has been possible to demonstrate that animals breeding at lower densities are more productive; while in the Shag, it has been shown that the young birds are prevented from going to good nest-sites by the social group bond, yet when a high proportion of the adult population is removed, these young animals select the good sites and are almost as successful breeders as their older members. This is not to deny that there is a selective advantage in social breeding, but in both species, under present conditions, less dense groups occupying good breeding sites are *more* productive. It is easy to argue from this that a population that was spread out in the manner of the small groups should be more productive than the crowded groups studied.

The situation studied in the Kittiwake is somewhat different, since the physical quality of the sites available were all equal. However, in this situation, the centrally breeding individuals were more successful. The reason for this is not clear; it is possible that the central site confers more stimulation to breed (note the lack of difference in breeding success in birds nesting for the first time on the edge and centre) or it could be a direct selection for the better individuals in the central sites.

There is a clear need for more work on the effects of social organisation, but in the meantime it is evident that the social properties of animals must be appreciated in detail when considering population dynamics and when applying measures either to conserve a species or to exploit or cull it in a scientific manner.

The effects of reduced productivity in larger social groups, as is apparent in the Grey Seal and the Shag, could be interpreted as a compensatory mechanism for a sudden or marked decrease in the numbers of breeding animals. Whether such effects are the reason for social breeding or merely the by-product of such evolution is not easy to decide. I do not consider it necessary to invoke group selection to explain their existence but, on the other hand, it is difficult to explain the present situation in the Grey Seal without suggesting that natural selection has not had time to eliminate or modify the social system which, at the new and high population size, has become a disadvantage. The main aim in this paper is to try to convince ecologists that such complex social effects do occur and need to be considered.

References

Coulson, J. C. & G. Hickling, 1964. The breeding biology of the grey seal, *Halichoerus grypus* (Fab.) on the Farne Islands, Northumberland. *J. Anim. Ecol.* 33: 485–512.
Coulson, J. C., G. R. Potts, I. R. Deans & S. M. Fraser, 1968. Exceptional mortality of Shags and other seabirds caused by paralytic shellfish poison. *Br. Birds* 61: 381–404.
Coulson, J. C., 1968. Differences in the quality of birds nesting in the centre and on the edges of a colony. *Nature* 217: 478–479.

Discussion

Participants: Coulson (Author), Bakker (K.), Dhondt, Frank, Huffaker, Kuenen, Murton, Perrins, Reynoldson, Scharloo, Southwood, Whittaker and Zahavi

In the case of the Kittiwake where there is such a large selective pressure against the edge birds, there must be a balance, a big adaptive value to adhere to that 'convention' and not to change it. Conventions in nesting colonies usually suggest that the centre is important although, theoretically, there is no reason why other places should not also be acceptable in terms of convention. It may be suggested that nesting colonies act as information centres about feeding sites, and this might have been the primary cause of their evolution. The convention in Kittiwakes, and in the other species described by Coulson, may be expected to hold so long as the advantage from holding that particular convention is greater than the loss of reproduction suffered by birds which are inhibited from breeding (Zahavi). I think this explanation is an over-simplification of the action of natural selection. Once an attribute is lost, it can often be very difficult for this to be regained by selection, particularly if it is complex in nature. Similarly, once an animal gives up the ability to breed in isolated pairs, it may be much more difficult to redevelop it despite selection pressure. To put the point in a different way; no animal is perfectly adapted, and there are always aspects of an animal's biology which could be improved and made more efficient. On the other hand, it has not yet been demonstrated that the observed differences in Kittiwakes are under genetical control (Author).

The explanation that communication of information about a food source is important makes most evolutionary sense. Are the foods of the three species fish that shoal? Is there any evidence of behaviour that could be such communication within these colonies? The

266

parallel between the system suggested by Zahavi for these vertebrates and that in social Hymenoptera is interesting (SOUTHWOOD). The food of all three species includes fish which shoal. I have no evidence of behaviour patterns in the seabirds or the seals which indicate a communication of information about food sources. Many shoals of fish are available to avian predators for only a short period of time because they can only be exploited while in the surface waters. I cannot see an advantage in communication at a seabird colony which may be 2–4 hours flying time from the food source. However, the actions and patterning of many diving seabirds obviously indicates the presence of food to other seabirds within vision (AUTHOR).

The food situation of the Kittiwake population studied is comparable to that of natural colonies; natural colonies on cliff site occur within three miles (AUTHOR to SCHARLOO).

The fallacy in the argument of Coulson is to make the interactions observed in the breeding colonies the central causative mechanisms, whereas they may only reflect the consequences of interactions occurring elsewhere. In the Wood Pigeon, it was shown that a failure to attend to nesting duties can be related directly to difficulties in finding food (MURTON). Although it is possible that interactions are taking place away from the colony, there is no reason to assume that what happens in the Woodpigeon should also apply to the Kittiwake. The Kittiwake, unlike the Woodpigeon, requires only a very short period of time each day to obtain food. It is a rapidly expanding species and food seems to be super-abundant during the breeding season. The mortality of chicks is very low in the Kittiwake; once hatched, the parents do not have difficulty in feeding the young; however, there is much evidence to suggest that it is the behaviour of the adults rather than food per se which is the causative factor in the Kittiwake and the Shag (AUTHOR).

The difference between individuals and their breeding success may be explicable in terms of their fitness. It was shown that some of the less successful Kittiwakes were lighter in weight; these may be less fit animals and might return to the colony later than fit ones, be less able to obtain central sites and be less successful at breeding. Hence, the colony and the individuals position in it may be irrelevant to this (PERRINS). This is not true in the Shag where similar quality birds improved in breeding success when competition for good sites was less. If it is true in the Kittiwake, then it must explain the way in which the difference becomes more pronounced in the older birds. Young recruits do equally well at the centre or at the edge of the colony when breeding for the first time. Having chosen a site, the males remain attached to it, and it is in subsequent years that most of the effects appear. On the other hand, there is no reason why a similar segregation should not occur in a non-colonial species (AUTHOR).

I bred about 100 Weasels and found a clear positive correlation between the social position which the animals gained in the earliest hierarchy in their litter and their length of life. Therefore I assume that the birds which gain the good breeding places in the centre of the colony were the a priori fitter and dominating ones, and that this must have a genetical basis (FRANK).

The mortality rates of adult Kittiwakes are estimated from the return of colour-marked adults together with an intensive search in colonies within 100 miles radius. In 15 years, only two breeding adults have moved colony, whereas 25% of marked, non-breeders have been found in the colonies searched (AUTHOR to MURTON).

In a growing colony, birds settling at the edge will be central birds some years later. Hence if birds become more dominant with increasing age and dominant birds breed in the centre, they would not have to change their breeding site to become centre birds (DHONDT). The social organisation puts a distinct brake upon the rate of colony expansion, and this is relatively slow. The shorter expectation of life of those at the edge means that very few survive to move from edge to centre as the colony grows, and those few which do are the 'better' edge individuals which approximate to a 'centre' bird (AUTHOR).

Would it be a critical experiment to investigate the performance of Kittiwakes which took over nests from which the dominant occupiers have been taken away (BAKKER)? or to set up new sites in the centre of the colony (WHITTAKER)? The recruitment is not restricted to the colony under consideration. Recruits come from a pool of several hundreds of individuals which will eventually breed in this or one of several other colonies. The removal of central birds (males) or the creation of new sites in the centre – which was done – will only result in potentially central-type birds being attracted from the pool, and the quality of the recruits cannot be assumed (AUTHOR).

What is the explanation for the fact that there are Kittiwakes which abstain from breeding rather than take a nesting site at the edge of the colony (BAKKER)? The social system restricts the amount of cliff on which recruits can colonize and hope to breed; they must be in very close contact with established birds. Accordingly, there is usually an excess of potential recruits and competition for the restricted number of sites imposed by the social convention. Younger and poorer quality birds fail to obtain a suitable site and often occupy sites further away from breeding birds and fail to breed (AUTHOR).

Is there any evidence that predation pressure is more intense at the edges, and could result in concentrating the animals at the centre (HUFFAKER)? In all three species, mortality from predation at the breeding site was small or non-existing (AUTHOR).

Coulson suggests that these three animals tolerate crowding rather than form a new colony in an apparently favourable situation. But many new colonies must be formed in time e.g. in *Fulmarus glacialis*, and until the conditions within the existing colony provide birds which form new colonies, it is difficult to interpret these data (REYNOLDSON). The formation of new colonies have been followed in the Kittiwake. These appear to be formed entirely by young birds (unless existing colonies are drastically disturbed) but it takes these birds several years before breeding occurs and even then, only a minority succeed in nesting. The potential quality of these birds it not known (AUTHOR).

What may be the advantage of breeding in a colony for the seal? The advantage in birds seems to be defence against predators (Kuenen). The Grey Seal is interesting since, apart from Man, it does not have, nor seems to have had, a predator which could attack it on its breeding islands. The only predator at the present time is Man and the Killer Whale, *Orca grampus*. The former is not likely to be deterred by the seals grouping, while the latter can only attack seals in the sea. Thus, social breeding in the Grey Seal does not seem to be an anti-predator device. It is possible to argue that the social group increases the pregnancy rate in breeding cows, but the Grey Seal is known to breed successfully at much lower densities. Hence, at the present time, there does not seem to be an advantage in being so highly social unless it gives the population stability and a reserve of breeding potential which can dampen the effects of increased mortality (AUTHOR).

268

Proc. Adv. Study Inst. Dynamics Numbers Popul. (*Oosterbeek, 1970*) *269–281*

On the modelling of competitive phenomena

C. T. de Wit

Department of Theoretical Production Ecology, Agricultural University, and Institute for Biological and Chemical Research on Field Crops and Herbage (IBS), Wageningen, the Netherlands

Abstract

It is shown that the dynamics of interfering species is most conveniently characterized on the basis of their relative abundances, which is defined as the ratio of the abundance of a species (measured as yield, number, etc.) in a mixture and in a monoculture under the same conditions, except for the competitive situation. This procedure is justified by the observation that under many conditions, species exclude each other; i.e. that the relative abundance total of the interfering species is equal to one. Examples of such situations are presented and discussed.

Subsequently it is shown that in situations where species exclude each other, it may be possible to simulate the growth of the species in a mixture solely on the basis of observations of the growth of the species in a monoculture. A simulation model of this situation, written in one of the continuous system simulation languages is presented.

The relative reproductive rate

Animals as well as annual plants have a definite life cycle so that successive generations may be easily distinguished. When, moreover, the individuals are ready distinguishable it is customary to express the performance from one generation to the other in terms of the reproductive rate, which is often defined as the ratio between the number of animals in two successive generations. It is then often implicitly supposed that a ratio of two means that the species is twice as abundant. But this only holds when the individuals of the successive generations are of the same phenotype, which is often not the case. A good example of this is given by Dempster in these Proceedings. In some years his Cinnabar moths are small and in other years large; these changes are accompanied by a range in fecundity of about 70 to 300 eggs per female.

When two species are coexisting, it is customary to characterize their dynamics with respect to each other with a double ratio, sometimes called the 'relative fitness', but for which the more explicit term 'relative reproductive rate' will be used here.

This relative reproductive rate of two species a and b in two successive years is defined by:

$$^{21}\alpha_{ab} = \frac{^{2}O_a / {}^{1}O_a}{^{2}O_b / {}^{1}O_b} \tag{1}$$

It is said that both species match each other when $^{21}\alpha_{ab} = 1$ and that species a gains on species b when its value > 1; it being again tacitly assumed that the individuals of each species are of the same phenotype in successive generations.

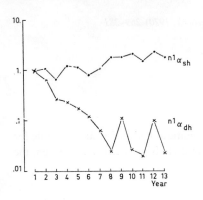

Fig. 1. 'Course lines' for the barley varieties White Smyrna (s) and Deficiens (d) with respect to Hannchen (h) calculated from the number of seeds in the yield of a mixture grown in Idaho (USA) (Harlan et al., 1938).

Without considerable experimental effort it is very difficult to prove or disprove the validity of the latter assumption. Hence, especially when the relative reproductive rate does not vary too much from one, it is always hard to conclude which species is actually gaining in a particular year.

An example is given in Fig. 1. This presents the results of a thirteen year experiment with some barley varieties done by Harlan and Martini. The species were sown in the first year in the same proportions and the harvested mixtures were resown in the following years. Even when the seeds of the species concerned are not the same in successive years, it is obvious that the cultivar Deficiens was much weaker than Hannchen in this situation. However, the cultivar Smyrna matched Hannchen fairly well over the 13 years.

An attempt can be made to correlate the relative decrease of Smyrna in, for instance, the 3rd, the 6th and 11th years with the particular circumstances in these years. But then it must be realised that the relatively bad performance of the cultivar Smyrna may be due either to a relative bad growth of the variety in those years or to the harvesting of relatively poor seeds of this variety in the preceeding year. It is impossible to distinguish between the possibilities without further observations and analyses.

These difficulties are amplified in ecological studies where perennial plant species or long living animals are involved and one is interested in their year to year performance. This will be illustrated by considering grassland plants in pastures and meadows. With these vegetative species the generation concept looses its meaning, whereas it is also often impossible to distinguish individuals. Harvests, if any, are not resown, but stubbles and roots are left over for regrowth. Moreover, each harvest grows under different circumstances so that it is even impossible to assume that one gram of yield from one harvest is the same as one gram of yield from the other. Unless changes are very drastic, it is very difficult to say which species gains or loses on the other within a certain period. We may revert to counting, for instance, the number of sprouts of each species at intervals, but then it appears again that these may change systematically several-fold in size and vigour during the course of even a short experiment.

The use of reproductive rates and relative reproductive rates in such situations may be very misleading, as is shown by the results of an experiment with *Lolium perenne* and *Anthoxanthum oderatum* grown in competition. In Fig. 2 the course lines for the mixtures, or the relative reproductive rates with respect to the fifth harvest on a logarithmic scale as a function of time are presented. Based on counts of the number of sprouts, it appears that the two species match each other to a large extent. But the experiment had to be termi-

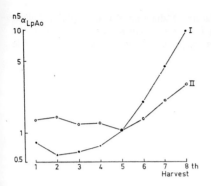

Fig. 2. The relative reproductive rate of *Lolium perenne* (Lp) with respect to *Anthoxanthum oderatum* (Ao), calculated on basis of dry matter yields (I) and number of sprouts (II) (de Wit et al., 1965).

nated at the ninth harvest, because *Anthoxanthum* had completely disappeared. The course line based on dry matter yields seems to reflect the situation much better, but this, of course, is a conclusion after the observation that the *Anthoxanthum* species has gone.

Thus, the conclusion of Harper (1961) may be reached that: 'if we neglect species which reproduce vegetatively and confine attention to those whose density is determined by the number of successful establishments from seed, we eliminate one of the most confusing factors in ecological analyses'.

The relative replacement rate

But Harper's conclusion is unduly pessimistic. It can be shown that many of the difficulties may be overcome by studying these vegetative species both in mixtures and in monocultures under the same conditions, and by comparing their performances not on an absolute, but on a relative value of abundance. This relative abundance is defined as the ratio of the yield, or the number of sprouts or any other abundance measure, in the mixture (O) and its comparative value (M) in the monoculture, grown under the same conditions except for the competitive situation, i.e. as:

$$r = O/M \tag{2}$$

As long as the influence of weather, nutrient status and so on are relatively the same on the species in the mixture and the monoculture, this relative yield is a truly dimensionless value and should be independent of the type of yardstick used for measurement of the abundance of the species.

The main justification for this procedure lies in the observation that after some period of growth of the species, they often exclude each other in the mixture. This follows from the observation that the relative abundance total:

$$RAT = r_a + r_b = O_a/M_a + O_b/M_b \tag{3}$$

is equal to one. This phenomenom, which characterizes a competitive situation for the same niche, is illustrated in Fig. 3 for a mixture of *Lolium perenne* and *Anthoxanthum oderatum*.

This situation, where two species are mutual exclusive, is automatically achieved with pasture species. irrespective of original seed or planting rates in mixture and monoculture and of the yield limiting factors. With annual crops it is, of course, possible to synthesize

271

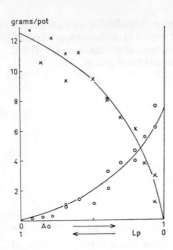

Fig. 3. A replacement diagram for the species *Lolium perenne* (Lp) and *Anthoxanthum oderatum* (Ao) with the relative planting frequency along the horizontal axis (de Wit et al., 1965).

the above situation in an experiment by planting a replacement series, i.e. by choosing the seed rates in the mixture in such a way that the sum of the relative seed rates is always one.

The relative abundance being defined, it is possible to define the relative replacement rate of species a with respect to species b for successive observation dates 1 and 2 by:

$$^{12}\rho_{ab} = \frac{^2r_a/^1r_a}{^2r_b/^1r_b} \tag{4}$$

It is obvious that the species neither gain nor lose in the mixture as long as the relative replacement rate is 1. If this relative rate is greater than one, species a gains space on species b and when it is smaller than 1, species b gains space on species a. The course lines based on the relative abundances, calculated from dry matter yields and number of sprouts, are presented in Fig. 4 for the *Lolium* and *Anthoxanthum* mixture. Contrary to the course lines based on the relative reproductive rate in Fig. 2, it appears that here the course lines are practically the same and, whether based on dry matter yields or counts of the number of sprouts, both lead to the conclusion that *Anthoxanthum* disappears.

Anthoxanthum, as measured on the basis of dry matter yields rather than number of

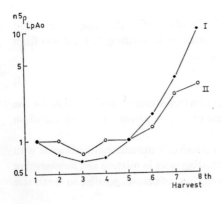

Fig. 4. The relative replacement rate of *Lolium perenne* (Lp) with respect to *Anthoxanthum oderatum* (Ao) calculated on basis of the relative abundance with respect to dry matter yield (I) and number of sprouts (II) (de Wit et al., 1965).

272

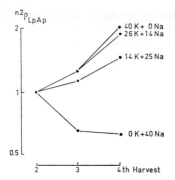

Fig. 5. The relative replacement rate of *Lolium perenne* (Lp) with respect to *Alopecurus pratensis* (Ap) at four K: Na fertilizer combinations in meq/pot (van den Bergh, 1968).

sprouts, still vanishes somewhat faster; but this is mainly due to clipping at 5 cm above the soil surface so that, especially at later stages, the small *Anthoxanthum* sprouts escape the treatment.

By using relative replacement rates it is now very easy to study quantitatively the effect of different conditions on the mutual interference of species. This is illustrated in Fig. 5, where the influence of the potassium-sodium ratio in the fertilizer on the relative replacement rate of *Lolium* with respect to *Alopecurus* is presented.

The relative abundance total

When the Relative Abundance Total (RAT) is one, it is good evidence of a situation where the species concerned compete for the same niche, to use an expression borrowed from animal ecology. In a replacement series, this phenomenon is reflected by the yield lines of the species concerned curving upward and downward to the same extent. As well as in Fig. 5, this is also illustrated in Fig. 6 for an experiment with oats and barley. It should be noted that in this experiment barley in monoculture yielded less kernels than oats, but also that in spite of this the yield line for barley is curved upward and that for

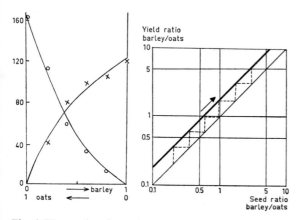

Fig. 6. The results of a replacement experiment with barley and oats and a frequency graph to illustrate that, in a case of repeated cultivation under the same conditions, the barley gains in spite of its lower yield in monoculture (de Wit, 1960).

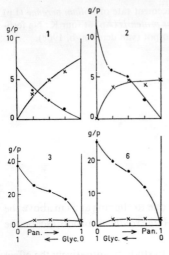

Fig. 7. Replacement diagrams for the dry matter yields in gram/pot of harvest 1, 2, 3 and 6 of *Panicum maximum* (P) and *Glycine japonica* (G), the latter being a leguminous grassland species (de Wit et al., 1966).

oats curved downward to such an extent that barley replaced oats in the mixture. This is illustrated in the frequency graph where the harvest ratio in the mixture is plotted against the seed ratio. The cause of this phenomenom is explained in the second part of this paper.

In plant mixtures it is often observed that a species gains in spite of its low yield. I do not know whether this is also the case with animals, but assumptions, as made for instance in Fisher's theory of natural selection or derivates from this theory, which implicitly state that the high yielding species always wins are certainly wrong.

Situations where two species are not excluding each other are easily recognized in replacement experiments, since then the yield lines are not curved up- and downward to the same extent so that the relative abundance total is larger than one. This is illustrated in Fig. 7, which concerns a replacement series of a leguminous and a non-leguminous grassland species, the former taking its nitrogen from the air and the latter from the soil. Course lines for various mixtures (Fig. 8), culculated as the ratios of the relative yields of both species, approach each other, revealing that these two species, which grow as far as their nitrogen is concerned in different niches, arrived at an equilibrium situation.

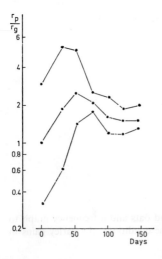

Fig. 8. Course lines for various mixtures of *Panicum maximum* and *Glycine japonica* (de Wit et al., 1966).

274

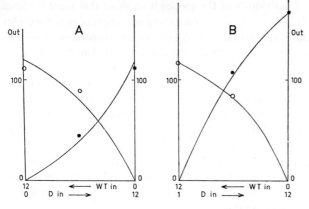

Fig. 9. Replacement diagrams for the *Drosophila* mutant 'Dumpy' (D) and 'Wild Type, (WT), taken from stock (A) and after selection for some generations in a competive environment (B) (Seaton et al., 1967).

The sensitivity of this type of analysis is very well shown by the results of an experiment by Seaton and Antonovics (1967) with *Drosophila* 'Wild Type' and 'Dumpy', presented in Fig. 9. A replacement experiment with these two strains, after growing them in monocultures for several generations, showed that they practically exclude each other. However, if a similar experiment is done with the two strains after growing them for only two generations in a mixture, it appears that both yield lines are curved upward. Hence, within two generations the varieties were able to find separate niches. That this is possible in half-pint milk bottles with a maize/treacle medium seeded with dried yeast and kept at 23 degrees in the dark, seems very surprising to me. But the experimental technique is sensitive enough to reveal the phenomenom.

These examples must serve to show us that in experimental population dynamics it is worthwhile to consider not only the behaviour of the species when they are growing in situations of mutual interference, but to study at the same time their behaviour in monocultures. In the laboratory, this may be done as well with plants as with animals. Since animals often have the unfortunate habit of moving about, it may be difficult for animal ecologists to realise experimental situations of this kind under field conditions. Plant ecologists are here at a definite advantage.

Stochastic and deterministic models

Numerical characteristics like relative yield, reproductive rate or replacement rate are approximations of the endpoint of a continuous and deterministic process of growth and development of the organisms involved. The use of these characteristics implies that we abstract from the underlying continuous process and simplify our world view by separating the phenomena in time. If the dispersion of the population in space is considered simultaneously, it is also necessary to separate the phenomena in space. As a consequence, it is impossible to analyse in detail the influence of the diversity of circumstances on the behaviour of the species, so that this diversity has to be accounted for by the introduction of stochastic elements.

If, moreover, the number of individuals of the species is so small that there is also a definite chance of extinction, it is necessary to consider many sequences of random events to arrive at meaningful conclusions regarding the abundance and dispersion of species. This stochastic approach is advocated by Birch, Reddingius and den Boer in these Proceedings.

Just as discrete and stochastic models abstract from the underlying continuous and deterministic growth processes, it is possible to abstract from the discrete and stochastic aspects and pay special attention to the continuous and deterministic processes.

A simple example may be used to illustrate this. In the first part of this paper, attention was drawn to the phenomenom that barley gains on oats in spite of the fact that in monoculture oats is the higher yielding species. This phenomenon can only be understood by considering the continuous process of growth and development, and since this can be done by means of an analysis which is an extension of the Lotka-Volterra approach in animal ecology, it is worthwhile to elaborate on this.

Growth analyses in a competitive situation

The yield of a plant species sown in monoculture depends on plant density and the length of the growing period. At earlier stages or within low density ranges, the yield is almost proportional to plant density, but later on and at higher plant densities a maximum yield will be approached. These saturation type of yield curves may be represented within a wide range of densities by:

$$O = \frac{B.S}{B.S+1} \, OM \tag{5}$$

where S is the density of sowing or planting, O the yield and OM the maximum yield which is obtained at very high planting densities (the condition where all space is occupied) and B is the space occupied by a single plant growing alone. Both B and OM are functions of time which may be determined by the periodic harvesting of a spacing experiment. The quotient:

$$SO = O/OM \tag{6}$$

is called the relative space (or yield) occupied at the seed density S. The relationship between B and time for barley and oats, obtained in a particular experiment, is presented in Fig. 10. In the case of barley, B at first increases rapidly, but remains constant during the second half of the growth period; whereas for oats B increases slowly at first but continues to increase at an age when the curve for barley has already flattened. Differentiating the equation:

$$SO = B.S/ (B.S + 1) \tag{7}$$

and expressing S in the resulting equation in terms of SO and B, results in:

$$\frac{d(SO)}{dt} = \frac{dB/dt}{B} \, SO \, (1-SO) \tag{8}$$

which is the well known differential equation for the logistic curve, except that here the equivalence of the relative growth rate, i.e. (dB/dt)/B, is a variable function of time.

276

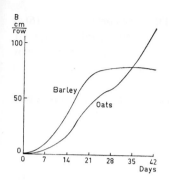

Fig. 10. The space (B) occupied by single row of barley and oats in relation to time, as calculated from periodically harvested spacing experiments (Baeumer et al., 1968).

If it is now assumed that barley and oats compete for the same niche in space, the Lotka-Volterra differential equations hold for the relative yield or space of each of the species:

$$\frac{d\,(SO)}{dt} = \frac{d\,B/dt}{B}\,SO\,(1-SUMSO) \tag{9}$$

in which SUMSO is the relative space occupied by both species together. The actual yield of each species is then found according to Eq. 6 with:

$$O = SO \cdot OM \tag{10}$$

A simulation model

It is impossible to obtain an analytical solution of these differential equations. Instead a solution is obtained by means of a simulation language, called Continuous System Modeling Program (CSMP), which is very suitable for the simulation of biological systems (Brennan et al., 1970). As an illustration, the whole program, as presented to the computer, is set out below.

```
MACRO    O,SO = GROWTH (BTBL, OMTB, SOI, DBI, SUMSO, DAY)    (1)
         SO = INTGRL (SOI,RSO)                                (2)
         RSO = RGR * SO * (1 – SUMSO)                         (3)
         RGR = DB/B                                           (4)
         B = AFGEN (BTBL,DAY)                                 (5)
         DB = DERIV (DBI,B)                                   (6)
         O = SO * OM                                          (7)
         OM = AFGEN (OMTBL, DAY)                              (8)
ENDMAC                                                        (9)
```

The mathematical behaviour describing the dynamic behaviour of one species in a mixture is presented in a MACRO called GROWTH. In line (2) it is stated that the relative space occupied by the species is the integral of its rate of occupation and in line (3) that this rate of occupation is the product of the relative 'growth' rate, the relative space which is occupied by the species and the space not yet occupied by any species, according to Eq. 9. Line (4) defines the relative growth rate as the quotient of DB and B, in which B is the absolute space occupied by a single plant and DB its rate of increase. In line (5) it is stated that B is a function of the number of days after emergence, and that the

277

function itself will be provided in tabulated form (BTBL). DB is then defined in line (6) as the derivative of B with respect to time. Line (7) calculates the yield according to Eq. 10. Line (8) states that the value of OM is again obtained from the day after emergence by means of the tabulated OMTBL. Line (1) defines the input and the output of the MACRO and line (9) its end.

At the start of the simulation the initial values of the relative space which is occupied (SOI) and the rate of increase of B (DBI) have to be calculated out of the seed rate (S). This is done with a MACRO called BEGIN.

MACRO   SOI,DBI = BEGIN (BTBL,S,START)

$$SOI = B * S/ (B * S + 1) \tag{1}$$

$$B = AFGEN (BTBL, START) \tag{2}$$

$$DBI = AFGEN (BTBL, START + 1) - B \tag{3}$$

ENDMAC

Line (1) calculates the initial space that is occupied by the species by means of Eq. 7 from the seed rate (S). Line (2) calculates B, and line (3) states that the rate of increase of B is equal to the difference between the values of B at the start of the simulation and one day later. Eq. 7 can only be used in the early stage, when the species on a field do not as yet interfere with each other.

The actual simulation program for a mixture of two species is now as follows:

INITIAL

SOI1, DBI1 = BEGIN (BTBL1, S1, START)

SOI2, DBI2 = BEGIN (BTBL2, S2, START)

These two lines calculate the initial values for species 1 and 2.

DYNAMIC

O1, SO1 = GROWTH (BTBL1, OMTBL1, SOI1, DBI1, SUMSO, DAY)

O2, SO2 = GROWTH (BTBL2, OMTBL2, SOI2, DBI2, SUMSO, DAY)

These two lines define the growth of the two species. The remaining variables are:

SUMSO = SO1 + SO2

and

DAY = START + TIME

Now the values of B in cm/row are tabulated as a function of the time after emergence in days (the first value between each pair of brackets) with:

FUNCTION BTBL1 = (0,0), (30,3), (35,5), (40,9), (45,16), (50,26), (55,38),...
                       (60,58), (65,88), (70,102).

FUNCTION BTBL2 = (0,0), (30,7), (35,13), (40,18), (45,28), (50,51),...
                       (55,82), (60,130), (65,175), (70,194).

and the values of OM in kg dry matter/ha with:

FUNCTION OMTBL1 = (0,0), (70,5600)

FUNCTION OMTBL2 = (0,0), (70,5600)

These are values for the barley varieties Alasjmoen (1) and NHT (2), as obtained from periodic harvests of a spacing experiment with the rows 25 and 75 cm apart. (The data are from the M. Sc. thesis of J. G. Blijenburg, 1971). The values of the maximum yield at high seed densities (OM) are the same for both species and increase linearly with time because they reflect the growth rate of a closed crop surface (de Wit, 1968). Alasjmoen is a naked barley and in the beginning has a slower growth rate that NHT.

The simulation has to be started before the species interfere with each other in the mixture. This is achieved by starting the experiment with

278

PARAMETER START = 10.

at the tenth day.

The seed rates are 1/50 row/cm if it is supposed that the species are sown alternatively in rows at a distance of 25 centimeter. These are introduced into the program with:

PARAMETER S1 = 0.02, S2 = 0.02

Now the simulation may proceed until the 70th day after emergence, because at that time the crops lodged seriously, whereas it is convenient to obtain calculated results every five days. This is achieved with:

TIMER FINTIM = 70   ,PRTDEL = 5

And the results to be printed are given by:

PRINT   DAY, SO1, SO2, SUMSO, O1, O2

Then the program is finished in the customary way with

END

STOP

The CSMP programming system is able to write, on the basis of this system description, a numerical integration program in FORTRAN in which the integration is performed according to a standard numerical integration technique; in this case according to the fourth order Runge-Kutta method with variable time step.

Conclusions

The simulated results, in terms of dry matter yield for the barley-oat mixture (basic data in Fig. 10) and the mixture of the two barley varieties (basic data in the program), are given in Fig. 11 and 12, respectively, together with the actual results of an experiment. The agreement between the calculated and observed curves is excellent; especially since the calculation used no information that was obtained from the competition experiment itself. It is seen that in spite of the species being sown in a 1:1 ratio, the barley performs much better than the oats and the barley variety NHT much better than Alasjmoen. This is a consequence of their better growth in the period directly after emergence.

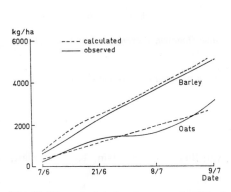

Fig. 11. The calculated and measured yield of barley and oats sown in a 1:1 ratio at normal densities (Baeumer et al., 1968).

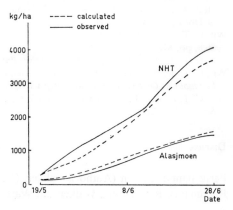

Fig. 12. The calculated and measured yield of the barley varieties Alasjmoen and NHT sown in a 1:1 ratio at normal densities (M.Sc. thesis J.G. Blijenburg, 1971).

More examples can be given to show that the classical Lotka-Volterra approach without the restrictions forced upon it by the lack of the technical equipment to obtain numerical solutions, is a very usefull tool in plant ecology. The models are deterministic and it is impossible to introduce stochastic elements. Instead, consequences of variability in the basic experimental parameters are studied by means of a sensivity analysis. In this analysis, runs are made not only with the average value of the experimental parameters, but also with the values of these parameters at their confidence limits. The sensitivity of a parameter is now judged by comparing the relative range of the output variables with the relative range of the input variables.

In more elaborate models, which cannot be discussed here, the analysis is not based on the observed behaviour of the species in a monoculture, but this behaviour is itself calculated from more basic physiological information obtained from experiments in the laboratory and under controlled conditions.

Statements to the effect that deterministic models are more oversimplified than stochastic models, or vice versa, do not have any foundation. There are modelling situations where it is more sensible to use stochastic models and other modelling situations where it is more sensible to use deterministic models; we should be versatile enough to use both or even combine them, when the necessity arrises.

References

Baeumer, K. & C. T. de Wit, 1968. Competitive interference of plant species in monocultures and mixed stands. *Neth. J. agric. Sci.* 16: 103–122.

Bergh, J. P. van den, 1968. An analysis of yields of grasses in mixed and pure stands. *Versl. Landbouwk. Onderz. (Agric. Res. Rep.) Wageningen* 714, pp. 71.

Bergh, J. P. van den & W. Th. Elberse, 1970. Yields of monocultures and mixtures of two grass species differing in growth habit. *J. appl. Ecol.* 7: 311–320.

Brennan, R. D., C. T. de Wit, W. A. Williams & E. V. Quattrin, 1970. The utility of a digital simulation language for ecological modeling. *Oecologia (Berl.)* 4: 113–132.

Harlan, H. V. & M. L. Martini, 1938. The effect of natural selection in a mixture of barley varieties. *J. agric. Res.* 57: 189–199.

Harper, J. L., 1961. Approaches to the study of plant competition. *Symp. Soc. exp. Biol.* 15: 1–39.

Seaton, A. P. C. & J. Antonovics. 1967. Population interrelationships. 1. Evolution in mixtures of Drosophila mutants. *Heredity* 22: 19–33.

Wit, C. T. de, 1960. On competition. *Versl. Landbouwk. Onderz. (Agric. Res. Rep.) Wageningen* 66.8, pp. 81.

Wit, C. T. de, 1968. Plant production. *Misc. Pap. LandbHogesch. Wageningen* No 3: 25–50.

Wit, C. T. de, P. G. Tow & G. C. Ennik, 1966. Competition between legumes and grasses. *Versl. Landbouwk. Onderz. (Agric. Res. Rep.) Wageningen* 687, pp. 30.

Wit, C. T. de & J. P. van den Bergh, 1965. Competition between herbage plants. *Neth. J. agric. Sci.* 13: 212–221.

Discussion

Participants: De Wit (Author), Bakker, (K.), van Biezen, Cavers, Jain, Kuenen, Platt, Reddingius, Rosenzweig, Walker and Watt.

Animals do compete for space but quite often it is known that ultimately competition is for food; moreover, contrary to plants, animals roam about. Therefore, a comparison between animals and plants will often be difficult or even impossible (KUENEN). Animals and

280

plants only behave analogously under certain circumstances. In order to be mutually ex-clusieve, it is not necessary that the food is the same. It may very well be that species A is limited by resource X and species B by resource Y. As long as the species cannot invade each other's territory, and the food does not roam about, both species are mutually exclusive. This is the situation that occurs with many plants and some animals. Other animals may not have territorial behaviour but move about, or may have territorial behaviour but their food may move about (e.g. some insects). In that case, they may only be mutually exclusive when they are living on exactly the same food (AUTHOR).

Whether in mutually exclusive species the response to shortages is the same or not is immaterial, although the competitive ability – as measured for instance by the relative replacement rate – depends on it. Hence, the behaviour of two species in a mixture may be described by parallel course lines even when their efficiency to a limiting growth factor is not the same, provided that the two species are mutually exclusive (AUTHOR to PLATT).

Of course there are many cases where two species are not mutually exclusive. Perhaps this occurs often in mixtures of two (plant) species which do not grow at the same time. The most obvious example being the growth of two monocultures in two successive years. In a forthcoming paper this situation will be further analysed on basis of experiments with potato varieties with different lengths of growing period, and planted at different times of the year. The analysis is then done on the basis that the two species in a mixture are only mutually exclusive during a part of their growing period. This situation occurs much more frequently with natural vegetation than in the field crop situation, because in the latter the species are often selected on basis of the length of the growing period. It may be remarked in passing, that two species with a different period of growth may still be mutually exclusive when a limiting resource, like N-fertilizer, is only supplied before the first species starts to develop (AUTHOR to CAVERS).

The results of a competition experiment in one year can only be used to predict the behaviour of a mixture in successive years when the genetic variability is low (BAKKER). This is indeed the case. However, the only straightforward example known to me is the *Drosophila* experiment discussed in the paper and here the effect of selection is perhaps too remarkable to be true. In an experiment with grass species over several years any effect of selection was absent (van den Bergh and Elberse, 1970) (AUTHOR).

REDDINGIUS then opened a discussion on the merits of stochastic and deterministic models to which WATT, ROSENZWEIG, JAIN, WALKER and van BIEZEN contributed. It was concluded, that there are two 'world views', a stochastic and a deterministic one, that both are abstractions which have their field of application and that students and ecologists should be exposed to and be familiar with both of them (EDITORS).

Proc. Adv. Study Inst. Dynamics Numbers Popul. (Oosterbeek, 1970) 282-297

The establishment of interspecific competition in field populations, with an example of competition in action between Polycelis nigra (Mull.) and P. tenuis (Ijima) (Turbellaria, Tricladida)

T. B. Reynoldson and L. S. Bellamy

Department of Zoology, University College of North Wales, Bangor, England

Abstract

Five criteria are suggested as appropriate evidence of interspecific competition in the field. These refer to comparative distribution and abundance, identification of the resource in short supply, the performance of the competing populations and the manipulation both of the populations and the resource.

These criteria are used to examine competition between *Polycelis nigra* and *P. tenuis* in natural populations. Opportunity was taken to follow the effects of competition between these two triclad species when *P. tenuis* colonised a lake previously occupied only by *P. nigra*. *Polycelis nigra* was reduced to a relatively small proportion (10%) of the total triclad population, and since the total *Polycelis* population remained approximately constant there was an actual replacement. This change had probably occurred within the period 1960 to 1970. By means of a serological technique, it was shown that the 'food refuge' of *P. tenuis* is not tubificid worms as previously suggested.

The particular focus of this paper is the result of our reading Southern's (1968) recent review of Miller's (1967) comprehensive paper on competition. We were lead by his remark that there are few well-established cases of competition in the field to consider the sort of evidence needed to demonstrate this beyond reasonable doubt. The usual type of evidence is based on comparative distribution of congeneric species, which is inadequate on its own. This has produced an understandable backlash from some ecologists who, predictably, have gone too far in the opposite direction. As one example of the sort of situation we have in mind, it has been claimed that the distribution of the stream-dwelling triclads, *Dugesia montenigrina* and *D. gonocephala* is, in part, the result of interspecific competition. This example appears in many ecological texts but it has been criticised justifiably by Andrewartha and Birch (1954). Miller (1967) makes the point that these authors do not offer an alternative explanation, but so little seems to be known of the ecology of these two triclads that, I am in no doubt, several equally feasible hypotheses could be offered. More recent work on stream triclads has also cast doubt on the relevance of competition in this context (Dahm, 1958; Wright, 1968). It is only fair to say that the explanation based on competition was offered tentatively by the original workers (Beauchamp and Ullyott, 1932) and it has often been translated into more dogmatic form in ecological texts and reviews. A second example refers to the comparative distribution of *Gammarus duebeni* and *G. pulex* in the British Isles (Hynes, 1954, 1955). This seemed to be one of the best established cases of interspecific competition in the field, yet recently, Sutcliffe (1967) has presented evidence to show that far from competing, the two species have yet to meet.

Criteria for establishing competition

Clearly, we need guide lines to what represents good evidence for competition and this has been discussed in part by Miller (1967). We propose to bring forward five criteria which together, in our view, establish competition beyond reasonable doubt. Before considering them, some comment on definitions of competition is necessary. Milne (1961) has written comprehensively on this topic and produced an acceptable definition (e.g., Varley, 1962; Dempster, 1967), but Miller's (1967) statement is more appropriate to the context of this discussion and describes the process in the sense in which it is used here. He says 'biological competition is the active demand by two or more members of two or more species at the same trophic level (interspecies competition) for a common resource or requirement that is actually or potentially limiting'. Perhaps a definition of wider generality can be based on the concept of energy, namely, that 'competition is occurring when an organism uses more energy to obtain (e.g. food) or maintain (e.g. living space) a unit of resource due to the presence of another individual, than it would otherwise do'. Such a definition applies equally well to intra- or interspecific competition. The five criteria we suggest are as follows:

1. The comparative distribution and/or relative abundance of the two potentially competing species should be amenable to explanation based on competition. This is indirect evidence and the situation may be explained in other ways, as already pointed out.
2. It is necessary to show that the competing species are utilising a common resource which may provide the basis of competition. This may seem an obvious pre-requisite but there are many examples of so-called competition which do not provide such evidence, among them the triclad case quoted earlier.
3. There should be evidence from the performance of the particular species populations in the field that intraspecific competition is occurring. This may relate to fecundity, survival, growth rate of individuals or some other appropriate parameter. This criterion assumes that if persistent interspecific competition is occurring then intraspecific competition must also be taking place.
4. Both the resource which is being competed for and the population should be manipulated separately in the field with predictable results based on the hypothesis that competition is occurring. It is insufficient to manipulate only the absolute amounts of a resource since its availability may be altered irrespective of the competition process. For example, many populations are likely to respond to an increase in food whether or not competition is occurring because the same amount (or more) may be obtained with less expenditure of energy. It should be unnecessary to mention that in any manipulation experiment either an adequate control or a good background history of the ecosystem is essential (e.g. Eisenburg, 1966).
5. Events following the introduction or removal (or reduction) of a competing species should be consistent with the competition hypothesis. This criterion differs from 4 since it concerns interspecific events only.

It might be pointed out that the range of possible situations involving competition between a pair of species (A and B) is one from where A excludes B, through co-existence to the situation where B excludes A. This does not include the case where co-existence is the result of repeated immigration of one species. Criteria 2 and 4 overlap in the sense that to be able to test 4, information on 2 is essential. Obviously, the strongest evidence of competition is provided if all five criteria can be shown to support the hypothesis. Although, in many populations, it will not be possible to obtain information on all because of technical problems, especially Criterion 4, nevertheless we consider that appropriate evidence for Criteria 1, 2, 3 and 5 demonstrates competition clearly enough. Obviously, the evidence becomes weaker and the conclusions more subjective the fewer it is possible to confirm. Such an extensive programme cannot be attempted for many species groups or ecosystems, but an effort should be made to study examples from a range of ecologically contrasted taxonomic groups in favourable and harsh environments. Refinements of this approach, especially the development of predictive models and their testing by field data is certainly one of the major fields of future ecological research. This aspect is dealt with by other con-tributors, but too many 'ecological castles' should not be built in this way without veri-fying in selected examples, that agreement between prediction and observation is causal and not spurious (Eberhardt, 1970).

If these arguments are reasonable then Southern (1968) was correct in saying that there are few convincing examples of competition in the field.

Evidence of interspecific competition between Polycelis nigra and P. tenuis

We propose now to look at the evidence of competition between *Polycelis nigra* (O. F. MULLER) and *P. tenuis* (IJIMA), two species of triclad with similar biology, in relation to the five criteria outlined earlier. Those aspects which have already been published are dealt with briefly.

Criterion 1: Comparative distribution and abundance

The distribution of the two *Polycelis* species has been observed in more than 2000 lakes and ponds situated mainly in northern Britain (Reynoldson, 1958, Fig. 2). In those geo-graphical areas inhabited by both species, *P. nigra* occurs alone most frequently in low calcium lakes, usually of low productivity. The species co-exist in the middle and higher ranges of calcium but *P. nigra* is sometimes absent in the richest calcium lakes of high productivity. Such a distribution is consistent with the occurrence of interspecific compe-tition, but could be explained equally well on other grounds. For example, each triclad species may be entirely dependent on a different prey organism and may reflect the latter's distribution. Rather more indicative of competition is the fact that in low calcium lakes usually one or the other species occurs alone; they coexist in only 2 out of 41 lakes although the evidence is that both can tolerate the physico-chemical conditions (Reynoldson, 1966). Most of the records of *P. tenuis* from low calcium lakes refer either to artificial habitats or to lakes in the north of Scotland, an area not yet reached by triclads in the course of natu-ral dispersal. Both situations have in common the fact that they have usually been stocked with fish and are often unusual in other aspects of their fauna which could be attributed to fish-stocking.

Considering abundance, it has been shown (Reynoldson, 1966, Fig. 6) that *P. nigra* is more abundant than *P. tenuis* only in low-calcium lakes. It reaches its maximum abun-dance in the middle part of the calcium range and then declines in calcium-rich lakes. *Polycelis tenuis* increases in numbers with calcium and surpasses *P. nigra* at a calcium level of 7.5 mg/l and above. Such a relative abundance is not inconsistent with interspecific competition, but again, it could also be explained in other ways. It might be pointed out here that the relation between calcium concentration and triclads is not causal, but indirect (Reynoldson, 1966) and simply offers a useful reference point.

More precise information is afforded by the distribution of these triclads on the island of Anglesey. *Polycelis nigra* is widespread in the lakes and ponds there while *P. tenuis* has reached the island relatively recently and is in process of dispersing. In 1952 it inhabited only 3 out of 21 habitats. This situation allows a comparison of numbers of *P. nigra* in lakes of broadly similar type in the presence (mainland lakes) and absence (Anglesey lakes) of *P. tenuis*. It has been shown (Reynoldson, 1958: Fig. 11) that although the overall *Polycelis* populations are similar in the two areas, supporting the idea of lake comparability, the *P. nigra* populations are significantly smaller in the presence of *P. tenuis*. It can be argued legitimately that there may be differences in other parameters which could account for this. However, the case for competition is made stronger by the fact that the two lakes on Anglesey which also support *P. tenuis* (Llyn Coron and Llyn Llygeirian) also have correspondingly small populations of *P. nigra*. These two lakes are close to others with typically large triclad populations but which contain only *P. nigra*. This situation is comparable with the stream triclad case discussed earlier, but there is the important difference that we know a great deal more about the ecology of the *Polycelis* species. On the basis of such knowledge it was predicted (Reynoldson, 1966) that most of the Anglesey lakes which are calcium-rich, productive habitats, could support *P. tenuis* and the other two common lake species, *Dugesia polychroa* (Reynoldson and Bellamy, 1970) and *Dendrocoelum lacteum*.

Criterion 2: A common resource

Extensive studies of the food of these two species by laboratory experiments, squashes of field specimens (Reynoldson and Young, 1963) and latterly by using a serological technique in which 2300 specimens from 12 lakes were tested (Reynoldson and Davies, 1970), have shown convincingly that there is considerable overlap in their diets.

Criterion 3: Performance of field populations

There are several pieces of evidence from two populations of each species that intraspecific competition for food is severe in all of them (Reynoldson, 1964). The shrinkage of adults when young appear in the population, the very low fecundity of adults compared with laboratory animals fed once weekly and the occurrence of the highest mortality in small individuals following recruitment, are all indicative of this. It has also been shown that such events are not interfered with by predation (Davies, 1967) except in special habitats (Davies, 1969) or by parasites (Reynoldson, 1966).

Criterion 4: Manipulation of resources

Two field populations, one of each *Polycelis* species, were sufficiently small in numbers and lived in a conveniently restricted habitat to allow manipulation. In one of these (*P. tenuis*), the food supply was increased over a period of several months just prior to and during the early part of the breeding season. In the other (*P. nigra*), the population was reduced to one third of its original size some months before the onset of breeding. In both cases the symptoms of intraspecific competition mentioned under Criterion 3 were either removed, reduced or delayed, consistent with the hypothesis that intraspecific competition was

285

regulating the population. The nature of these organisms and the habitat precluded control experiments, but there is a 5 year back-history of the populations for comparison. It would be stretching coincidence if such changes were regarded as events occurring by chance at the time of manipulation.

Criterion 5: Manipulation of species

This is treated in two parts, one dealing with deliberate introductions into water bodies within the geographical area of the species concerned; the second part considers 'natural' introduction and is dealt with more fully.

In 1952 a population of 2500 *P. tenuis* was introduced into Llyn Teyrn, a small shallow lake 2.5 hectares in area, at a height of 376 m in Snowdonia, N. Wales. The calcium content is 0.4 mg/l and the lake is unproductive. It contained a population of *P. nigra* with a few *Phagocata vitta* (DUGÈS). Although the introduction was relatively large, sampling in most years since 1952, including 1970, suggests that *P. tenuis* has not established itself; although it is possible that the population is exceedingly low. It would appear to have been eliminated as the result of competition from *P. nigra* since there is a great deal of evidence to show that the weather and physico-chemical conditions of the lake are suitable for *P. tenuis*. The second experiment concerned a very small (4 m) artificial spring fed pool with only three main triclad food organisms in it, viz. *Lumbriculus variegatus*, *Asellus meridianus* and *Potamopyrgus jenkinsi*. It contained only the triclad *P. tenuis*. The hypothesis explaining the distribution and abundance of triclads (Reynoldson, 1966; Reynoldson and Davies, 1970) predicted that *P. nigra* would not be able to co-exist with *P. tenuis* under such food conditions, while *Dugesia polychroa* and *Dendrocoelum lacteum* would be able to co-exist. We were able to introduce *D. polychroa* successfully but not *P. nigra*; the experiment with *D. lacteum* was not attempted at the time due to shortage of this species. Such a result is consistent with the hypothesis of interspecific competition between the *Polycelis* species.

The inter-action of Polycelis nigra and P. tenuis in Llyn Pen-y-parc

Introduction and methods

The second part concerns what might be called a semi-natural introduction since, as is argued later, man is probably involved, although not by a deliberate act. It is first necessary to consider the distribution of *Polycelis* spp. on Anglesey in the period 1948–52 when a survey was made (Reynoldson, 1956a). *Polycelis nigra* was found in all 21 lakes and ponds examined and also in many streams. *Polycelis tenuis* was restricted to the two lakes mentioned (p. 285) and also to one pond on Holy Island and a stream near Menai Bridge. *Dugesia polychroa* and *Dendrocoelum lacteum* were not found. This restriction of lake-dwelling species of triclad on Anglesey has been attributed to historical events. No further survey has been made since, but some of the habitats have been visited, at least annually, in the intervening 20 years. One of these, Llyn Pen-y-parc, originally a natural lake but operated as a public reservoir since 1913, has been visited 10–20 times a year since 1948 and several hundreds of thousands of triclads examined. Until recently they had all proved to be *P. nigra*, even the few brown species superficially resembling *P. tenuis* which occurred from time to time. The lake (Fig. 1) is small, 4.5 hectares in area, less than 5 m in depth

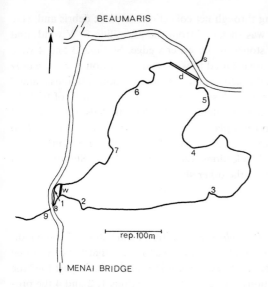

BEAUMARIS

Fig. 1. An outline of Llyn Pen-y-parc showing the position of the stations; d = dam, w = weir, s = piped outflow.

except near the dam and at an altitude of 50 m above sea level. At the west side there is a concrete wall, separating off a small area from the rest of the lake, containing a weir to regulate inflow and at the north end there is a large dam to control overflow. The water has a calcium content of 15 mg/l and the lake is moderately productive. The margin has a thin belt of deciduous trees and beyond these on most sides there are fields grazed by cattle and sheep. There is only one very small stream entering from the west which is about 75 cm wide and 25 cm deep. It is spring fed, arising 100 m to the west of the lake and the lower reaches often dry out in summer. There is considerable seepage of water into the lake during heavy rainfall from the steep eastern slopes. The lake level falls drastically during summer. Apart from the absence of fish, the lake contains a typical fauna and especially important from the viewpoint of triclad prey there are large populations of several species of *Naididae: Lumbriculus variegatus, Asellus meridianus, Gammarus pulex, Potamopyrgus jenkinsi, Lymnaea peregra* and *L. palustris*. It has been shown (Reynoldson and Davies, 1970) that the diet of *P. nigra* in this lake is normal, with oligochaetes forming the major food item. Llyn Pen-y-parc is a habitat in which all four main species of lake triclad might be expected to occur.

Polycelis tenuis was identified for the first time in August 1967 from a routine collection of *Asellus* taken by netting plant debris. A survey was then made to establish the distribution and numbers of *P. tenuis* and *P. nigra* in the lake by sampling at 7 stations around its perimeter. Similar samples were taken in December 1968, May 1969, December 1969 and June 1970. Two extra stations, one in the stream a few metres before it enters the lake, and the other 20 m upstream were added in May 1969. The positions of the sampling stations are shown in Fig. 1 and a brief description of them follows. Station 1 differs basically from the rest since it is separated from the main lake by the concrete weir which forms a little bay receiving the stream. This bay is very sheltered, subject to silting and consequently has a soft mud bottom. It contains a good growth of semi-emergent, floating and submerged vegetation including the following species, water horsetail (*Equisetum fluviatile*), starwort (*Callitriche verna*), *Potamogeton natans*, ivy-leaved duckweed (*Lemna trisulca*) and buck-bean (*Menyanthes trifoliata*). In addition there is heavy seasonal leaf fall of Sycamore and

Oak. Triclads were obtained by sorting through net collections of plant debris and were not sampled quantitatively. Station 2 was sheltered from the prevailing S–W winds and triclads were collected by hand from stones at the water's edge. Stations 3 and 4 were similar except that they were rather more exposed to wave action. Station 5 was the only shore with a large number of stones and it had the most exposed aspect; Stations 6 and 7 were sheltered and stones were scarce although sufficient to provide a sample of triclads. Station 8 was in the stream close to where it entered the bay and triclads were collected from the few stones available and also from plants. Station 9, further upstream, had no stones and triclads were obtained by searching the leaves of *Iris pseudacorus* plants which grew in the stream. Comparable, timed collections were only possible at Stations 2, 3, 4 and 5 because of the scarcity of stones at the other sites.

Results

Changes in the proportions of the two *Polycelis* species with time are shown for the individual stations in Fig. 2. The absence of data for Stations 6 and 7 in August 1967 was due to the low level of the lake which left the stones exposed. It is clear that in August 1967 the proportions differed at the several stations. For example, at Stations 1, 2 and 4 the proportion of *P. nigra* was high, 100 % at Station 4, whilst it was low at Stations 3 and 5. Such variation would be expected when one species was multiplying and possibly replacing another, since events are unlikely to occur at the same rate at all stations. It is striking that

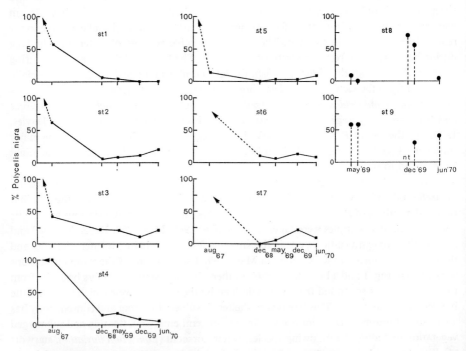

Fig. 2. The relative changes with time in the proportion of *Polycelis nigra* and *P. tenuis* collected at the nine stations in Llyn Pen-y-parc.

288

during the subsequent 16 months to December 1968, the proportion of *P. nigra* declined at all stations so that this species was uniformly, relatively scarce by this time, ranging only from 0% to 22% of the total *Polycelis* compared with 13% to 100% in August 1967. Furthermore, those stations which had high proportions of *P. nigra* in 1967 were not distinguishable from the remainder in December 1968. From the latter date onwards, the proportion of *P. nigra* remained uniformly low at all the lake stations. In three stations, 2, 6 and 7 there was a slight increase in the proportion of *P. nigra* between May and December 1969. In the period December 1969 to June 1970 three stations showed an increase (St, 2, 3, 5), three (St. 4, 6, 7) showed a decrease and one (St. 1) remained unchanged (Fig. 2). The average change in the proportion of the two species of triclad is shown in Fig. 3a. The most striking feature is the rapid decline in the relative numbers of *P. nigra* during the 18 months from August 1967 and the subsequent stability.

The two stream stations show distinct contrasts with those of the lake. At Station 8 the outstanding feature is the variation in the proportion of *P. nigra* from a low value in the

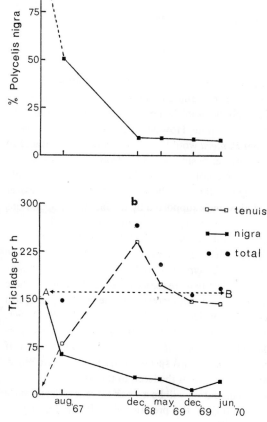

Fig. 3. (a) Average change in the proportion of *Polycelis nigra* with time in Llyn Pen-y-parc. (b) Average change in absolute numbers collected per hour of *Polycelis nigra* and *P. tenuis* with time in Llyn Pen-y-parc. The level A–B shows the average size of the *P. nigra* population before *P. tenuis* occurred.

Spring of 1969 to a high value in late 1969 and again to a low in May 1969. Since *P. nigra* is relatively more successful in streams and *P. tenuis* in lakes (Reynoldson 1956a), this station represents a fringe habitat for both. It would be expected therefore to show large changes, particularly if this stretch of the stream dries up during the summer, as it did in 1969. Dispersal of *P. nigra* to Station 8 would occur from upstream where the spring-fed stream is more permanent and dispersal of *P. tenuis* would be from the lake; this will provide a high potential for change. Station 9 is noteworthy for showing a permanently higher proportion of *P. nigra* than occurred in the lake, a result which would be anticipated from what is known of the ecology of the two species.

So far, we have deliberately referred only to proportions, since it is possible that the decline in *P. nigra* was only relative and due entirely to an increase in *P. tenuis*. If this is the correct explanation, then the total triclad population would have increased ten-fold; this has manifestly not occurred. Estimates of *P. nigra* before the advent of *P. tenuis* showed it to be present at a level of 160 specimens collected per hour. Using the quantitative data for Stations 2, 3, 4 and 5, it is possible to compare the absolute changes in numbers of both species and the total triclad population (Fig. 3b). This shows that *P. nigra* had declined from around 160/h to 64/h by August 1967, and during the next 18 months this trend continued to reach approximately 20 h; the population of *P. tenuis* had increased from zero to 81.5/h by August 1967 and then levelled off at 150 /h with a peak in December 1968 of 240/h. Thus it is appropriate to refer to the replacement of *P. nigra* by *P. tenuis*. The total triclad population showed a relatively sharp increase in 1968 when *P. tenuis* was at peak level, but fell again to the more usual value of 160/h by 1969.

Explanation and conclusions

The previous evidence of competition based on Criteria 1–5 provides an almost irresistable case for events in Llyn Pen-y-parc to be explained by interspecific competition between *Polycelis nigra* and *P. tenuis*. The probability of the appearance of *P. tenuis* and the decline of *P. nigra* coinciding by chance was remote. However, it is necessary to consider other possibilites. It might be argued that *P. nigra* would have declined in the absence of *P. tenuis*. This cannot be refuted by direct evidence since strict controls in the form of isolated parts of the lake devoid of *P. tenuis* were not maintained and, in any event, would have been difficult to provide. It is unlikely that there has been any change in climate over the last 20 years to account for events. This view is supported by the fact that populations of *P. nigra* in other nearby, comparable lakes such as Llyn Hendref and Llyn Llywenan (Reynoldson, 1956a) have not declined in numbers. Neither has there been any sufficient change in organisms important to triclads, such as prey species, in Llyn Pen-y-parc. Of the important triclad predators, the leech *Erpobdella octoculata*, *Odonata* (Dragonfly) nymphs and newt (*Triturus*) larvae (Davies, 1967), the last two are scarce except at Station 1 (where events were similar to the rest of the lake) and have not increased in the last few years; fish are absent. There is one point, however, to be considered in relation to *Erpobdella*. Davies, (1967) produced evidence, not entirely conclusive because positive results were few, suggesting the *E. octoculata* may feed relatively more on *Polycelis nigra* than on *P. tenuis*. If this is so, it would influence the proportions of the two species of triclads in Llyn Pen-y-parc irrespective of competition. However, the ratio of the leech to the triclad here is low, estimated at 1 to 70 so that any differential predation will be a weak force, especially since such leech predation is not heavy; only 10% of the predator population feeding on

Polycelis per day. If the extreme case of no interspecific competition is examined, and maximal preference by the leech based on Davies' data, the triclad population should stabilize as a result of predation at 1 *P. nigra* to 5 *P. tenuis*. As we have seen, the ratio established was 1 to 10. Perhaps more conclusive are the two following facts. In two natural productive habitats lacking *Erpobdella* and any other triclad predator, the *P. nigra/ P. tenuis* ratio was similar to that of Pen-y-parc. In several unproductive habitats with relatively large numbers of *Erpobdella*, *P. nigra* was the dominant species despite any possible preferential predation. Although the role of *Erpobdella* seems relatively insignificant compared with competition, it would tend to accelerate the rate of replacement of *P. nigra* by *P. tenuis* (especially in the later stages) in Llyn Pen-y-parc. Discussion of the role of *Erpobdella* demonstrates the difficulty of using relative distribution and abundance per se as evidence of competition.

In an attempt to decide whether or not the habitat was still favourable for *P. nigra*, two simple field experiments were set up. One of these was designed to test the continuing suitability of the lake water. Ten mature individuals of each species were kept in separate plastic cylinders 20 mm long and 6 mm in diameter with the ends closed by fine bolting-silk; five specimens of each species were kept together in a third cylinder. These cages were suspended in an open frame and the whole apparatus kept in shallow water at the edge of the lake. The triclads were fed at fortnightly intervals and survival was noted. The experiment was repeated. The first experiment extended over 5 weeks during cold weather in February-March 1970, the second for 8 weeks during April-May 1970; the results were similar in both. Survival was 50 to 80% except in the tube in the second experiment containing only *P. tenuis*; in this tube only one *P. tenuis* was found on the 8th week although two weeks earlier 8 healthy specimens were present. The cause of the mortality is unknown. Of the *Polycelis* surviving on the completion of both experiments 55% were *P. nigra* and 45% were *P. tenuis*. The departure from equality was due to the uncharacteristically high mortality in the one tube. Cocoons were deposited in all cages during the second experiment. The results show that the lake water influenced both species equally.

An attempt was made to isolate a part of the lake to observe the progress of a *P. nigra* sub-population in the absence of *P. tenuis*. Wave action breached the sealed-off area and spoilt the experiment.

One further interesting point remains. The fact that the total *Polycelis* population remained approximately the same after the replacement of most of the *P. nigra* suggests that despite the competitive superiority of *P. tenuis* this species does not noticeably exploit the ecosystem any more efficiently than does *P. nigra*. In an earlier comparison of approximately similar lakes (Reynoldson, 1966) there was some indication of more efficient exploitation of food by *P. tenuis*.

The time scale of events

It would have been more interesting if the presence of *Polycelis tenuis* in Llyn Pen-y-parc had been noted earlier and the replacement of *P. nigra* observed from the early stages. As second best, a crude estimate of the time taken for the two populations to become equal has been made on the basis of certain assumptions, namely: (a) that *P. tenuis* was introduced initially in small numbers, (b) that the population grew exponentially in the early stages at the maximum rate recorded in a field population of *Polycelis* (a 5-fold increase per year), and (c) that the total *Polycelis* population remained numerically stable, for which there is good evidence. Since the time at which equality was reached is known, the year of the introduction of *P. tenuis* can be estimated. Such a procedure required the total *Polycelis* population of the lake to be calculated. This has been attempted from a knowledge of the numbers collected per hour, the approximate area searched per hour and the length of the lake perimeter. The estimate is also based on the observation that triclads usually concentrate in shallow water although this is not always so, as we, and also Macan and Maudsley (1969), have noted; for example, they move temporarily into deeper water during an onshore wind. Such an estimate gives a total *Polycelis* population of 260,000 in the lake. It is likely to be an underestimate rather than the reverse because some individuals will live deeper than allowed for. However, if the population is twice this size it would make only one year's difference to the dates considered below. Based on an introduction of two adult *P. tenuis* (they are hermaphrodite and sperm in the receptaculum seminis can fertilise 20–30 eggs), these crude parameters suggest it was introduced 6–7 years prior to the time equality was reached with *P. nigra*; that is, about 1960. It would reach approximately 1/100 of the *P. nigra* population by 1964–65 and should have been detectable about this time; the chance of finding it earlier would be small. The fact that *P. tenuis* was not observed until 1967 can be attributed in part to our involvement from 1963 onwards with laboratory studies. Samples of lake animals taken from this time were obtained mainly by netting leaves from Station 1 for *Asellus* and *Gammarus* to feed laboratory populations of triclads. A second factor may have been the patchy distribution of *P. tenuis* in the early stages – it was still patchy by August 1967 (Fig. 2).

The dispersal of Polycelis tenuis to Llyn Pen-y-parc

The mechanism of dispersal is still one of the least understood phenomena in ecology and this is true of triclads. While some dispersal has probably occurred via mobile animals associated with aquatic habitats such as birds, especially from one watershed to an adjacent one, triclads undoubtedly spread within a watershed by their own locomotion. Man has also played some part by his trading activities and the introduction of the American triclad *Dugesia tigrina* into Britain and the Continent of Europe is believed to have been due to the aquarist trade (Reynoldson, 1956b). The introduction of *Dugesia polychroa* into North America (Ball, 1969) and *Planaria torva* into Britain (Sefton, 1969) have been tentatively attributed to trading, especially in the timber industry. There are several instances, not confined to triclads, where the fauna of a well-known and frequently stocked fishing lake has additional species to nearby, lesser known, unstocked lakes. Such species as *Polycelis tenuis*, *Asellus aquaticus* (Williams, 1962) and *Gammarus pulex* (Hynes, 1954) are probably transported along with fish. However, such explanations do not seem likely to account for the introduction of *P. tenuis* into Llyn Pen-y-parc. It has no fish population and is fed mainly by semi-permanent flushes of water. In the one small permanent stream (p. 287) there are no *P. tenuis* except near its entry to the lake, nor are there any records of this triclad in streams or ponds in the vicinity. Although transport by birds is possible it seems more likely that *P. tenuis* has been accidently introduced by students visiting the lake during courses in freshwater-biology. In the last decade the number of such courses and visits from schools and universities has multiplied greatly. As an example of this, I have noted a student setting off to do field work on Anglesey with a supposedly empty jar which, in fact, contained a specimen of *Dugesia polychroa* collected on a previous excursion to a mainland habitat.

292

Co-existence and the 'food refuge' concept

It has been shown (Reynoldson and Davies, 1970) that the *Polycelis* species, *Dugesia polychroa* and *Dendrocoelum lacteum* overlap substantially in their food niches, but each species preys to a greater extent on a different organism, designated a 'food refuge'. An attempt to quantify the minimal difference in food niche essential to allow co-existence suggests that it must be of the order of at least 30% of the total food intake. An unsolved problem concerns the basis of co-existence of *P. nigra* and *P. tenuis* in this context. It is clear from the events in Llyn Pen-y-parc that *P. tenuis* is competitively much superior to *P. nigra* in productive lakes. *Polycelis nigra* is therefore subject to severe selective pressure and relegated to a small proportion of the total triclad population. This means that its 'food refuge' may be provided by a prey organism which is not abundant and therefore may be difficult to identify. Consideration of the food of these two species based on squashing field specimens suggested that differences in oligochaete diet might provide a food refuge for each (Reynoldson and Davies, 1970). In particular *P. nigra* seemed to feed to a greater extent on *Naididae* (difference of 26%) while *P. tenuis* took *Tubificidae* and *Enchytraeidae* to a greater extent than does *P. nigra* (difference of 21%). To test this hypothesis an antiserum against tubificids was prepared and tested for specificity against the common prey organisms of *Polycelis*, especially oligochaetes. The antiserum cross-reacted only with the enchytraeid *Lumbricillis rivalis* and this reaction was removed by absorbing the serum with extract of *L. rivalis*. A total of 482 *P. nigra* from seven Anglesey lakes, some containing *P. tenuis*, and 390 *P. tenuis* from 4 Anglesey lakes, were tested for feeding on tubificids in July and October, 1969 with completely negative results. Such a definitive rejection of the hypothesis demanded a re-examination of the original data of feeding on oligochaetes by *Polycelis*. This revealed that all but 2 of the 33 cases of feeding on *Tubificidae* and *Enchytraeidae* came from a stony area of the Vaynol Park (Nr. Caernarvon) pond near the inflow of a heavily polluted stream. In this habitat there was a fauna of these oligochaetes quite unlike that of corresponding places in natural lakes. When these tubificid data are omitted, feeding on them becomes less than 5% of the total food and the difference between the *Polycelis* species is negligible in respect to these oligochaetes. *Naididae* still seem a possible 'food refuge' for *P. nigra* (difference of 23%) while *Lumbriculus variegatus* is eaten more by *P. tenuis* and is worth investigating further as a possible 'food refuge', especially since the available data are few. Future work will concentrate on these two features.

Acknowledgments

The senior author is grateful to the Natural Environment Research Council for providing a research assistant. We are also indebted to Dr. W. Hemmings and Mr Edgar Williams of the Agricultural Research Council Unit of Embryology at Bangor for advice and technical assistance with the serological work.

References

Andrewartha, H. G. & L. C. Birch, 1954. The distribution and abundance of animals. University Press, Chicago.

Ball. I. R., 1969. *Dugesia lugubris* (Tricladida: Paludicola), a European immigrant into North American fresh waters. *J. Fish. Res. Bd. Can.* 26: 221–228.

Beauchamp, R. S. A. & P. Ullyott, 1932. Competitive relationships between certain species of fresh-water triclads. *J. Ecol.* 20: 200–208.

Dahm, A. G., 1958. Taxonomy and ecology of five species groups in the Family Planariidae (Turbellaria Tricladida Paludicola). Malmö, pp. 241.

Davies, R. W., 1967. A study of predators of triclads by means of a serological technique. Unpublished Ph. D. thesis, University of Wales.

Davies, R. W., 1969. Predation as a factor in the ecology of triclads in a small, weedy pond. *J. Anim. Ecol.* 38: 577–584.

Dempster, J. P., 1967. Intra-specific competition and dispersal: as exemplified by a Psyllid and its Anthocorid predator. In: T. R. E. Southwood (Ed.), Insect abundance. *Symp. Roy ent. Soc. Lond.* No 4, pp. 160.

Eisenberg, R. M., 1966. The regulation of density in a natural population of the pond snail *Lymnaea elodes*. *Ecology* 47: 889–906.

Eberhardt, L. L., 1970. Correlation, regression and density dependence. *Ecology* 51: 306–310.

Hynes, H. B. N., 1954. The ecology of *Gammarus duebeni* LILLJEBORG and its occurrence in freshwater in Western Britain. *J. Anim. Ecol.* 23: 38–84.

Hynes, H. B. N., 1955. The reproductive cycle of some British freshwater Gammaridae. *J. Anim. Ecol.* 24: 352–387.

Macan, T. T. & R. Maudsley, 1969. Fauna of the stony substratum in lakes in the English Lake District. *Verh. Internat. Verein. Limnol.* 17: 173–180.

Miller, R. S., 1967. Pattern and process in competition. *Adv. Ecol. Res.* 4: 1–74.

Milne, A., 1961. Definition of competition among animals. *Symp. Soc. exp. Biol.* 15: 40–61.

Reynoldson, T. B., 1956a. Observations on the fresh-water triclads of North Wales. *Ann. Mag. nat. Hist.* S 12, 9: 612–622.

Reynoldson. T. B., 1956b. The occurrence in Britain of the American triclad *Dugesia tigrina* (GIRARD) and the status of *D. gonocephala* (DUGÈS). *Ann. Mag. nat. Hist.* S 12, 9: 102–105.

Reynoldson, T. B., 1958. The quantitative ecology of lake-dwelling triclads in northern Britain. *Oikos* 9: 94–138.

Reynoldson, T. B., 1964. Evidence for intra-specific competition in field populations of triclads. *J. Anim. Ecol.* (Jubilee Symp. Suppl.) 33: 187–201.

Reynoldson, T. B., 1966. The distribution and abundance of lake-dwelling triclads – towards a hypothesis. *Adv. Ecol. Res.* 3: 1–71.

Reynoldson T. B. & L. S. Bellamy, 1970. The status of *Dugesia lugubris* and *D. polychroa* (Turbellaria, Tricladida) in Britain. *J. Zool. Lond.* 162: 157–177.

Reynoldson, T. B. & R. W. Davies, 1970. Food niche and co-existence in lake-dwelling triclads. *J. Anim. Ecol.* 39: 599–617.

Reynoldson, T. B. & J. O. Young, 1963. The food of four species of lake-dwelling triclads. *J. Anim. Ecol.* 32: 175–191.

Sefton, A. D., 1969. The biology of *Planaria torva* (MÜLLER) (Tricladida Paludicola). Unpublished thesis, University of Wales.

Southern, H. N., 1968. Review of: J. B. Cragg (Ed.), Advances in ecological research, 4 (1967) *J. Anim. Ecol.* 37: 723–724.

Sutcliffe, D. W., 1967. A re-examination of observations on the distribution of *Gammarus duebeni* LILLJEBORG in relation to the salt content in fresh water. *J. Anim. Ecol.* 36: 579–597.

Varley, G. C., 1962. Review of: F. L. Milthorpe (Ed.), Mechanisms in biological competition, (1961). pp. 365. Cambridge Univ. Press. *J. Anim. Ecol.* 31: 167–168.

Williams, W. D., 1962. The geographical distribution of the isopods *Asellus aquaticus* (L.) and *A. meridianus* RAC. *Proc. zool. Soc. Lond.* 139: 75–96.

Wright, J. F., 1968. The ecology of stream-dwelling triclads. Unpublished thesis, University of Wales.

Discussion

Participants: Reynoldson and Bellamy (Authors), Bakker (K.), Cavers, Egglishaw, Frank, Gulland, Huffaker, Pimentel, Rabinovich, Rosenzweig, Walker, Williamson, Wolda, Zahavi and Zwölfer.

– The discussion mainly centered around the relative merits of mathematical and verbal definitions of competition –

The concept of competition is derived mainly from mathematics, and a mathematical definition has been implicit in all work since that of Lotka and Volterra. If A and B are the densities of two species, then they compete in a specific environment, if and only if, in that environment

$$\frac{\delta \left(\dfrac{d \ln A}{dt}\right)}{\delta B} < O \text{ and } \frac{\delta \left(\dfrac{d \ln B}{dt}\right)}{\delta A} < O$$

This definition shows the relationships between competition and the other population interactions of allelopathy and natural selection. It begs one to do perturbation experiments to prove the presence, and to measure the intensity, of competition, and it stresses the necessity for discovering just what changes occur when populations in nature are deliberately perturbed (ROSENZWEIG). Although, at the moment, there is unlikely to be any agreement on the definition of competition, we may be able to agree on the criteria to be used in deciding whether or not a particular situation is competition, and hence, we should follow the suggestions of Reynoldson (WILLIAMSON). There are technical difficulties in performing perturbation and manipulation experiments (my criterion 4) in many ecosystems. On the other hand I agree that they would provide the best evidence on the question of the existence of competition (AUTHOR).

Would the results of a computer similation study of such a manipulation be acceptable as a proof or disproof of the existence of a competition process (RABINOVICH)? That depends on the validity (premises) of the model. Most models are expected not to be sufficiently sophisticated to simulate natural ecosystems (AUTHOR).

Would Rosenzweig's formula also fit if external or internal factors affect the fitness of the two species differentially? If the fitness of the two species is reduced equally by a shortage of an essential requirement then biologically competition is occurring although according to the formula this would not be competition, because neither species won the competition (WALKER). It is unlikely that shortage of an essential resource would affect two different species equally. It is generally accepted opinion that no two species have identical needs (the same fundamental 'niche') (AUTHOR).

A 6th criterion for determining interspecific competition may be: character displacement (ZWÖLFER). I have not tried to give a complete list of possible criteria (AUTHOR). Character displacement is neither necessary nor sufficient as a criterion for competition. MacArthur and Levins have shown that if 'niches' overlap severely, character convergence may result. Moreover, character displacement may be the result of a need for species recognition in some cases (ROSENZWEIG).

A quantitative link between the mathematical inequality of Rosenzweig and the descriptive criteria may be given by what appears to be an example of competition in marine fish. In the California current, the sardine used to support a major fishery with catches reaching a peak of over 600,000 tons annually in the 1930's. Since then, the stocks have declined to very low level, while another pelagic species has increased greatly – as shown by the occurrence of eggs and larvae. Considering the sardine alone, there are two separate regressions, one showing a declining survival in the first two years of life, the other an increasing adult abundance; one covers the period up to about 1940, and the other the period of decline since 1940. If the survival is plotted against the combined abundance of sardines and anchovy, all the points (the whole period) fall on a single line. That is, survival of young sardines decreases with increasing anchovy abundance (GULLAND).

Are such closed hydrobiological ecosystems in lakes comparable with open terrestrial systems (FRANK)? Freshwater ecosystems are likely to show less physico-chemical variation than terrestrial ones, which may lead to more stable populations – but not necessarily so. Perhaps triclads are relatively favoured in this respect by having few predators, no lethal parasites and the ability to tolerate starvation for long periods (AUTHOR).

Competition can be observed directly in the interactions between individuals of related species when they meet. If supplemented with data on distribution it easily produces many examples of direct competition. Many such cases occur where faunas have met recently, and are especially clear in higher groups, e.g. vertebrates. Many examples occur in Israel among mammals, birds and reptiles (ZAHAVI). This depends on the definition used. Many may be trivial cases in which there is no major effect on the populations concerned. The paper referred to competition which has a large effect on the population. The definition based on energy covers all types of competition (AUTHOR).

There is a semantic problem: If we stick to Miller's definition it seems relatively easy to demonstrate the existence of competition in nature. One needs, in fact, only to show that (a) two species of the same trophic level have an active demand of a common resource, and (b) this resource is (sometimes) in short supply. In the paper, the result of competition – such as competitive exclusion – has been discussed. To clarify matters one should distinguish between a phenomenon and its effect, i.e. between competition and the possible results of competition (WOLDA). To know that competition is occurring you must have a result, and to demonstrate that a resource is in short supply you need to use criteria 3 and 4 (AUTHOR).

I do not agree with Reynoldson that only little evidence exists of interspecific competition in nature. As only one of many examples from the field of biological control: *Chrysolina quadrigemina* and *hyperici* were introduced in California to control the weed *Hypericum perforatum*. After both species had increased rapidly and had greatly reduced the weed, *C. quadrigemina* gradually completely displaced *hyperici* (HUFFAKER). This depends on how 'little evidence' is interpreted. Compared with the multitude of ecosystems and species existing, we have only little evidence (AUTHOR).

The unsuccesfull establishment of species A in a habitat occupied by B can only be ascribed to competition if A can easily colonize a habitat which is not occupied by B (BAKKER). All the evidence of laboratory and field experiments suggests conclusively that species A (*Polycelis tenuis*) can live in B (*P. nigra*)'s habitats in the absence of B. The Llyn Pen-y-Parc experiment showed that B (*nigra*) lived there before the arrival of A (*tenuis*) and then was drastically reduced in numbers when A was introduced. The actual mechanism of the replacement is under investigation, but not yet known. The suggestion of CAVERS, that some parasite may have been introduced in Llyn Pen-y-Parc with *P. tenuis* which had a much greater effect on *P. nigra* numbers than on those of *P. tenuis*, is not very probable, because triclads have only few parasites (*Sporozoa* usually) which are non-specific and less than 5% of British populations are parasitised (AUTHOR).

How was *P. nigra* able to hold on at a density of about 60 when the total reached 260, whereas the normal peak for *nigra* was about 150 (PIMENTEL)? The high total of 260 may have had several causes:

1. It may have been an overshoot of carrying capacity at the time of maximum interaction of the two species;
2. It may have been the result of a temporary change in prey numbers;
3. It is to be hoped that it was not the result of sampling errors! (AUTHOR).

There is no evidence of a change in quality of the individuals (mean weight, growth rate, etc.) of *P. nigra* when subjected to competition with *P. tenuis*, but there must have been some changes (e.g. behaviour in relation to competitive ability) (AUTHOR to EGGLISHAW).

Proc. Adv. Study Inst. Dynamics Numbers Popul. (Oosterbeek, 1970) 298–312

On the role of natural enemies in preventing competitive exclusion in some marine animals and in rain forest trees

J. H. Connell

Department of Biological Sciences, University of California, Santa Barbara, USA

Abstract

The following question is posed and discussed. Under what environmental conditions will the action of natural enemies prevent competitive exclusion between species of their prey? My studies on marine animal populations and rain forest trees both suggest that fluctuations in the physical environment and subsequent effects on the supply of resources reduce the effectiveness of natural enemies and allow the prey to increase to sufficiently high densities that they compete for resources. Fluctuations in weather may (1) reduce the populations of enemies more than their prey, (2) allow the prey to get a head start after an unfavourable season and (3) reduce the degree of specialization of the enemies. With lesser amplitude and/or more regularity of fluctuations, natural enemies are more effective in preventing competition. However, these conditions also lead to stronger defenses by the prey and greater effectiveness of the secondary enemies attacking the ones in question. In regions of very favorable physical conditions, the only defense against natural enemies seems to be rarity and widely scattered distributions, which together preclude competitive exclusion.

Interspecific competition is defined as the striving by members of two or more species, at the same trophic level, for the same requisite which is in short supply. It is often invoked to explain the organization of ecological communities, the evolution of closely related species, character displacement where ranges overlap, etc. While competitive interactions may be observed on occasion, the competitive exclusion or displacement of one species by another from a local area has seldom been documented clearly, as pointed out by Miller (1967). It is usually suggested that the reason why competitive exclusion is rarely seen is that in the past, competitors have evolved divergent strategies to share the contested resource. However, in many ecological communities, very similar species coexist with little obvious divergence in character. They often appear to be using completely the resource required; they seem to be competing, but not excluding each other.

An alternative hypothesis to explain such coexistence is that potentially competing prey populations are kept at such low numbers by very efficient predators that competition is greatly reduced. The prey coexist because no species reaches high enough density to exclude another in competition. There have been several experimental tests of this hypothesis, both in artificial populations such as crops, heavily grazed pastures or in the laboratory, and under more natural conditions. Probably the first experimental test of this idea was performed by Charles Darwin (1859, p. 67–68): 'If turf which has long been mown, and the case would be the same with turf closely browsed by quadrupeds, be let to grow, the more vigorous plants gradually kill the less vigorous, though fully grown plants; thus out of twenty species growing on a little plot of mown turf (three feet by four) nine species perished, from the other species being allowed to grow up freely.'

Harper (1970) has reviewed and discussed later experiments in which herbivores were removed from or added to highly modified vegetation, such as grazed pastures, sown swards and stands of introduced plant pests such as prickly pear or St. John's wort. The intensity and timing of grazing and the selection of prey had profound effects on the composition of the vegetation. In all these studies the implication was that grazing reduced the populations of certain species, allowing others to persist or enter.

In the laboratory, Slobodkin (1964) showed that when *Hydra* and *Chlorohydra* were kept in the light, *Hydra* became extinct. He then imposed 'predation' by removing a fixed percentage of both species. As the percentage of predation increased, so did the time to extinction of *Hydra*, until at 90% predation the two species were coexisting when the experiment was ended.

Under more natural conditions, removal of enemies has sometimes resulted in changes which are attributed to increased competition. Examples are the removal of rabbits from herbaceous stands in Britain (Harper, 1970), small mammals from herbaceous vegetation in young plantations of trees (Summerhayes, 1941) and marine grazers or predators from rocky shores (Connell, 1961b; Paine, 1966; Paine and Vadas, 1969).

In summary, it seems clear from these experimental manipulations in the laboratory, in simplified field situations such as crops and pastures, and in natural communities, that enemies can prevent competition between some of their prey species. The question is: Under what conditions will this happen in natural ecological communities? Since the most convincing case for the existence of 'organization' in an ecological community is the operation of interactions such as competition and predation, it is important to try to define the conditions that determine how and when these interactions operate effectively under natural conditions.

In the following case histories, I will provide some evidence concerning the conditions which determine whether predation will or will not be effective in preventing competition. These studies were made in largely undisturbed natural communities in which the species had their full complement of competitors, predators, parasites and food species.

Predation ineffective in preventing interspecific competition in intertidal barnacles

In a study of interspecific competition and predation in Scotland, I found that one species of barnacle excluded another species from most of the intertidal shore (Connell, 1961b). The losing species, *Chthamalus stellatus*, settled normally only in the upper half of the intertidal zone, and was displaced from it by direct crowding during growth of the winning species, *Balanus balanoides*. In this upper shore region, the predatory snail *Thais lapillus* attacked mainly *Balanus* but did so only after the prey were at least 6 months old (Connell, 1961a). By this time, much of the competition between the barnacles had already occurred, so that the predation could not lessen the competitive exclusion of *Chthamalus* by *Balanus*. At lower shore levels, *Thais* began to attack the barnacles when they were only about a month old. When I transplanted the competing barnacles to these lower shore levels, the predation was more effective in preventing competition. At each monthly census I made notes of which *Chthamalus* were being crowded by *Balanus*. Table 1 shows the mortality of *Chthamalus* caused by this crowding. Mortality from crowding was about the same at both levels when predators were excluded by cages, but in natural populations the predators reduced this crowding only at lower shore levels.

Table 1. The amount of mortality due solely to crowding in natural populations of *Chthamalus*, open to predation by *Thais* and protected from predation in adjacent cages. *Chthamalus stellatus* was competing with *Balanus balanoides*, the predator being *Thais lapillus*, at Millport, Scotland, 1954 (Connell, 1961b). *Chthamalus dalli* was competing with *Balanus glandula* and *B. cariosus*, the predators being *Thais emarginata* and *T. lamellosa* at Friday Harbor, Washington, USA, 1964.

	Chthamalus stellatus				*Chthamalus dalli*			
	upper shore		lower shore[1]		upper shore		lower shore	
	open	cage	open	cage	open	cage	open	cage
Number of sites	2	2	3	3	2	3	6	6
Number of *Chthamalus* in June	98	153	118	152	232	493	468	593
% mortality of *Chthamalus* by September, due to crowding by *Balanus*	31	39	13	32	6	22	10	37

[1] These barnacles were on pieces of rock from the upper shore, transpanted to the lower shore.

The question then is: Why weren't the predators so effective at upper shore levels? Why didn't they begin to attack the very young barnacles as they did at the lower levels? To answer these questions, I will describe another example, from a similar community in which the predators did this.

Predation effective in preventing interspecific competition in intertidal barnacles

On San Juan Island, Washington, USA, 3 species of barnacles live in the intertidal zone with 3 species of their principal predators, snails of the genus *Thais* (Connell, 1970). The vertical distribution of the two species of *Balanus* on San Juan Island is virtually identical with that at Millport, Scotland; adults of *B. glandula* were confined to a narrow band at the top of the intertidal zone, similar to *Chthamalus* at Millport. *B. cariosus* occupies the lower zone, like *B. balanoides* at Millport. But the reason why *B. glandula* only survived high on the shore on San Juan Island was not because it was excluded from the lower shore by competition with *B. cariosus* or any other competitor. Every year *glandula* settled throughout the lower shore but was quickly eaten by predators. The predators could not feed at the highest shore levels where adult *glandula* survived for several years. In situations where predators were absent, *glandula* survived throughout the intertidal zone. One such habitat was at the head of quiet bays, where both predators and other barnacles were rare (Connell, 1970).

In situations with at least moderate water movement, predators were common and fed heavily on both species of *Balanus* when the barnacles were young. With this intense predation the barnacles were seldom allowed to get dense enough to compete for space; I have seen crowding in *B. cariosus* occasionally, but never in *B. glandula*, or between the species. I several times attempted to exclude *Thais* with cages, as I did in Millport, but small *Thais* invariably got inside cages and attacked *B. glandula* preferentially. I have never managed to exclude predators for long enough to see which species of *Balanus* would win in competition. Since *cariosus* grows slightly faster than *glandula*, I would predict that *cariosus* would win.

Occasionally, a heavy settlement of *Balanus cariosus* survives at high shore levels, possibly because of unusually favorable cool weather during the settlement season. These may then crowd out the other species of barnacles because predation is much less intense at very high levels. This evidently happened to the 1963 settlement at the study area at San Juan Island. When this species reaches the age of 2 years, it becomes invulnerable to attack by *Thais* in the intertidal zone, and so survives a long time. Since this only happens occasionally, the age structure of the *B. cariosus* population consists of one or more 'dominant year classes', rather than the more evenly mixed age distribution of *B. glandula*.

Another species of barnacle, *Chthamalus dalli*, occurs scattered throughout the intertidal zone and not restricted to any particular level. In its small size and slow growth it resembles *C. stellatus* at Millport. I set up a series of cages to test the outcome of competition between *C. dalli* and the two species of *Balanus*, in the absence of predation. At each monthly census I made notes of which *Chthamalus* were being smothered, undercut or crushed by adjacent *Balanus*. Table 1 shows the mortality from this competition for the first summer when growth was most rapid. At both shore levels, mortality from crowding was much higher inside the cages. The predators outside were eating the *Balanus* and thus reducing the competition, as they did on the transplanted rocks at lower shore levels at Millport. But on San Juan Island, the predators were effective at almost all shore levels in keeping the barnacle populations below the point where they would compete for space. Only occasionally at very high levels did *B. cariosus* escape predation long enough to become dense and crowd out other competitors. Above this, in the narrow high band where adult *B. glandula* survived in a refuge above its predators, the barnacle population seldom occupied all the space (Connell, 1970, Fig. 8). Probably the harsh physical conditions at this high level kept the population sparse, as happened at Millport (Connell, 1961, Table 13).

The predator responsible for most of the predation at upper shore levels was *Thais emarginata*. It has a relatively thinner shell, larger opercular opening and shorter spire than either *Thais lamellosa*, which lives at low levels on San Juan Island, or *Thais lapillus* from Millport. As Kitching, Muntz and Ebling (1966) and Connell (1970, Table 17) have shown, the shell characteristics of the latter two species protect them from predation by shore crabs which feed at low shore levels. Evidently *Thais emarginata* has a refuge from crab predation at the higher shore levels, and does not require a heavy shell. Since it is reasonable to assume that constructing and carrying a thinner shell requires a lesser expenditure of energy, this saving may compensate for the disadvantages both of taking smaller sized prey and of having a shorter feeding period at high levels. Compared with *Thais lamellosa* from lower shore levels, *Thais emarginata* is smaller, has a thinner shell, reaches sexual maturity faster ($1\frac{1}{2}$ years as against $2\frac{1}{2}$ years for *T. lamellosa*) and lives a shorter time (3 to 4 years as against 8 or more years for *T. lamellosa*).

This specialized strategy has a price; *Thais emarginata* cannot retreat to lower shore levels if its food supply fails, because its shell structure renders it very vulnerable to predation by crabs. Therefore, it is dependent upon a very regular food supply. On San Juan Island *B. glandula* fulfills this requirement nicely; its recruitment is very regular (Connell, 1970, Fig. 4). Thus the prevention of competition at upper shore levels at San Juan Island is probably due to the presence of a specialized predator which harvests its prey very efficiently. The specialization is permitted by the existence of a dependable food supply, *B. glandula*.

In contrast, there is no such specialist predator at Millport, probably because the food supply is much more variable there. *B. balanoides* often reaches densities of 60 to 80 per cm^2, but in some years the settlement fails almost completely (Connell, 1961a). A high level specialist like *Thais emarginata* would occasionally starve in Millport. Apparently, the reason for the irregular barnacle recruitment in Scotland is due to the very short season of larval settlement. The population of *B. balanoides* liberates its larvae in two successive waves within one to one and a half months in early spring, in response to the phytoplankton bloom (Barnes, 1957). In some years, the first liberation perishes when the early bloom fails due to weather conditions. Occasionally both liberations perish and settlement is almost non-existent (Barnes, 1956; Connell, 1961a).

In contrast, the larval settlement of *B. glandula* on the Pacific Coast extends over six months. It is much less likely that weather catastrophes could completely eliminate the larval supply if settlement extends over six months, than if it occurs over a short period as in Scotland. As a consequence, recruitment of *B. glandula* was very regular.

Thus, the predator-prey system in Scotland is geared to a highly seasonal, rather undependable resource supply. There is a short intense spring bloom of phytoplankton, which demands close synchrony of liberation of the barnacle larvae, and there are occasional failures due to weather catastrophes. This system limits the degree of specialization of the predators, and decreases their efficiency in harvesting their prey in certain habitats. With less efficient predation and short intense recruitment of prey, strong competition develops between the prey species.

At San Juan Island, less seasonality in primary productivity probably allows a longer period over which larvae can be released into the plankton. This reduces the uncertainty of recruitment of prey to the shore population and permits specialization of the predator. It can keep up with the prey, thinning it out and preventing competition for space, as the predator *Pisaster* did in Paine's (1966) study.

On the prevention of competitive exclusion in rain forest trees

In contrast to the barnacles which were kept by their predators below the maximum level allowed by the resources available, trees in rain forests obviously compete for light and possibly for other resources. Their natural enemies, as a group, don't prevent competition between the trees. However, the enemies may prevent competitive exclusion of one species of tree by another, by preventing any one from forming a single-species aggregation and so displacing other species from the particular area.

The mechanism I suggest is that each tree species has host-specific enemies which attack it and any of its offspring which are close to the parent. The healthy parent tree supports a large population of these enemies without itself being killed, but the seedlings, whose growth is suppressed in the heavy shade, succumb to the attack of insects and other enemies which come from the parent tree itself or the soil below it. A similar hypothesis, though differing in certain details, has been proposed independently by Janzen (1970).

So the only way a species of tree can reproduce in these forests is to disperse its seedlings far enough from the parent to allow them to escape attack for long enough to reach the size when they can withstand attack by enemies. If all enemies of trees were removed from an entire forest, each species would probably form small groves, and the more rapidly growing species would gradually spread over the habitat it is best suited for, excluding the slower growing or less well adapted species in that area. The final result would be a lower 'pattern' diversity (less intermingling of the different species) and as a consequence, fewer species in any local area of forest.

The following is a preliminary account of work which I have done with J. G. Tracey and

L. J. Webb in rain forests in Queensland, Australia, in an effort to test this hypothesis (Connell, Tracey and Webb, in prep.). We mapped the trees in two rain forests, the larger ones (> 10 cm in diameter at breast height (DBH)) on areas of about 1.7 hectares, the smaller ones in strips within these plots.

Table 2 illustrates how the diversity increases with size and age of trees in the plot in northern Queensland. Seedlings up to 0.1 m high (less than about 4 years old) had a very low 'pattern diversity' (Pielou, 1966); that is, they tended to occur in single-species clumps rather than mingled with other species. (This sampling was done by taking the first and second nearest neighbours of each individual and recording the number of species in the 'triplets'.) In young trees of the next larger size class, 0.11 to 0.19 m high, the pattern diversity increased markedly, and by the time they were over 0.8 m high, their pattern diversity had approached that of the adult trees. Pielou's index of pattern diversity takes into account the number of species and their relative abundance. We have given reasons (Connell, Tracey and Webb, in prep.) why a high pattern diversity should lead to a greater species diversity and 'evenness' as shown in Table 2.

Table 2. Diversity of trees in rain forest at Davies Creek, North Queensland, Australia, lat. 17° S, elevation 850 m. Saplings less than 2.5 cm in diameter (breast height)were divided into five height classes as equal in number as possible. All the data refer to August, 1969, except those in the second column from the right, and for trees larger than 2.5 cm in diameter. Pattern diversity was calculated as shown in Pielou (1966): for trees 0.11 to 6.34 m high, the 1969 figures are from the same group of trees as in 1965, minus those which died in the interval.

Height class (m)	Number of trees	Number of species	Diversity H (base e)	Evenness J	Pattern diversity D Aug. 65	Aug. 69
0 –0.10	1080	71	2.05	0.39	—	0.51
0.11–0.19	1038	115	3.47	0.66	0.72	0.77
0.20–0.35	983	103	3.38	0.64	0.76	0.82
0.36–0.79	1040	111	3.60	0.68	0.87	0.89
0.80–6.34	1093	131	3.80	0.72	0.93	0.93
Diameter class (cm)						
2.5–9.9	956	116	3.79	0.72	0.96	—
10.0 +	1502	126	4.31	0.81	0.98	—

The pattern diversity increases not only with size but also with age, as shown in Table 2 by the changes between 1965 and 1969. The increase in pattern diversity was greater in the smaller size classes where mortality was greater. This suggests that mortality falls more heavily on trees which are next to others of the same species, than on those intermingled with other species. Since we had mapped every individual in 1965, we could test this hypothesis by tabulating for each tree whether its nearest neighbour was the same or a different species. As shown in Table 3, the small saplings having the same species as a nearest neighbour had a higher mortality rate than if they had a different species as neighbour. Larger saplings had a lower mortality and the species of the neighbour had no effect.

Adult trees also have a deleterious effect on smaller trees of the same species. We planted

Table 3. Mortality of tree saplings in rain forest in relation to the species of their nearest neighbour within the same size class. August 1965 to August 1969, Davies Creek, North Queensland, Australia, lat. 17° S, elevation 850 m.

Height class (m)		Species of nearest neighbour	
		same species	different species
0.11–0.19	Number living in 1965	64	148
	Number dying by 1969	24	27
	% mortality in 4 years	37.5	18.2
0.20–0.35	Number living in 1965	153	435
	Number dying by 1969	33	49
	% mortality in 4 years	21.6	11.2
0.36–0.79	Number living in 1965	100	548
	Number dying by 1969	11	36
	% mortality in 4 years	11.0	6.6
0.80–6.34	Number living in 1965	59	604
	Number dying by 1969	2	18
	% mortality in 4 years	3.4	3.0

seeds of *Planchonella sp. nov.* in four plots of 2 × 1 m each under two adjacent adult trees, and in four other plots nearby under adult trees of other species. In each place we cut the roots around 2 of the plots to eliminate competition for nutrients with the adult trees. Over 80% of the seedlings became established in all plots. The results in Table 4 indicate that mortality of the young trees during the next 3 years was much greater under adults of the same species than under those of other species. Removal of roots had no consistent effect; it certainly did not improve the survival under adults of the same species.

In other experiments we placed the seeds of other species on the surface instead of burying them, both under adults of the same species and of different species; some were protected by cages of 1 cm mesh chicken wire. To test the effect of density, we placed seeds one meter apart in a line through the forest as a 'sparse' treatment for comparison with the 'dense' treatments described above where the seeds were 100 per m². An insecticide spraying treatment wasn't effective; indications of insect attacks were as prevalent in

Table 4. Mortality between 2 February 1967 and 4 April 1970 of seedlings of *Planchonella sp. nov.* at Davies Creek, North Queensland, Australia, lat. 17°S, elevation 850 m. Seeds were planted under mature trees of the same species and under trees of other species. Each of the eight plots was 2 × 1 m and contained 98 seeds. Half of the plots were trenched, all roots being cut to a depth of 0.3 m.

	Number dying out of 98			
	under adults of the same species		under adults of a different species	
	plot 1	plot 2	plot 1	plot 2
Trenched	65	69	14	26
Not trenched	50	54	25	42

304

these plots as in the other treatments. Seeds of *Cryptocarya corrugata*, from the plot itself, and *Eugenia brachyandra*, brought from the other plot at 27° S, were used. None was used if it had already been attacked by insects. As shown in Table 5, almost every seed was killed within a year, regardless of its position or density. Since seeds were killed inside cages and since many seeds had holes caused by insect attack, it is probable that insects were the main cause of death. For these species, at least, the increase in pattern diversity evidently occurs after germination, not in the seed stage. That is, all seeds are probably killed most of the time, but in occasional years a seed crop may escape when, for some reason, the seed eaters are reduced. Then a great number of new seedlings becomes established in a patch, and these are attacked and thinned out over the succeeding years. The fact that both the evenness component of diversity and the pattern diversity were very low in the young trees which entered the population between 1965 and 1969 (Table 2, height class 0 to 0.1 m), is evidence that recruitment followed this pattern on the study site. This model differs from that proposed by Janzen (1970). He suggests that the probability of a fallen seed surviving is a function either of its distance from the parent or its population density. In the species I studied, neither was related to survival. However, we agree on the fundamental point that overall survival should be greater at greater distances from the parent. My data indicate that the mortality which increases pattern diversity occurs mainly after germination during the seedling and sapling stages.

Evidently, mortality is greater when individuals of the same species grow together than when they are intermingled with other species. At least three possible mechanisms could produce this effect. Firstly, each species might secrete toxins into the environment which poison individuals of its own species more than those of different species. Although this

Table 5. Survival of seeds of two species of rainforest trees, placed on the surface of the ground at the Davies Creek plot, North Queensland, 17°S. lat., 850 m. Seeds of *Cryptocarya corrugata* were from this plot. *Eugenia brachyandra* seeds were from South Queensland, 27°S. lat., 850 m. The figures are numbers of seeds at the start of the experiment in September, 1969, and of germinated seedlings in June, 1970.

	Under adults of same species		Under adults of other species	
	Sep. 69	June 70	Sep. 69	June 70
C. corrugata, 'dense', 100/m²				
Control, no treatment	134	1	130	0
Under wire mesh roof	75	0	75	0
Inside wire mesh cage	75	0	75	0
Insecticide, 0.1% Dieldrin	141	0	129	2

	Sep. 69	June 70
C. corrugata 'sparse', one seed every meter in a line through the forest	100	0
Eugenia brachyandra 'dense', 100/m²	100	0
'sparse', one every meter in a line through the forest	100	1

remains a possibility, it seems less likely than the others. The second possibility is that each species has such specialized requirements for nutrients that competition is more severe between plants of the same species than with plants of different species. However, the results of the experiment in Table 4 seem to exclude the possibility that intraspecies root competition with adults was more deleterious than interspecies competition. Competition between adults and young trees in these dense rain forests is probably primarily for light, not for soil nutrients or water. Competition for light should not be more severe within than between species, unless different species produce qualitatively different sorts of shade. On the basis of present evidence this mechanism seems less likely than the following one.

The third possibility is that attack by natural enemies is heaviest when trees live in single-species aggregations, rather than mixed with other species. There has been, to my knowledge, no direct experimental test of this hypothesis, but there is much indirect evidence (Gillett, 1962). For example, single-species stands such as rubber plantations were unsuccessful in their native Brazil where they were heavily attacked by disease. But, when introduced into Asia without their native enemies, they could be grown in plantations. In our own work (Table 4) there was much more grazing on the seedlings planted under adults of the same species than on those under other species.

For this mechanism to be effective the enemies must be both specialized in their choice of prey and not particularly mobile. Populations of insects or fungi centering their attention on an adult tree would probably be the most effective at producing the high pattern diversity we observed. Obviously, other factors, particularly heterogeneity in space and time, provide other opportunities for the maintenance of diversity in rain forest trees. I suggest that the role of predation is important in preventing trees from forming single-species groves, which is probably the only way in which one species of tree could exclude others by interspecies competition.

Conditions determining the effectiveness of natural enemies in preventing competitive exclusion in their prey

What circumstances determine whether natural enemies can prevent competitive exclusion between prey species? From the examples discussed above and from the studies of other workers, it seems clear that fluctuations in the physical environment decrease the effectiveness of natural enemies in several ways.

Firstly, prey populations are apparently less vulnerable to the direct effect of extreme fluctuations in weather, than are their enemies. For example, Michelbacher and Leighly (1940), Lord and MacPhee (1953) and DeBach, Fisher and Landi (1955) all found that extremes of weather killed a much higher proportion of the natural enemies than of their prey, herbivorous insects. Why this should be so isn't known, although it is probable that the enemy would be more exposed to the effects of weather when it was searching than would its prey, sheltered by the vegetation. However, this is not the whole story since much of the mortality occurred during winter when the parasite was a larva inside the hibernating host (Lord and MacPhee, 1953). On the intertidal shore, barnacles extend higher than their predators, evidently being better able to withstand the extremes of weather at the very high levels.

Secondly, fluctuations of the weather can reduce the effectiveness of natural enemies in less direct ways. After the reduction in numbers or activity of both predator and prey during an unfavorable season, the prey populations may recover and grow quickly to densities at which they begin to compete with each other before the predator populations have increased enough to control them. This evidently happens at high latitudes where phytoplankton blooms or huge swarms of insects occur in the spring. The favorable season may be so short that the natural enemies don't have time to increase enough to control their prey. In this respect the terrestrial high arctic resembles the high intertidal zone where there is too short a time for the predators to feed effectively. At the lower edge of the inter-tidal zone, the predators can feed almost continuously, as they can in those parts of the terrestrial wet tropics with little seasonal change. Even though the natural enemies have evolved to respond rapidly to such spring increases in their prey – as for example the re-lease of barnacle larvae in response to an increase in phytoplankton, or the spring migra-tion of insectivorous birds into the arctic – the prey may still outstrip them for a while.

Thirdly, irregular or unpredictable fluctuations in the physical environment may cause such unpredictable variations in the supply of some critical resource, such as the numbers of a species of prey, that the natural enemy cannot afford to specialize on it. This is prob-ably the reason why *Thais lapillus* has not specialized to the extent that *Thais emarginata* has, with the consequence that *T. lapillus* cannot attack the barnacles on the upper shore early enough to prevent competition. Whether specialist predators are usually more effec-tive in reducing their prey than generalists is hard to say at this time. In Paine's (1966) example, the large predatory starfish, *Pisaster ochraceus*, kept the mussel populations from competitively excluding other species. *Pisaster* is specialized in feeding if given several species of prey in equal abundance, showing a preference for mussels (Landenberger, 1968). Thus one would predict that when *Pisaster* first moved into a new area mussels would be common, and it would feed as a specialist on them, reducing their competitive effect. Thereafter, as shown by Paine (1966), it would feed more generally on a greater variety of the species of sedentary animals available. Thus when *Pisaster* was reducing the dominant prey it was acting as a specialist.

Other independent evidence that specialists are more effective than generalists in re-ducing their prey is, unfortunately, lacking. Although it is often stated (DeBach et al., 1964) that the best biological control of pests is done by highly specialized enemies, there has never, to my knowledge, been a test of this idea. Specialists are used in biological con-trol, not because they are known from independent evidence to be more effective than generalists, but because they are not likely to attack beneficial plants or animals after they are introduced to a new country.

Another example of differences in degree of specialization is the common observation that species nearer the 'top' of food webs tend to be less specialized in their choice of food. For example, Paine (1963, 1966) has found that whereas small predatory snails in the rocky intertidal habitat eat only a few species of suspension feeding or herbivorous grazing animals, the larger snails and starfish eat more species, including both the smaller pred-atory snails and their prey. Brues (1946) points out that herbivorous insects often feed on only one or a few species of plants, whereas many predatory insects attack many species of herbivorous insects. Also, he states that entomophagous parasitoid insects usually have fewer species of hosts than the hyperparasites, which often attack both the herbivorous host and the entomophagous parasitoid. If, as discussed earlier, unfavorable weather causes less fluctuation of populations at lower than at higher trophic levels, this would permit greater specialization of animals feeding on organisms at lower levels. Thus for several reasons, one might expect greater specialization and presumably greater effective-ness of natural enemies at lower trophic levels.

In summary, in the sort of environment with fewer irregular occurrences of extreme weather, and lower amplitude of variations in temperature, rainfall, etc., natural enemies will be most effective in preventing competitive exclusion in their prey. In such places the enemies should be more specialized, especially at lower trophic levels. There will be less chance for the prey to increase suddenly until it is beyond control of the predator, since the unfavorable seasons will be reduced in length and severity.

However, these same environmental advantages also work to diminish the effectiveness of natural enemies in at least two ways. Firstly, there will be strong selection on the prey to evolve defences which not only protect them from existing enemies, but also have the effect of reducing the number of species attacking them. Defences of the prey, for example plants with poisonous chemical substances or spines, or animals with armor, protective coloration, etc., require specialized methods of attack by the predator. Such a requirement for specialization must reduce the number of species of predator which can attack a particular species of prey. With fewer species of natural enemies there is a greater chance of the prey escaping. There is evidence for this from work in biological control; a pest of the olive, which was somewhat reduced during the cooler seasons by one species of enemy, was almost eliminated when another enemy species was introduced which attacked it in the summer (Huffaker and Kennett, 1966). Holling (1959) indicated that control of the European pine sawfly in Canada was more likely with several species of mammalian predators, each of which was most effective at a different prey density.

Secondly, such favorable environments also increase the effectiveness of the species of predators or parasites which attack the natural enemies in question. Since even large carnivores have parasites, and general predators feed on hyperparasites, no species is without its complement of natural enemies. For this reason, as natural enemies become more effective in more favourable climates, it becomes more difficult to predict whether, for example, plants will be reduced more significantly by herbivores than the herbivores by their predators or parasites. In some instances, such as in the rain forests I have studied, herbivores seem to be reducing competitive exclusion of the plants. But in the second growth of dry savannah woodlands in Central America, ants living on swollen-thorn *Acacia* trees kill both the herbivorous insects and the nearby competing vegetation (Janzen, 1966). In any event, in places with a more predictable or less fluctuating physical environment, attacks by natural enemies at all trophic levels would be expected to be more intense and continuous. The great increase in incidence and intensity of parasitism in humans as one approaches the equator is probably the best available evidence of this trend (LaPage, 1963).

In contrast, in areas with extreme and irregular fluctuation in climate the prey often excape their natural enemies and reach densities at which they compete for resources. As the amplitude and irregularity are reduced, natural enemies become more effective. In a completely constant benign physical environment, natural enemies should be very specialized and effective in finding almost all prey. In this situation, the only way in which any species could exist would be to be so rare and widely scattered that some individuals escape being found by their specialized natural enemies, at least until they are well established and reproductively mature. Because no environment is constantly benign, no ecological community is so organized. However, as one approaches such conditions in a tropical rain forest or coral reef, species certainly do become scarcer and more widely scattered amongst individuals of other species. I believe that increased effectiveness of natural enemies accounts for this trend.

Acknowledgments

Many people helped in these observations and experiments and criticized the manuscript. Together with those who arranged the meeting in Holland and who discussed the paper after I had delivered it, I would like to thank J. Choat, M. Hopkins, R. Knowlton, B. Menge, W. Murdoch, C. Peterson, D. Potts, T. Southwood, J. Tracey, L. Webb and J. White. The work was supported by grants from the John Simon Guggenheim Foundation, the Office of Naval Research and the National Science Foundation.

References

Barnes, H., 1956. *Balanus balanoides* in the Firth of Clyde: the development and annual variation in the larval population and the causative factors. *J. Anim. Ecol.* 25: 72–84.

Barnes, H., 1957. Processes of restoration and synchronization in marine ecology. The spring diatom increase and the 'spawning' of the common barnacle, *Balanus balanoides* (L.). *Ann. Biol.* 33: 67–85.

Brues, C. T., 1946. Insect dietary. Harvard University Press, Cambridge (Mass.), pp. 466.

Connell, J. H., 1961a. Effects of competition, predation by *Thais lapillus* and other factors on natural populations of the barnacle *Balanus balanoides*. *Ecol. Monogr.* 31: 61–104.

Connell, J. H., 1961b. The influence of interspecific competition and other factors on the distribution of the barnacle *Chthamalus stellatus*. *Ecology* 42: 710–723.

Connell, J. H., 1970. A predator-prey system in the marine intertidal region. I. *Balanus glandula* and several predatory species of *Thais*. *Ecol. Monogr.* 40: 49–78.

Darwin, Charles, 1859. On the origin of species. First ed. J. Murray, London.

DeBach, Paul (Ed.), 1964. Biological control of insect pests and weeds. Reinhold Publ. Co., New York. pp. 844.

DeBach, P., T. W. Fisher & J. Landi, 1955. Some effects of meteorological factors on all stages of *Aphytis lingnanensis*, a parasite of the California Red Scale. *Ecology* 36: 743–753.

Gillett, J. B., 1962. Pest pressure, an underestimated factor in evolution. In: Taxonomy and geography. *System. Assoc. Publ.* No 4: 37–46.

Harper, John L., 1970. The role of predation in vegetational diversity. *Brookhaven Natn. Lab. Symp. Biol.* No 22: 48–62.

Holling, C. S., 1959. The components of predation as revealed by a study of the small-mammal predation of the European Pine Sawfly. *Can. Ent.* 91: 293–320.

Huffaker, C. B. & C. E. Kennett, 1966. Biological control of *Parlatoria oleae* (COLVEE) through the compensatory action of two introduced parasites. *Hilgardia* 37: 283–335.

Janzen, D. H., 1966. Coevolution of mutualism between ants and *Acacias* in Central America. *Evolution* 20: 249–275.

Janzen, D. H., 1970. The role of herbivores in tropical tree species diversity. *Am. Nat.* (in press).

Kitching, J. A., L. Muntz & F. J. Ebling, 1966. The ecology of Lough Ine. XV. The ecological significance of shell and body forms in *Nucella*. *J. Anim. Ecol.* 35: 192–301.

LaPage, Geoffrey, 1963. Animals parasitic in man. Dover Press, New York.

Lord, F. T. & A. W. MacPhee, 1953. The influence of spray programs on the fauna of apple orchards in Nova Scotia. VI. Low temperatures and the natural control of the Oystershell scale, *Lepidosaphes ulmi* (L.) (Homoptera: Coccidae). *Can. Entom.* 85: 282–291.

Landenberger, D. E., 1968. Studies on selective feeding in the Pacific starfish *Pisaster* in southern California. *Ecology* 49: 1062–1075.

Michelbacher, A. E. & J. Leighly, 1940. The apparent climatic limitations of the alfalfa weevil in California. *Hilgardia* 13: 103–139.

Miller, R. S., 1967. Pattern and process in competition. *Adv. Ecol. Res.* 4: 1–74.

Paine, R. T., 1963. Trophic relationships of 8 sympatric predatory gastropods. *Ecology* 44: 63–73.

Paine, R. T., 1966. Food web complexity and species diversity. *Am. Nat.* 100: 65–75.

Paine, R. T. & R. L. Vadas, 1969. The effects of grazing by sea urchins, *Strongylocentrotus* spp., on benthic algal populations. *Limnol. Oceanogr.* 14: 710–719.

Pielou, E. C., 1966. Species-diversity and pattern-diversity in the study of ecological succession. *J. Theor. Biol.* 10: 370–383.

Slobodkin, L. B., 1964. Experimental populations of *Hydrida. J. Ecol.* 52 (suppl.): 131–148.

Summerhayes, V. S., 1941. The effect of voles (*Microtus agrestis*) on vegetation. *J. Ecol.* 29: 14–48.

Discussion

Participants: Connell (Author), den Boer (P. J.), Cavers, Clough, Jacobs, Jain, Kuenen, Murdoch, Pimentel, Rosenzweig, Solomon, Turnock and Watt

This work seems to be in keeping with a generalization, that in ecosystems which have evolved in stable environments for a long time, species maintenance is more by subtle behavioral or biochemical mechanisms than is the case in immature north and south temperate zone ecosystems in unpredictable environments. The fact that there are a great number of poisonous fish species in shallow coral seas, whereas these are absent in e.g. the Great Lakes, which are highly unstable, may bear on this (WATT). However, many poisonous species of fungi (mushrooms) are found in the subarctic Scandinavian forests; what is the position in the tropics (CLOUGH)?

The tropic zone may well be less variable than the temperate and arctic zones, but it is not clear that it is a more predictable environment (MURDOCH). The level of differences between seasons in arctic and boreal continental regions may be highly predictable. Moreover, in connection with the variability of tropic and temperate zones the influence of natural selection may have been such that animals in some tropic regions are about equally susceptible to the rather subtle weather changes prevailing there as are animals in temperate regions to more pronounced weather changes (DEN BOER). I agree with this (AUTHOR).

If one starts with a clumped distribution (as was the case with the small rain forest trees), and then allows mortality work at random, would not the spatial pattern diversity index increase towards 1? This would seem to mean that the supposed neighbourhood (intra-specific) competition is not needed to get an increase of spatial diversity with increase of tree size (JACOBS). This could easily be simulated. But random mortality should not kill trees with nearest neighbours of the same species more than those with nearest neighbours of different species, as was shown to be the case. And if mortality is random, pattern diversity should stay the same (AUTHOR).

It shown that species diversity and pattern diversity increase with tree height classes. But what is the possible effect of patterns of diversity between different tree heights on the changes in overall diversity measures (JAIN)? The neighbours used were all within the same height class. But the two nearest neighbours which were smaller than the central individual could be used to get some idea of the influence of larger trees on the pattern of smaller ones (AUTHOR).

How do you explain there being a higher number of species in the taller group than in the lowest height class, if only random mortality is involved (JAIN)? The height classes are not age classes, and the larger classes probably represent much longer periods of time. The smallest class are offspring only of those species which reproduced successfully over the past few years (AUTHOR).

Healthy phytophagous sawfly larvae on larch trees do not drop from trees, even during

310

rather violent storms, unless they have completed feeding or are depleting the foliage. Therefore, it seems unlikely that small trees under large ones, which support low densities of phytophagous species will be destroyed by this means (TURNOCK). In the tropics trees might 'declare a territory' by raining insects on their surroundings, by abscission of twigs and leaves having insects on them (ROSENZWEIG).

To explain a presumed non-random mortality of seedlings under a tree of the same species it is not necessary to assume the presence of specialized feeders. Each phytophagous insect coming down from the tree overhead will find seedlings of the same species more available than those of other species; moreover, it is very probable that even extreme generalists will show some preferences. There may be another complication; in temperate regions many phytophagous insects show a definite preference for small and young trees; to give an example: whereas nearly all leaves of the available young birches may be rolled up by *Deporaus betulae* (or other *Rhynchitini*), mature trees are hardly infested. How does this compare with the tropics? (DEN BOER). The problem is the meaning of 'more available'. Several species of young trees occur under a single large tree; if they are all of about the same size, they are equally available to any phytophagous insect. If the insects eat them without preference, i.e. in the same proportion in which they occur, those of the same species as the adult tree above need not be removed proportionately faster there than under adults of a different species. To produce the results shown in Table 4, the insects must specialize to some degree on young trees of the same species as the adult. Since most insects do show some preferences, this will probably happen. In regard to the second point, a greater rate of attack on young trees would intensify the removal of seedlings; I have no data on whether this tendency also occurs in the tropics, but I expect that it does. AUTHOR).

If something tends to prevent the growth of seedlings under a mature tree of the same species, this may be of advantage to the species, by giving preference to its seedlings a few meters away where the species has not depleted the soil of trace elements, etc., corresponding to its particular needs (SOLOMON). The experiment shown in Table 4 indicates that competition for soil nutrients between seedling and parent is not important in the species studied (AUTHOR).

There are examples of progeny arising only from the exact site of the parent plant. Koller and Roth (*Am. J. Bot.* 51, 1964) working with *Gymnarrhena* in the desert areas of Israel found that two kinds of seeds are produced (amphicarpy). One kind is light, aerial and wind dispersed. The other kind is heavy and is produced below ground; here the offspring actually grows up through the dead tissues of the parent plant. This site would be the most favourable for the species in a very unfavourable environment (CAVERS).

Is it not possible for two competitors to coexist although they are feeding on the same living resource if the food host can evolve differentially to the two competitors (PIMENTEL)? Perhaps, but this is not possible in plants whose food does not evolve. Probably it will occur in some animals, but the barnacles studied were competing for a resource which does not evolve either, namely space (AUTHOR). See also the discussion after the paper of Pimentel.

A few *Chthalamus* individuals survive and reproduce in the region of competition with *Balanus*, but they are smaller and so contain fewer larvae than uncrowded ones (AUTHOR to JAIN).

Could there be any selective pressure toward a greater heterogeneity of dispersion; compare Birch: *Cactoblastis-Opuntia* (JAIN). After a period in the plankton the offspring do not necessarily return to the habitat of the adults. Most of the offspring come from the upper shore zone where there is no competition with *Balanus*, and where this presumed selective advantage of aggregation would be less (AUTHOR).

Studying more cases and more species, experimentally, on rocky coasts may indeed upset some of the conclusions so far reached (AUTHOR to KUENEN).

Proc. Adv. Study Inst. Dyanmics Numbers Popul. (Oosterbeek, 1970) 313–326

Animal populations regulated to carrying capacity of plant host by genetic feedback[1]

David Pimentel and A. Benedict Soans

Department of Entomology, Cornell University, Ithaca, New York, USA

Abstract

An investigation was carried out, employing an animal (herbivore) and plant population system, to determine if the animal population numbeis could be adjusted and regulated to the surplus energy or carrying capacity of the plant-host population via the genetic feedback mechanism. The results demonstrated that feeding by an animal population became adjusted to the carrying capacity of its host plant population.

The mean density for the experimental animal population was 55, whereas the mean density for the control population was 228. The mean rate of increase per individual for the experimental animal population was 1.23, compared with 1.39 for the control population. The mean rate of population decline per individual for the experimental system was 0.26, compared with 0.44 for the control. Because of these differences in population characteristics, the amplitude of fluctuations in the experimental population system was significantly less than that in the control.

Initially, the plant population had frequencies of 0.20 resistant and 0.80 susceptible genes. In time and under animal feeding pressure, the frequency of resistant genes increased to between 0.60 and 0.74. Because of the increased proportion of resistant genes in the experimental system, the mean number of surviving plants gradually changed from 45 to about 85%.

The changes which the animal caused in the plant adds further evidence to support the idea that evolution in community systems is toward increased population stability and a balanced supply-demand economy between plant and animal.

Animal populations require a steady supply of food for their survival, and every living population has the innate tendency to increase and convert as much of the food resource into itself and its young as it can. Further, the majority of animal species feed on either living plants or other animals; only a few animals feed as scavengers. Although many animals are associated with decaying plant and animal matter, they seldom are saprophagous, but are herbivorous, grazing on bacteria and fungi present in the decaying matter.

In spite of their innate tendency to increase, natural animal populations seldom destroy their food-host populations. In nature, trees and other plants generally remain green and lush and only rarely is the feeding pressure on either plants or animals noticeable. Actually, the amount of protoplasm given up to herbivore populations by trees and other plants appears to be relatively small, compared with the quantity available. Support of this comes from the work of Bukovskii (1936), who reported that the herbivores (primarily invertebrates) feeding on the Crimean beech (*Fagus*) forest 'hardly destroyed more than

[1] This research was supported in part by a grant (GB 19239) from the National Science Foundation in Environmental Biology.

8 % of the leaf surface over a large area at any time, and usually destroyed much less.' Describing damage to Canadian forests, Bray (1964) stated that the mean yearly utilization of leaves by herbivores (primarily insects) over a 3-year period was: 10.6% for a xeric oak (*Quercus*) forest; 6.6% for a mesic maple-beech (*Acer-Fagus*) forest; and 5.9% for a moist maple-beech forest. Reichle and Crossley's (1967) investigation in a Tennessee forest agreed well with the results of Bray. They found the herbivores (again primarily insects) consumed a mean of 5.6% of the total leaf area of a tulip poplar (*Liriodendron*).

In a terrestrial ecosystem of an old-field in Georgia, Odum et al. (1962) reported that the granivore populations (primarily mice and birds) consumed from 10 to 50% of the annual seed crop, depending on animal numbers and the quantity of the seed crop. In contrast, the other herbivores (primarily insects) took from 4 to 20% of the annual above-ground vegetation. In Michigan, however, Wiegert (1965) found the feeding level of the primary consumer (grasshoppers) much lower than that reported by Odum. In fact, the herbivores ingested less than 0.5% of the net primary production of vegetation in 'old-field' and less than 2.5% of the 'alfalfa field' vegetation. Concerning a sericea-lespedeza ecosystem in South Carolina, Menhinick (1967) reported that the herbivores (primarily insects) consumed only about 1.0% of the net primary production. Van Hook et al. (1970), however, reported that herbivores (primarily insects) in a grassland ecosystem of Tennessee consumed 9.6% of the net primary production. They also reported that the associated predators consumed 16.5% of the herbivores.

Harvey (1950) reported that 11% of the producers were assimilated by herbivores (bivalves) found in the seas off Plymouth, England. On Eniwetok Atoll, Odum and Odum (1955) found that the herbivorous animals assimilated 18.9% of the biomass produced by the plants in the coral reef community. In a fresh-water ecosystem in Poland, Gliwicz (1968) reported that zooplankton consumed an estimated 25% of the algae. Based on Allen's data collected from 1919–20 on the Californian coast, Enright (1969) calculated that zooplankton grazed at least 40% of the standing crop of the phytoplankton. The dominant plant, *Spartina alterniflora*, in a salt marsh gave up about 7% of its annual net production to herbivores, primarily a grasshopper (*Orchelimum fidicinium*) and a leafhopper (*Prokelesia marginata*) (Smalley, 1959). However, in a later study of a *Spartina* salt marsh Teal (1962) reported that the primary herbivores (insects) assimilated only 4.6% of the net production of this marsh grass. Based on these studies of varied communities, herbivores assimilated about 10% (range < 0.5 to 40%) of the net primary production of their plant hosts.

That host plants give up only a small percentage of their protoplasm to feeding animals is not surprising, when the energy needed for growth, maintenance, and reproduction of the host plant is considered. For respiration alone, Odum (1959) calculated that the percentage of gross production lost in plants ranged from 13 to 58%. The small percentage of net productivity consumed by animals might be termed the 'carrying capacity' of the plant population, or the quantity of energy which may be harvested from the plant population without causing the host population to decline. We propose that via the genetic feedback mechanism animal feeding is limited to the carrying capacity of the food host population (Pimentel, 1961a, and Pimentel, 1968). The feedback mechanism functions to limit population numbers of the eating animal (herbivores, as well as predators and parasites) in the following way: high herbivore density creates strong selective pressures on its host-plant population, these selection pressures alter the genetic makeup of the host population to make the host more resistant to attack and, in turn, this feeds back negatively to limit the feeding pressure of the herbivore. After many such cycles, the numbers of the herbivore population are ultimately limited to the carrying capacity of the plant host and stability results.

Methods

The aim of this study was to determine if a herbivore population would adjust its feeding to the carrying capacity of the plant-host population via the genetic feedback mechanism. Specifically, this investigation was designed to answer the following questions:
1. How much genetic change takes place in a plant population under animal feeding pressure?
2. How rapid is genetic change in the plant population?
3. Will some equilibrium be reached between animal density and the genetic makeup of the plant?
4. If some equilibrium is reached, what will be the animal density and plant genetic makeup?
5. How much food will the animal population be removing from the plant population as the systems evolve?
6. What changes will take place in population fluctuations as the systems evolve?

In the herbivore-plant population system investigated, an artificial plant was used because no plant type could be found with a known genetic makeup of resistant characters. To use plants with unknown genetic resistance would have introduced several variables, thereby limiting the interpretation of the results to that particular plant population. Replicate experiments with limited variability were possible with an artificial plant of known genetic makeup, and the validity of making sound generalizations was increased. The artificial plant consisted of a glass vial (3 cm $\times$ 3 mm I.D.) filled with 'sap' (0.25 M (molar) sucrose solution) which provided the food resource for the animal. The open end of the vial was plugged with a small piece of plastic sponge. When the vial was inverted, the animal was able to feed on the 'sap'.

The resistant factors were added by introducing salt (NaCl) into the sap. Resistance in this case was quantitative and additive, with each additional resistant allele contributing 0.1 M of NaCl, with a maximum concentration of 0.6 M NaCl. For simplicity, a plant with a genetic make-up of 3 loci and 6 alleles was used. The genetic make up of the susceptible plant was A A B B C C. The genetic makeup of a plant with a single resistant allele was A′ A B B C C, A A B′ B C C, or A A B B C′ C. Assuming the resistance to be quantitative, the maximum level of resistance (A′ A′ B′ B′ C′ C′) was 0.6 M NaCl in the sap. Preliminary tests established that at the maximum level of resistance little or no animal feeding occurred.

Throughout the experiment to simulate natural reproduction of panmictic plants, the Hardy-Weinberg Law (Li, 1955) for random mating was used (1).

$$(p + q)^2 = p^2 + 2pq + q^2 \tag{1}$$

Also, an assumption was made that the development of a resistant allele in the plant reduced fitness, compared with the normal susceptible alleles, when animal numbers were low or absent. Therefore the resistant alleles carried a load of 1 − S where S in this experiment was 0.2. The surplus energy which each plant could give up and still survive was assumed to be less that 50%. Hence any plant that lost 50% or more of its sap was considered unable to reproduce. Although in this experiment the surplus energy of 'maximum carrying capacity' for each plant was higher than the overall 10% generally observed in nature, this 50% level provided greater accuracy in measurements and helped make the experimental manipulations easier.

The animal used in the population study was the female housefly (*Musca domestica* L.). On the 0.25 M sugar solution alone an average of 79% of the animals would live for 4 days, and 4 days was designated as the generation period for the experiment. On the various resistant plant genotypes animal survival for the 4-day period was as follows: 0.1 M NaCl = 82%, 0.2 M NaCl = 54%, 0.3 M NaCl = 43%, 0.4 M NaCl = 22%, and both 0.5 and 0.6 M NaCl = 0 survival. At the end of the 4-day generation period each surviving animal was assumed to reproduce and leave 2 offspring. Hence at equilibrium 50% of the animal population had to die each generation to have a 1:1 ratio between births and deaths.

The control plant population consisted of 100 vials filled only with 0.25 M sugar solution; no resistant genes (NaCl) were present. Because the animals could consume all the sap in each plant without affecting the reproductive survival of a genotype, more food was available to the control than to the experimental population.

The animal-plant populations were housed in cages consisting of transparent plastic boxes (5 × 10 × 14 in). The 100 plants (vials) were inverted and placed in holes in the lid with about 1/6th of the vial at the open end extending below the lid; thus, the vial opening plugged with plastic sponge was inside the cage, allowing the animal to feed on the sap if it so desired. The cages were uniformly illuminated from above.

Plant genotypes were located at random in the designated 100-plant locations in the lid. Initially, the following plant genotypes were introduced:

Genotype	Number
A A B B C C	20
A'A B B C C	17
A A B'B C C	17
A A B B C'C	17
A'A B'B C C	8
A A B'B C'C	8
A'A B B C'C	8
A'A B'B C'C	5
	——
Total	100

To start both the control and experimental systems, 50 newly emerged female flies of uniformly large size were introduced into each population cage. Temperature was maintained at about 78 °F ($\pm$ 5 °). Humidity was maintained at 95% ($\pm$ 3%) RH to limit evaporation from the sugar and salt solutions used in the 'plants'.

The control system had one variable; only animal numbers could change. In the experimental population system, however, there were 2 variables: (1) the genetic makeup of the plant population and (2) animal numbers. Therefore, in the experimental system genetic makeup of the plant population was determined by animal numbers and the genetic makeup of the plant, in turn, determined animal numbers; hence the genetic feedback mechanism could operate.

316

Results

The mean density for the experimental population from the 8th through the 30th generation was 55 animals, whereas the mean density for the animal population in the control was 228 (Fig. 1). The mean of 55 animals in the experimental population was slightly above the theoretical optimal carrying capacity of 50 animals. The control animal population density was 4 times greater than that of the experimental one because the total energy in each plant could be utilized.

The amplitude of the fluctuations in animal numbers was significantly less in the experimental than in the control population system. After the 8th generation, the density in the experimental population ranged from a mean low of 42 to a mean high of 67 animals; in the control, the fluctuations ranged from a mean low of 127 to a mean high of 295 animals. Note that at generations 5, 13, 19, 31, and 34 the control crashed from peak densities to extreme lows in just one generation.

The mean mortalities for both the experimental and control animal populations were approximately the same; in the experimental population it was 47.2% and in the control 40.7%. These high mortalities were expected if, as anticipated, the animal populations were no longer increasing but maintaining some degree of equilibrium.

The mean rate of population increase per individual for the experimental system was 1.23, compared with 1.39 for the control. The mean rate of population decline per individual for the experimental system was 0.26 compared with 0.44 for the control. Obviously, populations increasing and decreasing at the rates calculated for these 2 populations will behave differently. This was substantiated by the data on the amplitude of the population fluctuations of the two systems (Fig. 1).

NUMBER OF ANIMALS

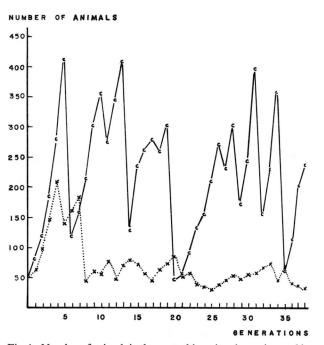

Fig. 1. Number of animals in the control (——) and experimental (. . . . .) systems at each generation.

317

The evolution which occurred in the plant population accounted for the changes observed in the experimental population system. Initially, the resistant genes in the plant population had a frequency of only 0.20, compared with 0.80 for the susceptible. Soon after the animals were introduced, they exerted an intense selective pressure on the plant population; this reduced the number of plants with susceptible genes and increased the number with resistant genes (Fig. 2). From the 3rd to the 8th generation, the number of resistant genes increased from 0.24 to 0.51, and from the 20th generation on, the frequency fluctuated between 0.60 and 0.74.

Because of the increase in proportion of resistant genes in the experimental system, the mean number of plants surviving gradually changed from about 45 to about 85% (Fig. 3). Even at equilibrium a small percentage of the plants was totally consumed. Some selective pressure from the animal was necessary to maintain the genetic makeup of the experimental plant population. In addition, the susceptible individuals provided more energy to the animal population than the more resistant plants. The susceptibles, which were fed upon heavily and destroyed, were sacrificed for the total plant population. Or, stated another way, the energy supplied to the animal population consisted of the entire contents of a few plants plus a limited amount of food from several of the more resistant genotypes. Under conditions of stability and with the animal populations at or above mean density, the mean percentage of total energy or sap removed from the plant population in the experimental system was estimated to be about 36%; in the control it was about 98%.

Hence in the experimental system the feeding pressure exerted by the animal on its plant

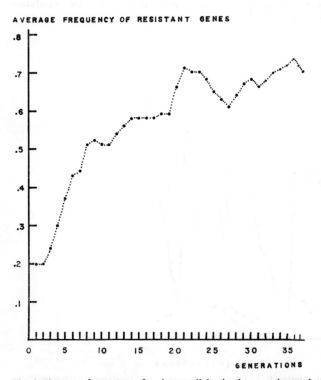

Fig. 2. Average frequency of resistant alleles in the experimental plant population.

318

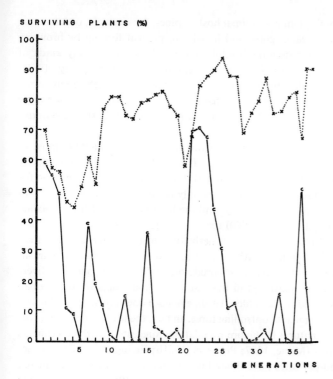

SURVIVING PLANTS (%)

GENERATIONS

Fig. 3. Percentage of surviving plants in the control (——) and experimental (. . . . .) population systems.

host evolved to a point at which it was limited to the carrying capacity of the plant population, or less than 50% of the total energy available.

Discussion

The results of the herbivore-plant interaction demonstrated that an animal population could adjust its feeding to the carrying capacity of the host-plant population via the genetic feedback mechanism. Animal feeding was adjusted almost perfectly to the carrying capacity or surplus energy of the plant population. The result of this adjustment was increased stability in the animal population and a balanced economy between the animal and plant.

Available evidence supports the thesis that animal feeding in nature is limited to surplus energy or the carrying capacity of its host population. A review of animal feeding on plants indicated that, in general, animals assimilated about 10% of the protoplasm available from their host plant populations. This is a small percentage, and it was surprising how similar the percentages were for a wide variety of species of plant hosts from many different terrestrial habitats. Zooplankton appear to be able to harvest a larger percentage (25 to 40%) than can terrestrial animals of the standing crop of plant hosts, and this may be due to the rapid rate of turnover characteristic of planktonic organisms (see Discussion). Animal feeding, in nature, appears limited to a small percentage of the total net productivity of its host plants. To limit animal feeding in nature, a variety of antifeeding mechan-

319

isms appear common to both plant and animal hosts. Spines, for example, occurring on many kinds of plants, such as cacti, gorse and hawthorn, prevent feeding by browsing animals (see Discussion). Toxins or growth inhibitors, which occur in many kinds of plants, also limit animal feeding; for instance, tannins in oak leaves (Feeny, 1966); cyanide in bird's-foot trefoil, a legume (Kingsbury, 1964); and nepetalactone in catnip (Eisner, 1964). Ricklefs (1970) also pointed out that antipredator adaptations were more highly developed in birds found in the tropics, where predation was a strong selective force.

With relatively little surplus energy available from hosts, animal numbers must of necessity be small compared with their food resource. If animal numbers are small relative to their food resource, how are their numbers limited to this low level? Competition for food appears to be an unsatisfactory explanation, mainly because of the large amount of food available to the feeding animal population and the little evidence of heavy feeding pressure by the animals. Hairston et al. (1960) reached the same conclusion when they reported that it was unusual for populations of herbivores to be limited by their food supply. These same authors discounted weather and suggested that predation and parasitism accounted for herbivore control. Although predators and parasites may effectively limit herbivore numbers, as was suggested in the case of the mule deer on the Kaibab (Russo, 1964, recently questioned by Caughley, 1970), evidence does not support the idea that natural enemies are the dominant controlling force. In fact, the low incidence of predator and parasite attack on natural herbivore populations suggests that these elements were seldom effective controls (Milne, 1957; Pimentel, 1961b; Errington, 1967). Further evidence that predators and parasites have limited effectiveness in controlling herbivore numbers is found in the biological control literature (Sweetman, 1958; Pimentel, 1963; DeBach, 1964); the number of successful cases of biological control has been small compared with the number of actual introductions made. We might also ask the question, why should the control mechanism for predators and parasites, which also live on surplus energy of their hosts, be different from herbivores? Logically, there should be no difference.

Barbehenn (1970) pointed out that the survival of parasites and their progeny depends upon the survival of their host. This principle also applies to the herbivore-plant system and to the predator-prey system. Animal (herbivore, parasite, and predator) feeding must be limited to the surplus energy of its host population. If an animal feeds upon the 'capital' (energy necessary for growth, maintenance, and reproduction), it will eventually destroy both its food resource and itself.

The functioning of the genetic mechanism automatically, through time, limits feeding of the animal to the 'interest' or carrying capacity of its host. For example, when animal numbers are high and capital is being sacrificed, many hosts are being destroyed. Those hosts eliminated first are the susceptible types and give up more than interest, leaving the more resistant host types to reproduce. The resistance in the host population will continue to increase until a suitably high level of resistance is reached and animal feeding is confined to only the 'interest' of the host population.

The level of host resistance will not continue to increase indefinitely because selective pressure decreases with a decline in animal numbers, and the development of resistant factors (thorns, etc.) costs the plant in energy. Energy is vital to all living systems. As Elton (1927) pointed out, 'the whole structure and activities of the community are dependent upon the questions of food supply' (energy). Thus one of the significant trends in evolution is the adaptation of demand by the feeding animal to the supply available from the

320

host. The resulting equilibrium is essential to the entire community system and the maintenance of its structure.

That the trend in the evolution of interacting eaten-eating species is toward stability is supported by the information gathered on the following parasite-host system. One of the outstanding examples of the genetic feedback mechanism functioning and the eventual evolution of stability in a natural population is the relationship between the myxomatosis virus and European rabbit population in Australia. After its introduction there in 1859, the European rabbit increased to outbreak levels for the next 20 years (Stead, 1935). To control the rabbit, the myxomatosis virus was obtained from South American rabbits and introduced in the rabbit population. In essence, this action was analogous to establishing a new parasite-host relationship, for the South American virus and the European rabbit never had been associated. The virus spread rapidly, and immediately virus outbreaks occurred in the rabbit population. During the first epidemic, myxomatosis was fatal to about 98 % of the rabbits; the second epidemic resulted in about 85 % mortality (Fehner, 1965); and now Meyers (these Proceedings) reports that the mortality was about 40%. Evolution took place in both the virus and rabbit populations, and Meyers reports that a state of equilibrium has been established, but that the system is still evolving.

An equilibrium evolved in the interaction of an experimental wasp parasite (*Nasonia vitripennis* WALKER) population with its housefly host (*Musca domestica*) population during nearly 3 years of interaction in the laboratory (Pimentel and Al-Hafidh, 1965). During the study measurable evolution took place in both parasite and host populations. The experimental host became more resistant to the parasite, as evidenced by a drop in the mean reproduction from 135 to 39 progeny per female wasp parasite and a decrease in their longevity from about 7 to 4 days. The results also suggested that, concurrently, the parasite population evolved some avirulence toward its host.

Coevolution has been observed in both a phage parasite and bacterial host (*Escherichia coli*) (Horne, 1970). Within a short period this parasite-host system evolved increased stability.

Although in these population systems evolution took place in both the eating and eaten species, evolution in our herbivore-plant model occurred, by design, only in the eaten species. In general, it is evident that evolution of a balanced economy and increased population stability by genetic feedback can take place via evolution in either the eating, eaten, or both species. This does not rule out the possibility that, under certain circumstances, the eating species may evolve to overcome host resistance and destroy its host.

At this point it is pertinent to review some evidence concerning natural populations and to suggest how the genetic feedback mechanism relates to this:

1. Outbreaks frequently occur in species populations newly introduced into foreign biotic communities because the introduced species are not genetically integrated into the new community. Examples: the European rabbit in Australia, the European gypsy moth in the USA, and the American gray squirrel in England;

2. Animal populations in natural communities seldom fluctuate widely in number, but are relatively stable; which agrees well with the trends observed in the experimental population system;

3. Characters which enable species to resist feeding by others are common in nature;

4. Most animal species are rare, and one would expect them to be rare relative to their food resource if the animal population is feeding on 'interest'.

There are several important biological implications of the genetic feedback mechanism:

1. It may regulate animal numbers and adjust the feeding of the population to only carrying capacity of the food host, as shown by the experiment described herein;

2. The interaction of herbivore-plant, parasite-host, and predator-prey via the genetic feedback mechanism may lead to a balance of economy between the eating and eaten species;

3. Under certain conditions of interaction, continuous cycles may occur in the populations of the herbivore, parasite, and predator.

4. Two competitors may coexist if they are feeding on the same plant or animal host;

5. Both population stability and coexistence of competitors will lead to increased diversity of species in the community;

6. The genetic feedback mechanism functions interdependently with other population control mechanisms such as competition and predation. In this case, the genetic feedback provides the 'coarse' adjustment, whereas competition and predation provide the 'fine' adjustment to an optimum equilibrium density.

References

Barbehenn, K., 1969. Host-parasite relationships and species diversity in mammals. An hypothesis. *Biotropica* 1: 29–35.

Bray, J. R., 1964. Primary consumption in forest canopies. *Ecology* 45: 165–167.

Bukovskii, V., 1936. The population of invertebrates of the Crimean beech forest (Transl. from Russian by J. D. Jackson, 1952, for the Bureau of Animal Population, Department of Zoological Field Studies, Oxford University. Trans. 241 F 159 B). *Trans. State Reserves (Series 2)*, 1: 5–103.

Caughley, G., 1970. Eruption of ungulate populations, with emphasis on Himalayan thar in New Zealand. *Ecology* 51: 53–72.

DeBach, P. H. (Ed.), 1964. Biological control of insect pests and weeds. Reinhold, New York.

Eisner, T., 1964. Catnip: Its raison d'être. *Science* 146: 1319–1320.

Elton, C. S., 1927. Animal ecology. Sidgwick and Jackson, London.

Enright, J. T., 1969. Zooplankton grazing rates estimated under field conditions. *Ecology* 50: 1070–1075.

Errington, P. L., 1967. Of predation and life. Iowa State Univ. Press, Ames, Iowa.

Feeny, P., 1970. Seasonal changes in oak leaf tannins and nutrients as a cause of spring feeding by winter moth caterpillars. *Ecology* 51: 565–581.

Fenner, F., 1965. Myxoma virus and *Oryctolagus cuniculus*: Two colonizing species. In: H. G. Baker and G. L. Stebbins (Ed.), The genetics of colonizing species pp. 485–499. Academic Press, New York.

Gliwicz, A. M., 1968. The use of anaesthetising substances in studies on the food habits of zooplankton communities. *Ekol. Pol. A.* 16: 279–295.

Hairston, N. G., F. E. Smith & L. B. Slobodkin, 1960. Community structure, population control, and competition. *Am. Nat.* 96: 421–425

Harvey, H. W., 1950. On the production of living matter in the sea off Plymouth. *J. marine. Ass. U.K.* 29: 97–137.

Horne, M. T., 1970. Coevolution of *Escherichia coli* and bacteriophages in chemostat culture. *Science* 168: 992–3.

Kingsbury, J. M., 1964. Poisonous plants of United States and Canada. Prentice-Hall, Englewood Cliff, N. J.

Li, C. C., 1955. Population genetics. University of Chicago Press, Chicago.

Menhinick, E. F., 1967. Structure, stability and energy flow in plants and arthropods in a sericea lespedeza stand. *Ecol. Monogr.* 37: 255–272.

Milne, A., 1957. The natural control of insect populations. *Can. Ent.* 89: 193–213.

Odum, E. P., 1959. Fundamentals of ecology. Saunders Co., Philadelphia.

Odum, E. P., C. E. Connell & L. B. Davenport, 1962. Population energy flow of three primary consumer components of old-field ecosystems. *Ecology* 43: 88–96.

Odum, H. T. & E. P. Odum, 1955. Trophic studies and productivity of a windward coral reef community on Eniwetok Atoll. *Ecol. Monogr.* 25: 291–320.

Pimentel, D., 1961a. Animal population regulation by the genetic feedback mechanism. *Am. Nat.* 95: 65–79.

Pimentel, D., 1961b. The influence of plant spatial patterns on insect populations. *Ann. ent. Soc. Am.* 54: 61–69.

Pimentel, D., 1963. Introducing parasites and predators to control native pests. *Can. Ent.* 95: 785–792.

Pimentel, D., 1968. Population regulation and genetic feedback. *Science* 159: 1432–1437.

Pimentel, D., & R. Al-Hafidh, 1965. Ecological control of a parasite population by genetic evolution in a parasite-host system. *Ann. ent. Soc. Am.* 58: 1–6.

Reichle, D. E. & D. A. Crossley Jr., 1967. Investigations on heterotrophic productivity in forest insect communities. *Proc. Work. Meet. Principles Methods sec. Productivity terr. Ecosystem (Warsaw, 1966)*, Vol. 2: 563–587.

Ricklefs, R. E., 1970. Clutch size in birds: Outcome of opposing predator and prey adaptations. *Science* 168: 599–600.

Russo, J. P., 1964. The Kaibab north deer herd: Its history, problems and management. *Ariz. Game Fish Dep., Wildl. Bull.* 7: 1–195.

Smalley, A. E., 1959. The growth cycle of *Spartiana* and its relation to the insect population in the marsh. *Proc. Salt Marsh Conf. (Sapelo Island, Georgia, 1958):* 96–100. Marine Institute of University of Georgia, Athens, Ga.

Stead, D. G., 1935. The rabbit in Australia. Winn, Sydney, Australia.

Sweetman, H. L., 1958. The principles of biological control. W. C. Brown, Iowa.

Teal, J. M., 1962. Energy flow in the salt marsh ecosystem of Georgia. *Ecology* 43: 614–624.

Van Hook, R. I., D. E. Reichle & S. I. Auerbach, 1970. Energy and nutrient dynamics of predator and prey arthropod populations in a grassland ecosystem. Oak Ridge Nat. Lab. ORNL–4509.

Wiegert, R. G., 1965. Energy dynamics of the grasshopper populations in old field and alfalfa field ecosystems. *Oikos* 16: 161–176.

Discussion

Participants: Pimentel and Soans (Authors), Bakker (K.), den Boer (P. J.), Beukema, Clough, Dempster, Eijsackers, Gulland, Jacobs, Jain, Kuenen, Lawton, Metz, Ohnesorge, Rosenzweig, Solomon, Southwood, Turnock, Varley and Zwölfer

Can experiments such as those described by Pimentel, with so many assumptions built in, ever be used as an argument for something which is happening in nature (KUENEN)? How far can one go in simplification before the experiment becomes senseless (BAKKER)? Do the experiments somehow refine our conceptual framework or broaden our insight in basic mechanisms any more than computer simulation could have done (METZ)? Even laboratory experiments closer to nature in design – which nevertheless are always highly artificial – have value only in illustrating how certain processes or mechanisms *may* work (BAKKER). The ultimate test of any hypothesis is nature. But then with how many species and in how many environments must the study be carried out for us to generalize about nature? No scientist would be foolish enough to believe that one experiment, either in laboratory or field, would answer all questions. I asked six important questions of my experimental population system and received six valuable answers. In the present laboratory experiment relative stability occurred in eight generations, whereas computer simulation showed that it took more than 100 generations to stabilize. Obvious conclusion: there is a difference between computer simulation and the response of living organisms (AUTHOR). – Some speakers were not convinced of the general occurrence of the genetic feedback mechanism in nature –

Leaf litter per se obviously cannot evolve in response to being fed upon, suggesting, on the basis of the model, that the structure of decomposer communities might be rather different from that of green-plant based systems. Although many decomposer animals 'graze' bacteria and fungi, many others may feed directly on the litter. Yet we do not observe massive outbreaks and great instability in litter systems – in fact, quite the reverse: great species diversity, coexistence of potential competitors and a balanced economy (LAWTON). Hence, the limitation of numbers to the 'interest' would not be possible where the resource itself cannot evolve, which would also be the case in carrion feeders. However, in these situations animals generally maintain high numbers, regularly compete intra- and interspecifically, and destroy the resource (SOUTHWOOD). On the other hand, it may be wondered whether rarity can be understood as a result of genetic feedback. Compare, for example, another case of evident mutual selection: specialized flowers and pollinators. Although the assumption of genetic feedback cannot supply an explanation for the keeping down of density in such cases (only a positive feedback is possible), such flowers and pollinators are often rare, especially in the tropics (DEN BOER). The genetic feedback mechanism does not apply in cases where a population and a non-living resource interact. The genetic feedback mechanism does not apply to pollinators and flowers because both organisms benefit in this interaction. The rarity of animals as defined in the paper means a scarcity of animals relative to their food resource (AUTHOR).

– Other aspects of the idea of genetic feedback were then discussed –

Is there not a bit of insinuation in using the word 'surplus'? It gives the impression that when that amount of vegetation, etc. is not eaten by predators, it is wasted energy (EIJSACKERS). It seems difficult to consider the feeding of Cinnabar Moth larvae on *Senecio* to be 'surplus'-feeding (DEMPSTER). How must 'surplus' and thus 'carrying capacity' be measured (VARLEY)? I define 'surplus' as the measurable amount of energy which can be harvested from the host population without causing the host population to decline. If the energy were not harvested by the animal, possibly the plant population could increase (AUTHOR).

The percentage of biomass available as 'surplus' energy will increase with an increasing ratio of production to biomass. Surplus energy is not necessarily a small amount; in zooplankton grazing on phytoplankton it may be mearly the total primary production (BEUKEMA). To avoid a misunderstanding: Slobodkin's 10% ecological efficiency is not a fraction of biomass consumed; he was referring to the biomass transferred from one trophic level to another (GULLAND).

It is stated that for the genetic feedback to be effective, the involved species would have to rely on the genetic diversity already present in the populations, i.e., mutation or gene immigration are unimportant. However, in the experiments only the 'plant' was allowed to 'evolve'. If the flies were given a chance to use their genetic variability for counter-evolution, the experiment would have ended up with a curve similar to the control curve; all 'plants' being salty, but all flies feeding on them (JACOBS). This would not happen because the animal cannot respond to resistance in the plant until the plant has evolved a degree of resistance. Experiments are in progress to investigate how rapidly the animal can adapt to change in its host plant (AUTHOR).

Apparently two very different time scales are involved in the development of plant resistance to herbivores. Plants that are poisonous or spiny show defenses that presumably

324

developed over a very long period. In the experiments, say 30 generations in duration, resistance can be developed only by selection from within the genetic variation that already exists; we have a situation like the development of insecticide resistance – rapid selection, but over a limited range (SOLOMON). Results under natural conditions comparable to the experiments are: resistance in the European rabbit to the virus in Australia and resistance in American elm trees to the Dutch elm disease fungus. Evolution in each of these cases is probably due to a recombination of available resistant genes (AUTHOR).

In the experiments, the model plants were started with an extremely low level of resistance. In nature there are several examples of the opposite situation. When the Douglas fir and the Ornarica fir, originating from a very remote mountain area in Southeast Europe, were introduced into Central Europe, they must already have had a high degree of resistance; they are to a much lesser degree attacked by insects than the indigenous conifer trees (OHNESORGE). In nature, the level of resistance may range from the extreme of nearly complete susceptibility, such as that of the American chestnut to the introduced fungus, to nearly complete resistance, as that of the ginko tree to pest insects and disease pathogens (AUTHOR).

The model suggests that there must be a selection pressure for herbivores to become polyphagous (ZWÖLFER). On the contrary, there is an advantage for a species to become highly integrated with its single host species. They both benefit from a balanced supply-demand economy. The polyphagous species is at a disadvantage in this sense (AUTHOR).

My general theory of the evolution of predatory systems differs in some ways from Pimentel's hypothesis: it predicts only that each predator-prey system has *an* equilibrium efficiency; this equilibrium may be unstable (and result in extinction), fluctuating, or stable. Unimportant predators may actually be losing their ability to use an unimportant prey, but at the same net rate their unimportant prey loses its ability to resist predation (ROSENZWEIG).

In the paper it is said that outbreaks usually are associated with newly introduced species which are not integrated with the system. But how does one explain the prevalence of short-term outbreaks, and the relative instability of arctic and sub-arctic plant and herbivore populations which have been together since the end of the Pleistocene Ice Ages? Could it be that 'outbreak' and 'constancy' should be considered on a very long time scale in which the Arctic communities could really be considered to have been the same for thousands of years (CLOUGH)? In the Arctic we do not observe the type of 'outbreak' which has been characterized for rabbits in Australia. In the Arctic the eating and eaten species will have a low degree of genetic integration because they suffer high mortality due to physical environmental factors, and hence populations are relatively unstable. In the favourable tropics mortality is primarily from biological factors, and there is a high degree of genetic integration between species and population stability (AUTHOR).

The model will have to be tested in nature by following the changes taking place between newly associated predator-prey, parasite-host, and herbivore-plant systems, e.g., those resulting from man's intentional or accidental introduction of species (JAIN). The two best models in nature are Myers' with the virus-rabbit association in Australia (in these Proceedings) and Turnock's with the parasite-larch sawfly association in Canada (see below) (AUTHOR).

The equilibrium between 'resistant' and 'susceptible' clones of the parthenogenetic larch sawfly *Pristiphora erichsonii* to the parasite *Mesoleieus tenthredinis* is determined by the amount of diversity in the parasites attacking the larch sawfly. Where *M. tenthredinis* is the only specific parasite, the resistant clone becomes overwhelmingly dominant. This natural population system clearly supports Pimentel's genetic feedback mechanism (TURNOCK).

Proc. Adv. Study Inst. Dynamics Numbers Popul. (Oosterbeek, 1970) 327–343

The phenomenon of predation and its roles in nature

C. B. Huffaker

Division of Biological Control, University of California, Berkeley, USA

Abstract

Predation plays several roles: shaping species' characteristics, determining their distribution and abundance, mediating intraspecific competition and contributing to community diversity and stability. The view that predators do not control their prey but take only surpluses is challenged. The average density of some invertebrate prey may be vastly less under predation. Predation by herbivores on plants, by invertebrates on other invertebrates and by vertebrates on vertebrates is discussed in relation to their comparative roles in nature. Territorialism is described as an essential feature if a predator is to optimize prey yield to itself; some parameters in territorial predation which contribute to a resilient regulatory role are discussed. Lastly, specific insect predators may well reduce their prey populations to levels 1/100 or less those prevailing in the absence of predators. Here, searching capacity seems to rule, and the prey population is commonly reduced to the point where closely competing predators which have lower searching capacities cannot subsist. The characteristics of predators and prey are evolved through the selective advantage to the individual of leaving progeny, but a specific, unstable, predator-prey link in a community may be removed by adverse effects on the capacity of the prey species to compete. Results from biological control of plants by weeds suggest that predation on plants may mediate plant competition; resulting in spacing out and increased species diversity.

Predation in its broad sense is the feeding of one organism on another. While it is customary to distinguish between herbivores, carnivores, parasites, parasitoids, and classical predators, we thereby lose perspective. I refer to all these categories as predators, but distinguish among them when relevant.

'How to get something to eat' and 'how to keep from being eaten' are among Nature's most fundamental demands. Such a ubiquitous force cannot fail to have a tremendous impact on organisms' structure, composition, abundance, and community integration. Predation may (1) shape the morphology, physiology and behavior of species, including mimics; (2) cause complete or local extinction or preclusion, affecting distribution; (3) cause suppression which is little related to population regulation; (4) do the regulating itself, or jointly with another agency; (5) mediate interspecific competition; and (6) enrich the diversity, structure and stability of communities. I attempt this overview inadequately and conjecturally.

It is useful to refer to predators as generalists or specialists, realizing that there are no true generalists and true monophagy is rare. The roles of generalists and specialists are different (vide infra).

Through predation, energy is channelled into a complex web of energy use, loss, and flow. Fig. 1 represents the loss in biomass from the browse consumed (1,156,400 lb) by

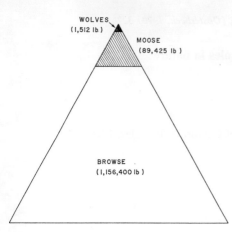

WOLVES
(1,512 lb)

MOOSE
(89,425 lb)

BROWSE
(1,156,400 lb)

Fig. 1. Pyramid of biomass: browse-moose-wolf system; based on biomass consumed only (After Mech, 1966).

moose (89,425 lb) which are, in turn, consumed by 22 wolves (1,512 lb) on Isle Royale (Mech, 1966). With the standing crop of browse (5,823,300 lb) producing the yield of moose as base, this is 3,851 lb per lb of wolf. If wolves regulate moose numbers as contended, they are a powerful force indeed.

Predators operate at all community levels. Some biologically control plant species such that they are 'spaced-out' (vide infra). But plants are variably protected from predators by carnivorous ones, and correspondingly escape destruction, persisting as resources for these and other less specialized feeders.

Vegetation results not only from direct competition for light, water and nutrients but from forces acting indirectly, including mediating predators and subtle genetic feedback between each plant and biological agent.

The Craigheads (1956) questioned Errington's (e.g. 1943, 1946, 1954) emphasis of the apparent fact that a large proportion of prey taken by a predator is doomed anyway. They noted that we miss the essential function if we view it in terms of predation on a single species or by a single species. The important point is not that a certain proportion is doomed but '... how they die, and that by their removal nature contrives to maintain population levels in harmony with the environment'. It matters greatly whether or not doomed individuals die from exposure or from predation, or whether or not carcasses are later eaten by a predator. The dead animal which does not nourish the predator does not extend the regulating force of predation; ones killed and eaten by predators, or eaten after death from other causes, do extend and perfect the mechanism.

We find all gradations in prey-specificity. The advantage of dietary range is obvious; selection for such is ever-present. But once begun selection for further specialization is often greater; the generalist is a poorer competitor for prey of the prey-specific predator. The latter is better attuned in its habits, haunts, life phases, nutritional needs, prey-finding and attack, and thus can maintain the prey at a density too low for the generalist. But conditions often prevail wherein specialization cannot proceed to a high degree of prey-specificity (Huffaker et al., 1969). If a 'specialist' prefers a given prey but utilizes others in emergency, it may have maximized its specialization consistent with the situation (maintained in greater numbers, better distributed and at hand to prevent irruptions). The use of alternative prey, if not excessive, may lessen the *individual* predator's control efficiency while increasing *population* control efficiency (Hoyt and Caltagirone, 1971; McMurtry and Scriven, 1966).

328

Predator control of prey populations

Errington (various papers) hypothesized that predators are simply by-products of prey populations, taking only surpluses, exhibiting no control. He applied this mainly to vertebrates; at least, he (1963b) came to consider vertebrate predation and invertebrate predation as quite different, the former rarely controlling, the latter commonly so. Correctly, Errington differentiated between predatized individuals which were doomed anyway to a pre-reproductive death, and those that would have reproduced. He stressed intrinsic inter-compensations. The death of one individual improves another's chances of survival. He saw in the muskrats (and quail) he studied great inter-compensations; predators only took habitat surpluses. But habitat capacity also meant 'cover' against predation, to *close-in* availability of food, and innate behavior. Yet, he saw exceptions, particularly in predation by canids on ungulates. He wrote, 'The most non-compensatory predation (on muskrats) occurred through the selective and specialized hunting tactics of red foxes which almost totally eliminated the exposed young...' But he regarded this as a rarity. His (1963b) statement, 'Never have I maintained that predation *cannot* be at some times and places a limiting factor with some prey populations', serves to emphasize his view. Errington's hypothesis was widely accepted – even generalized – for years, but is now challenged relative even to vertebrates.

The idea of predators taking only surpluses

Predators may take mainly surpluses, effecting no control. But there are two meanings of 'surplus'. One meaning is the 'doomed surplus' of Errington; i.e. those exceeding habitat capacity even if predation is absent. The second meaning applies to surpluses relative to equilibrium density; as may occur even when predation is regulating. On average, a regulating predator takes only surpluses even if it controls the prey at a density much lower than would prevail in its absence. Two regulating parasites of olive scale in California have reduced this pest to 1/1000 its former density, and now take only surpluses at the new equilibrium (Huffaker and Kennett, 1969).

Those who link the idea of a predator taking only surpluses with the idea of its exerting no control can mean only Errington's 'doomed surplus'. Protection from predators was part of the carrying capacity which Errington viewed as limiting, and he claimed that predators take only surpluses above capacity, but he defined that capacity at a level already depressed by predators below the capacity the prey could have in the predators' absence.

When predators reduce quails or muskrats in environments which are marginal mainly because of predator pressure, they are restricting the distribution and abundance of the species; and possibly also restricting more severe overpopulation repercussions. The removal of surpluses from favorable areas where normally behaving, socially well-integrated individuals are predator secure may foster control of other species or the same species at other times or other places.

The idea of predator rarity and feeding on surpluses

Pimentel (e.g. 1963a, 1963b, 1968) also views predators as taking only surpluses, i.e. 'interest', not 'capital' (breeding stock density). He recognizes that the capital (equilibrium density) may be reduced by predation itself. But he links some incompatible ideas. He says that since predators take only 'interest', they '... must be rare, especially relative to their food source'. He (e.g. 1963a, 1963b) also claims that predators having co-evolved with their prey are negligible controlling agents. Yet he (1963a) stated that co-integrative genetic changes involving new species to species contacts, adjusting relationships (I presume such that only 'interest' is taken), need not cause important increases in the prey.

The idea – that because a predator takes only 'interest' it must be rare – is wrong. Noncontrolling predators might take only interest items and be rare relative to the prey; but controlling predators may be abundant relative to the prey. The relative abundance depends on the prey necessary to yield the interest required to maintain the predator's capital stock. A predator requiring a high prey intake can only exist in low numbers, relative to its prey. For the 22 wolves of Isle Royale, the interest required was about 142 moose per year (25% of the capital stock of 600 in late winter). The ratio of wolves to moose is about 1:30 (Mech, 1966). The predatory mite *Metaseiulus occidentalis* requires 10 to 15 prey to develop, and exists at 1/8 to 1/15 the density of its tetranychid prey (Laing and Huffaker, 1969). Good controlling insect parasitoids that mature on a single host are more numerous than their hosts at breeding stock level. Olive scale in California is held by its two parasitoids at about one reproductive female/1000 leaves, while each parasitoid maintains about 3 to 6 times as many reproductive females.

The equilibrium density for a prey having a high r_m can be maintained only if a high interest is taken, whereas a low interest is sufficient for stabilizing a species having a low r_m. The densities at which these equilibrium mortalities occur are a function of the predator's searching ability and other parameters.

Good prey-specific predators may be much rarer than poor ones. Good ones maintain the prey at densities where both are rare; poor ones do not, and may exist simply as byproducts of abundant prey. Poor ones may be rarer than good ones for other reasons.

Pimentel's views (vide supra) are also based partly on the principle that, at the individual level, true parasitism progresses toward an amelioration of the severity of the parasitism. Huffaker et al. (1971) claim that his conclusions do not follow from this principle or from examples of it.

Control and regulation by invertebrate predators

The effect of efficient predators of phytophagous insects is to prevent overexploitation of food plants. Ecologically they often 'overdo' the job. Good ones do not permit anything near an optimum yield to the prey or, thus, to themselves. That some 250 or more stocks have yielded to partial or complete economic control (70 being complete control mainly by the introductions into adopted environments of their indigenous enemies) refutes the claim that predators do not control prey populations. Clausen (in press) lists efforts against 223 species with 120, or 55%, at least partially successful. Hagen et al. (1971) details examples of naturally occurring biological control in the western United States; MacPhee and MacLellan (1971) provide a similar list for Canada, and Rabb (1971) for the eastern United States. Complete biological control commonly means a density 1/25 to 1/100 of that prevailing without the controlling agents. The influence of predators on certain marine invertebrates (barnacles) is treated in these Proceedings by Connell.

Control and regulation by vertebrate predators?*

The hypothesis of non-control of vertebrates by predators was widely accepted for many years, or little contrary evidence was presented (e.g. Gabrielson, 1941; Presnall, 1950;

* Appreciation is expressed especially to Drs F. A. Pitelka and R. A. Skoog for many sources of information, and for their comments on them.

Leopold, 1954; Chitty, 1955, 1960). Illustrative of different viewpoints is the fact that Krebs' (1966) conclusions support the hypothesis relative to the California vole, although Pearson (1966) found predation losses as high as 25% (1963) and 88% (1961) in the same area during the same years. Many authors report predation as being unimportant for various vertebrates without subscribing to the general view that vertebrate predators take only surpluses (examples for rodents, ungulates, birds, etc. in Errington (1946), and others in the 1940's and 50's). Food, or territorial relationships and weather were thought to be the important factors, with predators rated of little importance: e.g. caribou in North America (Banfield, 1954; Cringan, 1947); reindeer on Pribiloff Islands (Scheffer, 1951); deer in Canada (Cowan, 1947), Wisconsin (Thompson, 1952; Dahlberg and Guettinger, 1956), New York (Cheatum and Severinghaus, 1950), California (Taber and Dasmann, 1957), USA (Leopold et al., 1947); elk in Washington (Buechner and Swanson, 1955) and Canada (Cowan, 1947); mountain goats in Idaho (Brandborg, 1955); bighorn sheep in western USA (Buechner, 1960); moose in Canada (Cowan et al., 1950) and, before the establishment of wolves, on Isle Royale (Murie, 1934); pronghorn antelope in Texas (Buechner, 1950); and vicuña and puma in Ecuador (Koford, 1957).

While many of these cases where predation had no apparent role are consistent with the hypothesis of non-control, they do not establish it. I do not suggest that other factors (habitat limitations, territoriality, food) do not limit many herbivores, but examples from wild ungulates in well-settled areas are irrelevant to this hypothesis although predators were found to be unimportant. The wolves, cougars, coyotes and bob-cats – key predators of ungulates, particularly deer which now seem to be food-limited – have been hunted and poisoned or driven from the habitats; they could not have their pristine roles. A predator cannot control an insect pest under insecticide applications against which the pest but not the predator is resistant!

Even for major vertebrates, studies in less disturbed areas suggest that an important role is being played by the predator. Also, even when vertebrate ecologists were denying a depressive role for predation (emphasizing mainly their improvement of the *quality* of prey populations), many of their colleagues disagreed.

Although re-stating the hypothesis as one of Gabrielson's (1941) principles of predation, Latham (1951) presented an illustration that is a clear denial. Brooks (1926) considered that deer populations in British Columbia were influenced by mountain lions and other predators. Murie (1944) concluded that wolves, interacting with weather, regulate Alaskan Dall sheep. Rasmussen (1941) felt that although deer on Kaibab Plateau, Arizona, were food-limited, predators exerted a strong influence. Klein and Olson (1960) noted that in wolf-free areas (Alaska) deer were food-limited (interrelated with weather), but in wolf areas wolves had a strong influence. Arrington and Edwards (1951) suggested that coyotes regulated antelopes in parts of Arizona and prevented re-establishment in other areas. Where coyotes were 'trapped out' many more fawns/100 does resulted than in untrapped areas.

Recently, Mech (1966), Shelton (1966) and Pimlott (1967) for wolves, Kruuk (e.g. 1970) for hyenas, and Schaller (1969, and pers. comm.) for lions in Tanzania, cast new light on canid and feline predation. Kruuk and van Lawick (1968) and Kruuk (1970) describe predation by hyenas in Ngorongo Crater and the Serengeti. Kruuk concluded that in the Crater hyenas exert a delicate regulation on certain major species, e.g. wildebeest (causing the death of most adults); on the Serengeti, where migrations of the abundant and 'preferred' prey (zebra and wildebeest) occur, they do not. The hyena packs protect territories.

The Crater population consists of 8 packs (about 420 adults). They are less restricted by their territorialism than the wolves of Isle Royale (Mech, 1966) or Algonquin Park (Pimlott, 1967). Wolves stabilized at 1/10 mile², or 10 for an area the size of the Crater. Even considering the food requirements, the hyenas are much more numerous. The resources in vegetation and prey are also apparently greater. Has not selection favored territorial behavior reflecting this?

Stevenson-Hamilton (1937), Guggisberg (1961) and Schaller (1969) describe the life of the African lion which rather fits the description of their being basically food-limited, although they are territorial. The mother eats first and gives a cub food only when she is well fed; she may abandon cubs when food is scarce. Young are killed seeking food out-of-turn. Cubs are left 24 hours at a time or even abandoned, and often fall prey to leopards or other lion prides. The more abundant and accessible the prey, the less the cubs are left subject to marauders. Schaller says the Serengeti harbors over a million hooved animals and might be expected to support more than the 1,000 or so lions present. But in periods when the abundant migratory prey are away, the available non-migratory prey are scarce and more formidable (buffalo) or speedier (impala). Schaller (1969, and pers. comm.) implies that food is then limiting, but the interaction is modified or stabilized somewhat by the lion's territorial behavior. Although he stated that lions help to prevent overpopulation which might lead to ruinous overgrazing and starvation, this may only apply to a limited degree to migrating zebras and wildebeests because territories must be large enough to permit survival during times of scarce prey. Migration can circumvent a controlling predation unless the predator moves effectively with the prey, which few can do, or unless the predator pressure is over the whole range. This applies to both vertebrates and invertebrates. The role of Hominids as possible key pristine predators here is a stimulating thought!

Unchecked by hunting (Cringan, 1957) or predators (Mech, 1966; Skoog, pers. comm.), moose and caribou overexploit and emigrate. With migrating species which move to areas where predators are man-restricted, the pristine role is elusive. Thus, studies in Ngorongo Crater and Isle Royale are most important, although unrepresentative since emigrating species are 'closed in' with their predators. On Isle Royale wolves and moose seemed in balance at about 1 wolf: 30 moose, with the wolf regulating. Pimlott (1967) also suggests that the role of wolves may be estimated upward if they are shown to depend on large prey rather than small ones in summer (which his data supports); he suggests also that wolf predation in Algonquin Park may have prevented major irruptions such as have occurred in many wolf-free ranges (Leopold et al., 1947).

Work on raptors and other birds also challenge the hypothesis of non-control by predators. Raptors are more migratory than many of their prey; the reverse is commonly true for canids. Raptors more easily shift to places of abundant prey. The Craigheads (1956) say that predation (collectively) lowers rates of increase in relation to prey density and before more drastic regulating forces (intraspecific strife, disease, emigration, starvation) become dominant. They do not adequately document this, but surely, where several species attack a prey population, the effect of one species is no basis for conclusions. Tinbergen (1946) considered that European sparrow hawks exhibit density-dependent concentration and probably regulate some passerines; if they were much decreased many small birds would increase. Southern (1954) suggests that the tawny owl controls certain prey. Also, while the work of Fitch et al. (1946) and Fitch (1947a, 1947b) indicates that ground squirrels are not controlled by predators, Fitch (1947b) partially accepts their importance for cottontail rabbits. Darrow (1947) claimed that by taking 'surpluses' pred-ators keep ruffed grouse within limits compatible with the habitat. About 39 % of nests were broken up, mainly by foxes; raptors were the main chick predators and horned owl and foxes preyed heavily on adults. Adult losses, 80 % of which was to enemies, averaged over half the fall population each year. The 'surplus' they mean cannot be Errington's 'doomed surplus', for a reduction of predators greatly reduced nest losses and, to an extent, adult losses. They noted that a control of the predator could not result in *continued* grouse increases!

Maher (1970) says that predators (weasels, jaegers, owls) can depress brown lemmings. Pitelka et al. (1955) suggest that they affect cycle periodicity, postponing 'highs'. Pearson (1966) says that predator pressure after the decline causes the extreme 'lows' and long de-lays in the increase phase in California voles. Maher (1970) suggests that avian predators mainly exploit and truncate brown lemming peaks; weasels and foxes may cause the big declines the winter following peaks, and '... this may be causing the population cycle.' Thompson (1955) noted extreme depressive effects of weasels on lemmings. Huffaker et al. (1963) describe similar predation on mites, and suggest that such action might synchronize cycle phase over a considerable area. Maher (1970) suggests that mammalian predators may possibly be the cause of a synchronous cycling of two lemming species (Krebs 1964, MacPherson 1966). Pitelka (1964) and Schultz (1964) stress lemming (food quality) soil nutrient interactions as the basis of brown lemming cycling which, if established, would mean that predators have a minor role.

Shaping the character of prey and the co-evolution of predators and prey

A predator's influence on the structure of a prey is an obvious fact of evolution, seen in the quills of porcupines, urticaceous hairs of caterpillars, shells of tortoises, and 'outlandish' mimicry. Errington (1954) also suggests that very long ago minks may have had a very real depressive influence on muskrats, forcing substantial changes in its behavior and way of life (habitat selection, home building, defense). In the co-evolution of predators and prey we may find the full roles of predation in community energetics. Territorial behavior and breadth and flexibility in dietary range are co-evolutionary results of selective ad-vantages. Sociality and territorialism have thus evolved as special forces in vertebrates.

For both social and non-social organisms, there are two principal means of countering overpopulation tendencies. One is the evolution of intrinsic characteristics; increasing overpopulation increases social intolerance, causing population reduction. The other is the evolution of prey-specific (and less prey-specific) enemies adapted to increase pressure on overly increasing prey, and including the co-evolution of sets of natural enemies and prey species whose lives are so enmeshed that extravagances are largely precluded. (However, local outbreaks may be normal to maintenance of species diversity and overall biome balance (Turnbull, 1969; Huffaker, 1971).) The species' characteristics must arise through selection at the individual level in leaving progeny. If a host specific phytophagous insect interacts violently with its host plant, the plant could not be a broadly successful competitor; both plant and insect might be excluded. With the co-evolution of an effective predator(s) of the insect, plant and insects could have secure niches. This relation could apply at other levels as well. Moreover, this does not preclude evolution of characteristics in social organisms that endanger the individual but benefit the group. A dominant male may by his leadership responsibilities expose himself to great danger defending the group, but if coupled with special sexual privilege selective advantage is obvious.

Territorialism has not been a strong force in the co-evolution of insect predator/prey relationships. In the absence of real territorialism, invertebrate predators lack any real tendency to optimize prey yield. Effective non-territorial predators reduce their prey far below the carrying capacity which is otherwise possible. Some plants are controlled by rather host-specific herbivores while predators of other similar herbivores often prevent such herbivore pressure. Some plants have developed effective resistance. Complexes of plants and herbivores persist as a mosaic of resources. Vertebrates also utilize this assemblage, have a role in its make-up and help to regulate it.

Although vertebrate predators have a broad flexibility in diet and may shift to prey species in proportion to their local abundance (vide supra), some heavily utilize only a few species. However, effective entomophagous insects are highly prey-specific (DeBach, 1964, Huffaker et al., 1971). If for no other reason than their vastly greater variety as terrestrial herbivores, the insects include far more relatively prey-specific species. When not limited by their own predators, many can mediate competition between plant species. Also, vertebrate herbivores, being larger and needing food in greater volume, cannot be so choosey if the plant species are spaced-out, as in mixtures. Thus insect herbivores and carnivores persist in an ancient role, acting as the more specific species-to-species links in community food webs, probably more intricately determining the co-evolutionary patterns and the kinds and abundances of plants that get through the 'grass-roots' sieve and are thus available to vertebrates (vide infra).

While insectan predators comprise many generalists which help to stabilize specific links and overall community relationships, canid predators are more characteristically generalists. The latter tend to be more linked with the collective energy resources of grasslands and range, and tend to regulate or dampen the extremes of overcropping, e.g. by ungulates, in pristine, mixed vegetation. They are 'overlord community predators' at a more encompassing level, but in a sense overlords of a system screened and shaped, historically and functionally, by lesser predators. However, entomophagous insects and pathogens seem to predominate over vertebrate predators at this level in their respective roles in the regulation of tree-strata vegetation.

Rodents pose an interesting case. Avian and other vertebrate predators may influence habitat occupancy and resource use, numbers and the timing and duration of 'highs' and 'lows' in rodent cycles. But by their modes of life rodents may have somewhat circumvented the most intense predator pressure. They have a highly developed self-limitation (Chitty, 1955, 1960), a good strategem if predation has been circumvented. But we cannot now generalize on the roles of predation vs. self-limitation for rodents as a group for all pristine situation (vide supra, Krebs, 1966; Pearson, 1966). Even the most self-limited species may have been less called upon to use the mechanism in pristine times.

Sociality, social intolerance and territoriality

Social behavior and organization arose in prey species partly as defense against predation, and in prey and predators for more effective food-getting. Sociality carries its own seeds of social intolerance, because as food-getting, protection from rigors of climate and defense against predators are perfected by group action, overpopulation becomes a by-product.

Territoriality is advanced social intolerance. Territorial spacing may greatly improve food-getting and breeding possibilities, or so reduce numbers that predators have less acute effects. Territorialism extended to other competing species further improves security. Territories are commonly compressible; this may vary extremely (Errington, 1963a). An upper limit to predator numbers may be set by the limit of territory compressibility.

If limited strictly by territorialism, for a predator to control its prey the territory size and compressibility must be such that, using the resilience in its functional and numerical responses, it normally prevents prey irruptions. It could not itself correct irruptions. Pimlott (1967) suggests that wolves could not control deer populations much exceeding 100:1 wolf; since they are territory limited, at their stable density (1/10 mile^2) wolves could not check further increase. Deer starvation could restore a ratio amenable to wolf regulation (similar situations are common for insects). Also, in pristine times when wolves, cougars, coyotes, lynxes, and lesser predators were not restricted by man, the resilience in a given primary predation (by virtue of wasteful feeding, territory compressibility, numerical response, and the shifting of attention to irrupting populations) is reinforced by other principal and lesser predators and by scavengers. Numerical responses are invoked most during times of instability; functional responses might largely regulate in times of stability. Territory size and compressibility may be evolved in relation to both the normal levels of prey and the accessory forces that increase the overall resilience of the regulative process.

Pimlott's (1967) remarks are apropos here: Considering deer and moose in particular, one may ask why intrinsic mechanisms have not evolved to prevent them from increasing beyond their food supply. It may be because they have had efficient predators, and selective pressures have kept them busy evolving ways, not of limiting their own numbers, but of keeping abreast of mortality factors. 'There is now great imbalance in environments. Environmental disturbances have been favorable for deer and moose, with great tracts of land cleared of trees and browse species appearing in great abundance... and populations are probably higher than they have ever been.' The pristine environments would not support high densities, and Pimlott suggests that the degree of territorial spacing of wolves, evolved under those conditions, suggests that in pristine times they had a capacity to regulate prey densities.

The evolution of territorial behavior in an overlord predator such as the wolf has arisen through trophic advantage. An over-expansive territory would be selected against since this would prevent him from having control over the prey; during the uncontrolled increase of the prey the latter's food supply would be endangered, and so also the wolf's – he and his progeny would pay. He would also have to prevent other predators (including parasites) from exerting, for him, a ruinous control effect; only by defending a resource could a predator do this. The wolf's antipathy to coyotes and the selective killing of diseased prey (even if coincidental) illustrates this possibility.

I suspect that the evolution of territory size and compressibility involved a selective advantage acting to develop an optimum yield to the predator. This could be through applying enough pressure on the herbivore to stabilize prey/vegetation interactions, but not enough to reduce the herbivore unduly. Slobodkin (1961) stated that a prudent predator should take yield organisms in a way such as to maximize its yield while also maximizing the population efficiency of the prey. He offered no explanation of how this could arise. He did not mention it in terms of territorialism. I do not know to what extent the yield to any predator has been optimized through territorialism, but such behavior would seem to be a prerequisite for yield optimization. If the territory were very small, advantages, except in physical protection, would be negligible. Interactions would be like non-territorial predator/prey interactions.

Non-territorial predators, however, can cause control and stability. Density-dependent

335

emigration of either predator or prey (Huffaker and Stinner, in press), extrinsic density-dependent actions on either species, intra-specific interferences, general or secondary predators, etc., can damp interactions. But the prey taken cannot be said to approach an optimized yield to the predator. The restriction in density is often great although both populations live in comparative security. Immature olive scales under control by parasitoids persist at about 4 to 16/1000 leaves, these yield both the host and parasitoid progeny. Scale densities in the absence of parasites are 200 to 1,000 or more times higher.

Entomophagous predators seem to lack an efficient territorial means of precluding inroads by competing predators; an essential requirement if they are to progress toward optimizing their yield. With the absence of territorialism, any lessened control opens up an opportunity for other, more effective predators to displace them. Success is determined largely by the degree of prey rarity that the predator can cause and still have security itself. Searching capacity, the primitive pre-territorial factor, is the main criterion (Huffaker et al., 1971).

If the territory is too large, a predator's combined behavioral and reproductive response is inadequate to regulate the prey. Selective pressure would oppose the defending a territory larger than that needed – wasting time and energy. Also, in the absence of another mechanism, the prey would overexploit the habitat. The system would break down. Wasteful feeding replaces part of the lack of numerical responsiveness that goes with territorialism. This, plus territory compression, some delayed numerical response, and the shifting to places of (or kinds of) abundant prey, presents marked intercompensations. Considering multiple complexes of predators – their kills are permitted in fat years to go to lesser predators and even scavengers, and they have an indifferent care of young in lean years – the intercompensations in the totality of predation seem substantial. Thus in lean years, a numerical response is counter-productive – called for only when the parents are well-fed. Even when the territory is compressed and saturated, and thus when recruits cannot be added although food is still abundant, the food utilized by the doomed young has a role – it absorbs more prey.

Territorial *prey* behavior which results in spacing-out may also tend to optimize the resource yield both to themselves and to a controlling predator. Spaced-out species of spider mites are subject to less violent predator/prey interactions.

An inadequate extension of territoriality to other competing species precludes true optimization of yield. The wolves, hyenas, and lions previously discussed hold fixed or sometimes moving territories. Wolves on Isle Royale are thought to be intolerant of coyotes, possibly causing their eradication (Mech, 1966). Lions commandeer the kills of cheetahs and hyenas.

Work of Huffaker et al. (1963) suggests the complexity of predator/prey relations and, by its absence, the value of territorialism. We studied a prey mite feeding on oranges and a predatory phytoseiid. In simple physical systems (massing of food), the predators quickly eradicated the system. Under conditions of an extensive dispersion of the orange supply, repeated population oscillations occurred. Significantly, when food units were equally dispersed but there was three times the quantity at each spot, the system was again quickly eradicated. With the usual reproductive lag in predator response, the prey increased to densities three times as high as previously before the predators caused a decline. The number of predators generated was six times as many as before. Although they had the same surface area to search, they overdid the job; the prey crash was severe and the predator population starved. This predator defends no territory, but in systems with the variables (above) appropriately balanced it regulates a rather stable system (see also Flaherty and Huffaker, in press; Hoyt and Caltagirone, 1971, for field populations). Hypothetically adding territorialism for this predator, the three-fold increase in the orange supply would probably not have caused annihilation. If they had been territory-limited, the predators could not have increased six-fold and would not so have overly exploited the prey.

All the above does not imply that territorial predators may not exist simply on surplus prey; some probably do.

Predation, species diversity, and community stability

Little is known about community diversity and stability, but I think that predation plays an important role in this. Ridley (1930) hypothesized that predation has an important role in species diversity; predation acting more intensely on either plants or seeds in one-plant associations than in species mixtures. He wrote, 'It is largely due to this ... that one-plant associations are prevented ...'. When stands of a weed are greatly reduced by biological control, replacement vegetation commonly consists of a greater mixture of species. Harper (1969) cited the case of biological control of prickly pears in Australia and also our work in California on St. John's wort, but for 3 of our 4 places the data quoted by him do not agree with our results.

Table 1 lists the corrected and extended (misc. species segregated) results. A single statistic is available prior to beetle control (full weed development at each site). Note that in spite of variation in weed dominance among the sites, the initial diversity at each site was the lowest of any year. A paired t-test of initial numbers of species against averages for the five post-control years gave values just under high significance. Such a comparison only suggests the important role of such predation for community diversity and stability. A single predator is involved. With the near-removal of one dominant species, some other aggressive species might take its place – as *Bromus mollis* tended to do here – unless it also

Table 1. Numbers of plant species dominant in microplot positions before the removal of St. Johnswort by beetles (1952, for Loftus; and, 1948 for other sites) and subsequent to removal.

Year	Loftus	Loomis	Blocksburg	Ft. Seward
1947	—	20	24	28
1948	—	23*	29*	34*
1949	—	—	—	—
1950	—	23	37	41
1951	19	22	28	31
1952	24*	—	—	—
1953	28	30	36	37
1954	32	—	—	—
1955	33	26	34	30
1956	27	—	—	—
1957	29	25	32	34
$\bar{x}$ of post-cont.	29.8	25.2	33.4	34.6

* The year the beetles removed the weed; there had not yet been sufficient time for much effect to show.

is under biological control. To envisage the full potentialities of predators, a complex of aggressive and less aggressive plants and effective, host-specific phytophagous predators should be studied in combinations.

Within a habitat, the outcome of competition between similar hosts may be mediated by their susceptibilities to a pathogen (Park, 1948), parasitoid (Utida, 1953) or predator (Brooks and Dodson, 1965; Paine, 1966; Connell, these Proceedings). Barbehenn (1969) extended this idea and hypothesized that true parasitism may mediate habitat division independent of the competitors' primary exploitive characteristics. Thus S_1, inherently able to replace S_2 in the absence of a common parasite, would be replaced by S_2, the more parasite-tolerant species, in that portion of the habitat conducive to the parasite. Thus species diversity for the larger habitat is increased.

Phytophagous insects and other herbivores have been shown to exert a great influence on the survival or dispersion patterns of surviving seeds or juvenile plants (Tevis, 1958; for some desert annuals; Manley and Butcher, 1967, and Cantlon, 1969; for *Melampyrum lineare*; and Janzen, 1967 and 1969: for bull's horn acacia; and others).

Paine (1966) restated the hypothesis that predation on plants in the tropics can explain the greater diversity of tropical vegetation. But this hypothesis rests on the assumption that there is an increased or more effective biological control in the tropics than in the non-tropics. Why should phytophagous predators in low humid tropics be better control agents of plants than their own carnivorous predators are of them? Janzen (1970) appears to believe this is so. He ignores the more favorable record of biological control of insect pests in the tropics and semi-tropics. Other factors than predation may be involved, e.g. greater total resource potential, time available since severe glaciations for a finer division of resources, and greater climatic stability and the spread in its favourability throughout the year (see also Pianka, 1966).

Thus, while phytophagous predators may account for some diversity, as Janzen (1969) notes, we know too little about the action of predators, especially on juvenile wild plants, to do more than suggest that they play an important role in the processes by which plant communities and their animal components of various complexity are determined.

References

Arrington, O. N. & A. E. Edwards, 1951. Predator control as a factor in wildlife management. *Trans. 16th N. Am. Wildl. Conf.* 179–191.

Banfield, A. W. F., 1954. Preliminary investigation of the barren ground caribou. Part II. Life history, ecology, and utilization. *Can. Wildl. Serv., Wildl. Mgmt. Bull. Ser.* 1(10B), pp. 112.

Barbehenn, K. R., 1969. Host-parasite relationships and species diversity in mammals: an hypothesis. *Biotropica* 1: 29–35.

Brandborg, S. M., 1955. Life history and management of the mountain goat in Idaho. *Idaho Fish Game Wildl. Bull.* 2, pp. 142.

Brooks, A., 1926. Past and present big game conditions in British Columbia and the predatory mammal question. *J. Mammal.* 7: 37–40.

Brooks, J. L. & S. I. Dodson, 1965. Predation, body size, and composition of plankton. *Science* 150: 28–35.

Buechner, H. K., 1950. Life history, ecology, and range use of the pronghorn antelope in Trans-Pecos, Texas. *Am. Midl. Nat.* 43: 257–354.

Beuchner, H. K., 1960. The bighorn sheep in the United States, its past, present and future. *Wildl. Monogr.* 4, pp. 174.

Beuchner, H. K. & C. V. Swanson, 1955. Increased natality resulting from lowered population density among elk in southeastern Washington. *Trans. 20th N. Am. Wildl. Conf.* 560–567.

Cantlon, J. E., 1969. The stability of natural populations and their sensitivity to technology. In:

Diversity and stability in ecological systems. *Brookhaven Symp. Biol.* 22: 197–205.

Cheatum, E. L. & C. W. Severinghaus, 1950. Variations in fertility of white-tailed deer related to range conditions. *Trans. 15th N. Am. Wildl. Conf.* 170–190.

Chitty, D., 1955. Adverse effects of population density upon the viability of later generations. In: J. B. Cragg and N. W. Pirie (Ed.), The numbers of man and animals. Edinburgh. pp. 152.

Chitty, D., 1960. Population processes in the vole and their relevance to general theory. *Can. J. Zool.* 38: 99–113.

Clausen, C. P. (Ed.), In press. A world review of parasites, predators and pathogens introduced to new habitats. U.S. Dept. Agric.

Cowan, I. McT., 1947. The timber wolf in the Rocky Mountain National Parks of Canada. *Can. J. Res.* 25: 139–174.

Cowan, I. McT., W. S. Hoar & J. Hatler, 1950. The effect of forest succession upon the quantity and upon the nutritive values of woody plants used as food by moose. *Can. J. Zool.* 28: 249–271.

Craighead, J. J. & F. C. Craighead, 1956. Hawks, owls and wildlife. Stackpole Co., Harrisburg, Penn. pp. 443.

Cringan, A. T., 1957. History, food habits and range requirements of the woodland caribou of continental North America. *Trans. 22nd N. Am. Wildl. Conf.* 485–501.

Dahlberg, B. L. & R. C. Geuttinger, 1956. The white-tailed deer in Wisconsin. *Wisc. Cons. Dept. Tech. Bull.* 14, pp. 282.

Darrow, R. W., 1947. Predation. In: G. Bump, R. W. Darrow, F. C. Edminster and W. F. Crissey (Ed.)The ruffed grouse,. Chap. 7: 307–350. New York State Conserv. Dept. pp. 915.

DeBach, P. (Ed.), 1964. Biological control of insect pests and weeds. Reinhold Publ. Corp., NY. pp. 844.

Errington, P. L., 1943. An analysis of mink predation upon muskrats in north-central United States. *Res. Bull. Iowa agric. Exp. Stn* 320: 797–924.

Errington, P. L., 1946. Predation and vertebrate populations. *Q. Rev. Biol.* 21: 144, 177, 221–245.

Errington, P. L., 1954. The special responsiveness of minks to epizootics in muskrat populations. *Ecol. Monogr.* 24: 377–393.

Errington, P. L., 1963a. Muskrat populations. Iowa State Univ. Press, Ames, Iowa. pp. 665.

Errington, P. L., 1963b. The phenomenon of predation. *Am. Sci.* 51: 180–192.

Fitch, H. S., 1947a. Predation by owls in the Sierran foothills of California. *Condor* 49: 137–151.

Fitch, H. S., 1947b. Ecology of a cottontail rabbit (*Sylvilagus auduboni*) population in central California. *Calif. Fish Game* 33: 159–184.

Fitch, H. S., F. Swenson & D. F. Tillontson, 1946. Behavior and food habits of the red-tailed hawk. *Condor* 48: 205–237.

Flaherty, D. L. & C. B. Huffaker, 1970. Biological control of Pacific mites and Willamette mites in San Joaquin Valley vineyards. I. Role of *Metaseiulus occidentalis. Hilgardia* 40: 267–308.

Gabrielson. I. N., 1941. Wildlife conservation. The MacMillan Co., NY.

Guggisberg, C., 1961. Simba. London. (From: Schaller, G. B., 1967, The deer and the tiger. Univ. Chicago Press, Chicago. pp. 370).

Hagen, K. S., R. van den Bosch & D. L. Dahlsten, 1971. The importance of naturally-occurring biological control in the western United States. In: C. B. Huffaker (Ed.), Biological control. Chap. 11. Plenum Press, NY.

Harper, J. L., 1969. The role of predation in vegetational diversity. Diversity and stability in ecological systems. *Brookhaven Symp. Biol.* 22: 48–61.

Hoyt, S. C. & L. E. Caltagirone, 1971. The developing programs of integrated control of pests of apples in Washington and peaches in California. In: C. B. Huffaker (Ed.), Biological control. Chap. 28. Plenum Press, NY.

Huffaker, C. B. (Ed.), 1971. Biological control. Plenum Press, NY.

Huffaker, C. B. & C. E. Kennett, 1969. Some aspects of assessing efficiency of natural enemies. *Can. Ent.* 101: 425–447.

Huffaker, C. B., P. S. Messenger, & P. DeBach, 1971. The natural enemy component in natural control and the theory of biological control. In: C. B. Huffaker (Ed.), Biological control. Chap. 2. Plenum Press, NY.

Huffaker, C. B., K. P. Shea & S. G. Herman, 1963. Experimental studies on predation: III. Complex dispersion and levels of food in an acarine predator-prey interaction. *Hilgardia* 34: 305–330.

Huffaker, C. B. & R. E. Stinner, In press. The role of natural enemies in pest control programs.

Huffaker, C. B., M. van de Vrie & J. A. McMurtry, 1969. The ecology of tetranychid mites and their natural control. *A. Rev. Ent.* 14: 125–174.

Janzen, D. H., 1967. Interaction of the bull's-horn acacia (*Acacia cornigera* L.) with an ant inhabitant (*Pseudomyrmex ferruginea* F. SMITH) in eastern Mexico. *Univ. Kans. Sci. Bull.* 47: 315–558.

Janzen, D. H., 1969. Seed-eaters versus seed size, number, toxicity, and dispersal. *Evolution* 23: 1–27.

Janzen, D. H., 1970. The unexploited tropics. *Bull. Ecol. Soc. Am.* 51(3): 4–7.

Klein, D. R. & S. T. Olson, 1960. Natural mortality patterns of deer in southeast Alaska. *J. Wildl. Mgmt.* 24: 80–88.

Koford, C. B., 1957. The vicuña and the puma. *Ecol. Monogr.* 27: 153–219.

Krebs, C. J., 1964. The lemming cycle at Baker Lake, Northwest Territories, during 1959–62. *Arctic Inst. N. Am. Tech. Paper* No 15.

Krebs, C. J., 1966. Demographic changes in fluctuating populations of *Microtus californicus. Ecol. Monogr.* 36: 239–273.

Kruuk, H., 1970. Interactions between populations of spotted hyenas and their prey species. In: A. Watson (Ed.), Animal populations in relation to their food resources. *Br. Ecol. Soc. Symp.* 10: 359–374.

Kruuk, H. & H. van Lowick, 1968. Hyenas, the hunters no one knows. *Natn. Geogr.* 134: 44–57.

Laing, J. E. & C. B. Huffaker, 1969. Comparative studies of predation by *Phytoseiulus persimilis* ATHIAS-HENRIOT and *Metaseiulus occidentalis* (NESBITT) (Acarina: Phytoseiidae) on populations of *Tetranychus urticae* KOCH (Acarina: Tetranychidae). *Res. Pop. Ecol.* 11: 105–126.

Latham, R. M., 1951. The ecology and economics of predator management. Penn. Game Commission, pp. 96.

Leopold, A., L. K. Sowls, & D. L. Spencer, 1947. A survey of overpopulated deer ranges in the United States. *J. Wildl. Mgmt.* 11: 162–177.

Leopold, A. S., 1954. The predator in wildlife management. *Sierra Club Bull.* 39: 34–38.

MacPhee, A. W. & C. R. MacLellan, 1971. Cases of naturally-occurring biological control in Canada. In: C. B. Huffaker (Ed.), Biological control. Chap. 13. Plenum Press, NY.

MacPherson, A. H., 1966. The abundance of lemmings at Aberdeen Lake, District of Keewatin, 1959–63. *Can. Field-Natur.* 81: 248–250.

Maher, W. J., 1970. The pomarine jaeger as a brown lemming predator in northern Alaska. *Wilson Bull.* 82: 130–157.

Manley, G. & J. W. Butcher, 1967. Insect predators of the Jack pine parasite *Melampyrum lineare* DESR. Mss. of paper presented at the 22nd A. Conf. Ent. Soc. Amer. (North Central Branch), March 23, 1967.

McMurtry, J. A. & G. T. Scriven, 1966. Studies on predator-prey interactions between *Amblyseius hibisci* and *Oligonychus punicae* under greenhouse conditions. *Ann. Ent. Soc. Am.* 59: 793–800.

Mech, L. D., 1966. The wolves of Isle Royale. *US Natn. Park Serv., Fauna Ser.* 7: pp. 210

Murie, A., 1934. The wolves of Isle Royale. *Misc. Publ. Mus. Zool. Univ. Mich.* 25: pp. 44.

Murie, A., 1944. The wolves of Mt. McKinley. US *Natn. Park Serv. Fauna Ser.* 5: pp. 238

Paine, R. T., 1966. Food web complexity and species diversity. *Am. Nat.* 100: 65–75.

Park, T., 1948. Experimental studies of interspecies competition. 1. Competition between populations of the flour beetles, *Tribolium confusum* DUVAL and *Tribolium castaneum* HERBST. *Ecol. Monogr.* 18: 265–308.

Pearson, O. P., 1966. The prey of carnivores during one cycle of mouse abundance. *J. Anim. Ecol.* 35: 217–233.

Pianka, E. R., 1966. Latitudinal gradients in species diversity: a review of concepts. *Am. Nat.* 100: 33–46.

Pimentel, D., 1963a. Introducing parasites and predators to control native pests. *Can. Ent.* 95: 785–792.

Pimentel, D., 1963b. Natural population regulation and interspecies evolution. *Proc. 16th Int. Congr. Zool. (Washington, DC)* 3: 329–336.

Pimentel, D., 1968. Population regulation and genetic feed-back. Science 159: 1432–1437.

Pimlott, D. H., 1967. Wolf predation and ungulate populations. *Am. Zool.* 7: 267–278.

Pitelka, F. A., 1964. The nutrient-recovery hypothesis for arctic microtine cycles. I. Introduction. In: D. J. Crisp (Ed.), Grazing in terrestrial and marine environments. pp. 55–56. *Brit. Ecol. Soc. Symp.* No. 4. Blackwell Sci. Publ., Oxford.

340

Pitelka, F. A., P. O. Tomich & G. W. Treichel, 1955. Ecological relations of jaegers and owls as lemming predators near Barrows, Alaska. *Ecol. Monogr.* 25: 85–117.

Presnall, C. C., 1950. The predation question-fact versus fancy. *Trans. 15th N. Am. Wildl. Conf.* 197–208.

Rabb, R. L., 1971. Naturally-occurring biological control in eastern United States, with particular reference to tobacco insects. In: C. B. Huffaker (Ed.), Biological control. Chap. 12. Plenum Press, NY.

Rasmussen, D. I., 1941. Biotic communities of Kaibab Plateau, Arizona. *Ecol. Monogr.* 11: 229–275

Ridley, H. N., 1930. The dispersal of plants throughout the world. L. Reeve and Co., Ashford, England. pp. 744.

Schaller, G. B., 1969. Life with the king of beasts. *Natn. Geogr.* 135: 494–519.

Scheffer, V. B., 1951. The rise and fall of a reindeer herd. *Sci. Mon.* 73: 356–362.

Schultz, A. M., 1964. The nutrient-recovery hypothesis for arctic microtine cycles. II. Ecosystem variables in relation to arctic microtine cycles. In: D. J. Crisp (Ed.), Grazing in terrestrial and marine environments. *Brit. Ecol. Soc. Symp.* No 4: 57–68. Blackwell Sci. Publ., Oxford.

Shelton, P. S., 1966. Ecological studies of beavers, wolves, and moose in Isle Royale National Park, Michigan. Purdue Univ., Lafayette, Ind. pp. 308.

Slobodkin, L. B., 1961. Growth and regulation of animal populations. Holt, Rinehard and Winston, NY. pp. 184.

Southern, H. N., 1954. Tawny owls and their prey. *Ibis.* 96: 384–410.

Stevenson-Hamilton. J., 1937. South African Eden. Cassell and Co. Ltd., London. pp. 311.

Taber, R. D. & R. F. Dasmann, 1957. The dynamics of three natural populations of the deer *Odocoileus hemionus columbianus. Ecology* 38: 233–246.

Tevis, L. Jr., 1958. Interrelations between the harvester ant *Veromessor pergandei* (MAYR) and some desert ephemerals. *Ecology* 39: 695–704.

Thompson, D. Q., 1952. Travel, range, and food habits of timber wolves in Wisconsin. *J. Mammal.* 33: 429–442.

Thompson, D. Q., 1955. The role of food and cover in population fluctuations of the brown lemming at Point Barrow, Alaska. *Trans 20th N. Am.* Wildl. Conf. 166–176.

Tinbergen, L., 1946. De sperwer als roofvijand van zangvogels. *Ardea* 34: 1–213. (English summary).

Turnbull, A. L., 1969. The ecological role of pest populations. *Proc. Tall Timb. Conf. Ecol. Anim. Control Habitat Mgmt.* No 1. Tallahassee, Fla., p. 219–232.

Utida, S., 1953. Interspecific competition between two species of bean weevil. *Ecology* 34: 301–307.

Discussion

Participants: Huffaker (Author), Bakker (K.), Frank, Hassell, Pimentel, Royama, Solomon, Tester, Watson, Zahavi

A number of speakers questioned whether or not the evolution of predation, stability of a community, 'natural control', etc. were considered 'purposeful'.

'Wolves have not evolved to fit in', but 'wolves fit in and thus evolved' (BAKKER). The 'biocoenosis' concept used is practically the same as that which Moebius developed in the beginning of the century; a concept of equilibrium in nature and of the mutual regulation of species which gives satisfaction by finding order, stability, and even harmony in nature (FRANK). It seems that stability through predation is considered the strategy of nature. But is not this strategy survival (PIMENTEL)? Of course, 'control' is not meant in a 'purposeful' way; it can be simply a temporary depressive effect, but it is used in the sense of 'regulation' over a long period of time. Neither a 'purpose' in predator evolution, nor an automatic 'super-organismal' regulating mechanism for a biotic community is intended.

I attempted to describe how the biotic communities have come to be what they are; by a process in which predation at all levels has had an important role. The origin and survival of the separate species and the development of any links among them would be according to genetic principles. Natural selection would operate, but the interactions (e.g. genetic feed-back) among the species would help to determine the relative selective advantage in progeny production of each species. Unstable or deleterious interactions will tend to be removed from the system. The proporties of the surviving interacting species and of the resulting processes will tend to be maintained under the same rules that produced the system. Thus, we have relatively highly stable biome systems which, however, are not immune to change. Survival or extinction is crucial to each species, but a complex biome can survive even though many specific component species (parts or links) are lost (Author).

If an animal species is evolved in order to maintain itself, this implies that group selection is involved (Royama). I did not mean to imply that a predator species has evolved 'in order to' maintain itself, and in general group selection is not suggested to be an underlying mechanism. However, a real possibility of a group sort of selection may be envisaged, for example, in a relatively closed society which exhibits strong dominance, with the sexual prerogative going to the defending leaders (Author).

To maximize energy transfer from prey (as surplus prey) to the predator, would it not be the best strategy for prey and predator to evolve a balanced supply-demand economy (Pimentel)? The surplus is that above the equilibrium density and its amount depends upon the parameters in the interaction equation. I suggest, that a non-territorial predator cannot tend to optimize its own yield. The prey will tend to evolve towards reducing the predator pressure as the predator evolves towards intensifying it. Moreover, the prey species could perfect its defence against a predator to the point of becoming a non-prey species. This tendency may be counterbalanced by the fact that the prey must face other challenges – e.g. defend itself against other natural enemies – and the total of these defense mechanisms may make too great a demand, genetically, or may even be mutually antagonistic. For generalist predators, the loss of a prey species is not too serious. It seems reasonable to suggest that a predator will develop some way to exploit its prey less severely. But genetic feedback has limits as to the effects it can produce, imposed by the evolutionary history and by the genetic adaptability possessed (Author).

We sometimes assume that an abundant species is more successful than a rare one, but the strategy of evolution does not always seem to lead in this direction. Competition between predator individuals tends to make the species increasingly efficient at finding and catching the prey, and this results in a reduced abundance of both prey and predator (assuming an interaction of a regulatory type). A predatory species will tend to displace a more abundant competitor species which is less efficient at reducing the density of the prey. The next evolutionary step for a highly efficient specific predator might conceivably be to extend its attentions to other species of prey. Predators that have a social organization or behaviour pattern which prevents an overexploitation of the prey and likewise defend the resource presumably escape the trend towards lower density (Solomon). I have the same view, except that for a specialist predator the prospective selective advantage in extending its attentions to other prey species could well be offset by a loss in its superiority as a specialist predator of its specific prey – i.e. that to which it has become so fully adapted. A predator can only maximize its degree of specialization according to the situation (AUTHOR).

Hence, predator-prey stability would depend on a balance between selection for greater searching efficiency and the resulting increased effects of interference (HASSELL). Stability due entirely to the intrinsic interaction would appear to depend on these two features being kept in balance, but the interaction can also be damped by actions other than the mutual interference between predators; for example, density dependent emigration of the prey itself can do so (Huffaker and Stinner, in press). But there is also a limit below which further reduction of the prey population and a greater perfection of those characters of the predator which produce the lowering effect offer no further selective advantage. An extreme rarity so created would lead to a greater chance of annihilation, and to increased severity of the effects of other mortality factors. On the other hand, this mechanism for lowering the prey density is also crucial in that such a predator is able to prevent other prey-specific predator species from coming in and exploiting the prey at a sufficient rate to displace it. Particularly in variable situations, however, other factors than searching power are also involved (AUTHOR).

Besides density, the distribution of the prey (unpredictable or more even) and the reactions of the predator (tendency to clumped distribution or territorial behaviour) may indeed be important features. Likewise, for some prey organisms, biomas, may be a much better measure than population numbers (AUTHOR to ZAHAVI).

Errington exaggerated the case for a lack of control by predators on his populations of muskrats and bobwhite quail. There are two main objections:
1. He said there were 'thresholds of vulnerability' between autumn and spring, and that when the populations exceeded these thresholds the 'doomed surplus' was removed by predation. But he gave no objective definition of these thresholds, and he determined them only a posteriori, once he knew how many 'surplus' animals had died. This is of course a completely circular argument.
2. He gave no criterion by which individuals of different social categories could be recognized. Although there was anecdotal information about certain individuals being attacked and forced to move on, the social differences were not quantitatively documented, the size of the surplus was not predicted, and generally the animals were not individually marked (WATSON).

Errington's hypothesis of non-control may be the result of his working mainly on species that were very abundant relative to the food requirements of the predators at the time he did his field observations. Today, with predator densities probably the same because of their territorial nature, but game populations much lower because of man's activities, the effect of predation may well be limiting on the same species and in the same area where Errington worked (TESTER).

This work was supported in part by a grant from U.S. Public Health Service, National Institutes of Health.

Proc. Adv. Study Inst. Dynamics Numbers Popul. (Oosterbeek, 1970) 344–357

Evolutionary significance of predators' response to local differences in prey density: A theoretical study

T. Royama

Forest Research Laboratory, Fredericton, New Brunswick, Canada

Abstract

Changes in the percentage predation or parasitism occur when predator or parasite species distribute themselves in accordance with the local variation of their prey or host species. To interpret these changes, we need a criterion which can be compared with the observed trend of changes. Such a criterion is deduced from an ideal situation in which the predator or parasite species tries to maximize its hunting efficiency. Any deviation from this ideal trend must be due to some counteracting factors. A model analysis is made with three examples from published field data.

Some observations have shown that the percentage predation or parasitism (i.e. the proportion of a prey population preyed upon) varies between localities with varying degrees of the prey density. But the way in which the percentage varies is somewhat complex.

Here, we have three published sets of observations (Fig. 1, 2 and 3). The first is Varley's (1941) study on a parasite, *Eurytoma curta* WALK, attacking its host, the knapweed gall-fly, *Euribia jaceana* HERING. The second is Gibb's (1958) observation on titmice of genus *Parus* (namely blue tit, *P. caeruleus* L., and coal tit, *P. ater* L.) feeding on the larvae of *Ernarmonia conicolana* (HEYL.) wintering in pine cones. The last is Holling's (1959a) study on the masked shrew, *Sorex cinereus* KERR, feeding on cocoons of the European pine sawfly, *Neodiprion sertifer* (GEOFF.).

Varley's data are shown in Fig. 1 in which the percentage parasitized is plotted on the

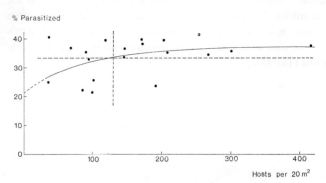

Fig. 1. *Eurytoma curta* (parasite) attacking *Euribia jaceana* (host) (after Varley, 1941). For the explanation of the solid curve and broken lines, see text.

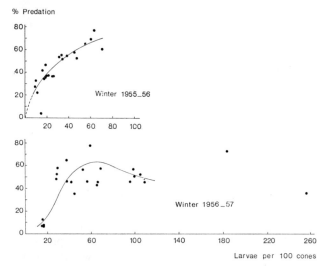

% Predation

Winter 1955_56

Winter 1956_57

Larvae per 100 cones

Fig. 2. Titmice of genus *Parus* feeding on *Ernarmonia conicolana* in pine cones (after Gibb, 1958). For the explanation of the curves fitted to the scattergram, see text.

vertical axis and the density of hosts on the horizontal axis. A variation in the percentage from low- to high-density areas is only slight, but there is an indication of an increase. Varley's interpretation is that a positive correlation, though weak, must be due to the parasites searching comparatively more intensely in areas where the host density was high, and less intensely where density was low.

Fig. 2 shows Gibb's observations. Here, the percentage predation by tits is plotted against the number of *E. conicolana* larvae per 100 cones, which is called 'intensity' and is considered to be the density with respect to available environment, i.e. pine cones. The upper figure is for the 1955-56 winter when the cone crop was exceptionally high. The lower figure is for the 1956-57 winter when the crop was unusually low so that, for the same larval intensity, the density of the larvae per acre of plantation was much less in the second winter than in the first. In both parts of the figure, the percentage predation increased from low intensity to the level of about 60 larvae per 100 cones. In the 1956-57 winter, some higher intensities than in the previous winter were involved, but the percentage predation did not increase appreciably for these high intensities and there is even an indication of a declining trend. Gibb's interpretation of the comparatively sharp increase in the percentage from low to intermediate intensities was similar to Varley's, but the interpretation of the levelling-off towards higher intensities was unique. Gibb (1962) postulated that the tits tended to stop tapping at a cone when an 'expected number' of larvae had been extracted from the cone, since the birds could not know how many larvae remained 'undiscovered' in the cone.

Holling's calculated curve is shown in Fig. 3. Holling took a direct measurement of the density of shrews and found that the density was high in areas where the cocoon density was high, but that at higher cocoon densities the shrew population levelled off. Holling also found that the number of cocoons collected by each shrew increased as the cocoon density increased, but again levelled off. Consequently, the precentage predation (Fig. 3)

345

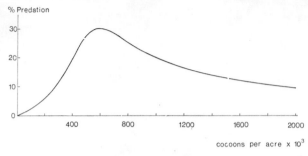

Fig. 3. *Sorex cinereus* feeding on *Neodiprion sertifer* (after Holling, 1959a).

increased to a maximum at localities with an intermediate cocoon density but began to decrease towards higher-density localities.

These three authors each interpreted their data as the predators distributing themselves, or allocating their hunting effort, in accordance with the local variation of the prey population. However, none of the postulates provides a single explanation of why the percentage predation in these observations varied in such specific patterns.

Formulation of the theory

It is my intention here to propose a general theory by which these observations become intelligible on the basis of an hypothesis developed primarily in my study of the great tit, *Parus major* L., (Royama, 1970). A brief account of the hypothesis is given below.

What is important from the predators' point of view is not the density of prey but rather the actual amount of prey that each predator can collect for a given time in a given hunting station. I call this amount the 'profitability' of a hunting station. The profitability, however, is not linearly related to the density of prey.

Let X be the density of a prey species at a given hunting station (Fig. 4, horizontal axis), and n the number of prey individuals taken by Y predators per unit area for time interval t (vertical axis). Let us assume here that in each station the prey density X is kept constant at a specific level, say X_A at station A, throughout the predation-period t. Let us also assume that Y and t are the same for all stations concerned in the figure.

Under these circumstances, (1) a predator can collect more prey at stations where the prey density is high than where it is low, and (2) the total number of prey taken at a given station is a linear function of the predator density. Here, the effect of social interaction among predators is not considered.

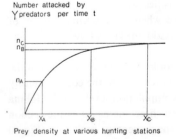

Fig. 4. Hypothetical relationship of predation to prey density in which X is not influenced by predation and Y and t are the same for all stations.

346

However, owing to a limited capacity of hunting and feeding by each predator, n will not increase indefinitely as X increases but will, sooner or later, level off. The point has been stressed by various authors (e.g. Ivlev, 1955; Holling, 1959b) and much supporting evidence has been reported. This curvilinear relationship between n and X is the starting point of my deduction.

Differences in profitability

Now, as the profitability is n/Yt by definition, the relationship between this factor and X is again represented by the curve in Fig. 4 since both Y and t are fixed for all stations concerned. Then, the difference in the profitability between stations A and B is large, whereas that between B and C is so small that it is not important from the predators' point of view.

This suggests that it will be more advantageous for the predators to choose station B rather than A, but not particularly advantageous to choose C rather than B. Consequently, if a predator tries to feed more efficiently within its capacity for movement and its ability to assess the profitability, we would expect the predator density Y to increase from low- to high-density prey stations, but no appreciable increase towards higher-density prey stations would be expected.

The above model assumes that the prey density at each hunting station remains constant during the hunting period t. This only holds, however, (1) when the prey population is replenished as fast as it is reduced by predation during t, or (2) when t is so short that a reduction in the prey population by predation can be neglected. These conditions are practically satisfied in the titmice predation on caterpillars during the breeding season. In the three examples cited earlier, however, neither condition is satisfied; the prey were not replenished during t, nor was the reduction during t negligible.

Let us assume a condition in which a prey population is subject to reduction by predation. The effect of a reduction in the prey population upon the rate of predation is taken into account in Fig. 5. Here, the number of prey taken per unit area is symbolized by z (to distinguish it from n in the first model) and is shown as a function of both the initial prey density, x_0, and the predator-hour, Yt.

Let us first look at the z-x_0 relationship in this figure. For a given value of Yt, z increases as x_0 increases but gradually levels off. This is because, as already pointed out in the first

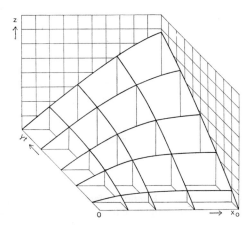

Fig. 5. Hypothetical relationship between z, Yt, and x_0 in which the prey density is subject to decrease by predation. x_0 = initial prey density; Yt = predator-hour; z = number taken per unit area.

347

model, the feeding capacity of each predator is limited. Unlike the n-Yt relationship in the first model, however, the z-Yt relationship is exponential, not linear; because the rate of predation progressively diminishes as an increase in the predator-hour, Yt, reduces the prey density. This idea had already been incorporated in the classical models proposed by Lotka (1925), Volterra (1926), and Nicholson and Bailey (1935) but has been entirely neglected in more recent models. The difference between the classical models and mine is that the former assumed a linear relationship between z and x_o, whereas in mine a curvelinear relationship is assumed.

Hunting surface

The surface in this figure, which I call a 'hunting surface', is calculated by combining Ivlev's (1955) equation for a curvilinear relationship between n and X with a generalized Nicholson and Bailey (1935) differential equation which yields an exponential relationship between z and Yt. The detailed process for the derivation of the surface in Fig. 5 is given in the appendix.

In Fig. 6, two stations A and B are assumed of an equal size and with initial prey densities of x_{o_A} and x_{o_B} respectively. If the distribution of the predator-hour between these two stations is Y_At and Y_Bt, the corresponding numbers of prey taken per unit area in stations A and B are z_A and z_B respectively.

Then the profitabilities of stations A and B are, by definition, z_A/Y_At and z_B/Y_Bt which are clearly tan α_A and tan α_B respectively. Thus, if $\alpha_A < \alpha_B$, a predator in station A can collect less prey than one in station B. Then, a predator capable of assessing the profitability of both stations would move into station B to increase its share. If, however, too many predators moved into station B, their share may decrease again. Then a reverse flow of predators would take place. Hence, there must be an equilibrium at which $\alpha_A = \alpha_B$. This suggests that each individual in both stations receives an equal share at the equilibrium distribution of the predator-hour.

The above situation can be expanded to one in which more than two stations are involved. But the equilibrium distribution of the predator-hour over the stations involved must again exist. This ideal distribution of the predator-hour, Yt, can be obtained graphically in Fig. 7.

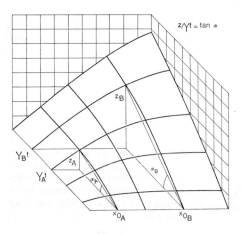

Fig. 6. Hunting surface as in Fig. 5 (for explanation see text).

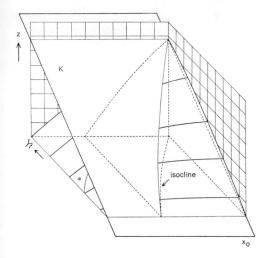

Fig. 7. A graphical method to obtain an isocline of profitability on all stations.

Isocline of profitability

Suppose there is a plane K which involves the x_o-axis; K's angle to the x_o-Yt plane being α. Then K intersects the hunting surface. The projection of the intersect onto the x_o-Yt plane forms an isocline of profitability along which all of the z/Yt values are equal to tan α. This isocline is therefore an ideal distribution of the predator-hour, Yt, over the stations concerned. The projection of the intersect on the z–x_o plane gives the relationship between the number of prey taken per unit area and the initial density of prey in each station when the predator-hour is ideally distributed.

In order to make my theoretical figure comparable with the data by Varley, Gibb, and Holling, the percentage predation, (i.e. 100 z/x_o instead of z), is plotted against x_o and Yt in Fig. 8. For any fixed value of Yt, the percentage predation is a decreasing function of the initial prey density. Further, the pattern of decrease changes as the Yt-value changes in somewhat complex way. Fig. 9 shows one example of the trend of the percentage preda-

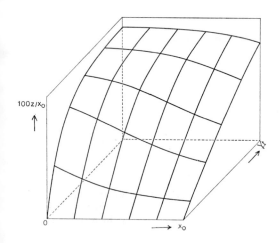

Fig. 8. As dig. 5 but with percentage predation on the vertical axis. 100 z/x_o = % taken.

349

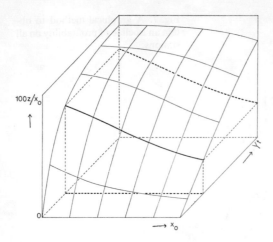

Fig. 9. An example of the change in percentage predation with a flat response by predators.

tion when the predators concerned do not respond to the local variation in prey density, so that the predator-hours are equally allocated between all the stations concerned. For this 'flat response' by the predators, the percentage predation is shown by the $100\ z/x_o$ coordinates on the constant Yt projected on the $100\ z/x_o$–x_o plane.

In Fig. 10, however, the predators' response is an ideal one. The isocline of profitability obtained in Fig. 8 is transferred to this x_o–Yt plane to read its $100\ z/x_o$ coordinates, the projection of which onto the $100\ z/x_o$–x_o plane gives changes in the percentage predation in accordance with changes in the initial prey density. Here, unlike the example in Fig. 9, the percentage predation is an increasing function of the initial prey density.

Fig. 11 repeats the relationships obtained in the last two figures, but the x_o–Yt and the $100\ z/x_o$–x_o planes are separated. The left-hand pair is for the flat response, and the right-hand one for the ideal response. It is noticeable that, in the ideal response, the curve for the percentage predation intersects the x_o–axis well above the origin of coordinates. This suggests that, in those stations in which the prey density is lower than the intersect, the profitability can never be larger than in those stations above the intersect no matter how low the predator-hour is. Consequently, if a predator spends any time in these low-density

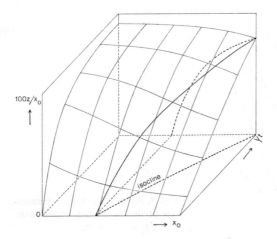

Fig. 10 An example of the change in percentage predation with an ideal response by predators.

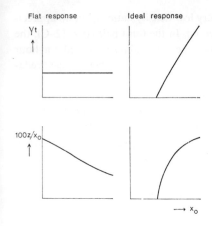

Fig. 11. Separate presentation of $Yt-x_0$ and 100 z/x_0-x_0 relationships derived from Fig. 9 and 10.

stations, it loses its share. Thus, ideally no predator should spend its time hunting in these stations.

Deviations from ideal responses

Practically, however, the ideal response will never be attained simply because predators will be unable to know the level of profitability of a station without sampling. This suggests that in any observed data some degrees of deviation should be expected. Particularly, there must always be some predator-hours observed in low-density stations. In other words, an observed relationship between x_0 and Yt should be an intermediate one between the flat and the ideal responses.

Various degrees of response in relation to the ideal response are assumed in Fig. 12. The first pair from the left (Fig. 12–A) shows a weak but positive response; its consequence on the percentage predation is a flat one. In the second pair (Fig. 12–B), the response becomes more strongly positive and the percentage curve begins to show an increasing trend. The

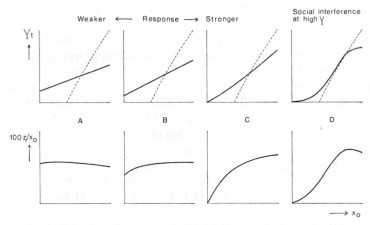

Fig. 12. As for Fig. 11 but with varying degrees between the flat and ideal (dashed line) predator responses.

351

increasing trend, however, is noticeable only for very low-density stations, but no appreciable increase towards high-density stations is observed. In the third pair (Fig. 12–C), the response is much stronger and closer to the ideal isocline. Also, almost no predator-hour is spent in stations where the prey density is extremely low. Hence, the percentage predation at such low-density stations is almost nil.

Now, my speculation is that differences between a weaker and a stronger response are a reflection of the evolutionary level of the predator species. Namely, if the predator species concerned has a limited capacity of movement and a less advanced central nervous system, its efficiency of response will be low. Whereas, if it is a highly advanced form, the response by the predator species will be more efficient, i.e. its response curve will be closer to the isocline than that of a less advanced form.

Interactions among predators

The last pair of figures (Fig. 12–D) represents a slightly more complex situation in which the response is very strong, but the curve deviates from the isocline towards very high predator densities. Some predator species have developed a tendency to maintain a certain minumum distance between individuals and, in an overcrowded state, fighting or physiological stress become apparent, which would result in a lower feeding efficiency. Hence, the distribution of individuals in such species could be sigmoid, levelling off towards high-density stations. A resulting percentage curve has a peak at intermediate-density stations.

The last three pairs of figures (Fig. 12–B, C, D) seem to correspond well to the observed data of Varley, Gibb, and Holling cited at the beginning of this paper. First, Varley's chalcid parasite must have responded weakly to the local variation of the host density, because the parasite's mobility and its ability to assess the profitability must be rather limited. Hence, the comparison of Varley's data with one of my theoretical figures (Fig. 12–B) seems appropriate. The fitting of this type of curve is justified in Fig. 1. The horizontal broken line is drawn at the average percentage, and the vertical broken line divides the scattered dots roughly into equal numbers. It is seen that more of the dots come below the average on the left-hand side of the vertical broken line than on the right-hand side; the difference is statistically significant at 5% level (tested by 2×2 table). Thus, a curvilinear relationship as suggested by the solid curve (fitted by eye) is justified.

In Fig. 2, a curve similar to Fig. 12–C fits Gibb's data for the first winter reasonably well. This suggests that the tits showed a strong response to the variation in the larval intensity in pine cones. As mentioned earlier, the cone crop in the first winter was exceptionally high so that the number of birds per cone was low, and the competition among the tits around a cone must have been low. Thus the adoption of Fig. 12–C is justified. In the second winter, however, the cone crop was unusually low so that competition among the birds around a cone must have been high. Thus Fig. 12–D involving social interaction, rather than Fig. 12–C, is suggested for the interpretation of the second-winter data (the bottom graph in Fig. 2). This again seems reasonable.

Now, it is reasonable to think that shrews have a strong tendency to avoid overcrowding, perhaps because they are potentially aggressive, which might induce physiological stress. Thus, the resemblance between Holling's curve in Fig. 3 and Fig. 12–D may not be coincidental.

My hypothesis suggests that variation in the pattern of percentage predation, as revealed by the three examples, cited, must have an evolutionary significance. There is, on the one hand, a selection to maximize the hunting efficiency of a predator by responding to a variation in the profitability of hunting stations but, on the other hand, there are practical difficulties in the attainment of the ideal, because of the limited capacity of the predator and also because of a counteraction from, say, social interactions among predators. Observations or experiments designed to test this suggestion are now needed.

Appendix. Derivation of the hunting surface in Fig. 5

Suppose there are Y predators and x prey per unit area, and each predator consumes the prey at the rate of f(x) per unit time (where f is a positive function of x). If there is no social interference or facilitation among the predators, and if the prey population is kept constant at $x = X$ during the hunting period t (i.e. the prey population is replenished as fast as it is depleted), then the number of prey taken (n) per unit area, by Y predators for time interval t, will be

$$n = f(X)Yt \tag{1}$$

If, however, the prey population is not replenished and so is only subject to decrease by predation, Eq. 1 holds only for a very short time interval, Δt. Hence, when the prey density at this instant is x, the correspondingly small number of prey taken (Δn) will be

$$\Delta n = f(x)\, Y\Delta t \tag{2}$$

and for $\Delta t \to O$ we have

$$dn/dt = f(x)\, Y \tag{3}$$

where dn/dt is positive. If, however, the rate of reduction in x, i.e. dx/dt, is considered, it is negative but its absolute value must be equal to that of dn/dt because the prey population is reduced as much as it is consumed. So we have

$$dx/dt = -f(x)\, Y \tag{4}$$

Let x_0 be the initial prey density at $t = O$, and the density is depleted to x after t. Then, integrating Eq. 4, we have

$$\int_{x_0}^{x} dx/f(x) = -Y\int_{o}^{t} dt \tag{5}$$

$$= -Yt \tag{6}$$

If we assume that f(x) is a linear function of x, i.e.

$$f(x) = ax \tag{7}$$

where a is a positive constant, then from Eq. 6 we have

$$\ln(x/x_o) = -aYt \tag{8}$$

and this can be solved with respect to $z = x_o - x$ as below,

$$z = x_o\,(1 - e^{-aYt}) \tag{9}$$

This generates the familiar Nicholson-Bailey (1935) 'Competition curve'.

353

Now, the assumption of $f(x) = ax$ is not reasonable as it contradicts some fundamental attributes of living beings such as the limited capacity of feeding and the time-limited activities. However, various observations have shown (see in the text) that $f(x)$ is a curvilinear function of x as shown in Fig. 4. Ivlev's (1955) function given below has proved to describe many such observed relationships reasonably well, i.e.

$$f(x) = b(1-e^{-ax}) \tag{10}$$

where a and b are positive constants. Substituting the right-hand side of Eq. 10 for $f(x)$ in Eq. 6, we have

$$\int_{x_0}^{x} dx/b(1-e^{-ax}) = -Yt \tag{11}$$

which yields

$$z = -(1/a)\ln\{(1-e^{-ax_0})e^{-abYt} + e^{-ax_0}\} \tag{12}$$

The hunting surface in Fig. 5 is generated by Eq. 12, in which both a and b are conveniently assumed to be unity. This convenient assumption does not influence the line of my argument, as the argument is concerned only with a general trend rather than with a strict quantitative comparison with observed data.

Equation 12 is, however, limited to predation and does not include parasitism. For those parasites which do not discriminate between parasitized and unparasitized hosts, the relationship in Eq. 1 holds for any t as there is no decrease in the host population during t. However, the probability of discovery of the unparasitised hosts diminishes as t increases. Let $P\{O\}$ be the probability of each host receiving no parasite eggs. Then the probability of a host receiving at least one parasite egg is $1 - P\{O\}$. If the total number of hosts present per unit area is X (this value is fixed during t as already pointed out), then the number of hosts parasitized per unit area, i.e. z, will be

$$z = X(1-P\{O\}) \tag{13}$$

Let us assume, conveniently, that the distribution of parasite eggs over hosts in each locality approximately follows the Poisson series. Then $P\{O\} = e^{-m}$ where m is the mean number of parasite eggs per host. As there are X hosts available per unit area, and the number of hosts attacked by Y parasites is n, m is equal to n/X. In the meantime, n is estimated by Eq. 1. So $P\{O\} = e^{-f(X)Yt/X}$. Substituting this relationship in Eq. 13, we have

$$z = X(1-e^{-f(X)Yt/X}) \tag{14}$$

If we use Ivlev's function for $f(X)$, we get

$$z = X(1-e^{-b(1-e^{-aX})Yt/X}) \tag{15}$$

Although Eq. 15 and 12 have different forms as shown above, they generate very similar surfaces. In my present argument, in which a general trend only is considered, the differences between Eq. 15 and 12 can be ignored.

References

Gibb J. A., 1958. Predation by tits and squirrels on the eucosmid *Ernarmonia conicolana* (HEYL). *J. Anim. Ecol.* 27: 375–396.

Gibb, J. A., 1962. L. Tinbergen's hypothesis of the role of specific search images. *Ibis* 104: 106–111.

Holling, C. S., 1959a. The components of predation as revealed by a study of small mammal predation of the European pine sawfly. *Can. Ent.* 91: 293–320.

Holling, C. S., 1959b. Some characteristics of simple types of predation and parasitism. *Can. Ent.* 91: 385–398.

Ivlev, V. S., 1955. Experimental Ecology of the Feeding of Fishes (English translation by D. Scott, 1961). Yale Univ. Press, New Haven.

Lotka, A. J., 1925. Elements of Physical Biology. Williams & Wilkins, Baltimore.

Nicholson, A. J. & V. A. Bailey, 1935. The balance of animal populations. Part 1. *Proc. Zool. Soc. Lond.* 1935, Part 3: 551–598.

Royama, T., 1970. Factors governing the hunting behaviour and selection of food by the great tit (*Parus major* L.). *J. Anim. Ecol.* 39: 619–668.

Varley, G. C., 1941. On the search for hosts and the egg distribution of some chalcid parasites of the knapweed gall-fly. *Parasitology* 33: 47–66.

Volterra, V., 1926. Variazioni e fluttuazioni del numero d'individui in specie animali conveiventi. *Mem. R. Accad. naz. Lincei, Ser. VI*, Vol. 2 (English translation in R. N. Chapman, 1931. Animal Ecology, p. 409–448. McGraw-Hill, NY and London).

Discussion

Participants: Royama (Author), Bakker (K.), Connell, Frank, Gradwell, Hancock, Hassell, Huffaker, Jenkins, Kuenen, Lawton, Turnock, Voûte, Wolda, Zahavi and Zwölfer

I support the suggestion that parasites spend very little time at low host densities, and strongly aggregate where the host density is high and where there is much social interference. *Nemeritis* does exactly like this when presented with a range of host densities. The result is an increase in percent parasitism with an increase in host densities of a form similar to that predicted by the model (these Proceedings) (HASSELL). This idea was also supported by ZWÖLFER: A. P. Arthur's work on *Itoplectus conquisitor*, by ZAHAVI: G. Smith's work on the Great Tit, by FRANK: work on the small weasel, and by HANCOCK: work on the oystercatcher feeding on cockles (these Proceedings).

The example of the tits feeding on *Ernarmonia conicolana* in cones may not be entirely comparable with the others, since the *conicolana* density was expressed as 'density per 100 cones'. The relationship shows within a year, but may not show between years when the cone crop is very different from year to year. (BAKKER). Certainly, 'intensity' and 'density' are not normally comparable to each other. However, if a predator is hunting only within the available environment of its prey, the argument will still hold since it is the profitability of available environment, rather than that of locality, which is important for the predator. In my example of tits, it was assumed that the available environment of the *conicolana* larvae, i.e. pine cone, is sufficiently conspicuous to the birds, and also that the birds can travel from cone to cone without losing much time in searching for the larvae in pine-cones. Under these circumstances, the tits are hunting practically within the available environment.

Incidentally, according to Varley, *E. jaceana* (host) occurs in the flower-head of knapweed (*Centaurea nemoralis* JORD.). But the number of host larvae per flower-head did not appreciably vary from locality to locality. Hence, it is the density of the larvae per locality, rather than intensity, which is of prime importance to the parasites (AUTHOR).

In his work on predation by the great tit on pine-forest insects, L. Tinbergen found a relationship between the percentage predation and prey density similar to the one Holling found in his shrews. Tinbergen's explanation, however, is not so much that there is a redistribution of predators over a variety of prey densities but rather that a searching image has to be formed at lower densities, and that at high prey densities the percentage drops because the tits learned to keep their diet varied. If such an explanation is correct, how would this affect the model (WOLDA)? What L. Tinbergen has shown is a pattern in the percentage predation by tits similar to that by the masked shrew observed by Holling. Tinbergen's theory of search images is, however, no more than one tentative and convenient explanation for this particular pattern. For various reasons given in my paper of 1970 (published in the *Journal of Animal Ecology*), I am reluctant to accept Tinbergen's idea, and the model proposed here is an alternative to the search image theory (AUTHOR).

An increase in the impact of the predator (Yt) can be achieved by more predators spending the same time hunting, or by the same predator spending more time hunting, (or a combination of both). The two extreme cases have biologically quite different implications (LAWTON). Indeed, if there is a social interaction among predators, factor Y and t are not complementary to each other. Under these circumstances, the shape of the hunting surface (as shown in Fig. 5) will change. This, in turn, influences the shape and position of the isocline. However, if we assume that animals in nature tend to avoid such an intense interaction (since it lowers the profitability), the simple model given here may still serve its purpose (AUTHOR).

The sigmoid relationship of Yt over x_0 at high levels of predators response is attributed to social interference. This explanation may well be applicable to breeding species with territorial behavior, but the same relationship has been demonstrated for non-breeding flocks of birds preying on larch sawfly (Buckner and Turnock, 1963). In such cases the upper asymptote would appear to be related to the number of birds close enough to respond to the food source (TURNOCK). I do not agree. If there is no counter force, such as social interference, the best strategy for the birds is to respond to the local variation in the food source as suggested by the isocline, or as close as they can. In that case there is no reason for the response curve to be sigmoid (AUTHOR).

Have you been able to test your model against your own data on the feeding of tits? The model may describe the best strategy to be adopted by a single predator; however, in the tits the breeding territories are established before the food for the brood becomes available. In this case, it seems probably that the population as a whole cannot respond to local abundances of prey which may be at a distance from many of the territories and thus not sampled by all the birds (GRADWELL). Similar objections were raised by VOûTE, and by HUFFAKER who suggested that the size of territories may perhaps be reshaped in order to agree better with local abundances of prey.

All these models embody the idea that predators respond only in relation to food – either availability of food, or interference with other predators while searching for food. But predators also behave in response to other factors beside food. The risk of death from physical factors such as weather, or from enemies, may greatly modify where they feed. The presence or absence of shelter may override the effects of degree of profitability of food alone. Thus local differences in prey density may not be equally profitable, if risk of death differs parallel with food profitability (CONNELL). Comparable objections were raised by KUENEN, and by JENKINS who refered to the work on the red grouse (in these Proceedings). I admit that the predators' distribution is not only determined by their response to the profitability of an area with respect to food, but also by their response to factors other than food. Indeed, social interference, which is considered in Fig. 12 D, is one such factor. If any factors other than food (territoriality, natural enemies, shelter, or what have you) are involved in an observed system, the percentage predation curve is bound to deviate from the one corresponding to the isocline; i.e. from an ideal pattern of the predators' distribution, expected as the best strategy for each predator if food is the only factor involved. I tried to show with the three examples that those factors, other than food, can be guessed at both by examining the pattern of deviations from the ideal response and by taking into consideration the mode of life of the species concerned. The model is not built for the purpose of drawing a final conclusion in terms of an agreement with the observation – which is of course a bold attempt. But I hope that a careful examination of disagreements between the ideal (a model) and the observed may provide some hints in future studies (AUTHOR).

Proc. Adv. Study Inst. Dynamics Numbers Popul. (Oosterbeek, 1970) 358–365

Simple elementary models in population dynamics

F. S. Andersen

Statens Skadedyrlaboratorium, Lyngby, Denmark

Abstract

Inspired by Hassell and Varley's model relating log 'area of discovery' of insect parasites to log of their density the author proposes a simpler model describing the efficiency and the fecundity as a linear function of the square root of the density. A different linear model involving the square root of the density is proposed for the granary weevil (*Sitophilus*). The models are deduced from simple and reasonable differential equations involving time and resting on assumptions on the physiology and behaviour of the insects.

Efficiency of simple models

Everybody will agree that the success of Galileo, Newton and Mendel was partly due to the fact that they used very simple mathematical models from which more complicated models could be deduced.

I am convinced that the use of mathematical models in population dynamics will be successful only if we deduce them from simple elementary models. Like Galileo, Newton and Mendel, we will have to derive these elementary models from very simplified experiments. The elementary models must be general in the sense that they have a wide application, but we can not expect generality from models derived from observations in the field where many special factors intervene.

I have suggested two such simple elementary models for the dependence of mortality and fecundity on density (Andersen 1957, 1960, and 1965):
1. If the animals interfere with one another, e.g. by fighting, we may expect the effect of this interference to be proportional to the number of animals interfering, that is to the number of animals per unit area. The percentage mortality and the number of eggs per female may therefore be expected to be linearly related to the density (N): $y = a - bN$. Also, the sex ratio may be linearly related to the density in some cases (Andersen, 1961).
2. If the animals do not interfere with one another but scramble peacefully for some requisite (e.g. food or oviposition sites), we may expect the percentage mortality and the number of eggs per female to be proportional to the amount of the requisite per animal and, therefore, linearly related to the reciprocal of the density (1/N): $y = a + b/N$.

Square root models

Until recently I thought these two models were exhaustive. In cases such as *Sitophilus*, where the graphs of fecundity plotted against density and its reciprocal were both curved,

I thought this was due to interference of the two models (Andersen, 1957, p. 18). I now know that this is not the case and that it is necessary to introduce two more models, namely a linear dependence of the total number of eggs or the number of eggs per female on the square root of the density.

So far I have found these models applicable only to fecundity. I got the idea for these models from the very interesting paper of Hassell and Varley (1969). They plot log 'area of discovery' of various parasites against log density of the parasite (p). I find that this is a weak test of models because almost anything looks like a straight line when log is plotted against log. When trying to find a stronger test, I noticed that the slope of the regression (b) was, in some cases, near to –0.5; Hassell and Varley use this figure in some of their simulations. I therefore decided to test the antilog of the equation of Hassell and Varley. Assuming that $b = -0.5$ their equation (5) becomes: $\ln (u_1/u) = a + b \sqrt{p}$, where u_1 is the total number of hosts and u the number of hosts not attacked. I found this equation satisfied by the experiments with *Dahlbominus* (Burnett, 1956) (cf. Fig. 1, a negative) and *Encarsia* (Burnett, 1958) (cf. Fig. 2, a negative), and not contradicted by experiments with *Cryptus* (Ullyett, 1949b) (cf. Fig. 3, a approximately zero; variance large). Also the figures for *Cyzenis*, kindly conveyed to me by Dr Hassell, could agree with the equation if some predator competed with *Operophtera* in eating the eggs of the parasite, especially in 1951, 1955, 1957, and 1960, and considering the fact that the percentage error of a parasite density of 0.1 is large; this density is equal to the lower limit of observation (cf. Fig. 4. Parasite density is in doubt for the point in brackets). However, the experiments with *Chelonus* (Ullyett, 1949a) fitted the equation $\ln(u_1/u) = ap - bp^2$; this is tested for linearity in Fig. 5 in the form $\ln (u_1/u)/p = a - bp$. The figures for *Nemeritis* (Huffaker and Kennett, 1969) were not available to me. These were all the cases studied by Hassell and Varley (1969).

That the 'area of discovery' may be constant is shown by the experiments of Wylie (1965) with *Nasonia* and 10 hosts, which is fitted by the equation $\ln(u_1/u) = bp$ (cf. Fig. 6).

Now, if the number of hosts is not too small (above 30), and the eggs or equal-sized clutches of eggs are distributed at random among the hosts, then $\ln(u_1/u)$ is equal to the mean number of eggs per host. In most of the experiments tested by Hassell and Varley (1969) the total number of eggs was known, and this is proportional to the mean number of eggs per host, as the number of hosts was kept constant in these experiments. I therefore subjected the figures to the more sensitive test by plotting the total number of eggs (y) against $\sqrt{p}$ and expected the straight line relationship $y = a + b\sqrt{p}$. In *Dahlbominus* (Burnett, 1956) the two straight lines (below and above 17.5 °C) were perfect. In *Encarsia* (Burnett, 1958) the graphs were slightly S-shaped and in *Cryptus* (Ullyett, 1949b) the graph seems slightly curved. These deviations may be partly due to experimental errors accentuated by the sensitive test. However, in *Chelonus* (Ullyett, 1949a) the number of eggs per female (z) did not deviate too much from the line $z = a - bp$, the total number of eggs approximating the parabola $pz = ap - bp^2$.

The model containing the square root of the density was also tested on data from the experiments by Richards (1947) with *Sitophilus* (*Calandra*) *granarius*. The grain pests, spending the whole of their immature life inside one kernel, are analogous to parasites, the kernels being analogous to the hosts. However, the grain was also the universe of the beetles, and their density was therefore defined as the number of beetles per grain (p/u_1). Using the figures from Richards' table XXX (1947, p. 34) I found that the number of

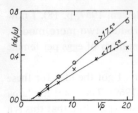

Fig. 1. *Dahlbominus fuscipennis*. Abscissa: the square root of the parasite density ($\sqrt{p}$). Ordinate: natural logarithm of the ratio of the total number of hosts to the number of hosts not attacked ($\ln(u_1/u)$) at temperature (1) below 17.5 °C (x and lower line) and (2) above 17.5 °C (o and upper line). Data from Burnett (1956).

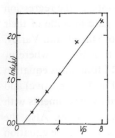

Fig. 2. *Encarsia formosa*. Co-ordinates as Fig. 1. Data from Burnett's (1958) experiments with equal spacing of hosts.

Fig. 3. *Cryptus inornatus*. Co-ordinates as Fig. 1. Data from Ullyet (1949b).

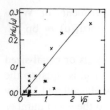

Fig. 4. *Cyzenis albicans*. Co-ordinates as Fig. 1. Data kindly conveyed to me by Dr M. P. Hassell (cf. Hassell and Varley, 1969).

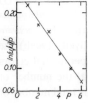

Fig. 5. *Chelonus texanus*. Abscissa: parasite density (p). Ordinate: natural logarithm of the ratio of the total number of hosts to the number of hosts not attacked, divided by the number of parasites (ln $(u_1/u)/p$ equal to 'area of discovery'. Data from Ullyett (1949a).

Fig. 6. *Nasonia vitripennis*. Abscissa: parasite density (p). Ordinate: natural logarithm of the ratio of the total number of hosts to the number of hosts not attacked ($\ln(u_1/u)$). Data from Wylie (1965).

360

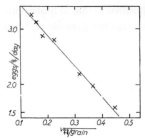

Fig. 7. *Sitophilus (Calandra) granarius*. Abscissa: square root of the number of beetles (♀♀) per kernel. Ordinate: number of eggs per female per day. Data from Richards (1947).

Fig. 8. *Sitophilus (Calandra) granarius*. Abscissa: mean number of eggs per kernel in 10 days calculated from the line fitted by eye in Fig. 7 ($y = 3.947 - 5.38 \sqrt{p/u_1}$) multiplied by 10 (days) and by the number of females (p) and divided by the total number of kernels (u_1). Ordinate: natural logarithm of the ratio between the total number of kernels and the number of kernels not infested. Data from Richards (1947).

eggs per female per 10 days (y) could be fitted by eye to a line $y = 39.47 - 53.8 \sqrt{p/u_1}$ (cf. Fig. 7). Multiplying y by the number of parasites (p) we get the total number of eggs, and dividing this total by the number of kernels (u_1) we get the mean number of eggs per kernel (host): eggs/u_1 = (p/u_1) $(39.47-53.8 \sqrt{p/u_1})$. Plotting $\ln(u_1/u)$ against eggs/u_1 (u being the number of non-infested kernels), we get a straight line through the origin and with a slope of 45° (cf. Fig. 8).

In this case the number of eggs per female was linearly related to the square root of the density. In *Dahlbominus* the total number of eggs was linearly related to the square root of the density (the number of eggs per female related to the reciprocal of the square root of the density). 1 think these two models will prove equally applicable to parasites as the linear relation to the density and its reciprocal has proved to other animals.

Deduction of the square root models

The models may be derived from simple and reasonable differential equations involving time. In the case of *Dahlbominus, Encarsia, Cryptus,* and *Cyzenis* we assume that the females scramble peacefully for oviposition sites and that oviposition is inhibited by the perception of eggs already laid. The instantaneous rate of increase in the number of eggs per parasite is therefore inversely proportional to the total number of eggs laid (= the number of parasites (p) multiplied by the number of eggs per parasite (x)) or to some linear function if it:

$dx/dt = c/(px + k)$

leading to

$(px + k) d (px + k) = cpdt$

and by integrating, as x = o at t = o,

$(px + k)^2 = 2cpt$

and

$px = \sqrt{2ct} \cdot \sqrt{p} - k$

However, if the number of hosts is constant and not too small, and the eggs or equal-sized clutches are distributed at random in them, then ln (u_1/u) is proportional to px and therefore linearly related to $\sqrt{p}$, as shown in Fig. 1–4.

In the case of *Chelonus* we assume that the inhibition of oviposition is due to mutual interference. The instantaneous rate of increase in the number of eggs per parasite is therefore linearly related to the number of parasites

$$dx/dt = c - kp$$

leading to

$$x = ct - ktp$$

and, by the above reasoning, to

$$\ln(u_1/u)/p = a - bp$$

as shown in Fig. 5.

In *Nasonia* the number of eggs per parasite is independent of density leading to

$$\ln(u_1/u) = bp \text{ (cf. Fig. 6).}$$

In the case of *Sitophilus* we assume that (1) the higher the frequency of meeting another weevil, the more the female will move to find a less crowded place and the less eggs it will lay, but also that (2) the more the oviposition has already been suppressed, the stronger will be the stimulus necessary to accomplish a further reduction in oviposition and the less will be the effect of meeting another weevil. The suppression of oviposition can be expressed as the difference between the potential number of eggs per female (x_0 = the number of eggs laid per unit time by an isolated female in a lot of grain) and the actual number of eggs per female per unit time (x). The instantaneous rate of increase in the number of eggs per female per unit time will therefore be directly proportional to the number of females (p) according to assumption (1), and inversely proportional to suppression of oviposition ($x_0 - x$) according to assumption (2):

$$dx/dt = - bp/(x_0 - x)$$

leading to

$$(x_0 - x)^2 = 2bpt$$

and

$$x = x_0 - \sqrt{2bt} \cdot \sqrt{p}$$

i.e. the number of eggs/female/unit time is linearly related to $\sqrt{p}$ as shown in Fig. 7.

The above differential equations are based on elements of the physiology and behaviour of parasites. Most of these elements are hypothetical and it remains to be seen if they can be verified, as was the case with the sleep of the flour moths (Andersen, 1965 and 1968).

References

Andersen, F. S., 1957. The effect of density on the birth and death rate. *A. Rep. St. Skadedyrlab.* 1954–1955: 56–78.

Andersen, F. S., 1960. Competition in populations consisting of one age group. *Biometrics* 16: 19–27.

Andersen, F. S., 1961. Effect of density on animal sex ratio. *Oikos* 12: 1–16.

Andersen, F. S., 1965. Simple population models and their application to the formation of complex models. *Proc. XII. Int. Congr. Ent. (London 1964)* 620–622.

Andersen, F. S., 1968. Sleep in moths and its dependence on the frequency of stimulation in *Anagasta kuehniella. Opusc. Ent.* 33: 15–24.

Burnett, T., 1956. Effect of natural temperatures on oviposition of various numbers of an insect parasite (Hymenoptera, Chalcididae, Tenthredinidae) *Ann. ent. Soc. Am.* 49: 55–59.

Burnett, T., 1958. Effect of host distribution on the reproduction of *Encarsia formosa* GAHAN (Hymenoptera: Chalcidoidea). *Can. Ent.* 90: 179–191.

Hassell, M. P. & G. C. Varley, 1969. New inductive population model for insect parasites and its bearing on biological control. *Nature* 223: 1133–1137.

Huffaker, C. B. & C. E. Kennett, 1969. Some aspects of assessing efficiency of natural ennemies. *Can. Ent.* 101: 425–447.

Richards, O. W., 1947. Observations on grain-weevils, *Calandra* (Col., Curculionidae). I. General biology and oviposition. *Proc. Zool. Soc.* 117: 1–43.

Ullyett, G. C., 1949a. Distribution of progeny by *Chelonus texanus* CRESS. (Hymenoptera: Braconidae) *Can. Ent.* 81: 25–44.

Ullyett, G. C., 1949b. Distribution of progeny by *Cryptus inornatus* PRATT (Hymenoptera: Ichneumonidae). *Can. Ent.* 81: 285–299.

Wylie, H. G., 1965. Some factors that reduce the reproductive rate of *Nasonia vitripennis* (WALK.) at high adult population densities. *Can. Ent.* 97: 970–977.

Discussion

Participants: Andersen (Author), van Biezen, Hassell, Rabinovich, Royama, Watt and Wolda

You said that more complicated models can be derived from the highly simplified models given. This probably means that it is hoped that eventually a model may be obtained which describes what happens in nature. But how are the complications to be entered in the simple models and how can we test the hypothesis that these simple models are suitable as a basis for such complex models (WOLDA)? If the behavioural assumptions could be verified, the elementary models could form a sound basis for deduction of field models, and this deduction will be easier the simpler the models are (AUTHOR).

Why are the linear models correct (VAN BIEZEN)? The linear models are good because they are simple. One should always prefer the simplest fitting model. Had Galileo plotted log s against log t he would probably not have found the law of falling bodies; he might have stated s $= \frac{1}{2}$ gt $^{1\cdot96}$ instead of the simpler equation s $= \frac{1}{2}$ gt^2 (AUTHOR).

Are these models general enough to apply to other than parasitic insects. Experiments with a sarcophagous fly (*Synthesiomyia nudiseta*) show that egg-laying rate increases with adult density without any drop, even at the highest densities (RABINOVICH). A more complex model will be needed (cf. Andersen, 1965) (AUTHOR).

Why should a model based on parasites showing a value of 0.5 for the interference relationship be the general case when this is not observed? Values available so far vary between about 0.3 and 0.7 (HASSELL). The examples Hassell and Varley (1969) used in their paper fit either 0.5 or a parabola (*Chelonus*) (AUTHOR).

Cyzenis does not avoid superparasitism since it oviposites principally around the edges of damaged leaves. Perhaps *Encarsia*, *Dahlbominus* and *Cryptus* change their searching behaviour after avoiding superparasitism, which would require changes in the basic equation: $\dfrac{dx}{dt} = c/(px + k)$ (HASSELL). I dit not assume that the parasites avoid superparasitism, but only that the presence of eggs of the species inhibits their oviposition (AUTHOR).

The integration of the first differential equation is incorrect (ROYAMA). I realise that the integration should result in $\sqrt{p + \dfrac{k^2}{2ct}}$, but k is small and k^2/2ct even smaller. The most serious problem is the biological interpretation of k (AUTHOR).

There is an extensive literature on models of this type, due to Ivlev, in fisheries, Gause, Thompson, Nicholson, Bailey and others. Many of these models are based on three simple ideas: that the probability of contact increases with density; that the attack capacity of parasites or predators can be saturated by large host numbers, and that the attack effectiveness per attacker declines at higher attacker (parasite or predator) densities. Andersen's formula is a special case of a more general formula, which can be shown as follows

N_a = number of hosts (or prey) that are attacked by parasites (or predators) during a time interval t,

N_o = numbers of hosts (or prey) exposed to attack at the beginning of a time interval t,

P = number of parasites (or predators) attacking during t,

K = the maximum number of hosts or preys that can be attacked during t, per attacker,

a = searching efficiency, and

b = coefficient of cooperation or disoperation amongst attackers,

then it is known (Watt, 1959, *Can. Ent.*) that

$$N_a = PK (1 - e^{-aN_o P^{1-b}})$$

Now from the Taylor's series we know that an exponent of form

$$e^{-x} = 1 - \frac{x}{1!} + \frac{x^2}{2!} - \frac{x^3}{3!}, \text{ etc., or to a first approximation,}$$

$$N_a = PK [1 - (1 - aN_o P^{1-b})] = aKN_o P^{2-b}$$

from which

$$\ln \left(\frac{N_a}{N_o}\right) = \ln (aK) + \ln P^{2-b}.$$

Translating this into the symbols used by Andersen, we have

$$\ln \left(\frac{u_1}{u}\right) = a + \ln p^{2-b}$$

$$= a + (2-b) \ln p \tag{1}$$

Over the range of values of p tested by Andersen, this function behaves like those tested. The widest range of values tested for the $\sqrt{p}$ transformation was that for *Dahlbominus*, where $\sqrt{p}$ varied from 3.5 to 20. The corresponding values of ln p and $\sqrt{p}$ in this range are

p	ln p	$\sqrt{p}$	1.4 ln p
12.25	2.5	3.5	3.5
100	4.6	10	6.4
400	6.0	20	8.4

It will be noticed in Andersen's Fig. 1, 2 and 4 that the points do not in fact fall along a straight line, but rather along a curve. From the figures and the above table, it will be seen that his data in fact describe equation (1) and not the $\sqrt{p}$ transformation (WATT). Watt is forced to plot log against log, which is a weak test, but in any case Watt's model does not fit as well as the square root model (AUTHOR).

364

The first of Watt's equation:

$$Na = KN_oP(1-e^{-aN_oP^{1-b}})$$

is incorrect, since

$$\lim_{p \to \infty} Na = 0 \qquad\qquad \text{when } b > 2$$

$$\lim Na = \text{constant } (aKN_o) \qquad \text{when } b = 2$$

$$\lim Na = \infty \qquad\qquad\qquad \text{when } 0 < b < 2$$

Under the last condition (i.e. $0 < b < 2$) the result (i.e. $\lim_{p \to \infty} Na = \infty$) is contradictory to the condition that N_a cannot exceed N_o (ROYAMA). However, b works in the range $1 < b < 2$ (WATT).

Proc. Adv. Study Inst. Dynamics Numbers Popul. (Oosterbeek, 1970) 366–379

Parasite behaviour as a factor contributing to the stability of insect host-parasite interactions

M. P. Hassell *

Hope Department of Entomology, University of Oxford, Oxford, England

Abstract

Many insect parasites are likely to concentrate their searching activities in areas of high host density. This should result in a density-dependent behavioural response as shown by *Cyzenis albicans*, a tachinid parasite of the winter moth.

Density-dependent responses were shown in the laboratory using the ichneumon *Nemeritis canescens* and its host, *Ephestia cautella*. These responses resulted from the aggregation of parasites in regions of high host density.

Increases in *Nemeritis* density resulted in a reduced searching efficiency per individual parasite. The form of this relationship between searching efficiency and parasite density suggests that such 'interference' is a function of encounters between parasite adults and/or encounters between adults and parasitised hosts.

Encounters between parasite adults ('contacts') increases the likelihood that one or both parasites involved will fly or walk away from that particular area. This accounts for a significant part of the observed interference.

Nemeritis adults tend to remain longer in an area containing healthy hosts. Thus, encounters with parasitised hosts have a similar effect to encounters with other adults.

Aggregation of parasites in areas of high host density is advantageous unless the percentage parasitism is such that parasitised hosts are frequently encountered. Interference is a mechanism causing parasites to disperse from such areas when a large proportion of hosts are already, or are likely to become, parasitised.

Simple population models suggest that interference such as observed for *Nemeritis*, would be important both to the stability of host-parasite interactions and to the coexistence of several parasite species on a single host species.

Insect parasites often play an important role in the natural control of insect populations. To understand how they do this we must study how the rate of increase of the parasite population changes from generation to generation with host density. Such changes will largely depend on the parasites' searching activities and especially on their responses to different host densities encountered during their searching lifetime.

The population models of Thompson (1922, 1924), Nicholson and Bailey (1935) and Hassell and Varley (1969) all make the very simple assumption that, irrespective of the host distribution, parasite individuals search at random. The advantage of such models is that they are simple enough for the necessary measurements to test them to be made in the field. However, because of their simplicity these models may well fail to describe some im-

* Present address: Department of Zoology and Applied Entomology, Imperial College, London, England.

366

portant aspects of host-parasite interactions. This paper is concerned with some observed features of parasite behaviour that may prove important to the development of population models.

Responses of parasites to host density

The work of Holling (1959a, b, 1961) has been most valuable in focussing attention on the relative efficiency of parasite individuals at different host densities. His functional response model for insect parasites (or predators) predicts that the individual parasite causes an inverse density-dependent mortality (a lower percentage parasitism at high host densities and vice versa). This is because as host density increases, the parasites or predators spend increasing amounts of time in 'non-searching activities' associated with encountering hosts – the 'handling time'. However, this model, which in its simplest form is represented by the 'disc equation' (Holling, 1959b), will only describe parasitism in the field if each individual tends to spend the same time in the areas of different host density that it encounters.

It is not uncommon to see some vertebrate predators, especially birds, spending more time searching for prey in areas where the prey density is high rather than where it is low. For example, in England flocks of starlings (*Sturnus vulgaris* L.) can be seen to concentrate on oak trees with the highest *Tortrix viridana* L. pupal densities. Goss-Custard (1970) has shown that the density of red shank – *Tringa totanus* (L.) – that he studied in Scotland is correlated with the density of its main prey, the amphipod *Corophium volutator* (PALLAS). The possibility that insect parasites may concentrate in areas of high host density has not been widely considered (but see Varley, 1941). However, it is to be expected that searching adult parasites will encounter different local densities of hosts, simply because hosts are never completely uniformly distributed. Phytophagous hosts, for example, are confined to their foodplants and one would expect there to be some variation in host density between individual plants, between areas of plants or between parts of plants.

Field evidence that individual parasites concentrate their searching activities in areas of high host density is mostly indirect. *Cyzenis* principally oviposits on the surfaces of damaged leaves, parasitism being effected by a winter moth larva eating an egg. Simple choice experiments have shown that the number of eggs laid on the foliage depends on the degree of leaf damage (Hassell, 1967). In the field this results in a density-dependent behavioural response by the parasite population (i.e. a higher percentage parasitism where host density is high and vice versa) as shown in Fig. 1 (Hassell, 1966, 1968). If each parasite had searched at random, tending to spend the same time on the different trees, one would expect the same percentage parasitism on the different trees, or an inverse density-dependent response if handling time or egg-limitation were important. It seems logical to expect a density-dependent behavioural response whenever parasites are strongly attracted by some feature related to host density. For example, Ullyett (1953) has observed that females of the ichneumon *Pimpla bicolor* BOUCHÉ will aggregate in swarms around a cocoon of its host *Euproctis terminalia* WALK. that has been broken open in the field. These parasites seem to be attracted to concentrations of scent from host pupae. Even if there is no long-distance attraction, parasite individuals may on average spend longer where there are abundant hosts if, after a successful encounter with a host, the behaviour changes to a more concentrated type of searching. Thus Laing (1937) found that female *Trichogramma evanescens* WESTW. change their behaviour following parasitism of a host

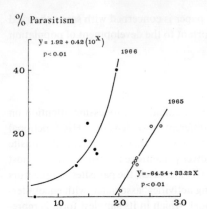

% Parasitism

$y = 1.92 + 0.42 \left(10^{X}\right)$
$p < 0.01$

1966

1965

$y = -64.54 + 33.22\,X$
$p < 0.01$

Log Winter Moth Density

Fig. 1. The behavioural responses of *Cyzenis* to its host, the winter moth, in two years at Wytham Wood, England. The percentage parasitism is plotted against the winter moth larval density per m^2 of canopy area in a stand of hazel, hawthorn and blackthorn.

egg by performing a number of turning movements in the same vicinity. She also found that an *Ephedrus* species behaved in a similar way after attacking green fly.

Laboratory experiments

Methods

It is a simple procedure to investigate in the laboratory the behaviour of parasites searching for an uneven host distribution. Instead of one or more parasites being exposed to each different host density for the same period of time on separate occasions, the parasites can be presented with the choice of a range of host densities at the same time. This allows one to measure the amount of time that the parasites spend searching at the different host densities.

The parasite and host species studied were the ichneumon *Nemeritis canescens* (GRAV.) and the larvae of the almond moth, *Ephestia cautella* (WALK.). Several authors have described the basic biology of these species (e.g. Diamond, 1929; Ahmed, 1936; Simmonds, 1943; Takahashi, 1961; Burges and Haskins, 1964; Corbett and Rotheram, 1965). *Nemeritis* is a thelytokous parasite. Females are attracted to areas containing hosts principally by some feature connected with the silk that is continually produced by the caterpillars during movement. Adult *Nemeritis* probe with their ovipositors in silked-up host food and, when a host larva is stabbed, an egg may be laid in the body cavity. Although *Nemeritis* tends to avoid superparasitism (Rogers, 1970), this avoidance is far from perfect and when superparasitism does occur only one of the progeny reaches maturity.

All the experiments were of a similar design. A given density of parasites searched for 24 hours for a fixed total number of hosts which were distributed in a clumped manner. The different host densities (see Table 1) were enclosed with some food (wheatfeed) in small circular containers (33 cm^2) which were covered with fine nylon netting and sunk flush with a layer of wheatfeed covering the bottom of a cage. The netting did not obviously affect the ovipositing behaviour of the parasites. Further experimental details are given in Table 1. After each experiment the adult parasites were removed and the hosts transferred to excess food. Later the numbers that were healthy or parasitised was ob-

Table 1. Details of experiments.

Experimental series	Size of cage (cm)	Replicates	Parasite density per cage	Total hosts	Host distribution. Number of containers with... hosts					
					4	8	16	32	64	128
1	71 × 71 × 15	5 at each parasite density	1, 2, 4, 8, 16	564	3	3	3	3	2	2
2	28 × 18 × 11	8 at each parasite density	1, 2, 4, 8, 16, 32	532	3	3	3	2	2	2

tained from counts of host and parasite pupae. The procedure for standardising the experimental material is described by Hassell (1971).

Results

In the first series of cage experiments parasite densities were varied between 1 and 16 per cage (0.5 m²; see Table 1). The behavioural responses shown in Fig. 2 were obtained from this experiment. Fig. 2a shows the outcome of a single parasite searching for the duration of the experiment. Parasitism is density-dependent: the higher the host density in the circular dishes, the greater is the percentage of the hosts parasitised. That this is due to the individual *Nemeritis* spending more time on the containers with many rather than those with few hosts is shown in Fig. 4 below, which compares the percentage of the total time spent by a parasite at the different host densities. Such behaviour has a selective advantage to the parasite compared with a random searching strategy throughout the whole host area, since each parasite will leave more progeny. This advantage of concentrating search in regions of high host density only disappears when the percentage parasitism in these areas is such that parasites are frequently encountering hosts which are already parasitised (see Discussion). Fig. 2a to 2e indicate that the density-dependent responses become somewhat stronger as parasite density in the cages increases, as shown by the increasing slopes. Equally important, however, is the fact that the responses for the higher parasite densities are not as strong as those predicted from a knowledge of the response of a single parasite (Fig. 2a). For example, if the 8 parasites (Fig. 2d) had each searched as did a single one, the percentage parasitism should have varied between 0% and 91.2% instead of between 0% and 38.5% as observed. Thus the average efficiency of a parasite is lower when more parasites are searching.

The same results can be expressed in terms of the total mortality for the different parasite densities. In this way it is possible to compare the average searching efficiency of a parasite at the different parasite densities. Slope 1 in Fig. 3 shows the changes in parasite efficiency, as measured by the 'area of discovery' (a) (Nicholson 1933), when parasite density (p) is varied. Both a and p are plotted on log scales. The area of discovery is calculated from:

$$a = \frac{1}{p} \log_e \frac{u_1}{u} \qquad (1)$$

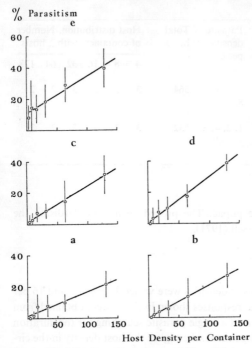

Fig. 2. The behavioural responses of *Nemeritis* to an uneven distribution of its host, *E. cautella*.
(a) 1 parasite; y = 1.02 + 0.16 x
(b) 2 parasites; y = − 0.20 + 0.21 x.
(c) 4 parasites; y = 1.25 + 0.23 x
(d) 8 parasites; y = 0.56 + 0.29 x
(e) 16 parasites; y = 10.75 + 0.24 x.
Data from first series of experiments. 95% confidence limits shown.

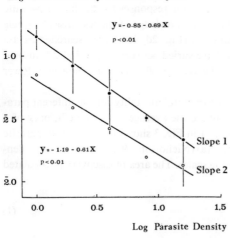

Fig. 3. Relationships between log searching efficiency and log *Nemeritis* density per cage. Searching efficiency is expressed as both area of discovery (slope 1) and area effectively searched (slope 2). Data from first series of experiments. 95% confidence limits shown for slope 1.

where u_1 is the initial host density and u is the hosts surviving parasitism. The relationship shows more clearly than Fig. 2 that the searching efficiency of an individual declines with increases in *Nemeritis* density.

Although the calculated areas of discovery will reflect changes in the average searching efficiency of a parasite, they do not in this case represent the proportion of the area effectively searched by a single parasite as defined by Nicholson. This is principally because each parasite is not searching at random but concentrating in regions of high host density (see Fig. 4). Thus slope 1 in Fig. 3 is based on the total percentage parasitism and expresses the areas that would have to be effectively searched at random to cause the observed mortality. Slope 2 in Fig. 3 has been obtained by using (in Eq. 1) the percentage parasitism in the different density containers to calculate the proportion of each container that has been effectively searched by each parasite. The values are smaller than for slope 1 because parasites searching where there are most hosts need cover a smaller area than if they searched at random to cause a particular mortality. However, in order to use these values in a population model for a host-parasite interaction, the model must be sufficiently sophisticated to predict the spatial distributions both of the hosts and of the percentage parasitism at the different host densities. The measurements necessary to build such a model would not be easy to make in the field. Although the areas of discovery (slope 1) may not represent the actual areas effectively searched, they do quite accurately reflect the real decrease in parasite efficiency. The outcome of the two different types of model, one based on means and using slope 1, and the other on spatial distribution and using slope 2, will only differ markedly if the behavioural response to the host distribution is very strong or differs markedly from generation to generation.

Smaller cages (0.05 m^2) were used in the second series of experiments. This made it easier to make the quantitative behavioural studies that were necessary to determine possible reasons for the inverse relationships in Fig. 3. The distribution of hosts was similar to that in the first series of experiments (see Table 1), but the containers of hosts were necessarily much closer together. Parasite density ranged from 1 to 32 per cage. Between the first and fourth hours of each experiment, a number of 15-minute observations of parasite behaviour were made. At the start of each observation period a parasite was selected at random and observed for seven and a half minutes. A tape recorder was used to note the time the parasite spent on the different host densities and the frequency and duration of its different activities. At the end of this time a second parasite was selected in the same way and observed for a further seven and a half minutes. When only one parasite was present, it was observed for the full fifteen minutes.

Fig. 4 is based on these direct observations of parasite behaviour and shows that, as previously mentioned, an individual *Nemeritis* spends more time in regions of high host density than where there are few hosts. When several parasites are in the cage, this behaviour results in more parasites searching on the containers with 128 hosts than elsewhere. Density-dependent behavioural responses similar to those shown in Fig. 2 are again obtained.

As in the first series of experiments, the area of discovery decreases as parasite density increases (Fig. 5, slope 1; see Discussion for explanation of slope 2). These relationships are of the same linear form as those shown by published data for several other species of parasite (Hassell and Varley, 1969; Hassell, 1971):

$$\log a = \log Q - m \log p \qquad (2)$$

where m is the 'mutual interference constant' (slope of log a on log p) and Q is the

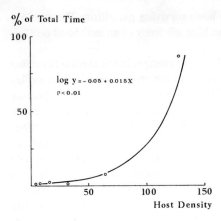

% of Total Time

Fig. 4. Relationship showing that a single adult *Nemeritis* spends a longer period of time (expressed as a percentage of the total time) on the containers with high host density compared with those of low host density.

'quest constant' (area of discovery when p = 1). Hassell and Varley used this relationship in simple population models for host-parasite interactions and showed that models in which the searching efficiency declines with increasing parasite density can be stable and allow the coexistence of several species of parasite on a single host species (see Discussion).

The inverse relationship between log area of discovery and log *Nemeritis* density indicates that there is some density-dependent factor influencing the adult parasite population. This is the same phenomenon as that deduced from Fig. 2 where the observed responses to host density were not as strong as those predicted from the behaviour of a single parasite searching on its own. Since there is the same relative drop in searching efficiency when parasite density is doubled from (e.g.) 1 to 2 per cage as when doubled

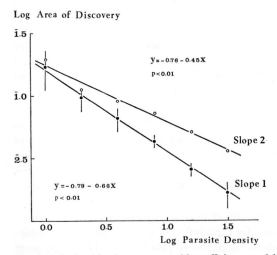

Fig. 5. Relationships between searching efficiency and log *Nemeritis* density per cage. Slope 1 represents the regression of log area of discovery on the log total number of *Nemeritis* present, while slope 2 represents the regression using the log number of *Nemeritis* searching at any one time. Data from second series of experiments. 95% confidence limits shown for slope 1.

372

from (e.g.) 8 to 16 per cage, the relationship cannot be a feature only of intense over-crowding of the parasites. Any change in the frequency of encounters either between searching adults or between an adult and a parasitised host is likely to be important in this respect.

Interference between adults

Adult *Nemeritis* visibly react to the presence of another individual nearby. When they are within one or two centimetres of each other on a container of hosts, one or both parasites often make a rapid backwards or sideways movement. There are several possibilities following such a 'contact'. The parasites may show no obvious change in behaviour, one or both may fly or walk off the container, or there may be a change in activity on the container (e.g. from probing to cleaning). The frequency of these contacts and the outcome of each one was scored during the observation periods.

Fig. 6 illustrates how the frequency of contacts between parasites increases as more parasites are present. The overall effect of this interference is important since, as shown in Fig. 7, it results in the proportion of parasites on the containers at any one time decreasing as parasite density increases. Note that in Fig. 7 the fall in the percentage of time spent by a parasite on the areas containing hosts is approximately linear when compared with the log parasite density. This is the form of the relationship to be expected if decreasing efficiency is dependent in some way on the frequency of encounters between parasites. Under natural conditions the tendency to fly or walk from an area after encounters between adults will cause some emigration of the parasites. This reduces the crowding of parasites in an area of high host density and ensures a more even exploitation of the different areas where hosts are relatively abundant.

These experiments have also indicated that the precise change in behaviour following some form of interference may well depend on where this interference occurs. Most interference between adult *Nemeritis* occurs on those containers with high host density where most parasites aggregate (Fig. 8). However, the effect of an encounter is much less where hosts are abundant than where there are few. This is shown in Fig. 9. The percentage of contacts that lead to one or both parasites flying or walking away is compared for the

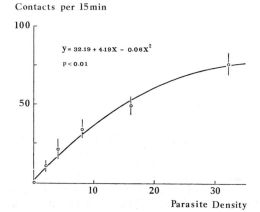

Contacts per 15min

$y = 32.19 + 4.19X - 0.06X^2$

$p < 0.01$

Parasite Density

Fig. 6. Relationship between the number of encounters between adult *Nemeritis* ('contacts') in a 15-minute period and the number of *Nemeritis* present in the cage. Data from second series of experiments. 95% confidence limits shown.

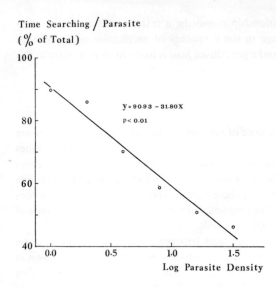

Time Searching / Parasite
(% of Total)

$y = 90.93 - 31.80X$

$p < 0.01$

Log Parasite Density

Fig. 7. The reduction in the proportion of time spent on containers of
hosts by an individual *Nemeritis* as the
Nemeritis density in the cage increases. Data from second series of experiments.

different host densities. At very low host densities approximately 80% of all contacts between adult *Nemeritis* lead to one or both leaving, whilst at the highest host densities less
than 30% of the contacts had this effect.

Interference between adults and parasitised hosts

Rogers (1970) has shown that the behaviour of adult *Nemeritis* also tends to change
following the detection of previously parasitised hosts. He found that individual parasites

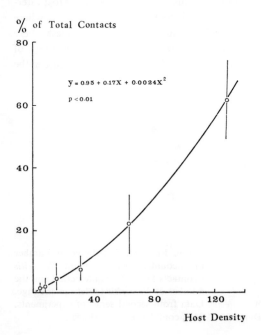

% of Total Contacts

$y = 0.95 + 0.17X + 0.0024X^2$

$p < 0.01$

Host Density

Fig. 8. Relationship showing that a larger proportion of the contacts between
adult *Nemeritis* occurs on containers
where the host density is high than where
it is low. Data from second series of experiments. 95% confidence limits shown.

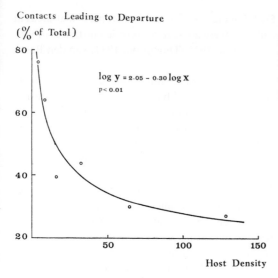

Contacts Leading to Departure (% of Total)

$\log y = 2.05 - 0.30 \log x$

$p < 0.01$

Host Density

Fig. 9. Relationship showing that the proportion of contacts between searching *Nemeritis* that lead to one or both parasites leaving a container is greater where host density is lowest and vice versa. Data from second series of experiments.

may spend several times as long in areas with unparasitised hosts as in areas where all hosts had been parasitised prior to the start of the experiment. Similarly, Laing (1937) found that female *Trichogramma* only perform the turning movements (see above) following successful parasitism of an egg. After encountering a host that had already been parasitised, the *Trichogramma* tended to leave the area in a more-or-less straight path.

Such changes in behaviour become important to the parasite whenever the percentage of hosts parasitised in an area is such that parasitised hosts are frequently encountered. These behavioural changes produce an effect similar to that caused by interference between adults and, under natural conditions, that is likely to be at least as important.

Discussion

The relative importance of the different effects of both types of interference is being investigated at present. The tendency for *Nemeritis* to try to emigrate from regions where parasite density is high (Fig. 7) is certainly one of the major factors responsible for the interference relationships obtained from the cage experiments. This is illustrated in Fig. 5. Slope 1 is based on the numbers of parasites introduced into the cage, while slope 2 shows the relationship after correction for the actual number of parasites searching at any one time. This is done by recalculating the area of discovery (Eq. 1), but now using the average number of parasites searching at one time instead of the total number of parasites present. The difference between the slopes indicates the proportion of the total interference that is explained by the increasing tendency to emigrate as parasite density it increased.

Parasites that aggregate in areas of high host density in the field are quite likely to come into contact with one another and therefore may interfere in some way with each other. There have been several reports in the literature of threat display and aggressive behaviour between female parasites (Hassell 1971, for review). The likely selective advantage of these types of behaviour is that they are one means of preventing a parasite remaining in a particular area after considerable parasitism has already occurred. This is especailly important for parasites such as *Nemeritis* which are attracted to concentrations of hosts

375

whether these are parasitised or not. Such high levels of parasitism on particular areas at certain times are not just laboratory artifacts; there are several recorded instances of very high levels of parasitism from the field (e.g. Salt, 1932; Thompson, 1934; van den Bosch et al., 1967; Embree, 1966; Hirose et al., 1968).

The behaviour of *Nemeritis* seems to be such as to take full advantage of an unevenly distributed host population. By aggregating in regions of high host density, the parasites are likely to leave more progeny than by searching at random. At high parasite densities interference is more likely. A parasite which now disperses and searches for less exploited areas of hosts, as a reaction due either to encounters with other parasite adults or with parasitised hosts, increases its chance of finding further unparasitised hosts. Kuchlein (1966) has shown that increasing densities of the predatory mite, *Typhlodromus longipilus* NESBITT, not only caused a reduction in the eggs laid per female mite per day, but also resulted in increased migration of the mites from the experimental leaf discs. Perhaps such changes in behaviour are widespread and provide a mechanism for local parasite dispersal.

There are two especially important features of host-parasite interactions in the field that need to be explained. Firstly, these interactions tend to be stable. Although oscillations are sometimes observed where parasitism is a key factor (e.g. Morris, 1959), there is no sign of the instability predicted by the models of Thompson (1924) and Nicholson (1933). Secondly, a single host species is commonly attacked by more than one species of fairly specific parasite. Nicholson (1933) and Nicholson and Bailey (1935) have considered this situation and their models predict very stringent conditions under which such coexistence could occur. These questions of stability and coexistence are both of the utmost importance to the practice of biological control.

The responses of *Nemeritis* to the host distribution and the occurrence of interference have a very important effect on the host-parasite interaction. A density-dependent behavioural response with no interference would contribute only a small amount to the stability of an interaction over a period of generations. This contribution to stability is (in effect) due to the low density areas of the host population being partially protected from parasite attack. Hassell and Varley (1969) have suggested that interference, if a widespread phenomenon, would be much more important in explaining both the observed stability of host-parasite interactions and the observed coexistence of several species of parasites on a single host species. Their models show that the greater the decline in searching efficiency with increases in parasite density – i.e. the higher the value for (m) the mutual interference constant – the more stable will be the interaction. Furthermore, it will be much easier for several parasite species to coexist on a single host species. Thus the model supports the practice of biological control workers in making multiple introductions of parasites to control a pest. Whether one or more parasite species become established, the outcome is likely to be beneficial if they show an interference relationship. The interaction will remain stable and the average density of the pest population will be reduced. There will be a further reduction if more parasite species become established.

Acknowledgments

I am very grateful to Professor G.C. Varley, Mr G. R. Gradwell and Dr David Rogers for their help in the preparation of this paper. The study was carried out during tenure of a Research Fellowship from the Natural Environment Research Council to whom I am very grateful.

References

Ahmad, T., 1936. The influence of ecological factors on the Mediterranean flour moth, *Ephestia kühniella*, and its parasite, *Nemeritis canescens*. *J. Anim. Ecol.* 5: 67–93.

Bosch, R. van den, C. F. Lagace & V. M. Stern, 1967. The interrelationship of the aphid, *Acyrthosiphon pisum*, and its parasite, *Aphidius smithi*, in a stable environment. *Ecology* 48: 993–1000.

Burges, H. D. & K. P. F. Haskins, 1964. Life cycle of the tropical warehouse moth, *Cadra cautella* (Wlk.), at controlled temperatures and humidities. *Bull. ent. Res.* 55: 775–789.

Corbet, S. A. & S. Rotheram, 1965. The life history of the ichneumonid *Nemeritis* (*Devorgilla*) *canescens* (Gravenhorst) as a parasite of the Mediterranean flour moth, *Ephestia* (*Anagasta*) *kuehniella* Zeller, under laboratory conditions. *Proc. R. ent. Soc. Lond. A.* 40: 67–72.

Diamond, V. R., 1929. The biology of *Nemeritis canescens*, a parasite of the Mediterranean flour moth. *Rep. ent. Soc. Ont.* 60: 84–89.

Goss–Custard, J. D., 1970. The responses of redshank (*Tringa totanus* (L.)) to spatial variations in the density of their prey. *J. Anim. Ecol.* 39: 91–113.

Embree, P. G., 1966. The role of introduced parasites in the control of the winter moth in Nova Scotia. *Can. Ent.* 98: 1159–1168.

Hassell, M. P., 1966. Evaluation of parasite or predator responses. *J. Anim. Ecol.* 35: 65–75.

Hassell, M. P., 1967. Studies of parasitism by some tachinid flies. D. Phil. thesis, Oxford.

Hassell, M. P., 1968. The behavioural response of a tachinid fly (*Cyzenis albicans* (Fall.) to its host, the winter moth (*Operophtera brumata* (L.). *J. Anim. Ecol.* 37: 627–639.

Hassell, M. P., 1971. Mutual interference between searching insect parasites. *J. Anim. Ecol.* 40: 473–486.

Hassell, M. P. & G. C. Varley, 1969. New inductive population model for insect parasites and its bearing on biological control. *Nature* 223: 1133–1137.

Hirose, Y., M. Shiga & F. Nakasuji, 1968. Interspecific relations among three hymenopterous egg parasites of the pine moth, *Dendrolimus spectabilis* Butler (Lepidoptera: Lasiocampidae) in the Japanese black pine forest. II. Spatial interspersion of the two egg parasites, *Trichogramma dendrolimi* and *Telenomus dendrolimi* in the pine crown. *J. Fac. Agric. Kyushu Univ.* 14: 459–472.

Holling, C. S., 1959a. The components of predation as revealed by a study of small mammal predation of the European pine sawfly. *Can. Ent.* 91: 293–320.

Holling, C. S., 1959b. Some characteristics of simple types of predation and parasitism. *Can. Ent.* 91: 385–398.

Holling, C. S., 1961. Principles of insect predation. *A. Rev. Ent.* 6: 163–182.

Kuchlein, J. H., 1966. Mutual interference among the predacious mite *Typhlodromus longipilus* Nesbitt (Acari, Phytoseiidae). I. Effects of predator density on oviposition rate and migration tendency. *Meded. Rijksfac. LandbWet. Gent.* 31: 740–746.

Laing, J., 1937. Host-finding by insect parasites. I. Observations on the finding of hosts by *Alysia manducator*, *Mormoniella vitripennis*, and *Trichogramma evanescens*. *J. Anim. Ecol.* 6: 298–317.

Morris, R. F., 1959. Single-factor analysis in population dynamics. *Ecology* 40: 580–588.

Nicholson, A. J., 1933. The balance of animal populations. *J. Anim. Ecol.* 2: 131–178.

Nicholson, A. J. & V. A. Bailey, 1935. The balance of animal populations, Part I. *Proc. zool. Soc. Lond.* 551–598.

Rogers, D. J., 1970. Aspects of host-parasite interactions in laboratory populations of insects. Ph.D. thesis, Oxford.

Salt, G., 1932. Superparasitism by *Collyria calcitrator* Grav. *Bull. ent. Res.* 23: 211–216.

Simmonds, F. J., 1943. The occurrence of superparasitism in *Nemeritis canescens* Grav. *Revue can. Biol.* 2: 15–58.

Takahashi, F., 1961. Studies on the fluctuation in the experimental population of the almond moth, *Ephestia cautella* Walker. *Jap. J. Ecol.* 11: 239–245.

Thompson, W. R., 1922. Théorie de l'action des parasites entomophages. Accroissement de la proportion d'hôtes parasites dans le parasitisme cyclique. *C. r. hebd. Séanc. Acad. Sci., Paris* 175: 65–68.

Thompson, W. R., 1924. La théorie mathématique de l'action des parasites entomophages et le facteur du hasard. *Annls Fac. Sci., Marseille* 2: 69–89.

Thompson, W. R., 1934. The development of a colony of *Aphelinus mali* Hald. *Parasitology* 26: 449–453.

Ullyett, G. C., 1953. Biomathematics and insect population problems. A critical review. *Mem. ent. Soc. S. Afr.* 2: 1–89.

Varley, G. C., 1941. On the search for hosts and the egg distribution of some chalcid parasites of the knapweed gall-fly. *Parasitology* 33: 47–66.

Discussion

Participants: Hassell (Author), Andrewartha, Coulson, Fransz, Jacobs, Krebs, Platt, Reddingius, Solomon, Watt, Williamson, Wolda, Zahavi and Zwölfer

How is a good model recognized? In plankton productivity it has been shown that equations based on erroneous assumptions may have good predictability. In Fig. 3 of the paper, where log area of discovery is plotted against log parasite density, a random search model (slope 1) is contrasted with a non-random, improved one (slope 2). The random model fits the data much better than the improved one. Which is the better model (PLATT)? Goodness of fit cannot be taken as a measure of how realistic a model may be, whereas the best model is that which describes the situation using more realistic parameters (AUTHOR).

Testing goodness of fit of a model should be done using an appropriate statistical test, for which a statistician must be consulted who is willing to try and design a test for this particular problem after carefully studying the biological background. (REDDINGIUS) Such a test – especially designed to test for an interference relationship – is available and was described by Hassell and Varley (1969) (AUTHOR).

Sometimes the choice of model must be dictated mainly by other considerations than goodness of fit to the data. It depends on what you want the model for. If it is to be only descriptive, a convenient summary of the data and/or a way of making predictions, then goodness of fit is the main criterion. But if you wish the model to express the causal relationships involved, you will aim for biological realism in the causal relations built into the model, and not primarily for goodness of fit, which you may hope to improve by further testing and modification of the model along lines you have shown to be biologically appropriate (SOLOMON).

I do not believe in the constancy of the quest and interference parameters. In order to produce models, which describe the situation and also predict reality, more factors will have to be incorporated into the model. How far can we extend models (FRANSZ)? In cases like this the model can be easily expanded to include such factors as:
1. Lack of synchronization between host and parasite;
2. Interspecific interference between adult parasites;
3. Different degrees of larval competition in cases of multiparasitism;
4. Independent mortalities acting on the host or parasite population (AUTHOR).
In the computer simulation of the model it seems that increasing m not only improves stability but also leads to higher mean densities. If one is trying to control mean density this would mean that a well stabilized system may be less satisfactory than a less stable one (WILLIAMSON). This is a special case: the average density increases only if Q is kept constant, and at the same time the mutual interference constant is increased (AUTHOR).

Concerning the straight-line relationship (on a log scale) depicting constant interfering coefficients: Which range of host density corresponds to natural conditions (JACOBS)? Densities of up to 10 parasites/m² are probably common in the field, although there may be cases of very high parasite densities. In these cases, there must be a threshold density at which encounters between adult parasites or between an adult and a parasitised host become unlikely and below which the line would have to level off (AUTHOR).

The lack of instability in field host-parasite systems is now predictable from existing theory in this domain (WATT). However, one cannot distinguish in the field between interference and density-dependent mortality of adult parasites if the latter acts between the sampling of the parasite adults and the searching of the adult parasites (AUTHOR).

I am surprised at the tendency of entomologists to argue from laboratory populations to possible field situations. In mammalian populations, laboratory situations have long since been abandoned because they provide results which are completely unrealistic by field standards (KREBS). It is difficult to understand the mechanism of parasite interference solely from field studies. Laboratory experiments can be most valuable if one checks the validity of the underlying ideas in the field (AUTHOR).

A varation in gregariousness in the parasite and/or the host may influence the relationships between parasite and host numbers. Suppose that some parasite individuals prefer localities with low host densities, because their searching efficiency is high enough to allow them to do this. Would not such parasites leave more offspring (they are hardly hindered by interference) and, therefore, be at a selective advantage? This might cause changes in the quality of the parasite population accompanied by changes in density. In the host, selection could operate on its variation in gregariousness via a variation in parasitism (WOLDA). I suspect that the time wasted by interference at high host densities would have to be very great to make it advantageous for a parasite to concentrate its searching activities in places of low host densities. On the other hand, it will often be impossible for hosts to disperse evenly, e.g. because they are confined to their foodplants (AUTHOR).

What is the quantitative relationship between the concentrating of parasites at high host densities and the leaving of parasites as a result of interaction. Which host density results in the maximum 'dispersion' of parasites (COULSON)? As an overall effect, most *Nemeritis* leave the areas of highest host density (AUTHOR).

The response to interference of *Nemeritis* is a process that promotes dispersal; similar processes were described by Gruys for *Bupalus* and by Way for *Brevicoryne* (both in these Proceedings). It is interesting that evidence for inbuilt dispersiveness, which is an outstanding feature of hypotheses that emphasize the importance of heterogeneity, arise from studies which are aimed primarily at studying the influence of density (ANDREWARTHA). This paper, like others read here, clearly shows that space is a resource, like matter and energy (WATT).

May the parasites themselves act as an attraction stimulus to other parasites, so that parasites are first attracted to others (to find oviposition sites) and only later, after close interactions, tend to fly away? Such mechanisms seem to affect the size of flocks of birds on food (ZAHAVI).

The proportion of time spent by a parasite searching for hosts and ovipositing varies greatly among parasite species. It would be interesting to relate these differences to the degree of mutual interference at an intraspecific and at an interspecific level (ZWÖLFER).

379

Proc. Adv. Study Inst. Dynamics Numbers Popul. (Oosterbeek, 1970) 380–389

A population study of the cinnabar moth, Tyria (Callimorpha) jacobaeae L.

J. P. Dempster

The Nature Conservancy, Monks Wood Experimental Station, Abbots Ripton, Huntingdon, England

Abstract

This paper describes a five-year study of a population of the cinnabar moth on Weeting Heath National Nature Reserve in Norfolk, England. This population fluctuates violently in size and periodically completely defoliates its food plant (*Senecio jacobaea*) over large areas.

Since 1966 the numbers of all stages in the life cycle of the moth have been counted and life tables are given.

Adult fecundity is dependent on the extent of larval crowding and so acts as a delayed density-dependent factor.

Larval mortality is weakly density-dependent due to the high mortality caused by starvation in years of high density. Of the other main causes of larval death, the parasite *Apanteles* appears to be acting as an inverse density-dependent factor and arthropod predation is density-independent.

There is a high mortality at, or immediately after, pupation due to predation by moles. This is independent of density.

This population does not appear to be regulated in the Nicholsonian sense. Its upward growth is limited by density-dependent competition for food, but no factor has been identified which could prevent extinction in years of extreme food shortage. The only buffer against extinction appears to be the heterogeneity within the population (timing) and the habitat (patchy abundance of *Senecio*).

Cinnabar moth has a single generation each year. In Britain, the adults emerge in May or early June and lay their eggs in clusters on the underside of the basal leaves of their food plant (principally ragwort, *Senecio jacobaea* L.). The eggs hatch after 2–3 weeks and, during their first instar, the larvae stay together on the leaf on which they hatched. At this stage, they are greyish green in colour. After their first moult they move to the top of the flowering shoots of the plant and feed on the developing flowers. By then they have developed their characteristic black and orange banding. There are five larval instars and development takes just over a month. The fully grown caterpillars leave the plant to pupate in the surface layers of the soil, often amongst moss or grass roots, or under a small stone. They remain as pupae throughout the autumn and winter and become adult in the following May.

Methods

Most of the data which I shall be giving come from a five-year study of a population of the moth on Weeting Heath National Nature Reserve in Norfolk (Dempster, 1971). This reserve is one of the last remaining fragments of the once extensive tract of sandy heath known as 'Breckland'. On the southern half of the reserve is an enclosure (19 ha = 47 acre) within which a large rabbit population occurs. This enclosure was built in 1956 in an attempt to maintain a rabbit grazing pressure similar to that on the reserve prior to myxomatosis. Ragwort is extremely abundant throughout the enclosure and it supports a cinnabar population which reaches very high densities in some years. Cinnabar caterpillars completely defoliated the ragwort throughout the entire enclosure in 1960 and 1961 and again in 1967 and 1968.

Since 1966, the numbers of the moth have been regularly estimated within a small plot (90 × 60 m) in the enclosure. Eggs and larvae were counted once a week by searching all ragwort plants within a set of 150-m² quadrats. Pupal numbers have been assessed by digging and sieving the soil to a depth of 5 cm (2 in) within fifty of these quadrats (25 in August and 25 in the following April). Adult moths have been studied by mark and recapture. From these counts a series of life tables have been constructed. For this, total egg numbers have been calculated by accumulating the records of new eggs over the egg-laying period. The number of first instar larvae has been estimated by counting the hatched egg shells; these normally stay on the leaf for several weeks after hatching. Since all larval stages may occur together, an indirect method of estimating total numbers was necessary. That described by Dempster (1961) was employed to estimate the total number of third and fifth stage larvae.

Population fluctuations

The population has fluctuated violently during the period of this study, from a maximum of 362 adults/150 m² in 1967–8 to 1.5 adults/150 m² in 1968–9. Egg numbers have varied to an even greater extent, from 17,110/150 m² to 62/150 m². Both fecundity and mortality have varied considerably.

In 1966 just over 2,000 eggs were laid in the quadrats. Egg mortality was low and about 1,800 hatched. By far the biggest cause of death in eggs was the chance destruction of leaves, or whole plants, by rabbits. Once the larvae had hatched the death rate increased, and in 1966 56% died during the first two instars; this was due mainly to arthropod predators. It is difficult to obtain quantitative estimates of predation, but precipitin tests identified nine species of predator which had fed on cinnabar during this early larval period. The most important of these was the mite, *Erythraeus phalangoides*. More intensive work at Monks Wood showed that arthropods were the main cause of early larval disappearance. By searching plants everyday, it proved possible to find a predator which had fed on cinnabar on just over 60% of the occasions when larvae were missing. Many of the species involved were nocturnal, so it is likely that an even higher percentage of disappearances would have been accounted for had searches been made more frequently than once a day.

As the larvae grow, they become immune from attack by these predators and so mortality is generally low during the third and fourth instars. There is another peak in the mortality during the fifth instar when the braconid parasite, *Apanteles popularis*, kills its hosts.

The last period of high mortality occurs at, or immediately after, pupation. Each year far more fully grown larvae than pupae were present. Thus, in 1966 it was estimated that 536 larvae left the plants to pupate, but a count of pupae showed only 108 present in August. A similar difference between larval and pupal numbers was found each year. In contrast, there was very good agreement between pupal numbers estimated in August and the following spring and adult numbers assessed by mark and recapture. This suggests that there is a period of high mortality at, or immediately after pupation, but that after August there is little mortality. This high early-pupal mortality is almost certainly due to vertebrate predators, particularly moles (see p. 384).

This then is the typical pattern of mortality: high death rates occur mainly in early-larval, late-larval and early-pupal stages. In 1967 and 1968 this picture was altered by starvation. Just over 100 adults/150 m² emerged in the spring of 1967, and these laid over 17,000 eggs in the quadrats. By 26 June, the larvae had completely defoliated the plants within many of the quadrats and larvae were wandering about on the ground in search of food. By 3 July there were only a few isolated patches of ragwort surviving, while a thorough search over the whole area one week later found no green remains of ragwort left. It is estimated that about 20 % of the larvae died from starvation. In spite of this, many adults emerged in the following year (362/150 m²) and 16,500 eggs were laid. Food was in even shorter supply in 1968, owing to the effects of defoliation in the previous year, and food was exhausted whilst there were still many young larvae and some unhatched eggs present. Probably close to 50 % of the caterpillars starved. Total mortality was estimated as 99.99 % and only 1.5 adults/150 m² emerged in 1969. Since this crash in the population the moths' numbers have slowly recovered, so that this year (1970) we found just over 3,000 eggs within the quadrats.

As has been found with many insects, fecundity of the adult cinnabar moth is closely correlated with its weight. Weight is determined by food intake and is, of course, markedly reduced by starvation. This means that fecundity is dependent upon larval density. In the laboratory, larvae kept crowded, but with excess food, developed into smaller pupae. This was presumably the result of mutual interference during feeding. When there is a shortage of food, the effects of crowding become bigger, and pupal size was greatly reduced in 1967 and 1968.

Table 1 shows the potential fecundity in each year calculated from pupal size. In both 1967 and 1969, the actual fecundity in the field was close to that expected from pupal size. This suggests that, in those years, size was the main factor determining fecundity; i.e. that adult mortality and dispersal played a minor role. In 1968 the actual fecundity was a good deal lower than that expected from pupal size. In that year, many adults were seen leaving the area and flying over cultivated land to the west of the enclosure. In 1970 the reverse happened and there was an immigration of adults onto the northern end of the plot from neighbouring areas in the enclosure. Because of the over-riding effect of size on the number of eggs laid, fecundity tends to be acting as a delayed density-dependent factor.

There are indications from the field data that many moths emigrated in 1968. In that year, adult numbers were exceptionally high and so laboratory experiments were carried out to study the effect of adult size, and of adult density, on flight activity. These ex-

Table. 1. Mean pupal size and fecundity 1966–70.

	Mean pupal width (cm)	Potential number of eggs/♀♀	Actual number of eggs/♀♀	Proportion of potential laid
1966–7	0.5213	297	285	0.9596
1967–8	0.4542	154	92	0.5974
1968–9	0.4254	83	73	0.8795
1969–70	0.5112	295	561	1.9017

periments showed that the size of the adult had no effect, but that increases in density markedly increased the incidence of flight by the moths. It seems probable, then, that emigration is density-dependent.

We have seen that total mortality varies considerably from one generation to another. Let us now look in more detail at the factors causing mortality.

Factors causing mortality

Larval mortality is large and variable and is caused by three important factors, arthropod predators, starvation and the parasite, *Apanteles*.

Larval predation

Arthropod predation is virtually confined to the first three larval stages. During the five years it is estimated that these predators have taken between 28–64% of the caterpillars (Table 2). This percentage appears to be independent of the density of cinnabar, and to be due mainly to large variations in the predators' populations. All of these predators are polyphagous, feeding on a wide variety of prey besides cinnabar moth.

Table. 2. Larval mortality 1966–70.

	Number of larvae/150 m²	Mortality from starvation (%)	Mortality from *Apanteles* (%)	Mortality from predators (%)	Failure to pupate (%)	Total mortality (%)
1966	1,861	0.0	9.1	60.7	1.4	71.2
1967	16,244	20.2	3.2	63.7	2.1	89.2
1968	14,324	48.5	1.7	47.8	1.5	99.5
1969	62	0.0	24.2	32.3	1.6	58.1
1970	2,829	0.0	16.8	28.6	3.8	49.2

Influence of ragwort abundance

In contrast, starvation is clearly density-dependent; although density in terms of numbers per quadrat is a poor measure of crowding, since plant numbers fluctuate enormously. Table 3 shows the weight of ragwort per larva present at the time of hatch in each year. This has varied from 0.04 g/larva to 162.1 g/larva.

Ragwort is normally a biennial, which passes the first year as a rosette and flowers in its second summer. If it is damaged and prevented from flowering, however, it can behave as a perennial, by repeated regeneration. This regrowth may take one of two forms. In the case of large plants, secondary flowering shoots may be formed from the crown of the plant in the autumn following defoliation. On the poor, sandy soil at Weeting, the plants

Table. 3. Estimated weight in grams of ragwort per larva present at the time of hatching.

Year	1966	1967	1968	1969	1970
Ragwort/larva(g)	1.36	0.14	0.04	162.07	90.37

Table 4. Number of ragwort/m² at Weeting Heath.

	Number of ragwort/m² on:						
	3/5/66	19/4/67	13/9/67	9/4/68	14/8/68	25/4/69	12/6/70
Rosettes	5.27	3.96	3.56	5.53	38.75	59.74	33.93
Flowering	4.39	4.14	1.42	0.05	0.00	8.36	18.38
Total	9.66	8.10	4.98	5.58	38.75	68.10	52.31
		Plants defoliated		Plants defoliated			

are small and secondary flowering is rare. Besides this regrowth from the crown of the plant, regeneration may also occur from root-buds (Harper and Wood, 1957). This type of regeneration is particularly vigorous from the roots of rosette plants. The small plants, resulting from regeneration from root-buds, are difficult to distinguish from seedlings, since the connection with the parent root is soon lost.

Differences in the percentage of plants in the rosette and flowering stages greatly alter the amount of food available. Table 4 shows the number of plants per quadrat during the five years. In 1966 there were approximately 10 plants/m², of which about half were of flowering size. Numbers dropped a little in the next year and these plants were then completely defoliated by the caterpillars. Few flowering sized plants survived so that, by the spring of 1968, almost all of the plants were small rosettes. These were then defoliated again. There followed a tremendous amount of regeneration, so that by September there were 39 plants/m² and by the following April (1969) there were 68 plants /m². This increase in plant numbers was probably entirely due to regeneration from root-buds. No seed had been set within the plot, or within a distance of ¼ mile (400 m), since 1966. Since 1969 the number of plants has started to drop as they have reached flowering size and then died. There is, then, a cycle in ragwort abundance which is dependent on the periodic defoliation brought about by the moth.

Larval parasitism

The third, important cause of larval mortality is the braconid parasite, *Apanteles popularis*. This has a single generation each year. The adult wasp lays its eggs in the very young caterpillars of cinnabar, and its larvae develop inside until the host is in its last instar. The parasite larvae then leave the caterpillar, killing it at this time. On average, 5–6 larvae develop per host, but this number was reduced to only 2.6/host in 1968 owing to the effects of starvation. Over the five years, the rate of parasitism has been inversely related to the density of cinnabar. That is *Apanteles* has killed a higher percentage of caterpillars when their density was low.

Pupal disappearance

Although the larvae and adults of cinnabar moth are distasteful to vertebrates, Windecker (1939) found that, shortly after pupation, pupae were acceptable to a wide range of vertebrates. Once they were about 4–8 weeks old, however, they were not eaten. It is probable that the early-pupal disappearance recorded at Weeting was due to vertebrate predators. Pupae put out in the field within 0.5-in mesh cages survived, but 40% of those

384

without this protection disappeared within 10 days. Attempts were made to determine whether the commonest vertebrate predators had fed on cinnabar pupae. Moles (*Talpa europaea*) and fieldmice (*Apodemus sylvaticus*) were trapped and their gut contents examined, but the results were inconclusive. Laboratory tests showed that both species opened the pupae and ate only the soft insides. The hard parts which are more easily identifiable, were not eaten. *Apodemus* fed by biting off each end of the pupae, while moles split the pupa longitudinally. During sampling, no pupal remains were found which showed the type of damage which was characteristic of *Apodemus* feeding, but many fragments were found which could have been the result of mole predation. There is another reason why I suspect moles to be the main predators of pupae. The ground at Weeting is criss-crossed by many superficial mole runs. At the time when cinnabar larvae are searching for pupation sites, many enter the ground through the soft, disturbed soil on the sides of these runs. Many larvae probably pupate within the mole-run itself. This early-pupal disappearance showed no correlation with density.

Key factors

So far, data are available for only three complete generations. Adult numbers were not assessed in the spring of 1966, so that fecundity is not known for that year; the 1970 generation is not yet completed. This makes a key factor analysis of rather little value. However, the data so far obtained are shown in Fig. 1. The results from this analysis support the conclusion that the key factors determining generation mortality are larval (k_{2-4}) and pupal (k_5) mortality. The only factors showing any density relationship are *Apanteles* which is acting in an inverse density-dependent way and fecundity (k_0) which is acting as a delayed density-dependent factor. Starvation is density-dependent and this has so marked an effect, that there is some density dependence in the total larval mortality (k_{2-4}). This correlation is not significant statistically, probably because starvation only operates at very high densities. In three out of five years there was probably no mortality from starvation. The correlation between larval mortality and density is closer to significance when density is calculated as number/kg ragwort, rather than number/m^2 (Fig. 2).

Causes of density fluctuations

The upward growth of the cinnabar population at Weeting Heath is limited by larval competition for food. The crash in numbers brought about by starvation has led to a cycle in the abundance of the moth and its food plant. On both occasions when a crash has occurred (1961 and 1968), it has taken two years of high density before lack of food brought the population down. Cameron (1935) records a similar two years of defoliation of ragwort by cinnabar moth on the Breckland in 1930 and 1931. The reason for this crash in the second year is that regeneration by ragwort leads to most of the plants being small rosettes and so to food supply being greatly reduced in the second year.

The rate at which the cinnabar population recovers depends on the rate of recovery of the food plants, and this is dependent on the rainfall during late summer. The plants made far better regrowth in the wet summer of 1968 than in 1967. Recovery by the moth is delayed by the inverse density-dependent action of *Apanteles* and by the effect of starvation on subsequent fecundity. The effect of crowding in 1967 led to fewer eggs being laid in 1968, as also did the emigration of adults in that year, but these could not prevent the

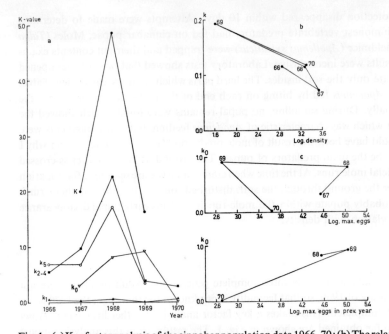

Fig. 1. (a) Key factor analysis of the cinnabar population data 1966–70; (b) The relationship between k (*Apanteles*) and larval density: r = 0.9476, P < 0.02, b = 0.0539; (c) The relationship between k_0 (fecundity) and maximum egg numbers: r = 0.9959, P < 0.005.
K = Total generation mortality, k_0 = reduced natality (i.e. adult mortality, dispersal and fecundity), k_1 = egg mortality, k_{2-4} = larval mortality, k_5 = pupal mortality.

subsequent crash in the population from starvation.

There appears to be nothing to prevent the local extinction of this moth in years when defoliation of the ragwort is particularly severe. Survival of larvae was better on some parts of the Heath than on others, and this heterogeneity, together with the huge area covered by ragwort, prevented complete extinction in 1968–9.

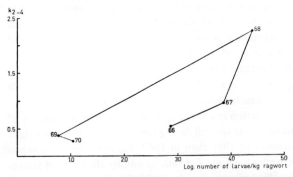

Fig. 2. The relationship between larval mortality (k_{2-4}) and larval density. r = 0.8195; 0.10 > P > 0.05.

386

Low density populations

These violent fluctuations in number only occur in some populations of cinnabar moth. Other populations persist at a low density and never eat out their food supply; such a population occurs at Monks Wood National Nature Reserve. This reserve is on a heavy clay soil and rabbit grazing is less marked than at Weeting. The vegetation is tall and dense and the density of ragwort is low. The lusher vegetation supports a larger population of predaceous arthropods than occurs at Weeting, and these take a higher percentage of the young caterpillars in each year. *Apanteles* does not occur at Monks Wood. Pupal survival at Monks Wood is very low (less than 2% each year) due probably to waterlogging of the soil. Cinnabar pupae can withstand a loss of about a third of their water, but excessive moisture soon leads to death.

With only two years' data from Monks Wood it is impossible to be certain that the population is not regulated by density-dependent factors. The population appears to be prevented from building up to a level where larval competition occurs by high mortality of the pupae. There is however no evidence to suggest that this mortality is density-dependent, but more work is required to be certain of this.

Survival of cinnabar moth

The results from this study raise, once more, the question of the validity of Nicholson's concept of population regulation about a stable equilibrium by density-dependent factors (Nicholson, 1954). The upper size of the cinnabar moth population is certainly limited by density-dependent competition for food, but lack of competition, alone, can not prevent extinction when the population is low. Competition only operates at very high densities, i.e. at densities above that at which the finding of its requirements by one individual starts to affect the chance of others doing likewise. Food is probably a limiting factor at Weeting, about once every seven years. It is frequently assumed that the effects of competition are relaxed immediately the population drops. This is not so for cinnabar moth, since the harmful effects of food shortage persist into the next generation, because of its effect on fecundity. In 1969, an exceedingly low fecundity prevented a rapid recovery of the population in the presence of a superabundance of food.

In this species the only factor which appears to buffer the population against extinction at the time of food shortage, is the heterogeneity present in the population and in the habitat. The earliest individuals obtain sufficient food in the small areas of ragwort which persist longer than others, i.e. where ragwort density is high and caterpillar density is low.

It might be argued that the population at Weeting is abnormal since it is within a man-made enclosure, which ensures overgrazing by rabbits. Similar fluctuations, involving the periodic defoliation of ragwort, do however regularly occur in many localities (van der Meijden, these Proceedings).

References

Cameron, D., 1935. A study of the natural control of ragwort (*Senecio jacobaea* L.) *J. Ecol.* 23: 265–322.

Dempster, J. P., 1961. The analysis of data obtained by regular sampling of an insect population. *J. Anim. Ecol.* 30: 429–432.

Dempster, J. P., 1971. The population ecology of the cinnabar moth, *Tyria jacobaeae* L. (Lepidoptera, Arctiidae). *Oecologia* 7: 26–67.

Harper, J. L. & W. A. Wood, 1957. Biological flora of the British Isles, *Senecio jacobaea* L. *J. Ecol.* 45: 617–637.

Meijden, E. van der, 1970. *Senecio* and *Tyria* (*Callimorpha*) in a Dutch dune area. These Proceedings.

Nicholson, A. J., 1954. An outline of the dynamics of animal populations. *Aust. J. Zool.* 2: 9–65.

Windecker, W., 1939. *Euchelia* (*Hypocrita*) *jacobaeae* L. und das Schutztrachtenproblem. *Z. Morph. Ökol. Tiere* 35: 84–138.

Discussion

Participants: Dempster (Author), Baltensweiler, Huffaker, Kuenen, Labeyrie, Pimentel, Reynoldson, Solomon and Zwölfer

The initial discussion concerned the role of density dependent mechanisms in the regulation of cinnabar populations.

Populations with density-dependent processes present are less likely to be at risk from extinction than populations where such processes are absent (REYNOLDSON, SOLOMON). Has anyone ever found a density-dependent mechanism that would prevent extinction? All that happens at low densities is that density-dependent influences relax or disappear until higher densities return (SOLOMON). The only density-dependent factor identified at Weeting was starvation. The effect of this on the population did not relax immediately the population dropped. Instead, because of its effect on fecundity, the harmful effects of food shortage lasted into the next generation, and this prevented a rapid recovery of the moth population. Whether or not one considers the population to be regulated depends on one's definition of the term. If regulation means the maintenance of a stable equilibrium in the classical Nicholsonian sense, then this population is not regulated. If, however, one just means that the upward growth of the population is limited, then I agree that regulation occurs. The two concepts are very different (AUTHOR). Compare with discussion after the paper of Solomon.

In the sand-dune area near Leiden, Netherlands, the population crash of the moth may take only one year. This happened in 1951 when there were so many caterpillars per plant that most failed to reach the pupal stage. The plants regenerated in the same autumn and seemed normal in the next year, when cinnabar numbers were extremely low (KUENEN). In California, where the insect had been introduced for biological control of the weed, the moth appears to exert a more constant pressure on the plant population, without the fluctuations described from Weeting Heath (HUFFAKER). The precise effect of the moth on the plant will vary according to grazing pressure, soil type and climate. The poor soil at Weeting led to few plants producing flowering stems in the autumn following defoliation, while the heavy grazing pressure enabled the plants to multiply by vegetative reproduction from root buds. This set up the cycle of abundance of the moth and its food plant (AUTHOR).

What is the importance of disease in the cinnabar moth? A latent virus has been found in the introduced stock prior to its release in Western Canada (HUFFAKER, ZWÖLFER). I had expected disease to be important at the time of stress from starvation, but none was found. The fungus, *Penicillium* sp., was present, but this was probably only weakly pathogenic. An unidentified bacterial disease was found in a laboratory culture of the moth in one year, but never in the field (AUTHOR).

Is there a possibility of changes in the quality of the plants and of the moth during the cycles of abundance and between the different localities. (BALTENSWEILER, LABEYRIE, PIMENTEL)? The limited experiments so far undertaken have failed to detect qualitative changes in the larvae with changes in density (AUTHOR).

Proc. Adv. Study Inst. Dynamics Numbers Popul. (Oosterbeek, 1970) 390–404

Senecio and Tyria (Callimorpha) in a Dutch dune area. A study on an interaction between a monophagous consumer and its host plant*

E. van der Meijden

Zoological Laboratory, State University, Leiden, the Netherlands

Abstract

In this paper the mutual influence of ragwort and the cinnabar moth is considered in relation to the importance of other influences on the numbers of these two organisms. It is concluded that the influence of *Tyria* on plant numbers is rather small in the situation studied: weather factors appear to be of far greater importance. Weather has a direct effect on the survival of healthy plants as well as an indirect effect on the ability of defoliated plants to regenerate.

The influence of ragwort on cinnabar moth numbers is dependent on the density of the cinnabar larvae in relation to plant biomass. Food shortage may result in a very high mortality due to starvation, in an increase of predation, and in a decrease in the fecundity of the moths. In a situation in which food shortage will occur, predation on the young larvae may have a favourable effect on the survival of those larvae which survive predation, since this prevents a more severe competition for food.

In 1907, the noted Dutch advocate of popularisation of natural history, Thijsse, described regular fluctuations in the population densities of *Senecio jacobaea* and *Tyria jacobaeae*. He supposed that these fluctuations were caused by defoliation of ragwort by cinnabar moth larvae, after which a large number of caterpillars died from starvation. He further assumed that as a result of this defoliation, the population density of ragwort was also severely reduced. After the catastrophe, the numbers of foodplant and consumer would gradually increase again.

Cameron (1935), working on the biological control of ragwort, came to the conclusion that *Tyria* could, indeed, be effective in controlling *Senecio*, 'provided that the attack is general and no secondary growth follows'. He stated that: 'when poor plants, growing on very inferior soil, are heavily and uniformly attacked by *Tyria*, the ragwort infestation should be wiped out'.

Hawkes (1968) described a biological control experiment in Fort Bragg (California). In 1959, a number of *Tyria* caterpillars was released. By 1963 numbers had increased to such an extent that complete defoliation occurred. Until 1966 virtually all the flowers were consumed. Hawkes wrote: 'between 1963 and 1965 the plant has been very substantially suppressed ... Although larval feeding may not have an outright killing effect on the plant, the larvae do consume the foliage and flowers from a high percentage of plants, thereby greatly reducing the amount of seed produced'. Apparently, however, another factor also

* This study has been made possible by a grant of the Netherlands Organisation for the Advancement of Pure Research.

played a role in the decline of numbers, viz. competition: 'the area of the [*Tyria*] population increase at Fort Bragg is not grazed at present, thus other vegetation, primarily grasses, can form a dense cover'.

It is the aim of our study to estimate the importance of the mutual interaction of *Tyria* and *Senecio* by measuring the whole complex of factors which determine the numbers of these two organisms. This study is not yet completed, but I will present some preliminary evidence to show that, though the influence of *Senecio* on *Tyria* may be very important in the determination of numbers, the influence of *Tyria* on *Senecio* is, in our research area, not so impressive as it was in the above-mentioned cases.

Ragwort in the Dutch dunes

In the Dutch dunes, ragwort generally occurs in clusters or pockets with solitary plants in between. These clusters may occupy areas of between a few and some hundred square meters; they occur in all types of vegetation, ranging from very poor communities with interrupted cover of mosses, lichens and very short grasses to tree-covered areas.

Ragwort is a biennial plant. The seeds germinate mainly in the autumn after seed formation, and in the following spring. In its first year the plant forms a rosette of leaves; in the second year the flowering stem is formed. Through this cycle the plant population is, in fact, subdivided into two groups (upper and lower part of Fig. 1). In principle, these two groups might be considered as separate populations because exchange of genes would be impossible. In practice, however, a number of factors intervene which prevent these two groups from becoming isolated (Fig. 1). One of these factors is defoliation by *Tyria*. When a second-year plant for some reason or another does not produce seeds, it may, in a number of cases, survive another winter. This prolonged life cycle may be due to a retardation in development, for instance by unfavourable weather conditions (Poole and Cairns, 1940). On the other hand, defoliation or other damage may have the same effect. When a plant is badly damaged, regeneration from root buds may occur. In these situations seeds will only be formed in the third year. (In some cases ragwort may flower again in the same year as that defoliation occurred. In most cases, however, the local situation is not suited for the setting of seeds late in the season, and a number of these plants continue to live into the next year.) Regeneration from root buds may result in a number of new shoots. For reasons of simplicity these systems are considered as to be one plant in this paper.

Factors determining the number of plants

Fig. 1 presents a schematic diagram of the factors which eventually determine the number of plants in a pocket. The effect of a number of these factors will be elaborated here.

Seeds

Wind dispersal. Since a cluster is of limited size and the adjacent areas have only low ragwort densities, a number of the seeds which are produced within the cluster will disappear out of it, and this is not compensated for by seeds coming in from outside. These seeds are therefore to be considered as a loss for the subpopulation. In fact, it would be important to have an estimate of the origin of new clusters in the vicinity of the seed producing area.

391

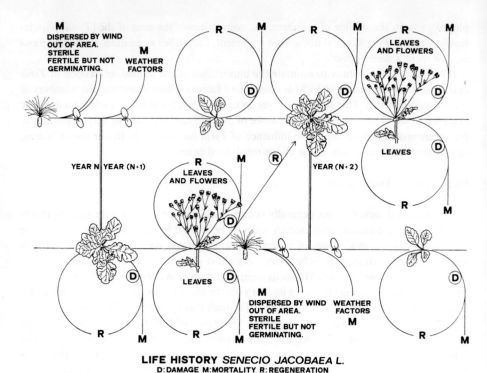

LIFE HISTORY *SENECIO JACOBAEA* L.
D: DAMAGE M: MORTALITY R: REGENERATION

Fig. 1. Schematic diagram of the life history of *Senecio jacobaea* L.

Sterility. A proportion of the seeds produced is sterile. Comparable figures for the different areas and years are obtained from germination experiments under identical conditions.

Not germinating though fertile. A very large proportion of the seeds fails to germinate in the field. Possible causes of this 'mortality' are:
1. a decrease in fertility with time,
2. consumption (predation) of the dispersed seeds,
3. an unfavourable microclimate in the site where the seed has fallen.

A life-table for one of the study areas, showing the quantities of capitula, seeds and seedlings, is presented in Table 1. The plants produce an enormous amount of seeds. Between the times of formation and germination of the seeds, however, there is a tremendous loss. The major part of this mortality takes place when the seeds have already been dispersed over the field. However, not all non-germinating seeds in this life-table can be classed under the heading of mortality, since data for the germination after August 1970 have not yet been included.

From field observations it is clear that the germination of seeds that have lain dormant in the field does not add very much to the total number of germinated seeds of the original crop; in a situation in which mortality of the seedlings of the main germination period is very high, however, their influence on the population can be very important.

In some cases germination of dormant seeds seems to be completely negligible; for instance, in Inner Forne and on Coquet Islands (Northumberland) where flowering only

Table 1. Life-table *Senecio jacobaea*. Seed production and germination (area II, 1969–1970). Number of mature plants in 1969: 112.

		Loss	Loss per stage (%)
Number of capitula 1969	23,437		
Incompletely developed		4,858	20.7
Damaged		14	0.1
Predated by *Pegohylemyia*		492	2.1
Total loss		5,364	22.9
Number of capitula left	18,073		
(Mean number of seeds per capitulum: 69.7)			
Total seed production	1,260,000		
Dispersed by wind out of area		475,000	37.7
Number of seeds fallen in area	785,000		
Sterile		93,000	11.8
Fertile	692,000		
Fertile seeds not germinated		681,200	98.4
Fertile seeds germinated			
in 1969	2,890		
in 1970 (up till August): 7,940			
Total germinated	10,800 = 0.9% of total seed production		

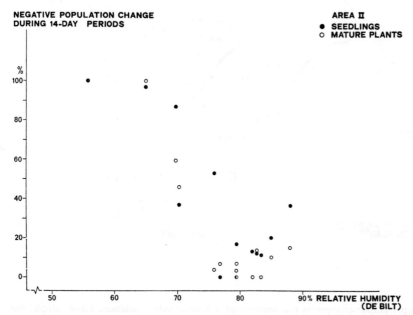

Fig. 2. The relationship between mean relative humidity of the air and the negative population change of seedlings and mature plants of ragwort over periods of fourteen days.

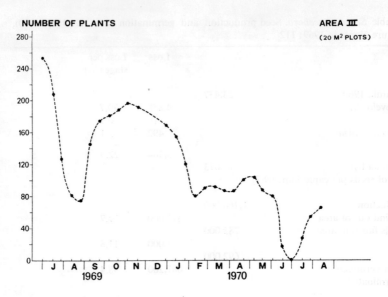

NUMBER OF PLANTS

AREA III

(20 M² PLOTS)

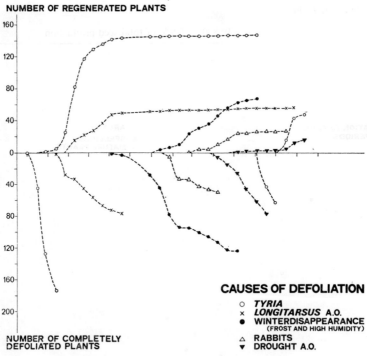

NUMBER OF REGENERATED PLANTS

CAUSES OF DEFOLIATION

○ *TYRIA*
× *LONGITARSUS* A.O.
● WINTERDISAPPEARANCE
   (FROST AND HIGH HUMIDITY)
△ RABBITS
▼ DROUGHT A.O.

NUMBER OF COMPLETELY
DEFOLIATED PLANTS

Fig. 3. Upper graph: changes in the numbers of a *Senecio* sub-population. Lower graph: the separate effects of a number of defoliating agencies and the subsequent regeneration (cumulative). Together, these effects are the cause of the population changes presented in the upper graph.

happens in alternate years. This suggests that the seeds of one year class of mature plants does not contribute to the other (J. C. Coulson, pers. comm.).

Immature plants

Seedling mortality. Adverse weather conditions like drought and frost may result in a strong decline in seedling numbers. In one of the study areas drought caused a total disappearance of the seedlings. The relation between the relative humidity of the air and the negative population change in this area is shown in Fig. 2. It can be seen that not only drought but also a high RH, which in our area often corresponds with low temperatures, results in an increasing negative population change.

Rosette-plant mortality. Defoliation or other damage may lead to mortality. Fig. 3 shows the fate of a rosette-plant population from July 1969 onwards (becoming second-year plants in 1970). The causes of the changes in total number are elaborated in the lower part of the graph.

A special case of defoliation is that by rabbits. Especially during winter, they dig up and consume the roots of ragwort plants, leaving the foliage unaffected. The causes of mortality in rosette-plants and mature plants are the same; however, they effect quantitative differences in the changes in numbers of the two groups.

Mature plants

As was the case in the younger stages, drought may be an important factor in limiting the number of mature plants (Fig. 2). No regeneration occurred afterwards in this case. These data were collected in a study area which consisted of bare sand sparsely covered with lichens, occasional tufts of *Corynephorus* and a few *Hippophae* shrubs. This type of vegetation occupies an important part of the dune area. In the extremely dry spring and summer of 1970, a high mortality rate caused by desiccation was noticed in many subareas. However, in areas with a denser vegetation, or in valleys, a fair number of plants may escape from the effect of drought.

The course of the *Senecio* population in one of the latter areas is represented in Fig. 3. The 1970 part of this graph shows the fate of a mature plant population in an area with a locally high vegetation of grass sheltered by white poplars. The life-table for this population is given in Table 2. Mortality as a result of defoliation by *Tyria* is certainly not the most important one. The last column of Table 2 shows the percentage mortality due to a certain factor in relation to the number of plants damaged by that factor. Apparently, defoliation by the cinnabar moth causes the lowest mortality value found; this, of course, is due to the fact that after this type of defoliation most plants are able to regenerate.

Weather factors, such as drought, not only may result in severe mortality, but, moreover, have an important effect on the ability to regenerate (Fig. 4). The same applies for frost when combined with a high relative humidity.

Influence of cinnabar moth larvae on plant numbers

Now, what is the significance of the role of *Tyria* in the whole complex? Apparently the influence on plant *numbers* is not very large. A large proportion of the defoliated plants

Table 2. Life-table *Senecio* (area III, 1969–1970). Initial number of plants on 1 July 1969: 253; on 12 August 1970: 66.

Causes of defoliation	Number of plants					
	present	defoliated	regenerated	died	died present × 100%	died defoliated × 100%
Tyria 1969	253	175	149	26	10	15
Longitarsus etc.	219	77	59	18	8	23
Winter disappearance (frost, high humidity)	150	115	68	47	31	41
Rabbits	116	50	28	22	19	44
Drought etc.	90	79	18	61	66	77
Tyria 1970	62	62	49	13	21	21

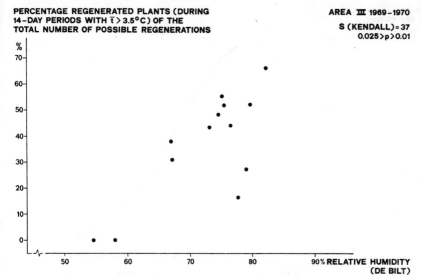

Fig. 4. The relationship between mean relative humidity of the air and regeneration of defoliated ragwort plants over periods of fourteen days.

regenerates. Of the mature plants that are prevented from flowering by the cinnabar moth larvae, a large proportion become third-year, or even fourth-year plants. We have not yet been able to estimate the effect of *Tyria* on seed production since this year there was again complete defoliation. If we look, however, at the biomasses of the individual adult plants in 1970, we see that on 15 May 1970 the average biomass amounted to 680 mg, while this was 570 mg on the same date in 1969. So, on the average, the biomass of a third-year plant is greater than that of a second-year plant. Since seed production in ragwort is positively correlated with biomass, we might assume that the plants with a prolonged duration of life due to defoliation would produce more seeds.

Factors determining cinnabar moth numbers

The life-cycle of the cinnabar moth is discussed extensively by Dempster (1971). The causes of mortality among the larvae can be divided into two groups:
a. mortality due to predation and parasitism,
b. mortality due to shortage of food.

For the calculation of these mortalities we used a modification of Dempster's method (1961). The method is based on the solving of a set of linear equations that are derived from the field data.

It is assumed that mortality resulting from food shortage will be a function of the biomass of the plants present. To estimate this biomass we constructed equations with which the biomass of a plant can be calculated from measurements of height, diameter and the number of leaves. These last features can be measured without damaging the plants. The equations were calculated by a method of multiple regression (Anon., 1969).

The change in biomass in one of the study areas is shown in Fig. 5. The increase is due to growth, the decrease is due to defoliation. As mortality due to food shortage was

397

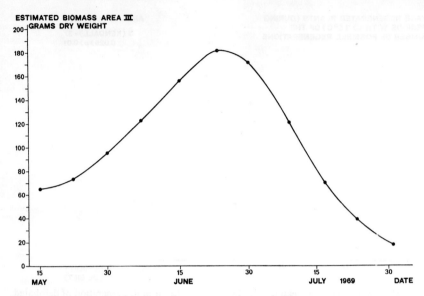

Fig. 5. Change in plant biomass of a ragwort sub-population.

assumed to be dependent on the plant biomass, the number of caterpillars found in a situation of starvation also will be dependent on the plant biomass. (The decrease in numbers with decreasing biomass is not only due to mortality within the area, but also to migration of the larvae out of the area. Mortality and migration are not separated here.)

The relationship between biomass and number of caterpillars is shown in Fig. 6. Since we assume mortality through predation to be linearly proportional to the number of caterpillars, $(\log B_{t_0} - \log B_{t_1})$ is proportional to the mortality caused by food shortage. This factor can be introduced into the set of equations and this set can then be solved.

Table 3 shows a life-table for one of the study areas in 1969. Mortality in the youngest two stages was very high, as it was in Weeting Heath (Dempster, 1971). In the example given, the calculated mortality due to food shortage amounted to about 20% of the total number of hatched eggs. Contrary to the British situation, we also found a high mortality among the older larvae which could not be ascribed to starvation. I will return to this point later.

Mortality caused by food shortage varied, roughly, between 20% and 80% in different years and in different study areas. It is quite obvious that a high mortality in the younger stages has a very favourable effect on the population of the cinnabar moth, because, due to this, a reduction is effectuated in the number of larvae reaching the fourth and the fifth instar in which about 90% of the total consumption takes place. When the population density of the older larvae is very high in relation to biomass, food shortage will occur very suddenly and reduce, or even eliminate, the population abruptly. High mortality in the early stages prevents a more severe competition for food later on. An example which illustrates this is shown in Table 4.

It is no exception that ragwort pockets are completely defoliated. We once found completely defoliated plants with many young larvae, only a small number of just moulted fifth-instar caterpillars, and still very many eggs. So, not only local *Senecio* populations, but also local *Tyria* populations may disappear.

398

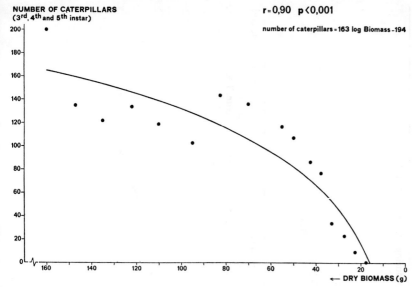

NUMBER OF CATERPILLARS
(3rd, 4th and 5th instar)

$r = 0,90$ $p < 0,001$

number of caterpillars = 163 log Biomass -194

← DRY BIOMASS (g)

Fig. 6. The fall-off in the number of caterpillars with decreasing plant biomass.

Pupation and migration of larvae

Shortage of food in a certain *Senecio* pocket, however, does not necessarily lead to the extinction of all the larvae. Fifth-instar caterpillars are able to pupate before they have reached their maximum weight. This ability, however, depends on the value of the body weight reached. Fig. 7 shows the relationship between the body weight of larvae at the time they were deprived of food, and the percentage of caterpillars still able to pupate. The 50% value is reached when the larvae have attained a body weight of about 185 mg. In a situation in which no food shortage occurs, the larva reaches this weight about four days after

Table 3. Life-table *Tyria* (area III, 1969).

Eggs laid		601
Hatched (instar I)		563
Mortality:		
(instar I and II)		
predation	290	
(instar III and IV)		
predation	49	
(instar V)		
predation	94	
parasitism *(Apanteles)*	7.5	
(instar III, IV and V)		
starvation	105	
total	545.5	
Number of pupae		17.5

399

Table 4. A calculated example of competition for food among larvae of *Tyria*, based on 100 eggs hatching at the same moment and an available plant biomass of 2500 units.

	Consumption per larva in plant biomass units	Consumption per instar in biomass units when food is not limiting	
		no predation	50% predation during instar I and II**
Instar I + II	1	100	75
Instar III + IV	19	1900	950
Instar V	30	3000	1500
Total consumption		5000	2525
Food deficiency in plant biomass		2500 (= 5000−2500)	25 (= 2525−2500)
Food units available for instar V		500 (= 2500− (100 + 1900))	1475 (= 2500− (75 + 950))
Number of pupations		0 − 17**	49
Mortality through starvation		83 −100%	2%

* 50% predation during instar I and II leads to a reduction of 50 larvae at some time during these instars. As this will happen only gradually, the consumption was calculated as if during these instars 75 larvae were present. From instar III on 50 larvae were used for the calculations.

** 500 plant biomass units are available for 30 Vth-instar caterpillars. If they consume equal parts of the total mass, none will pupate. The other extreme takes place when some larvae (17) consume 30 units each while the others get nothing.

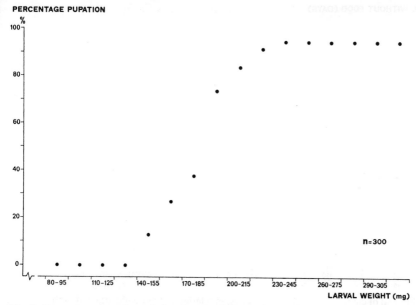

Fig. 7. Percentage pupation of cinnabar moth larvae in relation to the weight attained at the moment of food deprival.

it has moulted into the fifth instar; the total duration of this stage is 7 to 8 days. However, lighter larvae produce smaller pupae which give rise to moths with a lower fecundity.

The larvae that are not able to pupate because they have not reached the minimum pupation weight at the time when the food supply is exhausted, will not die immediately. They generally leave the defoliated plants and are able to cover large distances while searching for new food plants. The distance that these larvae may cover is supposed to be proportionally related to their ability to survive on the energy reserves laid down in the body. The relationship between survival and body weight is presented in Fig. 8. The heavier caterpillars may survive up to 18 days. A number of animals will succeed in finding new food plants during this period. However, it should be noted that, in this period, mortality due to predation will be high and proportional to the time that the animals are crawling around in the field.

Predation by ants

I promised to return to the subject of predation of the older larval stages. In order to determine the fate of the fifth-instar caterpillars and to localise the pupae, a dot of paint containing radioactive Ir^{192} was applied to a number of caterpillars. (Laboratory rearings did not show significant differences in pupation success between marked and unmarked larvae.) Out of some hundreds of larvae released, we only found a small number of pupae. The remaining radioactive marks were retrieved in the field still stuck to a small piece of larval skin; these were generally in the vicinity of nests of the ant *Lasius alienus* FÖRSTER. It therefore seemed very plausible that these larvae had been eaten by ants. For this reason this experiment was repeated in a number of areas in which the ant density was also estimated. The *Tyria* mortality was calculated by counting the number of marks retrieved in

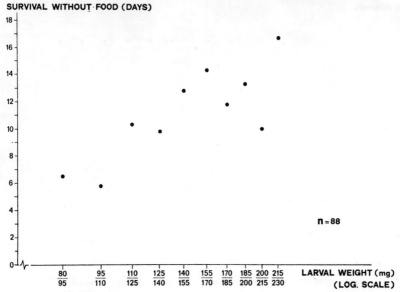

SURVIVAL WITHOUT FOOD (DAYS)

n = 88

LARVAL WEIGHT (mg)
(LOG. SCALE)

Fig. 8. Survival of cinnabar moth larvae, in days, in relation to the weight attained at the moment of food deprival (for larvae that had not reached the minimum pupation weight).

the field, and represents the geometric means of mortality occuring within a number of concentric circles round the release point; circles were drawn until the density of caterpillars dropped below one per m². The relationship between ant density and *Tyria* mortality is given in Fig. 9. Apart from the larvae searching for pupation sites, larvae that have left their defoliated food plants and are searching for fresh food also will be preyed upon heavily by *Lasius*.

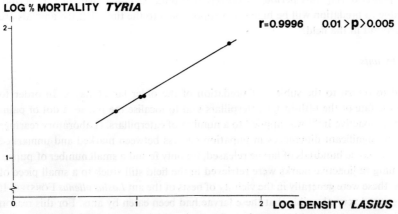

LOG % MORTALITY *TYRIA*

r=0.9996   0.01 > p > 0.005

LOG DENSITY *LASIUS*

Fig. 9. The relationship between density of *Lasius alienus* Förster and mortality of cinnabar moth larvae (instar V).

Conclusion

When considering only the number of ragwort plants, we see that the influence of the cinnabar moth is rather small. A considerable proportion of the plants regenerates. The effect on the seed production of adult plants is partly compensated for by the behaviour of ragwort which then forms seeds in the third year and, moreover, by the fact that seed production of these third-year plants may be higher than that of second-year plants. The number of plants which regenerate after being damaged by *Tyria* is not only dependent on the degree of damage done, but also on weather factors. It may be concluded that weather factors are the most important ones in determining the number of *Senecio* plants; at least, they were the most important factors in the two years that we have been studying the population.

The influence of ragwort on the cinnabar moth is strongly dependent on the density of the latter. Starvation may result either in mortality or a lower reproduction per female. In situations of high larva/foodplant ratios, predation on the younger larvae has a favourable effect, since it prevents a more severe competition for food later on. Finally, lack of food not only results in mortality through starvation, but also in an increase in mortality due to predation because larvae have to leave their defoliated food plants and are, hence, exposed to ants or other predators. This exposure may be of considerably longer duration than it is in the case of larvae which are searching for pupation sites.

References

Anonymous, 1969. Scientific subroutine package (PL/1). Program description and operations manual. IBM.

Cameron, E., 1935. A study of the natural control of ragwort (*Senecio jacobaea* L.) *J. Ecol.* 23: 265–322.

Dempster, J., 1961. The analysis of data obtained by regular sampling of an insect population. *J. Anim. Ecol.* 30: 429–432.

Dempster, J., 1971. A population study of the cinnabar moth *Tyria* (*Callimorpha*) *jacobaeae* L. In: P. J. den Boer & G. R. Gradwell (Ed.), Dynamics in population. *Proc. Adv. Study Inst. Dynamics Numbers Popul.* (Oosterbeek, 1970) 380–389.

Hawkes, R. B., 1968. The cinnabar moth, *Tyria jacobaeae*, for control of tansy ragwort. *J. econ. Ent.* 61: 499–501.

Poole, A. L. & D. Cairns, 1940. Botanical aspects of ragwort (*Senecio jacobaea*). *N. Z. Dep. sci. industr. Res.*, *Contr. Bull.* 82: 1–66.

Thijsse, J. P., 1907. Zomer. Verkade.

Discussion

Participants: Van der Meijden (Author), Beukema, Brussard, Cavers, Coulson, Dempster, Frank, Huffaker, Pimentel, Waloff, Way, de Wit and Zwölfer

Senecio may regenerate more from dormant seeds than from root buds (CAVERS). Despite the fact that dormancy may last from three to eight years, regeneration is probably more important than germination of dormant seeds (AUTHOR). I found that after two years germination was already very low (DEMPSTER).

The flowering of *Senecio* in alternate years only, on Inner Farne and Coquet Islands, Northumberland, is added evidence that the seeds remain viable for only a short time (COULSON). However, even a 1 % germination after a high production of seeds may be very important (CAVERS).

The work of Wilkinson et al. (1970) in British Columbia has shown that the regrowth of *Senecio* (after defoliation by *Tyria*) produces only about 600 seeds per plant (ZWÖLFER). It is difficult to draw conclusions about the influence of *Tyria* from the data mentioned by Zwölfer. In the first place, other factors than defoliation by *Tyria* influence seed setting. In the second place, it is necessary to study the behaviour of the plants after seed formation; a number of the plants that have flowered for the second time in the same year, after defoliation, continue to live into the third year (AUTHOR).

Does regeneration occur after the growing point of the plant has been eaten (DE WIT)? This is the case; plants cut off at ground level will regenerate from root buds which act as new growing points (AUTHOR).

May the regeneration of *Senecio* be influenced by the faeces of *Tyria* (FRANK)? No information is available on this (AUTHOR).

Has the influence of *Tyria* on *Senecio* been checked experimentally, e.g. by removing *Tyria* with an insecticide in some plots and comparing the effects on *Senecio* with the situation in plots containing *Tyria* (HUFFAKER)? One of the study areas is free from *Tyria*, so a comparison is possible. Insecticides were not used since this is prohibited (AUTHOR).

Is there any toxin in the roots of *Senecio* that may affect rabbits (PIMENTEL)? I know of no evidence for this. The main source of poisons is alkaloids in the leaves (AUTHOR).

What is the effect on the *Senecio* population of the larvae of the beetle *Longitarsus jacobaeae* and the seedfly, *Pegohylemyia seneciella* (ZWÖLFER)? I think that the seedfly is not important, since it only caused 2 % seed damage in the area studied. The influence of *Longitarsus* adults is shown in Table 2. The damage by the larvae is not known as they feed in the roots while only the upper parts of the plants could be examined without damaging the plant population. (AUTHOR).

Although *Lasius* is common at Weeting Heath in England, I only once observed *Tyria* larvae being attacked by ants. The different behaviour of the ants in the two localities may be explained by differences in the presence of different kinds of food (DEMPSTER). I agree with this, especially since we were able to show that ants fed on *Drosophila* in the laboratory would subsequently reject *Tyria* larvae (AUTHOR).

The periods when the ants are feeding their developing larvae – and are in highest need of protein – may differ in the two study areas. Is there a possibility that they are preying only on sick *Tyria* larvae (WAY)? I have observed *Lasius* preying on healthy larvae (AUTHOR).

Perhaps *Tyria* is most vulnerable to attack by *Lasius* at the time of moulting (WALOFF). Does any other predator remove last-instar larvae of *Tyria* (BRUSSARD)? They certainly exist, e.g. *Formica polyctena* (AUTHOR).

Is there any preference of *Tyria* larvae for first- or second-year plants (CAVERS)? The adult female *Tyria* prefers to oviposit on second-year plants, but this preference is soon masked by the tendency of the larvae to spread to all plants (AUTHOR).

Are there any observations on the distances travelled by larvae and adults of *Tyria*? Such movements could well be important because local populations of *Tyria* appear to be in high risk of extinction (BEUKEMA). Although the adult males are good fliers, this is not true of females. Thus, larvae constitute the main dispersive phase (AUTHOR). I also think the adults are not very migratory (DEMPSTER).

Proc. Adv. Study Inst. Dynamics Numbers Popul. (Oosterbeek, 1970) 405–418

The structure and effect of parasite complexes attacking phytophagous host insects

H. Zwölfer

Commonwealth Institute of Biological Control, Delémont, Switzerland

Abstract

Parasite (parasitoid) species exploiting the same phytophagous host insect compete with each other as far as larval food is concerned. To render possible the coexistence of such parasites, one or several parameters in the host-parasite system must be affected in such a way that the potential efficiency of the individual parasite species is reduced. The parasite complexes of *Operophtera brumata, Rhyacionia buoliana, Neodiprion sertifer, Thymelicus lineola* and *Choristoneura murinana* provide examples of mechanisms influencing the searching capacity of parasites (mutual interference), the behavioral response of parasite individuals (selection of host species available at high population levels) and the reproductive efficiency (encapsulation, superparasitism, multiparasitism, cleptoparasitism, hyperparasitism). Of particular importance is 'counter-balanced competition', a relationship allowing the coexistence of intrinsically inferior but well adapted parasites with less specialized parasites which are superior in cases of multiparasitism. The results of current biocontrol operations suggest that well synchronized and highly specialized parasites are often severely handicapped by systems of counter-balanced competition, but are able to use their full potentialities if introduced into an area where they can operate without such interactions. Where counter-balanced competition involves a potentially efficient parasite, biological control operations should proceed cautiously with the parasite species being introduced in a pre-determined sequence.

The structure of natural parasite complexes, i.e. the interactions between parasite species (parasitoids) and the interrelations between parasites and host insect, has been previously discussed by Zwölfer (1963)[1], and Pschorn-Walcher and Zwölfer (1968). The following is based on recent investigations made at the European Station of the Commonwealth Institute of Biological Control.

The problem of coexistence in multiple parasite systems

Parasite species (parasitoid species) exploiting the same population of a phytophagous host compete with each other as far as food and space for larval development is concerned.

[1] This paper has been the cause of some misunderstanding. Zwölfer (1963) has not 'claimed that the abundance of some of the moths arose from competition between the many parasite species' (Hassell and Varley, 1969). His paper simply states the following facts: In the large parasite complexes attacking *Choristoneura murinana* HB. and *Coleophora deauratella* ZELL. the biologically specialized and well-synchronized parasites are exposed to manifold interactions and are unable to prevent their hosts from building up high pupulations. However, the specialized parasites of *Paraswammerdamia* spp. and *Hydroecia* spp. operate without much interactions and are highly efficient against their host species.

Interactions between parasite species attacking the same host may lead to the competitive displacement of one species by another. This has been experimentally demonstrated and extensively discussed by DeBach and Sundby (1963), DeBach (1966) and Flanders (1966). It is now apparent that field populations of certain insect taxa such as moths or sawflies usually sustain numerous parasite species. How do such parasite species avoid competitive elimination? How do they manage to coexist in a multiple species system?

Certain mechanisms must exist to render possible the competitive coexistence of parasites. These mechanisms must affect one or several parameters in the host-parasite system in such a way that the potential efficiency of the individual parasite species is reduced if the number of competing parasites increases (Pschorn-Walcher and Zwölfer, 1968).

However, before discussing such mechanisms, we have to deal with a parameter which is perhaps the most important character of an insect parasite, host specificity.

Host specificity

In population models describing the dynamics of host-parasite systems, host specificity of a parasite is usually neglected and probably for the following reasons: (a) Population models are largely derived from experimental systems where only one host species is involved and where, consequently, host selection by the parasite could not enter into performance; (b) The introduction of host specificity as a parameter into population models may cause considerable difficulties with regard to mathematical formulation; (c) It is believed that unspecific parasite species are not used in biological control, a viewpoint recently taken by Hassell and Varley (1969).

However, biological control practices do include unspecific parasites, some of which have become successful biocontrol agents. Moreover, the classification of 'specific' and 'unspecific' parasites is a somewhat unrealistic simplification for the following reasons:
1. Between a strictly specific parasite (i.e. a monophagous parasite) and a completely unspecific parasite (i.e. a polyphagous species without any host preference) there is a wide range of intermediate forms. In many (if not in most) natural parasite complexes, the dominant role is played by such intermediate forms rather than by monophagous parasites.
2. Strictly specific parasites are rare and in many natural parasite complexes they do not occur at all. Ample evidence for this has been provided by the many projects dealt with at the Commonwealth Institute of Biological Control.
3. It may be argued that any species with a narrow host range as well as monophagous species belong to the group of specific parasites and that the former, in certain ecosystems, may behave like monophagous parasites and thus the research into their host-specificity could be neglected. However, field observations have shown that even in parasite species with a very narrow host range, host-specificity should not be neglected. The tachinid *Cyzenis albicans* (FALL.) is a highly specialized enemy of the winter moth, *Operophtera brumata* L., and is often cited as an example of a specific parasite, but in actual fact *C. albicans* does respond to other host species. Embree and Sisojevic (1965) have shown that in certain ecosystems, where winter moth is associated with other defoliators, lack of strict specificity in the oviposition response of *C. albicans* may have a detrimental effect on the efficiency of this parasite.
4. Within certain ecosystems, notoriously unspecific parasites (e.g. *Apechthis* spp., *Itoplectis* spp.) may show rather specific behaviour (Zwölfer and Kraus, 1957). Perhaps the best known example is the North American ichneumonid *Itoplectis conquisitor* (SAY); this

is potentially a very polyphagous species which regionally has become adapted to two phytophagous insects recently introduced to Canada. Arthur (1966) has shown that associative learning of parasite females is one factor in this process.

Instead of arbitrarily discriminating between specific and unspecific parasites, more differentiating systems of classification should be used. During parasite studies made at the European Station of the CIBC (e.g. Carl, 1968; Sechser, 1970; Zwölfer, 1961) the status of a parasite was determined by the following parameters:

a. *Host range*. This is the range of acceptable hosts. The host range is measured by the number of systematic categories of hosts which can be parasitized rather than by counting the number of host species (Pschorn-Walcher, 1957).

b. *Host preference*. This term indicates the status of a host species with regard to other acceptable hosts.

c. *Constancy*. This term refers to the presence of a parasite in the investigated host samples. It indicates the probability with which the parasite may be expected to occur in an individual sample.

d. *Abundance*. This term indicates the relative numerical importance of the parasite species within the parasite complex studied.

The values for 'constancy' and 'abundance' are calculated from the available samples of

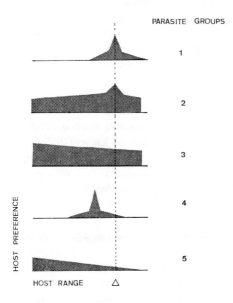

Fig. 1. Patterns of host range and host preference of some parasites of *Choristoneura murinana*. Abscissa: Range of acceptable host species. The triangle indicates the position of *C. murinana* within the host ranges of the five groups of parasites. Ordinates (height of shaded areas): Host preference.

Group 1: Stenophagous parasites with a preference for *C. murinana* (high constancy) (*Apanteles murinanae* Cap. & Zwölf., *Cephaloglypta murinanae* Bauer, *Phaeogenes maculicornis* Steph.).

(Group 2: An euryphagous parasite species with preference for *C. murinana* (high constancy) (*Itoplectis maculator* F.).

Group 3: Euryphagous parasites without particular preference for *C. murinana* (high constancy) (*Pimpla turionellae* L., *Apechthis resinator* Thunb., *Ephialtes inquisitor* Scop.).

Group 4: Stenophagous parasites with a preference for oak-tortricids, marginal parasites of *C. murinana* (low constancy) (*Phytodietus* sp., *Tranosema arenicola* Thoms., *Glypta*? *cicatricosa* Ratz.).

Group 5: Euryphagous parasites attacking occasionally *C. murinana* (low constancy) (*Itoplectis alternans* Grav., *Habrobracon brevicornis* Wesm.). (Details given by Zwölfer, 1961.)

the investigated host species, whilst host range and host preference have to be deduced from comparative field studies, experiments, and other sources of information.

Host range, host preference, constancy and abundance form combinations which characterize the position of a parasite species within the parasite complex studied. Fig. 1 shows this for some parasites of the European fir budworm (*Choristoneura murinana* HB.).

Such patterns which combine parasite species of different host specificity are widely distributed among parasite complexes of autochthonous host species. This fact has to be considered in the following discussion of competitive coexistence of parasites.

Parameters affected in multiple parasite systems

Our basic question is: Which mechanisms could affect the parameters of host-parasite systems to render possible the coexistence of different parasite species? Hence the parameters in host-parasite systems as discussed by Huffaker et al. (1968) are enumerated here:
a. 'Behavioral response' (i.e. responses in the behaviour of individual parasites);
b. 'Numerical response' (i.e. responses in the population trend of a parasite);
c. 'Heterogeneity of the host-parasite system' (i.e. existence of sub-populations, sub-habitats, etc.).

The 'numerical response' of a parasite population to numerical changes in the host population is usually taken as the most important parameter. Huffaker et al. (1968) state that the two basic ways in which an entomophagous insect may possess the ability of a 'numerical response' are: 'reproductive capacity' and – far more important – 'searching capacity'. The latter is often expressed in terms of the 'area of discovery'.

Searching capacity

By suggesting that the searching capacity of a parasite species is a density-dependent factor which declines exponentially as parasite density increases, Hassell and Varley (1969) have transformed the well-known population model of Nicholson. In the 'parasite quest theory', searching capacity is a function of a 'mutual interference constant' and progressive stability of host-parasite fluctuations is shown as the mutual interference constant is increased, thus giving a mathematical explanation for parasite species coexisting in multiple systems.

There is experimental evidence (Sechser, in preparation) to show that one of the two main parasites of the winter moth, the ichneumonid *Aptesis abdominator* GRAV., behaves according to the new population model. This parasite has a very low reproductive potential (daily oviposition rate: 2, total egg production 30–40), but also has a high searching efficiency combined with the ability to avoid hosts previously parasitized by *Aptesis*. The results from a series of cage experiments, where parasite density was progressively increased, have shown that there was a corresponding reduction in the parasite's efficiency. Sechser assumes that this is caused by mutual interference of the searching parasite females.

Hassell and Varley (1969) have analysed several host-parasite systems and conclude that the phenomenon of mutual interference among the individuals of a parasite species is very common. Dealing with multiple parasite systems one may ask the question whether mutual interference also occurs among individuals belonging to different parasite species. So far, we have not found such *interspecific* interference which would mutually affect the searching capacity of parasites. However, cases of non-reciprocal interference, e.g. of ants and parasites, certainly do occur.

Behavioral response

If a parasite could respond to variations in the population density of acceptable host species by attacking the most preponderant one, a mechanism would be provided to avoid over-exploitation of the host and to render coexistence of parasites possible. There is some evidence showing the occurrence of such behavioral responses which adjust host selection to the available supply of host species.

Pschorn-Walcher and Zinnert (1971) following population trends of the parasites associated with endemic populations of the European larch sawfly, *Pristiphora erichsonii* HTG., stated that in years of higher host densities the more polyphagous parasite species contributed to a proportionally greater extent of total parasitism (around one third), whereas in years of low host densities two monophagous parasites almost completely dominated the parasite complex. Schröder (in preparation) observed a similar phenomenon in the parasite complexes of pine shoot moth. Both cases suggest that the more polyphagous parasites show a behavioral response to host density. The North American ichneumonid *I. conquisitor* provides a striking example of a behavioral response influencing the searching image of the parasite. *I. conquisitor* became rapidly adapted to the introduced hesperid *Thymelicus lineola* OCHS. Arthur (1966) demonstrated that females of *I. conquisitor* possess the ability of associative learning and concluded that 'after finding and parasitizing a few hosts of a particular species, the female learns to associate certain characteristics of the oviposition site with the presence of hosts, and its host-finding ability is thus greatly increased'. Since the density of the host species determines the frequency of contacts between parasite and host, the ability of associative learning will direct the *I. conquisitor* female to host species which are present in high densities.

The parasite complexes of *T. lineola* offer another example which may be interpreted as a behavioral response. In Europe where *T. lineola* occurs only in low densities, Carl (1966) found, during his long-term study, only two marginal parasite species (i.e. euryphagous parasites which only occasionally attack *T. lineola*). In Canada, where the introduced *T. lineola* is locally abundant and causes extensive damage to meadows, 21 marginal parasite species are known to attack this hesperid (Table 1). It is noteworthy that two of these parasites also occur in Europe, but have never been reared from *T. lineola*. This impressive difference is not an artefact brought about by different sampling methods, etc., but a reflection of the true difference in behaviour of parasites in Canadian outbreak areas, compared with European regions of endemic host densities.

Reproductive efficiency

In natural host-parasite systems, there may occur various inherent mechanisms reducing the reproductive efficiency of a parasite by eliminating a certain proportion of its offspring, e.g. superparasitism, multiparasitism, hyperparasitism.

At constant host densities, the efficiency of two of these mechanisms – superparasitism and multiparasitism – increases with increasing parasite density. Some parasites, however, are able to discriminate between parasitized and unparasitized hosts and may thus avoid or reduce superparasitism or multiparasitism. Sechser (1971) has shown that *Aptesis*

Table 1. Composition of the parasite complexes of *Thymelicus lineola* in Europe and Canada. (Details given by Carl, 1968.)

	Europe	Canada
Status of host species	Native	Introduced
Status of parasites	Native	Native
Numbers of parasite species reared:		
Group 1 (euryphagous; preference, constancy and abundance low)	2	21
Group 2 (euryphagous; 'adapted' to host, preference, constancy and abundance high)	–	1
Group 3 (euryphagous; constancy high, preference and abundance moderate)	2	–
Group 4 (stenophagous; preference, constancy and abundance high)	1	–
Group 5 (stenophagous; preference?, constancy and abundance low)	1	–

The species belonging to group 4 (*Stenichneumon scutellator* GRAV.) will be released in Canada.

abdominator, one of the main parasites of the winter moth, is largely able to avoid super-parasitism, whilst *C. albicans*, another important parasite, does not possess this ability. Their ability to avoid multiparasitism has also been studied. It has been shown that the cocoon parasite, *A. abdominator*, parasitizes without discrimination and therefore multi-parasitism increases proportionally with the population densities of the two parasites. Since *C. albicans* is always eliminated in such case, multiparasitism is a density-dependent factor which reduces that rate of successful parasitism by *C. albicans*.

Pschorn-Walcher and Zinnert (1971) found quite a different situation arising with *Mesoleius tenthredinis* MORL. and *Olesicampe benefactor* HINZ, two highly specialized parasites of the larch sawfly, *Pristiphora erichsonii* HTG. These ichneumonids have a high searching capacity; *O. benefactor* attacks earlier host stages than *M. tenthredinis* and the latter shows partial discrimination between parasitized and unparasitized hosts. Multi-parasitism between the two species is one third of that which would occur in the case of random host selection. Although increasing parasite densities do not effect the *Mesoleius – Olesicampe* system by multiparasitism, their reproductive efficiency is reduced by other factors. The alpine populations of *Mesoleius* lose an average of 50% of their progeny by encapsulation (a defense reaction of their host), the rate of which varies from locality to locality and from year to year with a range from below 20% to over 95% (Pschorn-Walcher and Zinnert, 1971). There is no indication so far that encapsulation is a density-dependent factor. *Olesicampe* suffers an average loss of 40–50% of its progeny through elimination by a highly specialized and very effective hyperparasite, *Mesochorus dimidiatus* HLGR. Recent investigations in Canada made by Turnock and Muldrew (1970) have shown that this hyperparasite was able to follow a rapid population increase of its host *Olesicampe* by increasing the percentage hyperparasitism over 3 years from 0.4% to 8% and then to 61%. The available information strongly suggests that the hyperparasite *M. dimidiatus* has the ability of 'numerical response' to the population density of *Olesi-campe*. The role played by hyperparasites varies greatly in the different parasite complexes. Some primary parasites remain remarkably free of hyperparasites whilst others suffer heavy losses. So far, hyperparasites have been largely neglected in studies on the dynamics of host-parasite systems, but available information suggests that their influence on the re-productive efficiency of primary parasites is a major factor in some parasite complexes.

Systems of counter-balanced competition

It is a common phenomenon that the competitive inferiority of a parasite species in multi-parasitism (level of intrinsic[1] competition) is compensated by a superiority in searching efficiency or synchronization with the host (level of extrinsic[1] competition). Examples of such a counter-balanced competition are given in Table 2.

Current long-term studies on the interactions within the parasite complex of the European pine sawy, *Neodiprion sertifer* GEOFFR. by Pschorn-Walcher (Pschorn-Walcher, 1967; Pschorn-Walcher et al., 1969) have revealed complicated systems of counter-balanced competition rendering possible the coexistence of highly specialized ichneumonid parasites. Certain parasite species (*Synomelix scutulatus* HTG., *Lamachus eques* GRAV.) of the pine sawfly have a high searching capacity which enables them to find isolated host colonies whilst others, such as *Lophyroplectus luteator* THUNB. or *Exenterus abruptorius* THUNB., are less efficient in searching for hosts, being mostly attracted to foci of higher sawfly populations. The comparatively low searching efficiency, i.e. the inferiority in ex-trinsic competition, is compensated by an intrinsic superiority, i.e. by the ability to elimi-nate the other parasites in cases of direct competition (multiparasitism). This counter-balanced competition results in the phenomenon that the relative importance of the para-site species changes periodically and predictably with changing host densities.

Two important parasites within the complex of the European fir budworm, *Choristo-*

1 For details see Smith (1929).

Table 2. Some examples of counter-balanced competition between parasite species attacking the same host.

Level of competition	Examples of interactions	Superior parasite	Inferior parasite
I. Intrinsic competition (Efficiency of para-site in eliminating the competitor in a case of direct con-tact)	Elimination of competi-tor by territory behav-iour of first-instar larvae of parasite within host;	*Temelucha interruptor*	*Orgilus obscurator*
	Elimination of competi-tor by parasitizing (hy-perparasitizing) its larva;	*Itoplectis maculator*	*Cephaloglypta murinanae*
	Elimination of competi-tor by faster larval devel-opment and consump-tion of host	*Aptesis abdominator*	*Cyzenis albicans*
II. Extrinsic competition (Efficiency of para-site in exploiting the host population)	Differences in searching efficiency	*O. obscurator*	*T. interruptor*
	Differences in synchro-nization with host	*C. murinanae*	*I. maculator*
	Differences in reproduc-tive capacity (? and searching range)	*C. albicans*	*A. abdominator*

411

neura murinana, show a somewhat different type of counter-balanced competition. The highly specialized larval parasite *Cephaloglypta murinanae* BAUER is well synchronized with its host and shows a high searching capacity; but in all the samples investigated during the last 25 years and in all the observation areas it remained completely ineffective during outbreak conditions. The pupal parasite *Itoplectis maculator* F. is not very well synchronized with the host, but is the superior competitor in cases of direct contact with *Cephaloglypta*. It even shows a distinct preference for cocoons of *Cephaloglypta* over pupae of the host *C. murinana* (Zwölfer, 1961).

A very well documented example of counter-balanced competition occurs within the complex of *Rhyacionia buoliana* SCHIFF. Long-term investigations by the CIBC (Schröder, in preparation; Pschorn-Walcher et al., 1969), recent investigations carried out in southwest Germany by Bogenschütz (1969, 1970), investigations in Poland by Koehler and Kolk (1969) and extensive experimental studies by Arthur et al. (1964) bring about the consensus that the braconid parasite *Orgilus obscurator* NEES is the most specialized parasite of the pine shoot moth with the best potential for its control. However, *O. obscurator* is practically always eliminated in cases of multiparasitism with less specialized parasites. This multiparasitism is especially detrimental since it occurs in the form of cleptoparasitism (Arthur et al., 1964). Schröder (in preparation) found that the extrinsically inferior parasites *Temelucha interruptor* GRAV., *Eulimneria rufifemur* THOMS., *Campoplex mutabilis* HLMGR. and *Pristomerus* sp. selected pine shoot moth larvae already parasitized by *O. obscurator* and that from 80–90% of their larvae or eggs occurred together with a larva of *O. obscurator* (Pschorn-Walcher et al., 1969).

The potentialities of intrinsically inferior parasites

How can we measure the potentiality of an intrinsically inferior parasite such as *O. obscurator* which is exposed to heavy competition by extrinsically inferior species? Bogenschütz (1969) considered attempting artificial inhibition of the competitors. Such check-methods have been used in biological control (Huffaker and Kennett, 1966), but their application to the parasite complex of pine shoot moth obviously involves considerable difficulties. However, since pine shoot moth has been accidentally introduced to North America, there would have been a chance to test the potentiality of *O. obscurator* had it been introduced without its competitors. This was not the case. Parasite introductions into Canada resulted in the establishment of *O. obscurator* and the two competing species *Eulimneria rufifemur* and *Temelucha interruptor*. Since competition between *Temelucha* and *Orgilus* prevents the latter profiting fully from its high searching efficiency, the introduction of *Temelucha* may well be considered as a mistake (Arthur et al., 1964; Pschorn-Walcher et al., 1969).

The parasites established against the European pine shoot moth in Canada are, so far, unsatisfactory and the same applies to four parasite species established in Canada against the pine sawfly, *N. sertifer*. One of these is a highly specialized and well synchronized parasite (*Lophyroplectus luteator*) whilst others, e.g. *Dahlbominus fuscipennis* ZETT., are less specific. With regard to the latter, Pschorn-Walcher et al. (1969) state 'it would now seem as though its introduction into Canada was premature, in that its competition with larval parasites may perhaps be detrimental to the over-all mortality which could have been caused by the latter alone'.

Although, in the case of the pine shoot moth and the pine sawfly, the opportunity was missed for studying the effect of specialized parasites operating without competitors, there

412

are cases of biological control which elucidate the potentialities of such parasites. From six parasite species, recently liberated in Canada against the larch sawfly, *P. erichsonii*, only one, *Olesicampe benefactor*, has become successfully established. The parasite has shown a tremendous population build-up. Turnock and Muldrew (1970) conclude that 'the introduction of *O. benefactor* can be tentatively described as successful, giving every indication of reducing larch sawfly populations to a level where defoliation of larch with its subsequent losses will be substantially reduced'. *O. benefactor* is an intrinsically inferior parasite which in Europe 'often suffers quite heavily in competition with other parasite species'. Pschorn-Walcher et al. (1969) suggest that the absence of competition may be one of the reasons responsible for the rapid build-up of *O. benefactor* in Canada.

The successful biological control of winter moth in Canada by the introduced European parasites *C. albicans* and *Agrypon flaveolatum* GRAV. is a striking example showing the potentialities of intrinsically inferior parasites. Table 3 shows the composition of the parasite complex in winter moth as found by Sechser (1970) in Europe and as investigated by Embree (1966) and others in Canada. The rich European parasite complex provides unsatisfactory control, i.e. it cannot prevent the European winter moth populations from reaching pest status. The same is true for 19 native Canadian parasites occasionally reared in very low numbers from the Canadian winter moth populations (Sechser, 1970). However, the two introduced European parasites, especially the tachinid *C. albicans*, are very successful in Canada. Long-term population studies by Embree (1965, 1966) led to the conclusion that the two parasites, notably *C. albicans*, have been the key factor in bringing about effective control of the winter moth outbreak and that they appear also to be responsible for the present maintenance of the host at low population densities. *C. albicans* and *A. flaveolatum* form an ideal combination, the former being more active at high host densities, whereas the latter is effective at low densities (Embree, 1966).

It is a highly interesting phenomenon that operating alone in Canada, the two parasites are obviously much more efficient then in Europe where they operate within a large complex containing other primary parasites as well as hyperparasites. Sechser's (1971) studies have shown that in Europe the reproductive efficiency of the two parasites is reduced by

Table 3. Composition of the parasite complexes of *Operophtera brumata* in Europe and Canada. (Details given by Sechser, 1970.)

	Europe	Canada	Canada
Status of host species	Native	Introduced	Introduced
Status of parasites	Native	Native	Introduced
Numbers of parasite species reared:			
Group 1 (euryphagous; preference, constancy and abundance low)	15	19	–
Group 2 (euryphagous: preference low, constancy and abundance moderate)	1	–	1
Group 3 (euryphagous; preference and abundance moderate, constancy high)	8	–	–
Group 4 (stenophagous; preference, constancy and abundance high)	2	–	1

The two parasites introduced to Canada are *Agrypon flaveolatum* (group 2) and *Cyzenis albicans* (group 4).

multiparasitism (i.e. direct competition with other primary parasites) and hyperparasitism. Amongst the many species represented in the European parasite complex of winter moth *C. albicans* and *A. flaveolatum* are intrinsically inferior to all the other parasites; in multi-parasitism *C. albicans* is eliminated by 14–15 competitor species and *A. flaveolatum* is eliminated by 13 competitor species. Moreover *C. albicans* is exposed to 3–4 hyperpara-sites. So far the most plausible explanation for the difference in efficiency of the two para-sites in Europe and Canada is the absence of superior competitors as well as hyperparasites (Pschorn-Walcher et al., 1969).

Conclusions

The parasite complexes of winter moth (*O. brumata*), pine shoot moth (*R. buoliana*), pine sawfly (*N. sertifer*), larch sawfly (*P. erichsonii*), European skipper (*T. lineola*) and Europe-an fir budworm (*C. murinana*) are examples of the coexistence of parasite species sharing a common host species. We have discussed certain relationships found within these parasite complexes and we have omitted others e.g. the impact of the life history of the host on its parasites (Zwölfer, 1963) or the role of the location of the host (feeding-site, pupation-site) with regard to parasitism. For it was neither possible nor intended to give a full catalogue of interactions and interrelations determining a host-parasite system under field condi-tions.

However, even the restricted number of examples mentioned indicate the diversity of mechanisms reducing the efficiency of insect parasites: Mutual interference between para-sites may influence their searching capacity. The density of available host populations may affect the behavioral response of certain parasites by orienting them to hosts with high population levels. Defence reactions by the host (encapsulation), superparasitism, multi-parasitism and hyperparasitism are brakes put on the reproductive efficiency of many (if not most) parasite species. Counter-balanced competition allows the coexistence of ex-trinsically inferior parasites with others which are extrinsically superior but inferior in cases of multiparasitism.

The available evidence strongly suggests that parasites exploiting the same host species have different mechanisms at their disposal to render possible their coexistence. Such mechanisms are an essential part of the 'structure' of a parasite complex. The diversity of interactions in host-parasite systems, i.e. the diversity of structures, is perhaps the most striking feature of parasite complexes and renders any generalization difficult. Because of the diversity of interactions, there is no clear correlation between the number of parasite species attacking a host and the degree of control achieved by them. There are examples in biological control where successive introductions and establishment of parasite species increased the effectiveness of the parasite complex (Simmonds, 1959; Flanders, 1965) whilst the biological control of winter moth in Canada demonstrates that a small parasite complex may be more effective than a large one. There are cases where a relatively large number of parasite species are associated with host populations at a low density level (*P. erichsonii*; Pschorn-Walcher and Zinnert, 1971) and there are others where only few parasite species attack such a host species e.g. *Hydroecia petasitis* DBL. (Zwölfer, 1963). Host insects undergoing density fluctuations may, at periods of high population levels, have a less diversified parasite complex (*N. sertifer*; Pschorn-Walcher et al., 1969) or they may show a more diversified complex (*P. erichsonii*; Pschorn-Walcher and Zinnert, 1971). From such discrepancies it may be inferred that any generalization concerning parasite numbers and degree of control are misleading. Rather than stressing the quantitative element of a parasite complex, emphasis should be laid on qualitative aspects, i.e. on its structure as reflected by the interactions between the parasites, and the relationships between parasites and host. With regard to the strategy of biological control, the diversity of interactions in natural host parasite systems suggests that the following policies should be adopted (Pschorn-Walcher and Zwölfer, 1968):

a. Wherever possible pre-introduction studies in the donor country should clarify the interrelationships between the parasite species attacking the target host.

b. On the basis of such studies, parasite species should be introduced in a predetermined sequence so that, whenever counter-balanced competition within the parasite complex is indicated, the intrinsically inferior species (usually the more specialized one) would be introduced first. The unique opportunity of gaining additional information on host-parasite systems (Turnbull and Chant, 1961) would alone suffice to justify such a procedure, but such a practice would also help to avoid unnecessary parasite introductions and would help prevent irreparable mistakes.

Acknowledgments

I wish to express my gratitude to Dr H. Pschorn-Walcher, Dr K. Carl, Dr D. Schröder (Delémont, CIBC) and Dr B. Sechser (Basel) for their help concerning the problems dealt with in this paper and for permitting the inclusion of results hitherto unpublished. Sincere thanks are also due to Dr M. P. Hassell (Oxford University) and Dr W. J. Turnock (Winnipeg, Canada) for their comments and to Prof. G. C. Varley (Oxford University) and Dr H. Pschorn-Walcher for correction of the manuscript.

References

Arthur, A. P., 1966. The present status of the introduced skipper, *Thymelicus lineola* (OCHS.) (Lepidoptera: Hesperiidae), in North America and possible methods of control. *Can. Ent.* 98: 622–626.

Arthur, A. P., J. E. R. Stainer & A. L. Turnbull, 1964. The interaction between *Orgilus obscurator* (NEES) and *Temelucha interruptor* (GRAV.), parasites of the pine shoot moth, *Rhyacionia buoliana* (SCHIFF.). *Can. Ent.* 96: 1030–1034.

Bogenschütz, H., 1969. Interspezifische Beziehungen im *Rhyacionia buoliana* Parasitenkomplex des Oberrheingebietes. *Z. angew. Ent.* 63: 454–461.

Bogenschütz, H., 1969. Der Parasitenkomplex von *Rhyacionia buoliana* in verschieden stark befallenen *Pinus silvestris*-Kulturen der Oberrheinebene. *Z. angew. Ent.* 64: 104–107.

Carl, K. P., 1968. *Thymelicus lineola* (Lepidoptera: Hesperiidae) and its parasites in Europe. *Can. Ent.* 100: 785–801.

DeBach, P., 1966. The competitive displacement and coexistence principles. *A. Rev. Ent.* 11: 183–212.

DeBach, P. & R. A. Sundby, 1963. Competitive displacement between ecological homologues. *Hilgardia* 34: 105–166.

Embree, D. G., 1965. The population dynamics of the winter moth in Nova Scotia, 1954–1962. *Mem. ent. Soc. Can.* No 46.

Embree, D. G., 1966. The role of introduced parasites in the control of winter moth in Nova Scotia. *Can. Ent.* 98: 1159–1168.

Embree, D. G. & P. Sisojevic, 1965. The bionomics and population density of *Cyzenis albicans* (FALL.) (Tachinidae: Diptera) in Nova Scotia. *Can. Ent.* 97: 631–639.

Flanders, S. E., 1965. Competition and cooperation among parasitic Hymenoptera related to biological control. *Can. Ent.* 97: 409–422.

Flanders, S. E., 1966. The circumstances of species replacement among parasitic Hymenoptera. *Can. Ent.* 98: 1009–1024.

Hassell, M. P. & G. C. Varley, 1969. New inductive population model for insect parasites and its bearing on biological control. *Nature* 223: 1133–1137.

Huffaker, C. B. & C. E. Kennett, 1966. Studies of two parasites of olive scale, *Parlatoria oleae* (COLVÉE). IV. Biological control of *Parlatoria oleae* (COLVÉE) through the compensatory action of two introduced parasites. *Hilgardia* 37: 283–335.

Huffaker, C. B., C. E. Kennett, B. Matsumoto & E. G. White, 1968. Some parameters in the role of enemies in the natural control of insect abundance. In: T.R.E. Southwood (Ed.), Insect abundance, p. 59–75. Oxford.

Koehler, W. & A. Kolk, 1969. Studies on the significance of multiple parasitism in *Rhyacionia buoliana* SCHIFF. population dynamics. Prace Instytutu Badawczego Lesnictwa, No 374: 64–86.

Pschorn-Walcher, H., 1957. Probleme der Wirtswahl parasitischer Insekten. *Ber. 8. Wanderversamml. dt. Ent.* 11: 79–85.

Pschorn-Walcher, H., 1967. Biology of the ichneumonid parasites of *Neodiprion sertifer* (GEOFFROY) (Hym. Diprionidae) in Europe. *Tech. Bull. Commonw. Inst. biol. Control* 8: 7–52.

Pschorn-Walcher, H., D. Schröder & O. Eichhorn, 1969. Recent attempts at biological control of some Canadian forest insect pests. *Tech. Bull. Commonw. Inst. biol. Control* 11: 1–18.

Pschorn-Walcher, H. & K. D. Zinnert, 1971. Investigations on the ecology and natural control of the larch sawfly (*Pristiphora erichsonii* HTG., Hym.: Tenthredinidae) in central Europe. *Tech. Bull. Commonw. Inst. biol. Control* 14: 1–50.

Pschorn-Walcher, H. & H. Zwölfer, 1968. Konkurrenzerscheinungen in Parasitenkomplexen als Problem der Biologischen Schädlingsbekämpfung. *Anz. Schädlingskunde* 41: 71–76.

Schröder, D., 1971. A study of the interactions between the internal larval parasites of the European pine shoot moth (*Rhyacionia buoliana* SCHIFF.). In preparation.

Sechser, B., 1970. Der Parasitenkomplex des kleinen Frostspanners (*Operophtera brumata* L.) (Lep., Geometridae) unter besonderer Berücksichtigung der Kokon-Parasiten. II. Teil. *Z. angew. Ent.* 66: 144–160.

Simmonds, F. J. 1959. The successful biological control of the sugarcane moth-borer, *Diatraea saccharalis* F. (Lepidoptera, Pyralidae) in Guadeloupe, B. W. I. *Proc. 10th Congr. Int. Soc. Sugarcane Technol.* (Amsterdam) p. 914–919.

Smith, H. S., 1929. Multiple parasitism: its relation to the biological control of insect pests. *Bull. ent. Res.* 20: 141–149.

Turnbull, A. L. & D. A. Chant, 1961. The practice and theory of biological control of insects in Canada. *Can. J. Zool.* 39: 697–753.

Turnock, W. J. & J. A. Muldrew, 1971. *Pristiphora erichsonii* (HARTIG), larch sawfly (Hymenoptera: Tenthredinidae). *Tech. Commun. Commonw. Inst. biol. Control* 4: 175–194.

Zwölfer, H., 1961. A comparative analysis of the parasite complexes of the European fir budworm, *Choristoneura murinana* (HB.), and the North American spruce budworm, *C. fumiferana* (CLEM.). *Tech. Bull. Commonw. Inst. biol. Control* 1:1–162.

Zwölfer, H., 1963. Untersuchungen über die Struktur von Parasitenkomplexen bei einigen Lepidopteren. *Z. angew. Ent.* 51: 346–357.

Zwölfer, H. & M. Kraus, 1957. Biocoenotic studies on the parasites of two fir- and two oak-Tortricids. *Entomophaga* 2: 173–196.

Discussion

Participants: Zwölfer (Author), Bakker (K.), Cavers, Gradwell, Huffaker, Labeyrie, Lawton, Ohnesorge, Pimentel, Rosenzweig, Turnock, Varley and Wilbert

Empirical data, inductive and deductive models are converging to indicate that competitive co-existence leads to stable host-parasite interactions. Interference and searching coefficients can be estimated from existing population data using a trial and error computer programme. The data should be fitted to a form of the destructive equation:

$$\beta KP^{1-b} (1-e^{-aV})$$

in which P is parasite density, V is victim density, a is a search coefficient, β is a reproductive coefficient, b is the interference and K is the maximum rate of victims parasitizable by one parasite per unit time. A specific case of competitive coexistence was theoretically dealt with in *J. Mammal.* (Rosenzweig, 1966), in which P1 is superior in search and P2 is superior intrinsically because of operation at two trophic levels (Rosenzweig).

If life-table data on the three larch sawfly parasites are available, it would be valuable to check if a model gave an adequate description of the differing phase relations of the three parasites in relation to the host oscillations. Once we have a tested theoretical framework, biological and integrated control probably can become predictive sciences (Varley).

There is a danger of misinterpreting the data if we base conclusions about the outcome of competition by two species of parasites on incomplete life-tables for the parasites. At least measurements of the densities of the adult parasites searching are needed to interpret correctly the relative percentages of parasitism caused by the different parasite species (Gradwell).

In the case of parasites of *Neodiprion sertifer* (Pschorn-Walcher et al, 1969; Pschorn-Walcher, in preparation) it is indeed found that the effective parasitism of each parasite declines when its density increases. These interactions lead to predictable seasonal and long-term changes (Author to Wilbert).

The example of *Aphytis maculicornis* and *Coccophagoides utilis* attacking California olive scale shows that such interactions may be elucidated by the use of experimental check-methods (Huffaker).

Would it not pay to introduce relatively rare parasites, because it may be expected that hosts of such parasites would show a relatively low level of resistance (Pimentel)? I agree with this point of view. The importance of host resistance as a consequence of coevolution is shown by the case of the whoolly fir aphid (*Dreyfusia piceae*) which, in its native habitats in Europe, is controlled by an immunity reaction of its host, *Abies pectinata*. In North America, *D. piceae* came into contact with *Abies balsamea* – a potential host which has not built up an immunity against *Dreyfusia* – and, hence, is highly vulnerable to the attacks of *D. piceae* (Author).

It is important to have some standard of comparison to be able to conclude whether a host shows resistance (Pimentel). However, host specificity of a parasite may more easily be demonstrated by classifying immunity reactions by the hosts than by studying the behaviour of the parasite, because the latter in many cases depends on the environment (Labeyrie).

When many parasite species affect the same host, the development of specific defense mechanisms would not be expected. However, the specific resistance of larch sawfly (*Pristophora erichsonii*) to the internal parasite *Mesoleius tenthredinis* occurs both in alpine Europe and in Canada. In the former area where *M. tenthredinis* remains a major parasite, the proportion of resistant hosts is variable; whereas in Canada, where *M. tenthredinis* was initially the only effective parasite, resistant hosts increased to nearly 100%. As a consequence, *M. tenthredinis* became ineffective and even locally extinct (Turnock).

Biological control may indeed be confronted with serious problems by the increase towards monocultures of crop plants over large areas, and by the elimination of virtually all weeds associated with a crop. By doing this we are undoubtedly removing all the the phytophagous insects and their hosts (and the sources of nectar and honey-dew for parasites) except some very simple host-parasite systems accociated with the single crop plant, which systems are more likely to be disturbed than more complex systems (AUTHOR to CAVERS).

Why have host-parasite systems not evolved towards a single parasite being superior both extrinsically and intrinsically (LAWTON)? Such cases of displacement certainly may have happened in some parasite complexes. 'Balanced competition' may stabilize the system by optimizing the exploitation of the food (i.e. protecting the parasites from overexploiting the food supply). We have also to consider the possibility that the host species may exert stabilizing selection pressures on both parasite species (AUTHOR).

The range of parasitism in some cases is very variable in each species – e.g. in *Diadromus pulchellus* the threshold of the oviposition signals depends on the phenotype of the individual; some females have a very broad range, and others a much more restricted range of host specialization (LABEYRIE).

The phenomenon of cleptoparasitism may be interpreted as a special form of 'multiparasitism' as well as a form of 'ecological hyperparasitism'. The marking of the host by the parasite female is a type of territorial behaviour which avoids the necessity of territorial behaviour at the larval level (AUTHOR to OHNESORGE and BAKKER).

Proc. Adv. Study Inst. Dynamics Numbers Popul. (Oosterbeek, 1970) 419–439

The role of predators and parasites in a fishery for the mollusc Cardium edule L.

D. A. Hancock

Fisheries Laboratory, Burnham-on-Crouch, Essex, England

Abstract

Cardium edule L. is well suited for a study of population dynamics because changes in density can be monitored, and separate estimates can be made of mortality due to causes other than fishing. The paper describes studies of the stocks in the Burry Inlet, South Wales, from 1958 to 1970. Here, the cockles have become adapted to withstand the effects of alternating exposure to air and submersion by the tide, with accompanying fluctuations in temperature. Density levels are variable both in space and time, and the population is effectively regulated by density-dependent age-linked relationships, chiefly the inverse ones between density and growth and between density and recruitment.

Major contributions to mortality are (1) environmental causes and (2) predation, chiefly by oystercatchers and by man. At very high densities neither predation nor fishing seriously affects the percentage survival. At low densities both fishing and oystercatcher predation are reduced, the former more severely than the latter. It is at moderate densities that oystercatcher predation makes its greatest impact, chiefly on second-winter cockles; the resulting reduction in spawning stock gives recruitment at a level which allows only poor survival beyond the second winter.

The cockle, *Cardium edule* L.[1], is a sedentary, burrowing, intertidal, bivalve mollusc. It has proved well suited for a study of population dynamics because: (1) clearly defined growth rings (Orton, 1926) allow ready separation into age groups; (2) sampling in the intertidal zone is relatively straightforward; (3) tidal transport is restricted in the main to young individuals of up to 2 mm shell length during the first 4 weeks after settlement (Baggerman, 1953), and active movement by cockles older than this becomes reduced with age (Kristensen, 1957) and is primarily directed towards maintaining position in the substratum. Hence, changes in density can normally be monitored without too many complications of displacement or migration; moreover, it also becomes possible to make separate estimates of mortality due to causes other than fishing (Hancock and Urquhart, 1965), which is usually extremely difficult in most commercially exploited fish populations.

The observations described here form part of a study to investigate the decline during the 1950s of the quantities landed from the fishery in the Burry Inlet, South Wales, which, with the Wash and the Thames Estuary (Fig. 1), is one of the three traditionally most important areas for cockles in the United Kingdom. The study has been based on quantitative surveys from which population estimates have been made throughout the 13-year period 1958–1970, and which also provided information on distribution, age structure,

---

[1] Referred to as *Cerastoderma edule* (L.) by Tebble (1966), and Bowden and Heppell (1968).

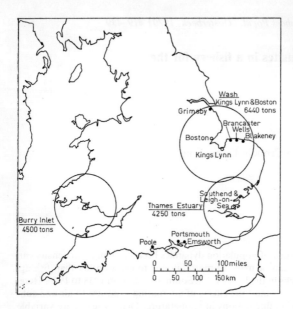

Fig. 1. Distribution of recorded landings of cockles in the United Kingdom (from MAFF Sea Fisheries Statistical Tables for 1969, published by HMSO, London).
● Ports with registered landings.

growth rates and mortality rates. Additional, more detailed, observations over selected areas were made to investigate special aspects of the general problem.

In the following sections the parameters of the population and the methods used to evaluate them are described briefly, the relationships between the parameters are discussed and, finally, the effect of predators, including man, on the various relationships are examined.

The general theme of the conclusions is that density levels of cockles have a variable distribution, both in space and time, and that this has contributed to a series of density-dependent age-linked relationships which effectively regulate population density.

Estimation of population parameters

Population and total mortality

Quantitative surveys have been based on systematic samples taken along fixed line transects. Although population estimates by this method are ineligible for statistical treatment, sampling could be systematically excluded from areas of low density (< about 50/m²) which occupy a large proportion of the intertidal zone in the Burry Inlet (Fig. 2A). By comparing population estimates from the same grid of samples taken at different times, usually in each November and May, but sometimes in February and August as well, changes in density (total mortality), distribution and size composition could be examined. Population estimates were calculated by relating sample densities to the areas sampled, and the results for the 13-year period 1958–1970 are given in Table 1 and Fig. 3. The low level of total stock in 1963 resulted from catastrophic losses during the severe winter of 1962–3, and the high level of stock in 1964 was a consequence of the exceptionally good recruitment which followed it (Fig. 3A). Total mortalities have been calculated on a 6-monthly basis, as instantaneous total mortality coefficients (Z), from the difference between the natural logarithms of numbers in half-yearly population estimates separately for

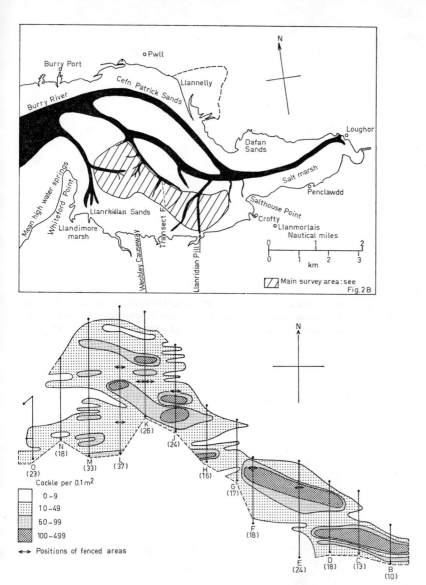

Fig. 2. A. Chart of the Burry Inlet, modified from Admiralty Chart No 1167, showing the position of the main survey area.

B. Representative contour map showing densities observed during a survey in May 1960, together with the positions of transects, numbers of samples per transect (in parentheses) and fenced areas.

first-year, second-year and older-than-second-year cockles (in the latter, all ages older than second year were grouped because in most years their numbers were small). The results (Fig. 4A) show how second-winter mortalities were highest before the winter of 1962–3, after which first-winter losses were highest. As a general rule, losses of cockles older than second winter were the lowest. During the summer months (Fig. 4B), second-summer cockles generally experienced higher losses than older ones.

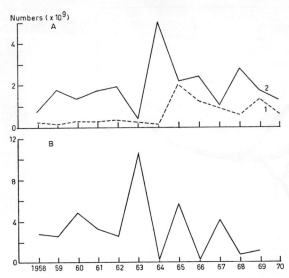

Fig. 3. A. Annual estimates of stock in May, 1958–70, showing (1) numbers of spawners (i.e. aged two years and older) and (2) total stock (i.e. numbers of spawners + immature one-year-olds). B. Numbers of O-group recruits in the November of their first winter, 1958–69 (from Hancock, in press).

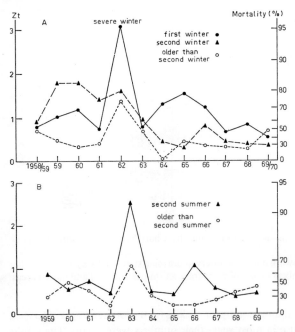

Fig. 4. Six-monthly losses expressed as instantaneous total mortality coefficients (Zt), where Z = instantaneous total mortality coefficient and t = $\frac{1}{2}$ year, for (A) winters 1958/9 to 1969/70, November to May; first-winter, second-winter and older-than-second-winter cockles are given separately, and (B) summers 1959 to 1969, May to November; second-summer and older-than-second-summer cockles are given separately.

Table 1. Summary of population estimates of Burry Inlet cockles from surveys in May and November 1958 to 1970. Numbers to the nearest million.

	Numbers in May				Numbers in November			
	1-year olds	2-year olds	older	total	first winter	second winter	older	total
1958	455	100	167	722	2,837	76	154	3,067
1959	1,667	40	92	1,799	2,578	922	72	3,572
1960	1,112	204	72	1,388	4,967	901	164	6,032
1961	1,474	153	116	1,743	3,296	846	155	4,297
1962	1,637	212	114	1,963	2,648	1,071	282	4,001
1963	102	204	61	367	10,615	10	104	10,729
1964	4,954	6	52	5,012	194	3,192	40	3,426
1965	54	2,019	38	2,111	5,717	33	1,775	7,525
1966	1,249	20	1,148	2,417	313	414	1,033	1,760
1967	87	174	727	988	4,169	49	652	4,870
1968	2,278	34	513	2,825	800	1,580	348	2,728
1969	362	1,109	265	1,736	1,213	229	796	2,238
1970	682	150	409	1,241				

Density distribution

Cockles were usually the dominant benthic organisms, but other species occurring in variable numbers included *Macoma balthica* (L.), *Scrobicularia plana* (DA COSTA), *Mytilus edulis* L., *Hydrobia ulvae* (PENNANT), *Corophium volutator* (PALLAS) and various annelids.

A representative contour map, based on about 300 samples of 0.1 m² (Hancock and Urquhart, 1965), is given in Fig. 2B to demonstrate the distribution of cockles. The frequency of numbers in samples showed a contagious distribution closely resembling a negative binomial (Saila and Gaucher, 1966). High-density patches were usually found towards the lower ends of transects, and in Fig. 5 (A and B) numbers in samples have been related to tidal height along a representative transect. Maximum densities were confined to an area between mean tide level and high-water mark of a poor neap tide. Above this tidal level numbers were regularly low, partly perhaps because there was less time for settlement, but also (see later) because survival there was poor. At the lower level the Burry River scours away the edge of the bank at low water, causing poor survival. Generally, the most successful settlement and early survival of cockles occurs in areas of reduced tidal flow, but there growth may not be good.

Mortality

Causes of mortality of cockles
These have been described in some detail by Hancock and Urquhart (1965) but are summarized here for completeness. They may be separated into four main groups, (a) environmental factors, (b) predators, (c) parasites and (d) fishing.

a. Environmental factors include the effect of wave action, particularly at very low temperatures, and exposure at low tide, especially at the higher levels of the shore during high and low extremes of temperature. Very severe winters have been responsible for catastrophic mortalities of cockles throughout Europe (Kristensen, 1957) and one in partic-

423

ular, 1962–3, was included in these observations; under such conditions survival was best amongst second-winter cockles, while younger and older individuals were almost wiped out (Hancock and Urquhart, 1964). Hot summer conditions seem to affect the older cockles particularly, maybe during weakness after spawning (Orton, 1933) or when they are heavily loaded with parasites (Kristensen, 1957).

b. Predators. Of the many and varied predators of cockles, only the few of particular importance to the Burry Inlet will be mentioned here. The shore crab *Carcinus maenas* (L.) can and does eat cockles of a size proportional to its own size, but relatively few crabs have been observed in the Burry Inlet. Shore crabs tend not to move into the intertidal zone in winter, during which feeding is also reduced. A flatfish, the flounder *Platichthys flesus* (L.), feeds on the cockle beds during high tide, taking a number of other organisms, including *Macoma* and small crustaceans, as well as newly-settled cockles up to their first winter (Hancock and Urquhart, 1965). During the winter months flounders move offshore to spawn.

Various seabirds, including gulls, appear to eat only moribund cockles or those broken by fishermen. One, however, the oystercatcher *Haematopus ostralegus* (L.), has emerged as by far the most serious predator in the Burry Inlet.

It is not intended to include a detailed account of the population dynamics of the oyster-catcher here – these have been dealt with fully by other authors (Davidson, 1967, 1968, pers. comm.; Dare, 1966, 1970) – but a short description is given of its relevant behaviour. The oystercatcher occurs throughout Europe, where it breeds in northern territories during the summer months, but overwinters in more southerly areas where it can find adequate concentrations of suitable food. It can eat a variety of foods, but tends to concentrate on areas where cockles and mussels occur in sufficient density to sustain the oystercatcher's large daily food requirement, which is normally in excess of 300 g wet weight of flesh per day. One of these areas is the Burry Inlet, where the oystercatcher has been found to feed preferentially on second-winter cockles but, when these are less plentiful, on younger and older cockles. *Macoma balthica* provides an alternative food but usually only when cockles are in poor supply. The feeding activities of oystercatchers can be clearly seen from the accumulated piles of broken shells, composed predominantly of second-winter cockles, 200 to 300 of which may be eaten per bird during a single daylight low tide. These piles result from the oystercatcher's habit of probing the exposed intertidal sand with its open beak, carrying the extracted cockle to an area of firm sand and probing the shell open with its beak. Smaller cockles may also be eaten in situ without being withdrawn from the sand; large older cockles of up to 6–7 years may be probed in situ, through the siphonal opening, in shallow water during the falling tide. Oystercatchers begin to arrive in the Burry Inlet from breeding grounds in Scotland, Norway, the Faroes and Iceland during August of each year. Flocks build up to a maximum in November/ December – the 1969 figure approached 19,000 birds – and from January onwards they leave the estuary in increasing numbers, leaving behind only a thousand or so mainly immature birds during May and June.

c. Parasites. Cardium edule is host to a wide range of parasites (Cole, 1956). Of these, only two which are clearly of importance to the population dynamics of the cockle will be mentioned here; both are trematodes, but unfortunately the life cycle of neither of them is completely known.

Cercaria bucephalopsis haimeana (Lacaze-Duthiers, 1854), a stage in the life of a bucephalid trematode, was recorded in up to 12% of Burry Inlet cockles (Hancock and Urquhart, 1965) in which they cause parasitic castration. Bowers (1969) believes the second intermediate host to be a gadoid fish and the final host the angler fish (*Lophius piscatorius* L.) or conger eel (*Conger conger* L.). Bowers suggested that the fall in percentage infection which he observed after 3 years of age was due to the death of infected cockles. Bowers and James (1967) found that the metacercaria stage of the second trematode, which they referred to as *Meiogymnophallus minutus* (Cobbold, 1859) occurred under the hinge of 100% of cockles older than one year in the Burry Inlet. Metacercariae are, accumulated individually over the years and may exceed 300 per cockle. The adult trematode lives in the oystercatcher and the common scoter. *Melanitta nigra* (L.). Bowers and James found no *Meiogymnophallus* in cockles of less than 6 months of age, but during the past two years Pistoor (1969) has found high infection rates and heavy losses of young cockles on Dutch cockle beds during the summer of settlement. It might be tempting to associate this with the recent increase in the number of oystercatchers in Europe, but, although the relationship between cockle and oystercatcher has been clearly established, the sequence between oystercatcher and cockle has yet to be worked out, because the first intermediate host has not yet been identified. Whether either of these two trematodes can be held directly responsible for the death of any cockles is not known, but they could well be an additional factor causing mortality at times of stress, such as in cold winters and hot summers.

d. Fishing. During fishing, a small amount of damage occurs to cockles which have not yet reached commercial size. When cockles are 15 months of age (i.e. in August/September) the largest, which usually occur towards the lower edges of the banks, reach fishable size. Fishing for the larger cockles of the year-class continues throughout their second winter, during which there is no increase in size, until the following May when growth recommences and most cockles soon enter the fishable stock. This contains the survivors of all previous age groups and is fished throughout the year.

In such a population, in which the known causes of mortality include exploitation and losses from a variety of predators and perhaps parasites, as well as environmental factors, it can be difficult to separate the quantitative effect of each. This is attempted in the following paragraphs.

Relationship between total mortality and tidal height
Fig. 5B shows how only relatively small numbers of an average year-class survived until the November beginning their second winter; it was only from the exceptional 1963 year-class that significant numbers survived into the following year on the selected transect. In Fig. 5 (A and C) total mortalities have also been related to tidal heights along Transect F. This shows clearly how losses of second-winter cockles were greater than those of other age groups at all levels of the shore, and it was concluded from enclosure experiments (see the section '*Estimation of natural mortality from fecend areas*') that this must have been due to selective feeding by oystercatchers. The consistently high mortalities of all ages on the upper part of the shore were most likely to have resulted from excessive exposure to air, especially during cold weather. At lower shore levels, tidal scouring may have contributed to the high losses. The central zone seems to favour better survival, but here settlement is relatively poor (Fig. 5B). Summer losses also tended to be greatest on the upper shore (Fig. 5D),

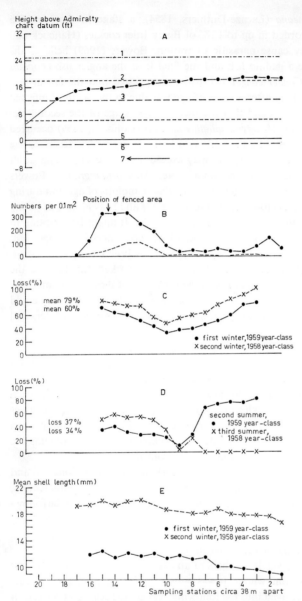

Fig. 5. A. Shore profile along Transect F (from Hancock and Urquhart, 1966). 1, mean high water springs; 2, mean high water neaps; 3, mean tide level; 4, mean low water neaps; 5, chart datum; 6, mean low water springs; 7, low water mark.

B. Numbers of cockles from samples of 0.1 m² along Transect F, showing 1959 year-class (O-group) in November 1959 (● — ●) and their survivors in November 1960 (— — —).

C. Percentage losses during the winter period from November 1959 to May 1960, smoothed in groups of five samples.

D. Percentage losses during the summer period from May to November 1960, smoothed in groups of five samples.

E. Mean shell lengths of cockles commencing their first and second winters, November 1959 (from Hancock, 1967).

426

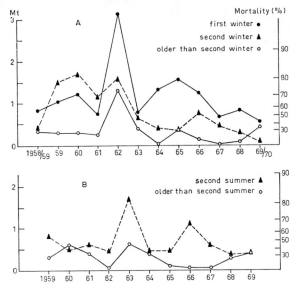

Fig. 6. Six-monthly losses expressed as instantaneous natural mortality coefficients (Mt), where M = instantaneous natural mortality coefficient and t = ½ year, for (A) winters 1958/9 to 1969/70 and (B) summers 1959 to 1969.

where cockles exposed to air continuously for several days on some neap tides would suffer adversely from high temperatures. The selectively greater losses of third-summer cockles on the lower shores were most likely to have resulted from fishing.

Estimation of natural mortality from population estimates
Information collected on the landings of cockles taken by fishermen has been combined with estimates of Z to calculate F, the instantaneous fishing mortality coefficient, from the expression formulated by Ricker (1958): Rate of exploitation (or fraction of the stock fished) = $(F/Z)(1-e^{-Zt})$; since $Z = F + M$, values of M, the instantaneous natural mortality coefficient, could be calculated. As natural losses comprise quite a large component of the total loss, the values of M (Fig. 6) do not differ markedly from those of Z given in Fig. 4. Additional information on the numbers of cockles fished annually is given in Fig. 12.

Estimation of natural mortality from fenced areas
The technique of sampling fenced areas in the Burry Inlet as a method of estimating natural losses independently from those due to fishing has already been described in detail (Hancock and Urquhart, 1965). The results from one of these areas situated on Transect F (for its position, see Fig. 2 and 5) are given in Fig. 7 to demonstrate the heavy losses of cockles during their second winter relative to those which are older and younger. These losses coincided with peak numbers of oystercatchers which had been observed to be selectively feeding on cockles of this age. The selective loss of second-winter cockles could be prevented by using netting enclosures (Fig. 8). Other fenced areas gave variable results which, as will be demonstrated later, appear to have been related to the density of cockles available in each area. The results described so far refer mainly to the period before 1963.

427

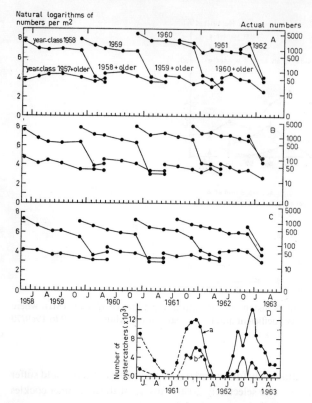

Fig. 7. Changes in natural logarithms of numbers per m² based on samples of 0.1 m², of cockles which settled each year on the area represented by Transect F; A. inside the fenced area (means of 10 samples), B. in nearby control samples, outside the fenced area (means of 10 samples), and C. along the transect (means of 17 samples). D. shows the numbers of oystercatchers counted at low tide by P. E. Davidson, (a) over the whole of the Burry Inlet, (b) from the area represented by Transect F only (adapted from Hancock and Urquhart, 1965).

First-winter cockles were then numerically most abundant, with somewhat fewer second-winter cockles; cockles older than this, relatively few of which survived the heavy second-winter losses, were the smallest component of the stock (Table 1). In this situation, the oystercatchers, while eating some cockles of all ages, often deliberately rejected or ignored other than second-winter cockles, for which they showed a marked preference. After 1963, the age composition was much more variable (Table 1) and this was reflected in the change in the pattern of mortality already noted (Fig. 4A and 6A).

Growth and age

Following settlement in June, shell growth continues until October, after which it ceases until early in May of the following year. In the Burry Inlet there is an inverse relationship between growth rate and tidal height (Fig. 5E), the largest cockles of each year-class being found at the lower end of each transect and particularly in the sandy north-western area

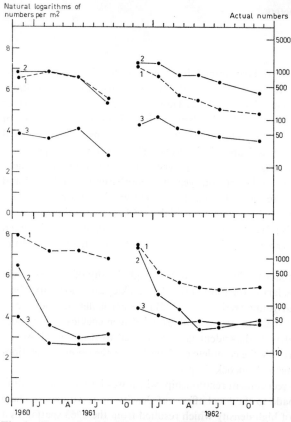

Natural logarithms of
numbers per m²

Actual numbers

Fig. 8. Changes in natural logarithms of numbers per m² based on samples of 0.1 m² taken inside (top; means of 8 samples) and outside areas (bottom; means of 10 samples) protected by netting. Broken lines denote the youngest age group in each series (i.e. commencing their first winter in November). Solid lines show age groups commencing their second (2) and subsequent (3) winters (adapted from Hancock and Urquhart, 1965).

of the cockle bed (see Fig. 4 of Hancock, 1967). The lifespan of cockles may exceed 10 years in the Burry Inlet (Hancock and Urquhart, 1965).

Recruitment

Egg production is related to size, varying from 5,600 to 52,000 eggs per female at 18 to 38 mm shell length respectively (Kristensen, 1957). In the Burry Inlet, although the largest one-year-olds may produce a few eggs, cockles normally mature at two years of age. Recruitment from year to year is extremely variable (Fig. 3B). Before 1963, recruitment was fairly regular but the severe winter of 1962–3 was followed by a spectacular settlement in 1963, and then recruit failure in 1964, 1966 and 1968 alternated with good recruitment in 1965 and 1967, but with relatively poor recruitment in 1969. The survival of recruits has been variable, with significant numbers reaching sexual maturity, or fully fishable size after the second winter, only when recruitment was specially good, e.g. the 1963 and 1967 year-classes (Table 1).

Relationships between the parameters

Density and recruitment

The relationship between stock size and recruitment has been discussed in detail in a recent publication (Hancock, in press). It was demonstrated that there was an inverse relationship between succeeding year-classes (Fig. 3 and 4 of Hancock, in press), which, together with the suggestion of a dome-shaped relationship between breeding stock and number of recruits (Fig. 2C of Hancock, in press), added up to an inverse relationship between total stock and recruitment (Fig. 5 and 6 of Hancock, in press). The practical consequence of this was that when there was a large number of spawners there was poor recruitment (1966) except when the O-group from the previous year was poorly represented (1965 and 1967) (Table 1). When there were fewer spawners, recruitment was heavy when O-group numbers were low (1963) but not when these were high (1964). The precise timing or operation of the control mechanism is not certain except that it occurs somewhere between the time of larval liberation, or perhaps even before, and 5 months after the time of settlement.

Although no study has been made of the larval phase, a high density of cockles might be expected to compete with the larvae for food, and adult cockles are known to inhale and kill larvae and newly settled young (Kristensen, 1957). In particular, the new year-class is unlikely to find sufficient space to survive and grow between cockles in high density, especially those in which density-dependent growth has led to stunting. However, none of these possibilities can provide the complete explanation for the observed relationship between stock and recruitment (Hancock, in press).

In the discussion of the stock/recruitment relationship, which was based on population estimates, reference was also made to the local effects of density on recruitment. These were most evident in the areas of high density which resulted from the 1963 spatfall as a marked inverse relationship between the density of cockles and the numbers of recruits (Hancock, 1969, in press).

Density and growth

The growth rate and density show a strong inverse correlation (Hancock, 1969, in press). In selected localities, increasing density was found to be associated with a gradually lowered growth rate, believed to result from competition for food. Reduction in growth was found to be most marked at densities approaching those of a maximum density curve (Fig. 3 of Hancock, 1969) derived from an experiment where cockles were extremely stunted and deformed from growing against each other: here competition for both space and food must occur. The integral effect of local overcrowding in the Burry Inlet was a general inverse relationship between annual population estimates and annual estimates of mean size of second-year cockles (Fig. 15 of Hancock, in press).

Density and mortality

Total mortality rates calculated from population estimates, of cockles up to the beginning of their second winter, were found to be independent of total numbers of all ages present when these cockles were spawned (Fig. 6–8 of Hancock, in press). Similarly, winter losses of first-winter recruits were found to be independent both of their own number and that of second-winter cockles present at the same time (Fig. 10 of Hancock, in press). There was, however, a correlation between the winter loss and the number of second-winter cockles, which took the form of a dome-shaped curve (Fig. 11 of Hancock, in press). The highest losses occurred during the four winters 1959/60 to 1962/63 when population estimates approached 10^9, but lower mortality rates were observed with both larger and smaller stocks. This was believed to be because low densities were uneconomic for predation by oystercatchers, whereas at high densities the full impact of predation generated only a small percentage loss from a larger stock. In Fig. 9B the same result was obtained from a consideration of losses from causes other than fishing (i.e. M = Z–F), and this shows also the very small number of survivors of the second winter in all years except 1964/65 and 1968/69. Summer mortalities of second-year cockles were not, however, correlated with their numbers (Fig. 9A). It is significant that during the summer of 1964 the exceptionally large stock of cockles from the 1963 year-class suffered a mortality rate which at 36 % (Mt = 0.45) was less than average (Fig. 9A). This was despite the fact that in locally overcrowded patches during the summer of 1964 losses exceeded 50 % (M = 0.7) due to squeezing out during the period of rapid growth. Even higher losses than that due to squeezing out would have been inevitable were it not for the tendency for lowered growth

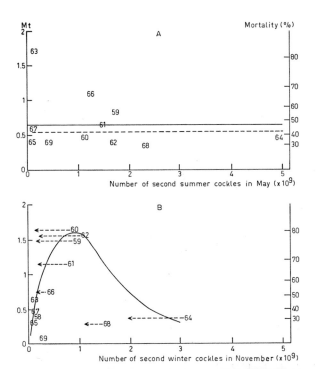

Fig. 9. Six-monthly natural losses related to the estimated numbers present at the commencement of the period. A. during the second summer (May to November) of 1958–1969 (—— mean excluding 1963 = 0.55; – – – mean including 1963 = 0.65); B. during the second winter (November to May) 1958/9–1969/70 (Line fitted by eye). The tip of each arrow represents the number of survivors each May.
Mt = M (= instantaneous natural mortality coefficient) × t (=$\frac{1}{2}$ year).

and stunting; as a result, larger numbers were able to maintain their position in the sand. It seems likely that high cockle density can have some survival value by changing the texture of the sand surface with accumulated pseudofaeces and mucus which would have a sealing effect against dislodging by the tide.

Density-related predation

During the period 1959/60 to 1961/62, when second-winter losses calculated from stock estimates were unusually high, observations were being made in a series of fenced areas similar to and including the one described earlier. In Fig. 10 the results from seven fenced areas (Fig. 2B) and their control samples have been pooled to demonstrate the relationship between percentage winter loss and initial density. Although there was no obvious correlation for first-winter cockles, there was a strong correlation between the rate of loss and density of cockles during their second winter; this was associated with the feeding of oystercatchers which were regularly observed in the areas of greatest loss. A regular feature of these observations was that by the end of each winter the number of survivors in

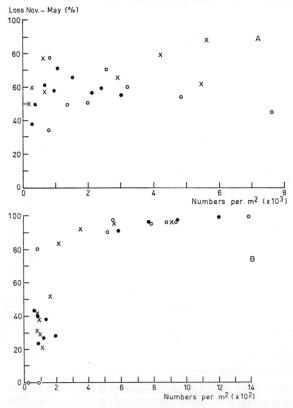

Fig. 10. Percentage losses during winter (November to May) related to mean density in November – based on samples taken inside and outside seven fenced areas during three years. A. first-winter cockles; B. second-winter cockles.
● 1959–60, × 1960–61, ○ 1961–62.

the heavily predated areas was usually less than in the areas where initially density was much lower.

The activities of the fishermen are usually also density-related, but the effects on density will be less pronounced, partly because fishing is size-selective and partly because fishing becomes uneconomic at densities of less than about 100 per m², whereas oystercatchers can feed successfully at densities of less than 20 per m² (Davidson, 1967).

Mortality and age

Fig. 11A relates the average annual losses (Z), calculated from population estimates, to cockle age. The rate of loss clearly decreases from year two to year four but numbers in older age groups were too small for analysis. The larger numbers provided by the 1963 year-class, however, allowed a more detailed analysis. Fig. 11B shows how the annual rate

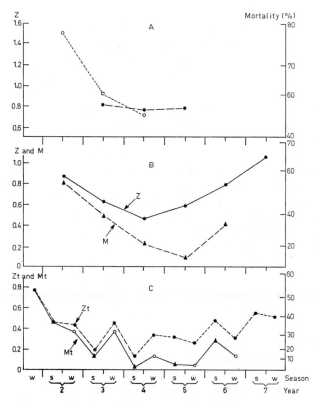

Fig. 11. A. Annual total losses, expressed as instantaneous total mortality coefficients, related to age. Each open circle represents the mean values, calculated from population estimates for the years 1958 to 1970 (May to May), excluding 1962/3, of cockles during their second, third and fourth years of life. The closed circles are values which also include all cockles of greater age (i.e. third year and older).
B. Values of annual total loss (Z) and natural loss (M), related to age for the 1963 year-class.
C. Six-monthly losses (Zt and Mt, where t = ½ year) related to age for the 1963 year-class.
S = Summer; W = Winter.

of total loss (Z) of the 1963 year-class also fell to year four and then rose steadily. When natural mortality was calculated separately, it was seen that this increase was partly due to increased exploitation, and that the rate of loss from natural causes alone fell to a minimum in year five before increasing in year six. On a half-yearly basis (Fig. 11C), it was found that the increase in the rate of loss after year five was contributed to by higher summer losses, as opposed to higher winter losses in the earlier years.

It has already been seen how feeding by oystercatchers made a significant contribution to second-winter losses before 1963, but, although second-winter losses represented a smaller percentage of the large 1963 year-class, winter losses in year three (1965–6) of the 1963 year-class were largely attributable to oystercatcher feeding in the virtual absence of second-winter cockles from the poor 1964 year-class. The increase in summer loss of older cockles of the 1963 year-class may have been associated with weakness after spawning, possibly affected by parasites.

Oystercatcher numbers, cockle stocks and landings

Before and during the severe winter of 1962–3, the mean number of wintering oystercatchers was around 8000 (Fig. 12; all oystercatcher counts are by courtesy of P. E. Davidson). This included a maximum count of 14,100 birds (Davidson, 1967). During the period 1959- 62, annual landings of cockles were low compared with those during the previous history of the Burry Inlet fishery (Hancock and Urquhart, 1966) and it was concluded that this was largely due to the depredations of oystercatchers which, each winter, were eating a quantity of cockles much greater than that taken by fishermen during the whole year. There was a sharp drop in the average number of birds to less than 4000 during the winter of 1963–4. This was interpreted as a temporary desertion of the area – due to lack of suitable food – at a time when the cockle stock, although numerically the highest recorded (Table 1), was dominated by first-winter cockles of unusually small size. This view was supported by the fact that during the three subsequent winters the oystercatchers returned in their previous numbers. The level of catches by fishermen during 1963 also reached a minimum (Fig. 12B and C). In 1967–8, the average wintering flock began to rise sharply to reach around 14,000 in 1969-70; this included a maximum count of 18,900 in January 1970. It is not known how much of this increase in the numbers of birds wintering in the Burry Inlet has resulted from the generally improved level of stocks of cockles older than O-group in the area since 1963, or whether it merely reflects the observed increase in oystercatcher numbers generally along the west coast of England and North Wales since 1967 (Dare, pers. comm.); the latter may well have been a consequence of improved survival of young oystercatchers during the period of greater availability of food, both cockles and mussels, in Northern Europe which followed the severe winter of 1962–3.

More or less in parallel with the increase in numbers of oystercatchers, there has been a steady improvement in the landings of cockles (Fig. 12B and C). The increase in landings began in 1965, when a larger proportion of the slow-growing crowded 1963 year-class reached fishable size, and soon accelerated as both market expanded and fishing effort increased. The increase in predation and in fishing in recent years was associated with a gradual overall decline in the size of the cockle population, though the proportion of individuals older than second winter remained higher than it was before 1963 (Fig. 12A and Table 1). In the winter of 1968-9, oystercatchers concentrated on the abundant second-winter cockles of the 1967 year-class, but also took some of the survivors of the

434

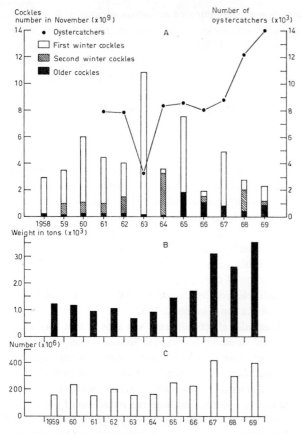

Fig. 12. A. Population estimates of cockles in the November of each year 1958 to 1969 (Table 1), together with the average number of oystercatchers in the Burry Inlet from counts made by P. E. Davidson during each winter.
B. Annual landings of cockles by weight.
C. Annual landings of cockles, by numbers, from the survey area during each year, December to November inclusive, following the surveys on which population estimates in graph A were based.

1963 year-class which were then in their sixth winter. In 1969-70, there were small numbers of second-winter cockles, and during August to November the birds fed selectively on the largest first-winter cockles from the 1969 year-class, but from November onwards they concentrated on the smaller third-winter cockles and on isolated patches of second-winter cockles. During each of these winters, oystercatchers feeding on the survey area alone were responsible for a quantity in excess of that by fishing during each full year.

Since 1965, the 'take-off' from the fishery has been controlled under a management policy which includes permitted daily quotas at a level predetermined from stock forecasts based on the trend of population estimates. After virtual recruit failure in two years (1968 and 1969) it became clear that the May 1970 stock (Table 1) would not be adequate to support both predation and fishing at the level recorded in 1968 and 1969. There are two alternative courses of action available to ensure the maintenance of steady catches throughout the year: either a reduction of predation or a reduction of catches; the first has, to date, not been allowed because of opposition from other interests, especially bird protection. In consequence, the only practical alternative was to reduce the quota levels permitted to each fisherman, a solution which was accepted with considerable misgivings by the cockle industry at a time when the demand for cockles was at a premium.

The effect of predators, including man, on the population dynamics of cockles in the Burry Inlet

The main effect of both fishing and predation will have been to produce a reduction in density. Since fishing is normally responsible for removing a relatively small proportion of the total stock (Fig. 12), its overall effect on population parameters would not be expected to be great, but the local reduction of higher densities may be important in allowing better subsequent growth and survival of the remaining cockles, perhaps even leading to an improved yield and biomass of individuals of larger size. Fishing is responsible for the selective removal of the largest cockles during their second year of life, but there is much less size selection in cockles older than this, most of which will have reached fishable size and which will form a variable proportion of the catch depending on their numbers. For the results of a detailed study of mesh selection by the sieves used during cockle fishing, the reader is referred to an earlier publication (Hancock, 1967).

Predation by oystercatchers differentially affects different age groups in a way which depends on their relative abundances. Selective feeding on second-winter cockles, as during the period before 1963, was very intensive, especially amongst locally high densities. After such periods any beneficial effect on the biomass or average size of individuals (due to improved growth and survival during the following summer, which might have resulted from thinning out) would not be apparent because the reduction of population was carried too far. It has been noted that in winters of unusually high or low density of second winter cockles the level of winter survival was relatively less affected by predation (Fig. 9); so in these cases too there would not be any influence of predation on growth rate, except perhaps locally. During winters when second-winter cockles were poorly represented and predation was concentrated on first-winter or older-than-second-winter cockles, the resulting reduction in density might be expected to lead to some improvement in the growth rate of the survivors, depending on the levels of density before and after predation.

From the observed relationships, the reduction in the number of spawners due to the combined activities of predation and fishing would normally be expected to result in a higher level of recruitment. This seems to have been the case during the period 1958 to 1962 inclusive when, largely as a consequence of oystercatcher predation, the numbers of spawners surviving the winter were relatively small and recruitment was regularly good (Table 1). This stable recruitment situation, however, supported fishing only at a low level. The severe winter of 1962–3 initiated a new sequence of events, with successful recruitment only every second year. From November 1963 onwards, the numbers in the total stock were highly variable (Table 1) but, in conjunction with differences in age composition from year to year, the resulting level of total biomass of cockles showed much less variation. At this time, instead of being able to maintain a preference for second-winter cockles, oystercatchers were constantly forced to vary the size and age of cockles eaten according to those predominating in the stock; this they appeared to do without difficulty except when only very small O-group cockles were available, as in winter 1963–4.

The better survival of cockles through their second winter, which was a consequence of alternating larger year-classes, provided a much sounder basis for the fishery.

At first, predation and fishing seemed to make little impact on the new pattern of recruitment, except perhaps locally, but gradually the intensity of both fishing and predation increased and together they exerted a greater proportional effect as total population became reduced. Failing some unusual circumstance, 1971 might be expected to mark the return of the more stable pre-1963 system of recruitment which provided the basis for heavy predation of second-winter cockles, with poor survival into the fishery. However, in view of the recently increased number of oystercatchers feeding in the Burry Inlet, the precise form in which the system is likely to settle down cannot be predicted with any confidence.

References

Baggerman, B., 1953. Spatfall and transport of *Cardium edule* L. *Archs néerl. Zool.* X (3) 315–342.

Bowden, J. & D. Heppel, 1968. Revised list of British mollusca. 2. Unionacea-Cardiacea. *J. Conch., Lond.* 26: 237–272.

Bowers, E. A., 1969. *Cercaria bucephalopsis haimeana* (LACAZE-DUTHIERS, 1854) (Digenea: Bucephalidae) in the cockle, *Cardium edule* L. in South Wales. *J. nat. Hist.* 3: 409–422.

Bowers, E. A. & B. L. James, 1967. Studies on the morphology, ecology and life-cycle of *Meiogymnophallus minutus* (COBBOLD, 1859) comb. nov. (Trematoda: Gymnophallidae). *Parasitology* 57: 281–300.

Cole, H. A., 1956. Benthos and the shellfish of commerce. In: M. Graham (Ed.), Sea fisheries: their investigation in the United Kingdom, pp. 139–206. London.

Dare, P. J., 1966. The breeding and wintering populations of the oystercatcher (*Haematopus ostralegus* LINNAEUS) in the British Isles. *Fishery Invest. Ser. 2, Lond.* 25 (5): pp. 69.

Dare, P. J., 1970. The movements of oystercatchers *Haematopus ostralegus* L. visiting or breeding in the British Isles. *Fishery Invest. Ser. 2, Lond.* 25 (9): pp. 137.

Davidson, P. E., 1967. A study of the oystercatcher (*Haematopus ostralegus* L.) in relation to the fishery for cockles (*Cardium edule* L.) in the Burry Inlet, South Wales. *Fishery Invest. Ser. 2, Lond.* 25 (7): pp. 28.

Davidson, P. E., 1968. The oystercatcher – a pest of shellfisheries. In: R. K. Murton and E. N. Wright (Ed.), The problems of birds as pests. *Inst. Biol. Symp.* 71: 141–155. Academic Press, London and New York.

Hancock, D. A., 1967. Growth and mesh selection in the edible cockle (*Cardium edule* L.). *J. appl. Ecol.* 4: 137–157.

Hancock, D. A., 1969. An experiment with overcrowded cockles (*Cardium edule*). Proc. Symp. Mollusca, (Cochin, 12–16 Jan. 1968), Symposium Series 3, Part II, Marine biol. Ass. India Symp. Ser. 3 Mandapam Camp, India, p. 396–402.

Hancock, D. A., in press. The relationship between stock and recruitment in exploited invertebrates. *Rapp. P.-v. Réun. Cons. perm. int. Explor. Mer.*

Hancock, D. A. & A. E. Urquhart, 1964. Mortalities of edible cockles (*Cardium edule* L.) during the severe winter of 1962–3. *J. Anim. Ecol.* 33: 176–178.

Hancock, D. A. & A. E. Urquhart, 1965. The determination of natural mortality and its causes in an exploited population of cockles (*Cardium edule* L.) *Fishery Invest. Ser. 2, Lond.* 24 (2): pp. 40.

Hancock, D. A. & A. E. Urquhart, 1966. The fishery for cockles (*Cardium edule* L.) in the Burry Inlet, South Wales. *Fishery Invest. Ser. 2, Lond.* 25 (3): pp. 32.

Kristensen, I., 1957. Differences in density and growth in a cockle population in the Dutch Wadden sea. *Archs néerl. Zool.* 12: 351–453.

Orton, J. H., 1926. On the rate of growth of *Cardium edule*. Part I. Experimental observations. *J. mar. biol. Ass. U.K.* 14: 239–279.

Orton, J. H., 1933. Summer mortality of cockles on some Lancashire and Cheshire Dee beds in 1933. *Nature, Lond.* 132: 314–315.

Pistoor, S. J., 1969. Broedval en groei van *Cardium edule* L. en *Macoma balthica* (L.). *Publ. Versl. Ned. Inst. Onderz. Zee* 1969–6. (Translated extract of p. 28–31).

Ricker, W. E., 1958. Handbook of computations for biological statistics of fish populations. *Bull. Fish. Res. Bd Can.* No 119: pp. 300

Saila, S. B. & T. A. Gaucher, 1966. Estimation of the sampling distribution and numerical abundance of some mollusks in a Rhode Island salt pond. *Proc. natn. Shellfish. Ass.* 56: 73–80.

Tebble, N., 1966. British bivalve seashells – a handbook for identification. *Publ. Trustees Br. Mus. (nat. Hist), Lond.* 647: pp. 212.

Discussion

Participants: Hancock (Author), Beukema, Korringa, Krebs and Reynoldson

Exceptional settlements of cockles were also observed in the Dutch Waddensea after severe winters, e.g. in 1947 and 1963; this has some times been attributed to the greater availability of space for settlement after adult stocks have been nearly wiped out. On the other hand, recent evidence on the importance of parasites, especially *Meiogymnophallus*, in reducing the numbers of cockles during their first year of life, might suggest that the possible wiping out of parasites or their intermediate hosts during severe winters might contribute to the success of the following year-class (BEUKEMA).

Solea vulgaris, Crangon crangon and *Polydora ciliata* reproduced successfully after stocks had been seriously reduced during the severe winter of 1962–1963. This may be ascribed to various causes including a shift in the season of reproduction, and the occurrence of unusually rich plankton due to the increased turn-over of organic matter, as well as to a reduction in the number of parasites or predators (KORRINGA).

There could be a number of factors contributing to the success of settlement after a severe winter. Kristensen (1957) believes that for a successful settlement the beds must be void of cockles and other organisms. This implies that more space is available and, possibly, that there is less predation on both the larval and the settled stage. If food is normally limiting, with a smaller number of adults there may be less competition for food amongst larvae, or between larvae and adults, and there might be a reduced amount of ingestion of larvae and newly settled young by adults (Kristensen, 1957). The relationship between *Meiogymnophallus* and cockles is not a direct one but through a first intermediate host. There was no adequate explanation for the high rate of loss of the 1965 year-class of cockles in the Burry Inlet (AUTHOR).

Intensive predation by sublittoral predators has usually been put forward as the reason for poorer survival below low-water mark. In years of heavy settlement of cockles and mussels better survival below low-water mark seems to reflect a surplus to normal predation of the young (AUTHOR to REYNOLDSON).

Although sublittoral populations of Holland are always rare and of low density, they have a great significance as a reservoir of larvae for repopulating tidal flats on which populations have been completely wiped out, e.g. during a severe winter; this is perhaps an example of 'spreading of risk' comparable with the case of the Australian rabbits mentioned by Birch (these Proceedings) (BEUKEMA).

In view of the heavy settlements and big losses (e.g. from oystercatchers) on tidal flats, transplantation to the sublittoral might prove rewarding (KORRINGA). I know of no attempts to do this, though I have made successful transplants in the intertidal zone (AUTHOR).

438

Is a 'rational' exploitation of the cockle fishery planned, or is it just planned to sit back and let things take their course, as in the case of the whales (KREBS)? If this remark implies taking control action against oystercatchers, this had become a vexed question with a long history involving many interests, an account of which is not relevant to the present discussion. An attempt has been made to gain an understanding of the dynamics of the cockle population, and a policy for management has been based on this. Oystercatcher predation has defeated the use of a number of legislative tools – such as minimum sizes and areas closed to fishing – and, in the present situation, the only permissible course of action was to take into account the observed relationships, including losses expected from predation, in order to predict a year or so in advance the quota levels for fishing (AUTHOR).

Proc. Adv. Study Inst. Dynamics Numbers Popul. (Oosterbeek, 1970) 440–449

Human intervention in the aquatic environment

P. Korringa

Netherlands Institute for Fishery Investigations, IJmuiden, the Netherlands

Abstract

Fluctuations in reproduction and variations in losses suffered through the activities of predators, parasites, and competitors are also in the aquatic environment the basis of population dynamics. If a man catches a fish, he is just an extra predator.

It is often wondered why even a light fishing intensity does not lead to extermination of the fish stocks, for before man intervened the fish stocks must have revealed the famous natural equilibrium, leaving no room for extra losses. That in reality fishery leads to a new, but lower level of the fish stocks, has often been explained in terms of an increased rate of reproduction in response to greater losses. No facts have been adduced to demonstrate this. Little attention has been paid to the fact that fishing means competition for other fish predators of different kinds, which are reduced by an intense fishery.

Nature, left to itself, does not necessarily lead to the greatest production of fish and shellfish. Striking cases of a positive effect of man's activities are oyster culture and mussel farming, in which considerably greater stocks than ever existed on the natural beds have developed through man's intervention in a bottle-neck in the biology of the organism. Several examples can be given of changes in the natural aquatic populations through man's multiple activities, changes leading to both increment and decrease in the stocks, and to serious shifts in the species composition of the body of water under consideration.

Every body of water reveals a given pattern of aquatic organisms. The difference in the patterns observed can be ascribed to factors such as *salinity* (ranging from fresh water to sea water, sometimes even to hypersaline waters), *temperature* (ranging from arctic to tropical conditions, and that with more or less seasonal aspects), *fertility* (ranging from oligotrophic via eutrophic to hypertrophic), *oxygen content* (ranging from saturation to anaerobic conditions), *light* (ranging from strong insolation with or without seasonal aspects to the almost complete darkness reigning at depths over 200 meter both in sea and in lakes; in turbid water even in lesser depths), *turbidity* (ranging from very clear water to water carrying so much silt and/or so much phytoplankton that a Secchi disc is out of sight a few cm below the surface), and also to certain *zoogeographical barriers* which hamper the migration of certain organisms to areas which would otherwise be habitable.

The pattern observed in a given body of water, determined by the factors mentioned above, seems to be quantitatively of a rather constant nature, but in reality this so-called natural equilibrium is of a very dynamic character. Every organism, plant or animal, small or big, faces a variety of risks, among which lack of food and predation preponderate. Every new-born organism has only a limited chance to complete its life-cycle, to die of old age after having given birth to a new generation. Every species observed has evidently eked out an existence and has avoided becoming extinct by reproducing so profusely that the losses suffered by adverse conditions, predators, diseases and parasites have always been duly compensated. Nature follows different pathways to reach this goal. Some organisms are biologically so well sheltered that a slow rate of reproduction suffices; others are so exposed to dangers of different kinds that they simply must produce countless juveniles to survive as a species. Fishes and commercially exploited invertebrates produce, as a rule, so many eggs per year that one is forced to conclude that the multiple dangers encountered before the new generation matures in its turn must be very serious indeed, since the stock under consideration does not increase perceptibly in the course of the years. Some species of fish produce modest numbers of rather big eggs which are well-stocked with reserve material; other species produce far greater numbers of eggs, which are considerably smaller and carry a lesser amount of yolk. Since both types just manage to keep up with the losses suffered, we are forced to conclude that large eggs means a reduction of risk or a better chance of survival, whereas fish larvae hatching from small eggs are evidently less strong and vigorous and must have a very small chance, indeed, to grow up. Species which produce few but large eggs, and also species which are viviparous, show, as a rule, rather limited variations in the success of their reproduction from year to year, whereas species producing countless eggs, of which an incredibly high percentage must perish, will show a greater variation in their success of reproduction. This is logical, for if multiple agencies levy a toll at various developmental stages there is almost automatically a chance of great variation in the net outcome, whereas annual fluctuations in the year-classes produced are usually much smaller in species producing small numbers of offspring. To give an example: the number of whale calves produced by a given whale stock will show a much smaller annual fluctuation than the numbers of codlings annually produced by a stock of cod.

Discussion on possible effects of exploitation

These considerations are of considerable importance when studying the effect of man's intervention on the stocks of various aquatic organisms. Fishery biologists have often wondered why fishing does not lead to complete annihilation of the fish stock under consideration. If one takes the concept of the natural equilibrium too literally, one assumes that for every fish which dies from natural causes, such as diseases and predators, just one will be produced to take the vacated place. If year after year only a little more or a trifle less were produced than just the required number to replace the losses suffered by natural causes, one would expect either a gradual and inevitable increment in the size of the fish stock under consideration, or a gradual and continuing decline until the stock has disappeared completely. Since a natural fish stock reveals a rather constant level and varies but little in the course of the years, one is inclined to assume that replacement is, indeed, perfectly adapted to the losses suffered.

What happens when man interferes, for instance by fishing? The fisherman himself firmly believes that nature will not and cannot notice that he takes a few fishes from the bounty of the sea. When he works on a little boat out of sight from the land, he feels so humble in the overwhelming vastness of the ocean that his brain refuses to believe the stories of the fishery biologists, who tell him that the fish stock does suffer from his activities. A fishery biologist, using the famous natural equilibrium as starting point for his considerations, is alarmed by fishing operations and fears that every fish taken by man will inevitably disturb that equilibrium so that sooner or later the stock will have disappeared completely. When the fish become so reduced in number that remunerative fishing is no longer possible, the fishermen will stop their activities, but how could the fish, left in peace, build up a new stock again if there is no mechanism to increase the reproductive rate to a level higher than that required to break even?

In reality, fishing operations do affect the fish stocks. In every area where serious efforts have been made to assess the size of the stocks in a large number of consecutive years, one can clearly demonstrate the adverse effects of fishing, the more so according as the fishing intensity is greater. In cases where the fishing intensity is kept constant for a longer period, one usually observed that sooner or later the fish stock shows no further decline, despite the continuous taking away of a great number of fishes through the activities of the fishermen. Fishing has led to a decline of the fish stock, but at a constant fishery pressure a new equilibrium, at a lower level, comes into being. The greater the fishing intensity, the lower the new level will be. But when the fishing intensity increases more and more, despite the smaller and smaller catches per hour fishing, one may all of a sudden observe a rapid decline of the fish stock, sometimes even leading to complete disappearance of the species from the area under consideration.

How can a fishery biologist explain these phenomena? That a new equilibrium will be established at a lower level when a constant fishery pressure is exerted was difficult to explain by those who firmly believed in the natural equilibrium based on commensurate replacement of the natural casualties. This led many biologists to the assumption that a fish stock, or in general a stock of any plant or animal, which suffers increasing losses, will respond by producing an increment in the number of its offspring. This may sound a rather logical thing to do for a stock in danger, but how could fish ever observe and record that the time has come to exert an extra effort to produce more offpsring? How could they become aware that their stock is in decline? Moreover, an increasing rate in reproduction should be perceptible to the fishery biologist, who would expect more eggs produced per fish and/or a prolonged season of reproduction. In the literature, observations of this nature have not been recorded for areas where fishing operations take place.

We should, however, not exclude the possibility that there is some relation between the density of the fish stocks and success in reproduction. It is certainly possible that smaller numbers of offspring are recorded per spawning female when the stocks are dense, but in a way different from that discussed above; when the stocks are very dense, lack of food or lack of space may adversely affect larval development and, moreover, increasing numbers of predators or parasites, attracted to and favoured by such rich feeding grounds, may lead to heavier losses than would occur in sparser populations of fish larvae.

If fish do not regulate the numbers of their offspring, what can then be the background for the new equilibrium in the fishing area? A fisherman should be considered as just an extra predator who levies a certain toll of the stock. This means nothing less than competition for other predators. When the stock under consideration declines to a lower level by fishing, many of the natural predators will notice this. A seal or a gannet, for example, can only collect fish during a limited number of hours per day and for as long as they can see the fish. If fish are plentiful, they can easily get the amount of food they need in part of that span of time. When fish becomes scarce, they have to use more hours to collect the food they need; but if scarcity becomes more serious still, they cannot possibly get the quantity of food in the maximum time available. This means that they must either turn to another type of food, or migrate to areas richer in fish. If they fail to follow either of these pathways, the consequence is starvation and ultimately reduction in their numbers. The same reasoning can be followed for other fish predators. Man's interference leads to a new pattern of predation. The more he takes, the less remains for the other predators and in due course a new equilibrium will be established, containing fewer natural predators than before. Similar things have been described for the terrestrial habitat as well; when a stock of a certain plant or animal declines by whatever cause, this will in due course result in a decline in the number of its predators and parasites which, in its turn, means reduced losses and better chances to build up the stock again. On the other hand, a noticeable increment of a stock of any plant or animal will, in due course, inevitably lead to increasing numbers of parasites and predators and/or to shortage of food, and thereby to greater losses which ultimately will bring back the stock to its old level. This explains the true nature of the natural equilibrium, and a man fishing means nothing more than just another factor in this dynamic pattern.

Regulation of fisheries

The main duty of a fisheries biologist is to produce material of scientific character on which to base a sound regulation of the fishery. This does not mean that he should aim at the highest possible level of the fish stocks but rather at the optimum sustainable yield. In the early days of scientific advise on fishery matters, one thought it sufficient to adduce evidence on the size at which fish begins to participate in reproduction and to ensure, by adequate regulation of the mesh size of the nets that every fish gets a chance to reproduce at least once before it is caught. Another aspect of scientific assistance to the fishery were, at that time, the many hatcheries where great numbers of eggs of fish and lobsters were given due protection until they hatched; then the new-born larvae were set free in the natural habitat, because it was cumbersome and costly to feed them adequately under artificial conditions. All this was done on the assumption that it would lead to a noticeable increment in the fish stock, compensating for the losses the stocks suffered by the fishery. However, one rarely observed positive results of the hatchery work.

We can hardly blame the old fishery biologists for this first approach and for their lack of quantitative insight. We know now that quantitative information on the success of reproduction, on growth and age of the fish, on the so-called natural mortality and on the losses brought about by fishing (together with exact information on their migrations, which complicate the picture) is the only sound basis for a fishing theory. Beverton and Holt's book on the dynamics of exploited fish stocks meant a big step forward, indeed. Guided by this magisterial work, fishery biologists of our time can collect enough evidence on the population dynamics of the exploited fish stocks under their care to advise their governments on an adequate system of regulation of the fisheries; aiming either at the optimum sustainable yield or, if so preferred, at the optimum sustainable profit. Basing their calculations on the given size of a certain year-class, they demonstrate how the total weight of that year-class increases, despite a continuous loss in the number of fishes, first rapidly, later more slowly, until the maximum weight has been reached. In some species of fish this maximum is observed one or two years after birth, in other species much later. An anchovy year-class will show its maximum weight after one year, a herring year-class after about 4 years (a herring can easily reach an age of well over 10 years, but does not grow much after 4 or 5 years), whereas a year-class of plaice may reach its maximum weight after about 10 years. The fishery may expect the greatest yields when fishing focusses on the time of the maximum weight of the year-class. This means that usually the fishes will have participated more than once in reproduction before they are caught.

Though the scientific basis for an adequate regulation of the fisheries has now been developed, it must be admitted that this does not mean that all countries have regulated their fishery accordingly. When more than one nation fishes in a given body of water, international agreement is required on the measures to be taken, and on an international system of control. This is not an easy matter. If regulation of the mesh sizes of the nets and/or the minimum legal size of the fish landed was itself sufficient to produce close to the optimum sustainable yield, the situation would not be as disappointing as it now is on most of the traditional fishing grounds. The fishing industry invariably tries to make up for declining catches by introducing more ships, stronger engines, better nets, and more sophisticated electronic equipment to locate concentrations of fish; in short, by increasing the fishing effort. Without appropriate regulation of the fishery intensity, all efforts to raise and to stabilize the catches by means of minimum mesh sizes and minimum legal sizes for landed fish are to a large extent nullified by this tendency. Overfishing is evident on many of the traditional fishing grounds, the symptoms are decreasing average age and size of the fish caught, decreasing catches per unit of effort and, in serious cases, even decrease of the total landings.

Observed effects of exploitation

Another aspect of overfishing is an increasing degree of fluctuations in the annual catches; a head-ache for the fish trade. This too belongs to the realm of population dynamics. As has been said, a great number of eggs are produced by a fish, and a high percentage of losses brought about by multiple agencies means a great variation in the net output; this is the more so according as the eggs produced are smaller and more numerous. The fishery biologist speaks about strong and weak year-classes. He does not always know which factors lead to success or failure in reproduction, but there is evidence that not only simple factors like water temperature determine how many of the larvae will develop into juvenile fishes, but that in many cases the availability of the right type of food in sufficient quantities is the decisive factor which may lead to a large year-class. There is little one can do in this phase in the life of a fish, but one could reduce the commercially adverse effect of fluctuations in the strength of the consecutive year-classes by smoothing them out through catching a greater number of year-classes simultaneously. Where fishing exerts not too great a pressure on a fish stock, one observes a large number of year-classes in the catches, and therefore the effect of one very strong or one very weak year-class is hardly noticed by the fishing industry and is seen only by the biologist who analyses the catches. Such a situation was responsible for the remarkably constant level of the total landings of herring from the North Sea during a prolonged period; this pattern was drastically destroyed by the recent sudden increase in fishing intensity in this area. Now, one or at most two year-classes are found in the catches in numbers worth mentioning, instead of about ten, as observed in the former period. The same unfavourable development is observed in other fisheries with too heavy a fishing pressure.

When the adult stock is composed of only a very few year-classes, the fluctuations in the strength of the year-classes may lead to noteworthy fluctuations in the total number of eggs produced per year, whereas the total number of eggs did not fluctuate much when a greater number of year-classes participated in reproduction. Formerly, fishery biologists assumed that the total number of eggs produced per season would never be a limiting factor, and had little or nothing to do with the ultimate strength of the year-classes, but in our time it is open to doubt whether this assumption is correct. If only one, or at most two, year-classes participate in reproduction, and if it so happens that two weak year-classes occur in succession, the total number of eggs produced will automatically be very small. When most of the factors involved are favourable during the early development of the species of fish under consideration, a small number of eggs may still produce a reasonably good year-class. Statistically seen, it is clear that the starting point, the total number of eggs produced, must exert an influence on the net output. Several cases have been observed where a stock shows a sudden decline and may even dwindle to insignificance after a period of very heavy fishing pressure. This is explained in terms of a drastically reduced egg production and unfavourable conditions in the larval period. It is unwise to assume that the factor 'egg production' is unimportant for the maintenance of a fish stock.

The case of the European flat oyster, *Ostrea edulis*, grown on large scale in the Ooster-schelde (Netherlands) may serve as an example. Quantitative data on the size of the stock over a long period (1870–1962) and on the number of larvae produced in the course of the summer season (1935–1962), clearly demonstrate that when there is a great stock of oysters, settlement of spat will be good in a year with average water temperatures, and profuse in a warm summer; it will be unsatisfactory only if the summer is unusually cold. In periods with a small stock of adult oysters, on the other hand, settlement of spat was only satisfactory in warm summers. For the years 1935 to 1962 there appeared to be a rather close relationship between the number of adult oysters and the number of larvae observed per 100 l of water throughout the summer season. Evidently, environmental conditions such as water temperature, food organisms, and predators determine what *percentage* of the larvae will reach the stage of settlement. Hence, the *total number* of larvae produced by the adult oysters must be a factor of importance in determining the net output. There is no reason why this should be fundamentally different in fishes. The ultimate effect of the total number of eggs produced will be greatest in species producing rather small numbers of eggs. Therefore, American investigations on *Crassostrea virginica*, which produces far more eggs than do flat oysters, failed to show such a close correlation between parent stock and spat production as that observed in the Oosterschelde.

Fishery exerts not only an influence on the size of the stock one is fishing for, but indirectly also on many other denizens of the sea. Taking great numbers of fish away from the sea can lead to a food shortage for its natural predators and, therefore, to changes in the size of their stocks; but the effect can at the same time be a lower degree of predation or grazing on its favourite prey and hence, to a positive effect on these stocks. The fishing industry, therefore, has a much greater effect on the entire pattern of aquatic organisms than one is inclined to believe at first sight. Fishes like rays become very scarce in areas where trawls fish for demersal fish because their shape leads to an early capture in the nets. Intensive fishing for hake in the waters of the North African continental shelf led to a surprisingly great increase in the number of squids. Depletion of the California sardine through serious overfishing led to an explosion of anchovies. These examples demonstrate that the interrelationships are of rather a complex nature.

Positive influences

When there is no fishing at all, one generally assumes that the level of the fish or shellfish stock is optimal for the given pattern of environmental conditions. This may be true, but it does not necessarily mean that nature, left to itself, leads to the greatest possible production of fish and shellfish. Often the primary production would enable a far greater number of fish and shellfish to thrive in a given body of water than one encounters in reality. In such cases too, man can exert an influence on the aquatic population dynamics. Several examples can be adduced to demonstrate that man can exert a positive influence on the size of the stocks by taking adequate measures. The natural oyster beds in the Oosterschelde produced year after year some half to three-quarters of a million marketable oysters. The introduction of adequate cultivation techniques in the years following 1870 soon led to the development of a far greater stock of oysters than ever existed on the natural beds. A limiting factor was evidently the scarcity of material on which the full-grown larvae could settle. By offering sufficient settling places of various descriptions, a far greater percentage of the larvae ready to settle could find a suitable place than under the former fully natural conditions. In due course, one produced year after year 25 to 30 million oysters in an area which once produced less than one million oysters. Evidently food was not the limiting factor here. Efforts to increase the stock still further failed. Evidently food became the limiting factor when more than 100 million adult oysters were grown in the Basin of the Oosterschelde (about 1 oyster per 4 m^3 of sea water). Food shortage inevitably leads to poor growth and increasing mortality.

Man's positive handling led in this case to a marked increment in the stock. His negative handling by fishing too intensely on natural oyster beds in the Firth of Forth led to complete extermination of the oyster in this formerly very productive area. Fishing oysters led to a reduced production of larvae (commensurate with the size of the stock) and at the same time to a serious reduction in the quantity of suitable settling sites (collectors: the clean new growth shoots of the shells of adult oysters). Moreover, oyster spat which had settled on the shells of the adult oysters was destroyed when the latter were fished and marketed. Soon the population became so scanty that a revival was impossible.

Another striking case is mussel farming in the ria's of North Western Spain. Wild mussels (*Mytilus edulis*) could be found on the rocks in the intertidal zone, but mussels of good size and of a quality acceptable on the market were rarely found. Evidently the places where the young mussels settled did not offer them suitable conditions for growth and fattening. A system of mussel farming has recently been developed in this area. The small mussels are detached from the intertidal rocks and fixed to ropes hung from rafts in the plankton-rich waters of several of the ria's. Rapid growth and excellent fattening, leading to the production of marketable mussels within 10 months time, is the result. This area of Spain now produces per year some 200 million kg of marketable mussels. Here again is a case of man's interference in a positive way. The area was potentially rich enough, but the mussels foolishly settled in the wrong places. This is often a feature in oyster farming too: oyster spat settles in places with very limited current velocities, but growth and fattening is much better in places where strong currents prevail. Man interferes by transplanting young oysters to places where currents are stronger and where the water is rich in food.

Many other cases could be cited to show that nature, left to itself, does not necessarily lead to the optimum development of stocks of fish and shellfish.

Conclusion

All the examples cited warrant the conclusion that human intervention in the aquatic environment exerts a much greater influence on the population dynamics under water than one could believe at first sight. The oceans may seem unbounded and man's fishing boat a mere dot, but most of the fishes and shellfish of commercial importance can thrive only on the continental shelves, and usually show a certain number of distinct populations which live in very limited sections of the waters above the continental shelves. The influence that man exerts in these limited areas is so far reaching that other predators may be greatly reduced, and whole populations of fish and shellfish are in due course destroyed by the wasteful exploitation of these natural resources. On the other hand, adequate cultivation techniques lead to a far greater production of some species than nature, left to itself, would have given.

Discussion

Participants: Korringa (Author), Bakker (K.), Birch, den Boer (P. J.P), Gulland, Hancock, Reddingius, Varley and Waloff

Theoretical exercises suggest that there may be two types of populations:
1. Populations the density of which is kept between rather narrow limits, or around an equilibrium level, by governing or regulating factors (competition, maybe predators).
2. Populations the density of which fluctuates up and down, natality and mortality on the average cancel each other, limitation of population density occurring occasionally.

If this is correct, a population is exploitable, and the optimum yield problem can be solved only if we have the first type of population. Otherwise we would just add another mortality factor and this would lead to extinction of the population. Therefore it seems that stock-recruitment curves are very important, and it is striking that they are usually fitted through a bunch of points through which any other curve could be drawn (REDDINGIUS). Regulation and exploitation seem to be so closely related, that it is hardly possible to separate them (BAKKER and BIRCH). As far as I can see, competition and predation are nearly always important factors regulating the size of the stock. When a new fishery is started we should know whether the species under consideration grows fast enough to warrant a sufficient annual weight increase of the stock. *Sebastes norvegicus*, the red fish, on which the German fishery focussed its attention in the post-war years, grows so slowly that even at a modest fishing intensity the stock declines in a few years to a level which is no longer exploitable. One should come back after leaving the stock in peace for quite a few years. Only rapidly growing fish species with sufficient reproductive potential can be used for a sustainable commercial exploitation (AUTHOR).

I agree with Reddingius that the stock-recruitment relationship is vital in determining the intensity of exploitation that can be sustained. Historically most fish populations have behaved as though recruitment were independent of adult density. This, of course, implies that the survival from egg to recruitment is, on the average, inversely proportional to adult abundance. The difficulty in studying any individual fishery is that there is a great deal of noise in the system which obscures the precise shape of the mean stock-recruitment curve. Also the critical events occur in the pre-recruit phase – eggs, larvae and juvenile fish – which are difficult to observe, and behave quite independently of the adult fish (GULLAND).

Korringa's point boils down to the desirability of delaying exploitation until enough is known about population dynamics of the species concerned. Unfortunately, this requires

447

extensive research and probably we only know enough about a very few species e.g. plaice and sole. FAO and similar bodies have therefore to keep a very narrow balance between the need to expand fishing to feed developing countries, and the need for prior research (GULLAND). This is perfectly true. Fishery biologists have to produce scientific material to be used in framing regulations of the fishery. If they are perfectionists, the advice for regulation of the fishery may come too late to save that fishery from its own deleterious effects, at least for a great number of years. On the other hand, too hasty and superficial a view may lead to undesirable financial losses for the industry. A good fishery biologist should have sufficient imagination, should feel how much data he needs to grasp the essentials of the underwater truth, and should dare to advise his government before he has the feeling that he is in all details on perfectly safe ground (AUTHOR).

How many complete life-tables are, by now, available for the most important marine fish (WALOFF)? Out of the 30,000 fish species we have chosen a few which are economically so important for our fishery, that we can afford to study them in greater detail: herring, sole, cod, haddock, mackerel, plaice, eel, brown shrimp, mussel, oyster. For those few, we study year-class fluctuations, growth, recruitment, natural mortality, fishery mortality, and migrations. A complete life-table, including all losses suffered since early youth would be ideal, but is not necessary for a forecast of the catches or for framing regulations for ensuring the optimum sustainable yield. For the oyster, *Ostrea edulis*, we come very close to a complete life-table for we have collected quantitative information on the events during pelagic and early sedentary stages (AUTHOR). There are no *complete* life-tables for commercial fish – even for the plaice there are still gaps. Small fish are exceedingly difficult to observe quantitatively (GULLAND).

The fact that after starting exploitation of a population of fish the population stabilizes at a new lower level is explained by assuming that natural mortality had decreased. If this natural mortality is supposed to be due to predators, would it be possible that fisheries have removed the predators – or at least some of them – together with their prey, i.e. the fish exploited (BAKKER)? Every fishery has a certain effect on the fish stocks. At constant fishery pressure the fish stock will show in due course a new but lower level. The more intensive the fishery, the lower the level. Some of the fish predators are indeed removed by fishing with a non-specialized gear such as a trawlnet, but not predators such as seals, porpoises, sharks and seabirds, whereas more specialized gear will not lead to any removal of predators (AUTHOR). Unless there is an all-out effort at pest control, this could even work the other way. Anyone who has watched the process of fishing will see that, in general, a fisherman selects the catch he requires, and then throws back the remainder. The trash can include unwanted species of fish, bottom predators such as starfish, gastrol pods, etc., all of which could affect part of the chain involved in the food of commercia-fish (HANCOCK).

But what about the intensive exploitment of fishes like cod, haddock, hake? The removal of such predators may importantly influence the proportion of recruitment of smaller fishes (e.g. herring) that reaches the exploitable age. And what is known about the influence of intensive fishing of pelagic species (e.g. herring) on the survival of larvae of the same and of still smaller species (DEN BOER)? Certainly fishing has a greater effect on the whole aquatic community than just removing species of economic importance; the whole food-web may be affected. Also cannibalism may be important, as was found in the cod: the appearance of a rich year-class of cod greatly increases amounts of codlings found in the stomachs of big cods; the same happened to the pike-porch in the IJsselmeer. In both cases the chance of encountering small specimens of the same species among other prey had obviously increased. By this mechanism strong year-classes are 'creamed off' by their own species (AUTHOR).

In many a fishing area one has observed increases and decreases of species of vertebrates and invertebrates as secondary effects of the fishery, but it is not easy to collect quantitative information on such phenomena, since one should then clearly distinguish the often considerable natural fluctuations from the effects of the fishery. The trawl fishery in the Gulf of Thailand is an interesting example of an area about which there was information both before and after fishing, and for which changes in species composition of the stocks can be demonstrated. Here, there was a steady decline in total biomass in the area, but while some species declined greatly, including most of those preferred by the fishermen, others increased – including the shrimp, possibly due to the removal of their predators. The increase in squid catches off North Africa mentioned by Korringa could have reflected a diversion of the fishing effort from hake to cephalopods rather than greater abundance (GULLAND).

To what extent was the extinction of oysters in the colder parts of their range helped by the introduction of spat from more southern waters (VARLEY)? Oysters are a well-known example of a species which can be completely exterminated by a fishery. They cannot move from the spot, occur very locally on natural beds, and can be caught with simple and cheap equipment. The introduction of spat or half-grown oysters usually did not lead to revival of depleted beds, since there are marked hereditary differences between the various stocks, both in respect of the required minimum temperature for larval development (14°C in Galicia, 15°C in the Firth of Forth and in Germany, 18°C in France and in Zeeland, 25°C in Norway) and in resistance to low winter temperatures. Low temperature breeders which are at the same time 'winter–proof' are now extinct (Slesvig-Holstein, Firth of Forth, Waddenzee). Transplantation may lead to good growth and fattening, but will rarely lead to a revival of the local stock (AUTHOR).

Proc. Adv. Study Inst. Dynamics Numbers Popul. (Oosterbeek, 1970) 450–468

The effect of exploitation on the numbers of marine animals

J. A. Gulland

Department of Fisheries, FAO, Rome, Italy

Abstract

Exploitation by man has increased the mortality rate among the larger individuals of many species of mammals and fish. Many populations of whales and seals have, in the absence of controls and regulations, been reduced to near extinction, but under proper management other stocks, e.g. the fur seals in the North Pacific, have shown their ability to maintain their number under moderately heavy exploitation.

In the Antarctic the catches of whales have been controlled for some quarter of a century, but until recently the limit set was greater than the sustainable yield. This sustainable yield is rather less than 10% of the population, and is the surplus of net recruitment over natural mortality, which results from maturity at an earlier age and a rather greater pregnancy rate in the present stocks.

Most fish stocks have proved more resilient to exploitation. This appears to be connected with their high fecundity. The mortality of young between egg-laying and the time of recruitment to the fishery is very high. Small density-dependent changes in the average level of this mortality can give the results, often observed, of approximately constant numbers of recruits over a wide range of adult densities.

The dynamics of the numbers of marine animals have been studied intensely for a long time. This is because many natural populations support economically important fisheries (a term which, in common usage, covers the exploitation of whales and seals, as well as fish in the correct biological sense). In addition to providing incentives to the fundings of research, commonly carried out in Government laboratories, these fisheries are themselves valuable sources of data to the scientists studying the stocks. Statistics of the catch provide information on one major cause of death, often with data on the date and location of capture, and on the sizes of the animals concerned. Also data on the catches per unit amount of fishing (e.g. numbers of whales killed per day's work by a standard catching vessel) provide a reasonable index of abundance of the population, which can be used to study changes from year to year.

The study of the dynamics of marine animal populations has therefore advanced far; in some respects further than corresponding studies on land. On the other hand, progress in some aspects has been slow due to the special difficulties of marine research. Observations at sea require expensive research vessels. Quantitative sampling of most animals is difficult; they are either active enough to avoid the nets, or are small enough to pass through the meshes. Another difficulty is that, due to the commonly wide movements and

---

[1] The views expressed here are those of the author and not necessarily those of FAO.

migrations, large populations have to be analysed as a single unit (e.g. the albacore tuna in the whole North Pacific from Japan to California are part of a single stock). This means that any evaluation of the effect of, say, environmental factors (e.g. temperature) on juvenile survival has to be based on one pair of figures per year. This, plus the near impossibility of any direct experimental approach, makes progress in some directions slow.

Another difference between most situations on land and on sea is the objective of man's operations. On sea, this is essentially hunting; thus the objective is to kill as many of the preferred species as possible while leaving sufficient alive to provide good catches for next year. On land, most of the natural populations are considered as pests to be killed off as completely as possible. The cropping of game animals and birds, whether for sport or, as is being increasingly done in parts of Africa, for food has many features in common with marine fisheries.

The direct effect of exploitation

The effect of exploitation on marine animals by man is basically extremely simple. Fishing operations are highly selective, being directed towards certain preferred species or groups of species and for certain size – usually those above a certain size set by market demand, technical limitations or by regulations. Within the preferred range of size, fishing often acts effectively at random and may be represented simply as an additional source of mortality. This mortality expressed as a rate (the proportion removed per unit time), will be proportional to the fishing effort – the amount of fishing in some standard terms.

Except when the animals leave the sea, e.g. seals on the breeding grounds, or salmon going up the spawning streams, there is a practical limit to the fishing mortality that is set by the amount of fishing it is economically possible to carry out.

This limit can, however, be very high compared with other causes of mortality. For instance, at the peak of Antarctic whaling 30% or more of the adult fin whales were being killed each season. Estimates of the natural death rate vary but it is almost certainly lower than 10%, and could well be lower than 5% per year. In fish stocks (in the proper sense) an equal dominance of fishing over natural mortality has also been observed. In the North Sea, about 50% of the larger plaice (*Pleuronectes platessa*) are caught each year, while the natural death rate is about 10–15% per year.

With such a formidable additional mortality, often of several times, exploitation would soon decrease the population to a very low level if there were not some compensatory changes in the population – in growth, other causes of mortality, or in reproductive rate. Fortunately such changes do occur, to a greater or lesser extent, and thus allow a greater or lesser degree of cropping which can be maintained indefinitely without further depletion of the stock.

The main objective of research into the population dynamics of exploited marine animals is to study these changes, either in detail or in their overall effect, and thus determine the possible patterns of sustained cropping. In particular, there will be some intermediate cropping rates which will give the 'optimum' results – the maximum physical catch, or a large catch at low cost.

Until recently these analyses could reasonably be made species by species, treating each separately, since the species concerned generally made up only a small element of the ecosystem. Now a much wider range of species are being exploited – in many areas virtually all the conveniently sized animals (greater than say 10 cm long). Studies therefore have to be made of the interactions of several species (and the fisheries on them), either as predator and prey (e.g. cod or dogfish and herring), or as competitors at the same trophic level and filling similar ecological niches, e.g. sardine and anchovy in the California Current, both of which are zooplankton feeders.

To study the immediate effects of fishing, two general techniques have been used. First, to consider the overall effect on the abundance, considering the population has been adequately represented by a single measure of its biomass without being concerned by its age or other structure. The population will have an intrinsic rate of natural increase, which is a function of the biomass. Changes in the population then follow the simple laws of population growth as set out, e.g., by Volterra (1928) and Schaefer (1954, 1957). This approach has given useful descriptions of fisheries, after exploitation has had a significant effect, but gives little insight into the processes concerned.

The other approach consists in measuring the parameters of growth and mortality in the exploited part of the stock (Ricker, 1958; Beverton and Holt, 1957; Gulland, 1969). Relatively simple calculations can then give the abundance of the population, the catch and any other characteristics (e.g. average size of fish) as functions of these parameters, e.g. the catch from a cohort of fish will be given as:

$$Y = \int_{t_1}^{t_2} F_t\, N_r\, S_t\, W_t\, dt$$

where t_1 to t_2 = the range of ages over which fishery acts; F_t = fishing mortality on fish of age t; N_r = number of recruits, i.e. the number of individuals in the cohort at the time they enter the fishable stage of life, assumed to be at age t_r; S_t = survival from age t_r to age t; W_t = average weight of an individual of age t.

Also $S_t = \exp - \left\{ \int_{t_r}^{t} (F_t + M_t)\, dt \right\}$

where M_t = natural mortality of fish of age t.

Using this expression, with adaptations depending on the precise form used for the weight etc., the yield for any pattern of fishing (fishing mortality, and the range of sizes over which it operates) can be calculated, if changes in the other non-fishing parameters can be ignored. The common experience of fisheries has been that, to a reasonable first-order approximation, changes in mortality and growth due to fishing (or more precisely due to fishery induced changes in population abundance) can be ignored. Changes in N_r, the number of recruits, are more complex; N_r will be equal to the number of mature females times their average fecundity times the survival from births (or the time of egg production) to recruitment. In this, there is an important difference between marine mammals with low fecundities (one every other year in the case of large whales) and high survival rates, and most fish with high fecundities and very low survival rates (a large female cod may produce a million eggs). For fish, it seems (again as an acceptable first-order assumption) that as fishing (or other causes) decreases adult abundance, there is a small but sufficient increase in survival among the young animals to maintain the number of recruits. For mammals, the mortality of the young is less, giving less opportunity for reduced mortality of the young to compensate for increased mortality among the larger animals. Thus, mammals have proved more sensitive to exploitation than fish, as is illustrated by the contrasting trend in catches of Antartic whales (Fig. 1), and of cod and haddock in the North Sea (Fig. 2). The difference between the successive declines of each of the main

452

whale species, and the oscillation about a fairly constant level by cod and haddock, are even more obvious in Fig. 3 and 4. These show the estimated abundances of each species, calculated as the catch per unit fishing effort.

Marine mammals

The history of the exploitation of marine mammals has generally been an unhappy one. Exploitation has steadily decreased the stock and, in the absence of strong conservation measures, this has continued until the animals become so scarce that catching no longer becomes worthwhile; i.e. the stock becomes commercially, if not biologically, extinct. Several great whale fisheries have followed this pattern. The earliest commercial whale fisheries were on the right whales (the 'right' whales to hunt because they were slow and easy to kill, and floated after being killed).

These supported the great Arctic fisheries from England, Scotland and Holland. At their peak several hundred vessels took part, but by the middle of the nineteenth century only a handful remained, and these had great difficulty in finding any whales. Even now, after a century without exploitation the North Atlantic right whale remains extremely rare.

The end of the Arctic right whale fishery coincided with the peak of the next great whale fishery – that conducted out of New England for sperm whales. This covered all the warmer oceans; as the hunters of the right whales were the first to penetrate in number into Arctic regions, the hunters of the sperm whales were the first Europeans to appear in numbers in many parts of the South Pacific. Though reduced by exploitation, the sperm whales were not so seriously depleted as the right whales. The discovery of petroleum as a better source of oil for lighting etc., destroyed the main market for the products, and the industry declined for outside economic reasons (also hastened by events of the American Civil War) before the stocks were seriously threatened.

The early fisheries were conducted from open boats, and the whales were killed by harpoons thrown by hand. With the development of the harpoon gun, man could go after the great blue and fin whales; the last and greatest era of whaling came with the development of the Antartic pelagic fishery some half century ago.

The trends in the catches of the main species in the fishery are shown in Fig. 1. This shows that there has been a succession in the main species sought, first blue whales, then fin whales and finally sei whales. The peak catches of blue whales (even omitting the exceptional season of 1930/31, when 41 factory ships and 230 catching vessels took part) were only maintained for a very short period. There was a rather longer period (1953 to 1962) of high catches of fin whales; this was a time when catches were restricted by the International Whaling Commission – though the quota set turned out to have been too high. More recently, more stringent restrictions have been imposed which include a complete ban on the killing of blue and humpback whales, and it seems that the present low levels of catches could be maintained indefinitely.

Better evidence of the ability of marine mammals to provide substantial catches under conditions of enlightened management is provided by the history of the North Pacific fur seal (*Callorhinus ursinus*). These breed on a limited number of islands in the Bering Sea and adjacent waters; the biggest herds being on the Pribilof Islands. By 1911, unrestricted exploitation both on the breeding islands and on the high seas had brought the stocks to a very low level. Under a treaty signed in 1911 (and subsequent agreements) between the

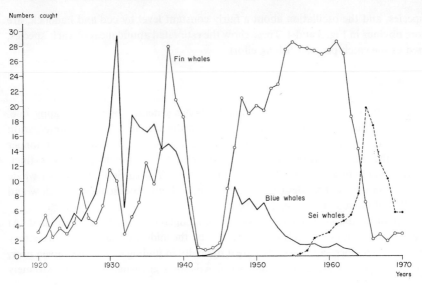

Fig.1. Total catches (× 1000) of the major species of baleen whales in the Antarctic, 1920–1970.

USA, Japan, the USSR and Canada (in the first treaty the UK acted for Canada), exploitation has been strictly controlled by an International Commission. Catches, mainly of young males, are limited to the breeding islands, and are carried out by the governments concerned (USA and USSR); these hand over a proportion of the skins thus obtained to Japan and Canada in consideration for their abstaining from catching fur seals in the high seas.

Antarctic whales

For the Antarctic whales, virtually complete and fairly accurate data of the catches are available from about the beginning of the fishery. These data include the information on the number and species of all whales caught and the location of each capture (strictly the noon position of factory ships on the day of capture). Data on the sizes of the whale, whether if female, it was pregnant and, if so, the size of the foetus, are also available for all but the earlier years. Studies on the population dynamics of whales have been carried on for several decades (e.g. Hjort, Jahn and Ottestad, 1933), but more detailed analysis mainly dates from 1960. At that time, the International Whaling Commission, disturbed by what was believed by many, but not all, of its members to be a serious decline in whale stocks, and by the lack of clear scientific advice as to what was happening and what should be done, set up a special Committee of Three (later Four) Scientists who were specialists in population dynamics. The report of this Committee (Anon., 1964), the subsequent reports of the Scientific Committee of ICW, and papers presented to the Scientific Committee, describe the current knowledge of the status of the Antartic stocks.

The most important data that are not available for a long period are those on the age of whales. A number of methods of age determination have been used. Initially counts were made of the ridges on the whale-bone (which is only suitable for young whales) and counts of the corporea lutea (only possible for mature females). Recently, counts have been made of the laminations on the ear-plug, but not until 1968 (Anon., 1968) was it clearly shown that only one lamination was laid down each year.

Before examining the scientific aspects of the population dynamics, it is worth reviewing briefly the status of the whaling industry, and especially the successes and failures of conservation actions. As Fig. 1 shows, a decline in blue whales was clearly in progress before the Second World War. Action was taken in the 1930's towards forming a regulatory body and a related and most valuable step was also taken by the Norwegian Government in setting up the Bureau of International Whaling Statistics. International conferences were held in 1937, 1938, 1939, 1944 and 1945 which set increasingly strict controls on whaling; finally, the International Whaling Commission was set up by a conference held in Washington at the end of 1946. This Commission has set limits on the total Antartic catch, which varied during the period 1947–1963 between 14,500 and 16,000 Blue Whale Units (1 blue whale = 2 fin whales = 6 sei whales = $2\frac{1}{2}$ humpback whales). In the 1960/61 and 1961/62 seasons, while negotiations were in progress on the division of the total quota between countries, no limit was set, but the catch remained in the same range.

The catch quota was originally set without any sophisticated scientific calculations as to what it should be. Later analysis shows that the quota was not very different from the combined sustainable yields of the stocks immediately after the war. There were, however, two serious shortcomings – first the general quota provided no differential protection for the various species, and second there was no immediate or semi-automatic provision for a revision of the quota – particularly for a reduction if there were a decline in the stocks.

When the quota system was introduced, the blue whales had been already severely reduced, as had been most of the local stocks of humpback whales, while the fin whales were only moderately exploited and the sei whales were virtually untouched. Extra measures for the former two species were introduced – a shorter open season for blue whales in 1953/54 and later seasons, and for humpbacks a separate quota (1,250) from 1949/50 to 1952/53 followed by a limited 4-day open season in 1953/54 to 1958/59 – though there is reason to believe that this latter was not strictly observed. However, as Fig. 1 and 3 show, these measures were not sufficient to prevent a steady decline in the blue whale

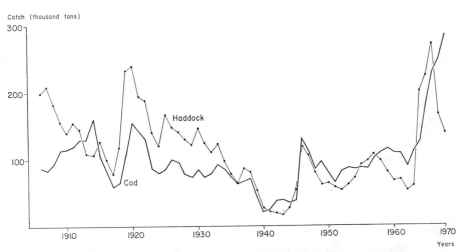

Fig. 2. Total international catches of cod and haddock in the North Sea, 1906–1969.

455

stock. The data for humpback whales are not shown, since they form a number of independent stocks exploited both in the Antartic and in the southern waters along the coasts of Australia, New Zealand, etc. All these stocks have been greatly reduced, though the declines have not been exactly contemporaneous in all stocks.

Fig. 3 also suggests that there was actually an increase in the apparent abundance of fin whales between 1950 and 1956. This is an artefact of the method of estimation. The figures plotted are the numbers of whales caught per catcher-ton-day, i.e. the total catch divided by the number of days operating by catcher vessels (approximately the product of the number of catchers and the length of the season) multiplied by the average tonnage of the vessels. The tonnage is included as a correction for the increasing efficiency of the vessels. Between 1945 and 1968, the average gross tonnage increased from 310 to 769 tons. During the same period, the efficiency has increased for a number of reasons – the ships are faster, they are equipped with sonar so they can follow the underwater movements of the whales, etc. – the effects of which are very difficult to quantify. However, it is generally believed that the trend in efficiency is fairly well reflected in the (measurable) trends in tonnage.

The other difficulty in estimating the abundance of any one species is that there are some (but not complete) geographical separations of the species. The expeditions go to the areas where the preferred species (blue whales in 1945–48, fin whales in 1955–65, sei whales in 1966–68) are most abundant. Thus, the apparent increase in fin whales up to 1956, and in sei whales up to 1966, is due to the shift of attention of the expeditions from blue to fin, and fin to sei whales respectively.

The best measure of the general overall abundance of whales is, therefore, the total catch per unit effort in blue whale units. The trend in this measure, as shown in Fig. 3, exhibits four distinct periods – a short period of rapid decline immediately after the war, a level period between 1950 and 1955, another period of steady decline between 1955 and

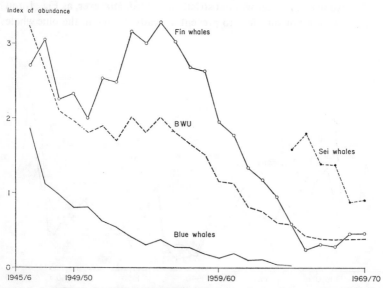

Fig. 3. Indices of abundance of baleen whales in the Antarctic, as estimated as the number caught by 1000 catcher-ton-days.

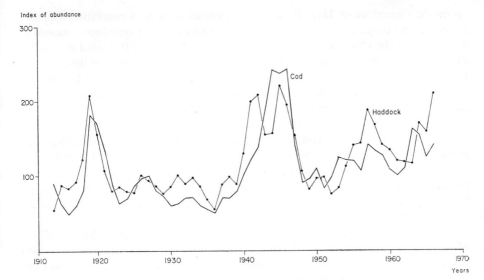

Fig. 4. Indices of abundance of cod and haddock in the North Sea, as estimated by the catch per unit fishing time by English and Scottish trawlers (for cod and haddock respectively).

1966, and a final period of some 4 years up to the present with again little change in abundance.

These changes may be interpreted first as a period during which the blue whales decline to a level at which they were no longer of major economic importance. In the second period, the catch quota was only slightly greater than the sustainable yield and any slight decrease in stock was masked by changes in efficiency. After 1955, the difference between catch and sustainable yield widened, leading to progressively faster declines, until the catch quota was again brought into accord with the (much reduced) sustainable yield in 1966/67. Thereafter the combined stocks of fin and sei whales seem to have remained about constant.

The period between 1959 and 1967 was one of intense political and scientific argument. One phase of the political argument concerned the division of the quota between the various countries. Without such allocation, each country had to scramble for its share – the so-called whaling olympics – sending as many vessels to the Antartic as possible. As a result, the length of the open season became progressively shorter reaching to a minimum of 58 days in 1955–56, and the operations became increasingly uneconomic. Disagreements over the allocation resulted in the failure to set a definite quota in the 1960/61 and 1961/62 seasons, but agreement was reached in 1962 and some form of allocation has been in operation ever since.

The more serious arguments concerned the desirable level of the total quota. By 1955, the decline in stocks was becoming clear to both the whale gunners in the Antartic and to the scientists. However, there was no complete agreement on the extent (or even for some time even on the existence) of the decline. Certain scientists maintained that the decline in catch per day of the catcher vessels did not represent a true decline in the stocks. It was this failure of its scientific advisors to give clear and agreed advice which led the IWC to set up the Committee of Three (later Four) Scientists, experts in population dynamics but not directly concerned with whale research, to advise it. This Committee presented its final report at the 15th meeting of the Commission in June 1963. It showed that, at the existing low level of stocks, the current quota was about three times greater than could be taken without further depleting the stocks. Though the validity of the conclusions were generally accepted – an acceptance that was helped by the coincidence between the actual catches by pelagic expeditions in 1963/64 (13,780 fin whales) and those predicted (14,000, compared with 18,668 in 1962/63) – it was not at all easy to agree on an immediate cut in the quota to the extent recommended (any industry finds it difficult to cut its activities by two-thirds in one year). However, by the 1966/67 season the quota had been reduced almost to the level of the combined sustainable yields of fin and sei whales, though there has been some disagreement concerning the precise values of these sustainable yields. Since then, the estimated combined abundance of the Antarctic whale stocks has changed little (see Fig. 3).

This paper is not concerned with the extensive arguments over the blame for the collapse of Antarctic whaling, but it is worth pointing out that the common picture of destruction brought about by short-sighted greed is wrong. The whaling industry has supported and adhered to conservation regulations for a quarter of a century. Certainly it failed to accept the very drastic measures that were shown to be necessary around 1963, but another critical failure was that of the scientists to provide clear advice to the industry around 1955–60 when a reduction in quota was necessary, but would have involved much less drastic reductions in catches. This, in turn, was due to failure of the Governments concerned to ensure the right kind of competence – in quantitative methods and especially in population dynamics – among their scientists concerned with whale research. An important lesson of the whaling story is, therefore, the need of adequate and timely research.

Estimates of sustainable yield

In estimating the sustainable yield, both groups of methods described earlier have been used (Anon., 1964). For blue whales, an adaptation of the Schaefer method could be used. The data covered a very wide range of levels of population abundance, over most of which the blue whale was a sufficiently important objective of the industry for the catch per catcher-ton-day to be a reasonable index of abundance.

The first problem was to relate this index to the absolute abundance. The principle method used was that of De Lury (1947). This relates the reduction in the index (catch per unit effort) to the numbers removed. In the simple form, the assumption is made that catches are the sole cause of change in the population, but modifications were introduced to allow for the fact that the number of whales dying of natural causes was less than the number of young whales recruiting, the latter being the off-spring of the rather more numerous adult population some years previously. With various adjustments, this method gave estimates of the blue whale population in 1963/64 of from 9 to 14 thousand. This agrees reasonably well with estimates, obtained from sightings of whales from research vessels (Mackintosh and Brown, 1956), of about 20–50 thousand blue whales in 1933/34–1938/39. Like other estimates based on sightings, these latter estimates depend firstly on accurate identification by the observers, and then on the assumption that all, or some specified proportion, of whales in a strip of some determined width at each side of the vessel's track are seen and recorded. Further, and perhaps critically, the density of whales

458

along the ship's track should be the same as in other parts of the Antartic.

Once the abundance of the stock in each season can be expressed, in absolute terms, the natural rate of increase of the population, Y (births less deaths from non-fishery causes) can be estimated as the algebraic sum of the increase in the stock (which will be mainly negative) and the catch, C; $Y = \Delta P + C$ where P is the population (in numbers) and, in the simple model, it is assumed that the natural rate of increase is a simple function of the population; $Y = f(P)$.

In practice, since the catches only come from the exploitable stock – excluding the very young animals – most of the data refer only to that part of the total population. The above equations should, therefore, be re-stated in terms of the exploitable population. The natural rate of increase of this part of the population will be the difference between the natural deaths and the number of recruits – young animals reaching the size at which they become exploited.

Following Schaefer (1954), the values of Y for any year can be estimated as the sum of the catches in that year and the observed change in the population, as derived from the catch per unit effort. Since it is difficult to estimate the catch per unit effort at an instant of time, the catch per unit effort (and hence the population) at the beginning of one year is generally estimated as the mean of those observed in that year, and the previous year.

The results of applying the method to the data for blue whales are shown in Fig. 5 (from Anon., 1964). The curve has been fitted by eye, through the plotted points, and through zero at zero population, and at a population of 210,000 whales – the estimated unexploited population. The fit is reasonably good at lower population sizes, when the sustainable yield is 0.1 times the population – whereas the catches in the post-war period were some three times this. Fig. 5 is adequate to give an explanation in general terms of what has happened to the blue whale stock, and to provide fairly precise guidance to the IWC on the management of the stock. However, there is no explanation provided for the shape of the

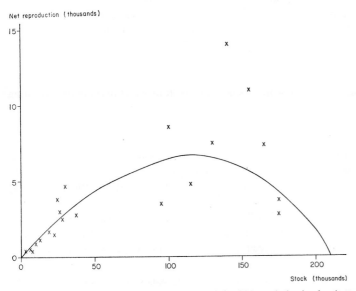

Fig. 5. Net reproduction (or sustainable yield) of blue whales in the Antarctic.

459

curve – which incidentally appears not to be symmetrical, as would be suggested by the simpler population theories. Without such explanation it is difficult to derive the comparable curve for the stocks of other species of whales for which the data are not so complete.

Analytic models

The numbers, N, of whales in the exploited parts of the population can be expressed, in terms either of instantaneous rates or of changes during a year, as the algebraic sum of recruitment, natural deaths and catches.

i.e. $\dfrac{dN}{dt} = (r - M - F)\,N$

where r = recruitment rate, or number of animals reaching exploitable size per unit time, as a proportion of the existing stock, and M,F = natural and fishing mortality coefficients. Clearly the population will not change if F = r − M, and the annual catch (= sustainable yield or net natural rate of increase) will be FN = (r − M) N.

The expressions on the right hand side are not constants, but are functions of the population size – not only the current population, but of previous populations. However, the range within which r and M can vary is not large.

The recruitment rate, r, is limited by the reproductive biology of whales; it can be expressed as:

$r = p \cdot q \cdot n \cdot e^{-M'T}$

where p = proportion of females in the exploitable stock, q = proportion of females which are mature, n = average number of young produced per unit time by a mature female, M′ = mean natural mortality coefficient among the pre-recruit animals, T = age at which whales enter the exploitable stock.

As a result of exploitation p has varied. Extensive data on the sex of unborn young show almost exactly equal numbers of males and females; the same was probably also true of the unexploited adult population. Initial catches included more males than females because mothers with calves were protected; as a result the proportion of females in the stock increased. If the stock consists of a limited number of survivors of heavy exploitation, then even the proportion in the catch may rise above 0.5. For instance, in 1964/65 the proportion of females in the Antartic catches was as follows (International Whaling Statistics, Vol. LVI):

Fin whales (after a long period of heavy exploitation)   0.54
Sei whales (first year of very heavy exploitation)   0.44

Therefore, in a heavily exploited stock p might be about 0.6. Most of the whales in the exploitable stock in the Antartic are mature, but there is a small proportion of immature whales between the ages of recruitment (about 4–5 years), and first maturity (6–7 years; Lockyer, 1970), q may therefore be taken as about 0.9.

An upper limit to n is set by the fact that baleen whales produce only one young at a time (among fin whales about 1 % of the births are twins, and very rarely triplets or more), with a normal cycle of pregnancy and feeding of young of two years, i.e. n < 0.5, but may approach this level.

No direct estimate of natural mortality among young whales is available. As pointed out by Chapman (1970), this is almost certainly greater than that for adult animals –

estimated for the present fin whale stock as around 0.04. The age at recruitment is about 4–5 years.

Using these values, the corresponding value of the recruitment rate for fin whales is:

$$r = 0.6 \times 0.9 \times 0.5 \times e^{-0.04 \times 4}$$
$$= 0.27 \times e^{-0.16}$$
$$= 0.23, \text{ which will be an upper limit.}$$

Considerably lower values have been estimated directly e.g. by Allen (1970). These, as reviewed by Chapman (1970), give a mean value from 0.06 to 0.095.

Subtracting the natural mortality (say 0.04) gives an upper limit to the value of F in a stable situation of about 0.19, and more likely values of 0.02 to 0.055. These rates, equivalent to an annual harvest of between 2% and a little less than 15% of the stock and which have been largely based on data from fin whales, may be compared with the left hand side of Fig. 5. This suggests that for blue whales at lower stock levels, a sustainable yield of around 10% can be taken. Since the relevant biological characteristics (age at maturity, number of young, frequency of breeding, etc.) of the two species are similar, the agreement with the figures derived from these characteristics (considered as an upper limit) is good, but that with the observed recruitment rates of fin whales is less good.

Several explanations are possible for this discrepancy: errors in determining the recruitment rate of fin whales, the possible cropping rates of blue whales, real differences between blue and fin whales, etc. These are being carefully examined, since the problem is very critical in relation to the levels of quota set by the ICW. However, the agreement is good enough to show that by determination of the parameters of age at maturity, birth and death rates, a reasonable first approximation of the slope of the left hand part of the curve of sustainable yield (net natural rate of increase) as a function of population size, can be obtained.

The rest of the curve – the rate at which it bends over, the position of the maximum, etc. – will be determined by the way in which r and M vary as a function of population size. Presumably as a result of competition for food, etc. r will decrease with population size (except possibly at very low levels, when it may be difficult to find mates), and M increase.

There is no evidence of changes in natural mortality, and the only good estimate of natural mortality is that obtained from the age composition of the unexploited stock – particularly for sei whales, for which Doi et al. (1967) estimated M as 0.065 on the average. For exploited stocks, only the total mortality can be estimated directly from age composition data; from such estimates the natural mortality may be derived by subtracting the fishing mortalities. The range of possible errors on these estimates is large, rendering the estimate of natural mortality even more imprecise.

There is much better evidence of changes in the recruitment rate. The most interesting is that of Lockyer (1970a). He showed that there was a change in the pattern of the layer laid down in the ear-plug which occurred at sexual maturity. From ear-plugs of old fin whales caught in 1958–1965 (up to 50 years old) the age of maturity could be determined for whales born as early as 1910 and which matured in the 1920's and 1930's (before exploitation had any significant effect on the fin whale stock). Though there is some degree of bias in his data as presented for the most recent samples, since no whale born in 1952 and maturing older than 6 years could appear in the 1958 data, there is a very clear decline in the age of maturity – from about 9 years for the whales born before about 1930, to some 4–5 years for those born most recently. The decline in age at maturity since 1956/57, as

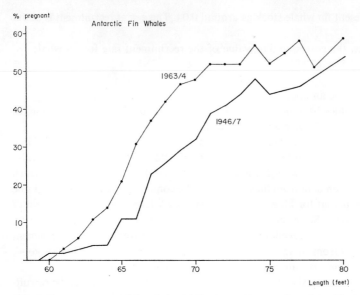

Fig. 6. Pregnancy rate of fin whales in the Antarctic, as a function of length.

determined by direct biological examination of the animals on the factory ships, has also been shown by Ohsumi (1970).

Contemporary evidence of change in breeding rate is also provided by the data on pregnancy provided for most seasons since 1932/33 in the International Whaling Statistics. In Fig. 6 the data for the 1946/47 and 1963/64 seasons are presented in terms of the percentage of each length of female fin whales in the catches which were observed to be pregnant. Some caution is needed in interpreting these data, since they were mainly collected by non-scientists, and the smaller foetuses may have been overlooked.

In both years there is a steady increase in the proportion pregnant with length. There are two important differences; the clearest is that the curve for 1963/64 is displaced to the left, so that compared with the years 1946/47 the percentage of whales of a given size that were pregnant was about the same as whales of some 5 ft (1.5 m) longer in the earlier year when whales were more abundant. The other difference is a suggestion that the curve for 1963/64 is flattening out at a higher level around 55% compared with some 45–50% in 1946/47. That these two years are part of a more general trend is shown in Fig. 7. This shows that the percentage of pregnant female fin whales at a given length in the catches increased in the pre-war period, dropped during the war, and increased thereafter.

These changes can be fitted into the previous expression for recruitment rate. In this, a low figure for natural mortality was used for providing an upper limit to the present value for r. A more reasonable value for M' (the average natural mortality coefficient among the young whales) and one which would agree better with observed recruitment rates, might be M' = 0.15.

The value used for n (the mean number of young per year; the reciprocal of the interval between births) was also rather high. A more reasonable value for the present stock might be 0.4; the changes in the limiting percentage shown in Fig. 6 suggest that this would be lower in the unexploited population, say 0.35.

462

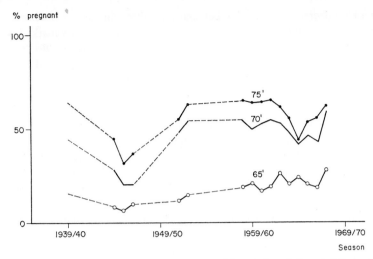

% pregnant

Fig. 7. Changes in the percentage pregnant of female fin whales of different lengths.

The sets of values for the present, and unexploited populations, might therefore be:

	Present	Unexploited
p	0.6	0.5
q	0.9	0.9
n	0.4	0.35
M′	0.15	0.15
T	4	9
r	0.119	0.041
M	0.04	0.04
r − M	0.079	0.001

Subtracting the same natural mortality (0.04) from the recruitment rates gives a sustainable harvesting-rate of nearly 8 % for the present stock, and nearly zero in the unexploited population. Clearly only a small adjustment in the values used for the parameters would give the equality between recruitment and mortality expected in a stable unexploited population.

Fisheries

Fish stocks, unlike mammal stocks, have proved extremely resistant to exploitation. Following an initial period of decline when exploitation starts, the abundance normally settles down at a new lower level. Further, as soon as man's pressure is removed, the stocks recover rapidly to their old level. These tendencies are shown clearly in Fig. 2 and 4, which give for the cod and haddock of the North Sea the basic statistics of total catch, and the index of abundance as estimated from the catches per hour fishing of English and Scottish trawlers (for cod and haddock respectively). The series, though covering over half a century, do not begin until some time after the North Sea trawling had become fully developed (around 1890). However, the drop in catches, and increase in abundance during both wars (especially between 1939 and 1944), is clearly marked for both species. Both

463

figures also show a high degree of correlation between the indices for the two species in addition to the gross effects of the war time changes in the fishery. Particularly marked is the increase in catch, and to some extent also abundance for both species since 1964. The immediate cause of this is a succession of good year-classes, such as the 1962 and 1968 year-classes of haddock, though why there should be such a succession is not known.

Any population which maintains itself for a long period within moderately narrow bounds, and especially which can remain within such bounds despite the addition of extra mortality must, as often pointed out, be subject to some kind of density-dependent or regulating effect. In the North Sea demersal stocks this effect must be large, since the additional mortality due to fishing would, if there were no other changes, be expected to reduce the stock abundance by between 50% and 90% each generation. Some density-dependent changes in growth and mortality among the adult fish have been observed, but they are not nearly sufficient, even if mortality from all causes other than fishing fell to zero. The fishing mortality alone would often be considerably higher than the total mortality in the unexploited stock.

The change that does occur, and that is sufficient to maintain the stock in the presence of heavy fishing pressure, is in the survival during the pre-recruit phase, i.e. in the first few months or years of life. This phase is very difficult to study quantitatively, and all that can commonly be observed is the number of recruits; hence, dividing by the number of eggs (which can be estimated either directly, or from a knowledge of the size of the adult stock), the survival during the whole of the pre-recruit phase can be estimated. Among most fish species which have very high fecundities, this survival is very low; of the order of hundredths of a percent. Clearly a small difference in mortality, say from 99.998% to 99.996%, can make a big difference in survival. That is, if there was only a weak link between pre-recruit mortality and abundance, either of adult or young, it would result in density having a big effect on pre-recruit survival.

It appears that in many fish stocks the number of recruits is, over a substantial range of adult stocks, independent of the abundance of adults. This has, for example, been clearly shown for the North Sea plaice by Beverton (1962). For most other stocks this is less easy to demonstrate because the data extend over only a few years, and the number of recruits fluctuates widely, from causes other than changes in adult stock. Typical plots of number of recruits against adult stock are shown in Fig. 8; for Antarctic fin whales in terms of annual recruitment (from Allen, 1970), sockeye salmon (*Oncorhyncus nerka*) (from Dahlberg, 1970), and Pacific halibut (from Cushing and Harris, 1970). The relation for whales departs only slightly from proportionality. For the two fish species a horizontal line has been suggested in the figure; i.e. the number of recruits is independent of adult stock, and the average pre-recruit survival is precisely inversely proportional to adult density. In fact, the points are so scattered that a range of relationships could easily be suggested. For the above argument, it is sufficient to note that a strictly proportional line (implying that pre-recruit survival is independent of adult density) does not fit the points.

The precise shape of the curve does, however, have considerable practical importance in relation to problems of conservation and management of fisheries. If the average recruitment decreases (but less than proportionally) with decreases in adult stock, then management measures must be aimed at keeping the adult stock large.

In practice the precise form is very difficult to determine. For this reason, and also to study the large, apparently random density-independent fluctuations in recruitment, increasing attention is being paid by fishery scientists to the pre-recruit phase. The results

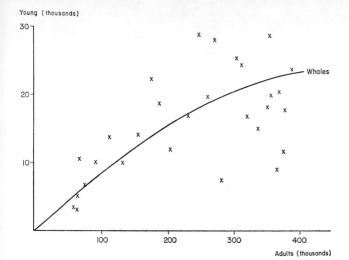

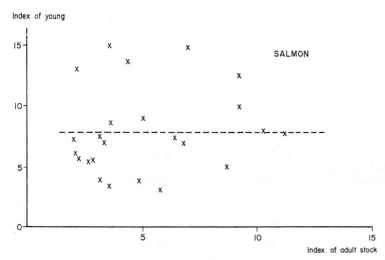

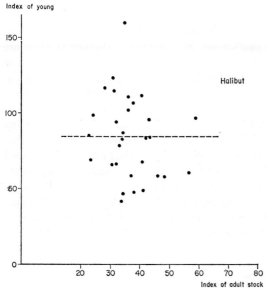

Fig. 8. Relation between adult stock and numbers of recruits for Antarctic fin whales, sockeye salmon, and Pacific halibut.

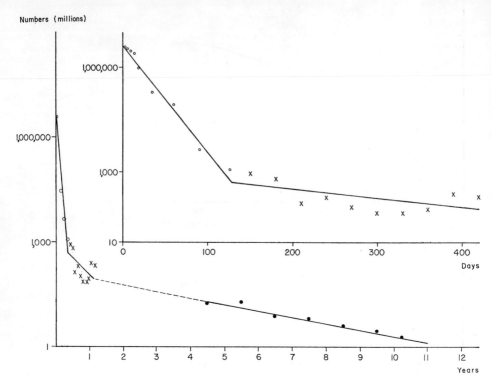

Fig. 9. Changes in numbers of the 1963 year-class of plaice in the North Sea. (Figure beyond 6 years extrapolated assuming similar trends as in previous year classes.) Data from plankton surveys (open circles), inshore surveys (crosses), and commercial catches (full circles).

of some existing studies are shown in Fig. 9, in which an attempt has been made to construct a complete life-table for the North Sea plaice, specifically for the 1963 year-class. The numbers of eggs and larvae have been taken from the data of plankton surveys of Harding and Talbot (1970), and those of the adult fish from data of English commercial landings (Anon., 1970). The numbers for ages beyond 6 have been obtained by assuming the same mortality as in the pre-1963 year-classes. No estimates of absolute numbers are available for the intermediate phases. Corlett (1966) gives data on the relative numbers of young plaice along part of the coast of the Irish Sea. If the mortalities of these stages of plaice in the North Sea are similar to those in the Irish Sea, then the absolute numbers must be approximately as shown.

This diagram shows several things. First, the complexities and varieties of sampling methods involved in studying the whole life-cycle; second, the enormous mortality that occurs in the earliest stages, and which obscures the relatively minor effects being studied – the density-dependent effect, covering no more than a two-fold range, and the density-independent effect controlling year-class fluctuation; thirdly, that despite these difficulties a fairly consistant picture emerges. This gives some hope that studies of the early stages will give some quantitative insight into the processes involved. It is likely that during the next few years much of the research into the population dynamics of fishes will be concentrated in this field.

References

Anonymous, 1964. Final report of the Committee of Three Scientists. *Rep. int. Commn. Whal.* 14: 39–92.

Anonymous, 1968. Report of the meeting on age determination in whales, Oslo, 26 February to 1 March 1968. Paper presented to the Annual meeting 1968 of the International Whaling Commission (mimeo).

Anonymous, 1970. Fishing prospects 1970–71. United Kingdom, Ministry of Agriculture, Food and Fisheries. pp. 40.

Allen, K. R., 1970. Analysis of the stock-recruitment relation in Antarctic fin whales (*Balaenoptera physalis*). Paper presented to the Symposium on Stock and Recruitment, organized by ICES, FAO and ICNAF, held in Aarhus, Denmark, 7–10 July 1970.

Beverton, R. J. H. & S. J. Holt, 1957. On the dynamics of exploited fish populations. *Fishery Invest. Ser.2 Lond.* 19: pp. 533.

Chapman, D. G., 1970. Review of the analysis of southern baleen whale stocks. Paper presented to Fin Whale meeting, International Whaling Commission, held in Hawaii, March 1970 (mimeo).

Corlett, J., 1966. Mortality of O-group plaice in the Irish Sea. Paper presented to the International Council for the Exploration of the Sea, Annual Meeting 1966, Near Northern Seas Committee. Doc. CM 1966/C.6 (mimeo).

Cushing, D. H. & J. G. K. Harris, 1970. Stock and recruitment and the problem of density dependence. Paper presented to the Symposium on Stock and Recruitment, organized by ICES, FAO and ICNAF, held in Aarhus, Denmark, 7–10 July 1970.

Dahlberg, M., 1970. Stock and recruitment relationships of sockeye salmon returns to Chignik Lakes, Alaska. Paper presented to the Symposium on Stock and Recruitment, organized by ICES, FAO and ICNAF, held in Aarhus, Denmark, 7–10 July 1970.

Doi, T., S. Ohsumi & T. Nemoto, 1967. Population assessment of sei whales in the Antarctic. *Norsk Hvalfangsttid.* 56 (2): 25–41.

Gulland, J. A., 1969. Manual of methods for fish stock assessment. Pt. 1. Fish population analysis. *FAO Man. Fish. Sci.* 4: pp. 154.

Harding, D. & J. W. Talbot, 1970. Recent studies on the eggs and larvae of the plaice (*Pleuronectes platessa* L.) in the Southern Bight. Paper presented to the Symposium on Stock and Recruitment, organized by ICES, FAO and ICNAF, held in Aarhus, Denmark, 7–10 July 1970.

Hjort, J., G. Jahn & P. Ottestad, 1933. The optimum catch. *Hvalråd. Skr.* 7: 92–127.

Locker, C., 1970. Revision of age of sexual maturity in southern fin whales. Paper presented to Fin Whale meeting, International Whaling Commission, held in Hawaii, March 1970 (mimeo).

Locker, C., 1970a. A new method of estimating age of sexual maturity on southern fin whales. Paper presented to Scientific meeting, International Whaling Commission, 1970. Doc. SC/22/19 (mimeo).

Lury, D. B. de., 1947. On the estimation of biological populations. *Biometrics* 3: 145–167.

Mackintosh, N. A. & S. G. Brown, 1956. Preliminary estimates of the southern populations of the larger baleen whales. *Norsk Hvalfangsttid.* 45 (9) 469–480.

Ohsumi, S., 1970. Yearly changes in age and body length at sexual maturity in the Antarctic fin whale. Material presented to the 1970 session of the Scientific Committee of the International Whaling Commission (unpubl.).

Ricker, W. E., 1958. Handbook of computations for biological statistics of fish populations *Bull. Fish. Res. Bd Can.* 119, pp. 300.

Schaefer, M. B., 1954. Some aspects of the dynamics of populations important to the management of commercial marine fisheries. *Bull. inter-Am. Trop. Tuna Commn* 1 (2): 26–56.

Schaefer, M. B., 1957. A study of the dynamics of the fishery for yellowfin tuna in the eastern tropical Pacific Ocean. *Bull. inter-Am. Trop. Tuna Commn* 2 (6): 247–285.

Volterra, V., 1928. Variations and fluctuations of the number of individuals in animal species living together. *J. Cons. perm. int. Explor. Mer* 3 (1): 3–51.

Discussion

Participants: Gulland (Author), Coulson, Frank, Gradwell, Korringa, Murdoch and Voûte

Several possible explanations were put forward to explain the observed change in the reproductive rate of the fin whale which enable it to stand an exploitation rate of some 5–10 % –

1. Decreased territoriality (KORRINGA).
2. In such different mammals as seals and rodents it is found that the number of old females may strongly influence the age at which young females start to reproduct. This is due not to competition for food but to social pressure; e.g. by preventing the young females from landing in the breeding places (seals) or suppressing their oestrous (rodents). Under high density conditions, this mechanism restricts the reproduction to those members of the population which have already passed the filter of selection (FRANK).
3. At higher densities, competition for food may make the young females pregnant at a later age (VOÛTE).
4. It may be selection. Even with a slow breeder like a whale, 50 or 60 years seems enough to produce such a shift, if selection is heavily age-dependent – as it is in fishing for whales (MURDOCH).
5. In some long-lived marine vertebrates there is considerable variation in the age at first breeding. It is possible that those individuals which start breeding at a greater age also survive longer. Thus the evidence from 50-year-old whales could be heavily biased (COULSON).

There are as yet insufficient data to accept or reject any of these hypotheses. The important practical point is that these changes have occurred, and presumably as a result of exploitation. Only Coulson's point seems not very probable; if it were, one would expect a difference between very old animals (born in 1910), and middle age animals (born in 1930), and this does not seem to occur (AUTHOR).

That the post-war blue whale catches continued exactly on the pre-war line is accidental. The Committee of Three estimated, from detailed catch-per-unit-effort data, that the blue whale stock did increase during the war at about 4,000 individuals per year. Apparently, this effect was compensated for by the very different number of expeditions before and after the war (AUTHOR to GRADWELL).

Proc. Adv. Study Inst. Dynamics Numbers Popul. (Oosterbeek, 1970) 469–477

The effect of human intervention on the distribution and abundance of Chondrilla juncea L.

A. J. Wapshere

CSIRO Chondrilla Biological Control Unit, Centre National de la Recherche Scientifique, Montpellier, France

Abstract

Theoretical considerations based on Andrewartha's and Birch's (1954) contention that distribution and abundance are both aspects of a population's ability to survive, reproduce and grow in abundance, suggested that, where conditions favour rapid population growth, the habitat range of a plant in terms of climate, soil type, competitive situations and different cultivation methods should be larger than when conditions are less favourable. Comparison of the habitat range of *Chondrilla juncea* L. in Australia, where methods of wheat cultivation and lack of biological control organisms favour the plant, with that in Europe, where methods of wheat cultivation and certain biological control organisms reduce plant populations, confirm the hypothesis. Conversely, when situations are found in Europe which resemble the Australian situation closely, the habitat range and population level of *Chondrilla juncea* approaches that observed in Australia.

Introduction

Chondrilla juncea L., skeleton weed, is an important weed in wheat-fallow cultivations in the Mediterranean type climatic areas of Australia. It is most abundant on light friable or sandy soils (Moore, 1964).

A study of the organisms attacking *Chondrilla juncea* has been undertaken in Europe to discover whether any of these organisms could serve as biological control agents for the plant in Australia. During this study various observations have been made on the effect of human intervention on *Chondrilla juncea* populations.

Theoretical considerations

The study of the effects of the biological control organisms on the plant under conditions similar to those in Australia has tested the hypothesis of Andrewartha and Birch (1954) that the distribution and abundance of organisms are both aspects of the ability of populations to survive, reproduce successfully and grow in abundance.

Clearly, if distribution and abundance are related as in Fig. 1, then in situations or places where one or more factors (including the effect of biological control organisms) were reducing reproductive success and survival, there should be a corresponding reduction in habitat range and abundance. Conversely, in situations where increased survival and reproductive success occur, there should be increases in abundance and at the same time extensions of the plant's habitat range.

In testing the above hypothesis two measures have been used. The first is a measure of

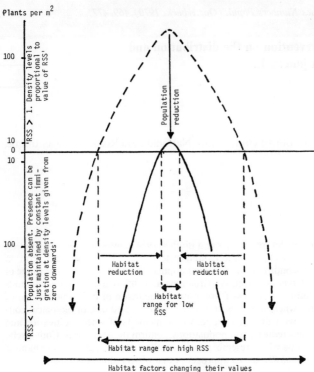

Plants per m²

Fig. 1. Diagram illustrating the relation between the habitat range of a plant and its level of reproductive success and survival (RSS).

Density levels for high RSS would apply to *Chondrilla juncea* (— — —) if plant competition and attacking organisms were not able to act. Those for the low RSS (——) would apply to *Chondrilla juncea* under pressure by plant competitors and biological control organisms.
— — — — Population level at high level of reproductive success and survival
———— Population level at low level of reproductive success and survival

the population abundance of *Chondrilla juncea* (skeleton weed) in a wide variety of situations in both Australia and Mediterranean Europe, and the other is a series of observations on the habitat range in terms of climatic range, of soil type, of non-competitive or competitive situations, of cultivation methods etc.

In Australia, Groves and Hull (1970) have been measuring the plant's densities in various representative parts of its range using numbers of permanent and semi-permanent quadrats. In Mediterranean Europe, due to the exigencies of the biological control programme with which the study was combined, two less time consuming methods have been used. The first, described by Wahba (1970), based on a method by Parker (1954), is a long transect of a given length and width within which plant densities in terms of rosette centres or central flowering stems can be easily counted.

At the same time and in the same places, visual observations were made of plant densities in closely adjacent fields under different methods of cultivation and land utilisation. For this purpose an approximately logarithmic ranking scale was used between 1, indicating *Chondrilla juncea* just present (= 0.001 plants/m² or less), and 5 for densities up to 100 plants/m².

In the following discussion, *Chondrilla juncea* densities in Australia are from the data of

470

Groves and Hull (1970) and the densities in Europe are those recorded by Wapshere, Hasan, Wahba and Caresche (unpublished data) between 1968 and 1970.

The plant

Chondrilla juncea is essentially a plant of climates with a certain but not excessive summer drought, such as occur in Eurasia in the continental climates of this type in southern Russia (Ukraine and Turkmanistan etc.) and in the Mediterranean climates of Europe. In Australia its initial establishment and rapid spread and population build-up occurred in the inland Mediterranean type climates of eastern Australia, but it has recently spread northwards into summer rainfall climates (McVean, 1966). It is an extremely polymorphic triploid apomict. The plant produces a rosette during the autumn and spring, and a flower shoot in early summer. The rosette then dies off and the shoot flowers throughout the summer, dying back completely by the autumn. The rosette then regenerates from the perennating vertical rhizome. The seeds germinate rapidly and have no dormancy.

Once populations are well established, both in Europe and in Australia the year to year replacement of rosettes is mainly from the perennating rhizomes and should these be cut or the rosette destroyed, rapid replacement regeneration takes place. Seedling establishment in these populations plays a less important role than rhizome regeneration.

The effect of wheat cultivation methods on the distribution and abunbance of Chondrilla juncea

The most obvious difference between the Mediterranean and Australia is the far greater importance of *Chondrilla juncea* as a weed within wheat cultivations in Australia. For this reason we compared the wheat growing methods in Australia with those used in the Mediterranean. This indicated how the Australian method of cultivation could greatly increase the population level of the weed. Table 1 summarises this comparison, the main points being as follows:
1. The smaller quantity of wheat sown per unit area in Australia reduces competition against *Chondrilla juncea*, thereby increasing the weed's survival and reproductive success

Table 1. A comparison of the cultivation methods for autumn-sown wheat in Mediterranean Europe and in Mediterranean climates of Australia.

Parts of the cultivation methods compared	Mediterranean Europe	Mediterranean Australia
Amount of seed sown (kg/ha)	180	66
Fertilizer/crop		
Phosphorus (P_2O_5 in kg/ha)	36–72 (mean 45)	38
Various nitrogen compounds (kg/ha)	250	rarely used
Depth of ploughing (cm)	20–35 (mean 25)	10
Type of plough	plough share	disc
Type of rotation	2–5 year wheat, pasture or sown crops, etc. Fallow rare	2 or 3 year wheat, fallow and/or sown pasture

These data were compiled from correspondence with agronomists in Europe and in Australia as well as personal discussions in the field with farmers.

compared with that in Europe where three times more wheat seed is sown per hectare.

2. Nitrogen fertiliser is used rarely in Australia and its absence, although reducing the growth of *Chondrilla juncea*, reduces the competitiveness of the wheat crop to a greater extent, thereby increasing *Chondrilla* success in Australia.

3. The shallow ploughing in Australia cuts roots just below soil level and induces multiple regeneration of rhizome buds which rapidly reach the soil surface as rosettes, thereby greatly increasing reproductive success via vegetative regeneration.

4. The Australian disc plough cuts the roots and allows the cut portions of roots to regenerate in the soil, thereby again increasing vegetative reproduction. The European plough share lifts up the cut plants to the soil surface where they die.

5. The two-year wheat/fallow rotation, which was the customary rotation in Australia from the early years until about 1940 and is still practised in many areas, allows the *Chondrilla juncea* seedlings to establish during the short fallow phase and to grow rapidly with reduced competition from other plants and, once established, to maintain itself more strongly during the wheat phase. With this method of cultivation the reproductive success and survival of *Chondrilla juncea* is extremely high. In most places in Europe such a rotation has long been superseded; here the typical rotation is wheat, sown fodder crop and sown weeded crop, such as beet. Under these conditions competition is maintained, cultivation is more frequent and establishment and survival of *Chondrilla juncea* is minimal. In some places, the same field is sown every year with wheat and this more frequent cultivation reduces skeleton weed populations.

With the cultivation practices used in Australia, it is not surprising that *Chondrilla juncea* spread rapidly in wheat cultivations from its original centre of establishment near Wagga Wagga (New South Wales) and in the thirty years between the 1920's and the 1950's had invaded most of the wheat growing areas of eastern Australia (McVean, 1966). At the same time the plant increased rapidly in abundance in these areas. At the present time there are still many infestations in wheat crops of 100 to 300 plants/m² (Groves and Hull, 1970). Observations in the Taranto and Gargano regions of southern Italy give some confirmation of the above interpretation. In this area, climatically similar to the Australian areas of infestation, wheat is grown with a similar wheat/fallow rotation, and on occasional areas of light sandy or light friable soils there are heavy infestations between 40 to 140 plants/m² of *Chondrilla juncea* in these wheat/fallow cultivations. Here, as in Australia, the fallow phase is grazed by sheep and it seems likely that grazing plays a role in increasing the success of *Chondrilla juncea* by reducing competition and by burying the seeds below the soil surface where they germinate more readily. McVean (1966) also commented on the importance of this type of soil disturbance in Australian infestations.

Observations in the field have shown that the various organisms which attack *Chondrilla juncea* in Europe do not control the plant in these short wheat/fallow rotations, since the length of time between ploughings is not enough for the organisms to reduce plant populations sufficiently. These organisms are either absent from Australia or not present in the *Chondrilla juncea* infested areas. For the same reasons other competing plants do not act sufficiently continuously to be effective.

Population increases of the size observed, due presumably to large increases in reproductive success and survival, should theoretically produce corresponding increases in habitat range compared with Europe. There are several good examples. For instance, *Chondrilla juncea*, which in Europe is almost restricted to very light sandy or light friable soils in cultivations, has increased its soil range in Australia to such an extent that Kohn,

472

Storrier and Cuthbertson (1966) and Cuthbertson (1969) were able to carry out herbicide experiments on dense stands on clayloams, a soil type on which the plant occurs extremely rarely, and only at low densities in Europe. Moore (1964) also notes that the plant has become established, i.e. has extended its range, to all but the heaviest clays in Australia. Similarly, the data of Groves and Hull (1970) show that *Chondrilla juncea* has spread with the wheat/fallow method of cultivation into dry Mediterranean climate areas of the Victorian and South Australian Mallee (350 mm average annual rainfall) at very high densities (100–200 plants/m²); whereas in Mediterranean Europe and North Africa it is seldom found in such dry areas, and even then densities are seldom greater than 5 plants/m² in wheat fields. It has also spread into the hot summer rainfall areas (average annual daily temperature 18 °C) into which, in Australia, the wheat belt continues northwards, with densities up to 11 plants/m². As confirmation of the relationship between wheat cultivation and the abundance of the plant in these dry and summer rainfall areas, *Chondrilla juncea* is found only in the wheat and not on the roadsides (McVean, 1966).

Thus, these comparisons strongly suggest that the method of wheat cultivation in Australia so increases the survival and reproductive success of *Chondrilla juncea* that it is able to establish and maintain itself at high densities in soil and climatic situations which would be regarded as unsuitable in Europe.

The effects of other cultivation practices on Chondrilla juncea populations

Because the various organisms attacking, or plants competing with *Chondrilla juncea* do not function as population controlling agents in cultivations, the most important population level determinant of the plant for a given climate and soil type is the frequency and type of cultivation itself. Furthermore, since each type of cultivation should affect the reproductive success and survival of the plant by a given fixed amount, its population levels under the same environmental conditions (soil, climate, etc.) should, for a given method and type of cultivation, be the same in Europe and in Australia. For instance, in a wheat/fallow, cultivated thoroughly about once a year, *Chondrilla juncea* populations in Australia vary between 80 and 180 plants/m² and in southern Italy between 40 and 160 plants/m². Under continuous wheat or barley, cultivated about once every six months, densities in Australia vary between 8 and 80 plants/m² and in southern Italy between 3 and 50 plants/m². In vineyards in Mediterranean Europe, which are cultivated at least once every two months, *Chondrilla juncea* populations were rarely 1 plants/m² and often lower than 1 plant/100 m².

It is quite clear that as frequency of cultivation increases so *Chondrilla juncea* populations decline, and that for each type of cultivation there is a corresponding characteristic level of abundance. This result is readily explained since plants whose rosettes are continuously destroyed cannot lay down reserves in their rootstocks, and seedling establishment is drastically reduced.

The effect of competing plants and the organisms attacking Chondrilla juncea on its distribution and abundance

Competing plants and biological control organisms begin to be effective in *Chondrilla juncea* populations once cultivation has stopped.

Skeleton weed, both at the seedling and at later stages, has been found to succumb readily to shading by other plants (McVean, 1966). In Australia, where there are no arthropods or fungal pathogens attacking the plant, the main biological control method is the use of sown pastures particularly of Subterranean Clover (*Trifolium subterraneum* L.) (Moore, 1964). Other clovers, lucerne and *Medicago* species are also being used. This method of control is particularly effective in the region around Wagga Wagga (average annual daily temperature 16.7 °C, average annual rainfall 490 mm). Here the average density of *Chondrilla juncea* in wheat/pasture rotations with Subterranean Clover varies from 8 plants/m² to 30 plants/m², whereas in other regions where competition is less effective *Chondrilla juncea* populations of between 80 and 300 plants/m² are found.

The important difference between Europe and Australia is the level at which *Chondrilla juncea* maintains itself in these competitive situations. In the Vieste (Gargano) and Taranto regions of southern Italy which are climatically similar to the Wagga region, *Chondrilla juncea* although common at high densities in wheat/fallow cultivations is very rare or absent from any site where pasture has developed, and is found only at densities below 20 plants/m² in abandoned cultivations where competition is less intense.

In Australia, judging from observations and experiments conducted in the Canberra, Wagga and Mallee regions, *Chondrilla juncea* initially declines sharply in competition with pasture plants, but later is able to maintain itself for many years at a relatively high level. For instance, Kohn, Storrier and Cuthbertson (1966) used for their experiments at Wagga Wagga fields which had been four to five years under clover pasture before sowing to wheat. These still had sufficient *Chondrilla juncea* to obtain increase grain yields by spraying the plant with herbicides. Moore and Robertson's (1963) experiment with a sown pasture of the grass *Lolium rigidum* Gaud. and *Trifolium subterraneum* L. showed a reduction from 188 to 96 plants/m² (51 % of the original density) in two years, followed by the maintenance of *Chondrilla juncea* population levels at this reduced level for at least two further years and, apparently, for an even longer period after cropping of the same field. *Chondrilla juncea* populations at such high densities have not been found during four years research in Mediterranean Europe in such competitive pasture situations as those produced by Moore and Robertson. The level of competition from these sown pastures is certainly higher than that produced by the common weed species which are found in the abandoned field situations in Europe where *Chondrilla juncea* populations are considerably lower. Ability to withstand competition appears to be definitely enhanced under Australian conditions, and this is yet another example of the greater habitat range of the plant in Australia compared with Europe. There would not seem to be sufficient differences in soil texture and mineral nutrient composition to explain the greater part of this difference, particularly since the investigation sites in Europe have been chosen for their similarity to Australian areas of infestation. Nor does the heavy grazing occurring at some sites in Australia explain it, since heavily grazed sites in Europe often have lower *Chondrilla juncea* densities.

Since observations have shown that several organisms damage the plant sufficiently to cause population reduction (Wapshere, Hasan, Wahba and Caresche, unpublished data) and since these organisms either do not exist in Australia or, if they do, are ineffective in the *Chondrilla juncea* infested areas, it is reasonable to infer that the reduced ability of the plant to persist at high densities in competitive pastures and abandoned cultivations in Europe is due to the action of the organisms attacking it.

The most important of the organisms attacking *Chondrilla juncea* in Europe is the rust, *Puccinia chondrillina* (Bubek & Syd.), which destroys seedlings and rosettes, heavily

474

damages flowering shoots and reduces seeding (Hasan, 1970; Wapshere, 1970). Two other fungi, both powdery mildews, also play a role. One is *Leveillula taurica* ARNAUD form *chondrillae* JACZ., which severely damages the flower shoot and reduces seed production and the other, probably a form of *Erysiphe cichoraceorum* Dc. (Hasan, pers. comm.), destroys rosettes and seedlings. *Aceria chondrillae* CAN., an eriophyid gall mite, may have a slight population effect by reducing seed production (Caresche, 1970; Wapshere, 1970). Finally, various Mediterranean snails also damage plants severely. In Greece, as well as the organisms mentioned above, there are also two insect species with population reducing capabilities. They are a cecidomyid gall midge (*Laubertia schmidtii* Low. or a *Cystiphora* species), which can cover the plant with galls and reduce seed production, and the root feeding caterpillar of the moth *Bradyrrhoa gilveolella* TR. which can destroy thin-rooted plants and reduce rosette regeneration.

The *Puccinia* rust, the cecidomyid and the eriophyid gall makers and the root feeding moth are not present in Australia, but the powdery mildews and the most important of the Mediterranean snails (*Theba pisana* MULLER) already occur there but for various reasons are not present or not effective in the *Chondrilla juncea* infested regions.

Discussion

From the above account, it will be realised that the population dynamics of *Chondrilla juncea* can be understood in terms of a balance between, on the one hand, increasing survival and reproductive success with decreasing frequency of cultivation, and on the other hand, the decreasing survival and reproductive success with the increase of plant competition and increased effectiveness of the biological control organisms after cultivation has stopped. Apparently the wheat/fallow method of cultivation practiced by the Australian farmer gave maximum advantage to this plant in terms of the above balance. It produced disturbance sufficiently often to reduce competition to a low level, and at the same time the cultivation was not frequent enough to stop the establishment and rapid population build-up of the plant.

Conclusion

By comparing the population dynamics of the weed *Chondrilla juncea* in Mediterranean Europe and Australia under different levels of cultivation, competition and damage by infesting organisms, the hypothesis that the habitat range of a plant should increase as its reproductive success and survival increase has been tested and confirmed.

Acknowledgments

I wish to thank other members of the Chondrilla Biological Control Unit, Dr S. Hasan, Mr W. K. Wahba and Mr L. Caresche, for the use of a small part of the data collected during the field surveys. These data are being prepared for publication elsewhere. The opinions presented here are those of the author and are not necessarily held by the other members of the *Chondrilla* unit.

I thank also Dr R. H. Groves and Miss V. Hull for carrying out the density measurements in Australia, for access to their data before publication and for the frequent exchange of information and ideas.

The work described above was carried out whilst members of the Chondrilla Biological Control Unit were enjoying the hospitality of the Centre d'Etudes Phytosociologiques et Ecologiques (CNRS), Montpellier, and the INRA Station de Recherches Cytopathologiques, Alès, and I would like to express my thanks to Professor Sauvage and Professor Vago for the use of laboratory facilties and equipment.

References

Andrewartha, H. G. & L. C. Birch, 1954. The distribution and abundance of animals. University of Chicago Press, Chicago.

Caresche, L., 1970. The biological control of *Chondrilla juncea* L.: Entomological aspects. *Proc. first int. Symp. biol. Control Weeds, March 1969.* CIBC, in press.

Cuthbertson, E. G., 1969. *Chondrilla juncea* in Australia. 2. Preplanting weed control and wheat production. *Aust. J. exp. Agric. Anim. Husb.* 9: 27–36.

Groves, R. H. & V. Hull, 1970. Variation in density and cover of *Chondrilla juncea* L. in southeastern Australia. *Rec. CSIRO Div. Pl. Ind. Field Stn* (December).

Hasan, S., 1970. The possible control of skeleton weed (*Chondrilla juncea* L.) using *Puccinia chondrillina* (BUBEK and SYD.). *Proc. first int. Symp. biol. Control Weeds, March 1969.* CIBC, in press.

Kohn, G. D., Storrier & E. G. Cuthbertson, 1966. Fallowing and wheat production in southern New South Wales. *Aust. J. exp. Agric. Anim. Husb.* 6: 233–241.

McVean, D. N., 1966. Ecology of *Chondrilla juncea* L. in south-eastern Australia. *J. Ecol.* 54 (2): 345–365.

Moore, R. M., 1964. *Chondrilla juncea* L. (skeleton weed) in Australia. *Proc. seventh Br. Weed Control Conf.* 2: 563–568.

Moore, R. M. & J. A. Robertson, 1963. Studies on skeleton weed. Control by competition. *Rec. CSIRO. Div. Pl. Ind. Field Stn* 3.

Parker, K. W., 1954. A Method for measuring trend in range condition on national forest ranges. *Adm. Stud. Forest Serv. USDA, Revised Memo* pp. 26.

Wahba, K. W., 1970. A method to measure the percentage attack of organisms in the field. *Proc. first int. Symp. biol. Control Weeds, March 1969.* CIBC, in press.

Wapshere, A. J., 1970. The assessment of the biological control potential of the organisms attacking *Chondrilla juncea* L. *Proc. first int. Symp. biol. Control Weeds, March 1969.* CIBC, in press.

Discussion

Participants: Wapshere (Author), Cavers, Laughlin, van der Meijden, Myers, Pimentel and Solomon

The spread of skeleton weed in Australia affords an interesting comparison with the spread of the rabbit. Both had previously evolved in the Mediterranean and behaved similarly in invading at first the same soil types and climatic regimes as in Europe and afterwards spread to other environments (Myers). Has skeleton weed reached the limit of its possible range in Australia (LAUGHLIN)? McVean believes that it has reached its limit in Eastern Australia. It has recently arrived in Western Australia and attempts are being made to exterminate all the isolated populations (AUTHOR).

Chondrilla juncea occurs throughout Europe; why have you concentrated your studies in the southern part of its range (CAVERS)? This southern Mediteranean region is climatically closely similar to the heavily infested areas in Australia (AUTHOR).

Chondrilla appears to be definitely perennial but its rosette and flowering shoot are annual (AUTHOR to VAN DER MEIJDEN).

The rest of the discussion was on the possible control of *Chondrilla* –

In the reports about *Chondrilla juncea*, it appears that the plant is most vulnerable for biological control at the early seedling stage before the long root has extended (CAVERS). Any control at this stage would be effective, whether by frequent cultivation, by competing plants or by biological control organisms. Control is more difficult in Australia because dense, long-rooted infestations are already well established (AUTHOR).

Is the plant useful as pasture for stock, and wouldn't they be able to control it? Can the plant be killed by herbicides (SOLOMON)? The plant is eaten especially in dry seasons by stock, but they generally prefer the other competitive plants. Herbicides are not readily translocated into the rootstock and are not effective enough to be used economically over much of the plant's distribution (AUTHOR).

Even in southern Italy the endemic fungi are not able to control *Chondrilla*, because in these wheat/fallow rotations the length of time between ploughings is too short (AUTHOR to MYERS).

Is there any resistance of the plant to the fungus (PIMENTEL)? Hasan, our mycologist, has found that there are many different forms of *Puccinia chondrillina* and that different *Chondrilla juncea* clones show differential resistance to the various forms (AUTHOR).

Also in this aspect *Chondrilla* may be compared with the rabbit. The biological control of the rabbit used a virus (myxomatosis) from a different genus of rabbits, *Sylvilagus*, which had been separated in the American sub-continent from the Asian rabbit, *Caprolagus*, and the European rabbit, *Oryctolagus*, for a long time. Other parasites are known on all these rabbit genera and the biological control of the rabbit with myxomatosis is only a start in the right direction (MYERS).

Proc. Adv. Study Inst. Dynamics Numbers Popul. (Oosterbeek, 1970) 478–506

The rabbit in Australia

K. Myers

Division of Wildlife Research, Commonwealth Scientific and Industrial Research Organization, Canberra, Australia[1]

Abstract

The progeny of a dozen wild rabbits released in south-eastern Australia in 1859 now inhabit an area of some 1,500,000 mile^2, and live in environments which include arid, stony deserts, sub-alpine valleys, wet coastal plains and sub-tropical grasslands.

Reproductive patterns and survival rates vary markedly in both magnitude and duration between the different areas.

The interplay between reproduction and mortality results in populations which have different age-sex structures and different powers of increase. The most productive populations occur in areas with climates resembling that of the Mediterranean.

The rabbit in Australia possesses no inbuilt physiological or behavioural mechanism to control its numbers. The rabbit evolved in a system where extrinsic mortality factors (mainly predation) are necessary to maintain population stability. Its main responses to an increase in density – a decrease in reproduction and socially stimulated movements away from more favourable habitats – nevertheless indicate that intrinsic responses to density were probably important factors in the area where the rabbit evolved.

Until the advent in 1950 of the virus disease myxomatosis, population numbers rose and fell in direct correlation with the favourability of climate despite the destruction of millions of animals by man. Since myxomatosis, numbers have fluctuated about relatively low levels, except in those habitats where disease transmission is sporadic or limited.

The rabbit in Australia represents a problem common in the world today – that of a broadly adapted species transplanted from a system in ecological balance – stochastically speaking – to one where ecological chaos ensues. Other examples include the rat and the mouse, and man himself.

The history of the rabbit in Australia begins with the colonization of the continent by white European settlement in 1788, when five domestic rabbits entered Sydney harbour with the first fleet. By the middle 1800's the colonies (of people) were well established. In order to make the country inhabitable, acclimatization societies sprang up in most centres of population; these were dedicated to introducing and spreading all manner of animals and plants – blackbirds, sparrows, pheasants, foxes, hares and, amongst countless others, the rabbit. On Christmas day 1859, the brig 'Lightning' arrived in Melbourne with about a dozen 'wild-type' rabbits, bound for 'Barwon Park', a property in western Victoria. There the species prospered, and further 'liberations' followed.

In 1863 a bush fire destroyed the fences enclosing one colony of rabbits, and initiated a series of events which helped change the whole economy of nature in southern Australia.

---

[1] Present address: Department of Zoology, University of Guelph, Ontario, Canada.

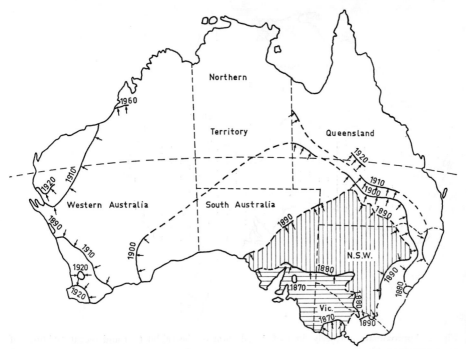

Fig. 1. Pattern of spread of the rabbit in Australia, 1870–1960 (after Stodart, unpublished).

The species spread with amazing rapidity. From two small centres of distribution in 1870 it had dispersed 1,000 mile to the north and the west by 1900 (Fig. 1).

The spread has been well documented by Rolls (1969) and Stodart (in prep.), but lack of data, and human interference, deny the modern ecologist any real understanding of the biological basis of the phenomenon. Records exist suggesting that trappers, spurred on by the booming fur trade of the later 1800's, carried rabbits in their saddle-bags to seed down new colonies ahead of the main wave of infestation. Man undoubtedly continued to play an important part in the spread of the species long after the exulting shouts of the hunter and trapper had given way to the despair of pastoralist and government alike. The rabbit ate grass!

Today the rabbit inhabits the southern half of the continent, an area of some 1,500,000 mile^2, living in environments ranging from arid stony deserts with an annual rainfall of four inches or less, to subalpine valleys, subtropical grasslands, wet coastal plains, and a whole array of habitats possessing mediterranean characteristics. The northern line of distribution more or less coincides with the Tropic of Capricorn (Fig. 2; Myers and Parker, 1965).

The problem of control of the rabbit represents one of the most complex of its kind, and for the past decade research on this species in Australia has been deliberately oriented towards trying to understand the ways in which it is meeting the challenge of colonizing new environments. The studies have been long term in nature, and have been carried out at both experimental and field population level; utilizing purely laboratory techniques, the manipulation of experimental populations in quasi-natural surroundings, the examination of over 7,000 rabbits collected at night by spotlight and gun from a diverse variety of

479

Fig. 2. Approximate northerly limit of distribution of the rabbit (—) and recent sightings of unknown status (*).

geographical situations in nature, regional surveys, and the study of living animals in natural populations, and various methods of capturing, marking, and observation for gathering data pertinent to the programme.

In this paper I will be mostly concerned with data obtained between 1962 and 1967 from 6792 rabbits shot in samples of about 50 at approximate intervals of six weeks, at four sites: Snowy High Plains – subalpine south-eastern New South Wales; Mitchell – subtropical Queensland; Tero Creek – semi-arid north-western New South Wales; and Urana – temperate mediterranean New South Wales. Several extra samples relating to special climatic circumstances were taken at later dates. A similar, smaller series of samples was collected from 1966 to 1968 at Mogo, a temperate, coastal site in southern New South Wales by a colleague, Dr J. D. Dunsmore, who has kindly permitted me to make use of the data from that source in some of the following analyses. In all, 7482 rabbits were collected in 123 samples. Statistical analyses relating to the data will be presented elsewhere.

Surveys of patterns of distribution

Numerous surveys have shown that within each of the major habitat types, rabbit populations are distributed discontinuously, relative to topography, soils, and plant cover.

In subalpine areas, rabbits are mainly confined to open, grassy high valleys (Myers and Parker, 1965). In areas of mediterranean-type climates, they inhabit the edges of rocky and forested hills, wooded river and creek frontages, and lightly forested sand-hills (Myers, 1960). This distribution pattern has hardly changed during the past 20 years (Myers and Hale, in prep.).

480

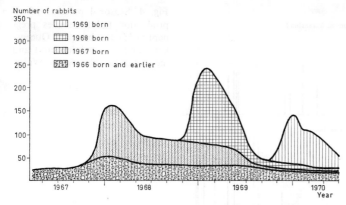

Fig. 3. Regular, annual fluctuations in the number of rabbits in a subalpine population, in the snowy plains of subalpine New South Wales (Dunsmore, unpublished).

Some habitats remain favourable for years on end, yielding relatively regular annual patterns of fluctuation in numbers (Fig. 3, Dunsmore unpublished). In others, favourability may be reversed within a short period of time causing dramatic changes in both numbers and distribution. This is especially evident in the more arid regions (Table 1; Birch, in these Proceedings). Present studies in these latter areas are showing that the most favourable refuge of all is the deep warren, in hard soils, near large swamps (Parker and Myers, unpublished; Wood and Hall, unpublished).

Table 1. Changes in population indices in three different habitats in arid north-western New South Wales

Year	Sand dunes (55 mile²)		Margins of large swamp (30 mile²)		Stony hills (42 mile²)	
	number of warrens	mean number of active entrances per warren	number of warrens	mean number of active entrances per warren	number of warrens	mean number of active entrances per warren
1963	1649	4.98	–	–	717*	6.37
1965	648	0.12	929	1.06	1025*	0.20
1966	2	0.00	47	1.28	1251	0.05
1967	13	0.23	74	2.12	1436	1.16
1968	23	2.22	266	2.63	971	3.45
1969	322	3.36	437	4.68	1420	3.97

* Areas less than 42 mile² (Parker and Myers, unpublished).

Reproduction

Patterns of reproduction vary markedly in both magnitude and duration in the different areas (Fig. 4). The most sharply defined breeding season (and the shortest), measured in terms of percentage of adult females pregnant per sample, occurs in the subalpine region.

481

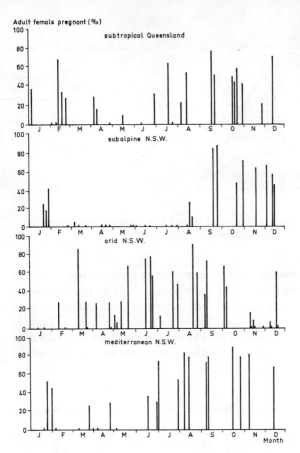

Adult femals pregnant (%)

subtropical Queensland

subalpine N.S.W.

arid N.S.W.

mediterranean N.S.W.

Month

Fig. 4. Seasonal patterns of reproduction (adult females pregnant in %) in subtropical Queensland, and in subalpine, arid and mediterranean New South Wales.

Here reproduction is sharply limited to the late spring and early summer months. In the mediterranean site, reproduction occurs during most months of the year, although there is a prominent peak in the spring. Most of the samples which contain no pregnant females occur there at the beginning of the year.

Table 2. Average productivity in different sites (means)

	Subtropical Queensland	Subalpine N.S.W.	Arid N.S.W.	Mediterranean N.S.W.	Coastal N.S.W.
Number of females > 3 months of age	548	636	937	412	301
Pregnant (%)	32.1	24.1	24.9	43.4	26.6
Lactating (%)	46.4	33.5	24.9	41.0	36.5
Litter size	4.80	4.53	4.49	5.65	5.23
Average productivity per female per year	15.4	10.9	11.2	24.5	13.9
Loss in productivity (%)	46.0	44.7	34.5	21.2	41.1

482

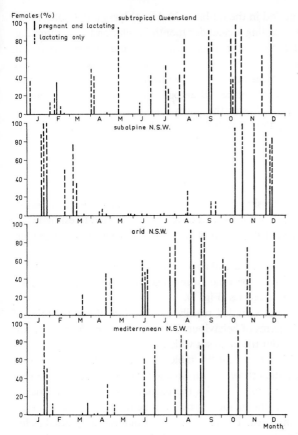

Fig. 5. Seasonal patterns of reproductive success (adult females pregnant and lactating) and reproductive failure (adult females lactating only) both expressed as percentages, in subtropical, Queensland, and in subalpine, arid and mediterranean New South Wales.

The overall proportions of females pregnant in the different sites also differ significantly Whereas 43.4 % of the adult females collected at Urana were pregnant, only 24.1 % were pregnant in subalpine New South Wales.

There are also large and significant differences between the sites in relation to reproductive failure, measured as the proportion of adult females in the samples in breeding condition, but lactating only; i.e. females which either did not conceive post-partum or lost embryos during early stages of development (Fig. 5). The physiological aspects of these data are to be analysed and discussed more fully elsewhere (Hughes, unpublished). The largest loss occurs in the subtropical site where 27.4 % of breeding females show this condition. Only 11.7 % of breeding females in the mediterranean site show apparent loss. The low rate of reproductive failure during the spring months in the latter environment is especially significant, as opposed to the high losses at the same time in subtropical Queensland.

In addition to the above differences, large differences also occur in mean size of litters (in embryo) both in relation to age and season. The overall means are tabulated in Table 2. In this table, females three months of age and over are included, to incorporate all pregnancies.

The figure quoted for average productivity of young per female per year is based on the fortunate fact that the gestation period in the rabbit is 30 days (Myers and Poole, 1962), which I am, for practical purposes, calling a calendar month in relation to the sampling. In the 821 pregnancies examined during autopsy, only two total resorptions were noted. Forty four partial resorptions were recorded; in these cases only the viable embryos were included in the analyses. Despite the large rates of embryonic losses in rabbits which have been reported by other workers in other places (Brambell, 1944; Poole, 1960; Watson, 1957), I thus have little reservation about using the embryonic data as a reliable indication of the young actually produced. Lloyd's (1963) findings would, I think, support this premise.

Age structure

The overall age distributions in all the sites were measured as frequency distributions of oven-dried weights of the crystalline eye lens, which have been calibrated to estimate age up to two years (Myers and Gilbert, 1968). Two of the distributions (arid and mediterranean N.S.W.) are shown in Fig. 6.

The two oldest populations occurred in the arid zone and subtropical Queensland. The differences, highly significant by χ^2 tests, become more apparent when the total samples are broken up into their major age categories (Fig. 7).

The 0–3 months age group was not sampled readily by shooting. Present studies of marked populations explain this in terms of behaviour. The data collected from such animals have therefore been omitted from the analyses which follow.

Using standard methods, provisional vertical life-tables have been drawn up to compare survival rates of rabbits older than three months in each population. Since the rabbits were all collected by identical means and, with the partial exception of the coastal area, during the same period of time, the method appears to be the most sensible to use to bring out the main differences involved. The lx curves thus obtained are plotted as log lx against age expressed, as previously mentioned, in terms of dried lens weights (Fig. 8). The differences between the sites are clear, and highly significant.

There are also significant differences, both within and between sites, in the apparent survival rates of males and females, in relation to age (Fig. 9). In the arid zone the older females survive better than the males. In the mediterranean site this trend is reversed.

Fig. 8 and 9 actually approach log × log curves. When lx is plotted against derived age (in months) it can be seen that survival rates in adults change fairly sharply at about the two year mark (Fig. 10). This represents the second breeding season, when those animals still alive become dominant and secure in their social setting (Myers and Poole, 1961; Mykytowycz, 1960). In this graph it should be noted that the last two points, representing the tail of the lx curve, are fitted according to Myers and Gilbert (1968) and from unpublished observations of present studies of natural populations. They are not accurate, but are sensible biological approximations. The eye lens technique is of little use beyond two years of age. For the construction of provisional life-tables from these data, equal rates of mortality were assumed within the 2 to 3, and 3 to 6 year periods as shown in Fig. 10. Observations from the live studies do not negate this assumption.

Data from the dead samples are also instructive in demonstrating that survival rates of rabbits during their first year of life differ markedly from site to site. In Fig. 11 the mean monthly age distribution of rabbits up to 12 months of age is compared with the average annual production of young, expressed as a percentage per month. In arid New

484

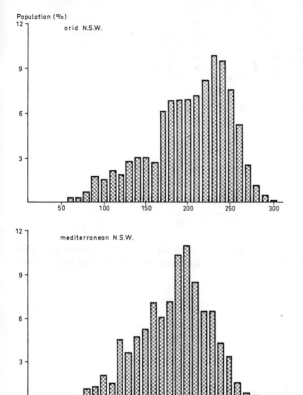

Population (%)

arid N.S.W.

mediterranean N.S.W.

Age (lens weight in mg)

Fig. 6. Frequency distributions of oven-dried weights of the crystalline eye lenses from the total samples taken in arid and mediterranean New South Wales.

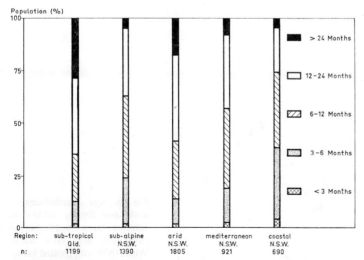

Population (%)

> 24 Months

12 – 24 Months

6 – 12 Months

3 – 6 Months

< 3 Months

Region:	sub-tropical Qld.	sub-alpine N.S.W.	arid N.S.W.	mediterranean N.S.W.	coastal N.S.W.
n:	1199	1390	1805	921	690

Fig. 7. Age distributions of samples taken from subtropical Queensland and subalpine, arid, mediterranean, and coastal New South Wales.

485

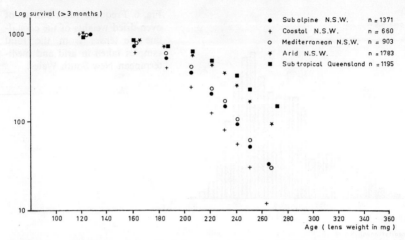

Fig. 8. Age distributions plotted as log cumulative frequencies of dried eye lenses of rabbits from subtropical Queensland and arid, mediterranean, subalpine and coastal New South Wales.

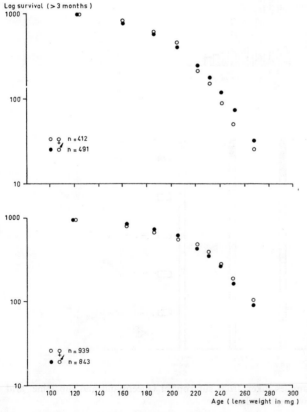

Fig. 9. Age distributions of male and female rabbits in samples from mediterranean (top) and arid New South Wales (bottom), plotted as log-cumulative frequencies of dried eye lenses.

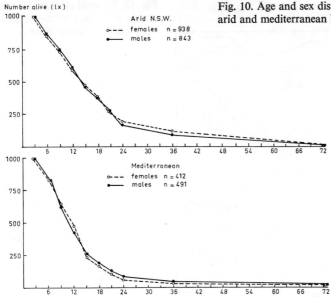

Fig. 10. Age and sex distributions of rabbits from arid and mediterranean New South Wales.

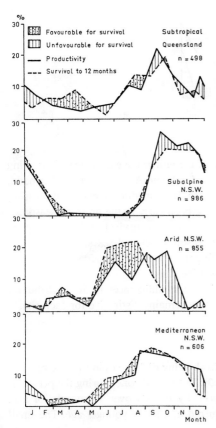

Fig. 11. Graphs of mean monthly production (——) and survival (– – –) of rabbits to 12 months of age in subtropical Queensland and subalpine, arid and mediterranean New South Wales.

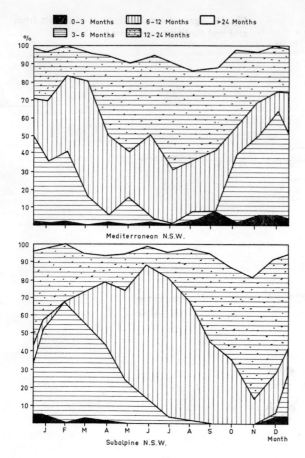

Fig. 12. Seasonal changes in age structure in mediterranean and subalpine New South Wales.

South Wales, rabbits born between September and December have a chance of surviving of approximately 1 in 2. If they are born between March and August, on the other hand, their chance of surviving to 12 months is almost 2 to 1. In mediterranean climates also, enhanced rates of survival accompany those young born early in the breeding season.

The net result of the interplay between reproduction and survival outlined above results in populations with significantly different seasonal age and sex structures in the different sites (Fig. 12). Fig. 12 illustrates the different patterns of changing age structure, month by month, in the mediterranean and subalpine sites.

Although, within each site, analyses show significant differences in age distribution patterns from year to year, the basic annual pattern remains distinctive for each site.

Productivity

The reproductive data collected are instructive in showing differences in average productivity between the sites in relation to age (Table 3). In the arid zone, during the period of sampling, over 50% of the young were produced by rabbits over 18 months of age. In the mediterranean site, peak production occurred at a much younger age. The small

488

Table 3. Age specific reproduction in two sites

Age (months)	Number of females > 3 months	Number of females (% of total)	Females pregnant (%)	Mean litter size (in embryo)	Production per female	Production per group (%)
Mediterranean						
3–6	73	17.72	23.29	4.38	1.81	7.4
6–12	148	35.92	43.24	5.60	8.70	35.4
12–18	125	30.34	52.80	5.89	9.43	38.4
18–24	44	10.68	45.45	5.85	2.84	11.5
> 24	22	5.34	54.54	6.18	1.80	7.3
Totals & means	412	100.00	43.45	5.65	24.58	100.00
Arid						
3–6	131	13.98	4.58	3.80	0.24	2.18
6–12	248	26.47	14.52	4.66	1.79	16.06
12–18	203	21.66	31.53	4.56	3.11	27.94
18–24	180	19.21	37.22	4.33	3.09	27.76
> 24	175	18.68	34.29	4.53	2.90	26.06
Totals & means	937	100.00	24.87	4.48	11.13	100.00

differences between the means in Tables 2 and 3 are due to the rounding off of figures in the additional operations in Table 3. The data in this table represent an average annual natality, for the period sampled, and are referred to as such from here on.

If production of young is expressed in terms of mean monthly pregnancy rates and litter sizes (in embryo), an annual estimate of productivity is obtained which is based on reproduction under more favourable conditions, possibly approaching the maximum to be

Table 4. Correlation matrix – productivity at two sites

	Day of year	Day length	Rain in previous 12 weeks	Rain departure from normal	Evaporation over 8 weeks	P/E $^{0.7}$	Body weight (g)	Kidney fat index	Pituitary weight (mg)
Mediterranean (n = 339)									
Ovary weight (g)	0.68	—	0.61	0.65	−0.43	0.72	0.66	—	0.80
Pregnancy (%)	0.78	—	0.62	0.59	−0.66	0.80	0.77	—	0.70
Lactation (%)	0.58	—	0.62	0.62	−0.47	0.65	0.68	—	0.66
Production	0.80	—	0.60	0.61	−0.62	0.81	0.72	—	0.70
Loss of production	—	—	0.44	−0.56	—	−0.32	0.36	—	0.41
Subalpine (n = 553)									
Ovary weight (g)	—	0.75	—	—	0.45	—	—	−0.64	0.51
Pregnancy (%)	0.61	0.57	0.43	0.39	—	—	—	−0.41	0.40
Lactation (%)	—	0.89	0.41	—	0.59	—	—	−0.74	0.64
Production	0.62	0.64	0.48	0.41	—	—	—	−0.48	0.43
Loss of production	—	0.87	0.33	—	0.74	—	—	−0.75	0.5

expected in each of the areas. These figures, for comparison with those quoted in Table 2 are:

Subtropical Queensland:	16.0	young/year
Subalpine N.S.W.:	13.8	young/year
Arid N.S.W.:	16.8	young/year
Mediterranean N.S.W.:	27.3	young/year
Coastal N.S.W.:	15.6	young/year

They represent high rates of natality, and are referred to in such terms from here on.

Although few statistical analyses are included in this paper, I would like to draw attention to the highly significant way in which all of the productivity data correlate with weather indices in the mediterranean study area (Table 4). Although as the various graphs indicate, there is a lot of curvilinearity present in many of the relationships, when day of year and day length are added together in a multiple regression analysis for all sites, most of the curvature disappears and for predictive purposes two or three of the weather indices then account for significant portions of the variability involved.

Capacity for increase

Using the lx curves from the provisional life-tables of rabbits older than three months, it is possible, by varying mortality rates in the 0–3 months age group and reproductive rates from 0.1 to 2.0 litters per three-month period, to derive an array of tables showing net reproduction rates for all the conditions of births and deaths proposed, and to calculate an approximate average capacity for increase, r_c (Laughlin, 1965). Two such models are presented in Fig. 13 and 14.

The point 2.0 litters per three months was taken as the upper limit of reproduction since it has been shown elsewhere (Mykytowycz, 1959) that a female rabbit can produce seven litters in a year. In nature, this figure is rarely reached even under the most favourable conditions. The range of conditions on the graphs where $r_c = 0$ is indicated by the heavy line. The differences between the two populations are readily obvious.

For comparison between the sites I have tabulated a series of data which bring out clearly the differences in their inherent abilities to increase, allowing for both average and high natality (Table 5). It is clear that the population in the mediterranean habitat possesses an outstanding superior capacity for increase – almost double that of its nearest rival in subtropical Queensland. The latter population's challenge resided in the fact that it alone, of all those studied, remained free of human predation for a number of years and had reached a stage of relative stability with a high proportion of breeding adults (Fullagar, unpublished). Under the conditions measured, the mediterranean population required the highest mortality amongst the young for the maintenance of stability.

The data in the model are more strikingly presented as curves of interaction between juvenile mortality and reproduction where $r_c = 0$ (Fig. 15). I have inserted on the respective graphs those points representing the field measurements of average and high natality. The small range of interaction between mortality and reproduction within which the coastal and subalpine populations can manoeuvre are evident. Imposed mortality on the subtropical population by human activity would undoubtedly lower the graph of that population well below that of the mediterranean area. The outstanding strengths of the

490

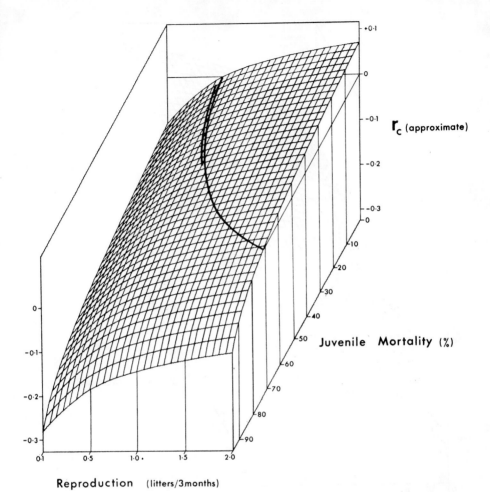

Fig. 13. Solid model showing relationships between reproduction, juvenile mortality (0–3 months age group) and capacity for increase, r_c, in subalpine New South Wales. The curved line joins those points on the plane where $r_c = 0$. The other thick line represents the measured rate of reproduction.

Reproduction (litters/3months)

population in the mediterranean climate are again emphasized.

The model also permits comparison of life-table data on different aspects of population in the different sites (Table 6), thus suggesting further fertile areas of research. In the data presented here, the apparent mortality in young females about the end of the first breeding season, and the increase in expectancy of life from the second breeding season appear to be common to all sites, and thus probably represent something real in the life of the rabbit in nature. The differences between the sites are again obvious.

Processes

Ecology is not a study of reproduction and survival, but of those processes which affect them. In attempting to explain the differences between the populations just described, my

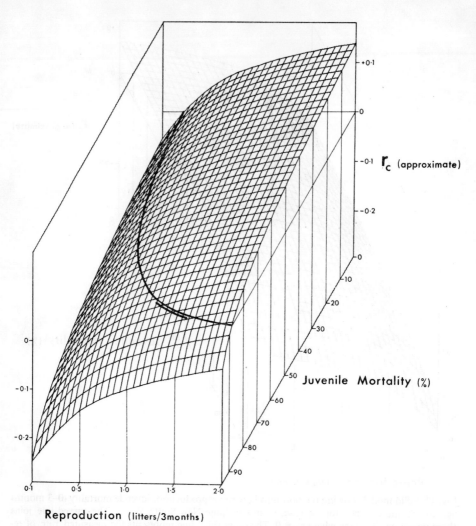

Fig. 14. Solid model showing relationships between reproduction, juvenile mortality (0–3 months age group) and capacity for increase r_c, in mediterranean New South Wales. The curved line joins those points on the plane where $r_c = 0$. The other thick line represents the measured rate of reproduction.

colleagues and I have spent considerable time in obtaining data on the array of variables shown in Table 7. This work is still in progress and it would be premature for me to proffer, at this stage, dogmatic generalizations arising therefrom. It is already clear, however, that the variables listed, either alone, or in relationship with each other, assume different degrees of importance, depending upon the habitat and population in which they operate. Some of the differences are reflected in the crude means included in Table 8.

Other analyses show that food, as a factor for growth and survival, rarely appears to limit the populations in the subtropical, subalpine and coastal areas. Food for reproduction, on the other hand, importantly affects subtropical, subalpine and arid populations.

Table 5. Maximum capacity for increase

	Number of litters per year	Ro	r_c (3 months)	Young mortality $r_c = 0$ (%)	Generation time (months)
Average natality					
Subtropical	3.2	3.542	0.055	72.0	22.92
Subalpine	2.4	1.035	0.002	3.0	17.47
Arid	2.5	1.752	0.024	43.0	22.95
Mediterranean	4.3	4.609	0.098	78.0	15.64
Coastal	2.7	1.267	0.017	21.0	14.06
High natality					
Subtropical	4.0	4.427	0.065	77.0	22.92
Subalpine	3.4	1.553	0.025	36.0	17.47
Arid	4.0	2.920	0.047	66.0	22.95
Mediterranean	6.0	6.286	0.118	84.0	15.64
Coastal	4.8	2.171	0.055	54.0	14.06

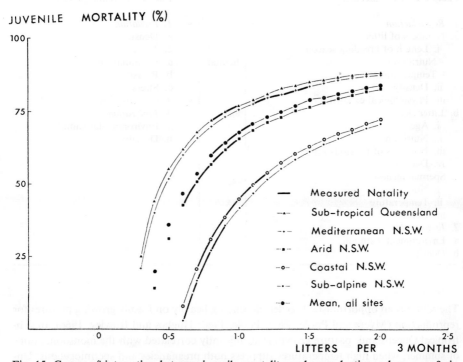

Fig. 15. Curves of interaction between juvenile mortality and reproduction, where $r_c = 0$, in subtropical Queensland and mediterranean, arid, coastal and subalpine New South Wales. The range of natality, as measured in the samples from each population, are inserted on each graph as a thicker line.

493

Table 6. Female derived life table – Average natality ($r_c = 0$)

Pivotal age (months)	Mediterranean				Arid			
	lx	dx	ex (months)	1000qx	lx	dx	ex (months)	1000qx
1.5	1000	780	3.97	780.0	1000	430	11.12	430.0
4.5	220	39	9.76	177.0	570	80	15.38	140.0
7.5	181	41	8.54	227.2	490	69	14.64	140.7
10.5	140	38	7.61	270.4	421	82	13.80	196.2
13.5	102	52	6.87	508.6	339	75	13.80	218.9
16.5	50	15	9.44	298.2	264	49	14.25	185.3
19.5	35	14	9.81	406.2	215	59	14.15	275.1
22.5	21	9	12.50	442.1	156	50	15.95	321.2
*25.5	12	1.4	18.22	122.6	106	11.3	19.79	106.2
*37.5	6	0.49	18.00	83.3	61	5.1	17.98	84.0
*49.5	4	0.49	12.00	125.0	41	5.1	11.99	125.0
*61.5	2	0.49	6.00	250.0	20	5.1	5.99	250.0
*70.5	0.5	0.49	1.5	1000.0	5.08	5.1	1.50	1000.5

* Beginning of 12-month periods only, for economy of space.

Table 7. Population numbers

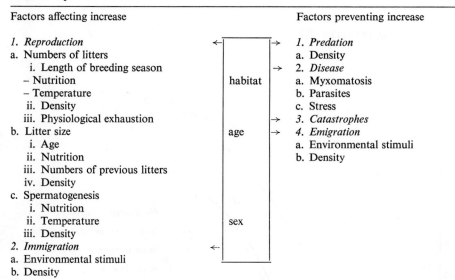

Factors affecting increase		Factors preventing increase
1. Reproduction	←	*1. Predation*
a. Numbers of litters		a. Density
i. Length of breeding season	→	*2. Disease*
– Nutrition	habitat	a. Myxomatosis
– Temperature		b. Parasites
ii. Density		c. Stress
iii. Physiological exhaustion	→	*3. Catastrophes*
b. Litter size		*4. Emigration*
i. Age	age →	a. Environmental stimuli
ii. Nutrition		b. Density
iii. Numbers of previous litters		
iv. Density		
c. Spermatogenesis		
i. Nutrition		
ii. Temperature	sex	
iii. Density		
2. Immigration	←	
a. Environmental stimuli		
b. Density		

The rabbit is an opportunistic breeder, depending heavily on freshly growing pastures for reproduction (Myers and Poole, 1962; Poole, 1960; Hughes and Rowley, 1966). In subtropical Queensland, pasture growth is significantly correlated with the monsoonal rains of summer, when high temperatures suppress both pregnancies and spermiogenesis. Under such conditions small deteriorations in pastures severely affect reproduction (Hughes, unpublished). It has now been demonstrated on several occasions that the highest rates of reproduction in the rabbit in Australia occur in areas which possess a high probability of

Table 8. Regional differences in adult male rabbits (age corrected)

	Subtropical (n = 765)	Subalpine (n = 443)	Arid (n = 765)	Mediter-ranean (n = 423)	Significance of differences d.f. 3/2433
Weight (g)	1350	1304	1245	1304	0.001
Ear length (mm)	82.05	77.64	80.74	78.60	0.001
Foot lenth (mm)	92.01	89.38	90.76	89.65	0.001
Spleen (mg)	329	419	272	380	0.001
Pituitary (mg)	35.8	37.0	32.9	38.2	0.001
Adrenals (mg)	340	354	232	253	0.001
Gonads (g)	2.87	2.69	2.29	3.11	0.001
*Liver (g)	33	39	26	32	0.001
*Kidneys (g)	10.4	8.8	11.3	9.8	0.001
*Packed cell volume	38	35	30	37	0.01
*Serum protein (g/100 ml)	5.6	5.4	5.2	5.4	0.01
Kidney fat index	1.26	1.61	1.93	1.40	0.001

*After Casperson (1968).

winter-spring rains, followed by a summer drought which undoubtedly causes heavy mortality in the early developmental stages of endoparasites.

The arid zone suffers severely in all respects, as evidenced by the differences in mean body weights and in weights of organs, along with other indices which point to differences in rates of growth and of physiology. Note also that the rabbits from the warmer regions have longer extremities than those from cooler regimes. Stodart (1965) has shown that arid zone rabbits have a yellower coat, and Regnery (unpublished) has measured differences in blood groups between rabbits from warmer and cooler regions. Genetic changes may thus be involved in some of the differences measured.

In subalpine areas, except during periods of infrequent catastrophic falls of snow, the protein content of the available food remains fairly high, but rabbits in that habitat have to contend with a very low sodium content in their diet. During the spring and early summer months they become hungry for sodium and avidly devour soft wooden pegs impregnated with sodium salts (Myers, 1967, 1968). The appetite for salt almost disappears during the winter months. The behaviour is accompanied by a dramatic broadening of the zona glomerulosa of the adrenal gland, especially in lactating females.

Analyses of soils and mixed plants show that they are low in Na^+ (< 1 meq/kg dry weight) during the spring and summer, but that this increases in plants during the autumn and winter. In spring and summer the mountain rabbits excrete a urine virtually free of sodium. In autumn and winter the sodium content of the urine increases. The concentration of peripheral blood aldosterose is greatly elevated in rabbits, especially in lactating females in the spring (Blair-West et al., 1968; Scoggins et al., 1970). At the same time the concentration of renal renin is high. In other areas, the zona glomerulosa, although fluctuating in size, remains relatively narrow throughout the year, and appetite for sodium is absent (Myers, unpublished).

At birth, a rabbit weighs about 40 g and total body sodium is about 5 meq. Nestling rabbits, under favourable conditions, grow by about 9 g/day. If the doe provides 100 g of milk of normal composition each day (of which the ash content is 2.5%, and sodium is 5% of the ash; Baxter 1961) about 20% of the sodium content of the circulating plasma would be required daily for normal lactation to feed a litter of 4 or 5 young. The low levels of sodium present during the breeding season of subalpine rabbits could only provide about 5% of the sodium content of the circulating plasma in a week's intake of food. On normal pasture, on the other hand, sodium equivalent to 10–25% of the plasma content is ingested each day. The tremendous stress on sodium homeostasis in rabbits in the subalpine habitat is thus evident, and undoubtedly affects reproduction significantly.

In addition to the acute shortage of environmental sodium, subalpine rabbits are heavily infested with endoparasites (Dunsmore, 1965a,b; 1966; Dunsmore and Dudzinski, 1968; Stodart, 1968), adding further to their physiological problems. This phenomenon they share with rabbits in coastal populations (Dunsmore, unpublished), which, even in the presence of a copious supply of food, exhibit high rates of reproductive losses (see Table 2). There is little doubt that the abnormally high parasite burdens are playing some part in causing mortality of the young, and in suppressing reproduction.

The role of predation and other factors remains to be evaluated in the light of work in progress. It is nevertheless clear that the most important predators of the rabbit throughout most of its range in Australia are two other imported mammals, the European fox and the feral cat. Predation is of particular importance in the arid and mediterranean areas where it can account for up to 80% of the annual crop of young.

Density

Special attention has been paid to the role of population density itself as a factor affecting numbers. In confined populations, increase in numbers leads to marked changes in behaviour and physiology. Rates of aggression increase, and there is an increase in the number of breeding groups. Territory size decreases (Myers and Poole, 1961). There is a large loss in body weight, and changes in the weights of index organs vitally concerned with metabolic function. The kidneys become inflamed, pitted and scarred with lesions caused by a systemic disease similar to that in other mammals where it has been shown to be ACTH-induced (Christian et al., 1965, 1967). There is an impairment in reproductive condition, and the zonation and morphology of the adrenals alters to favour increased secretion of glucocorticoids and suppression of mineralocorticoids, probably causing natriuresis, and upsetting Na: K ratios in the body. The adrenal cortical tissue reorganizes into alveoli separated by prominent sinuses. There is a significant increase in the formation of adrenal cortical nodules and a decrease in the lipid precursors of adrenocortical hormones (Table 9) (Myers, 1967; Myers et al., 1971).

The same syndrome is elicited when rabbits are challenged with graded doses of longacting ACTH; measurements of circulating corticoids from such animals have yielded highly significant regressions showing that the indices listed in Table 9 are indicative of adrenocortical exhaustion (Myers, unpublished).

This aspect of the work has been most enlightening in several respects:

i. Stress, as indicated in Table 9, is a graded phenomenon, and operates more at an individual than a population level. Some of the response to stress is undoubtedly genetic (reviewed in Myers, 1966; Myers et al., in press). Some of the response has developmental origins (Table 10). Thus rabbits born into high or low density populations exhibit differences in behaviour and physiology as adults. Adult patterns of neuroendocrine activity regulating ACTH secretion and affecting some aspects of behaviour, appear to be formed

496

Table 9. Relationships between indices of condition, behaviour and survival in male rabbits (confined populations)

Variable	Type of death				
	sacrificed at end of experiment (n = 87)	social perse-cution (n = 17)	pathological symptoms (n = 23)	unknown (n = 3)	significance of difference between means; d.f. = 3/127
Survival (%)	100	50.5	63.4	64.2	P < 0.001
Weight (g)	1469	1156	1150	1066	P < 0.001
Weight change (%)	−6.1	−24.9	−26.1	−29.8	P < 0.001
Adrenals (g)	0.45	0.62	0.56	0.64	P < 0.001
Kidney disease (index 1–8)	2.82	4.06	5.33	5.67	P < 0.05
Lipid in adrenal (index 1–10)	9.07	5.18	5.44	4.25	P < 0.001
Median cross section adrenal area (mm²)	31.56	40.48	36.62	40.63	P < 0.001
Area zona glomerulosa (% total)	10.2	7.0	7.0	7.5	P < 0.001
Area zona fasciculata-reticularis (% total)	83.9	87.5	87.7	89.1	P < 0.001
Adrenal nodules	1.25	0.41	0.44	−	P < 0.01
Alveolation of cortex (index 1–12)	7.44	10.12	10.35	8.50	P < 0.01
Aggressive behaviour (acts/minute)	0.055	0.035	0.070	0.017	P < 0.01
Sex behaviour (acts/minute)	0.079	0.020	0.073	0.016	P < 0.05
Status (1–3) 1 = dominant	2.05	2.74	2.04	2.35	P < 0.05

Table 10. Origin and adult biology (male rabbits)

Variable	Born in medium to high density (confined) (n = 16)	Born in low density (confined) (n = 12)	Born in low density (natural) (n = 102)	Significance of differences d.f. = 2/128
Survival (%)	72.5	84.4	86.8	P < 0.01
Body weight (g)	1215	1389	1375	P < 0.01
Weight change (%)	−21.5	−9.1	−12.0	P < 0.05
Relative adrenals (g/kg)	0.450	0.315	0.363	n.s.
Adrenal lipids (index)	5.70	8.33	8.07	P < 0.001
Zona glomerulosa (% total area)	8.4	9.2	10.3	P < 0.02
Nodules on adrenals	0.25	0.83	1.08	P < 0.02
Alveolation of adrenals (index)	9.70	9.42	8.01	P < 0.02
Aggression (acts/minute)	0.101	0.072	0.039	P < 0.02
Total activities	0.260	0.227	0.173	P < 0.01
Testis weight (mg)	1996	1944	1615	P < 0.02

very early in life during sensitive periods in development. Recent papers, which show that the hypothalamus takes up circulating corticosterone differentially (Zarrow et al., 1968) and that morphological changes occur in the hypothalamus when stress hormones are administered neonatally (Palkovits and Mitro, 1968), point the way to promising developments in this field in the near future.

ii. Stress operates differently in the sexes, and differentially in relation to reproduction. Non-breeding male and female rabbits do not succumb to stress in the way outlined above. Priming by gonadotropins appears to be required before either ACTH, or the corticoids, have their effects. Thus, in the non-breeding season high densities in rabbit populations have little effect on health, provided food is not limiting (Myers, unpublished). In this period, there is a minimum of aggression (Myers and Poole, 1961). During the breeding season females are affected more than males (Myers et al., in press).

iii. Stress operates differently in different environments. Rabbits taken from subalpine (sodium-deprived) and coastal (sodium-replete) populations when challenged with ACTH respond quite differently. The sodium-replete rabbits exhibit the typical symptoms as described by Robb et al. (1968), with massive fluid accumulation, ascites, enlargement of the liver, adrenals and kidneys and the development of the other indices described earlier. The sodium-deficient rabbits, on the other hand, lose weight more rapidly, and the female adrenal, unable to respond to the stimulus, actually decreases in size. Most females thus challenged succumb within 21 days (Table 11), apparently due to a loss of the ability to regulate sodium metabolism.

The kidneys of the sodium-replete animals possess large medullae; these are indicative of water retention. The sodium-deficient animals possess small medullae indicative of water loss, thus allowing valuable Na^+ to escape (Myers, unpublished).

Recent experimental evidence has shown that restriction of dietary sodium intake results in altered hormone secretion by the adrenal cortex (Eisenstein and Hartroft, 1957). Under the stimulation of ACTH, the secretion of glucocorticoids is suppressed and that of aldosterone increased (Müller and Huber, 1969). In view of Aumann and Emlen's (1965) and Aumann's (1965) records of an apparent correlation between the relative abundance of sodium in the soil and the peak densities reached by microtine rodents in North America, and of our unpublished observations mentioned briefly above and in Myers et al. (in press), the suggestion that inadequate adrenocortical regulation of sodium metabolism under conditions of crowding is an important factor in population history appears likely to be true.

In natural populations of rabbits in Australia, evidence of the stress syndrome, as described above, occurs, but varies from habitat to habitat; in general it does not appear to be significant over large proportions of the rabbit's range.

In our experiments, it has been clearly evident that stress is most severe in its effects when living space is decreased. Although stress is elicited as reaction to rise in population numbers, in the individual it is not a response to group size per se, but to some form of spatial restriction either in the form of space itself, or animal behaviour in space. Decrease in the size of territory appears to be all that is necessary to stimulate the stress response (Myers et al., 1971).

Our work so far does not suggest that the rabbit in Australia possesses any inbuilt behavioural or physiological mechanisms capable of controlling its own numbers. The evidence collected supports the thesis that the rabbit evolved in a system where extrinsic mortality factors (mainly predation) are necessary to maintain population stability. Its main responses to increase in density – a decrease in reproduction (Myers and Poole, 1962; Mykytowycz, 1960) and movement away from more favourable to less favourable habitat – nevertheless indicate that intrinsic responses to density are part and parcel of its biology and undoubtedly assume more importance in this evolutionary setting.

498

Table 11. Affects of injection of long-acting ACTH for 21 days into adult rabbits from a natural population suffering severe sodium deficiency

Variable	Males				Females			
	ACTH 10 I.U. in 0.2 ml per 48 h (n = 11)	distilled H_2O 0.2 ml per 48 h (n = 8)	free-living controls (n = 10)	significance of differences (d.f. 2/28)	ACTH 10 I.U. in 0.2 ml per 48 h (n = 12)	distilled H_2O 0.2 ml per 48 h (n = 7)	Free-living controls (n = 10)	significance of differences (d.f. 2/28)
Weight (g)	1028	1065	1650	$P < 0.001$	963	1054	1676	$P < 0.001$
Weight loss (%)	−17.3	−12.4	—	$P < 0.001$	−15.5	−13.9	—	$P < 0.001$
Kidney (g)	6.24	5.85	8.95	$P < 0.001$	6.13	6.36	8.68	$P < 0.001$
Spleen (g)	1.91	2.05	3.46	$P < 0.001$	1.75	2.31	4.35	$P < 0.001$
Adrenals (g)	0.45	0.38	0.34	$P < 0.001$	0.36	0.38	0.50	$P < 0.001$
Area median cross section adrenals (mm²)	29.63	27.70	27.99	n.s.	25.84	26.76	31.25	$P < 0.05$
Area zona glomerulosa (% total)	13	22	23	$P < 0.001$	31	28	36	n.s.
Area zona fasciculata (% total)	82	72	70	$P < 0.001$	62	65	60	n.s.
Sodium in urine (meq/l)	0.20	0.45	0.95	n.s.	0.93	0.68	0.14	$P < 0.001$

The large areas in southern Australia with climates similar to the western Mediterranean where the rabbit evolved, and also the lag factor inherent in the formation of new biological interactions between colonizing and resident species, automatically assured the rabbit of pest status in Australia.

Control

Until the advent in 1950 of the virus disease myxomatosis, population numbers of rabbits rose and fell in direct correlation with the favourability of climate for reproduction and survival, despite the mass destruction of millions of animals by trapping, poisoning, fumigating and so on. Recurrent plagues were a common event (Fenner and Ratcliffe, 1965).

Since myxomatosis, numbers have fallen dramatically and now fluctuate about relatively low levels, except in those habitats where disease transmission is sporadic or limited.

There is no comprehensive set of data available to quantify the actual effect of myxomatosis on the Australian rabbit population. There has been a dramatic decrease in the quantities of rabbit skins exported from Australia since 1950 (Fig. 16) and in four study areas, where population indices were collected in 1950 (Myers, 1954), the present (1970) numbers of rabbits are clearly less than 1% of their 1950 levels (Table 12).

It should be noted that the studies reported in this paper have been carried out during the past decade in populations of low to medium levels of density, when compared with those of the 1940's and earlier.

Attempts at control in Australia are still relatively unsophisticated and based on methods of undirected, massively imposed mortalities. Data collected in the eastern Riverina of New South Wales (temperate mediterranean) during the past 20 years (Myers and Hale, unpublished) show that man is acting merely as a facultative predator, varying his effort in direct correlation with ease of access to rabbit populations, and with changes in the degree of infestation (Fig. 17).

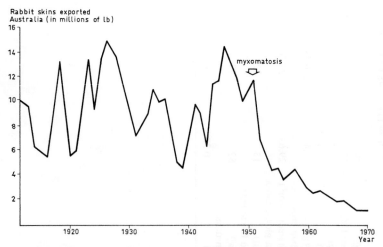

Fig. 16. Quantities of rabbit skins exported from Australia during the past 65 years, showing the rapid decline since the advent of myxomatosis (data from Bureau of Census and Statistics, Canberra). (Note the depressions caused by World Wars I and II.)

500

Table 12. Rabbit population indices

Area and index	Before myxomatosis (1950)	After myxomatosis (1970)
Rutherglen, Vic., 13 acres		
Number of warrens	15	0
Warrens/acre	1.15	0
Number of rabbits	1000	3
Rabbits/acre	77	0.23
Active burrows	850	4
Coreen, N.S.W., 17 acres		
Number of warrens	26	0
Warrens/acre	1.5	0
Number of rabbits	400	2
Rabbits/acre	24	0.12
Active burrows	600	2
Balldale, N.S.W., 17 acres		
Number of warrens	150	5
Warrens/acre	8.8	0.3
Number of rabbits	300	20
Rabbits/acre	18	1.18
Active burrows	1250	17
Urana, N.S.W., 30 acres		
Number of rabbits	5000	11
Rabbits/acre	167	0.37

The work described in this paper, however, indicates the way to a better understanding of the nature of the problem, and suggests biologically oriented ways of dealing with it.

The rabbit in Australia represents a problem common in the world today – that of a broadly adapted species transferred from a system in ecological balance – stochastically speaking – to one where ecological chaos ensues. Other examples of the same class include the rat and the mouse, and man himself.

The rabbit 'learnt its biological rules' in the western mediterranean. Its basic physiology is in tune with the physical aspects of a vast area of southern Australia, and it is also

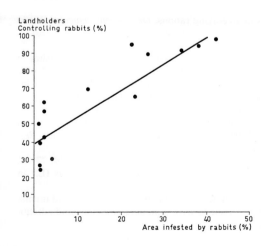

Fig. 17. Relationship between numbers of landholders carrying out control and size of area infested by rabbits, in 300 mile^2 of mediterranean New South Wales (Myers and Hale, unpublished). Area 200,000 acres. Arcsin transformed. $y = 37.76 + 0.9x$; $F = 46$; d.f. $= {}^1/_{12}$.

managing to cope with many marginal habitats with varying degrees of success. The outcome of its adjustments to its biological environment, both exotic and indigenous, however, is yet to be decided. This study merely documents a phase in that process.

Acknowledgments

I want to thank those of my colleagues who may recognise some of their data in this paper, especially Dr J. D. Dunsmore, and Mr B. S. Parker for assistance with the solid models.

The original analyses and unpublished data mentioned throughout will appear elsewhere in the near future.

References

Aumann, G. D., 1965. Microtine abundance and soil sodium levels. *J. Mammal.* 46: 594–604.

Aumann, G. D. & J. T. Emlen, 1965. Relation of population density to sodium availability and sodium selection by microtine rodents. *Nature, Lond.* 208: 198–199.

Blair-West, J. R., J. P. Coghlan, D. A. Denton, J. F. Nelson, E. Orchard, B. A. Scoggins, R. D. Wright, K. Myers & C. L. Junquiera, 1968. Physiological, morphological, and behavioural adaptation to a sodium-deficient environment by wild native Australian and introduced species of animals. *Nature, Lond.* 217: 922.

Blaxter, K. L., 1961. In: S. K. Kon & A. T. Cowie (Ed.), Milk: the mammary gland and its secretion, Vol. 2, p. 305. Academic Press, New York.

Brambell, F. W. R., 1944. The reproduction of the wild rabbit, *Oryctolagus cuniculus* (L.). *Proc. zool. Soc.* 114: 1–45.

Casperson, K., 1968. Influence of environment upon some physiological parameters of the rabbit, *Oryctolagus cuniculus* (L.) in natural populations. *Proc. ecol. Soc. Aust.* 3: 113–119.

Christian, J. J., 1967. ACTH-induced treatment on maturation of intact female mice. *Endocrinology* 74: 669–679.

Christian, J. J., J. A. Lloyd & D. E. Davis, 1965. The role of endocrines in the self-regulation of mammalian populations. In: Recent progress in hormone research, Vol. 21. Academic Press, New York.

Dunsmore, J. D., 1965. Nematode parasites of free-living rabbits, *Oryctolagus cuniculus* (L.) in eastern Australia. I. Variations in the number of *Trichostrongylus retortaeformis* (ZEDER). *Aust. J. Zool.* 14: 185–199.

Dunsmore, J. D., 1965. Nematode parasites of free-living rabbits, *Oryctolagus cuniculus* (L.) in eastern Australia. II. Variations in the numbers of *Graphidium strigosum* (DUJARDIN) RAILLIET and HENRY. *Aust. J. Zool.* 14: 625–634.

Dunsmore, J. D., 1966. Nematode parasites of free-living rabbits, *Oryctolagus cuniculus* (L.) in eastern Australia. III. Variations in the numbers of *Passalurus ambiguus* (RUDOLPHI). *Aust. J. Zool.* 14: 635–645.

Dunsmore, J. D. & M. L. Dudzinski, 1968. Relationship of numbers of nematode parasites in wild rabbits, *Oryctolagus cuniculus* (L.) to host, sex, age, and season. *J. Parasitol.* 54: 462–474.

Eisenstein, Albert B. & Phyllis Merrit Hartroft, 1957. Alterations in the rat adrenal cortex induced by sodium deficiency: steroid hormone secretion. *Endocrinology* 60: 634–640.

Fenner, F., & F. N. Ratcliffe, 1965. Myxomatosis. Cambridge University Press.

Hughes, R. L. & Ian Rowley, 1966. Breeding season of female wild rabbits in natural populations in the Riverina and Southern Tablelands districts of New South Wales. *CSIRO Wildl. Res.* 11: 1–10.

Laughlin, R., 1965. Capacity for increase: a useful population statistic. *J. Anim. Ecol.* 34: 77–91.

Lloyd, A. G., 1963. Intra-uterine mortality in the wild rabbit, *Oryctolagus cuniculus* (L.) in populations of low density. *J. Anim. Ecol.* 32: 549–563.

Müller, Jüng & Rolf Huber, 1969. Effects of sodium deficiency, potassium deficiency and uremia upon the steroidogenic response of rat adrenal tissue to serotonin, potassium ions and adrenocorticotrophin. *Endrocrinology* 85: 43–49.

Myers, K., 1954. Studies in the epidemiology of infectious myxomatosis of rabbits. *J. Hyg.* 52: 47–59.

Myers, K., 1960. A survey of myxomatosis and rabbit infestation trends in the eastern Riverina, New South Wales, 1951–1960. *CSIRO Wildl. Res.* 7: 1–12.

Myers, K., 1966. The effects of density on sociality and health in mammals. *Proc. ecol. Soc. Aust.* 1: 40–64.

Myers, K., 1967. Morphological changes in the adrenal glands of wild rabbits. *Nature, Lond.* 213: 147.

Myers, K., 1968. Physiology and rabbit ecology. *Proc. ecol. Soc. Aust.* 3: 1–8.

Myers, K. & N. Gilbert, 1965. Determination of age of wild rabbits in Australia. *J. Wildl. Mgmt* 32: 841–849.

Myers, K., C. S. Hale, R. Mykytowycz & R. L. Hughes, 1971. The effects of varying density and space on sociality and health in animals. In: Aristide H. Esser (Ed.), Behaviour and environment, p. 148–187. Plenum, New York.

Myers, K. & B. S. Parker, 1965. A study of the biology of the wild rabbit in climatically different regions in Eastern Australia. I. Patterns of distribution. *CSIRO Wildl. Res.* 10: 1–32.

Myers, K. & W. E. Poole, 1961. A study of the biology of the wild rabbit, *Oryctolagus cuniculus* (L.) in confined populations. II. The effects of season and population increase on behaviour. *CSIRO Wildl. Res.* 6: 1–41.

Myers, K. & W. E. Poole, 1962. A study of the biology of the wild rabbit, *Oryctolagus cuniculus* (L.) in confined populations. III. Reproduction. *Aust. J. Zool.* 10: 225–267.

Mykytowycz, R., 1959. Social behaviour of an experimental colony of wild rabbits, *Oryctolagus cuniculus* (L.). II. First breeding season. *CSIRO Wildl. Res.* 4: 1–13.

Mykytowycz, R., 1960. Social behaviour of an experimental colony of wild rabbits, *Oryctolagus cuniculus* (L.). III. Second breeding season. *CSIRO Wildl. Res.* 5: 1–20.

Mykytowycz, R., 1961. Social behaviour of an experimental colony of wild rabbits, *Oryctolagus cuniculus* (L.). IV. Conclusion. *CSIRO Wildl. Res.* 6: 142–155.

Palkovits, M. & A. Mitro, 1968. Morphological changes in the hypothalama – pituitary – adrenal system during early postnatal period in rats. *Gen. comp. Endocr.* 10: 253–262.

Poole, W. E. 1960. Breeding of the wild rabbit, *Oryctolagus cuniculus* (L) in relation to environment. *CSIRO Wildl. Res.* 5: 21–43.

Robb, Charles A., James O. Davis, Colin I. Johnston & Phyllis M. Hartroft, 1968. Effects of cortisone on renal sodium excretion in rabbits. *Endocrinology* 82: 1200–1208.

Rolls, Eric C., 1969. They all ran wild. Angus and Robertson, Australia.

Scoggins, B. A., J. R. Blair-West, J. P. Coghlan, D. A. Denton, K. Myers, J. F. Nelson, Elspeth Orchard & R. D. Wright, 1970. The physiological and morphological response of mammals to changes in their sodium status. *Mem. Soc. Endocr., Cambr.* 18: 577–602.

Stodart, Eleanor, 1965. A study of the biology of the wild rabbit in climatically different regions in eastern Australia. III. Some data on the evolution of coat colour. *CSIRO Wildl. Res.* 10: 73–82.

Stodart, Eleanor, 1968. Coccidiosis in wild rabbits, *Oryctolagus cuniculus* (L.) at four sites in different climatic regions in eastern Australia. *Aust. J. Zool.* 16: 619–628.

Watson, J. S., 1957. Reproduction of the wild rabbit, *Oryctolagus cuniculus* (L.) in Hawke's Bay, New Zealand. *N.Z. Jl Sci. Tech.* B 38: 451–482.

Discussion

Participants: Myers (Author), Huffaker, Jacobs, Pimentel, Southwood, Vlijm and Watson

It seems that at present much of the population change can be explained in terms of the reproductive rate as influenced by the resource of 'food quality', together with mortality due to parasites and predators. It would also seem that space cannot be a limiting resource. Or was space formerly limiting and monitored through behaviour, whereas now available space is restricted through an epidemiological parameter (SOUTHWOOD)?

Mosquitoes which are important in the transmission of myxomatosis occur only rarely in the arid region, hence myxomatosis seems not to be an important controlling factor in the arid environment (PIMENTEL).

Previous to myxomatosis, could the refuge warrens in arid areas maintain much higher densities, and therefore, is the number of refuge warrens limiting (SOUTHWOOD)?

Is it right to look at the heterogeneity of the environment – in relation to the number of rock holes serving as a really secure refuge base for some rabbits – as a primary regulating factor itself rather than as a conditioning factor (HUFFAKER)?

The point is that each population is a case history in itself, and that the variables measured assume different degrees of importance depending upon the environment in which they operate. The different habitats exert their individual effects both on the rabbit itself, and on those biological factors which form important components of its life system. Some factors are density-related; others are not. To this extent it is not possible to generalize other than to reiterate that the rabbit is clearly best adapted to environments akin to that of the mediterranean region.

The ecological situation in the arid zone appears to be simpler than elsewhere in Australia. During drought years warrens in sandy habitats are destroyed, but there is a select group of warrens which remains permanently situated in or near swamps, or in stony habitats with a shrub-steppe vegetation. The number of these warrens seems to bear no relation to present population size. They are fixed components of the environment and are not fully inhabited in drought years. Although a necessary resource, they are not a limiting one. Many of them were probably excavated by the burrowing marsupial, *Bettongia lesueur*. They are deep and cool and assist the rabbit to meet problems related to high loss of body water. The limiting factors are undoubtedly food and water.

After rain when food again becomes plentiful over large areas, rabbits can recolonize the sandy habitats fairly rapidly. In sand, the excavation of new burrows is possible even though predators constitute a formidable obstacle. The numbers of warrens in sand are thus a function of the numbers of rabbits present. In good years, the 'refuge areas' appear to be no more favourable than other areas. The data, in fact, suggest that they support a smaller population than the sandy habitat because of the quality and quantity of food available.

Myxomatosis occurs infrequently in arid zone populations, and thus operates as a dampener of fluctuations rather than as a strong regulator.

In other areas the rabbit faces problems more closely related to the biological aspects of its environment, and in these places the 'refuge areas' are undoubtedly those areas of favourable physical environment which afford special protection from predators and disease. This protection is afforded by direct physical barriers, such as rough, rocky terrain, or climate which is unsuitable for parasites and vectors of disease.

Space per se is certainly not limiting, but the reduced number of warrens now available to the rabbit everywhere forms an obstacle to the recolonization of areas which it occupied prior to the introduction of myxomatosis. In other words, it is difficult for rabbits to build new warrens outside their refuge areas; part of this difficulty is due to the greater ability of predators to kill nestlings in new burrows, which are built as short, shallow stops. Following the drastic reduction in rabbit numbers, the predator population itself is now exerting a sufficient pressure to prevent rabbits from increasing, thus counterbalancing the declining effects of myxomatosis.

I think it is possible that a sudden change in climate may upset the balance now in evidence in a way which will either surfeit the predators or affect in another way their ability to hold the number of rabbits down. Food might then again become the limiting resource (AUTHOR).

In the paper you said that territory size fluctuates greatly, and is not related to food. This could simply be a reflection of population density and have nothing to do with population limitation. It is not clear how territorial behaviour can be a limiting factor unless (a) it is related to space or food (either in quantity or quality) or (b) the emigration rate of less dominant individuals is higher at higher population densities as a result of territorial behaviour of the dominants (WATSON). I did not intend to suggest that territorial behaviour is related to population limitation in the rabbit in Australia. It was shown that the depression of reproduction and enforced emigration of some segments of the population are both results of a reduction in size of territory. Until recently, movements of this nature in Australia usually shunted rabbits from one area to another because of the large amount of favourable habitat available. Under such conditions, territorial behaviour in the rabbit merely structures local populations of a social and gregarious species to permit successful reproduction; it helps to protect nestling young from other members of the same species as well as from other kinds of animal. This pattern of behaviour evolved in another system under selection pressures different from those operating in Australia. It becomes meaningful, ecologically speaking, only if set in its evolutionary context of a heterogeneous environment and complex herbivore-grass predator-prey relationships (AUTHOR).

Are any of the differences observed in length of legs, ears, etc. between rabbits of different areas inherited (PIMENTEL)? There was a tremendous dispersal of rabbits during the last century. How can a genetic gradient arise in the face of such strong mobility? Have rabbits stopped moving about, or are dispersing rabbits prevented from establishing themselves because of rabbits already established (JACOBS)?

Evidence is accumulating that genetic changes are occurring in the different populations under study. The black band in the agouti pattern is becoming larger in the subalpine rabbit and smaller in the semi-arid rabbit. Regnery of Stanford University has measured differences in blood groups between the rabbits in colder and warmer areas. Allen's rule appears to help explain the reason for the observed phenomenon of shorter extremities in the cooler and longer extremities in the hotter climates. More recently, geographic variation in glucose-6-phosphate dehydrogenase concentrations in the blood was established. Although no attempt has been made yet to delineate the genetic component in the variations measured, there is little doubt that we are seeing speciation in action.

Movement of rabbits, on a regional basis now appears to be very limited. Genetic isolation of populations is a reality. The early spread of the rabbit makes sense only in terms of human participation and population growth in an unlimited environment. Neither process operates today (AUTHOR).

Is there any competition for food between rabbits and sheep? Could there be, for example, some areas in which some nutrients are deficient for both but where these are stored in sheep to such an extent that this could effect rabbit populations (VLIJM)? There is little doubt that rabbits and sheep have similar nutritional requirements, and where they coexist they compete very strongly. The ability of the sheep to walk long distances for water gives it a marked advantage over the rabbit in more arid areas. Rabbit populations collapse very quickly in competition with sheep under such conditions. The outcome of such competition in more temperate regions cannot be predicted, but one can suspect that the rabbit in a high class habitat, where food and water are less likely to limit, would be a more formidable adversary; the rabbits' ability to dig for roots would give it a decided advantage there (AUTHOR).

Proc. Adv. Study Inst. Dynamics Numbers Popul. (Oosterbeek, 1970) 507–523

Regulation of numbers in populations of Great Tits (Parus m. major)

H. N. Kluyver

Institute of Ecological Research, Arnhem, the Netherlands

Abstract

Great Tits are territorial songbirds of woods and gardens. They often produce two broods a year. The number of young birds leaving the nest largely outnumbers the annual mortality of adults. Many young die soon after fledging. The early disappearance (mortality or emigration) is greater the later in the season the young are born, when even enough food is available. The late-born young are more inclined to emigrate than the early ones; the more so when the density of early young and parents is higher.

On the island of Vlieland, the artificial reduction of the reproductive capacity (number of eggs laid) to about 40% of the normal value resulted in about a doubling of the annual survival rate of the adults.

The regulation of the population is mainly accomplished in early autumn, i.e. at a time when a shortage of food could not be limiting. The mechanism for this has to be sought in intraspecific strife, rather than in food.

Great Tits are territorial songbirds of woods and gardens. A young tit usually claims its territory in the September after hatching, often very near to the place where it hatched. The settled parents defend their territories succesfully against yearlings and possible immigrants.

The Great Tit is a hole-nesting bird. If we put up enough suitable nestboxes, virtually all pairs present will accept them for breeding. Moreover, a large part of the birds present will use these boxes as a sleeping place in winter.

The Great Tit inhabits oak woods, which are rich in food for tits, up to an average density of 33 pairs per 10 ha. In Scots pine – poor in food – only about 4 pairs per 10 ha are found. The numbers in the two habitats, however, never show any constancy in the course of the years, but fluctuate about an average, showing no significant trend (Fig. 1).

It is this process of the apparent adjustment of population density to carrying capacity, which might be brought about by a density-dependent mechanism. This mechanism is likely to be some form of competition, which either raises mortality and emigration or reduces reproduction and immigration if the population density increases.

We may tackle the problem round these phenomena experimentally by putting the question: Is it possible to demonstrate any correlation between rate of reproduction and rate of survival to population density? If one doubles the mortality of eggs or nestlings, does the population decline to a lower level; or is this increased mortality counterbalanced either by an increased survival of adults as a result of reduced intraspecific competition, or by increased reproduction in the subsequent year, or by both? And if so, what is the mechanism of the processes involved?

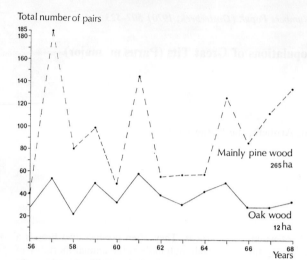

Total number of pairs

Fig. 1. Breeding population of the Great Tit, 1956–1968 in oak and pine wood.
– – – – Hoge Veluwe; 265 ha, mainly pine wood, with some birch, beech and oak; average density: 4 pairs per 10 ha.
——— Liesbos; 12 ha, oak wood; average density: 33 pairs per 10 ha.

Reproduction

I established the role of density-dependence in both reproduction and survival of the Great Tit in a study on the estate ONO (182 ha) by a nearly complete annual census of the pairs present in the breeding season and by ringing all parents as well as nestlings (Kluyver, 1951).

Within one habitat, the frequency of large clutches is higher in years when population density is low than in years when it is high. The difference, however, is small and statistically barely significant. On the other hand, the average clutch-size of first broods is more or less similar in oak and pines, in spite of the fact that the population density in oak is much higher than in pine. Thus, though a high population density tends to decrease clutch-size, an abundant food-supply – as found in oak woods – on the other hand has an increasing effect. In fact, the food factor often predominates.

More important than this density-dependent effect on clutch-size is the effect of density on the number of clutches produced in one breeding season. All pairs start laying in April or May, and the young of these broods leave the nest in late May or early June. After early June, some pairs start a second clutch; more pairs do so in thin populations than in dense ones (Kluyver, 1951, 1966).

However, the numerical contribution of this variability in reproductive rate to the regulation of population density is immaterial, because it only varies a naturally very high progeny surplus. Great Tits usually have clutches of 8–12 eggs, and each pair raises 8 nestlings a year on an average. Reproduction thus amounts to 400% per individual parent per year, whereas the annual mortality of the adults averages only 50%.

This means that there is a large surplus of offspring. To prevent overpopulation a greater part, more that 80% of the individuals fledged, has to die or emigrate at an early stage.

508

Hence, more important than a density-dependent reproduction rate, is a density-dependent survival rate.

Local survival

Perrins (1965) studied the ecology of the Great Tit in a deciduous wood in England where these birds are only single brooded. He is of the opinion that soon after fledging many young suffer severely from a shortage of food. He supposes that it is the survival of the newly fledged late young which determines the size of the breeding population of the next year. He observed that the local recovery percentages of ringed young were smaller the later in the season they were born. Also, the body weight of the young at fledging decreased during this period and he concludes from this that the amount of food available in the habitat decreases at the end of the breeding season.

In Holland, the decrease in the local recovery rate of late hatched young birds is also very striking; as shown in Fig. 2 for pine- and oakwood. This does not coincide, however, with a decrease of the available food supply as is shown for pine woods by L. Tinbergen's study (de Ruiter, 1960, p. 336), from which I made Table 1. The larvae of *Acantholyda* and *Panolis* are both common and highly valued prey of the Great Tit. Expressed as individuals they consitute together with spiders 58 % of the food brought to the young in a pine wood in June and July. Moreover, these prey species increase in size from May until the end of July, more than do the rest of the insect-fauna.

Hence, in pine plantations in Holland a shortage of food for the young is, in general, not probable in June and July. In fact, Kluyver (1950) and Gibb and Betts (1963) showed that in pine woods Great Tit nestlings of the second brood get much more food from their parents than do the nestlings of the first brood. In general, there is enough food available; hence, especially in pine woods, many of the pairs have a second brood immediately after their first one.

In order to study the survival of the young after fledging (expressed as the local recovery

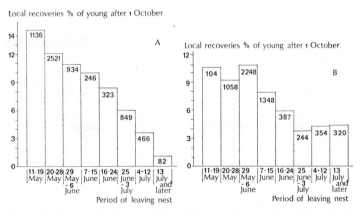

Fig. 2. Period at which young Great Tits left the nest in relation to local recoveries after 1 October. Numbers refer to ringed young.
A. Mainly pine wood; Hoge Veluwe, 1955–1966; coniferous and mixed wood.
B. Oak wood; Liesbos, 1955–1965; deciduous wood.

Table 1. Number of faecal pellets (over 0.6 mm) found by L. Tinbergen c.s. on frass collectors of 0.25 m² in 1954 and 1955 in a plantation of Scots Pine.

Date	Acantholyda		Panolis	
	1954	1955	1954	1955
27–V	0.2		0.0	0.0
7–VI		2.0	0.0	0.4
11–VI	6.3		1.4	
16–VI		3.9		0.0
23–VI	7.1		4.7	
24–VI		7.8		2.8
1–VII	2.8		23.1	
6–VII		12.0		16.9
9–VII	7.1		26.4	
20–VII	39.0	169.0	35.7	134.8
29–VII	33.1	156.4	35.1	110.0
4–VIII		36.9		43.7
6–VIII	31.9		68.7	
11–VIII		10.6		31.5
16–VIII	20.0		51.3	
24–VIII		5.8		18.9
30–VIII	4.7		15.5	
5–IX		4.2		5.4

rate of ringed individuals) I divided the season in two parts; an early period including all first broods ending 15 June, and a late period including the second broods.

Young of the second brood appeared to survive locally less well after fledging than first-brood young; the recovery rate in the breeding area after at least three months averaged 8.75 % for first- and 5.30 % for second-brood young (Table 2; see also Table 7) In all areas under investigation, the difference tended in the same direction. However

Table 2. Ringed fledglings recovered after 1 October at a distance of less than 1 km from the place of hatching.

Area; overgrowth; and years	Young fledging			
	up to 15 June inclusive (early period)		after 15 June (late period)	
	ringed	recovered (%)	ringed	recovered (%)
ONO; mixed; 1935–40, 1946–57	4743	7.3	1867	4.2
Hoge Veluwe; mainly pine; 1955–63	2781	11.6	1367	7.0
Liesbos; oak; 1955–63	3329	9.8	1133	4.3
Kreel-Waterberg; pine; 1955–58	719	7.4	404	5.3
Total	11572	8.75	4771	5.3

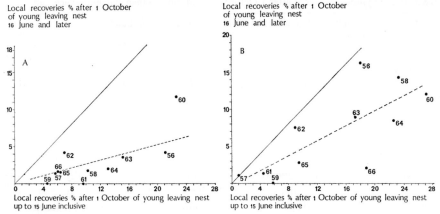

Fig. 3. Local recoveries of early and late hatched young, 1956–1966.
A. Liesbos, oak wood; B. Hoge Veluwe, mainly pine wood.

there was a wide annual variation in these percentages. On Hoge Veluwe (pinewood, Fig. 3B) these values vary from 0.9% to 27.0% for the first brood, and from 0.0% to 16.0% for the second brood; in Liesbos (oakwood, Fig. 3A) from 4.5% to 23.0% for the first brood, and from 0.0% to 11.8% for the second brood.

The annual values for first and second brood were closely correlated, as is seen in the scatter diagrams (for Hoge Veluwe, r = 0.747, P < 0.005, and for Liesbos r = 0.757, P < 0.005). This suggests that for both pine- and oakwood a similar mechanism is determining the local recovery rate of early and late young. Because the young of the second brood leave the nest six weeks later than those of the first brood, and because they find a quite different prey fauna, it is improbable that feeding conditions soon after fledging influence the local recovery of all young equally.

Does the local recovery rate being higher for the young of the first brood point to a smaller local mortality of the young of the first brood? This may partly be true, because the young of the second brood, more than the early nestlings, are parasitized by larvae of the fly *Protocalliphora* which attack the young in the nest. Though the parasitized young do fledge, many of them die soon afterwards (Kluyver, unpublished).

Dispersion

Further, however, the second-brood young disperse on the average farther away than those of the first brood. Dutch Great Tits, in contrast to English ones, are not fully resident. Some of them even undertake trips of up to 500 km in a south-west direction from their birth-place.

In imitation of Dhondt and Hublé (1968) I differentiated between the birds that emigrated and those that were recovered on the place where they hatched. In Table 3 I summarize all our local and distant recoveries of ringed young, grouped into first and second broods. Unfortunately, the percentages are very low because we have to rely on incidental records. Nevertheless they are instructive. The recovery rate in the hatching area is higher for the first-brood young. We now see that for distances up to 4 km the recovery rates for early and late young are equal, but at distances of from 4–25 km and over 25 km the recoveries

Table 3. Ringed young recovered after 1 October at and outside their hatching-place.

Fledging period	Number ringed	Recovered at different distances from hatching-place			
		<1 km	1–4 km	4–25 km	>25 km
Before 16–VI (early)	11572	1013 (87.54⁰/₀₀)	41 (3.54⁰/₀₀)	12 (1.04⁰/₀₀)	11 (0.95⁰/₀₀)
After 15-VI (late)	4771	253 (53.03⁰/₀₀)	16 (3.35⁰/₀₀)	14 (2.93⁰/₀₀)	9 (1.89⁰/₀₀)

of the second-brood young preponderate (both differences are statistically significant). From this one may conclude that the young of the second brood disperse to greater distances. Possibly the urge to disperse is more pronounced. To me, however, it seems more likely that the young of the second brood are the inferiors in territorial quarrels with the young of the first brood which are on the average six weeks older; the second-brood young are expelled by the first-brood young and the older birds from early September onward.

Now, what happens to the second-brood young when few first-brood young are present? In 1955 we had the opportunity to observe this. May and June of this year were abnormally cold and wet and the development of insect larvae was very much retarded. Lack of food for the nestlings of the first brood resulted in a high mortality among them; the number of fledglings leaving the nest was lower than in any other year. Moreover, since the cold weather persisted for another three weeks many of the few first-brood young present most probably died soon after fledging. However, the temperature rose early in July and the second broods developed under normal conditions. Hence, in September 1955 the second-brood young experienced much less competition from the first-brood young than normally. After October, the percentage of local recoveries of the young of the second brood was extremely high, when contrasted with that of the young of the first brood which was below average (Fig. 4). In view of this, I set up an experiment in 'Hoge Veluwe' in 1967 and 1968; I removed up to 90% of the first broods with young on the verge of fledging. This resulted, in 1968 and 1969, in many more second-brood young being recovered as local-born breeding birds – 16% and 18% against an average of 6% in normal years (Fig. 5A).

This proves that it is the number of first-brood young present which determines to a considerable degree the number of second-brood young that are able to remain in the area where they were hatched. The surplus either has to die or to disperse. It has already been shown that, for a large part, they disperse.

In this context, it is of course important that the parents are also present in the area. On the average they have a 50% survival from year to year and moreover they are virtually tenacious to the place where they have once bred.

In Fig. 5B, which is actually the same as Fig. 3B, I have added for each year the number of breeding birds. It is evident that in years with a high number of breeding pairs the percentage of young both of the first and the second brood, locally recovered after 1 October, is low. A low number of breeding birds nearly always corresponds to a high local recovery percentage of the young. The number of breeding pairs present in the years with a low recovery percentage of the young averaged 122, as against 63 in the years with a high recovery percentage. This difference is statistically significant ($0.01 < P < 0.025$).

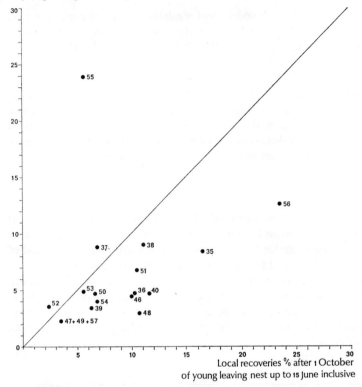

Fig. 4. ONO (Oranje Nassau Oord, Renkum), 1935–1940, 1946–1957. Local recoveries of early and late hatched young.

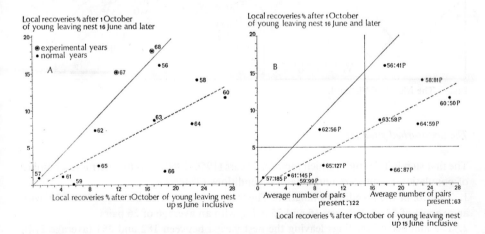

Fig. 5. Local recoveries of early and late hatched young.
A. Hoge Veluwe. Experimental years 1967 and 1968 have been added.
B. The influence of the number of breeding birds. Hoge Veluwe, 1956–1966. P = number of pairs present. See text p. 512 for further explanation.

Density-dependent regulation

These data form a clear case of density-dependent regulation of a local population; i.e. (next to weather, abundance of food and other environmental factors which of course affect the survival rates of young and old Great Tits) it is their own density which acts as a regulative agency.

Owing to the fact that the older and stronger birds expel the younger and weaker ones from the hatching area, a small proportion of the young of both first and second brood are still present in the autumn after a breeding season with many breeding pairs, and more young remain after a breeding season with a low breeding population. The second-brood young being the youngest and weakest are expelled most of all. It is birds in this category which are to be found at larger distances from the place of hatching.

Vlieland

For a further study of these problems, I chose the island of Vlieland (Fig. 6). Vlieland is the most remote of the Dutch Frisian Islands. Its total area amounts to 5000 ha; 292 ha of these are covered by wood suitable for Great Tits. This wooded area is comprised of one large wood covering 214 ha and four small ones of 78 ha together.

Within a distance of 20 km this habitat is surrounded by sand dunes, mudflats and sea, all of which are of course not suitable for tits. Therefore, few immigrants are to be expected. Moreover the woods on Vlieland were not under normal forestry management; i.e. hardly any trees were cut down and replaced by young trees which are unsuitable for tits for the first couple of years.

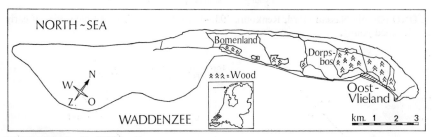

Fig. 6. The island of Vlieland.

The undisturbed situation

The first step in this study, which took four years (1956–1960), was to determine a number of population parameters under natural conditions (Table 4).

1. The size of the breeding population. The total number varied between 32 and 70, with an average of 52, or between 16 and 35 pairs, with an average of 26 pairs.

2. The number of nestlings leaving the nest varied between 182 and 364 (average 274). This means a reproductive rate of 11 young per breeding pair, which is very high for tits.

3. Annual adult local recovery rates averaged 27% on the island, whereas local recovery rates on the continent averaged 50%.

Table 4. Experiment on the regulation of the population in the first 8 years of the investigation on Vlieland

Year n	Breeding birds				Young leaving nest			Year n + 1	Recovered in breeding season n + 1					
	total	ringed	sum	a.av.¹	total	sum	a.av.¹		adults total	sum	yearlings a.av.¹(%)	total	sum	a.av.¹(%)
Normal years														
1956	36	25			219			1957	12			41		
57	70	40	156	39	364	1097	274	58	6	42	27	11	103	9
58	32	31			182			59	12			37		
59	68	60			332			60	12			14		
60	40	38												
Exp. years														
61	68	68			89			61	20			32		
62	54	54	200	50	135	440	110	62	31	104	52	12	88	20
63²	42	41			115			63	27			14		
					101			64	26			30		

¹ Annual average   ² Fledglings taken, not eggs.

4. The annual local recovery rate of ringed nestlings proved to be high, an average of 9%
was observed as contrasted with 4% on the continent.

Reduced reproduction

After these four years of observation I set up an experiment. The number of fledglings was
limited by taking eggs, and the influence of this interference on population density was
studied. The experiment started in 1960 and was continued for four seasons. The fledglings
were reduced to about 40% of the normal average.

What was the effect of this reduction of fledglings on the population? In the subsequent
years, the number of breeding birds stayed at approximately the same level, or even increased somewhat as compared with the normal situation. Furthermore, this lack of
decrease was not due to any increase in the number of unringed immigrants or young
'illegally' born on the island outside the nestingboxes. This percentage remained about the
same, namely 29% and 21%. This means that the artificial birth control must have been
compensated for by an increase in the survival rate of the residents.

The next question is whether it was the survival either of the yearlings or of the adults,
or of both which was effected. Our figures ('black dots' in Fig. 7A) for the yearlings suggest
a negative correlation between the number of fledglings in a certain year n and their recovery rate in the next year $n + 1$. However, the correlation is not statistically significant
$(r = - 0.425, P > 0.05)$. The survival of the adults after having been 27% in the normal
years, rose to 52% in the experimental years.

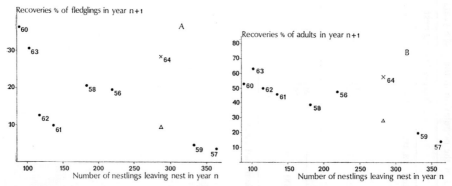

Fig. 7. Vlieland, Great Tit. Number of nestlings leaving their nests in year n, and
A. Recoveries of fledglings in breeding season $n + 1$;
B. Recoveries of adults in breeding season $n + 1$.

Thus, the reduction of the reproduction resulted in a doubling of the annual survival
rate of the adults. This is clearly demonstrated in Fig. 7B. The four black dots at the right
represent the 4 normal years and the group of 4 at the left hand the experimental years
$(r = 0.926, P < 0.0005)$. Thus, the survival of the adults is influenced by the number of
young that the population produced in the preceding breeding season, and in such a way
that a reduced reproduction increases the survival of the adults; in other words, producing
few young raises the chance of an adult's further survival.

516

Increase of carrying capacity

In 1964, I gave the Vlieland Great Tits the opportunity to raise 283 fledglings in order to see if the recovery-rate of adults would indeed mount up to about 27%, as was to be expected from the graph in Fig. 5B ('triangle'). To my amazement this was not the case. By 1965 the breeding population had risen to twice the maximum number in any of the preceding years. The percentage of recoveries of adults rose to 58% ('cross'). The yearlings also showed a much larger rate of recovery than was to be expected (Fig. 5A).

At first I could not explain this unexpected phenomenon. One striking point, however, was that the increase was not due to a higher immigration of 'foreigners', but was entirely due to a better survival of yearlings and of old autochtons of Vlieland.

After this the birds were allowed to reproduce undisturbed for another two years, after which, once more, the number of young was limited to about 40%.

Meanwhile, I found the solution of the puzzling increment of the tit population. It was due to a sudden and considerable improvement of the habitat for Great Tits. In 1961 a new forester had succeeded his predecessor and, contrary to expectation, after one year he started to thin out a part of the woods by cutting down many of the thirty-year old conifers. As a result of this, many small oaks which had been planted simultaneously with the conifers or a few years afterwards, but which had never grown up through lack of light, now got more light and grew up luxuriously improving the Great Tit habitat and thus increasing the carrying capacity of the wood for this bird. Fig. 8 shows the number of pairs which occupied the nesting-boxes in the thinned and the unmanaged parts of the woods; the number doubled in the former part but did not change in the latter.

The intensification of the thinning-campaign took several years, culminating in 1963–64. The course of the Great Tit population with natural and limited numbers of young before, and after the intensified thinning is summarized in Table 5. The better survival of both young and old tits in untreated woods during the years with restricted production of young is clearly visible; survival of yearlings increased from 9% to 17%, that of the adults from 27% to 49%. Moreover, both yearlings and adults showed a high survival in the years with intensive thinning of the wood, but normal reproduction; the recovery percentages increasing from 9% to 14% for the yearlings and from 27% to 42% for the adults. These increases are doubtless due to an increase in the carrying capacity of the habitat.

Number of pairs breeding

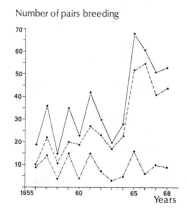

Fig. 8. Vlieland. Number of pairs occupying the nest-boxes in the thinned and the unmanaged parts of the woods.
—— total numbers;
– – – – numbers in the part where woods were thinned in 1963 and later (214 ha);
–.–.–. numbers in the part where woods were not thinned in 1963 and later (78 ha).

517

Table 5. Vlieland: Yearlings and adults ringed in the breeding season and the percentage recoveries in the next breeding season, classified in years before and during intense thinning of the woods and in normal years and years in which reproduction was reduced to 40% of normal. Recorvery percentages have been calculated from the totals for the three or four corresponding years.

Structure of wood	4 (resp. 3) normal years		3 years reprod. + 40%		χ^2	Significance
	ringed	recovered	ringed	recovered		
Yearlings						
untreated	56/57:219 57/58:364 58/59:182 59/60:332 } 1097	41 11 37 14 } 103 = 9%	60/61: 89 61/62:135 62/63:115 } 339	32 12 14 } 58 = 17%	14.674	P < 0.001
thinned	64/65:283 65/66:526 66/67:383 } 1239	81 53 34 } 168 = 14%	63/64:101 67/68:157 68/69:162 } 418	30 25 27 } 82 = 20%	8.394	P < 0.005
χ^2 Significance	8.981 P < 0.005		0.745 P > 0.30			
Adults						
untreated	56/57:25 57/58:40 58/59:31 59/60:60 } 156	12 6 12 12 } 42 = 27%	60/61:38 61/62:68 62/63:54 } 160	20 31 27 } 78 = 49%	15.997	P < 0.001
thinned	64/65:55 65/66:137 66/67:120 } 312	32 52 47 } 131 = 42%	63/64:41 67/68:104 68/69:103 } 248	26 52 43 } 121 = 49%	2.544	P > 0.10
χ^2 Significance	10.108 P < 0.005		0.034 P > 0.80			

As expected, the increase in the number of breeding birds obviously lagged behind the improvement of the habitat. In 1963/64 no increase took place, whereas it demonstrated itself most clearly in the figures for 1964/65 (see Table 5 and Fig. 8).

In years with reduced reproduction, the recovery percentages of the yearlings only increased from 17% to 20%, while for the adults it was 49% in both untreated and thinned wood. Probably this means that in thinned wood the percentage survival had nearly reached its maximum.

Dhondt (1970, p. 84) established the important influence of air temperature during the breeding season on the percentage of survival of the young after leaving the nest. On Vlieland the breeding seasons of 1956, 1960 and 1964 were relatively warm (Maandelijks overzicht der weersgesteldheid in Nederland, 1957–68) and, indeed, it was the young born in these seasons which showed the highest recoveries in the next season. This points to the probability that the recovery percentage of the yearlings was influenced not only by the number of young produced and by the improvement of the habitat, but also by the air-temperature in the preceding breeding season.

Clearly, a better survival of the adults must alter the age-composition of the breeding population. In fact this can be demonstrated convincingly through a comparison of the age-composition of the breeding populations of 1959, 1960 and 1966, 1967 – the years immediately preceding each of the two experimental interferences – with 1963, 1964and 1968, 1969 respectively, which were the last years of each experimental period (Table 6). Only the last experimental years are of interest for this comparison, because in the first experimental years the birds had not yet had the opportunity to reach an older age. During the normal years, first and second-year birds together formed 87% of the population; during the experimental years they constitute only 62%, whereas the higher age classes formed 14% of the population in the normal against 38% in the experimental years.

Table 6. Age composition of the breeding population on Vlieland in normal and experimental years.

Age (year)	Normal years						Experimental years					
	1959	1960	1966	1967	sum	%	1963	1964	1968	1969	sum	%
1	34	12	56	35	137	50	14	26	26	27	93	36
2	10	13	40	37	100	37	9	11	30	16	66	26
3	2	0	6	16	24	9	10	6	23	12	51	20
4	0	0	4	3	7	3	5	4	11	11	31	12
5	1	0	3	3	5	2	2	4	3	6	15	6
Sum					273	101					256	100

The absence of regulation in the breeding season

Now, why is it that a repression of the reproduction lengthened the average life both of the adults and of each new generation that was produced?

As to the second point the improvement in the survival of the yearlings Gibb (1950) has shown that, in England, nestlings in large broods show competition for the food brought in by the parents to such an extent that per individual the young in the large broods get less food than those in the small broods. In large broods, the parents are unable to cover the total need for food of the young. At fledging, a young from a large brood weighs less than one from a small brood. Moreover, during the winter Perrins (1965) retrapped relatively less young from large broods than from small broods. Therefore, he assumed quite rightly that a higher percentage of the large-brood young dies shortly after leaving the nest. Is it possible to explain the better survival of the young during the experimental years along this line?

In normal years great differences in brood-size exist. There are a few with 1–3 young, many in the middle groups of 4–6 and 7–9 young and less of 10–12 young. In the experimental years, the latter two groups fell out because in most broods egg number was reduced to 3 or 4. Table 7 summarizes for the normal years the percentages of recovery of young from broods of different sizes, differentiated into early and late fledging period.

Table 7. Number of young of different brood sizes ringed in the breeding season and recovered after 1 October on Vlieland in normal years

Ringed per brood	Fledged up to 15 June		Fledged after 15 June	
	ringed	recovered (%)	ringed	recovered (%)
1– 3 young	30	30	42	14
4– 6 young	277	29	319	12
7– 9 young	865	30	399	14
10–12 young	285	32	60	12

It is clear from these data that the young from the smaller broods had no better survival than those from the larger broods.

In 1963 we reduced reproduction by taking young immediately before fledging; previously we had taken eggs. During the complete nestling period the 101 young which left the nest had endured the normal competition of their fellow nestlings. Yet their recovery percentage in 1964 was the highest but one of the whole series of observations.

All these figures give no indication whatever that young from a small brood would have a higher post-fledging survival than those from a large brood. This is the reason why, in my opinion, the better survival of the yearlings in the experimental years was due not to reduced competition during the nestling period, but to reduced competition in the period after they had left the nest.

With respect to the adults, it may be supposed that the rearing of many nestlings might exhaust the parents so that their chance of subsequent survival was decreased. Our figures concerning this aspect are summarized in Table 8.

Table 8. Vlieland. Recovery of adults between 1 October and 31 December of normal breeding years, according to the size of brood they had reared.

Brood size	0	1–4	5–6	7–8	9–10	11–12	13–14	15–16	17–21	0–21
Adults ($\female + \male$) ringed	3	41	70	131	74	40	31	25	21	436
Adults recovered	0	21	43	68	40	24	14	8	5	223
Recovered (%)	–	51	61	52	54	60	45	32	24	51

The survival of parents in the undisturbed population (i.e. with the complete range of numbers of seasonal offspring) was 51%, that of parents with a total offspring of 7–21 young (first and second broods together) was 49% and those with 0–6 young was 56%. Hence, when in the experimental situation we left the parents only 6 or less young to rear the average recovery percentage of all adults was expected to increase only from 51% to 56%. However, as a result of our experimental interference, the recovery rate of the adults increased to about twice the value found for the normal years (see Table 9). Therefore, it is concluded that the better survival of the adults resulting from the experiment has to be attributed not only to a greater ease in feeding a smaller number of young, but also, and even to a greater extent, to some other factor coming into action, viz. intra-specific competition after the breeding season is over.

Table 9. Vlieland: Yearlings and adults ringed in the breeding season and present in the next December classified in years before and during intense thinning of the woods, and in normal years and years in which reproduction was reduced to 40% of normal.

Structure of wood	3 normal years		3 years reprod. ± 40%		χ^2	Significance
	ringed	recovered	ringed	recovered		
Yearlings						
untreated	'56: no December inspection					
	'57: 364 ⎫	14 ⎫	'60: 89 ⎫	37 ⎫		
	'58: 182 ⎬ 878	26 ⎬ 57 = 6%	'61: 135 ⎬ 339	14 ⎬ 74 = 22%	59.901	P < 0.001
	'59: 332 ⎭	17 ⎭	'62: 115 ⎭	23 ⎭		
thinned	'64: 283 ⎫	74 ⎫	'63: 101 ⎫	33 ⎫		
	'65: 526 ⎬ 1239	61 ⎬ 176 = 14%	'67: 157 ⎬ 418	37 ⎬ 97 = 23%	18.407	P < 0.001
	'66: 383 ⎭	41 ⎭	'68: 162 ⎭	29 ⎭		
χ^2		31.269		0.223		
Significance		P < 0.001		P > 0.50		
Adults						
untreated	'56: no December inspection					
	'57: 40 ⎫	6 ⎫	'60: 38 ⎫	22 ⎫		
	'58: 31 ⎬ 131	13 ⎬ 34 = 26%	'61: 68 ⎬ 161	36 ⎬ 91 = 57%	28.807	P < 0.001
	'59: 60 ⎭	15 ⎭	'62: 55 ⎭	33 ⎭		
thinned	'64: 55 ⎫	43 ⎫	'63: 41 ⎫	31 ⎫		
	'65: 137 ⎬ 312	76 ⎬ 193 = 62%	'67: 104 ⎬ 248	72 ⎬ 177 = 71%	5.514	P < 0.02
	'66: 120 ⎭	74 ⎭	'68: 103 ⎭	74 ⎭		
χ^2		47.543		9.581		
Significance		P < 0.001		P < 0.005		

Regulation in autumn

We know from recoveries in autumn and winter that the size of the breeding population is determined before the winter sets in. In late autumn and winter many Great Tits sleep in nestboxes. By one night inspection of all boxes in the early winter (preferably in December before the frost sets in) we get a reliable random sample of the birds present, though not a complete census as is the case in the breeding season. These samples when taken each year in exactly the same way are comparable. The results of these night-inspections are given in Table 9.

Before the extensive thinning of the habitat, we found 6% of the ringed young sleeping in the boxes in December of normal years compared with 22% in the experimental years. For the years after the wood had improved (through thinning) the values were 14% and 23% respectively. This means that the surplus of young in normal years had already been eliminated by December.

The effect of the improvement of the habitat on the yearlings was clearly visible in the normal years (6% against 14%) but not in the experimental years (22% against 23%). Most probably 22% was near to the maximum survival possible. There is evidence that there is a high percentage mortality immediately after fledging (Perrins, 1965, p. 633).

The recovery rate of the adults, however, was clearly influenced positively by the improvement of the habitat in both situations; it increased from 26% to 62% in the normal years and from 57% to 71% in the experimental years. All of these differences are statistically significant.

Hence, a density dependent determination of population level in the Great Tit takes place in the period between fledging of the young (i.e. from May to June) and December.

The agency active in regulation

Both the improvement of the habitat, by a thinning-out of conifers which resulted in an increase of the carrying capacity for the Great Tits, and the reduction of their reproduction, by which fewer individuals, parents as well as young, had to be dislodged, influenced the number of breeding birds. This regulation of numbers is effected in autumn, i.e. at a season when the birds presumably do not suffer from any lack of food. They do suffer from a certain lack of food in winter, the season when they often visit the feeding places erected for them by bird loving people. Thus, in autumn the birds anticipate the maximum number of pairs which the habitat can sustain optimally in the future.

The fact that this regulation does not take place in winter, but has already taken place in autumn, is of importance in view of the theory of population regulation. Especially in the last few years there has been a brisk discussion going on in Great Britain in which Lack (1966) stands for the idea that regulation is the outcome of direct competition for food, during which the weaker part of the population is eliminated through undernourishment. Contrary to this concept Wynne-Edwards (1962) believes that population regulation in birds and other higher animals takes place before any lack of food becomes evident; he assumes, that the regulatory mechanism acts by intensifying the mutual aggressiveness among the individuals as the habitat becomes overpopulated. An intensification of emigration will be the consequence. This emigration results in the arrival of many individuals at unsuitable places, where many of them die. Wynne-Edwards is of the opinion that this is an adaptation of the species to prevent the undernourishment of all of the individuals, which would come into force if the regulation process was delayed until the lack of food actually arose.

In the Great Tit, winter is doubtless the season of the severest lack of food. Hard winters, which require a high metabolism, often take a heavy toll of the tit population. Most probably this toll is positively correlated with the density of the tits, though up to now this is uncertain; and if so, it is not the only process acting. Our December inspections showed that population regulation has already been accomplished before the winter sets in. This indicates that Wynne-Edwards' theory may also be applicable. The results of our investigation on Vlieland allude to the probability that the mechanism of population regulation in this bird has to be sought, at least partly, in intra-specific strife. Population regulation proved to be highly influenced especially by strife, in early autumn, a season when food is still abundant.

In view of this strife, the composition of the population in September is of interest; it is the numerical ratios of adults, juveniles from the first brood and those from the second brood which are important factors in the regulation process.

I do not give an opinion on how this form of regulation may have come into being. I do not endorse Wynne-Edwards's view that this must be due to group selection, but I agree with Wiens's (1966) opinion that 'the theory of population regulation through social mechanisms advanced by Wynne-Edwards is certainly worthy of much serious study, and it should not be discarded simply because it appears to rely on group selection'.

References

Anonymus, 1955–1969. Maandelijks overzicht der weersgesteldheid in Nederland. Koninklijk Nederlands Meteorologisch Instituut no. 94a.

Dhondt, A., 1970. De regulatie der aantallen in Gentse koolmeespopulaties (*Parus m.major* L.). Verh. tot het behalen van de graad van doctor in de Wetenschappen, Rijksuniversiteit Gent, pp. 169.

Dhondt, A. & J. Hublé, 1968. Fledging-date and sex in relation to dispersal in young Great Tits. *Bird Study* 15: 127–134.

Gibb, J., 1950. The breeding biology of the great and blue titmice. *Ibis* 92: 507–539.

Gibb, J., 1954. Feeding ecology of tits, with notes on treecreeper and goldcrest. *Ibis* 96: 513–543.

Gibb, J. & M. M. Betts, 1963. Food and food supply of nestling tits (Paridae) in breckland pine. *J, Anim. Ecol.* 32: 489–533.

Kluyver, H. N., (1950). Daily routines of the great tit, *Parus m. major* L. *Ardea* 38: 99–135.

Kluyver, H. N., 1951. The population ecology of the great tit, *Parus m. major* L. *Ardea* 39: 1–135.

Kluyver, H. N., 1966. Regulation of a bird population. *Ostrich* 38, Suppl. 6: 389–396.

Lack, D., 1966. Population studies of birds. Oxford.

Perrins, C. M., 1965. Population fluctuations and clutch-size in the great tit, *Parus major* L. *J. Anim. Ecol.* 34: 601–647.

de Ruiter, L., 1960. Appendix (In L. Tinbergen, The natural control of insects in pine woods). *Archs. néerl. Zool.* XIII: 336–343.

Wiens, J. A., 1966. On group selection and Wynne-Edwards' hypothesis. *Am. Scient.* 54: 273–287.

Wynne-Edwards, V.C., 1962. Animal dispersion in relation to social behaviour. Edinburgh and London.

Discussion

This paper is discussed, together with Perrins's and Dhondt's papers, on p. 544.

Proc. Adv. Study Inst. Dynamics Numbers Popul. (Oosterbeek, 1970) 524–531

Population studies of the Great Tit, Parus major

C. M. Perrins

Edward Grey Institute, Botanic Garden, Oxford, England

Abstract

Among the factors known to affect populations of the Great Tit, those which are reasonably well established include:

1. Clutch size. This is adaptive, inherited and can be modified in response to the environment (the ability to respond to change is also adaptive and, presumably, inherited).
2. The survival of the young. This is the main factor causing the year to year changes in numbers; the period shortly after they leave the nest seems to be critical. The variations in mortality are probably caused by variations in the food supply.
3. Spring territorial behaviour. This has the effect of limiting the density in optimal habitats, but it does not act in a density-dependent fashion nor, apparently, does it result in 'outcast' birds that are unable to breed at all.

Clutch size and hatching success are the only factors which have so far been shown to vary in a density-dependent fashion; these are sufficient for regulation.

Points that are very poorly understood include:

1. The general ecology of the young birds after they have left the nest. A fuller study of the food at this time is necessary as is, if possible, the discovery of the link between juvenile survival and the beech crop.
2. The proximate mechanism whereby the clutch size is adjusted in relation to density.
3. The relative importance of different factors in different populations; since the densities of breeding birds vary markedly between populations. This is illustrated in particular, by the relatively greater number of young raised on the Continent, and by the higher winter mobility of Continental compared with British birds.

This paper summarizes some of the factors known to affect changes in numbers in populations of the Great Tit, together with some of the more recent findings in the study made at Oxford, England. For fuller details of earlier work see Kluyver (1951), Lack (1966) and Perrins (1965).

The Great Tit is a very common species of small passerine, it is largely resident and is territorial in the breeding season. It nests readily in nesting boxes where the young are relatively safe from predators (compared at least with species in open cup nests); hence not only can the nests be easily found, but large numbers of young birds can be ringed for study of survival rates. In addition, the adults can be easily caught as they visit the nesting boxes and do not normally desert as a result of this disturbance. As a consequence, many workers in Europe have made studies of this species. This paper is concerned primarily with a study of the bird in Oxford, and it is necessary to point out two main differences between the British birds and those that breed in Continental Europe. First, the latter birds (a named race *Parus major major*, which is some 15% lighter in weight than the British *P. m. newtoni*) show more tendency to move about during the winter than their British counterpart; in some winters, a proportion of the population may undertake irruptive movements on a large scale (Ulfstrand, 1962; Perrins, 1966). Secondly, the Continental birds have a higher tendency to have second broods than the British race; in consequence, more young are usually raised per pair on the Continent than in Britain.

Since the annual adult mortality in the two areas is similar, it follows that, in a stable population, more young must die before reaching breeding age in the former than the latter area. Consequently one might expect any possible competition for necessary resources to be more intense on the Continent than in Britain.

Population fluctuations

Some broad generalisations can be made from those censuses of Great Tit numbers that have been made over long periods in different parts of Europe. Firstly, there is a tendency for at least some of the major changes in numbers to occur simultaneously over wide areas of Europe. In 1961, for example, high breeding numbers were recorded from Sweden to southern Germany and from Britain to Poland. Hence, at least the major changes observed in the relatively small study areas are meaningful in the sense that they are not random changes in small populations, but indicative of changes that have occurred over much wider areas.

The numbers of Great Tits in a study area show marked changes from year to year – though these are small compared with changes in numbers of other animal groups such as some insects (see e.g. Kluyver, 1951, p. 113). There is no sign of a regular 'cycle' in these fluctuations, but there is a marked tendency for the population to decline in numbers the year following a sharp rise in numbers.

Only one striking correlation has been shown between changes in numbers and any changes in the habitat. Spring numbers tend to be higher than those in the previous year when there has been a good crop of beech seed *Fagus sylvatica* in the intervening winter; conversely breeding numbers tended to be lower than in the previous year after winters when there was no crop of beech seed (Perrins, 1965). Since the beech never has good crops of seeds in successive years – but may have in alternate years – the supply of seed available in winter for the birds may be the cause of the, at times, regular oscillations in numbers of Great Tits. Further, the fruiting of the beech is greatly affected by climatic conditions (Matthews, 1963) and tends to be synchronised over large areas of Europe; this could be responsible for the synchronous changes in numbers of Great Tits over this area. A similar correlation of changes in numbers with the beech crop is found in the Blue Tit, *Parus caeruleus*.

Two points, however, show that the relationship cannot be wholly causal. The birds feed heavily on the seed when it is available, but there are areas where beech does not occur in which the Great Tits also show fluctuations synchronous with those where there is beech. Further, the survival of the young (see below) varies markedly from year to year and the critical period for the young appears to come before the seed is available for them, yet their chances of survival are correlated with the crop of beech. The crops of many other species of fruiting tree and shrub occur in the same years as those of the beech (Hyde, 1963) because, at least in part, they are all influenced by the same climatic factors (Matthews, 1963). Hence, it seems possible that the survival of young Great Tits in areas where beech does not occur, and in the period before the beech seeds are available, is influenced by the fruiting of other trees. The beech crop, therefore, can only be considered as an indicator of general food abundance.

As mentioned, the proportion of the young which survive after leaving the nest has a marked effect on the annual changes in breeding numbers. Perrins (1965) produced evidence pointing to the probability that much of this mortality occurred shortly after the birds left the nest and might be related to the food supply at this time. In a recent reanalysis of some of the Great Tit data, Krebs (1970) showed that the juvenile loss (Krebs' k_4) after leaving the nest was the 'key factor' (Varley and Gradwell, 1960). If the data for one year was excluded, Krebs was unable to show satisfactorily that this large mortality could be related to density[1]. Neither the proportion of young which survive from the time of leaving the nest until autumn, nor the proportion that survive from autumn until the following spring (see Krebs, 1970, Fig. 4a and 4b), seem to be affected by density. However, since the population tends to be low in the year prior to a beech crop (because there was no crop for the birds in the preceding winter) and, conversely, high prior to a winter without a beech crop (because often there was crop in the preceding winter), there is at least some tendency for numbers to decline when high and rise when low. Hence, since it may be said that the 'carrying capacity' of the habitat changes from year to year, caution must be exercised in relation to calculations as to whether density-dependent mortality does or does not occur.

Krebs (1970) also measured the k-values for several other components of the reproductive rate: namely, the variation in clutch size, the egg mortality and the nestling mortality. These were calculated in the following manner:

$$\text{variation in clutch size} = k_1 = \log \frac{(\text{potential maximum clutch}^2 + 2)N}{(\text{observed clutch} + 2)N}$$

$$\text{egg mortality} = k_2 = \log \frac{(\text{clutch} + 2)N}{(\text{hatched} + 2)N}$$

$$\text{chick mortality} = k_2 = \log \frac{(\text{hatched} + 2)N}{(\text{fledged} + 2)N}$$

The variation in clutch size was measured because the mean clutch varies markedly from year to year; the highest recorded figure being a mean of 12.3 in 1948 and the lowest a mean of 7.8 in 1951. Hence, in many years the Great Tit lays a smaller clutch than that which, at least at other times, it is capable of laying (see also Southern (1970) for an example of a species in which eggs – particularly whole clutches – not laid have a major effect on reproductive rate). It has been shown by many workers, starting with Tollenaar (1922), that various factors affect the size of the clutch, and Krebs' analysis confirms that clutch size is markedly affected by the density of breeding pairs. Reduction of the clutch by 5 eggs lessens the period for which the nest is at risk to predation by about 10%.

[1] The plot of k_4 on initial populations was just significant, but was only so because of one point. If this one point were removed, the remaining 20 points show no significant relationship; hence, the biological importance of the correlation seems highly questionable. Statistically, such a plot is not a convincing demonstration without others (see Southwood, 1966, p. 303) which, in this case, showed no significance.

[2] Arbitrary value which does not affect future calculations.

While Krebs was unable to show any effect of breeding density on the mortality of the nestlings, he demonstrated that egg losses were related to density. This was apparently due not to a higher rate of 'infertility' with increase in density, but to an increase in the number of nests taken by predators as the number of breeding pairs increased. Krebs suggested that this was because the predators (weasels, *Mustela nivalis*) are more likely to take a nest if they have already found another one nearby. Hence the higher the density (= the closer the nests) and the larger the clutch, the greater the chance that the nest will be taken.

As density increases, the smaller clutches and increased predation lead to fewer young being raised per pair (Kluyver, 1951, and Lack, 1964). These authors pointed out that, although many fewer young per pair were raised in years of high breeding densities, the total number of young produced per unit area was larger in years of high than low density; the reduction in reproductive rate did not compensate for the increase in the number of breeding pairs. In addition, Perrins (1965) showed that the main losses of young occurred after they had left the nest and, although very variable, was not apparently related to density; therefore it seemed that the smaller variations in the numbers of young leaving the nest were not likely to be important.

Krebs has challenged this view. He calculated the survival for each year using the relevant figures derived from: 1. the density-dependent effects on clutch size (k_1); 2. the density-dependent effects on hatching success (k_2); 3. the average mortality from hatching to fledging (k_3 treated as a constant); 4. the average mortality from fledging to breeding the following year (k_4) (also treated as a constant); and 5. the average annual mortality of the adults. Using these data in a model for an imaginary population of 60 pairs, Krebs (Fig. 3) showed that the numbers in the population declined rapidly at first and then levelled off at a number not far from the average observed in the study area. Hence, the variations in clutch size and hatching success may be extremely important in the regulation of the numbers of Great Tits even though they precede even larger losses which occur after the young have left the nest.

Krebs showed that stability is achieved even more rapidly if mortality after leaving the nest is also density-dependent. However, such additional density-dependent mortality may not be necessary for regulating the breeding numbers in the population, since that occurring up to the point of leaving the nest is sufficient to do so. At first sight it may seem surprising that regulation can be achieved in spite of more young being raised per unit area under conditions of high than of low density. However, only a relatively small number of the young survive to breed. For stability to occur, enough young must survive to replace those adults which die each year (some 50%). As the breeding population increases the number of young raised per breeding adult decreases so that, at the higher densities, the number raised becomes insufficient to produce an average of 0.5 surviving young per adult: the figure needed to maintain a stable population. This statement is, of course, only true on average since stability of the form shown in Krebs' figure is not observed in nature but, rather, quite wide oscillations occur around it. This is because the observed survival rates vary quite widely about the average figures which Krebs used as constants; this does not affect the arguments put forward here.

Clutch size

As mentioned above, the mean clutch of the Great Tit varies markedly in relation to the density of breeding pairs. However, clutch size is also known to vary in relation to the age of the female, the habitat in which the birds are breeding and the date at which they lay. Perrins (1965) provided evidence that the survival of the young birds tended to be higher under those conditions when higher clutches were laid and suggested that such variations in clutch size were adaptive. It has also been shown (Lack et al., 1957; Perrins, 1965) that there is evidence that the most productive clutch was often that which was most frequently laid; hence, the clutch size observed must be a result of natural selection favouring maximum production of young.

For this last statement to be true, at least some of the variation in size of clutch must be inherited from the parents. Perrins and Jones (in prep.) have recently shown that, when the known effects of the environmental factors mentioned above have been allowed for, the clutches laid by the same individuals in successive years have a lower variance than that of those laid by the population as a whole – in other words, successive clutches of an individual tend to be similar in size. Further, the correlation between the clutch size of mothers and those of their daughters accounts for about half the tendency of each individual to have a consistent size of clutch. Hence clutch size is inherited. However, since individuals lay clutches of different sizes under different conditions, the inherited tendency cannot be to lay a fixed number of eggs but, rather, to vary the clutch about a certain mean. Thus, a female which lays clutches that are above the average for prevailing conditions is likely to produce young that lay clutches which are also above average size regardless of the conditions.

The most common number of eggs laid by the individuals in a population will correspond to the most productive clutch size only if there is no differential mortality of females that lay clutches of different sizes. If, for example, birds that raised larger broods suffered higher mortality than those which raised smaller ones, then selection would tend to favour the production of smaller broods. However, analysis of survival rates of females from one breeding season to the next in relation either to their initial clutch size or to the number of young actually raised give no indication of such differential mortality (Perrins, unpublished). The only breeding birds that had a lower than average chance of survival were those which failed to raise a brood at all and, since most broods that fail do so because they are taken by predators, the most likely explanation for this is that some of the females of such broods are also taken by the predators at the same time.

Territorial behaviour

Some Great Tits, particularly adults (birds that have bred in previous seasons), take up territories during the autumn, largely relinquish them during winter (October-January) and take them up again during warmer weather in spring (February–May). Other birds, particularly first-year ones, do not appear to take up territories in the autumn, but remain in flocks during this period. During the winter though they may roost in their territories, many move out of them to feed over a much wider area of woodland; they may come into gardens to feed at bird tables.

Since the density of breeding pairs varies markedly from year to year, it follows that the birds hold territories of different sizes in different years. However, at least in some years when the density is low, there may be areas of suitable but unoccupied woodland between territories (Hinde, 1952). In woodland, territorial pairs removed by Krebs (1971) in spring were quickly replaced by other, mainly first-year, birds moving in from territories in adjacent hedgerows which were, presumably, of poorer quality (breeding success is lower in such places). The vacated territories in the hedge rows were not refilled. Preliminary observations with Great Tits caught in another area of woodland and moved into the study area in spring (Perrins, unpublished), showed that some of these birds (of both sexes) settled to breed in the area where they were released. However, it was not possible to observe whether they took up territories between established birds or whether they evicted these.

At present, it appears that territorial behaviour results in spacing the birds and causing some to breed in poorer habitats (see also Kluyver and Tinbergen, 1953) but, at least in the spring, does not prevent any birds from obtaining a territory. Whether or not one considers that this behaviour has any density-limiting effect, depends entirely on the area which one is talking about. If one considers only the compact areas of woodland within the estate, some birds are prevented by the territorial behaviour of others, from breeding there. If, on the other hand, one considers the whole estate, which includes large areas of hedgerows and other marginal habitat, all birds appear to get territories; therefore, territorial behaviour does not limit the total number of birds in optimal and suboptimal habitats taken together. It would be of considerable interest to know what would happen if there were no suboptimal habitat. Would some birds be forced out of the population altogether, or would they try harder and so get themselves territories in the better habitats?

Further support for the suggestion that territorial behaviour may not limit breeding numbers comes from the fact that the mortality from the time the young leave the nest until the next spring (see above Krebs 1970, Fig. 2d and p. 320) does not appear to be density-dependent. In calculating this mortality, birds that survive, but failed to obtain territories would be represented as lost. Hence, one would expect that, if territory limited the numbers that could settle to breed, a greater proportion of birds would be excluded from holding territories in years of high breeding density, and therefore that such a calculation would show a density-dependent relationship. That this cannot be shown may be because the data are inadequate or because territorial behaviour results in the exclusion of a constant proportion of the birds regardless of actual numbers, but were it to have a strong density-dependent effect one might have expected it to show up in such calculations.

If territorial behaviour spaces but does not limit the number of Great Tits, what is its function? Krebs (1971) has shown that the further a pair of birds nest from the next pair, the more likely they are to raise their young; he suggests that the function of territory may be simply to obtain the maximum spacing possible in order to reduce the risk of predation.

Since it appears that the key factor causing the changes in numbers from year to year is the survival of the young shortly after they leave the nest in mid-summer, a more detailed study of the survival in the post-fledging period is needed. If large numbers survive to this point, the breeding population is likely to be high the following year, but the total number raised per pair to the point of fledging is largely dependent on the breeding success which is, in turn, greatly affected by the number of breeding pairs in the area.

The fact that the tendency to lay a clutch of a certain size is partly inherited as well as influenced by enivronmental factors, means that the average clutch in a certain area, or in a certain year, will be influenced by the breeding success in the area previously. If, for example, large broods are more successful than smaller ones for a series of years, then birds tending to lay large broods will become progressively more common and the average clutch size will rise. Although there is some tendency for birds to move from place to place, the average distance moved between the birth place and the place of breeding is small, and in any one area a proportion of the birds will have been raised in that place;

529

hence, one factor affecting the mean clutch in any area will be the recent effects of natural selection for the most productive brood size.

It is necessary, therefore, to ask why the birds vary their clutch in relation to varying conditions, and what is the mechanism whereby they achieve this variation? As mentioned above, Perrins (1965) provided evidence that some of the variation in clutch size could be related to the chances of raising young and was therefore adaptive; older, more successful breeders lay larger clutches than younger inexperienced birds and are more successful in raising them. In addition, birds have larger clutches in richer than in poorer woodland since the chances of raising the young there are greater; they also lay larger clutches early than late in the season, since there is more food available then and the young can be raised more easily. However, the evidence is less good for the reduction of clutch size with increase in density being adaptive. Such an adaptation is suggested, mainly, by the data for one year with exceptionally high density of breeding pairs, in which parents not only had difficulty feeding their young but also there was an unusually high nestling mortality.

However Kluyver (1966, and in preparation) has recently made two important series of experiments which clearly demonstrate that some form of interaction occurs between young after they leave the nest and, at about the same time, between young and adults; whatever this interaction is, it has a very important effect on the survival of the birds. Since food is scarcer at this time, the parents may find it harder to care for their young after they have left the nest than when they are in the nest. Royama (1966) has also provided evidence to suggest that this period may be the most critical. However, it is not easy to make accurate measurements of all the many components which contribute to the mortality at this time of year. The large, apparently density-independent, mortality that occurs shortly after the young become independent of their parents obscures any density-related processes which might be occurring at the same time.

At the present stage of our knowledge of the Great Tit, it is not easy to speculate on the mechanism whereby a bird lays a clutch of a different size under different conditions. However, it seems unlikely that the birds are normally prevented from laying more eggs because they are short of food. The birds must collect most of the food necessary to form the eggs during the laying period and, with the possible exception of limitation by some essential trace element, the amount of food they have stored at the start of laying does not seem likely to control the number of eggs laid. Further, if the nest of a bird is taken by a predator, it quickly lays another clutch and the total number of eggs laid is considerably larger than the average clutch. Hence, the number of eggs laid in the clutch appears to be a result of a positive reaction of the bird rather than to the birds simply running short of resources. If so the mechanism is entirely unknown, though important to the understanding of the regulation of numbers in the Great Tit.

References

Hinde, R. A., 1952. The behaviour of the Great Tit (*Parus major*) and some other related species. *Behaviour* Suppl. 2: 1–201.

Hyde, H. A., 1963. Pollen-fall as a means of seed prediction in certain trees. *Grana Palynologica* 4: 217–230.

Kluyver, H. N., 1951. The population ecology of the Great Tit. *Ardea* 9: 1–135.

Kluyver, H. N. & L. Tinbergen, 1953. Territory and the regulation of density in titmice. *Archs néerl. Zool.* 10: 266–287.

Kluyver, H. N. 1966. Regulation of bird populations. *Ostrich* 38 Suppl. 6: 389–396.

Krebs, J. R., 1970a. Regulation of numbers in the Great Tit (Aves: Passeriformes). *J. Zool., Lond.* 162: 317–333.

Krebs, J. R., 1971. Territory and breeding density in the great tit *Parus major* L. Ecology 52: 2–22.

Lack, D., 1964. A long-term study of the great tit *(Parus major) J. Anim. Ecol.* 33, Suppl.: 159–173.

Lack, D., 1966. Populations studies of birds. Oxford.

Lack, D., J. A. Gibb & D. F. Owen, 1957. Survival in relation to brood-size in tits. *Proc. zool. Soc. Lond.* 128: 313–326.

Matthews, J. D., 1963. Factors affecting the production of seeds by forest trees. *For. Abstr.* 24(1) 1–13.

Perrins, C. M., 1965. Population fluctuations and clutch size in the Great Tit *(Parus major). J. Anim. Ecol.* 34: 601–647.

Perrins, C. M., 1966. The effect of beech crops on Great Tit populations and movements. *Br. Birds* 59: 419–432.

Perrins, C. M. & P. J. Jones. The inheritance of clutch size in the Great Tits (in prep.).

Royama, T., 1966. The breeding biology of the Great Tit, *Parus major*, with reference to food. Oxford, Ph. D. thesis.

Southern, H. N., 1970. The natural control of a population of Tawny owls *(Strix aluco). J. Zool., Lond.* 162, Part 2.

Southwood, T. R. E., 1966. Ecological methods. Methuen, London.

Tollenaar, D., 1922. Legperioden en eierproductie bij eenige wilde vogelsoorten, vergeleken met die bij hoenderrassen. *Meded. LandbHoogesch., Wageningen* 23 (2) 1–46.

Ulfstrand, S., 1962. On the nonbreeding ecology and migratory movements of the Great Tit *(Parus major)* and the Blue Tit *(Parus caeruleus)* in Southern Sweden. *Var Fagelvarld* Suppl. 3: 1–45.

Varley, G. C. & G. R. Gradwell, 1960. Key factors in population studies. *J. Anim. Ecol.* 29: 399–401.

Discussion

This paper is discussed, together with Kluyver's and Dhondt's papers, on p. 544.

Proc. Adv. Study Inst. Dynamics Numbers Popul. (Oosterbeek, 1970) 532–547

The regulation of numbers in Belgian populations of Great Tits

André A. Dhondt

Laboratory of Ecology, Ghent State University, Ghent, Belgium

Abstract

Answers are sought to three main questions relative to the regulation of numbers in Great Tit populations. The data reported come from a ten-year study of different habitats in and around Ghent (Belgium).
1. It is shown that juvenile survival is correlated with temperature during the breeding season and with breeding density. Yearly fluctuations in juvenile survival are caused mainly by temperature variations when the young are in the nest (via food availability) and are damped through density.
2. Autumn territorial behaviour causes density-dependent emigration of juveniles out of all habitats; more second-brood than first-brood young take part in these movements.
3. Spring territorial behaviour can limit numbers breeding in optimal habitats. The subordinate birds, which are forced to leave, will settle and breed in marginal habitats. Hence spring territorial behaviour does not limit overall numbers.

Major contributions to an understanding of the factors responsible for the regulation of numbers in populations of Great Tits (*Parus major* L.) have been made by Kluyver (1951, 1957, 1966), Kluyver and Tinbergen (1953), Gibb (1965), Lack (1955, 1958, 1966) and Perrins (1963, 1965, 1966). However, two important questions remain unanswered. The first concerns the factors responsible for the varying proportion of young surviving each year and in this Kluyver (these Proceedings) has shown that density plays a role. The second concerns the effect of autumn and spring territorial behaviour; Kluyver (1966) thinks that social behaviour before winter is very important and Kluyver and Tinbergen (1953) believe spring territorial behaviour also to be important. This latter suggestion is rejected by Lack (1966) who does not believe that, in Wytham Wood, spring territorial behaviour limits the numbers of pairs breeding (p. 79).

In this paper I discuss: a. the factors affecting juvenile survival; b. the effect of autumn territorial behaviour; and c. the influence of spring territorial behaviour.

The results are based on data collected since 1961 in study areas in and around Ghent (Belgium). These are Zevergem (oak wood), Maaltepark and Maria-Middelares (mixed deciduous parks), Hutsepot (beech wood) and COO (coniferous wood). The study area Citadelpark (a very poor urban park) will also briefly be referred to. The first three study areas are considered to be good breeding habitats for tits; the last three are poorer. These catagories are based on differences in breeding densities, with higher densities occurring in better habitats. The study areas were described in more detail by Hublé (1962), and Dhondt and Hublé (1968a, b), who also described the methods used. The special methods concerning spring territories and the sexing of the young in the nest were described by Dhondt (1966, 1970).

In the preceding paper (these Proceedings), Perrins shows that the reproductive rate is inversely related to density. This was also demonstrated by Kluyver (1951), and is further confirmed by the Ghent data (Dhondt, in prep.). I agree with Kluyver (1951) and Lack (1966) that this density-dependent factor is not sufficient to regulate the numbers in Great Tit populations because (a) although the reproductive rate decreases with increasing density, within the range of observed densities, the total number of young fledging is greater at higher densities than at low ones, and (b) the variance of the mortality in the other part of the year (between fledging and the next breeding season) is high compared with the density-dependent effect on production.

Factors affecting the survival of juveniles

A bird is considered to have survived if it was recaptured at least three months after fledging. In the Ghent data it is not necessary to take into account the higher dispersal of second-brood young compared with first-brood young. Many of the birds that left their birth place were later recovered and it was possible to show that the recovery rate of first and second-brood young did not differ; hence it was supposed that their survival did not differ either (Dhondt and Hublé, 1968a).

Perrins (1963, 1965) has shown that, in England, heavier young survive better. My data lead to the same conclusion (Fig. 1), but show a difference between males and females. Also, if we divide the breeding season into shorter periods, my results become quite different from Perrins' observations. In Fig. 2 the average weight of the nestlings at fifteen days and their survival is plotted. It can be seen that the average weight of the nestlings fluctuates during the breeding season; early young are heavier, later young of first broods and early repeats average lighter weights, but young from early second broods (end of June) are again heavy. It is also clear that even first-brood young in 1968 were very light, and that a sudden fall in weight occurred in July 1969. These periods of lighter weights are also periods of lower recovery rates.

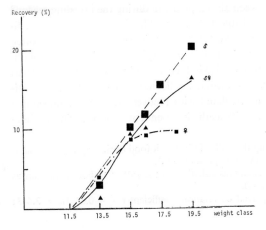

Fig. 1. Recovery (%) of 15-day-old Great Tits in relation to their weight class.

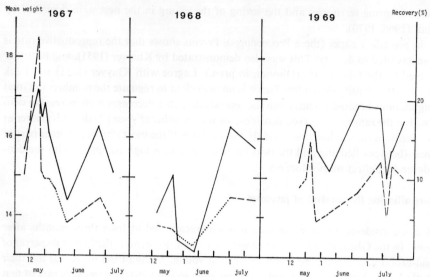

Fig. 2. Relationship between the mean weight of 15-day-old Great Tits in different periods of the breeding season, and their recovery. Weight (——) and survival (– – – –) vary in parallel. Note that young fledging in July are again heavy.

What can be the cause? It is normally accepted (e.g. Lack, 1966) that the condition of the young is influenced by the amount of available food, but since I have not – nor did most other people – measured the food supply, this supposed correlation leads no further.

A possible factor affecting food is weather. Like Kluyver (1951) I found mortality in the nest to be correlated with air temperature during the nestling period. Hence it might be supposed that air temperature, affecting food availability[1] and therefore the condition of nestlings, would ultimately affect their subsequent survival. This possible influence of temperature on weight and survival is also supported by the low weight and poor survival of nestlings in May 1968 and by the sudden fall in weight and in survival in July 1969, since both these periods could be related to periods of low temperatures. Therefore I have calculated the correlation coefficient between air temperature during the breeding season[2] and survival of the young after fledging (Table 1, Fig. 3b). The linear correlation coefficient is low, but significant ($r = 0.67$; $t_7 = 2.388$; $P < 0.05$). In Fig. 3a survival is plotted against breeding density; although the correlation coefficient is very low and not significant ($r = -0.37$) it suggests that density might also influence survival because the aberrant points coincide with years of extreme temperatures (as indicated with arrows).[3] The multiple correlation coefficient was therefore calculated with recovery rate as the dependent variable and temperature and breeding density as the independent variables. This correla-

[1] The activity of arthropods, which make up the bulk of Great Tit food during spring and summer, is strongly influenced by temperature (Varley, pers. comm.).
[2] The temperature during the breeding season was calculated in a rather elaborate fashion as will be explained elsewhere (Dhondt, in prep.).
[3] This is supported by the significant partial correlation coefficient $r = -0.83$ ($t_6 = 3.613$; $P < 0.02$).

Table 1. Survival of young Great Tits in relation to temperature during the breeding season and density. Notes: Data from Maaltepark, Zevergem and COO were used for the years 1961–1969; from 1964 onwards the data from Hutsepot were included. Density rates and recovery are averages for all the areas. See also text and Fig. 3.

Year	% Young recovered	Temperature (°C)	Density p/10 ha
1961	1.3	14.3	15.7
1962	2.7	11.3	11.6
1963	8.4	13.9	8.7
1964	10.0	16.7	13.8
1965	5.4	14.7	17.0
1966	4.3	14.0	14.6
1967	8.4	15.1	12.9
1968	4.2	13.1	12.5
1969	8.7	14.7	12.2

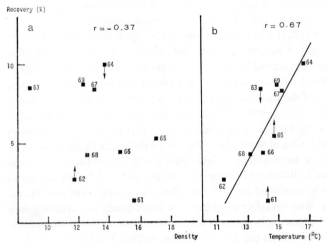

Fig. 3. Recovery in relation to breeding density (a) and temperature (b) during the breeding season (see text).

tion coefficient is high and significant ($r = 0.91$; $F_{2.7} = 14.153$; $P < 0.01$).

I would therefore suggest that survival of the young is strongly and mainly influenced by two independent variables. The main cause for the yearly fluctuations in juvenile survival is a strongly fluctuating climatic factor, but a density-dependent factor also influences these fluctuations and in such a way that they are damped. This latter is a true regulatory mechanism.

The influence of autumn territorial behaviour

It has been shown that a higher proportion of young from second than from first broods emigrate (Dhondt and Hublé, 1968a). I agree with Perrins (1963, 1965) that this, obviously,

Table 2. Autumn recoveries of juvenile Great Tits. The percentage of local recoveries of males and females. The percentage of males recovered decreases during September, whereas it remains constant in females. This suggests an emigration of the males because of autumn territorial behaviour.

Period	♂		♀	
	number recovered	% local	number recovered	% local
20.VIII–5.IX	19	58		
6–15.IX	14	64	26	19
16–20.IX	24	42	30	17
21–30.IX	20	50	22	18

is true only for the surviving young; the light young dying, the heavy young surviving. Like Perrins, I did not find a difference in the average weights of the young at fifteen days, as between those remaining close to their birth places and those emigrating.

I also agree with Kluyver (1951) that the emigration of a higher proportion of young from second broods is a result of autumn territorial behaviour. In September, when this behaviour is intense, young from second broods have not yet finished moulting and hence are in a subordinate position. I have one set of not very convincing data to illustrate this. It stems from a comparison of the percentages of emigrating males and females as shown by recaptures of juvenile birds in autumn. Table 2 illustrates the fact that the dispersal of the juvenile males continues as autumn progresses, whereas that of the juvenile females has stabilized before the beginning of September. This sexual difference in dispersal is evidence in favour of the effect of territorial behaviour, since it is the males that are involved in it. However, we also see a difference in male and female dispersal before territorial activity sets in. This might be explained through the subordinate position of the juvenile females in skirmishes over food (possibly resulting in a stress condition) resulting in a higher proportion of them emigrating in search of areas where food is more readily available. Finally, Löhrl has commented (in the discussion) that in Coal Tits kept in aviaries a sharp period of restlessness can be observed in September. This could be the proximate mechanism causing dispersal and emigration at that time of year.

Arguments suggesting that the proportion emigrating is density-dependent are twofold. It has been suggested by Lack (1954,p. 236) that large-scale emigrations, which occasionally occur in Great Tit populations, are stimulated by high numbers. Berndt and Henss (1967) have shown that such irruptions occur in years after high breeding densities. Perrins (1966) has shown that the amount of food available in the subsequent winter (measured by the beechmast crop) is also correlated with invasions, and Cornwallis and Townsend (1968) have concluded that irruptions occur in years after high breeding densities and with poor beechmast crops. However, since irruptions take place before the Tits feed on beechmast, and even in areas where it is absent, I would suggest that irruptions occur in those years when breeding densities are high and, because of high temperatures during the breeding season, survival of the young good. These combine to give high numbers in autumn.

The second argument suggesting that dispersal and short-distance emigrations are

536

Table 3. The percentages of immigrants and of all juveniles in the winter population and the percentage of young recovered in different years (see also Table 1). The data come from the same study areas as those in Table 1. It is clear that when survival is good many juveniles appear in the study areas.

Winter	Young recovered from previous breeding season (%)	Immigrants in the winter population (%)	Juveniles in the winter population (%)
1963/64	8.4	61.4	67.8
1964/65	10.0	60.1	69.4
1965/66	5.4	22.4	28.8
1966/67	4.3	40.7	46.5
1967/68	8.4	62.2	67.8
1968/69	4.2	38.0	43.3

density-dependent is that I find a significant correlation between the percentage of young surviving and the percentage of immigrants in the winter population (Table 3) ($r = 0,81$, $t_4 = 2.762$, $P < 0.05$). This means that when more young survive more will emigrate, since the birds that immigrate into my study areas must have left another place. It also suggests that the same factors are responsible for juvenile survival in the areas not studied.

It is known that densities of Great Tit populations tend to fluctuate parallel over a wide geographical area, and parallel fluctuations were also observed in my study areas. If we assume that most of the Great Tits appearing in my study areas come from the immediate surroundings and have undergone similar temperatures, then we should find a significant correlation between the percentage of immigrant birds in the winter populations and temperature and density during the previous breeding season. We should also find a significant correlation between the percentage of all juvenile birds, immigrants and residents, in the winter population and these factors. This is in fact what is found; the multiple correlation coefficients are 0.94 and 0.95, respectively ($P < 0.05$).

The conclusions which can be drawn concerning the data presented, is that in autumn a density-dependent emigration occurs in all areas, the mechanism being, at least partially, autumn territorial behaviour. Any extra mortality suffered as a result of this emigration must also be considered to be density-dependent and, hence, we have found a density-dependent factor limiting numbers.

The effect of spring territorial behaviour

During winter, mortality occurs in all groups of birds. Since immigrant juveniles are more mobile, their numbers will decrease more rapidly in the populations studied but their overall mortality may be similar to, or only slightly higher than, that of other groups. Kluyver (1951) has shown that, when densities are high, winter mortality is influenced by cold temperatures.

The main fluctuations in the size of the winter populations are caused by varying numbers of immigrants (Kluyver, 1951; Dhondt, in prep).

Table 4 shows the percentage of immigrants in the winter populations in different habitats. The fluctuations are in parallel (Kendall coefficient of concordance $W = 0.59$; $s = 146.5$; $P < 0.01$). This means that when many immigrants appear we will find them in

Table 4. The percentage of immigrants in the winter populations of different study areas. When many juveniles are present they will occur in all study areas (W = 0.59; P < 0.01 for 1964/65–1968/69).

Winter	Maaltepark	Zevergem	Hutsepot	COO
1963–64	68	55	—	63
1964–65	66	56	75	45
1965–66	31	16	29	19
1966–67	58	32	44	26
1967–68	67	63	62	54
1968–69	49	32	45	27

all habitats. It was previously shown that their numbers are correlated with temperatures and density in the previous breeding season. It should also be noted that in some winters the percentage of immigrants in the winter population is high (60% or more) whereas in other winters this percentage is much lower (40% or less). The first type of winter will hereafter be called high-density winter (1963/64, 1964/65 and 1967/68), the second type low-density winter (1965/66, 1966/67 and 1968/69). This division is made simply for practical reasons and does not imply that, if data from many years of observations were available, we would not find intermediate values.

There is no difference in the percentage of immigrant males found in the winter populations of good and bad breeding habitats. However, a difference is seen when we compare the percentage of immigrant males, both in good and poor habitats, in winters of high and low density (Table 5). A study of survival from October until the breeding season was based on the bimonthly evening controls of roosting birds in the good habitats. I compared survival in the different age and sex groups, and this separately for high- and low-density winters. Only in 'immigrants' was a difference found between the two types of winter. This is illustrated in Fig. 4 where survival is plotted against time (the data for all winters are lumped; those for immigrant juveniles are lumped separately for high- and low-density winters). It can clearly be seen that survival of adults and resident juveniles is approximately constant throughout winter. This is probably also true for the immigrant juveniles in low-density winters, but the slope for immigrants is greater because their

Table 5. The percentage of immigrant males in the winter population. There is no significant difference between habitats; comparing winters however the percentage of immigrant males is significantly higher in high-density winter.

Notes: high-density winters: 1963–64, 1964–65, 1967–68; low-density winters: 1965–66, 1966–67, 1968–69. Optimal habitats: Maaltepark and Zevergem; marginal habitats: COO and Hutsepot.

Habitat winter	Optimal		Marginal		χ^2
	number	% immigrants	number	% immigrants	
High density	233	57	140	54	0.306 n.s.
Low density	154	32	495	30	0.061 n.s.
All winters	387	47	235	44	0.481 n.s.
χ^2	22.751	P < 0.001	12.388	P < 0.001	

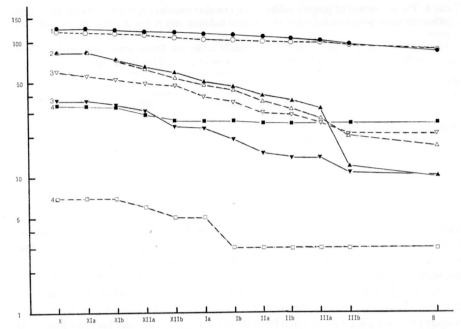

Fig. 4. Survival of different age and sex groups from October until the next breeding season. 1 = resident adults; 2 = immigrant juveniles in high-density winters; 3 = immigrant juveniles in low-density winters; 4 = resident juveniles. Open symbols are ♀♀, filled symbols ♂♂. Note the sudden loss in the group of immigrant ♂♂ at the beginning of March in high-density winters.

mobility is greater. However, in high-density winters, the immigrant juveniles – and especially the males – show a sudden decrease in numbers during the first half of March. This sudden decrease in the numbers of subordinate males after high-density winters suggests that it is due to increasing territorial activity, which occurs during the same period (personal observation). If this sharp decrease in numbers was caused by mortality, we should expect to find it occurring in the group of immigrant females as well, since these are subordinate even to the immigrant males.

If one accepts the hypothesis that the disappearing young males do not suffer wholescale mortality but emigrate out of good habitats, one must expect to find them breeding in marginal habitats; although it is clear that during their dispersal from good to bad habitats they will undergo some mortality. Unfortunately I have no direct proof of this; I have no recoveries of birds which disappeared from the good habitats which show them breeding in a marginal one. There is, however, some indirect evidence. It was earlier shown that the percentage of juvenile birds in the winter population does not differ between good and bad breeding habitats. Table 6 shows the percentages of first-year males in breeding populations of good and bad habitats. Comparing winters we find that in good habitats the percentage of first-year males in the breeding population is not significantly higher after high- than after low-density winters, although such a difference was found to exist during winter. This confirms the conclusion that after high-density winters some birds left the good habitats. Also, in poor habitats, the percentage of juvenile males is higher after

Table 6. The percentage of juvenile males in the breeding population. After high-density winters, significantly more young males occur in marginal habitats, this is not the case after low-density winters.

In marginal habitats, significantly more juvenile males are found after high-density winters than after low-density winters, whereas this is not so in optimal habitats. Note: see Table 5.

Habitat winter	optimal		marginal		χ^2	P
	number	% juveniles	number	% juveniles		
High density	74	47	45	71	5.518	< 0.02
Low density	77	38	75	51	2.106	n.s.
χ^2	1.067		4.032			
P	n.s.		< 0.05			

higher-density winters than after low-density winters. Since this difference already existed in winter, it does not prove anything by itself. Comparing habitats we find that, after low-density winters, the percentage first-year males in the breeding population does not differ between good and bad habitats. However, it does differ after high-density winters; significantly more juvenile males breed in poor habitats. This was not so during winter. This last result is conclusive. Together with the other facts, it shows that after high-density winters juvenile males leave optimal habitats when territorial activity becomes important, and breed in marginal habitats.

Gompertz, studying Great Tits in England, has direct evidence of this. She has observed that young, subordinate males were driven away from the best parts of her study area, and settled in marginal parts (comments at the XVth I.O.C., The Hague, 1970). I believe the evidence strongly suggests that territorial activity in spring limits breeding populations in optimal habitats in a density-dependent way. This provides the mechanisms needed in the hypothesis of the 'buffer mechanism' formulated by Kluyver and Tinbergen (1953). My data also show this buffer mechanism to be effective in the Belgian populations.

The buffer hypothesis formulated by Kluyver and Tinbergen (1953) explains the greater amplitude of the fluctuations in breeding densities in marginal habitats compared to optimal habitats, birds being attracted by suitable habitats but being repelled by high densities. When the good breeding habitats are 'filled up', potential settlers 'spill over' from them into marginal ones. This hypothesis is not generally accepted (Lack, 1966; Brown, 1969). I believe the Ghent data provide additional evidence to support this hypothesis. It is possible to check the hypothesis in two ways; by comparing the amplitude of the yearly

Table 7. Coefficient of variation of densities in different habitats: it is higher in poorer habitats.

Habitat	Coefficient of variation (%)
Zevergem	19.3
Maaltepark	18.1
COO	24.7
Citadel	37.5

540

fluctuations in the breeding densities of good and poor habitats, and by comparing the rate of increase of breeding numbers in good with that in bad habitats. This can be done by plotting against one other the yearly breeding densities in the two habitat types.

Table 7 summarizes the calculated coefficients of variation in the different habitats of this study. It is clear that with diminishing quality the coefficient of variation increases. In Fig. 5, 6 and 7 I have plotted the number of breeding pairs per year for the different types of habitat. The lines lie as expected if the buffer hypothesis is correct. Comparing a poor habitat (COO, Hutsepot) with a good one (Maaltepark, Zevergem) gives a regression line cutting the ordinate at a point lying significantly above the origin. Comparing good and bad habitats with one another gives regression lines not deviating significantly from the origin. These results show that in the habitats in and around Ghent the buffer mechanism

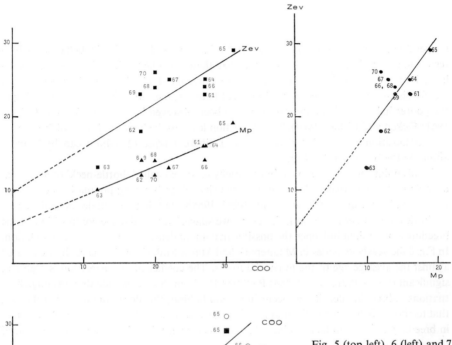

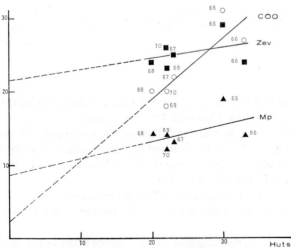

Fig. 5 (top left), 6 (left) and 7 (top right). The relationships between the numbers of Great Tits breeding in different habitats. The extrapolated calculated regression lines for COO/Maaltepark, COO/Zevergem, Hutsepot/Maaltepark and Hutsepot/Zevergem deviate significantly from the origin. Hutsepot/COO and Maaltepark/Zevergem do not deviate significantly from the origin. COO and Hutsepot are poor habitats for Great Tits, Maaltepark and Zevergem good habitats.

541

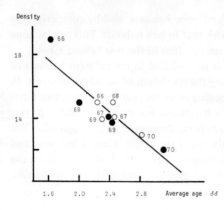

Fig. 8. The relationship between the average age of territorial males in Maaltepark (○) and Maria-Middelares (●) (1966–1970), and breeding density. It is suggested that fluctuations in breeding density could be caused by changes in the age composition of territorial males.

is operating. Earlier, I showed that the mechanism involved is territorial behaviour which results in emigration from good habitats when these are 'filled up'. At high densities such behaviour will not limit the overall number of breeding birds, but the birds present will merely distribute themselves over all kinds of habitats, the subordinate males breeding in the poorer habitats. This latter fact has also been observed in other species (e.g. Orians, 1961; Ficken and Ficken, 1967). This deduction leads to the hypothesis that differences in age composition of breeding males between different types of habitat can be brought about by the buffer mechanism.

At this point I would like to comment briefly on the so-called 'bottle-neck' of territorial behaviour, to show that it does not limit the size of the breeding populations to a fixed maximum. It was shown (Dhondt and Hublé, 1968b) that first-year males defend smaller territories than older males and, therefore, we suggested that the age composition of the breeding males might influence the possible maximum density of the breeding population. In Fig. 8 the yearly densities in Maaltepark and Maria-Middelares (10 ha each) are plotted against the average age of the territorial males. The coefficient of correlation is high and significant ($r = -0.91$; $t_8 = 6.288$; $P < 0.001$). From this I conclude that although fluctuations in breeding density do occur in a good habitat, this does not contradict the idea that territorial behaviour limits numbers in such a habitat; and a large part of the changes in breeding density can be explained through yearly variations in the age composition of the territorial males.

Conclusions

I believe that reasonable evidence has been presented to conclude that the following factors play a role in the regulation of numbers in Great Tit populations:
1. Factors affecting reproductive rate; these are not discussed in this paper, but see Perrins (these Proceedings); in my view these factors are not sufficient to regulate numbers
2. Factors affecting juvenile survival; it has been shown that the influence of temperature is important, and that density acts in a regulatory fashion;
3. Autumn territorial behaviour affects emigration in a density-dependent way;
4. Survival during winter is influenced by extreme temperatures at high densities (Kluyver, 1951);
5. Spring territorial behaviour results in the emigration of subordinate males out of good

habitats. This has a limiting effect on density in good habitats, but no limiting effect on the overall population density.

More general conclusions can also be drawn. Firstly, concerning the effect of spring territorial behaviour, it can be argued that around Ghent, where the environment is heterogeneous, there is a selective advantage for subordinate males to leave good breeding habitats in spring when these are crowded. If they are able to breed in a less crowded environment of a poor habitat, they will produce more offspring than they would have been able to do in a poorer and smaller territory in a good habitat.

Secondly, in contrast to most case histories presented in these Proceedings, there seems to be some safeguard against extinction of local populations since it has been shown that at low densities, juvenile survival is better than expected. This means that young of poorer condition, which would have died at higher densities, will survive when density is low.

Summing up it can be said that many factors affect the numbers in the Great Tit populations studied, but that only one true regulatory factor was found, namely the density-dependent survival of young. The other factors either vary at random (climatic factors) or only limit either the overall population or local populations, or result in the spacing out of surviving birds.

Acknowledgments

The author is indebted to Prof. Dr J. Hublé who supervised the work and originated the project; to Mr R. de Waele and Mr P. Bekaert for help in the field.

Part of this work was carried out while the author was holding a fellowship of the Belgian National Foundation for Scientific Research.

References

Berndt, R. & M. Henss, 1967. Die Kohlmeise, *Parus major*, als Invasionsvogel. *Vogelwarte* 24: 17–37.

Brown, J. L., 1969. The buffer effect and productivity in tit populations. *Am. Nat.* 103: 347–354.

Cornwallis, R. K. & A. S. Townsend, 1968. Waxwings in Britain and Europe during 1965/66. *Br. Birds* 61: 97–118.

Ficken, M. S. & R. W. Ficken, 1967. Age-specific differences in the breeding behaviour and ecology of the American Redstart. *Wilson Bull.* 79: 188–199.

Dhondt, A. A., 1966. A method to establish boundaries of bird territories. *Giervalk* 56: 404–408.

Dhondt, A. A., 1970. The sex ratio of nestling Great Tits, *Parus major* L. *Bird Study* 17: 282–286.

Dhondt, A. A. & J. Hublé, 1968a. Fledging-date and sex in relation to dispersal in young Great Tits. *Bird Study* 15: 127–134.

Dhondt, A. A. & J. Hublé, 1968b. Age and territory in the Great Tit (*Parus m. major* L.). *Angew. Orn.* 3: 20–24.

Gibb, J., 1950. The breeding biology of the Great and Blue Titmice. *Ibis* 92: 507–539.

Hublé, J., 1962. The population density of Great and Blue Tits in two municipal parks (1958–1961). *Giervalk* 52: 344–352.

Kluyver, H. N., 1951. The population ecology of the Great Tit *Parus m. major* L. *Ardea* 39: 1–135.

Kluyver, H. N., 1957. Roosting habits, sexual dominance and survival in the Great Tit. *Cold Spring Harb. Symp. quant. Biol.* 22: 281–285.

Kluyver, H. N., 1966. Regulation of a bird population. *Ostrich* 38, Suppl. 6: 389–396.

Kluyver, H. N. & L. Tinbergen, 1953. Territory and regulation of density in titmice. *Archs néerl. Zool.* 10: 265–289.

Lack, D., 1954. The natural regulation of animal numbers. Oxford.

Lack, D., 1955. British tits (*Parus* spp.) in nesting boxes. *Ardea* 43: 50–84.

Lack, D., 1958. A quantitative breeding study of British tits. *Ardea* 46: 91–124.

Lack, D., 1966. Population studies of birds. Oxford.

Orians, G. H., 1961. The ecology of blackbird (*Agelaius*) social systems. *Ecol. Monogr.* 31: 285–312.

Perrins, C. M., 1963. Survival in the Great Tit, *Parus major. Proc. 13th Int. orn. Congr.*: 717–728.

Perrins, C. M., 1965. Population fluctuations and clutch size in the Great Tit, *Parus major* L. *J. Anim. Ecol.* 34: 601–647.

Perrins, C. M., 1966. The effect of beech crops on Great Tit populations and movements. *Br. Birds* 59: 419–432.

Discussion of the papers of Kluyver, Perrins and Dhondt

Participants: Dhondt, Kluyver and Perrins (Authors), van der Aart, Andrewartha, Bakker (K.), den Boer (P. J.), Frank, Jacobs, Jenkins, Löhrl, Royama, Solomon, Southwood and Zahavi.

Whether or not an effect on the reproductive rate is density-dependent depends on the proportional effect, not just on the absolute numbers involved. A numerically small reduction in reproduction or survival may play an important role in regulation if there are other, large mortalities in the life cycle. To illustrate with a simple model: Suppose there are initially 150 young at high density and 100 at low density, and that a high density-independent mortality of 90% operates in both. Suppose this is followed by a density-dependent mortality such that 20% die when the remaining population is 10, and 50% die when it is 15. Then:

$$150–90\% = 15, \text{ less } 50\% = 7.5, \text{ and}$$
$$100–90\% = 10, \text{ less } 20\% = 8$$

Whether or not a density-dependent mortality has this effect depends on the strength of the density-dependent relationship (a very strong one was assumed here), and on the amount of the mortality contributed by other factors (the 90% mortality here) (SOLOMON).

It is not realistic to assume deterministically density-independent factors. The variances of the influences has to be taken into account. Crudely speaking: if, in some adequate transformation, the overall effect of the density-dependent factor is stronger (take into account also its variance!) than the variances of the density-independent influences, it may be possible (but not necessary) that it 'regulates' in such a way. Otherwise its influence generally will go down in the multitude of other variable influences (DEN BOER) (See also the discussion after the paper of Solomon).

A possible density-dependent relationship between numbers and survival over the winter may be masked by non-density-dependent mortality in part of the winter, or such a relationship may only occur when the population density exceeds a certain level. In the first case, mortality soon after the young are fledged may be density-independent while mortality at the time when the birds all take up territories may be density-dependent (JENKINS). There is no evidence that 'losses' were higher in years with very high densities (PERRINS, AUTHOR).

Dhondt said that within each study area he considers the population is regulated by emigration. What is the regulating mechanism for the total population – favourable and marginal areas? Is it death after emigration or, if they breed in marginal areas, the effect of density on reproduction (SOUTHWOOD)? In my view, the main factor influencing the total population is juvenile survival (DHONDT, AUTHOR).

544

Most of the work on the Great Tit seems to be directed towards how the birds that succeed in establishing a territory effectively use a resource in the exploited area. What determines the abundance of this resource? The emphasis placed on density-related processes that do not lead to a negative feedback has obviously lead to a concentration of effort on counting animals, and to overlooking the rest of the environment. It would be interesting to learn about food and about a possible feedback between density and food during either winter or summer. It would be interesting to know about nesting sites as a resource for a natural population; i.e. one not provided with an excess of boxes. Perhaps closely related species or predators are important (ANDREWARTHA). With respect to food, some measurements I have made suggest that at the time when the young are in the nest larvae of the winter moth are so abundant that the tits cannot make a substantial effect on them; also, in winter when the beech crop is abundant, the tits cannot eat them all and many seeds germinate. At other times presumably food is limited – see Gibb's work in pine forests (PERRINS, AUTHOR). I would refer you to L. Tinbergen's study in *Archives Neerlandaises de Zoologie*, 1960 (KLUYVER, AUTHOR).

The higher summer emigration of female tits found by Dhondt suggests that feeding problems are involved. Direct experiments in changing food availability may solve the problem of to what extent territorial behaviour limits the reproduction of tits much quicker than long series of observations. Through experiments on food within wagtails' territories it was easy to show that territory size is related to food, and that females pair in winter to avoid emigration when there are difficulties in encountering food. The fact that many tits pair in winter suggests that they have feeding problems in winter (ZAHAVI). I did such an experiment in two study areas by providing a surplus of fat to the birds during the winter of 1965–66. In these two areas, densities were higher in the breeding season 1966 than in 1965, whereas they were lower in all other areas. In 1966 it was estimated that in these two areas about half of the territories were of normal size, whereas the other territories were either smaller or located in less favourable parts of the area. On the average the birds with 'good' territories did not lay bigger clutches than those with 'bad' territories, but the former fledged about twice as many young as the latter. This would suggest that when the 'carrying capacity' of the habitat is surpassed a good territory has survival value, and that possibly food plays an important role (DHONDT, AUTHOR).

Can the time of laying clutches be correlated with the condition of the females, e.g. will adults entering the breeding season in poor condition tend to lay late? Would the young in these broods be expected only to survive when the food is particularly good (JENKINS)? I indeed expect late young to survive when late food is good. The condition of a female to some extent depends on its size, the smaller ones breeding first (PERRINS, AUTHOR).

Whose natural resource are the tits? The artificial nesting sites used in all three studies possibly cut out one whole trophic level, viz. the predators (except some weasels) and also perhaps parasites. What is their function in natural tit populations (JACOBS)? In Ghent predators are almost completely absent (DHONDT, AUTHOR). In Oxford the only known serious predator is the weasel, though newly fledged young may be taken by avian predators (PERRINS, AUTHOR). At Arnhem weasels are not important. Many young tits die soon after fledging as delayed victims of the parasitic fly *Protocalliphora*. Some adult tits are caught by owls and sparrow-hawks (KLUYVER, AUTHOR).

Breeding success is to a high degree box-dependent. The conditions in boxes are very much better than in natural tree holes and it may be assumed – from a study of some broods in natural holes – that the reduction in the number of eggs in Kluyver's experiment was more natural than that affecting 'normal' broods in boxes. The nestling mortality in tree holes seems to be much higher than in boxes. Experiments show the birds to have a significant preference for large boxes, which also results in a significant increase in clutch size. The extremely favourable conditions in boxes result in the great number of fledglings observed in the studies discussed here (LÖHRL).

It was shown that after years with an extremely high density of breeding pairs there always was a great crash. Could this be due to an increase in the mean territory size of the two-year old birds? What is known about the age distribution in years of high density and the year following it (BAKKER)? There are indeed fewer young birds in the breeding population the year after a 'crash'. The annual adult mortality seems to be higher in the 'crash' years than in the increase years, but on the whole the mortality variations are relatively small in adults, 40–60% (PERRINS). In a year with high density there are generally many one-year old breeding birds (locally ringed as nestlings the year before). In the following year such birds are nearly absent because many more have died or emigrated (KLUYVER, AUTHOR).

In Great Tits, individuals in different breeding stages differ in their degree of intolerance, i.e. individuals in the same stage are most intolerant of one another. As there are considerable differences between individuals at the breeding stage, the influence of territoriality on a local population must be rather complex. How does this complexity influence the buffering of density (ROYAMA)? In years when both optimal and marginal habitats are 'filled' to capacity, the unsettled birds can do one of two things: either they do not breed and become 'floaters', or they do breed. They will probably settle in all habitats, and can do this because the complete territory is only defended during a short period (with a maximum of interactions just before egg-laying), so that later, the 'floaters' will be able to settle in the undefended areas (DHONDT, AUTHOR).

The building up of a new territorial system in autumn has already been discussed by Kalela (1958). He found evidence that the integration of the young birds into the resident population becomes easier due to a decrease in the aggressiveness of the adults – due to decreasing gonad activity, and by a striking increase in the aggressiveness of the young due to a temporary activation of the gonads. A mechanism of this kind is found in the carnivorous mammal *Mustela nivalis*. What is known about this in the Great Tit (FRANK)? A study of the endocrinology of the Great Tit has been started at Ghent and also in Groningen by Drent (DHONDT, AUTHOR).

It seems that 'territorial behaviour' in September is pronounced in Holland and Belgium, but not in Oxford. This parallels the situation in English grouse – sometimes territories are taken up in autumn and sometimes not till February. In the Red Grouse this difference is related to altitude and snow fall – in all cases territories are abandoned in snow. Presumably, the time of taking up territories in grouse depends on the relative priorities of either spending most of the time feeding or being aggressive. What is the situation in Great Tits? Perhaps Holland and Belgium, with two broods and autumn territorial behaviour, must be regarded as better-class environments than England with only one brood and no autumn territorial behaviour. Although Red Grouse are never double brooded, an interesting comparison with Great Tits is possible; the continental tit areas being like low altitude grouse areas and English tit areas like high-altitude grouse areas. What is known about the total resource situation in the two areas (JENKINS)?

I have no evidence on total resources. One possible reason for the greater territorial behaviour in Holland and Belgium could be that since the birds raise two broods there (as opposed to one in England) the population – per pair of adults – is greater; 'Oxford' produces say 6–8 young per pair and 'Holland' up to 12 or more (PERRINS, AUTHOR).

The predictive value of the multiple linear regression model used by Dhondt must be shown on data other than those used for calculating the regression equation. Perhaps the data can be split into two parts, one part for making the analysis and calculating the equation, and the other part for testing the equation; either that, or the study has to be extended for another 10 years to test the predictability of the equation (VAN DER AART). I did not intend to prove anything with the 'model', it is only used as an illustration. Recently, the proposed splitting up of the data into two parts was accomplished: the model appears to have predictive value for the second part of the data, one year in advance (DHONDT, AUTHOR).

Proc. Adv. Study Inst. Dynamics Numbers Popul. (Oosterbeek, 1970) 548–564

Key factor analysis, density dependence and population limitation in red grouse

Adam Watson

Nature Conservancy, Blackhall, Banchory, Kincardineshire, Scotland

Abstract

A key factor analysis of numerical data on red grouse populations is compared with the results of empirical experiments aimed at understanding underlying causal mechanisms. Winter loss on one area was the key factor contributing most to variations in spring population between years, but losses at the egg and chick stage were also substantial. On a second area, winter loss and breeding production losses were both key factors, with production losses greater in some years. Most k values for periods of loss showed delayed density dependence, with heavier losses during declines than at the same density during increases.

A reasonable interpretation would be that breeding stocks were determined by winter mortality, probably mostly due to starvation and predation. However, the experimental work showed that breeding stocks were determined by the territories chosen the previous autumn. Overwinter mortality fell almost entirely on grouse that did not have territories; and it was secondary, occurring only after certain changes in social behaviour. Hence winter losses were irrelevant to population limitation, even though they appeared to be a key factor. A few similar examples in other species are discussed, particularly with reference to the problem of compensatory changes.

A long-term research project has been done by a small team studying the population dynamics of red grouse (*Lagopus lagopus scoticus*). The two main questions asked are: what determines annual fluctuations within areas, and what causes differences in mean abundance between areas? The specific aim of this paper is to compare a key factor analysis with an empirical programme of observations and experiments on the mechanisms underlying changes in numbers. The comparison illustrates how a difference of approach or methodology in population ecology can lead to different interpretations. This may be important if different theoretical positions held by different people can to some extent be explained by their different initial approaches to the problem. It may seem a tautology in science to say: the results one gets depend on the methods one uses. Population ecology is in an even more difficult state because so many of the arguments are about different interpretations, which depend heavily on the particular kind of analytical methods used.

The key factor analysis

In using this analysis I assume, for the present argument, that the only data available are counts of the number of animals at different times of year – a similar position to that in many population studies. For the results from the other method, considered more fully in the next section, I assume there are available the data on behaviour-food-population relationships that have been built up largely from experimental work.

Using the key factor method, I analysed population counts already published (Jenkins, et al., 1963, 1967), and included further counts up to the present date. The method has been found fruitful for the study of insect populations (Varley and Gradwell, 1968, 1970), and a good example of its use for a bird is the study by Blank et al., (1967) on the partridge (*Perdix perdix*).

With this method, one plots for the successive periods 1, 2, 3, etc. the disappearances or losses k1, k2, k3 etc. (logarithms) which are additive to a total annual loss of K. In red

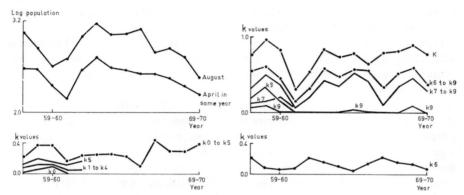

Fig. 1. Key factor analysis of data on red grouse populations at Glen Esk in Angus.

Notes

$K = k_0 + k_1 + k_2 + k_3 + k_4 + k_5 + k_6 + k_7 + k_8 + k_9$.

k_0: potential natality loss. This is the logarithm of (adult population + maximum potential of eggs) − logarithm of (adult population + actual number of eggs laid). The maximum potential of eggs is the mean clutch size in the one year of the study when this was largest, multiplied by the number of hens in the spring population;

k_1: eggs taken by us, nil in most years. The greatest loss in Glen Esk was 0.0139 in one year, and at Kerloch 0.0473, i.e. small or negligible compared with other production losses;

k_2: egg predation;

k_3: eggs lost by the hen deserting the nest; k_2 and k_3 are not necessarily successive and may occur at any time in incubation;

k_4: loss of eggs which failed to hatch due to infertility or embryo death.

There is an error in the life table data given for Glen Esk in Jenkins et al. (1963, Table 28). The figure for hatching success is applied to all eggs laid, whereas it should be applied (Table 20) only to the number of eggs left after predation, desertion and earlier losses;

k_5: loss of chicks from hatching to being full-grown;

k_6: loss due to shooting;

k_7: loss from after shooting to midwinter;

k_8: loss from midwinter to spring;

k_9: loss due to unmated cocks that do not pair up with hens. Late-winter loss is $k_8 + k_9$, as in Blank et al. (1967). The April population in Fig. 1 and Fig. 5 includes unmated cocks.

In a given year, the August figure is for the August following the April figure vertically underneath it. When comparing losses from August to the following April, one should therefore look at the April figure one year to the right.

At Glen Esk from 1962 on, only a part of the original area was counted. However, the number counted was multiplied by a conversion factor based on acreage, so that all densities here are comparable.

grouse, which breed once a year, total K is the logarithm for the maximum total for the year (adults in summer + number of eggs) minus the logarithm for the minimum (adult stock of pairs in the next spring). The individual k values are plotted for the years when population data are available. One can then tell which of these individual k values contributes most to the variation in total K and thus to population variations between years. The mortality factor concerned, the 'key' factor, is useful for predicting future population changes up to the next spring.

The following figures are available for each year: number of adult cocks and hens before egg laying, maximum potential clutch size (the mean clutch in the one year of the study when this was at a maximum), mean clutch for the year, number of eggs failing to hatch due to predation, desertion, infertility and embryo mortality, total numbers of adult cocks, hens and young when the young are full-grown at 12 weeks, number shot, number after shooting, number in mid December, and number next spring.

Data were used from two study areas in Scotland: Glen Esk in Angus and Kerloch in Kincardineshire. Each area was divided into several parts which were counted separately (since separate analyses might possibly show local differences), but the parts are combined for this preliminary analysis. At Glen Esk, populations in August were positively correlated (Fig. 1) with those in the following April ($r = +0.77$, $P < 0.001$). Fig. 2a suggests that in the first five years when the data were absolute figures and not samples, shooting took a higher proportion at high densities than at low ones, but there is a less clear relationship when data for all years were considered. Winter loss is the key factor (Fig. 1) contributing most to variations in spring population between years. Winter loss (including the loss due to unmated cocks not pairing up) is closely correlated with total K ($r = +0.74$; $P < 0.01$).

There is a suggestion of direct density dependence in a few k values (Appendix), but, as an example, the k for winter loss at Glen Esk is not correlated ($r = +0.385$, n.s.) with the logarithm of the population after shooting. In the first five years when, as mentioned, the data were based on absolute figures and not on samples, there is no direct density dependence (see Appendix for fuller details). Individual k values for other periods of loss are not directly or inversely correlated with the logarithm of the density at the beginning of the appropriate period of loss (Fig. 2b and 3). Instead, when points for successive years are joined they show an anti-clockwise spiral. This indicates 'delayed density dependence' (Varley and Gradwell, 1970), which is a feature of cyclical fluctuations. It suggests that the cause occurred earlier, but continues to influence population dynamics in later years due to a strong lag of one or two years. Another feature of such cycles is that when log N_{t+1} is plotted against log N_t in the previous year, the result is a clockwise spiral (Fig. 4).

The usual procedure is to plot each k value against the logarithm of the population density on which it acts (Varley and Gradwell, 1970). In some cases, such as winter loss, this is completely valid. In others, such as the k for chick mortality, it may perhaps seem inappropriate to plot it against the logarithm of hatched chicks plus number of adults, as was done by Blank et al. in the partridge, and possibly better to plot it against the logarithm of the number of hatched chicks only. Both plots (Fig. 3) show a similar anticlockwise spiral, but with hatching loss the relationship is much less clear-cut in the graph where adults are excluded.

There was little or no shooting at the second area, Kerloch. Winter loss is again a key factor (Fig. 5), but so also is production loss at the egg and chick stage. Indeed, in five years out of eight production loss is larger than winter loss. As in Glen Esk, delayed density dependence can be demonstrated for most k values when each is plotted against the

550

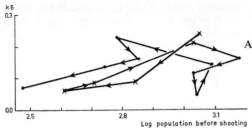

Fig. 2. Individual k values at Glen Esk plotted against densities at the beginning of the appropriate period of loss. See also the notes of Fig. 1. Left: x = first five years (absolute figures, not samples), r = + 0.446; 0.05 < P < 0.1.

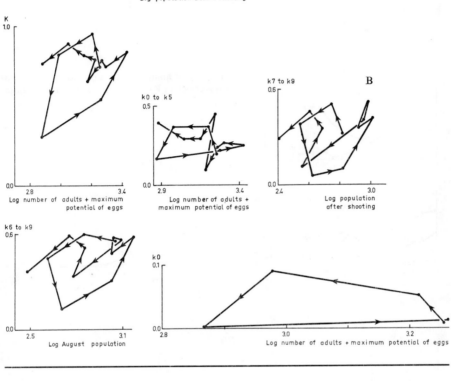

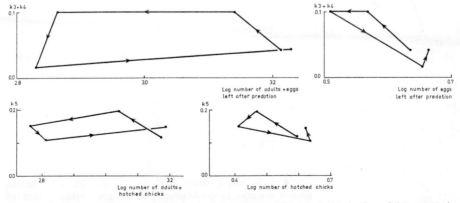

Fig. 3. Individual k values at Glen Esk plotted against densities at the beginning of the appropriate period of loss; k_2 and k_3 are not necessarily wholly successive. See also the notes of Fig. 1.

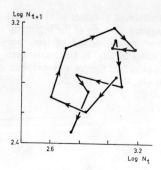

Fig. 4. Population density in year t + 1 at Glen Esk plotted against density in year t. N = August population. See also the notes of Fig. 1.

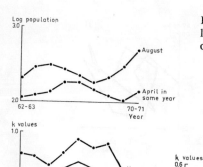

Fig. 5. Key factor analysis of data on red grouse populations at Kerloch in Kincardineshire. See also the notes of Fig. 1.

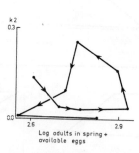

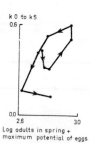

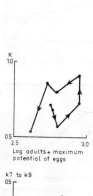

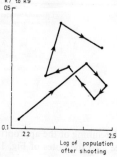

Fig. 6. Individual k values at Kerloch, Kincardineshire, plotted against densities at the beginning of the appropriate period of loss; k₂ and k₃ are not necessarily wholly successive. See also the notes of Fig. 1.

552

logarithm of density at the beginning of the appropriate period of loss and the points are joined in a time sequence (Fig. 6).

Different k values are stated (Blank et al., 1967) to be additive. One could conclude that spring stocks of red grouse were determined mainly by winter losses, but that losses at the egg and chick stage contributed further – sometimes a lot further – to reducing spring numbers. Shooting also contributed a lot on one area.

Summary of long-term work on population dynamics of red grouse

A key factor analysis is simply a way of analysing a series of population counts, and studies of individual behaviour and experiments may give a fuller picture. The differences with this other approach are:

1. It uses intensive studies of the behaviour, survival, mortality, migration and reproduction of individually known red grouse, rather than enumerating totals for all individuals combined; and

2. It consists largely of experiments aimed at discovering underlying mechanisms, instead of simply following natural changes in abundance. The experiments concentrate on population-behaviour relationships, on the effects of altering food by using fertilisers and by burning, and on various features of behaviour, nutrition and reproduction in captivity that in turn give ideas for new work in the field.

A little background information is necessary. Heather (*Calluna vulgaris*) is the predominant plant and forms the birds' main food. The total quantity of it vastly exceeds requirements at all times, and there are few signs of grazing by red grouse. However, they sometimes select heavily for nitrogen and phosphorus (Moss, 1967), especially when the nutrient content of what is generally available is low. Another important point is that each cock is exclusively dominant over all other cocks on a fixed territory of heather moor. Here he courts hens, and here the hen that eventually pairs up with him nests. Territories become redistributed annually in October-November; they are held until late May, though only in early mornings until January-February. Within an area, bigamous cocks have significantly bigger territories than cocks with one hen which, in turn, have bigger territories than unmated cocks (Watson and Miller, 1971). The more aggressive cocks have larger territories; also territory size is secondarily related to cover or visibility, being smaller on hillocky than on open ground (Watson, 1964). An androgen implant makes a cock take a bigger territory and an oestrogen implant makes a cock lose his hen, show less territorial behaviour and eventually give up his territory (Watson, 1970).

Population changes within areas

Breeding success

Annual variations in numbers of young red grouse reared per adult cannot be explained by weather conditions after hatching. When eggs are taken from the wild, rearing success in captivity parallels that in the wild stock (Jenkins et al., 1965). Hence the number reared per adult is largely predetermined by egg quality. Breeding success is related (Jenkins et al., 1963, 1967) to parental condition in spring, the state of the heather in spring, winter, and the previous summer, and in one area to weather in the previous summer. Some of these

553

points have been tested by an experiment increasing the heather's nutritive value by fertiliser (Miller et al., 1970), whereupon grouse reared bigger broods.

Breeding stock

The density of the breeding stock is determined by the territories taken by cock grouse in October (Watson and Jenkins, 1968). Many birds fail to get territories, but they can take territories, survive well and breed if vacancies either occur naturally through death or are made experimentally by removing established territory owners. Very few grouse migrate to settle and breed elsewhere, so populations are largely self-contained and most birds either get a territory or die within 1 km of where they were hatched.

Nearly all birds that fail to get a territory die during winter. This mortality is secondary, as these birds survive very well up to the time of certain changes in strife and social organisation described by Watson (1970). Birds that are territorial and surviving well in one year may lose their territories at the next annual contest and thereafter they soon die (Watson, 1967). The proximate cause of death may be predation, accidents or other causes, but social behaviour is the initial limiting factor (Watson and Moss, 1970).

As all the heather moorland is occupied every year, differences in spring density between years are inversely related to changes in mean territory size (Watson and Miller, 1971). Territorial cocks from year classes hatched during a decline took bigger territories, both as young birds and in a later year as old birds, than territories taken at the same time by cocks from other year classes (Watson and Miller, 1971). They also survived better and were more aggressive.

The question is: what are changes in territory size between years related to? They are not related to either (i) changes in the length of current year's shoots grown in summer, used as an index of the potential quantity of green heather in autumn; or (ii) the number of competitors, since the birds that fail to get territories are not a constant proportion of the total (Watson and Moss, 1971); or (iii) the density of competitors in a density-dependent sense where a higher proportion fails to get territories at high densities (this paper). Instead, the proportion that fails shows delayed density dependence.

There is some evidence that territory size is related to the viability of year classes, and is therefore related to nutrition, but only indirectly via egg quality and maternal nutrition. Miller et al. (1970) showed that when residents were all shot, colonists reared elsewhere did not take smaller territories on fertilised ground, where the heather's nutritive value was better, than on a control area. However, more recent experiments where residents were left unshot, show that cocks on fertilised ground do take smaller territories in their first autumn there than on control areas. This is evidence of a direct reaction to quality of food, either by an adjustment of territorial behaviour at the time when territories are chosen, or by behaviour being affected through the bird having been on a better plane of nutrition. Inherited changes may also be involved, either genetic (Chitty, 1967) or phenotypic, and this is now being studied.

A model of population limitation in red grouse is given in Watson and Moss (1971). The main feature is a chain of causal factors operating at different points in time and often correlated with one another. Weather may be the initial factor triggering off changes. Theoretically, weather could bring out-of-phase populations into phase (Chitty, 1969), but it is uncertain to what extent weather is an initial trigger in red grouse or merely a coordinating tendency.

Differences between areas

Some areas have consistently more grouse than others, even in the same region where climate and amount of heather are similar. Over base-rich rocks, where the heather is of higher nutritive value, grouse stocks are larger, fluctuate less in amplitude, and show better breeding success, than over base-poor rocks (Miller et al., 1966; Jenkins et al., 1967; Moss, 1969).

Comparison of interpretations from the two methods

Red grouse

Many grouse are found dead in winter, mainly killed by predators but often suffering a non-violent death, emaciated and often parasitised (Anon., 1911; Jenkins et al., 1963). An interpretation of this could be that, in winter, predation and starvation from food shortage appreciably reduced breeding stocks below the size of the post-shooting population. This would be partly speculative, but not unreasonable if the only data available were counts of animals, as often occurs in population studies and in key factor analyses of them. However, this interpretation is refuted by intensive observation and experiments with individually marked grouse. The experimental work shows that breeding stocks are already determined by the pattern of territories chosen in the previous October, and it is the many birds failing to get territories which die over the winter, while the others survive extremely well. Winter loss is therefore irrelevant to the determination of the spring population, even though it is a key factor.

Although key factor analysis implies that other losses are additive and this is sometimes stated explicitly (Blank et al., 1967), experiments on red grouse show that some losses are cancelled by later compensatory changes. For example, grouse on an unshot part survived no better than on a shot part (Jenkins et al., 1963, Table 32), so post-shooting mortality on the unshot part was compensatory. The shooting loss, which might otherwise have appeared additive, was not so. In other words, some losses may be a sufficient condition to explain changes in numbers, but are not a necessary condition.

These apparent criticisms of key factor analysis may seem unfair as the method was used only after a detailed programme of experiments and observations on individuals had already been done, whereas ideally it should perhaps be a preliminary way of looking at numerical relationships and testing them statistically with a view to more detailed follow-up work. However, criticism of this useful method developed by Varley and Gradwell (1968) is not justified and is certainly not intended here, provided it is used as just stated. One point of the comments in the previous two paragraphs is to warn against possible misuse of the method, for example in cases where it is thought that a short-term preliminary numerical analysis for density dependence or key factor determination is best followed by doing counts for more years, or that a more thorough analysis based on a longer period is in itself sufficient to allow conclusions that imply causation.

Examples from other species

Another point of the comments three paragraphs above is to illustrate how a difference of initial approach could reasonably provide different speculative interpretations over a matter of some importance to population theory. For example, the speculative interpretation that winter mortality, to a large extent due to starvation, reduces breeding stocks of grouse is the same as Lack (1966) made in the great tit (*Parus major*), where some numerical details of population relationships from late summer through to spring are similar (Watson and Moss, 1970, p. 204; Krebs, 1970) to those in red grouse. The question is whether this mortality in great tits is really reducing breeding stocks, or whether it is secondary as in red grouse. There is no way of telling this one way or the other from a key factor analysis or any other numerical analysis of counts. The only way of finding out is to take the different initial approach of studying individual behaviour and doing experiments. This has now been done in the great tit by Krebs (1970). His paper is another demonstration, paralleled by that in this paper, that a numerical analysis alone can readily lead to interpretations which may be at odds with the results attained by experiments.

The previous section gave an example of compensatory change in red grouse. Kluyver (1971) gave another at this conference. The removal of 60% of the production of young great tits made no difference to the breeding population next year. Yet Krebs (1970) has shown by a key factor analysis followed by a tested model that density-dependent variations in production in a population near Oxford are sufficient to account for regulation (i.e. maintaining the mean level of spring population observed). Kluyver's conclusion is subject to the important qualification that there was no untreated control area nearby, but his result seems difficult to refute since he found that individually marked birds survived much better than usual (i.e. compensatory survival) on the depleted area. Similarly, several studies with rodents in the wild have shown compensatory changes in mortality, survival and migration when individuals were removed or added (references in Watson and Moss, 1970, p. 185, 193).

Of course it is possible to explore the problem of compensatory changes by using key factor analysis. If a series of mortalities is largely compensated for, they ought not to show up as key factors or at least the analysis should show that the effects of highly variable key factors have been reduced by compensation (G. R. Gradwell, pers. comm.). For example, Varley and Gradwell (1968) found in winter moth (*Operophtera brumata*) that k values for pupal predation in the soil appeared to be compensating, to some extent, for changes in the k values for winter mortality which was the key factor. One difficulty is that this kind of compensation may be difficult to detect by counts alone (a) unless counts are made at many different intervals of time, which is often difficult or impossible in many species, and (b) if the mortalities involved are not a key factor but nevertheless may seem important by appearing to be additive. However, rather than involving ourselves in increasingly sophisticated testing of numerical data for compensation, I consider it more useful to do empirical experiments on the subject.

In some cases it is implied that finding correlations between certain demographic parameters is sufficient to provide firm conclusions about what determines populations. For example, an analysis by Blank et al. (1967) in the partridge showed that chick mortality was the key factor and was density-dependent. Shooting was also density-dependent, and they stated (p. 533) that 'undoubtedly the contrived density dependence of this artificial mortality factor has prevented the demonstration of any natural density-dependent regulation through migration and behavioural mechanism'. However, after shooting there is still a big and variable winter loss, and Blank et al. gave no data against the possibility that this might involve social behaviour, whether density-dependent or not, although Jenkins (1961) had given descriptive evidence suggesting that much of the winter loss might be due to agonistic behaviour. In fact, in every year the post-shooting k values are much greater than the k values for shooting. It is not certain yet what determines spring populations in this species, and firm conclusions must await the experiments which have not yet been attempted.

General problems

Key factor analysis and numerical methods involving density dependence indicate periods of loss. Such methods may be useful for prediction, and are an effective way of laying out data and looking for relationships. These may be important steps, but they are only first steps which do not necessarily identify or measure the underlying mechanisms behind changes in numbers. Eberhardt (1970) has questioned the use of correlations and regressions for showing density-dependent regulation, and has illustrated the caution that is needed by generating from a series of random numbers a model with a correlation coefficient similar to that cited as demonstrating density dependence. I support his conclusion (p. 309) that 'trustworthy inferences about population regulation must come from an understanding of the mechanics of the underlying processes and their direct effect on population dynamics.'

Furthermore, the terms 'factor' or 'mortality factor' in numerical studies may be misleading. What is generally involved is a period of change of numbers or period of loss, where the loss is a disappearance – not necessarily a mortality – and where the method usually cannot (except in some cases like shooting) attribute the loss to specific causal factors. A proper understanding of the underlying causal mechanisms is likely to come only from experiments.

Acknowledgments

I am grateful to Prof. G. C. Varley who persuaded me to use key factor analysis, and to him and Dr D. Jenkins for making useful comments on the manuscript. I particularly thank Mr G. R. Gradwell for his interest in the work and his valuable comments on the manuscript.

Appendix

Samples and absolute counts

In the first five years at Glen Esk, the counts are absolute figures. In later years the figures for shooting and for the number of young reared are based on samples; the spring count is an absolute figure, as is the calculated spring total of adults + maximum potential of eggs. This means that the k values for production losses, shooting and post-shooting winter loss are less reliable in the later years, whereas the estimates of K are as good as in the first five years. This may account for the facts that:

i. k for shooting loss at Glen Esk suggests clear density dependence in the first five years, but there is a big scatter in later years;

ii. k values for total production loss, August-April loss and its component of winter loss, all show a clear anticlockwise spiral (delayed density dependence) in the first five years at Glen Esk, but there is a much less clear spiral in later years;

557

iii. K, which does not depend on sample counts, shows a fairly clear anticlockwise spiral for all years at Glen Esk;

iv. At Kerloch, where the counts are absolute figures in all years, there is always a fairly clear anticlockwise spiral in K (total production loss). Winter loss shows no clear relationship.

The total August population was counted and separated into adults and young. The number of adults in August was sometimes greater and sometimes less than the number in spring, due to local movements, but was usually very similar (Jenkins et al., 1963, Table 12). For convenience of analysis, the August population used here is based on the spring population of adults + an estimate of the number of young. The estimate of young is based on the observed proportions of young and adult in the total counts made in August, thus the adult population in spring multiplied by the number of young per adult in the August count equals the number of young in August.

The post-shooting population was calculated as the August population minus the number shot.

Density dependence and delayed density dependence

There is a suggestion of direct density dependence at Glen Esk in the plots of K, k_6–k_9 inclusive and its component of post-shooting winter loss. However, there is a big scatter in points, and in K the apparent association depends on only one point and so has not been tested. Also the k value for winter loss (k_7–k_9 inclusive) is not significantly correlated ($r = + 0.385$, $P > 0.1$) with population density after shooting, thus refuting a direct density-dependent relationship. However a delayed density-dependent relationship appears when the points for the first five years (when the data are absolute figures and not samples) are joined in a time sequence. The apparent density dependence thus depends on the later and less reliable set of data. At Kerloch, where all the data are absolute figures, there is again a suggestion of direct density dependence in the plot for production losses, but delayed density dependence is suggested when the points are joined in time sequence. Perhaps both are involved in some cases. The answer should become clearer with a few more years' data from absolute figures at Kerloch.

References

Anonymous, 1911. The grouse in health and in disease, 2 vols. Committee of Inquiry on Grouse Disease, London.

Blank, T. H., T. R. E. Southwood & D. J. Cross, 1967. The ecology of the partridge. I. Outline of population processes with particular reference to chick mortality and nest density. *J. Anim. Ecol.* 36: 549–556.

Chitty, D., 1967. The natural selection of self-regulatory behaviour in animal populations. *Proc. ecol. Soc. Aust.* 2: 51–78.

Chitty, D., 1969. Regulatory effects of a random variable. *Am. Zool.* 9: 400.

Eberhardt, L. L., 1970. Correlation, regression and density dependence. *Ecology* 51: 306–310.

Jenkins, D., 1961. Population control in protected partridges (*Perdix perdix*). *J. Anim. Ecol.* 30: 235–258.

Jenkins, D., A. Watson & G. R. Miller, 1963. Population studies on red grouse, *Lagopus lagopus scoticus* (Lath.) in north-east Scotland. *J. Anim. Ecol.* 32: 317–376.

Jenkins, D., A. Watson & G. R. Miller, 1967. Population fluctuations in the red grouse *Lagopus lagopus scoticus. J. Anim. Ecol.* 36: 97–122.

Jenkins, D., A. Watson & N. Picozzi, 1965. Red grouse chick survival in captivity and in the wild. *Trans. Int. Un. Game Biol.* 6: 63–70.

Kluyver, H. N. 1971. Regulation of numbers in populations of Great Tits. In: P. J. den Boer and G. R. Gradwell, Dynamics of population. *Proc. Adv. Study Inst. Dynamics Numbers Popul.* (Oosterbeek, 1970): 507–523.

Krebs, J. R., 1970. Regulation of numbers in the great tit (Aves: Passeriformes) *J. Zool.* 162: 319–333.

Lack, D., 1966. Population studies of birds. Oxford.

Miller, G. R., D. Jenkins & A. Watson, 1966. Heather performance and red grouse populations. I. Visual estimates of heather performance. *J. appl. Ecol.* 3: 313–326.

Miller, G. R., A. Watson & D. Jenkins, 1970. Responses of red grouse populations to experimental improvement of their food. In: A. Watson (Ed.), Animal populations in relation to their food resources, p. 323–335. Oxford & Edinburgh.

Moss, R., 1967. Probable limiting nutrients in the main food of red grouse (*Lagopus lagopus scoticus*). In: K. Petrusewicz (Ed.), Secondary productivity of terrestrial ecosystems, p. 369–379. Warszawa & Krakow.

Moss, R., 1969. A comparison of red grouse (*Lagopus l. scoticus*) stocks with the production and nutritive value of heather (*Calluna vulgaris*). *J. Anim. Ecol.* 38: 103–112.

Varley, G. C. & G. R. Gradwell, 1968. Population models for the winter moth. In: T. R. E. Southwood (Ed.), Insect abundance, p. 132–142. Oxford & Edinburgh.

Varley, G. C. & G. R. Gradwell, 1970. Recent advances in insect population dynamics. *A. Rev. Ent.* 15: 1–24.

Watson, A., 1964. Aggression and population regulation in red grouse. *Nature, Lond.* 202: 506–507.

Watson, A., 1967. Social status and population regulation in the red grouse (*Lagopus lagopus scoticus*). *Proc. R. Soc. Popul. Study Grp* 2: 22–30.

Watson, A., 1970. Territorial and reproductive behaviour of red grouse. *J. Reprod. Fert.*, Suppl. 11: 3–14.

Watson, A. & D. Jenkins, 1968. Experiments on population control by territorial behaviour in red grouse. *J. Anim. Ecol.* 37: 595–614.

Watson, A. & G. R. Miller, 1971. Territory size and aggression in a fluctuating red grouse population *J. Anim. Ecol.* 40: 367–383.

Watson, A. & R. Moss, 1970. Dominance, spacing behaviour and aggression in relation to population limitation in vertebrates. In: A. Watson (Ed.), Animal populations in relation to their food resources, p. 167–220. Oxford & Edinburgh.

Watson, A. & R. Moss, 1971. A model of population dynamics in red grouse. *Proc. Int. orn. Congr.* 15 (in press).

Discussion

Participants: Watson (Author), Bakker (K.), Brussard, Clough, Coulson, Dhondt, Frank, Gudmundsson, Jacobs, Lawton, Murton, Pimentel, Rosenzweig, Turnock, Varley, Watt, Way, Williamson and Zahavi

The pattern of fluctuations in game birds would appear to be that of an autocorrelated time series with density at any time dependent on density at – at least – two previous times: $\ln N_t = b_0 + b_1 \ln N_{t-1} + b_2 \ln N_{t-2}$ (N_t: density in year t).

This was shown by P. A. P. Moran (*Aust. J. Zool.*, 1953) to describe the lynx cycle very well, with residuals being due to weather. Large clusters of residuals are due to lowered global temperature caused by effects of volcanic eruptions on atmospheric turbidity: see W. J. Humphrey's article in *Bull. Franklin Inst.* (1913) and his 'The physics of the air'; K. Watt's article in *Brookhaven Symp. Biol.* (1969) (WATT). Is this valid in the lynx cycle, in view of Moran's demonstration that the residuals differ in the up and down phases of the cycle (WILLIAMSON)? Clusters of negative residuals follow volcanic eruptions with a lag of six to eight years, and these residuals are larger than any corresponding positive clusters (WATT). But the driving force in the lynx-hare cycle remains to be explained; Pitelka's data on lemmings suggest that nutrient content of vegetation is important for

mammals (ROSENZWEIG). The driving force is some causal pathway of fundamentally density-dependent character as explained by Schultz in 'The ecosystem concept in resource
management' (Academic Press, edited by Van Dyne). The carry-over of environmental
effects for more than one generation or year is probably via maternal rather than genetic
inheritance. Using the data of Green and Evans on Minnesota hare survival, it appears
that a principal reason for the hare cycle is year-to-year variations in the survival of
young hares during the first 18 months of life. It can be shown that this, in turn, is due to
year-to-year fluctuations in the depth of snowfall to which their mothers were exposed
(WATT). The length of the lag within the population cycle depends partly on the animals'
survival rate. In the red grouse in one intensively studied fluctuation, the territorial cocks
that were reared during the decline survived better. They also took bigger territories than
did other year-classes both during the decline and during the start of the subsequent increase – i.e. first as young birds and later as old birds. Until such a year-class has died out,
a considerable lag is introduced (AUTHOR).

For the last 8 years I have been working on the rock ptarmigan (*Lagopus mutus*) in
Iceland, which is subject to a predictable 10-year cycle reaching a peak about the middle
of each decade. When the population was increasing the annual survival of young was
17–24%, but after the peak in 1966 it dropped to 3–4% and has remained at this level for
the past four years. This – mainly due to different winter mortality – was found to be the
population parameter that results in by far the greatest variations in numbers. So far I
have not been able to correlate these variations with any variations in environmental
factors (climate, food) or with the behaviour of the birds themselves. When ptarmigan are
scarce territories are large, and when ptarmigan are abundant territories are small. Hence,
territoriality appears to function chiefly as a spacing mechanism, although in a few areas
where ptarmigan reach an exceptionally high density, territoriality may put a ceiling on
population size, only resulting in overflow to less favourable or marginal habitats
(GUDMUNDSSON). Although in various details there are differences between Iceland and
Scotland, one should, if possible, look for common features. Both in Iceland and Scotland
the key period of loss is over the winter, and there are clear signs of variations in the
viability of different year-classes (AUTHOR).

Watson's paper starts with the questions:
1. What causes the fluctuations from year to year?
2. What sets the mean level of abundance?
In view of the violent yearly fluctuations shown by the data, the 'mean level of abundance'
seems a rather uninteresting statistic (BRUSSARD). I think the 'mean level of abundance' is
a difficult concept anyway, even without violent changes. However, it may be a handy
term, provided that its conceptual limitations are clearly realized. For instance, differences
between areas can be enormous, with some low-density areas never remotely approaching
the densities of high-abundance areas (AUTHOR).

How would the difference in the amplitude of fluctuations between areas of high and
low mean abundance be explained (DHONDT)? I see two possibilities:
1. When numbers are relatively high in high-density areas some birds are moving to lower-
density areas;
2. Populations in the two areas are self-contained, and the higher-density areas stay
higher because the nutrient content of the food is better and because a high proportion of
the locally reared birds get territories there.

560

I favour the second possibility, although the first cannot be fully refuted. I go on the assumption that some of the explanation of annual fluctuations is not essentially different in red grouse from that for different mean abundance between areas. In this connection, the following hypothesis is currently being tested: In a high-density area the nutrient content of the food is nearly always high, and the population of locally reared birds stays high. In a poor year the nutrient content of the food may fall, and then even the population in the best area should also fall. If these events do not coincide, the hypothesis will be refuted (AUTHOR).

Is there migration between adjacent areas with:

a. high population level, but low amplitude fluctuations, and

b. lower level, but high amplitude fluctuations?

Does the possibly small amount of migration vary with time and is it related to population level (TURNOCK)? I have no evidence of any such migrations between areas; on the contrary, the populations appear to be largely self-contained. A very few hens do move long distances, but not necessarily from high- to low-density areas. I doubt whether the small amount of migration varies between years either at different or at the same densities, but the data are not yet specifically analysed on this point.

Were there differences in genetic variability between peaks and lows of population density, and could such differences give a clue to the key factors responsible for the density fluctuations (JACOBS)? In a current experiment where birds are reared in the laboratory from eggs taken in the field, the aim is to test whether any form of inheritance is involved in these annual fluctuations. If there is any, it will not yet be known – from the technique used – whether it will be maternal or genetic inheritance (AUTHOR).

Were there marked differences in breeding succes between different year-classes in any one year, which cannot solely be explained in terms of there being an improved breeding with increase in age; so that either genetical or maternal inheritance of breeding success will play some part (COULSON)? There is no obvious increase in breeding success with age, but red grouse live a very short time and hardly any hens breed more than twice (AUTHOR).

Was there an increase in body weight or in fat deposits in the increase phase or at the peak of the grouse cycle? Such an increase in body weight at the peak of the 3–4 year cycle in microtine rodents has been found by Chitty, and is often considered a good overall indicator of health and general condition (CLOUGH). I found a positive correlation between adult body weight in summer and breeding success in the same year during one fluctuation. Adult body weight in summer was lower in years of decline (AUTHOR).

The role of the food in the fluctuations of numbers of the red grouse

1. Do the birds select for the quality (nutrient content) of the food (PIMENTEL)? The nutrient content of the food eaten by the birds varies according to their degree of selection, because it depends on which part of the plant is eaten. A similar part will vary in nutrient content within the same plant, between plants of the same age, and between different ages of plants. So it becomes difficult to define what 'food' is for red grouse, far less to measure how much is present (AUTHOR).

2. Does the quality of the food change from year to year (FRANK)? In spring – which is thought to be a critical time, when the hen is laying down material for her eggs – the nutrient content varies a lot from year to year. This depends mainly on the current weath-

er, which brings on highly nutritious new growth in a mild spring but no new growth at all in a late spring. The nutrient content in late autumn also varies between years, even when measured after growth has ceased (AUTHOR).

3. The youngest leaves on a shoot will be the most nutritious, but as they grow tannins will accumulate which can inactivate digestive enzymes. If birds on 'poor' food were to compensate by taking more, this would increase the amount of the poisonous tannin ingested (VARLEY). The youngest-growing leaves of heather are the most nutritious in N and P content. If tannins were toxic it would be expected that grouse would select against them. However, an experiment by Moss showed that, if anything, there was a significant selection ($P < 0.05$) for tannins (AUTHOR).

4. Was the density of animals correlated with the genetic type of plants surviving (PIMENTEL)? This was not studied, but only about 5% of the total amount of potential food gets eaten by the birds in a year (AUTHOR).

5. Is there any evidence that the time available for feeding is limiting? Is the short part of the day when they feed all the time they have available? Food has to be digested, and the birds have to do many other things as well as feed (LAWTON). Red grouse spend much of the day resting, and feed intensively only before dusk. However, there may be a limit to the amount of material which can be processed through the gut in 24 hours. Nevertheless, the spring population is determined – sometimes within a few days in autumn – at a time when heather is still growing and when there is an abundance of other foods such as ripe oats, grass seeds, weeds, etc. What happens after this seems unimportant, as the non-territorial birds all die and the territorial ones nearly all survive. But to avoid a dogmatic or simplistic view of food shortage, J. Savory, a Ph. D student, is studying these time-intake relationships (AUTHOR).

6. Although food supply appears to be more than sufficient for all individuals, some bird species may be faced with food shortage because they have conventions – important in other respects – which set limits on the way they can exploit their food. Therefore, it might be misleading to state that it is unlikely that red grouse will be affected by food shortage. The wood-pigeon may be an example. The birds are forced to feed in flocks and interactions within the flocks set limits on how many birds can maintain adequate feeding rates. Hence, the availability of food and its total abundance are obviously different in the wood-pigeon, and may be so in the red grouse. For instance, the height of heather may be important; tall heather would prevent the grouse seeing or reaching nutritive shoots, short heather would perhaps expose them to predators. Again, the females perhaps need special resources while incubating or for some special season which could be quite brief (MURTON). The nutritive value of the food certainly affects grouse, but the statement was that there was no shortage in the total quantity of potentially edible vegetation. Availability is another thing, and height of heather may well be important in determining the relationship between the birds' spacing behaviour and their total food supply. Savory is now studying these aspects. However, we see virtually no starvation mortality in autumn, when the main social events that determine the breeding population occur (AUTHOR).

7. Does territory size vary according to the quantity and quality of the food (PIMENTEL)? Large territories have much more total quantity of potential food than small territories, but it is again difficult to examine quality in a way that is realistic to the birds. However territories are smaller after the nutrient content of the heather has been greatly increased by fertilizer (AUTHOR).

8. What is the selective value of territorial behaviour in the red grouse? Is there any evi-

dence that territorial behaviour minimizes feeding damage to the heather that might otherwise affect the quality or quantity of food in the following season? That the red grouse is feeding at not much below the limits of its food supply is surely indicated by the population changes in one of the study areas where the numbers fluctuated in relation to seasonal variation in vigour of the heather (WAY). The question whether territorial behaviour minimizes damage to future food resources can not be answered, because of the difficulty of defining food. However, the main differences in nutritive value occur between different springs, and are due largely to spring weather. Possibly an increase in the territory size could allow a bird a better selection of the minute amount of new growth in April. The selective value of territorial behaviour is a difficult problem because the arguments are speculative. Considered teleologically, territorial behaviour could be of selective value because: a) it allows birds to survive; b) courtship, pairing and breeding do not occur without previous territorial behaviour; c) it limits the breeding population; d) it may allow uninterrupted mating, though nothing is known about the importance of this; e) it is a fixed address where cock and hen can find each other quickly after being separated; f) it ensures an exclusive food territory for the pair in late winter and spring; g) it probably allows the birds to get acquainted with their home ground very well, and this may be one reason why they are less vulnerable to predators than non-territorial birds. These are not given in any order of importance because such an order cannot be assessed (AUTHOR).

9. The type of territory in the red grouse can be shown, by a comparative behaviour study of different species, to be related to feeding behaviour. Species which eat food that has a homogeneous distribution tend to split their habitat into feeding territories. When we want to examine how the individual birds relate their territory size to the feeding capacity of the area we may be misled by a study of aggression. By making an animal more aggressive by hormone implants and correlating this with the attainment of a larger territory, one may miss the natural mechanism. If an animal attacks another from a further distance and we call it a higher aggressiveness, the real mechanism may be that the same amount of aggression is released by a different releasing stimulus. If the whole population is selected for aggression, but resources are not limiting, over a short time they may develop behavioural mechanisms to be able to live as a dense crowd at the higher aggressive level. What may really happen is that aggression often stays at the same level, but that birds under different conditions aim at different territory size (ZAHAVI). The trouble about these evolutionary arguments is that they are so speculative, and thus can be used as confirmatory evidence for many possible hypotheses. Individuals within areas vary in territory size and social status, and experiments with hormone implants are a useful way of exploring this variation in the quality of individuals. Experimentation with food is another useful way. The problems of aggression and individual quality become difficult if one is comparing differences between years or between areas, using field observations. I am now trying to get over this by using a standard stimulus in the field and by testing in a standard way in the laboratory (AUTHOR).

The disadvantage of an increased aggressiveness may very well be the disturbance of the balance between 'aggression' and 'sex' in the behavioural pattern of the bird. This may make it impossible for the male to court the female. This problem is being studied in the three-spined stickleback at the Department of Ethology at Leiden. An attempt is being made to select strains for high and for low aggressiveness, with the hypothesis that a highly aggressive male will have difficulties in courtship, and a male of low aggressiveness will have difficulties in getting a territory (BAKKER). I have just started to study some of these points by trying to breed for high and low aggressiveness with captive red grouse and ptarmigan (AUTHOR).

Proc. Adv. Study Inst. Dynamics Numbers Popul. (Oosterbeek, 1970) 565–567

Some general remarks on the concepts 'population' and 'regulation'*

K. Bakker

Zoological Laboratory, State University of Leiden, the Netherlands

In his paper Andrewartha stated that it would be worthwhile to discuss the question of what we are talking about when using the term population. Solomon then answered that he had no special need for formal definitions, since everybody studying populations will have a perfectly clear idea about what he means by some term. This may be so, and I agree with his remark that when two population ecologists are discussing their work together, they will understand each other perfectly well on this point, albeit after some time. However – and I confess that this is one of my idiosynchrasies – I feel that the problem of how to delimit a population is very fundamental, and cannot be bypassed.

A growing number of ecologists recognize that the delimitation of what one takes as a population entirely depends on the problem one wants to study, and, because ecologists may study widely different problems, their delimitation of a population will also be very different. I am quite willing to consider the parasites which are competing for the food supply in one host larva as a population, or the nestlings in one nest of a bird, or the aphids on a certain bean plant, or the bunch of isopods hiding under the bark of a tree during a particular day, as long as the problems one wants to solve on these populations are biologically meaningful. The same applies to one colony of birds, or one pocket of ragwort plants in the dunes, or the herring in the North Sea. However, when one studies population *dynamics*, it is clear that the population studied must exist for longer than one generation. A population is a biological unit for study, with a number of varying statistics (e.g. number, density, birth rate, death rate, sex ratio, age distribution) and which derives a *biological* meaning from the fact that some direct or indirect interactions among its members are more important than those between its members and members of other populations. These interactions may consist of utilization of the same food resource or of the same suitable space, or of being subjected to the same predator or parasite, or of collective action to protect the members against desiccation, etc. Questions pertaining to these interactions may be entirely valid scientifically, but they are studied on populations which are very different in size and longevity.

A lot of confusion can arise when problems pertaining to populations on different scales are discussed.

I will try to illustrate this with the well-known beautiful experiment done by Huffaker on the interaction between a phytophagous mite, feeding on oranges, and a predatory

---

* This paper was prepared during the conference on request of a number of participants as a personal reaction on a few points raised.

mite. When he released the prey on one or a small number of oranges, the prey increased rapidly. But some time after introduction of the predator, the prey population began to decrease and both prey and predator became extinct. Certainly, no predator-prey oscillations resulted in these small populations. However, by increasing the number of oranges and by *lumping* the numbers of prey and predators counted on all of them, Huffaker got a fine predator-prey oscillation, going on for about three cycles. This was due to the fact that not all oranges were colonized by the prey and the predator *at the same time*, and, as in the prickly pear and *Cactoblastis*, the two organisms played 'cat and mouse' with one another. Nevertheless, there was still some synchronization in the system and after the third cycle both populations died out. Now we may predict that if the number of oranges had been increased say 10–fold, and the numbers counted on them had been lumped as before, one would have found that the populations did not show oscillations, but would fluctuate irregularly around a more or less stable mean.

One may call this a fine case of 'regulation', but it is difficult to see any advantage in doing so, since the mechanism which is responsible for this apparent regulation can be perfectly understood from the processes taking place in the various subpopulations – the animals on the separate oranges – and from the statistics of the system. I hasten to add that this is *not* meant to imply that *all* predator-prey oscillations are due to a similar mechanism, but only to illustrate the importance of scale effects. Nor do I want to deny the importance of density-dependent processes.

Another point I want to make is on the nature of population regulation. As an example I will take the importance attributed to territorial mechanisms for the regulation of numbers. I think there is an error in our thinking when we state that territorial behaviour has evolved to avoid overexploitation of a habitat, although this may be the result. I firmly believe that selection acts on the individuals in a population, and that any advantage from the development of some kind of territorial behaviour should be sought for on the level of the individual organisms' chances to live and multiply and transfer its genes to the next generation. This means that the regulation of population density is only a beneficial by-product of natural selection, which has its point of attack at the individual level. This does not reduce the problem of regulation to being a relatively unimportant problem! However, I feel that 'regulation' is *not* a *property* of a population in the way that homeostasis may be a physiological property of an individual organism. Here we come to the very fundamental problem of the extrapolation of properties from the level of the individual organism to that of the population, or even to that of the community; this was touched upon during the discussion following Huffaker's paper. The extrapolation of analogies to another level of organization is very dangerous, and I am afraid that we may readily fall into this pitfall. For this reason, I always get worried if someone speaks about the 'functions' of a community (or uses similar expressions) as if the community were an entity comparable to an individual organism. Instead of clarifying our thoughts I think that it may confuse us.

I strongly advocate a thorough analysis of the terms used in ecology. At least, we may expect an author to give a definition of the terms he uses – as Varley emphasized. Well-defined terms and agreement on them are prerequisites for the development of a synthetic ecology.

Concluding, I may ask: What is ecology, and what are ecologists? Clearly, ecology is not yet a unified science, studying the fundamental processes of life as is done in biochemistry and cell biology. On the other hand, we will not be satisfied with being described as a

566

bunch of naturalists – albeit scientific naturalists as Elton once said – studying a bewildering variety of interesting biological phenomena on the supra-individual level. What is the common aim of the thoroughly studied case-histories on cinnabar moths, pine loopers, kittiwakes, aphids, grouse, etc.? Are we continuing these studies for their own sake, because they are interesting, or do we have a hope, however faint, that some genius like Darwin will unify ecology in a general theory on animal and plant numbers? Our colleagues studying problems in applied ecology are better off; they may easily point out the relevance to human society of what they are doing, even when they feel the same lack of synthesis in ecological theory as the pure scientists do.

I sincerely hope that as a result of this conference we will be now able to get somewhat nearer to an answer to these questions.

For me, the synthesis has already been laid, by Darwin; my personal interest lies mainly in the various ways organisms try to secure 'a place in the sun'.

Proc. Adv. Study Inst. Dynamics Numbers Popul. (Oosterbeek, 1970) 568–580

Dynamics of populations: A synthesis

K. E. F. Watt

Department of Zoology, University of California, Davis, USA

Abstract

This paper proceeds to a synthesis of data and theories about population dynamics through five steps. At first, we briefly survey the present situation in this field, hopefully from a sufficiently broad perspective to be able to discern fundamental deficiencies in the present state of our understanding. Second, certain sample phenomena are discussed which provide clues about how we might improve our understanding. Third, we briefly sketch an approach for arriving at a small set of powerful principles which can provide a satisfactory theoretical basis for this subject. Fourth, we review the properties that would be desirable in a set of such principles. Finally, we present and explain some of the basic principles, show how they relate to each other, the material presented in this meeting and, very briefly, the affairs of mankind.

The present situation

This meeting has presented us with a representative sample of the current situation in the ecological literature. A great number of facts, theories, and rules have been discussed, but it takes a tremendous mental effort to comprehend all of this material as expressions of a small number of powerful general principles. It would appear that after about 30 years of intensive effort, ecology at present is having its forward progress impeded by six fundamental problems. Before we attempt any novel synthesis, it is important to identify these problems.

One dominant impression of the state of this science is that theoretical developments have been remarkably influenced by data from a relatively small group of species. Most of these species happen to be of great economic importance. If economically important species happen to be biologically unusual as a group, in any way, then our theories are biased to that extent. It should be noted that a great many of the species in the world are so rare that they have attracted little attention, and also may be quite stable in numbers, which would also prevent them from attracting attention.

Also, the great influence on theory of a small number of species has a deeper significance. When research is focussed on one, or a small number of species, this has a subtle but profound influence on the type of hypothesis being tested. In effect, the hypotheses have often been related to the question: 'Why does this species fluctuate from time to time the way it does?' It is remarkable how we seem to have forgotten that probably the most famous and intellectually important environmental scientist of all time was Darwin, and he used a quite different research approach. His hypotheses were related to the comparative studies of many and quite different species. The central research question was: 'Why do these species differ the way they do?'

Ecology is remarkably short of long runs of data. If one wishes to study patterns of fluctuation over long periods of time in order to determine the relative impact of density-dependent and -independent factors – such as volcanic eruptions – on population dynamics, he needs data of a type which were collected long ago, but less frequently now. The current system of financing research puts great emphasis on short-term results. The resulting data are of no use in examining many kinds of issues.

I believe that a preoccupation with changes in numbers through time has blinded us to many other kinds of phenomena which should have received more attention. It appears to be the product of laboratory studies, where densities are often so unnaturally high that a large number of incidents occur per unit time and space. In the field, I am impressed not so much by great density as being a common phenomenon, but great rarity. Thus, I am much more impressed by the significance of the great distance that often occurs between nearest neighbors, and the effect this has in lowering the probability of an event.

The fifth problem that disturbs me deeply is the current highly fragmented state of ecology as a science. Several different foci of research effort can be distinguished, and there is danger that the links between these activities are weakening. This Institute is primarily concerned with numbers; other groups are concerned with energy flow in ecosystems, the theory of diversity and stability, the role of space in ecology, qualitative changes, and so on.

My sixth and most basic concern is that I do not see a tremendous effort underway to develop a strong theoretical core that will bring all parts of this science back together. If this is not done, we shall all be washed out to sea in an immense tide of unrelated information.

Clues about future directions

Many studies provide clues about where we should go from here. Work by Hamilton and his colleagues (1967, 1969, 1970) on starling roost dispersal considered the various energy strategies being followed by starlings that fly each day different distances out from the roost. Those that fly out only a short distance lose little energy in flight, but meet great competition for food. Those that fly out a long distance gain in reduced competition, but lose in the increased energy cost of flight. Ultimately, the distance flown is so great that the increased fuel cost of flight and the decreased time for feeding can not be compensated for by decreased competition. The conceptual models required by this type of study link together matter, energy, space, time and information. Information enters in several senses, including the species diversity and pattern diversity of the starlings' food.

Recent studies on hunting prides of big cats in Africa also point to the fact that space, time and information are resources in the same sense as matter and energy. The destructive efficiency of mammalian carnivores is so great that there must be some important resource limitation that prevents them from annihilating their prey. The limited resources are their energy, which they burn up in abundance while involved in tremendous exertion traversing space to catch their prey, and the time available in which to catch prey before their energy reserves are so low that they are not strong enough to kill. It is noteworthy that stalk and pursuit of a buffalo by three adult female lions has been clocked at 45 minutes (Trimmer, 1962), and a big lion can become sufficiently exhausted to be killed by its smallest prey, all of whom have their own armament (Trimmer, 1961).

Finally, the papers already given here by Birch and den Boer focus attention on the role of space and environmental diversity as resources in ecology. I would include environmental diversity in the broad category of information, including also species diversity and the negentropy of genetic information.

An approach to arriving at general principles

I have been trying to arrive at a small set of powerful general principles underlying animal, plant and human ecology for a new text on environmental science. Briefly, the approach has been to first review the literature to statements of principles, and data which clearly imply principles. All principles which could thus be discovered were then written on slips of paper, and classified into groups. Finally, all principles were compared to make sure they were not restatements of other principles in the same, or another group. Finally, by using flow charts, I attempted to discover logical relationships between these principles, analogous to those between Euclidean theorems.

Desirable properties in a set of ecological principles

Such a set of principles should meet four desiderata. First, the set itself should be expressed in such a fashion that logical relationships between different principles in the set are exposed. That is, it should be demonstrated that the data in this field are expressions of a powerful underlying general theory which has an internal logical structure of its own, as in physics of chemistry. Second, the body of theory should be both a deductive and an inductive system. In addition to it being possible to deduce the principles from preceding principles in the system, or theory in other branches of science, the principles should be supportable by data and useful in accounting for data. Third, the principles should be stated in a sufficiently fundamental, general fashion that many existing principles can be derived from them as corollaries, or special cases. In other words, it should be possible to reduce the total number of generalizations, by stating principles so as to expose fundamental analogies between apparently different types of situations. Finally, such a body of theory should be deliberately designed to be practical. It should be clearly indicated by this theory how one should proceed in building specific models to rationalize any given set of data.

The core principles of environmental science

In my view, the most important of the core principles of environmental science number about 40. However, space here is inadequate to explain more than 15 (Fig. 1). These have been selected as being particularly relevant to this Institute, and to indicate the character of the entire set. I have deliberately excluded principles which belong to other sciences as well as ecology, such as the first and second Laws of Thermodynamics.

1. The rate of energy flow through all living organisms, populations and ecosystems is determined by the availability of five categories of resources: matter, energy, space, time and information.

Inorganic and organic chemistry, and thermodynamics provide the deductive basis, and plant physiology the data showing that this principle applies for matter and energy

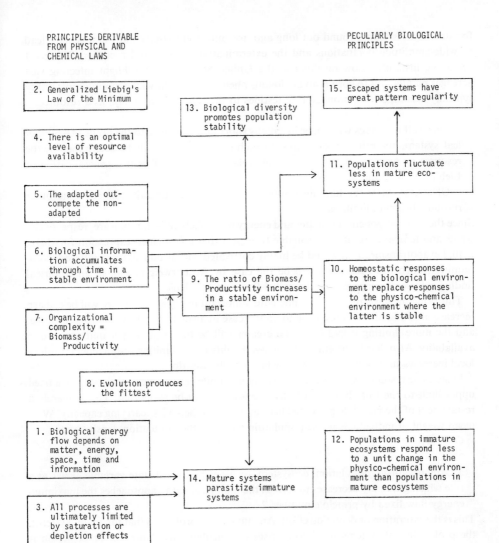

2. Generalized Liebig's Law of the Minimum

4. There is an optimal level of resource availability

5. The adapted out-compete the non-adapted

6. Biological informa-tion accumulates through time in a stable environment

7. Organizational complexity = Biomass/ Productivity

8. Evolution produces the fittest

1. Biological energy flow depends on matter, energy, space, time and information

3. All processes are ultimately limited by saturation or depletion effects

13. Biological diversity promotes population stability

9. The ratio of Biomass/ Productivity increases in a stable environ-ment

14. Mature systems parasitize immature systems

15. Escaped systems have great pattern regularity

11. Populations fluctuate less in mature eco-systems

10. Homeostatic responses to the biological environ-ment replace responses to the physico-chemical environment where the latter is stable

12. Populations in immature ecosystems respond less to a unit change in the physico-chemical environ-ment than populations in mature ecosystems

Fig. 1. Flow chart of logical relationships amongst 15 core principles.

However, space operates in the same way. If the concentration of fluorides is too low or too high, this is harmful. If the space to the nearest neighbor is too great in a population of fecund females and prospective mates, the probability of fertilization will be too low; if this distance is not great enough, interference will depress egg laying rate per female, as we were shown here by Hassell and others. The papers of Dempster and Birch brought out the role of space as a resource.

Holling's work demonstrates that time itself is a resource, not just an independent variable. Several remarks of Birch here support this view. For example, whether or not rabbits can migrate from site to site depends on whether they have the energy to keep them moving for a long enough time at mean cruising velocity to cover the minimum distance to another favorable site. Den Boer's environmental heterogeneity is clearly a prerequisite for stability. As Gause found out long ago, too much environmental homogeneity lead to wide-amplitude fluctuations and the extermination of prey and predator. The great economic instability now resulting in the United States from the blight infecting vast acreages planted out to corn is an analogous phenomenon. The wide-amplitude instability typically accompanying monoculture testifies to the role of information as a resource.

2. Since all resources will not be in equally short supply relative to the needs of a biological system, the rate of energy flow through the system will only be determined by the resource or resources in shortest supply relative to needs. This is a generalization of Liebig's Law of the Minimum.

Of course, once the limiting resource is available in superabundance, some other resource becomes limiting.

Since the two components of matter and energy most likely to be limiting are, respectively, water and temperature, it is reasonable to expect that a combined expression for these, actual evapotranspiration, would be highly correlated with productivity in different communities. Such has been shown to be the case by Rosenzweig (1968), in an empirical finding sufficiently important to be called Rosenzweig's Rule.

This principle has a number of immediate important implications. There will be a sharp increase in productivity in response to an increase in availability of the limiting resource, and the more limiting it had been, the greater will be the response per unit increase in availability. Also, local concentrations in availability of the limiting resource will produce local increases in productivity. This is what greenhouses do.

Since some resource will always be limiting in a finite environment, there will be a fixed upper limit to the total biomass of any species that can be supported. This is merely a restatement of the principle presented here by White. Where C = carrying capacity, $\overline{W}$ = mean weight of individuals in the populatoin and p = the population density, then

$$C = \overline{W}p^{3/2}$$

3. Any organism, population, ecosystem, or other biological state variable grows at a rate which gradually decreases to zero as the biological entity approaches the maximum energy flow fixed by principle number 2.

This is the saturation or depletion effect. An immediate corollary is that for many systems, the probability of systems breakdown rises exponentially as saturation or depletion is approached. Thus Smeed (1964) has shown that an increase of 1% in automobile traffic on a freeway system causes a vastly greater impact on the probability of system congestion when the system is already 90% saturated than when it is 50% saturated. This principle is violated or ignored in much long-term planning at present, particularly economic planning, which assumes that everything can grow at x % forever, even in a finite planet.

4. For all categories of resources except time, there is an optimum availability of the resource for any given biological system. Thus, for availability of the resource either below or above the optimum amount, appropriately selected biological state variables will show reduced values.

This is the fundamental explanation for density-dependent regulating mechanisms. Interestingly, it is not a peculiarly biological principle, because the rate of physical and chemical reactions also will be maximal at some intermediate, optimal set of environmental conditions.

572

Stating this principle differently, there will be an intensification of the struggle for existence as the supply of resources per individual declines, or a relaxation as the supply increases. Consequently, excessive population density leads to population decline, and unusually low population density leads to population increase. It is clear from the papers of den Boer, Birch and others that dispersal must be included as a density-dependent compensatory mechanism, along with rates of birth, growth and death.

For the reasons stated, population densities must fluctuate about some equilibrium value. This need not imply that they are pulled back to it after short departures. It need only imply that large upward departures sharply increase the probability of decline, and large downward departures sharply increase the probability of subsequent increase.

This is the principle which explains the evolutionary advantage to clumping in space (aggregation of individuals in high-density rookeries, roosts, or colonies). There is an optimal space between individuals for a variety of reasons. These reasons have to do with such phenomena as information communication, feeding efficiency, decreasing per capita vulnerability to predators. The key idea in the last point is that attack capacity of predators or parasites can be saturated. If each attacker can only generate K attacks per unit time at the most, and there are N attackers, then any prey in excess of NK must escape per unit time. This makes intense selection pressure for large prey aggregations. It was also the reason for making convoys as large as possible in the second world war: percentage losses were minimized by saturating the attack capacity particulairy of submarines. This principle is also the driving force which creates the organized society of men, ants and bees.

5. Species and communities characteristic of particular environments are able to persist because they make more efficient use of the resources there than any prospective invaders. This is the first principle stated here that applies peculiarly to living systems, and is the principle of adaptation.

It follows that if conditions change, a different species may be better adapted. For example, different parasite species seem to have different degrees of tolerance to high density in their own species, that is to available space in the sense of distance to the nearest neighbor. A parasite which performs well at low host densities because of high searching efficiency may be replaced at high host densities by other species for whom the optimal space to the nearest neighbor is smaller.

One specific implication is that individuals, species, and ecosystems evolve or develop mechanisms to make energy use as efficient as possible. Allen's and Bermann's rules would appear to be examples.

6. The information content of any biological system increases through time so long as the stability of the physical environment makes this possible. This is a restatement of the time-stability hypothesis of Slobodkin and Sanders (1969), and follows from the definition of time as a resource in principle number 1. The rate of increase will decrease to zero as space becomes saturated with diversity, in accord with priciple number 3. This is probably the most central single principle of modern biology; all others are related to it.

What we mean here by 'stability' is pattern regularity. There can be a big difference between night and day, or the coldest and hottest days of the year. However, if the physical environment is exactly the same from a particular time in one cycle to the corresponding time in the next cycle, this is a perfectly predictable pattern and the organism can evolve a response to it. What organisms can not evolve a fixed response to is, for example, the situation in which the coldest month one year has a mean monthly temperature 40 °F lower than that for the coldest month in the same place the preceding year.

7. The organizational complexity of any individual, population, trophic level or community is equal to the biomass divided by the productivity.

Morowitz (1968) has given two separate arguments by which this principle can be deduced from thermodynamic theory. Margalef (1969) has presented a graph showing that the primary productivity per unit of biomass is a decreasing function of diversity in ecosystems. Carlander (1955) has shown that the standing crop of fish in different reservoirs was an increasing function of the number of species present.

Another way of stating this principle is to note that the energy efficiency of biological systems increases with increasing organizational complexity. That is, the energy cost of maintaining a unit of biomass decreases with organizational complexity, or information content.

8. The struggle for existence, on average, results in the selection of the fittest, or best adapted to a particular environment.

9. The ratio of biomass to productivity increases through time so long as the physical stability of the environment makes this possible. This follows immediately from 6, 7 and 8. If organizational complexity (O) increases through time (6) and $O = B/P(7)$, then B/P must increase through time. This is an extremely important principle, because it implies that biological systems evolve in the direction of increased efficiency of energy use. That is, if P is fixed by incoming solar radiation, but O and B increase through time, then a quantum of light energy is being used to support more biomass, and a higher degree of organizational complexity.

As Royama has speculated here, there may be selection for maximization of hunting efficiency in bird predators. We would expect to see in mature communities the employment of distribution and dispersal patterns which make the most efficient possible use of energy.

A trophic level, or a community can be kept immature by wide amplitude weather fluctuations, predation by man or other animals, unpredictable flooding, or other perturbations.

10. High levels of energy efficiency in stable ecosystems and trophic levels develop by replacing homeostatic mechanisms for response to physical changes by those responding primarily to the biological and social environment. This follows from number 9. If energy efficiency is to increase with increased time in a stable environment, then efficiency must be obtained somehow. This can only be done by avoiding energy expenditure where it is not necessary. Thus, it follows that in mature ecosystems that have evolved in a stable environment, there will be no need for homeostatic responses to wide-amplitude physico-chemical fluctuations, and such responses will be replaced by sensitive behavioral and biochemical adjustments to the biological environment.

Evolution in a highly unpredictable environment calls for the maintenance of a highly plastic response on the part of the population. This implies a high degree of heterozygosity. Evolution in a highly stable but biologically complex environment equates success with a perfect, highly complex but rigid response to an information-rich set of environmental cues.

Way has shown us here that there is evidence of biochemical interactions between insects and plants that can only be expected in a mature community after long co-evolution.

Connell has reported here that the unpredictable barnacle supply in Scotland had a general predator whereas the predictable supply of Washington State had a specialist. The perfect, but rigid predator is the product of greater stability in its environment.

His additional report of tropical tree species killing their own offspring indicates the importance of biochemical adjustments in a mature community.

11. Populations fluctuate less in mature ecosystems or trophic levels. This follows from number 6, which indicates that physico-chemical environmental stability is a prerequisite for ecosystem maturity, and 10, which states that sensitive adjustments will have evolved to the biological environment – the only other thing which can fluctuate. Thus, in mature ecosystems one cause of fluctuation is absent and the other is modulated by sensitively balanced adjustments. This also follows from number 9, concerning the relation between maturity (high O) and efficiency of energy use. High efficiency implies minimal waste, and wide-amplitude population fluctuations are made possible by a high rate of biomass turnover $(r - m)$ which is a measure of waste. Consequently, wide-amplitude fluctuations are characteristic of immature ecosystems, trophic levels or populations. The very large fluctuations described by Baltensweiler occurred in forests of remarkably low tree species diversity.

12. However, populations in immature ecosystems are less sensitive to a unit change in the physical environment than are populations in mature ecosystems. This follows from number 10, which states that populations in environments with physico-chemical stability for a long time lose their ability to adjust to it.

The populations in mature ecosystems are vulnerable to being exterminated by catastrophic changes in the physical environment because of their genetic rigidity mentioned in 10. Thus, an important consequence of living in a highly predictable environment is that it leads to irreversibility, because selection pressure places a premium on perfection, and hence rigidity of response. Since there is little free energy available in a mature community to adjust to great environmental perturbations, the latter may cause a totally unsuspected magnitude of response. This is particularly true because of the complex system of control mechanisms jointly linking all species in the community. Such mechanisms mean that a perturbation applied somewhere in the causal web will produce shock waves through the system. Because many of the control mechanisms are exponential, and have threshold effects, cumulative effects, and interaction effects, some consequences of the original perturbation may have much wider amplitude deviation from mean values than the perturbation itself. This is the amplifier effect. The Crown of Thorns starfish may be an excellent example.

13. It follows from number 6 that because of the increase in organizational complexity, or diversity of a mature ecosystem, there will be a great increase in the number of species, and the variety and complexity of control systems and trophic pathways in the community. This will lead to an increased degree of stability within the ecosystem, provided there is a persistent high degree of stability in the physico-chemical environment.

This principle is well understood by field biologists, and was stated formally in the context of information theory by MacArthur (1955). Interestingly, it has been rediscovered independently by the architectural writer Jane Jacobs (1969). She contrasts the Manchester Detroit type of city with the Birmingham-Cambridge, Massachusetts-Palo Alto type. The economies of the former are dominated by a small number of very large industries, and hence are not assured of long-term stability. The latter type have a very large number of small industries, and therefore what den Boer (1968) called spreading of risks, and probably long-term stability. However, the parallels with the natural world are not perfect. In man's world, the large industry cities have great efficiency of energy use, because of economies of scale, which are lacking in small industries. As in the animal-plant world, however, great efficiency is linked to rigidity, irreversibility, and vulnerability to catastrophic change. It is man's conversion from dependence on a flow energy source (the sun) to dependence on stock energy resources (fossil fuels) that has broken down the natural relationship between the number of energy flow pathways and the efficiency of energy use. In the world of man, efficiency of energy use is not regarded as being as important a desideratum as maximization of energy throughput. This type of thinking clearly supposes that unlimited energy resources will be available indefinitely.

Huffaker has presented at this Institute an interesting example of a regulatory mechanism in mature communities. Predators can enrich the diversity of lower trophic levels by an increased cropping of any prey species that begins to increase in numbers relative to other prey species. Thus, predators' functional responses are a mechanism for constantly maximizing the information content per individual (species diversity) at the prey trophic level. Predators damp wide-amplitude fluctuations in mature communities. The exceptions, as in lemming, hare and spruce budworm outbreaks, would appear to be characteristic of immature communities; where the species diversity and pattern diversity is too low, herbivores erupt and 'escape' from regulation by their predators.

In view of the importance of this principle, the way in which mankind is decreasing both the species diversity and pattern diversity of the planet is frightening. Professor Westhoff, Department of Botany, Nijmegen University, has reported that half the higher plant species of Holland have disappeared during the last four decades. Dr Beukema informed me that the number of butterflies in the Netherlands is about 10% of what it was four decades ago.

14. Mature ecosystems, trophic levels and populations parasitize energy, biomass, and information from their immature counterparts. This follows, in part, from number 1. Because information is a resource, the accumulation of information facilitates the accumulation of still more information, up to a maximum, as indicated by 3. It also follows in part from 9, which states that increasing information in a system implies increased efficiency of energy use. One way to increase efficiency of energy use is to constantly gather up energy, biomass and information from some other place, or some other part of the system. This is a surprisingly widespread phenomenon, pointed out by Margalef (1963, 1968) in connection with flow in plankton systems along a gradient of increasing information content. But in addition, young people move from farms, villages, and towns to big cities, birds take food from fields surrounding a woodland to their nests within it, ants and bees take energy back to their highly organized nests, and top predators in trophic pyramids have a higher degree of energy efficiency than the animals in lower trophic levels that they eat. This principle implies that those parts of

systems which have a high degree of organizational complexity actually suppress development of organizational complexity in other parts of the system, and thus prevent them from attaining maturity, with its associated information richness.

This principle also explains the curious phenomenon pointed out here by Huffaker, that wolves have a territory limited to one tenth of a square mile, which keeps the wolf population too low to prevent prey explosion. As Huffaker stated, the size of the territory and its compressibility may be an evolved response to the typical mean food density. In terms of principle 13, this may mean that the wolves have evolved a higher degree of order than their food, because constant predation by wolves and other predators keeps the prey trophic level immature, and hence low in information content. I believe this is the interpretation that would be used by Margalef.

15. The degree of pattern regularity in population fluctuations increases with the relative importance for population trend in any generation of the state of the population-environment system two and more generations previous.

Some populations in vast land areas with homogeneous, optimal food supply and wildly fluctuating weather may increase so rapidly that they 'escape' normal controlling factors. This is another way of saying that the factors which control them operate with long time lags, because, of course, all populations must ultimately be controlled. Where the controlling system has 2 or 3 or longer step time lags, the trend in population density at any point in a cycle has a high degree of inertia built into it, and the result is extraordinary pattern regularity in the fluctuating system. Predators which follow such prey have an even longer number of lagged steps connecting the ultimate causes of their fluctuation with the fluctuations themselves. Thus, we have a graded series of pattern regularity in fluctuations, going from most irregular, with least lag, to most regular with longest time lag. The lynx is longest of all and most regular; Baltensweiler's larch bud moth is quite a long-sequence control system, and almost as regular as the lynx.

Since man has escaped normal controls more than any other species, through increasing dependence on fossil and nuclear fuels, the implications of this principle are ominous. A catastrophic trend to higher density can become self-promoting because of long time lags.

References

Boer, P. J. den, 1968. Spreading of risk and stabilization of animal numbers. *Acta biotheor.* 18: 165–194.

Carlander, K. D., 1955. The standing crop of fish in lakes. *J. Fish. Res. Bd Can.* 12: 543–570.

Hamilton III, W. J., W. M. Gilbert, F. H. Hepner & R. J. Planck, 1967. Starling roost dispersal and a hypothetical mechanism regulating rhythmical animal movement to and from dispersal centers. *Ecology* 48: 825–833.

Hamilton III, W. J. & W. M. Gilbert, 1969. Starling dispersal from a winter roost. *Ecology* 50: 886–898.

Hamilton III, W. J. & K. E. F. Watt, 1970. Refuging. *A. Rev. Ecol.* 1 (in press).

Jacobs, Jane, 1969. The economy of cities. Random House, New York.

MacArthur, R., 1955. Fluctuations of animal populations, and a measure of community stability. *Ecology* 36: 533–536.

Margalef, Ramon, 1963. On certain unifying principles in ecology. *Am. Nat.* 97: 357–374.

Margalef, Ramon, 1968. Perspectives in ecological theory. University of Chicago Press, Chicago.

Margalef, Ramon, 1969. Diversity and stability: a practical proposal and a model of interdependence. *Brookhaven Symp. Biol.* 22: 25–37.

Morowitz, H. J., 1968. Energy flow in biology. Academic Press, New York.

Rosenzweig, M. L., 1968. Net primary productivity of terrestrial communities: prediction from climatological data. *Am. Nat.* 102: 67–74.

Slobodkin, L. B. & H. L. Sanders, 1969. On the contribution of environmental predictability to species diversity. *Brookhaven Symp. Biol.* 22: 82–93.

Smeed, R. J., 1964. The traffic problem in towns. *Town Planning Rev.* 35: 133–158.

Trimmer, C. D., 1961. Uganda national parks report for the quarter ending 31 December 1960.

Trimmer, C. D., 1962. Uganda national parks report for the quarter ending 30 September 1962.

Discussion

Participants: Watt (Author), van der Aart, Andrewartha, Bakker (K.), Birch, den Boer (P. J.), Gulland, Jacobs, Krebs, Lawton, Reddingius, Rosenzweig, Varley, Vlijm, Walker, Williamson, de Wit and Zwölfer

Watt has presented his views from another level of organization than that on which most of us are working. In his paper de Wit distinguished the level of the *population* from that of the *community* and, just as de Wit stressed, Watt tries to interrelate and explain processes on the level of the community with the aid of the separate processes in the populations (the next underlying level of organization). Therefore, Watt's views are not those of a population ecologist but the views of a community ecologist and, however interesting these may be for biological synthetic theory, they will not help people studying the 'minor problems' in population ecology. Please note that this is *not* a criticism (BAKKER). Similar comments were made by ANDREWARTHA, BIRCH (there are missing links between populations and communities) and DE WIT. However, all principles discussed by Watt *are* population principles (ROSENZWEIG). Hence, it should be concluded, that a community has to be considered as a kind of 'compound population', and *not* as a distinct higher level of organization with its principles, differing (although possibly derivable) from those of populations (DEN BOER).

Watt's attempt to develop a general theory does not satisfy the requirement of a powerful mathematic system that most principles follow from a few basic theorems, in the manner of a bunch of bananas, rather than from a long sequence of theorems, like a string of sausages (GULLAND). I assume that the 15 or 40 'principles' are thought to be eventually based on some *biological* concept which combines matter, energy, time and space, and might be some 'third law of thermodynamics' taking up 'information' as a kind of negative entropy (VLIJM).

There seem to be two types of 'general principles' in Watt's scheme: (1) Deductive principles, like No. 8, which are strictly logical once the assumptions are stated and accepted, and (2) Empirical rules of thumb, like No. 7, which although it may have some deductive reasoning in it, also has difficulties regarding precise wording and controversial evidence, and which also try to put several observations under one heading. Rules such as No. 7 should be followed by systems the actual *causal* elements of which (in terms of organismal physiology, etc.) may be quite different. Such principles have to be clearly distinguished from 'general principles' in physics and chemistry which are the expression of certain *exact set of causal elements* by which one can explain the diversity of physics and chemistry at higher levels of organization. The question is then: Why, in spite of the diversity of causes, we do have general ecological principles? This may have to do with the general applicability of principle No. 8 by means of which the population level acts on the molecules, viz. the genetic make-up of the individuals (JACOBS).

Watt states 'space is distance'. Organisms, however, 'translate' space (distance) into energy, and something similar applies to 'information'. Therefore, there seems to be only *one* resource: energy-matter (VLIJM).

Information can be understood most easily as a resource if we imagine that an organism, whose best strategy is to obtain it, loses time during its search for matter and energy. Information competes with matter and energy for the attention of organisms. This is an example of an additional general principle which it is hoped Watt will include in his list: The more generally adapted organism is less proficient at each separate task than a specialist would be (ROSENZWEIG).

The inclusion of 'information' in the essential categories of energy flow demonstrates the necessity for more research on 'information flow' in population dynamics and studies of community diversity. Three different levels of information flow should be considered: (1) genetic information flow, (2) information flow between individuals of a population, and (3) interspecific information flow (ZWÖLFER).

Many participants were reluctant to extend the concept of 'information' so as to allow it to include phenomena such as diversity, organization, complexity, etc.

How do we measure the increasing structural and pattern diversity in terms of increasing 'information'? Unless we can actually measure it, the use of a term like 'information' only means that something has been given a sophisticated name in order to cover our ignorance of how to measure it, and this may restrict further advance (LAWTON). One thing that has to be carefully considered in the future development of ecology is the way we measure things, especially if we are to arrive at, or to depart from, general principles. In this connection, the concept of 'information' can be very difficult because of the confusion that may arise between information in every-day sense and information as entropy defined by Shannon's formula (REDDINGIUS). The every-day and Shannon's meanings *can* be equivalent (AUTHOR). In the case of Shannon's formula, we must have a fixed alphabet as well as a well-defined source, a channel, and a sink. We may have strong suspicions about the validity of this mathematical information theory to communities, and must be on guard against the danger of using incompatible measures. Information in an every-day sense can be: Signs in the environment which can give animals clues as to how to utilize the environment (including other animals), it can be stored in a memory, can be used as 'experience' and can result in learning. Information can also be stored in genes, and – via natural selection – can result in evolution (REDDINGIUS).

Breaking biological structures and processes down into bits leads to situations such as (as illustrated by Wasserman) that so and so many millions of bacteria have the same 'information content' as a human being. In other words, it leaves us with a bag full of identical units whilst the specific structure has disappeared. Therefore, the second law of thermodynamics seems to be of no help at all in understanding either populations or individual organisms. Weiss gave a different and, probably, a more useful definition of 'organization', namely, the repetition – or rate of repetition – of thermodynamically highly improbable patterns; but note that the rate of repetition would *not* be given in terms of probability (WALKER).

As a continuation of Reddingius' comment, many complex relationships are included in Watt's concepts, and it may be feared that in some instances the same basic measurements (with its errors) may be hiding in both coordinates. This will need careful study (VARLEY).

Some of Watt's relationships may in fact be tautologies, No. 9 states that the ratio of bio-mass/production tends to increase with time. The example given was top predators. These are indeed more efficient because of their reduced area/volume ratio – which is a function of their size – i.e. top predators are big and efficient. But how has *Mustela* evolved so many species (VARLEY)?

Saying that the B/P ratio increases in more mature ecosystems is only saying that more mature ecosystems are storing more non-living material (e.g. carbon) in relation to photo-synthetic biomass. This stored material then leads to increasing pattern diversity (LAWTON). What is a 'mature ecosystem' in this connection? In many cases the storage of non-living material seems to result from a disturbance of 'turnover' which causes the material to be withdrawn from further turnover. Does the storage of non-living material in e.g. a peat-moor lead to increasing species and pattern diversity (DEN BOER)?

$O = B/P$ cannot be measured in bits, which is dimensionless, while $O = B/P$ has the dimension of time (GULLAND).

Some of Watt's principles are almost true rather than completely true. For example, (1) it is possible to have stable, homogeneous population systems, (2) the concept of stability should surely include measures of amplitude as well as of pattern regularity, and (3) there are some cases in which selection does not lead to adaptation (WILLIAMSON).

I think it important to distinguish between natural and man-made systems. Stable, homogeneous systems, as in brewing, involve an energy subsidy from fossil fuels, as do agricultural systems (AUTHOR).

Are the populations of Andrewartha and Birch that are 'short of time' for increase exempted from principle 4 and, if so, does this exclude these populations from all the following principles too? Is principle 5 inherent in the theory of natural selection, or is it an additional theorem to Darwin (KREBS)?

What should ecologists do, or investigate in the near future (VAN DER AART)? Where shall we have to 'lay our eggs' in the coming 20 years (KREBS)? People who make advances are those who are able to say what is the next step (VARLEY).

Proc. Adv. Study Inst. Dynamics Numbers Popul. (Oosterbeek, 1970) 581–583

Final remarks

D. J. Kuenen

Research Institute for Nature Management, Arnhem, the Netherlands

The essence of a two-week meeting of this kind is the discussion which it provokes. It is therefore questionable whether there is any sense in one person standing up and trying to review what has been happening during this Study Institute. It is exactly the discussion of the different aspects, the shock of opinions of people from different backgrounds coming together, which we need for furthering our aims. I find that, particularly during these two weeks, I have been struck by the very great difficulty which people have of even understanding what other have been saying – let alone in agreeing. I believe that this must be due to the great heterogeneity in the material with which biologists are working.

If you have subjects of study for which you use a mass spectograph, or if you study the structure of hydrocarbons, or are concerned with electron spin – or whatever it is physicists or chemists are doing – the material and your apparatus itself tends to draw you together. But biologists, due to the fact that they are studying at least two and a half million species at the same time, tend to be drawn apart. This is because each species has its own particular characteristics and, besides, we very nearly always have to deal with more than one species at the time. This further increases the specific aspects of our work and further increases the centrifugal tendency of our research. I am sure that is one of the problems with which we are faced and which has been quite evident during our discussions. What is happening in biology is that, on the one hand, we want to have general theories which will pull us together and, on the other hand, we want the definite data which are going to push us apart. But whether we continue to study problems of detail or look for general principles, we need words and generally accepted definitions in order to communicate our ideas. Now there, we are in very grave danger, as has been formulated by Hardin: 'The history of science is littered with the carcasses of discarded panchrestons: the Galaenic humors, the Bergsonian élan vital and the Drieschian entelechy are a few biological examples in point. A panchreston which "explains" all explains nothing'. Because of the enormous diversity of the material and things we are working with, we are very certainly in danger of falling into this trap. If we start to abstract and try to get to something which is useful for everything, we loose our contact with reality. We must insist on facts. We certainly do not lack theories and models and, as has even been formulated in a resolution, we have heard repeatedly that what we need is long-range research to get those data on which we can really build our theories and models. We cannot get there the easy way. We may be in a great hurry, but we cannot reduce the generation time by artificial models. We cannot try to do things which we could better theorize over behind our tables. It is much better to state a good idea straight forward and ask people whether they will please hurry up and do the experiments. If we are afraid we will not have the time to really finish the experiment, then we must assure that the experiment or series of observations is so good that someone else will finish them. We must be patient and we must be persevering.

Obviously, quite a number of people do not like to relinquish their 'idée préconçue', their preconceived ideas. They try to stick to their definitions, to their formulations, to their ideas. Even if experimental evidence gives some people the impression that one thing is proved, other people may not always be convinced. I think we need not worry too much about that. Some of you may remember the controversy between Huygens and Newton as to whether light was a wave or a corpuscle, and it was proved beyond doubt in favour of Huygens that light consisted of waves. It took another threehundred years to show that, after all, perhaps Newton was to a certain extent right.

Now, I do not expect you all to sit around for threehundred years waiting to see whether or not your particular idea comes to fruition in some far ahead general theory. As long as we have stated quite clearly what we think and put it down clearly on paper, we then can just wait for the solution to come and we need not continue to harp on theoretical aspects. This does not mean that theories are not important but, to quote O. W. Richards, we should try to discuss these questions with more light and less heat.

Now the question, of course, is: What are our aims, where are we trying to go? Again and again the discussion comes up whether we should do fundamental or applied research. This has been mentioned several times during this meeting. In my opinion the relationship between the two is very close. When we make an investigation we generally start with an observation and think about it, and then we try to get some facts to confirm or contradict our thinking. This leads to another formulation. We keep on switching from facts to concepts as our investigation progresses. The only difference between those who do pure research and those who do applied research, is that in applied research one stops at a fact, while in pure research one stops at some idea or concept. But however different the two aims of research – which, of course, may be very firmly inbedded in one individual – the methods of work are not different.

At this meeting, where both applied and non-applied people have been together, the question is: What is the use of a meeting like this? It is certainly not to just ventilate our ideas. That can be done much more efficiently by writing them up and sending them out. It is certainly essential to listen; but the difficult thing is that some people have so much to say that they have no time to listen. Others have talked so much that they no longer know how to listen! On the other hand, some people have been listening so much that it is very boring to be in their company, because they never say anything. We must remember that if we want other people to listen to us, we must give them the example by also being prepared to listen to them.

I get the impression that the extremes have not been too evident during this meeting, and while wandering through these rooms my observations have been that in many places conversations were going on, and it was not orators who were speaking. My conclusion, therefore, is that it has been a successful meeting.

But we do not only have our fellow biologists to talk to. There are others for whom we have a message; some of you have explicitly mentioned it, others have considered it implicit in what they have been thinking and talking about. I am sure that the application of population dynamical principles to the problem of the human population, if we find the right way to express ourselves, can help the future of mankind. 'Our lives will not be regulated by science or research, our future depends upon the way we make use of our knowledge'. I think it is an apposite quotation and exceedingly important. On one evening we heard some people explain how they thought other people were making use of their knowledge, and I think that we should take that warning to heart. We should all consider how we are going to use our knowledge. We all have a fairly fixed pattern of behaviour. Even the youngests in this room are at the stage when their central nervous system is beginning slowly to deteriorate; this implies, of course, that it becomes more and more difficult to learn new things. We must be careful not to blame those who fail to apply our knowledge for the betterment of the future of mankind because they cannot; but those who can, should do their very best to build a dependable future.

We have been talking about facts and theories, and, every now and then when facts fail and theories do not conform to what we hoped they will, it was obvious that we still have some faith. Although there is very little to show that the human race will survive the next few decades, I think we all, in spite of our knowledge, have faith in the survival of mankind. I sincerely hope that this faith will carry us through the very difficult period ahead of us. We can help to increase the chances for survival of mankind.

Species index

fruit –, see: *Dacus, Drosophila*
gall –, *344, 355*
green –, 368
house –, see: *Musca domestica*
sarcophagous –, 363
seed –, *393, 404*
tsetse –, see: *Glossina*
Formica polyctena (Hym. ant) 404
fox (carn. mammal) 478
European – 496
red – 329, 333
foxglove, see: *Digitalis purpurea*
frog (amphibian) 100
fruitfly, see: *Dacus, Drosophila*
Fulmaris glacialis (bird, fulmar) 268
fungus 388
mildew – 475, 477, 572
poisonous – 310
rust – 474, 475, 477

Galium (dicot.) 42
gallfly, see: fly
Gammarus (amphipod)
– *duebeni* 282
– *pulex* 282, 287, 292
gannet (bird) 442
gastropod *33, 100, 103, 104,* 287, 423, 448,
475. See also *Cepaea nemoralis, Thais*
ginko (dec. tree, gymnosperm) 325
Glossina (Dipt. tsetse) 177
– *morsitans 38*
Glycine japonica (dicot.) *274*
Glypta cicatricosa (Hym. ichneumonid) 407
goat (ung. mammal), mountain – 331
Gonyaulix (protozoan) 261
grain 48, *49,* 270, 273, *276–279,* 471–475, 572
grass 44, *46,* 47, *49–50,* 53, 56, 58, 62, *169,*
270–273, 274, 337
grasshopper 314
grouse (bird) 567
black – *24–25*
red –, see: *Lagopus lagopus scoticus*
ruffed – 333
gull (bird) 424
Gymnarrhena (dicot.) *311*

Habrobracon brevicornis (Hym. braconid) 407
haddock (fish) 448, 452, 453, *455, 457, 463–464*
Haematopus ostralegus (bird, oystercatcher)
355, *424–425,* 427, 428, *431–439*
hake (fish) 445, 448, 449
halibut (fish) *464, 465*
Halichoerus grypus (carn. mammal, grey seal)
258–261, 265–266, 268

Hannchen, see: barley
hare (rodent) 255, 478, *559, 560,* 576
Harmonia arixidis (Col. coccinellid) 132
hawk (bird), sparrow – 332, 545
heather, see: *Calluna vulgaris*
Helianthus annuus (dicot.) *46,* 49
Hemiptera, see: aphid, corixid, leafhopper,
olive scale. See also: *Nezara*
herbaceous dicotyledon 42, 44, *45, 46,* 48, 49,
50, *51, 54–57,* 58, 117, 128, 236, *274,* 296,
299, *311, 337,* 338, 355, 474. See also: bean,
beet, cactus, clover, cucumber, egg plant,
lucerne (alfalfa), pepper, potato, ragwort,
skeleton weed, tomato
herring (fish) 443, 444, 448, 452
hesperid, see *Thymelicus lineola*
Holcus mollis (grass) 58
hominid 332
housefly, see: *Musca domestica*
Hydra (coelenterate) 299
Hydrobia ulvae (gastropod) 423
Hydroecia (Hym.) 405
– *petasitis* 414
hyena (carn. mammal) 331, 332, 336
Hymenoptera, see: ant, bee, braconid, chalcid,
ichneumonid, sawfly, scelionid
Hypericum (dicot., St. John's wort) 299, *337*
– *perfoliatum* 296

ichneumonid 325–326, 355, *359–361,* 363,
367–376, 378, 379, 406, 407, *408–412, 413,*
414, 417, 418
insect, see: beetle, Diptera, Hemiptera, Hymenoptera, Lepidoptera, Odonata, Orthoptera
insectivorous mammal, see: mole, shrew
isopod 286, 287, 292
Itoplectis (Hym. ichneumonid) 406
– *alternans* 407
– *conquisitor* 355, 406, *409*
– *maculator* 407, *411–412*

jaeger (bird) 333
Juglans regia (walnut tree) 240

kangaroo, red –, see: *Megaleia rufa*
kittiwake, see: *Rissa tridactyla*
knapweed, see: *Centaurea nemoralis*

ladybird, see: *Coccinella septempunctata*
Lagopus (bird)
– *lagopus scoticus* (red grouse) 356, *546,*
548–558, 560–564
– *mutus* (rock ptarmigan) *560*

Myzus persicae (Hemipt. aphid) 233, *235–237*

Naididae (annelid) 287,293
Nardus stricta (grass) 58
Nasonia vitripennis (Hym. chalcid) 321, *359–360*, 362
Nebria brevicollis (Col. carabid) 83
nematode 26
Nemeritis canescens (Hym. ichneumonid) 355, 359, *368–376*, 378, 379
Neodiprion sertifer (Hym. pine sawfly) 128, 308, *344–346*, *411*, 412, 414, 417
Nezara viridula (Hemipt. 'Southern green stinkbug') *190–191*, 195

oak, see: *Quercus*
oat (grain) *273*, *276–277*, *279*
Odonata (dragonfly) 290
Olesicampe benefactor (Hym. ichneumonid) *410*, *413*
olive (dec. tree) 308
  – scale (Hemipt.) 329, 330, 336, 417
Oncorhyncus nerka (fish, sockeye salmon) *464*, *465*
Operophtera brumata (Lep. winter moth) 359, *367–368*, *406*, 408, 410, *413–414*, 545, *556*
Opuntia (dicot., prickly pear) *111–113*, 127, *128*, 233, 299, 311, 337, 566
  – *inermis* *111*, *128*
  – *stricta* *111*, *128*
orange (dec. tree) *565–566*
Orca grampus (killer whale) 261, 268
Orchelimum fidicinum (Orthopt. grasshopper) 314
Orgilus obscurator (Hym. braconid) *411*, *412*
Orthoptera, see: grasshopper, mantid
Oryctolagus cuniculus (rodent, rabbit) 21, *113–116*, *127*, *192–196*, 198, 299, 321, 325, 381, 387, *394–396*, 438, 476,'*477*, *478–506*, 571
Ostrea edulis (lamellibranch, oyster) *445–446*, 448, *449*
owl (bird) 333, 545
  horned – 333
  tawny – 332
Oxychilus cellarius (gastropod) 100
oyster, see: *Ostrea edulis*
oystercatcher, see: *Haematopus ostralegus*

palm (monocot.), oil – 48
Panaxia dominula (Lep. moth) 118
Panicum maximum (grass) *274*
Panolis (moth) 509, 510
parasitic insect *190–191*, 195, 196, 321, *359–360*, 362, 405–407, *410–414*, 418, 511, 545.

See also: braconid, chalcid, ichneumonid, tachinid
Paraswammerdamia (Hym.) 405
partridge, see: *Perdix perdix*
Parus (bird, tit) 196, *345*, *355–356*
  – *ater* (coal tit) 344, 536
  – *caeruleus* (blue tit) 344, 525
  – *major major* (great tit) 345, 355, *507–522*, *524–530*, *532–547*, *556*
  – *major newtoni* 525
pear, prickly –, see: *Opuntia*
Pedicularis condensata (dicot.) 57
Pegohylemiya seneciella (Dipt. seedfly) *393*, 404
Penicillium (fungus) 388
pepper, (dicot.), red – 131
perch (fish), pike – 448
Perdix perdix (bird, partridge) 549–550, *556*
Peucedanum pschavicum (dicot.) 57
Phaeogenes maculicornis (Hym. ichneumonid) 407
Phagocata vitta (triclad) 286
Phalacrocorax aristotelis (bird, shag) 258, *261–262*, *265–268*
pheasant (bird) 478
Phytodietus (Hym. ichneumonid) 407
Picea (conifer) 53
pigeon (bird), wood – *267*, *562*
Pimpla (Hym. ichneumonid)
  – *bicolor* 367
  – *turionellae* 407
pine, Scots –, see: *Pinus*
pine-apple (monocot.) 48
pine looper, see: *Bupalus piniarius*
pine shoot moth, see: *Rhyacionia buoliana*
Pinus (conifer, pine) *507–511*
  – *cembra* *214*, 216
Pisaster (echinoderm, starfish) 302
  – *ochraceus* 307
plaice, see: *Pleuronectes platessa*
Planaria torva (triclad) 292
Planchonella (rain forest tree) *304*
plant, see: dicotyledon, fungus, monocotyledon, tree
Plantago erecta (dicot.) 117
Platichthys flesus (fish, flounder) 424
Pleuronectes platessa (fish, plaice) 443, 448, 451, *464*, *466*
Poa annua (grass) 44, *46*
Polycelis (triclad)
  – *nigra* *284–293*, 296, 297
  – *tenuis* *284–293*, 296, 297
Polydora ciliata (annelid, polychaet) 438
Polygonum carneum (dicot.) *56*, *57*
porpoise (whale) 448
Potamopyrgus jenkinsi (prey of *Polycelis*) 286, 287

Subject index

More important reference numbers are given in italics

parasite(s)
attraction of –, see: attraction
– behaviour, see: behaviour
coexistence of – species, see: coexistence
– complexes   405–418
– constancy   407, 408, 410, 413
defence against –, see: defence
efficient/unefficient –   405, 406, 408, 409–, 411, 413, 414
handling time of –, see: time
–/host systems (heterogeneity), see: heterogeneity
marginal –   407, 409
primary –   410–411, 414
resistance to –, see: resistance
specialization of –, see: specialization
superior/inferior –, see: competition
synchronization of – and host, see: synchronization
see also: parasitation
partitioning, see: hypothesis
patchy (fragmentary, discontinuous), see: aggregation, clustering, distribution, diversity, habitat, heterogeneity, method (stratified sampling), sub-population
pathogenes, see: parasitation
pattern, see: activity, age, diversity, fluctuation, mortality, predation, recruitment, reproduction
perfection. See also: adaptation, selection, specialist/generalist
irreversibility by –   575, 576
persistence
– of individuals   55. See also: survival
– of populations, see: population
– of sparse populations, see: population
pest, see: control
pheromone marking   191, 193–194, 203
phenological, see: variation
phenotype, phenotypic, see: frequency, morphotype, polymorphism, variation
plankton   438
phyto –   220–221, 222, 302, 307, 314, 324, 440
zoo –,   314, 319, 324, 452
see also: production, productivity
plasticity (flexibility), see: adaptability, diet, genetic, growth, regeneration, response
pleitropic effects   107, 256
poisonous, see: defence
pollution   22, 27, 227, 293
polymorphism   100, 214, 216, 471
biochemical –   119, 249–253. See also: genetic markers
genetic –   62, 107, 249, 254, 256
seed –   44, 311
somatic –   44

wing (flight) –   152, 157, 235–238, 241. See also: activity, dispersal
see also: balance, heterogeneity within the population, morphotype, variation
polyphagous (euryphagous) 93, 135, 325, 383, 406, 407, 409, 410, 413. See also: diet, preference, specificity
population(s)
aggregated –, see: aggregate, colonial animals
concept of –   183–184, 187, 189–190, 197, 565–566
delimitation of –   565–566
– density, see: density
– as element within a system, see: element
exchange between –, see: exchange, recovery
extinction of –, sub – 23, 24, 37, 66–67, 116, 118, 386, 387, 398–399, 417, 438, 449, 543, 566, 575. See also: risk
fenced/unfenced –   244–246, 253, 254, 425, 427–429
– fluctuations, see: fluctuation
founding of –, see: colonization, dispersal
–/genetic processes, see: genetic
heterogeneity within –, see: heterogeneity, morphotype, polymorphism, variation
local (sub) –   78–88, 109–118, 129–146, 189–190, 566. See also: heterogeneity
management of –   22–25, 26, 27–28, 173, 435, 439, 453, 459, 464. See also: exploitation
manipulation of –   43, 286, 295
– models, see: model
persistence of –   32, 37, 58, 69, 78, 94, 96, 387. See also: regulation, stabilization
– ratio, see: (net) rate of reproduction
refuge –, see: refuge
seed –   46, 47, 53
sparse –   77–78, 91–94, 237, 301, 308. See also: persistence
stable/instable –, see: stable/instable
– statistics, see: statistics
– turnover 42, 52, 319
turnover of –   96. See also: colonization, extinction
population dynamics   19, 29–35, 41–59, 565
the aim of –   20–21, 98, 582
definition of –   19, 20
definitions in –   197, 283, 295–296, 565–566, 581. See also: appropriate use of concepts, concept
descriptive studies in –   30
hypotheses in –, see: hypothesis, model
the needs of –   10, 30, 35, 43, 59, 72, 99, 146 199, 208–209, 568–569, 581–583
principles in –, see: principles
theories in –, see: theory

protection
- against enemies *93*, 195, 204, *206–207*, 223, *238*, 328, *329*, *504*. See also: defence, refuge, resistance
- from parasite attack 376. See also: defence
physical – 334, 335. See also: aestivation, diapause, hibernation, refuge
- of wildlife (conservation) *21–23*, 173, 436, 455. See also: preservation
protective coloration, see: defence
protein, see: shortage

quality of individuals, see: condition
quest
- constant 372, 378
- theory 408
see also: interference, searching
quota (of exploitation) 435–436, 439, 453, *455, 457–458*, 461

random
- (host) attack 410. See also: selection
- distribution *359*. See also: clustering
- fluctuations 67, 464, *525*. See also: fluctuation
- processes *40*. See also: stochastic processes
- mortality *310–311*. See also: mortality
- numbers *147, 557*
- searching 366, 367, *369, 376, 378*. See also: searching
range, see: abundance, fecundity, fluctuation, habitat
rare (sparse) species, rarity 77, 97, *308, 321, 324, 329–330*, 342, *343*, 417, 453, *568, 569*. See also: distance, persistence, sparse populations
realistic/unrealistic, see: hypothesis, model
recapture, see: recovery
recognizable/unrecognizable (sub-sets), see: method of stratified sampling
recovery (recapture)
- rate (percentage) *135–137, 509–513*, 514, *515*, 516–*518*, 519, *520–521, 533–537*. See also: exchange, method, migration, model
recruitment 52, 54, 133, 159, *227, 229, 264–265*, 268, 285, 301, *302*, 305, *429–430, 436–437, 447*, 460, *464*
pattern of – 437
pre – ⟨larval) phase 430, *447, 464*
- rate *460–463*. See also: growth
-/stock relationship *430*, 436, *445, 447, 464–465*
see also: age, maturity, production, reproduction, settlement

redistribution 145. See also: migration
- of territories *553*. See also: territorialism
refuge (shelter) *116, 169, 171–172*, 195, 356–357, *504*
- area *504*. See also: heterogeneity
food – *293*. See also: coexistence
heat – *169, 171–172*. See also: seasons
- populations *115, 117, 120*. See also: heterogeneity
- for predators *301*. See also: coexistence
see also: protection
regeneration *383–384*, 385, 386, 390, *392, 394*, 395, *396–397*, 403
- from dormant seeds *403*
- from rhizome *471–472*, 475
- from root-buds *384, 391, 403, 404*
- by secondary shoots *383–384*
see also: predation on plants, seed
regression, see: analysis
regularity
pattern – *218, 573, 577*, 580
see also: predictability of environmental conditions, rigidity of response, stability
regulation 19, 20, 22, *24–27*, 29, *39–40*, 51, 527, 530, *532–533, 542, 544, 556, 557, 566*; (model) *184*, 187; (operation doubtful) 156, 216, *387*, 442, 504, 508; (predators) *328–332, 335, 447*
concept of – *387, 388, 522, 566*
- by density-dependent factors 9, 22, *31–33, 36–39, 387, 388*, 464, 507, *514, 522*, 535, *543, 544, 556, 557, 572–573*
- of exploitation (fisheries) *443–444*, 448, 451, 453, *455, 457–458*
- by genetic processes *38–39*, 255, 322. See also: genetic feed-back
mechanism of – *40, 156*, 195, 206, 507, *522*, 535, 544, *566*, 576
mutual – of species *341*
physiological – *498*
self – *38*, 96, *195*, 199, *206, 232–241*
see also: balance, carrying capacity, control, density, equilibrium, feed-back
related, see: density
age –, see: dispersal
closely –, see: species
density –, see also: dispersal, mortality, predation
re(dis)placement 288, 290, *291, 296*, 298
competitive – 50, *299, 302*, 342, *343, 406*, 410, *411*, 412, *418*
relative – rate 50, *271–275*, 281
see also: interspecific competition, exclusion
reproduction, reproductive *50–51*, 54, *56–58, 441–442*, 487, *488–492*, 507, 508; (infl. by aggregation) *234, 237–238, 261–262, 264–266*, 505; (infl. by condition) 202, 204, 494–